American Literary Scholarship
1984

American Literary Scholarship

An Annual / 1984

Edited by J. Albert Robbins

Essays by Philip F. Gura, Rita K. Gollin, Kent P. Ljungquist, Brian Higgins, Jerome Loving, Louis J. Budd, Robert L. Gale, Hugh Witemeyer, Linda W. Wagner-Martin, Michael S. Reynolds, William J. Scheick, David J. Nordloh, John J. Murphy, Louis Owens, Jerome Klinkowitz, James K. Guimond, Lee Bartlett, Walter J. Meserve, John M. Reilly, Michael J. Hoffman, F. Lyra, Marc Chénetier, Rolf Meyn, Gaetano Prampolini, Maria Vittoria D'Amico, Hiroko Sato, Mona Pers

Duke University Press   Durham   North Carolina   1986

© 1986, Duke University Press. Library of Congress Catalogue Card number 65–19450. I.S.B.N. 0–8223–0666–2. Printed in the United States of America by Heritage Printers, Inc.

Foreword

As editor of the 22nd volume of *American Literary Scholarship* I welcome three new contributors. Chapter 1 (Emerson, Thoreau, and Transcendentalism), done for eight years by Wendell Glick, is written by Philip F. Gura of the University of Colorado, Boulder. Chapter 4 (Melville), previously contributed by Robert Milder, is covered by Brian Higgins of the University of Illinois at Chicago. Chapter 10 (Fitzgerald and Hemingway), done for four years by Scott Donaldson and for one by Jackson Bryer, is prepared by Michael S. Reynolds of North Carolina State University, Raleigh. We appreciate the good work of our alumni and welcome the newcomers.

For *ALS 1985* there will be two changes of personnel. After a two-year leave, Karl Zender (University of California, Davis) resumes the Faulkner chapter. Our thanks go to Linda W. Wagner-Martin for covering Faulkner and to James K. Guimond for surveys of Poetry, 1900 to the 1940s, in the 1983 and 1984 volumes. The poetry chapter will be written by Timothy A. Hunt (Indiana University–Purdue University, Fort Wayne).

Our useful coverage of foreign contributions (chapter 21) varies from time to time. For reasons of health or academic duties there are volumes that lack a foreign essay or two. Last year, in *ALS 1983*, we had no essays from East Europe or Italy. This year we have a full complement of six foreign essays, plus an extra one from Italy, by Gaetano Prampolini, for 1983. We thank Professor Prampolini for his good work in past years and welcome his successor, Maria Vittoria D'Amico of the University of Catania, whose first appearance is an essay covering Italian scholarship in 1984.

Warren G. French, who edited *ALS 1983*, was to have edited *ALS 1985*, but early retirement and plans to live abroad necessitated his giving up this commitment. I will edit *ALS 1985*. We thank Warren for his work on *ALS 1983* and hope for the pleasure of his mind and company when he comes back to this country from time to time.

Although we have noted this before, I would like to remind readers that, in the large part, we use the system of periodical abbreviations used in the *Modern Language Assn. Bibliography*. A list of these abbreviations can be found in any issue of *MLAB*. More details about many of these periodicals can be found in the *MLA Directory of Periodicals*, published bienially.

A current authority for publishers' addresses is the list in *Books in Print, 1985–1986*, volume 6.

Beginning with *ALS 1985* we are making an adjustment in coverage of the three chapters reviewing 20th-century fiction. Previously chapter 13 covered three decades; chapter 14, two decades; and chapter 15, three and one-half decades. This allotment placed undue stress upon Jerome Klinkowitz, who has been reviewing fiction since the 1950s (chapter 15). Not only did his chapter cover three and one-half decades (1950 to 1984), but it grew fatter year after year because of the sheer quantity of scholarship on contemporary fiction. We have given him some relief by moving the decade of the '50s to chapter 14, reviewed by Louis Owens.

We urge authors to send books and offprints of articles either to the editor, who will forward them to the appropriate *ALS* contributor, or directly to that contributor. The former is more certain for, from time to time, *ALS* people are on leave and away from their home campuses.

J. Albert Robbins

Indiana University

Table of Contents

Key to Abbreviations

Festschriften, Essay Collections, and Books
Discussed in More Than One Chapter

(Alternative) Literary Publishing / Sally Dennison, *(Alternative) Literary Publishing: Five Modern Histories* (Iowa)

American Literature and Social Change / Michael Spindler, *American Literature and Social Change: William Dean Howells to Arthur Miller* (Indiana, 1983)

The American Narcissus / Joyce W. Warren, *The American Narcissus: Individualism and Women in Nineteenth-Century American Fiction* (Rutgers)

American Poetics of History / Joseph G. Kronick, *American Poetics of History from Emerson to the Moderns* (LSU)

American Procession / Alfred Kazin, *An American Procession* (Knopf)

American Renaissance / Walter Benn Michaels and Donald E. Pease, eds., *The American Renaissance Reconsidered: Selected Papers from the English Institute, 1982–83* (Hopkins, 1985)

The American Short Story / Philip Stevick, ed., *The American Short Story, 1900–1945: A Critical History* (Twayne)

American Theories / Sergio Perosa, *American Theories of the Novel, 1793–1903* (NYU, 1983)

The Bang and the Whimper / Zbigniew Lewicki, *The Bang and the Whimper: Apocalypse and Entropy in American Literature* (Greenwood)

Between Women / Carol Ascher, Louise DeSalve, and Sara Ruddick, eds., *Between Women: Biographers, Novelists, Critics, Teachers, and Artists Write About Their Work on Women* (Beacon)

Black Women Writers / Mari Evans, ed., *Black Women Writers, 1950–1980: A Critical Evaluation* (Doubleday)

California Writers / Stoddard Martin, *California Writers* (Macmillan, 1983)

Chicago and the American Literary Imagination / Carl S. Smith, *Chicago and the American Literary Imagination, 1880–1920* (Chicago)

Contemporary Approaches / Anthony Mortimer, ed., *Contemporary Approaches to Narrative* (Tübingen: Narr)

Critical Essays / Scott Donaldson, ed., *Critical Essays on F. Scott Fitzgerald's* The Great Gatsby (Hall)

The Diagonal Line / August J. Nigro, *The Diagonal Line: Separation and Reparation in American Literature* (Susquehanna)

The Dialectic of Discovery / John D. Lyons and Nancy J. Vickers, eds., *The Dialectic of Discovery: Essays on the Teaching and Interpretation of Literature Presented to Lawrence E. Harvey* (French Forum)

The Echoing Green / Carlos Baker, *The Echoing Green: Romanticism, Modernism, and the Phenomenon of Transference in Poetry* (Princeton)

Exiles at Home / Daniel Marder, *Exiles at Home: A Story of Literature in Nineteenth Century America* (University Press)

Exorcising Blackness / Trudier Harris, *Exorcising Blackness: Historical and Literary Lynching and Burning Rituals* (Indiana)

Faulkner IP / Doreen Fowler and Ann J. Abadie, eds., *Faulkner: International Perspectives* (Miss.)

Fifteen American Authors Before 1900 / Earl N. Harbert and Robert A. Rees, eds., *Fifteen American Authors Before 1900: Bibliographic Essays on Research and Criticism*, rev. ed. (Wisconsin)

Flawed Texts / Hershel Parker, *Flawed Texts and Verbal Icons: Literary Authority in American Fiction* (Northwestern)

God Be With the Clown / Ronald Wallace, *God Be With the Clown: Humor in American Poetry* (Missouri)

Great American Adventure / Martin Green, *The Great American Adventure* (Beacon)

The Great Circle / Beongcheon Yu, *The Great Circle: American Writers and the Orient* (Wayne State, 1983)

Hagiographie / Serge Ricard, ed., *Hagiographie et Iconoclastie: Modèles Américains* (Actes du GRENA, 1983)

Hawthorne, Melville, and the American Character / John P. McWilliams, Jr., *Hawthorne, Melville and the American Character: A Looking-Glass Business* (Cambridge)

History and Tradition / Günther H. Lenz, ed., *History and Tradition in Afro-American Culture* (Frankfurt: Campus)

Hollywood / *Hollywood: Réflexions sur l'écran* (Actes du GRENA)

The Image of the Prostitute / Pierre L. Horn and Mary Beth Pringle, eds., *The Image of the Prostitute in Modern Literature* (Ungar)

Kierkegaard and Literature / Ronald Schleifer and Robert Markley, eds., *Kierkegaard and Literature: Irony, Repetition, and Criticism* (Oklahoma)

The Land Before Her / Annette

Kolodny, *The Land Before Her: Fantasy and Experience of the American Frontiers 1630–1860* (N. C.)

Link Festschrift / Ulrich Halfmann, Kurt Muller, and Klaus Weiss, eds., *Wirklichkeit und Dichtung: Studien zur englischen und amerikanischen Literatur: Festschrift zum 60. Geburtstag von Franz Link* (Berlin: Duncker & Humblot)

Literature of Tennessee / Ray Willbanks, ed., *Literature of Tennessee* (Macon: Mercer Univ.)

Los Angeles / David Fine, ed., *Los Angeles in Fiction: A Collection of Original Essays* (New Mexico)

Melville: Reassessments / A. Robert Lee, ed., *Herman Melville: Reassessments* (Barnes & Noble)

Money and Fiction / John Vernon, *Money and Fiction: Literary Realism in the Nineteenth and Early Twentieth Centuries* (Cornell)

Mothering the Mind / Ruth Perry and Martine Watson Brownley, eds., *Mothering the Mind: Twelve Studies of Writers and Their Silent Partners* (Holmes & Meier)

Mothers and Others / Wilma Garcia, *Mothers and Others: Myths of the Female in the Works of Melville, Twain, and Hemingway* (Lang)

Mythologizing of Mark Twain / Sara deSaussure Davis and Philip D. Beidler, eds., *The Mythologizing of Mark Twain* (Alabama)

Naturalism in American Fiction / John J. Conder, *Naturalism in American Fiction: The Classic Phase* (Kentucky)

New Directions / Doreen Fowler and Ann J. Abadie, eds., *New Directions in Faulkner Studies* (Miss.)

The Origins / Tibor Frank, ed., *The Origins and Originality of American Culture* (Budapest: Akadémiai Kiadó)

Poetic Prophecy / Jan Wojcik and Raymond-Jean Frontain, eds., *Poetic Prophecy in Western Literature* (Fairleigh Dickinson)

Portraits of Marriage / Anne C. Hargrove and Maurine Magliocco, eds., *Portraits of Marriage in Literature* (Macomb: Western Ill. Univ.)

Prairie Frontier / Sandra Looney, Arthur R. Huseboe, and Geoffrey Hunt, eds., *The Prairie Frontier* (Nordland)

Problematic Fictions / Judith L. Sutherland, *The Problematic Fictions of Poe, James and Hawthorne* (Missouri)

Psychological Perspectives / Joseph Natoli, ed., *Psychological Perspectives on Literature: Freudian Dissidents and Non-Freudians* (Archon)

Realism and Naturalism / Donald Pizer, *Realism and Naturalism in Nineteenth-Century American Literature*, rev. ed. (So. Ill.)

Religion in the American Novel / Leo F. O'Conner, *Religion in the American Novel: The Search for Belief, 1860–1920* (Univ. Press)

Revolution and Convention / Donald E. Stanford, *Revolution and Convention in Modern Poetry: Studies in Ezra Pound, T. S. Eliot, Wallace Stevens, Edwin Arlington Robinson, and Yvor Winters* (Delaware)

Richard Wright / Richard Macksey and Frank E. Moorer, eds., *Richard Wright: A Collection of Critical Essays* (Prentice-Hall)

Society in the Novel / Elizabeth Langland, *Society in the Novel* (N. C.)

Study and Writing / Wauneta Hackleman, ed., *The Study and Writing of Poetry: American Women Poets Discuss Their Craft* (Whitston, 1983)

The Texas Tradition / *The Texas Literary Tradition: Fiction, Folklore, History* (Texas, 1983)

The Transcendentalists / Joel Myerson, ed., *The Transcendentalists: A Review of Research and Criticism* (MLA)

Translation Perspectives / Marilyn Gaddis Rose, ed., *Translation Perspectives: Selected Papers, 1982–1983* (Binghamton, N. Y.: Translation Research and Instruction Program, SUNY Binghamton)

A Usable Past / Paul Mariani, *A Usable Past: Essays on Modern and Contemporary Poetry* (Mass.)

The Uses of Fiction / Douglas Jefferson and Graham Martin, eds., *The Uses of Fiction: Essays on the Modern Novel in Honour of Arnold Kettle* (Milton Keynes, Eng.: Open Univ. Press, 1982)

Die Utopie / Hartmut Heuermann and Bernd-Peter Lange, eds., *Die Utopie in der angloamerikanischen Literatur* (Düsseldorf: Schwann-Bagel)

Women Writers and the City / Susan M. Squier, ed., *Women Writers and the City: Essays in Feminist Literary Criticism* (Tennessee)

Women Writers of the West Coast / Marilyn Yalom, ed., *Women Writers of the West Coast: Speaking of Their Lives and Careers* (Capra, 1983)

Women Writing in America / Blanche H. Gelfant, *Women Writing in America: Voices in Collage* (New England)

Writer in Context / James Nagle, ed., *Ernest Hemingway: The Writer in Context* (Wisconsin)

Periodicals, Annuals, Series

A&E / *Anglistik & Englischunterricht*

AAF / Anglo-American Forum (Peter Lang)

ABC / *American Book Collector*

ADE Bulletin (Assn. of Departments of English)

Aevum

Agenda

AI / *American Imago*

AIV / *Atti del R. Instituto Veneto di Scienze, Lettere ed Arti*

AJES / *Aligarh Journal of English Studies*

AL / *American Literature*

ALR / *American Literary Realism, 1870–1910*

ALS / *American Literary Scholarship*
AmerP / *American Poetry*
AmerS / *American Studies*
AmerSS / *American Studies in Scandinavia*
AmSI / *American Studies International*
Amst / *Amerikastudien*
AN&Q / *American Notes and Queries*
AppalJ / *Appalachian Journal*
APR / *American Poetry Review*
AQ / *American Quarterly*
ArAA / *Arbeiten aus Anglistik und Amerikanistik*
Arbor: Ciencia, Pensamiento y Cultura (Madrid)
Arc / *L'Arc* (Aix-en-Provence)
Arcadia: Zeitschrift für Vergleichende Literaturwissenschaft
ArielE / *Ariel: A Review of International English Literature*
Arnoldian: A Review of Mid-Victorian Culture
ArQ / *Arizona Quarterly*
ASInt / *American Studies International*
ATQ / *American Transcendental Quarterly*
AuLS / *Australian Literary Studies*
BAAAS / *Bulletin of the American Academy of Arts and Sciences*
BALF / *Black American Literature Forum*
BForum / *Book Forum*
Biography: An Interdisciplinary Quarterly
BIS / *Browning Institute Studies*
BJRL / *Bulletin of the John Rylands Univ. Library of Manchester*
Boundary / *Boundary 2*
BSUF / *Ball State Univ. Forum*
BuR / *Bucknell Review*
Callaloo: A Black South Journal of Arts and Letters
CCrit / *Comparative Criticism: A Yearbook*
CE / *College English*
CEA / *CEA Critic*
CentR / *The Centennial Review*
CeS / *Cultura e Scuola*
ChiR / *Chicago Review*
CIEREC / Centre Interuniversitaire d'Etudes et de Recherches sur les expressions contemporaines

CL / *Comparative Literature*
CLAJ / *College Language Assn. Journal*
CLC / *Columbia Library Columns*
CLQ / *Colby Library Quarterly*
CLS / *Comparative Literature Studies*
Clues: A Journal of Detection
CollL / *College Literature*
Comparatist
CompD / *Comparative Drama*
ConL / *Contemporary Literature*
Courier
CQ / *Cambridge Quarterly*
CRAA / Centre de Recherche sur l'Amerique Anglophone
CRCL / *Canadian Review of Comparative Literature*
CRevAS / *Canadian Review of American Studies*
Crit / *Critique: Studies in Modern Fiction*
CritI / *Critical Inquiry*
Criticism: A Quarterly for Literature and the Arts
CritQ / *Critical Quarterly*
CS / *Concord Saunterer*
CVE / *Cahiers Victoriens et Edouardiens*
Dada / *Dada Surrealism*
DeltaES / *Delta: Revue de Centre d'Etudes et de Recherche sur les Ecrivains du Sud aux Etats-Unis* (Montpellier, France)
DGQ / *Dramatist Guild Quarterly*
DicS / *Dickinson Studies*
DLB / Dictionary of Literary Biography (Gale)
DQ / *Denver Quarterly*
DQR / *Dutch Quarterly Review of Anglo-American Letters*
DR / *Dalhousie Review*
Drama (London)
DrN / *Dreiser Newsletter*
EA / *Etudes Anglaises*
EAL / *Early American Literature*
EAS / *Essays in Arts and Science*
EAST / *Englisch-Amerikanische Studien*
ECent / *The Eighteenth Century: Theory and Interpretation*
ECLife / *Eighteenth-Century Life*
EdWN / *Edith Wharton Newsletter*

EEAS / European Assn. for American Studies
EGN / Ellen Glasgow Newsletter
EIC / Essays in Criticism
ELH / English Literary History
ELN / English Language Notes
ELWIU / Essays in Literature (Western Ill. Univ.)
Epoch
ES / English Studies
ESA / English Studies in Africa: A Journal of the Humanities
ESC / English Studies in Canada
ESQ: A Journal of the American Renaissance
EuWN / Eudora Welty Newsletter
Expl / Explicator
Extrapolation
FictI / Fiction International
Field: Contemporary Poetry and Poetics
FR / French Review
FRAN / Facteur Religieux en Amérique du Nord
Frontiers, A Journal of Women Studies
FSt / Feminist Studies
Genre
GPQ / Great Plains Quarterly
GRAAT / Groupe de Recherches Anglo-Américaines de Tours
Granta (Cambridge, Eng.)
GRENA / Groups d' Etudes et de Recherches Nord-Américaines (Aix: Université de Provence)
HemR / Hemingway Review
Hispania
Hispano / Hispanófila
HJ / Higginson Journal
HJR / Henry James Review
HLB / Harvard Library Bulletin
HSE / Hungarian Studies in English
HSN / Hawthorne Society Newsletter
HudR / Hudson Review
IJAS / Indian Journal for American Studies
IR / Iliff Review
JAC / Journal of American Culture (Bowling Green, Ohio)
JAmS / Journal of American Studies
JASAT / Journal of the American Studies Assn. of Texas

JEP / Journal of Evolutionary Psychology
JGE: The Journal of General Education
JHI / Journal of the History of Ideas
JISHS /Journal of the Illinois State Historical Society
JML / Journal of Modern Literature
JNT / Journal of Narrative Technique
JPC / Journal of Popular Culture
KN / Kwartalnik Neofilologiczny (Warsaw)
KR / Kenyon Review
LALR / Latin American Literary Review
LAmer / Letterature d'America
Lang&S / Language and Style
LCUT / Library Chronicle of the Univ. of Texas
LFQ / Literature/Film Quarterly
LGr / Literaturnaya Gruzia (Tbilisi, USSR)
LHRev / Langston Hughes Review
LitR / Literary Review
LitSw / Literatura na Świecie (Warsaw)
LJHum / Lamar Journal of the Humanities
LOS / Literary Onomastics Studies
LPer / Literature in Performance
MarkhamR / Markham Review
M.D.
MD / Modern Drama
Meanjin
MELUS: Journal of the Society for the Study of the Multi-Ethnic Literature of the United States
MFS / Modern Fiction Studies
MHLS / Mid-Hudson Language Studies
MHRev / Malahat Review
Mid-AmerR / Mid-American Review (Bowling Green, Ohio)
MiltonQ / Milton Quarterly
MissFR / Mississippi Folklore Register
MissR / Missouri Review
MissRev / Mississippi Review
MLN / Modern Language Notes
MLQ / Modern Language Quarterly
MLS / Modern Language Studies
MMisc / Midwestern Miscellany
ModA / Modern Age

Mosaic: A Journal for the Inter-disciplinary Study of Literature
MP / *Modern Philology*
MQ / *Midwest Quarterly*
MQR / *Michigan Quarterly Review*
MR / *Massachusetts Review*
MSE / *Massachusetts Studies in English*
MSEx / *Melville Society Extracts*
MSpr / *Moderna Språk*
MTJ / *Mark Twain Journal*
N&Q / *Notes and Queries*
NCarF / *North Carolina Folklore Journal*
NCF / *Nineteenth-Century Fiction*
NConL / *Notes on Contemporary Literature*
NDQ / *North Dakota Quarterly*
Neophil / *Neophilologus*
NEQ / *New England Quarterly*
New Criterion (New York)
NewRep / *New Republic*
NHJ / *Nathaniel Hawthorne Journal*
NMW / *Notes on Mississippi Writers*
NOR / *New Orleans Review*
Novel: A Forum on Fiction
NYRB / *New York Review of Books*
NYTBR / *New York Times Book Review*
Obsidian: Black Literature in Review
OhR / *Ohio Review*
ON / *The Old Northwest*
P&L / *Philosophy and Literature*
PAAS / *Proceedings of the American Antiquarian Society*
Paideuma: A Journal Devoted to Ezra Pound Scholarship
ParisR / *Paris Review*
PCL / *Perspectives on Contemporary Literature*
PCP / *Pacific Coast Philology*
PerfAJ / *Performing Arts Journal*
Phylon: The Atlanta University Review of Race and Culture
PLL / *Papers on Language and Literature*
Ploughshares
PMHS / *Proceedings of the Massachusetts Historical Society*
PMLA: *Publications of the Modern Language Assn.*

PMPA / *Publications of the Missouri Philological Assn.*
PNotes / *Pynchon Notes*
PoeS / *Poe Studies*
Poesis: A Journal of Criticism
Poétique: Revue de Théorie et d'Analyse Littéraires
Prospects: An Annual Journal of American Cultural Studies
Proteus (Shippensburg, Pa.)
PRR / *Journal of Pre-Raphaelite Studies*
PrS / *Prairie Schooner*
PSt / *Prose Studies*
QL / *La Quinzaine Littéraire*
QW / *Quarterly West*
RaJAH / *Rackham Journal of the Arts and Humanities*
RANAM / *Recherches Anglaises et Américaines*
Raritan, A Quarterly Review
RCEH / *Revista Canadiense de Estudies Hispanicos*
RCF / *The Review of Contemporary Fiction*
REAL / *Re: Artes Liberales*
Renascence: Essays on Value in Literature
Rendezvous
RFEA / *Revue Française d'Etudes Américaines* (Paris)
RLMC / *Rivista di Letterature Moderne e Comparate*
RS / *Research Studies* (Pullman, Wash.)
RSA / *Rivista di Studi Anglo-Americani*
SA / *Studi Americani* (Rome)
SAF / *Studies in American Fiction*
Sage: A Scholarly Journal on Black Women (Atlanta)
Sagetrieb: A Journal Devoted to Poets in the Pound–H. D.–Williams Tradition
SALit / *Chu-Shikoku Studies in American Literature*
Salmagundi
Samtiden: Tidsskrift for Politikk, Litteratur og Samfunnsspørsmål
SAP / *Studia Anglica Posnaniensia*
SAQ / *South Atlantic Quarterly*

SAR / *Studies in the American Renaissance*

SB / *Studies in Bibliography*

SCB / *South Central Bulletin*

SCCEA / *Round Table of the South Central College English Assn.* (Lafayette, La.)

SCR / *South Carolina Review*

SECC / *Studies in Eighteenth-Century Culture*

SELit / *Studies in English Literature* (Tokyo)

SHR / *Southern Humanities Review*

Signs: *Journal of Women in Culture and Society*

SIR / *Studies in Romanticism*

SLitI / *Studies in the Literary Imagination*

SLJ / *Southern Literary Journal*

SN / *Studia Neophilologica*

SNNTS / *Studies in the Novel* (Denton, Texas)

SoAR / *South Atlantic Review*

SoQ / *Southern Quarterly*

SoR / *Southern Review*

SoSt / *Southern Studies*

Soundings: *An Interdisciplinary Journal*

Southern Exposure (Durham, N. C.)

SR / *Sewanee Review*

SSEng / *Sydney Studies in English*

SSF / *Studies in Short Fiction*

StAH / *Studies in American Humor* Standpunte

StTCL / *Studies in Twentieth Century Literature*

StuMed / *Studies in Medievalism* (Oxford, Ohio)

Style

SubStance: *A Review of Theory and Literary Criticism*

Sulfur

SWR / *Southwest Review*

TCL / *Twentieth-Century Literature*

TCW / *Turn-of-the-Century Women*

TDR / *Drama Review*

TEAS / *Twayne's English Authors Series*

Thalia: *Studies in Literary Humor* Thought

ThS / *Theatre Survey*

ThSw / *Theatre Southwest*

TJ / *Theatre Journal*

TLS / *Times Literary Supplement*

TriQ / *TriQuarterly*

TSLL / *Texas Studies in Literature and Language*

TUSAS / Twayne United States Authors Series

TWA / *Transactions of the Wisconsin Academy of Sciences, Arts, and Letters*

TWN / *Thomas Wolfe Newsletter*

UDR / *University of Dayton Review*

UES / *Unisa English Studies* (Pretoria, S. Africa)

UMSE / *University of Mississippi Studies in English*

UTQ / *University of Toronto Quarterly*

VisC / *Visions Critiques* (Paris)

VLU / *Vestnik Leningradskogo Universiteta*

VMHB / *Virginia Magazine of History and Biography*

VMU / *Vestnik Moskovskogo Universiteta, Serija 9 Filologija*

VP / *Victorian Poetry*

VQR / *Virginia Quarterly Review*

WAL / *Western American Literature*

WCPMNewsl / *Willa Cather Pioneer Memorial Newsletter*

WE / *Winesburg Eagle: The Official Publication of the Sherwood Anderson Society*

WHR / *Western Humanities Review*

WiF / *William Faulkner: Materials, Studies, and Criticism* (Tokyo)

WMQ / *William and Mary Quarterly*

WQ / *Wilson Quarterly*

WS / *Women's Studies*

WSJour / *Wallace Stevens Journal*

WVUPP / *West Virginia Univ. Philological Papers*

WWR / *Walt Whitman Quarterly Review*

WWS / *Western Writers Series* (Boise, Idaho)

XUS / *Xavier Review* (formerly *Xavier Univ. Studies*)

Yeats: *An Annual Publication of Critical and Textual Studies*

YER / *Yeats Eliot Review*

YES / *Yearbook of English Studies*

YR / *Yale Review*

Publishers

ALA / Chicago: American Library
Assn.

Alabama / University: Univ. of
Alabama Press

Alberta / Edmonton: Univ. of
Alberta Press

Archon / Hamden, Conn: Archon
Books

Arte Publico / Houston, Tex.: Arte
Publico Press

Associated Faculty Press (Port
Washington, N. Y.)

Barnes and Noble (Totowa, N. J.)

Basic Books (New York)

Basil Blackwell (New York)

Beacon / Boston: Beacon Press

Belknap / Cambridge, Mass.: Belknap
Press of Harvard Univ. Press

Bolchazy-Carducci (Chicago)

Borgo / San Bernardino, Calif.:
Borgo Press

Bowling Green / Bowling Green, Ohio:
Bowling Green State Univ., Popular
Press

Bruccoli Clark (Columbia, S. C.)

Bucknell / Lewisburg, Pa.: Bucknell
University Press

Calif. / Berkeley: Univ. of California
Press

Cambridge / Cambridge and New
York: Cambridge Univ. Press

Campus / Frankfurt: Campus Verlag

Capra / Santa Barbara, Calif.: Capra
Press

Carl Winter (Heidelberg)

Chicago / Chicago: Univ. of Chicago
Press

Clarendon / Oxford: Clarendon Press

Columbia / New York: Columbia
Univ. Press

Cordelia / Santa Barbara, Calif.:
Cordelia Editions

Cornell / Ithaca, N. Y.: Cornell Univ.
Press

Cowley / Cambridge, Mass.: Cowley
Publications

Crown / New York: Crown Publishers

Delaware / Newark: Univ. of
Delaware Press

Doubleday / New York: Doubleday
and Co.

Drama Book Publishers (New York)

Duke / Durham, N. C.: Duke Univ.
Press

Dutton / New York: E. P. Dutton

Ecco / New York: Ecco Press

Faber / Winchester, Mass.: Faber &
Faber

Fairleigh Dickinson / Madison, N. J.:
Fairleigh Dickinson Univ. Press

Farrar / New York: Farrar, Straus and
Giroux

Florida / Gainesville: Univ. Presses
of Florida

Florida State / Tallahassee: Florida
State Univ. Press

Fordham / Bronx, N. Y.: Fordham
Univ. Press

French Forum / Lexington, Ky.:
French Forum Publications

Gale / Detroit: Gale Research Co.

Garland / New York: Garland
Publishing Co.

Georgia / Athens: Univ. of Georgia
Press

Greenwood / Westport, Conn.:
Greenwood Press

Grove / New York: Grove Press

Hall / Boston: G. K. Hall & Co.

Hamish Hamilton (London)

Harcourt / New York: Harcourt Brace
Jovanovich

Harper / New York: Harper and Row

Harvard / Cambridge, Mass.: Harvard
Univ. Press

Holmes and Meier / New York:
Holmes and Meier Publishers

Holt Rinehart / New York: Holt, Rinehart & Winston

Hopkins / Baltimore: Johns Hopkins
Univ. Press

Houghton Mifflin / Boston: Houghton
Mifflin Co.

Humanities / Atlantic Highlands,
N. J.: Humanities Press

Illinois / Urbana: Univ. of Illinois
Press

Indiana / Bloomington: Indiana Univ.
Press

Int'l. / New York: International
Universities Press

Iowa / Iowa City: Univ. of Iowa Press

Kent State / Kent, Ohio: Kent State Univ. Press

Kentucky / Lexington: Univ. Press of Kentucky

Knopf / New York: Alfred A. Knopf

Lang / Frankfurt: Peter Lang

Library of America (New York)

Little, Brown / Boston: Little, Brown & Co.

LSU / Baton Rouge: Louisiana State Univ. Press

Lyle Stuart (Secaucus, N. J.)

Macmillan (New York)

McFarland / Jefferson, N. C.: McFarland & Co.

McGraw-Hill (New York)

Majority Press (Dover, Mass.)

Mass. / Amherst: Univ. of Massachusetts Press

Methuen (London)

Michigan / Ann Arbor: Univ. of Michigan Press

Minnesota / Minneapolis: Univ. of Minnesota Press

Miss. / Jackson: Univ. Press of Mississippi

Missouri / Columbia: Univ. of Missouri Press

MLA / New York: Modern Language Assn.

Morrow / New York: William Morrow & Co.

Mysterious Press (New York)

Narr / Tübingen: Gunter Narr

N. C. / Chapel Hill: Univ. of North Carolina Press

Nebraska / Lincoln: Univ. of Nebraska Press

Nelson-Hall (Chicago)

Nevada / Reno: Univ. of Nevada Press

New Directions / New York: New Directions Publishing Corp.

New England / Hanover, N. H.: Univ. Press of New England

N. Mex. / Albuquerque: Univ. of New Mexico Press

Nordland / Sioux Falls, S. D.: Nordland Heritage Foundation

Northeastern / Boston: Northeastern Univ. Press

North Point / San Francisco: North Point Press

Northwestern / Evanston, Ill.: Northwestern Univ. Press

Norton / New York: W. W. Norton & Co.

NYU / New York: New York Univ. Press

Ohio / Athens: Ohio Univ. Press

Ohio State / Columbus: Ohio State Univ. Press

Orenda / Berkeley, Calif.: Orenda Publishing / Unity Press

Oxford / New York: Oxford Univ. Press

Paget / Santa Barbara, Calif.: Paget Press

Pantheon / New York: Pantheon Books

Penn. / Philadelphia: Univ. of Pennsylvania Press

Penn. State / University Park: Pennsylvania State Univ. Press

Performing Arts / Beverly Hills, Calif.: Performing Arts Network

Performing Arts / New York: Performing Arts Journal Publications

Permanent Press (Sag Harbor, N. Y.)

Peter Lang / New York: Peter Lang Publishing Co.

Philos. Lib. / New York: Philosophical Library

Pilgrim Press (New York)

Pittsburgh / Pittsburgh, Pa.: Univ. of Pittsburgh Press

Pluto Press (London)

Praeger / New York: Praeger Publishers

Prentice-Hall / Englewood Cliffs, N. J.: Prentice-Hall

Princeton / Princeton, N. J.: Princeton Univ. Press

Purdue / West Lafayette, Ind.: Purdue Univ. Press

Putnam's / New York: G. P. Putnam's Sons

Random House (New York)

Routledge / London: Routledge and Kegan Paul

Rutgers / New Brunswick, N. J.: Rutgers Univ. Press

St. Martin's / New York: St. Martin's Press

S. C. / Columbia: Univ. of South Carolina Press

Scarecrow / Metuchen, N. J.:
  Scarecrow Press
Scholars Press (Chico, Calif.)
Scribner's / New York: Charles
  Scribner's Sons
Scripta Humanistica (Potomac, Md.)
Secker & Warburg / London: Secker
  and Warburg
Sherwood Sugden (Baton Rouge, La.)
So. Ill. / Carbondale: Southern
  Illinois Univ. Press
Square Circle / Corte Madera, Calif.:
  Square Circle Press
SUNY / Albany, N. Y.: State Univ. of
  New York Press
Susquehanna / Cranbury, N. J.:
  Susquehanna Univ. Press
Swallow / Athens, Ohio: Swallow Press
Syracuse / Syracuse, N. Y.: Syracuse
  Univ. Press
TCG / New York: Theatre
  Communications Group
Temple / Philadelphia: Temple
  Univ. Press
Tenn. / Knoxville: Univ. of Tennessee
  Press

Texas / Austin: Univ. of Texas Press
Twayne / Boston: Twayne Publishers
  (G. K. Hall & Co.)
UMI / Ann Arbor, Mich.: University
  Microfilms International
UMI Research Press / Ann Arbor,
  Mich.: UMI Research Press
Ungar / New York: Frederick Ungar
  Publishing Co.
Universe / New York: Universe Books
Univ. Press / Lanham, Md.: Univ.
  Press of America
Viking / New York: Viking Press
Virginia / Charlottesville: Univ. Press
  of Virginia
Vision / London: Vision Press
Wayne State / Detroit: Wayne State
  Univ. Press
Wesleyan / Middletown, Conn.:
  Wesleyan Univ. Press
Whitston / Troy, N. Y.: Whitston
  Publishing Co.
Wis. / Madison: Univ. of Wisconsin
  Press
Yale / New Haven, Conn.: Yale Univ.
  Press

Part I

1. Emerson, Thoreau, and Transcendentalism

Philip F. Gura

Keeping in mind Thoreau's witty comment that "some circumstantial evidence is very strong, as when you find a trout in the milk," it is clear that 1984 was rewarding for those interested in Emerson, Thoreau, and transcendentalism. The publication of *The Transcendentalists: A Review of Research and Criticism* by the Modern Language Association in its centennial year is cause enough for celebration; but in fact there appeared many other significant books and essays, items varied enough to convince both literary historians and critical theorists that antebellum Concord still can be the center of one's intellectual universe.

By my tally, there were four important book-length studies of Emerson and two of Thoreau, in addition to the appearance of the second volume of the latter's *Journal* in the Princeton edition. Equally significant, this year saw the third volume (of a projected five) of Margaret Fuller's complete correspondence, as well as a splendid one-volume selection of Elizabeth Palmer Peabody's letters. Lawrence Buell contributed a comprehensive review-essay, a model of its kind, on the last decade of Emerson scholarship; and Thoreau was particularly well served by Leonard Neufeldt's essay on his political language and ideology, a provocative effort which proves how valuable it is to know what words meant to their user, a lesson now too infrequently impressed upon graduate students.

i. Bibliographies, Edited Texts, General Studies

The event of the year, and arguably the single most important contribution to the study of the subject since Perry Miller's *The Transcendentalists: An Anthology* (1950), was the appearance of *The Transcendentalists: A Review of Research and Criticism* (MLA; hereafter referred to without subtitle) under the general editorship of Joel Myerson. Myerson, best likened to a queen bee at the swarming center of any and all projects Transcendental, marshaled a highly capable group of contributors and elicited judicious and thorough work from them all. The volume begins with Lawrence Buell's 36-page essay, "The Transcendentalist Movement," in which he reviews bibliographies, early histories, reminiscences, modern views of the subject from various critical and ideological perspectives, particular aspects of the movement (such as its adherents' interest in religious and social reform, and their aesthetic theory), source studies, and the movement's legacy in American life and thought: no small order! But as becomes the author of so seminal a work as *Literary Transcendentalism* (1973), Buell carries the occasion so completely that this essay now becomes the starting point for any serious consideration of its subject. His essay is followed by Myerson's "Transcendentalism: The Times," a solid treatment of the movement within its historical context; Conrad Wright's "Unitarianism and Transcendentalism," a summary of the movement's relationship to 19th-century American Christianity; Carol Johnston's "Transcendentalist Communities," a thorough review of the extensive literature generated by Brook Farm and Fruitlands; and Donald F. Warders's "Transcendentalist Periodicals," which treats not only such obvious journals as the *Dial* and *Western Messenger* but also the *Present* and the *Radical*, among others.

This section is followed by essays on 28 individuals identifiable as the core participants in the Transcendentalist movement. These efforts range from a two-page piece on Charles King Newcomb (by Myerson) to a 32-page essay on Emerson (by Robert E. Burkholder and Myerson). Each essay includes discussion, where applicable, of bibliographies, manuscripts, editions, biography, criticism, and suggestions for further research. Because of space restrictions in this essay, I can only highlight this part of the book, but for the benefit of future researchers I also list all the essays and their authors. Frederick C. Dahlstrand, author of the definitive life of Amos Bronson Alcott, provides a handle for the often abstruse thought of Emerson's "tedious Archangel." Robert N. Hudspeth, editor of Margaret Fuller's letters, judiciously guides us through the literature on this significant woman; he is particularly helpful in his discussion of the various ways her biography has been written, given her multifaceted personality. Burkholder and Myerson, faced with the most difficult task in this section, somehow manage to confine their slippery Proteus long enough for us to comprehend why Emerson was so much to so many different people; their treatment of the criticism that has accumulated around his work is especially valuable. Michael Meyer's piece on Thoreau derives from his recent work as coeditor of *The New Thoreau Handbook* (1980); it is a fine distillation of the indispensable larger work. David Robinson, one of the best of the new generation of interpreters of the relationship between transcendentalism and Unitarianism, writes on Christopher Pearse Cranch and Jones Very, two of the movement's more unusual personalities; he makes one want to pay more attention to these polar opposites—an extrovert and an introvert—to learn how transcendentalism could appeal to people of such different dispositions.

But these essays are only the beginning. Who remembers Charles Timothy Brooks, author of the not-yet-immortal *Aquidneck* (1848) and other poetry, perhaps the most assiduous translator of German literature among the Transcendentalists? Read Elizabeth McKinsey's piece herein. Or Samuel Johnson? Not *the* Samuel Johnson, nor even the American Samuel Johnson who defected from Yale to the bosom of the Episcopal church in 1722 and later became president of King's (Columbia) College, but the Transcendentalist Samuel Johnson who authored books on India, China, and Persia in a series on *Oriental Religions and Their Relation to Universal Religion,* and who believed that transcendentalism provided the faith that would unify Eastern and Western religious thought. Read Roger C. Mueller's essay. And what of John Sullivan Dwight, America's first professional music critic? William G. Heath discusses that aspect of his career as well as his association with Brook Farm. This book thus is a delight to leaf through, if only to discover such fascinating minor players on transcendentalism's main stage. Others who make appearances of varying length are Cyrus Bartol (Heath), William Ellery Channing II (Francis B. Dedmond), William Henry Channing (McKinsey), James Freeman Clarke (Leonard Neufeldt), Moncure Daniel Conway (Burkholder), Convers Francis (Guy R. Woodall), Octavius Brooks Frothingham (J. Wade Carruthers), Frederic Henry Hedge (Neufeldt), Thomas Wentworth Higginson (Howard N. Meyer), Sylvester Judd (Dedmond), Charles Lane (Myerson), Theodore Parker (Gary L. Collinson), Elizabeth Palmer Peabody (Margaret Neussendorfer), George Ripley (Charles Crowe), Sarah Dana Ripley (Crowe), Franklin Benjamin Sanborn (Burkholder), John Weiss (Burkholder), and Charles Stearns Wheeler (Myerson).

The third section of the volume, "The Contemporary Reaction," discusses (as Myerson puts it in the preface) those "who influenced, were influenced by, or reacted against the Transcendentalists." The approach in these briefer essays is a bit different, particularly for such prominent writers as Hawthorne or Melville, who have received extensive bibliographic treatment elsewhere; the emphasis quite rightly falls on those parts of their writings or careers which relate in some way to the Transcendentalist movement. Among this group are George William Curtis (W. Gordon Milne), Emily Dickinson (Paul J. Ferlazzo), Hawthorne (Myerson), James Russell Lowell (Thomas Wortham), Melville (Brian Higgins), Poe (Ottavio M. Casale), and Whitman (Jerome Loving). We also find those who at one time or another were fellow-travelers on the movement's celestial railroad. Thus, for example, Leonard Gilhooley treats Orestes Brownson, who by the mid-1840s already was on the track that eventually led him to the bosom of the Roman Catholic church. As befits a historian of the Unitarian movement, David Robinson writes on William Ellery Channing and offers a detailed look at how this important clergyman has been treated by those interested in America's literary, cultural, and religious history. Finally, those two harbingers of the Transcendentalist movement, James Marsh and Sampson Reed, receive their due in essays by Douglas McCreary Greenwood and Elizabeth A. Meese, respectively. Anyone interested in the former will want to pencil in a reference to Peter C. Carafiol's *Transcendent Reason* (1982), the first book-length treatment of Marsh; and I wish that Meese had provided more guidance through the mystery of Swedenborgian publications for those interested in Reed. All in all, though, this section is as solid as the previous one is definitive.

This book concludes with a 118-page bibliography, a fitting capstone to this important project. Now anyone who wishes to "know" transcendentalism as well as Thoreau knew beans can turn to this reference source, which lists all the secondary literature on transcendentalism and its main figures, as well as the requisite editions of the latter's works. Myerson and his coworkers have painstakingly provided the foundation for what we long have needed, a full-scale history of the movement in all its phases, something akin to Perry Miller's work on Puritanism and which could be called *The New England Mind: Transcendentalism*. In the meantime, we all should heartily applaud *The Transcendentalists*. Given the kind of book it is, the prose is eminently readable, the editing meticulous, the typography a pleasure, the knowledge herein encapsulated a marvel. The book is quite simply invaluable.

Two other essays deserve mention at this point. Lawrence Buell's "The Emerson Industry in the 1980s: A Survey of Trends and Achievements" (*ESQ* 30:117–36) is, as I already have mentioned, a first-rate piece of work. Buell covers textual scholarship, biographical studies, "The De-Transcendentalization of the Emerson Image," "Emerson and the Ideology of Gender," and "Emerson the (Re)Writer." Buell is equally at home with the most avant-garde theoretical methodology as well as with more traditional types of scholarship, and his evaluations are judicious and apt, not at all tainted by bias. This essay is a must for anyone trying to find his way through the many significant books and essays that marked one of the most productive decades of Emerson scholarship. William J. Scheick's "Emerson the Poet: A Twenty-Year Retrospective" (*AmerP* 1, iii:2–19) is more limited in scope but still well worth one's time. Noting that previous scholars of Emerson's verse have struggled to appreciate its aesthetic dimensions even as they acknowledge the problems Emerson had in working in this form, Scheick systematically discusses what critics of the last two decades have said about Emerson's imagery, structure, and voice in the poetry. He then closely reads "Blight" and argues that what he sees therein is indicative of most of Emerson's verse. Specifically, "particular imagery gives way to general abstraction, the linear structure eventuates in the poet's reach for an abstract truth, and the poetic voice tends to arrive at a 'frozen' moment which evinces less the stillpoint of truth than the failure of language."

The most important edition to appear was the second volume of Thoreau's *Journal* in the Princeton series, edited by Robert Sattelmeyer; this volume includes much material not included in the 1906 "Walden" edition of Thoreau's works—most notably, the April–December 1846 notebook now in the Berg Collection of the New York Public Library. Covering the years 1842–48, including the time Thoreau spent at Walden Pond, as well as when he was working on a first draft of *Walden* and completing *A Week*, this edition also restores much material that went into these two books but which had not been published by Bradford Torrey and Francis H. Allen in the 1906 *Journal* because the passages already had appeared in his published works. In his "Historical Introduction" Sattelmeyer nicely places the volume in the context of Thoreau's literary career, and in the "Textual Introduction" explains the difficulty of establishing a text so heavily revised, whether on the first level of manuscript or upon later copying of it. As with the earlier volume of the *Journal* already published in this edition, in most cases only the first level of composition in the document is reproduced, through the rationale that "Thoreau's later revisions are actually preliminary versions of his literary works and are thus no longer related to the Journal itself." The exception is pp. 3–116 in this volume, those sections of the so-called Long Book which are transcriptions from the earlier journals of passages for *A Week*, around which Thoreau left space so that he might add to them. As Sattelmeyer puts it, "In that section of the Journal in which Thoreau was compiling material for *A Week*, all his compilation is reproduced," but not later revisions which went beyond such expansion. Such decisions clearly will not please all scholars all of the time, but we still have to be grateful to the editors of this edition for their arduous labors in establishing a more complete text than we hitherto have known.

While on the subject of the *Journal*, I dutifully note that the Peregrine Smith publishing company has reprinted the 14-volume 1906 edition in paperback; given how long it will be before the Princeton edition is complete, Thoreau scholars will find this set a good investment. A 15th volume to the set contains Ray Angelo's "Botanical Index to the Journal of Henry David Thoreau," an exhaustive and invaluable list which provides the English and Latin names to every botanical reference in the journals. Angelo also describes "Thoreau as Botanist" in the same volume. Both of these items also appear as volume 15 of the *Thoreau Quarterly* (dated 1983 but appearing in 1984). Three other items may be of interest to Thoreauvians. Francis B. Dedmond's "Thoreau as Seen by an Admiring Friend: A New View" (*AL* 53:331–43) treats James Watson Spooner of Plymouth, fragments of whose previously unpublished journal of the 1850s speak to his friendship with Thoreau when the latter visited the South Shore for lectures, and also record Spooner's subsequent visit to Concord. Edmund A. Schofield and Thomas Blanding present "E. Harlow Russell's Reminiscences of Thoreau" (*CS* 17, ii:6–14); Harlow's lecture, written in 1891, describes his and Thoreau's sole meeting in Worcester in 1860 and also provides an estimate of his character. Schofield adds a lengthy essay on Russell, "Time Recovering Itself: E. Harlow Russell's Thirty Years (and More) with

Henry D. Thoreau" (*CS* 17, ii:14–47). Though Russell, a school-teacher, met Thoreau only once, he is important because of his close friendship with H. G. O. Blake, who left all of Thoreau's manuscripts to him in 1898; Russell was instrumental in getting the journals published by Torrey and Allen in 1906.

The only significant primary material on Emerson was Elizabeth Maxfield-Miller's "Elizabeth of Concord: Selected Letters of Elizabeth Sherman Hoar to the Emerson Family, and the Emerson Circle (Part One)" (*SAR*, pp. 229–98), a lengthy biographical essay of this fiancée of Charles Chauncy Emerson, who died before they could be wed. An intimate friend of Margaret Fuller and neighbor of the Thoreaus, Elizabeth Hoar always was close to the center of Concord's intellectual life. In this, the first of three scheduled installments, Maxfield-Miller establishes the chronology of Hoar's life and gives a calendar of all her known letters. The correspondence itself will be published later.

Robert N. Hudspeth continued his important editorial labors with publication of *The Letters of Margaret Fuller, Volume III: 1842–1844* (Cornell). Covering the years when she left the editorship of the *Dial*, traveled to the West, wrote both *Summer on the Lakes* and *Woman in the Nineteenth Century*, and finally moved to New York to become a book reviewer for Horace Greeley's *New-York Daily Tribune*, this volume displays Fuller taking complete charge of her life, making decision after decision which decreased her dependence on the Concord circle. As in the first two volumes, Hudspeth's annotations, at the end of each letter, are succinct yet informative. Surely this edition, when completed, will rival Ralph Rusk's edition of Emerson's letters in importance. Another scholar who has done much for Fuller's reputation in the last decade is Joel Myerson, whose "Supplement to *Margaret Fuller: An Annotated Secondary Bibliography*" (*SAR*, pp. 331–86) updates his 1977 volume through 1982, adding 108 new entries published between 1844 and 1975, and 143 more from 1975 and 1982, the latter testimony to Fuller's resurrection as an important cultural figure. In *Nineteenth-Century Literary Criticism, Vol. 5* (Gale; pp. 153–74) the editors print excerpts "from the first published critical appraisals to current evaluations" of Fuller's works. (They do the same for Thoreau's in volume 7 [pp. 346–414].)

More importantly, this new interest in women Transcendentalists has led to further study of Elizabeth Palmer Peabody, too long in Fuller's shadow. Bruce A. Ronda has published *Letters of Elizabeth Palmer Peabody: American Renaissance Woman* (Wesleyan), a selection of 154 items from her correspondence from 1820 to 1890, letters that range from the period of her schoolteaching days with Bronson Alcott at the Temple School, to her ownership of the West Street bookstore, her discovery of Froebel and her subsequent interest in the Kindergarten movement, to her attendance at the Concord School of Philosophy. It is not too much to claim that Peabody's life constitutes an inner history of 19th-century New England liberalism, and Ronda has done a great service by publishing this tantalizing volume which should send other scholars back to the archives to read more. In addition to his informative footnotes, he also provides a lengthy biographical introduction, probably the best single modern essay on Peabody in relation to her times. Margaret Neussendorfer, who is preparing Peabody's biography, added to Ronda's selection by publishing "Elizabeth Palmer Peabody to William Wordsworth: Eight Letters, 1825–1845" (*SAR*, pp. 181–212).

Those interested in the theological dimension of Transcendental reform should turn to Helen R. Deese's "Selected Sermons of Jones Very" (*SAR*, pp. 1–78), in which she prints 11 sermons and a calendar of Very's preaching engagements. In addition, she has written a solid introduction in which she treats the content and style of his sermons as well as his ministerial career. It may surprise some, for example, to learn that Very's "effective years" did not end in 1840, for between then and the Civil War he remained a committed Unitarian preacher whose 100 extant manuscript sermons display him solidly within the tradition of Unitarian pietism. Deese also has given us "Unpublished and Uncollected Poems of Jones Very" (*ESQ* 30:154–62), in which she surveys and criticizes previous editions of his poems and then gives a description and sampling of those that remain uncollected, particularly the verse that appeared in local newspapers and in religious periodicals, as well as unprinted verse in several major libraries.

In "An Annotated List of Contributors to the *Western Messenger*" (*SAR*, pp. 93–180), Robert D. Habich provides a valuable reference tool by listing the titles of all contributions with their authors (as can best be ascertained); there is as well an alphabetical list of the contributors with brief biographical information. Habich also published "The 'Spiral Ascending Path' of William Henry Channing: An Autobiographical Letter" (*ESQ* 30:22–26), a missive which Channing

sent to O. B. Frothingham in 1882 but which the latter did not publish in his biography of Channing, presumably because it was "too
personal" a document. The letter offers a vivid description of the
three spiritual crises that marked its author's life. Stephen Garrison
and Joel Myerson have edited 16 of "Elizabeth Curson's Letters
from Brook Farm" (*RALS* 12:1–28). These epistles, to her mother
and sister, offer good descriptions of the daily round of affairs at the
farm in the period 1845–47; unfortunately, Curson has little to say
about the adoption of Fourierism or the constantly escalating financial crisis in those years. Finally, in "Theodore Parker and the
Unitarian Controversy in 1837" (*ESQ* 30:211–19), Gary Collinson
reprints Parker's first known polemic against Unitarianism. The 4
November 1837 issue of the *Christian Register* carried Parker's "Reasons Why a Clergyman Should Not Study the Scriptures Carefully
and Critically," a sarcastic piece which ridiculed ministers for not
accepting the Higher Criticism. Antedating Emerson's "Divinity
School Address" by a few months, the dialogue indicates the kind of
mounting criticism faced by conservative Unitarians at the time
the Transcendentalist movement was emerging.

There was one important general study published this year. In
his "Transcendentalism and Urbanism: Concord, Boston, and the
Wider World" (*JAmS* 18:361–81) Robert A. Gross argues that the
heyday of transcendentalism coincided with the time when Concord
became a *bona fide* suburb to Boston; that is, a place away from an
urban environment to which people were both attracted and repelled, and from which they could make periodic forays into the
city without having to accept it as a home. Gross sees Emerson as
the major articulator of this profoundly middle-class and capitalist
suburban vision, and argues that his example was typical of the
Transcendentalists' response to urbanism—they embraced the city
while evading it, and assisted in the consolidation of middle-class
culture even as they attacked it.

ii. Emerson

Most of the attention to Emerson came in the form of book-length
studies, though there were a few first-rate essays. John McAleer, un-
daunted by Gay Wilson Allen's *Waldo Emerson* (1981), provided a
mammoth biography, *Ralph Waldo Emerson: Days of Encounter*
(Little, Brown). Thankfully, his is a different enough book that the

two works need not compete for space on one's shelf. Allen still will provide us with the strict chronology of Emerson's life, while Mc-Aleer offers a portrait that is structured around "those 'days of encounter' which constituted for [Emerson] spiritual, ethical, intellectual, ideological, emotional, or physical crises advancing the progress of the soul." In most cases this methodology yields graceful and informative vignettes—the book has 80 chapters—of people and events that shaped the life and work of Emerson as we now know them. Put another way, McAleer works in mosaic-like fashion, his bits of colored glass such people as Harriet Martineau, Convers Francis, or Fredrika Bremer, and such occurrences as "The Cherokee Expulsion," "The Waterville Oration," or "The Burns Centennial." Assembled within the frame of Emerson's life, they do indeed combine to make a new portrait of Emerson which derives color, tone, and intensity as much from their own juxtaposition as from each one's relation to the whole. McAleer's is a refreshing biographical style.

The most challenging book on Emerson was Julie Ellison's *Emerson's Romantic Style* (Princeton), in which she argues that Emerson's self-confidence as a writer came only when he realized his power as a reader or interpreter of texts. Grounding her argument in the recent scholarship that has linked the Higher Criticism of the Bible to both English and American romanticism, Ellison demonstrates, from early journal entries through the great essays, Emerson's growing awareness that it was the responding reader and not the text's authority that constituted the true source of power in interpretation of any literature. Discussing at length the influence on Emerson's thought and style of the study of comparative religion, notions of the sublime, and the aesthetics and psychology of irony, she also argues that Emerson's development from timid student to powerful critic typified that of all writers of nonfiction prose in the Romantic period, particularly Carlyle, Coleridge, and Schlegel. Most pleasing is Ellison's sure grasp of Emerson's intellectual context, so that, while her writing clearly reflects training and interest in contemporary critical theory (particularly as articulated by Harold Bloom), she is never in danger of forgetting that she has before her a real text that was assembled at an ascertainable point in time. Blessedly, there is none of what one witty reviewer has called "the new ignorance" that marks the work of some theorists who don't know their history.

Bloom's influence is more evident in two essays of Julie Ellison closely related to her book. In her piece on "Aggressive Allegory" (*Raritan* 3:100–115), which unfortunately is a bit more jargon-laden than her book, she argues that Emerson's prose demonstrates the aggressive potential of the allegorical mode as it has been described, most recently, by Bloom and Paul de Man, and thus also is characterized more by the oppositions within it than by its essence. In "The Laws of Ice: Emerson's Irony and 'The Comic' " (*ESQ* 30:73–82), she continues this mode of analysis, noting that for Emerson the comic always subverts critical energy and thus becomes another form of the aggressive thought so common in his writing. In his essays, Ellison observes, laughter and humor have to do primarily with the dichotomy of authority and freedom, as well as with self-control and self-assertion, and as such are profoundly disjunctive forces. She locates in his "comic" moments the times when humor, violence, and the physical body are most frequently conjoined; irony allows for transition from these, either for its own sake or to suggest the redemptive power of the Reason. Thus, far from being harmless, irony is a critical mode that introduces conflict into Emerson's prose, as it does, she again stresses, in that of the European Romantics.

In *Emerson's Demanding Optimism* (LSU), Gertrude Hughes challenges the commonly accepted argument that as Emerson matured, the ebullience of his early years was eclipsed by a somber, more realistic mood, his voice in turn becoming more skeptical or ironic. Reversing our expectations and beginning with *The Conduct of Life*, she leads us backward in Emerson's work to *Nature*, pointing out that the philosophical tone we find in the later work was in fact present throughout his career. What most readers have overlooked, she claims, is that from *Nature* on, Emerson's frequent affirmations functioned not to reassure but to challenge himself and his audience; the promises he offers do not comfort but rather make demands on us. Thus it is the cost of one's faith, the human toll it exacts and which the strong individual knows he must pay—as Emerson did through the loss of his first wife and his son—that signals its true vitality. With this in mind, Hughes locates two complementary voices in the essays, one affirming, the other confirming, with the latter revealing the true tone of the former. But despite such insights, this study finally lacks the consistent novelty that makes Ellison's work so provocative. In Hughes's book, once the cards are on the table (so to speak), we know how the rest of the hand will be played. This is probably why her chapter on *The Conduct of Life*, coming as it does so early in the study, strikes me as the most rewarding.

Robert J. Loewenberg's *An American Idol: Emerson and the "Jewish Idea"* (Univ. Press) offers a critique of liberalism in part through a re-evaluation of Emerson's notions of freedom and equality, ones which he regards as atheistic and antisemitic. "By independence," Loewenberg writes, Emerson understood "that most radical freedom which encompasses both non-dependence (equality) as well as liberty or autonomy." "The source of this idea," he continues, "is the founding doctrine of modern thought, the state of nature, according to which each man is his own judge"; further, because "the goal of independence has the effect of encouraging centralization in the state as the means to individual liberation," all other "mediating institutions between the individual and the central power"—e.g., religion—are threatened. Because "Emerson understood better than any previous American and most later ones that the obstacle to freedom was none other than Judaism," Loewenberg thinks that we should reconsider, say, why Nietzsche so admired Emerson, and the consequences of the latter's substitution of the poet, a "liberating god," for the older, Judaic concept of the deity. This book has four chapters on Emerson framed by others which treat the "Jewish Question" in contemporary scholarship. Not all readers will agree with Loewenberg's particular emphases but probably will admit to a fascination with the new twist he gives to Andrews Norton's claim that Emerson's was "the latest form of infidelity."

Emerson figured in four larger studies of American literature. In *American Procession* Alfred Kazin devotes two chapters to him, but his treatment holds no surprises. Kazin stresses first that Emerson had a mission to emancipate the individual and so to change society by making him aware of himself; and second, that though the 19th century consistently rejected Emerson's message, it insisted on idolizing him as America's premier man of letters. This particular enigma can bear more investigation than Kazin devotes to it, but this should not be held against an author whose book offers a major, sustained reading of two centuries of American literary history.

More provocative for Emersonians is Joseph G. Kronick's *American Poetics of History* in which there also are two chapters on Emerson, whom Kronick sees at the head of a long line of American writers whose anxieties over the problem of a national literature emerged most clearly in their works in an obsession with history. "In order to create," he tells us, Emerson had to forget all that was "anterior"; but for him, as for his successors, this "question of originality has been bound up with the question of place," which is another way of saying that American exceptionalism remains the key issue. In Kronick's view, then, American literature from Emerson on is "less a beginning than a continual destruction of the old," a fact which has made it full of the aggression and irony that Ellison finds among the European and American Romantics more generally. For those not used to traveling the paths of critical theory, reading Kronick can evoke the same response that *Pilgrim's Progress* did in Huck Finn, who noted that its "statements was interesting but tough"; I would, however, urge persistence. Kronick has important things to say, for example, about the Transcendentalists' attempts to possess a language that moves beyond mere mediation, and his notion of a "poetic of history" as "the rhetorical interplay that poses history as a problematic of reading wherein temporal relations are generated by a linguistic process of exchange," is one that should be tested by those scholars who devote their time to contextual readings in the Emersonian circle.

Joyce W. Warren, in *The American Narcissus*, claims that 19th-century theories of individualism, particularly those strengthened by Emerson and other Transcendentalists, left no room for acknowledgment of the *other* person—i.e., most often women, blacks, and Native Americans. Thus the American dreamer, she concludes, is Narcissian at his core. As we shall see, Warren views others besides Emerson as being stricken by this selfishness, but in his writings and personal relations she finds its epitome. Unfortunately, this is the kind of book that gives feminist criticism a bad name, for her argument is reductive at best and skewed at worst. After reading McAleer's biography of Emerson, for example, what can one do but reject outright Warren's claim that "Emerson's view of the individual leaves no room for the individual's relation to other people"? I can accept the fact that the American self as expressed by Emerson and others was self-obsessed, and that quite often women were only secondary characters in the drama of American individualism; but if I want to explore how this situation in fact affected women in the 19th century, I will turn to the sophistication of an Annette Kolodny (see below).

In *The Great Circle* Beongcheon Yu devotes a chapter to Emerson's orientalism, in which he reviews previous studies of Emerson's interest in Eastern thought and then discusses how Indian religion and philosophy influenced the development of Emerson's ideas. Too brief to be more than suggestive, this chapter still has to be supplemented by reference to the earlier studies of F. I. Carpenter (1930) and Arthur Christy (1932). Finally, in *Creativity in American Philosophy* (SUNY), Charles Hartshorne devotes a brief chapter to "Emerson's Secularized Calvinism and Thoreau's Approach to Anarchism" (pp. 34–49). He reminds us that in American philosophy Emerson is important for keeping before us the importance of the "private experience of transcendent values," but also that his philosophical reasoning from that point contains significant inconsistencies. (Hartshorne's treatment of Thoreau is too cursory to warrant further mention.)

In his substantial essay, "Emerson on Nature: Philosophy Beyond Kant" (*ESQ* 30:201–10), A. J. Cascardi observes that Emerson's chief obligation to philosophy in *Nature* was to "discover the relationship of the mind to nature, to find out whether nature is eternal to man, and to show whether, and how, nature conforms to our experience," a very Kantian formulation. Arguing that Emerson's understanding of that German thinker was in fact more profound than we often give him credit for, Cascardi goes on to claim that Emerson, both attracted to and repelled by idealism, resolved his dilemma by joining that idealism to pragmatism and thus moving beyond Kant. "The pragmatic development of idealism," by which Cascardi means that nature is good when it is an object for human use, "is certainly Emerson's most American, if not also his most original, revision of Kant." This is a closely argued and stimulating essay, with pregnant references to Rousseau and Marx.

In "Emerson's Tragic Serenity and Unamuno's Tragic Sense of Life" (*ELWIU* 11:77–93), Kenneth Marc Harris takes a crack at another chestnut, Emerson's supposed insensitivity to the painful aspects of life. Harris claims that, from Stephen Whicher and Newton Arvin on, all who approach this topic have neglected to go to the source of the phrase "tragic sense of life" in Unamuno. Having done that, Harris finds Emerson and the Spanish writer in essential agreement in their willingness to confront their own deaths and to develop a philosophical position from that encounter. Though not likely to shake most readers from the earlier view of Emerson's "serenity," Harris's essay is well argued and worth considering.

In "Emerson and Deconstruction: The End(s) of Scholarship"

(*Soundings* 67:379–98) David L. Smith discusses how Emerson anticipated contemporary critical theorists' description of ours as a "decentered" world in which all that is left the individual is enjoyment of the game of endlessly interpreting texts. A remarkably clear essay, this effort, which equates, among other things, the Deconstructionists' notion of "play" with the project of Emerson's "active soul," is recommended reading for anyone who wishes to understand why so many theorists have focused on Emerson as a 19th-century man central to their concerns. Robert E. Abrams, in "Emerson and the Limits of Metaphysical Psychology" (*PCP* 18:14–22), notes how difficult it was for Emerson to claim "a radically *self-formulated* consciousness of the self" even as he argued that the self is related to the ultimate ground of being. He concludes that Emerson's attempts "to trace conscious processes back to a reassuring fount of Godhead becomes problematic and provisional at best," with metaphysical assurance always sought but never reached.

Kevin Van Anglen, in "Emerson, Milton, and the Fall of Uriel" (*ESQ* 30:139–53), takes us back to another 17th-century radical to resolve our continuing confusion over whether to read "Uriel" as a scarcely veiled biographical statement or as a philosophical position paper which deals with the Reason and Understanding. By looking closely at how Emerson uses his Miltonic source, Van Anglen concludes that it is not an either/or proposition; Emerson moved away from the standard Unitarian reading of Milton as a poet who defended liberty and freedom of expression to an understanding of him as a deliberately satanic, yet angelic, character, one who possessed a potentially subversive force (the imagination) to be used for the good of mankind. The poem, then, is both biographical *and* philosophical, and must be seen as the result of "its author's long and profound meditation on the significance of John Milton." In "Emerson's Essay 'Immortality': The Problem of Authorship" (*AL* 56:313–30), Glen M. Johnson discusses whether *Letters and Social Aims* (1875) was assembled primarily by James Elliott Cabot and Ellen Emerson rather than by Emerson himself. Close examination of the extant manuscript of the essay "Immortality" as well as related documents indicates just that: because those two individuals thought the lecture disjointed as it stood, they reorganized the text in such a way as to shift some of Emerson's statements from the context in which he had put them, a procedure that made his religious ideas look more moderate than he had intended. Emerson clearly wrote the essay,

Johnson concludes, but in its final form it was indeed a collaborative effort; and this may have been the case with the entire book. And in "Emerson's Italian Journey" (*BIS* 12:121–31) Robert D. Richardson describes the first part of Emerson's trip to Europe in 1833, which culminated in his decision, reached after a moment of illumination in the Jardin des Plantes in Paris, to abandon theology for natural history. Emerson's months in Italy, Richardson argues, "crystallized his sense of history, confirmed the integrity of his American eye, and turned him toward natural history."

David Baldwin, in "The Emerson-Ward Friendship: Ideals and Realities" (*SAR*, pp. 299–324), studies one of Emerson's friends in the 1840s, Samuel Gray Ward, a wealthy Bostonian. Based in large part on Emerson's letters to Ward (his to Emerson are not extant), Baldwin indicates that, try as he might, Emerson could not introduce Transcendentalist ideas to this acquaintance with any degree of success. In "Emerson and the Angel of Midnight: The Legacy of Mary Moody Emerson" (*Mothering the Mind*, pp. 218–37), Evelyn Barish adds more substantial lines to the portrait of the relationship between Emerson and his aunt that has emerged in the last few years. Using Emerson's letters to her that were omitted in part from Rusk's edition and *in toto* from the *Journals and Miscellaneous Notebooks*, but parts of which did appear in the earlier edition of the *Journals*, as well as a gothic story about one "Uilsa" that appears in his journals in the early 1820s and whose main character purportedly was modeled on his relative, Barish reconstructs the influence Mary Moody Emerson exerted over her nephew at a critical juncture in his intellectual development. In particular, she notes Uilsa's incessant search for transcendent experience and her capacity for prophecy; both her ideas, then, as well as her visionary stance, clearly had their origin in Emerson's understanding of his remarkable aunt. Finally, Madeleine B. Stern, in "Emerson and Phrenology" (*SAR*, pp. 213–28), discusses the March 1854 issue of the *Phrenological Review*, which contained a lengthy piece on Emerson (including a reading of his head). As Stern points out, Emerson, like many others, was interested in this pseudoscience because it promised self-knowledge and was so a potential path to self-improvement, but he never actually sat for a phrenological examination. This particular reading, reprinted in full, was done by someone who had carefully studied his portrait and observed him from a distance. The phrenologist found Emerson of the "bilious-nervous temperament," sometimes called the "motive-mental," and, in a description that brings to mind Bronson Alcott on vegetables, he observed that "all his faculties *ascend*." "Such a head," the phrenologist continues, "will never carry its followers downward toward the gross, but always upward." Finally (Thoreauvians take note), of "Agreeableness" Emerson "seems to have less in Phrenology than we supposed belonged to him."

iii. Thoreau

We had no phrenological reading of the Concord saunterer, but we did have what some critics of psychohistory would consider its modern counterpart, Richard Lebeaux's *Thoreau's Seasons* (Mass.), the sequel to his previous biography of Thoreau's formative years, *Young Man Thoreau* (1977). Lebeaux's new book again is heavily psychological; in addition to his patron saint, Erik Erikson, he most often invokes Daniel Levinson and William Bridges, two other students of the human life cycle. But though some may argue that a biography with such a weighty and controversial infrastructure may go the way of Henry Seidel Canby's *Thoreau* (1939), there is no denying that Lebeaux's two books offer the most detailed interpretation of Thoreau's works and days we have and as such will stand with Walter Harding's *The Days of Henry Thoreau* (1966) and Sherman Paul's *The Shores of America* (1958) as standard references, particularly because Lebeaux has incorporated into his books the many facts about Thoreau's life that we have learned since the publication of the other studies. Still, there will be those who wince at such passages as the one in which he describes Henry and John re-entering the Merrimack River through the Middlesex Locks. They were allowed through, Lebeaux writes, "not by a threatening, castrating figure who would bar the way for initiative" but an "approving father-figure whose 'duties . . . did not require him to open the lock on Sundays.'" Once Lebeaux has them launched on the river, he notes that "at this point, in the intrusive mode linked to the phallic stage, the brothers enter the state of New Hampshire." Moreover, "the Merrimack River itself, Thoreau informs us, was formed by the flowing together—a sort of sexual union—of two rivers." If one can take such readings with a grain of salt, there is much else to make this exploration of Thoreau's later years (the book begins with the Walden period) an enlightening experience.

The only other book on Thoreau was Victor Carl Friesen's *The*

Spirit of the Huckleberry: Sensuousness in Henry Thoreau (Alberta), a study he admits is for the "general" reader. For those who might come to this straight from Lebeaux's book and thus be alert to veiled sexuality in Thoreau's works, be forewarned: Friesen knows and respects the difference between sensuousness and sensuality. He defines the former as the ability to "perceive the world around him with his senses, an ability depending upon the acuity of the senses and upon their wide use," and sets out "to show that sensuousness accounts for the essential Thoreau." The book is well written and thankfully not overstated, as it easily might have been. It will please those whose Thoreau is best defined not by his language or ideology but his response to the natural world, as well as those who wish to argue against Joel Porte's notion, expressed in *Emerson and Thoreau* (1966), that in his later years, as his impending death became a grim reality, Thoreau lost his sensuous appetite for life.

The same authors who treated Emerson in their book-length studies of American literature or culture also treated Thoreau. In *American Procession,* Kazin discusses Thoreau's relation to Nature and in particular how he tried to forge a language equal to his experience—a life in words, so to speak. He also focuses on Thoreau's problematic relation to the state, which, try as he might, he could not bend to his will; Kazin uses Thoreau's antislavery writings to good purpose in this section. As with his Emerson chapters, though, there are few surprises. Kronick, in *American Poetics of History*, explores the tempting subject of language in Thoreau through the lens of contemporary critical theory and concludes that he adheres to the traditional metaphysics of "presence" more than Emerson does. As in other studies that rely heavily on the formulations of contemporary theorists, there are brilliant insights amidst many statements either infuriatingly dense or merely laughable. Consider as an example of the latter this assertion. Thoreau's "objection to speech is that it is common—he must learn it from others." So far so good, then we encounter this. "But by writing, he gains the mastery of the pen, which we might call a phallus, and in rewriting history, he inscribes his own origin. The master of the pen/phallus becomes his own father."

At least Kronick's work is challenging. Not so Warren's *American Narcissus.* Given how she treats Emerson, her section on Thoreau is utterly predictable, and even more simplistic. How can anyone who claims to have read Thoreau's *Journal* argue that "except for occasional references to William Ellery Channing, there is no record of any real interaction between Thoreau and other people" in it? Certainly we can agree that Thoreau's individualism was peculiarly exclusive, more so than Emerson's, but to explain it only by reference to a myth onto which one has grafted his/her particular ideology is not the way to explore its origins or implications. One would do much better to read Lebeaux on the subject. Finally, Beongcheon Yu, in *The Great Circle*, briefly discusses Thoreau's orientalism; but, as in his discussion of Emerson's thoughts about the East, offers no more than a quick survey of the subject.

Thoreau fared very well in the many essays devoted to his thought and writings; two are particularly significant. In "Henry Thoreau's Political Economy" (*NEQ* 57:359–83), Leonard Neufeldt argues that to understand Thoreau's politics we have to consider his age's continuing devotion to the ideology and language of Revolutionary republicanism, particularly to such concepts as virtue, culture, law, corruption, liberty, and conspiracy. Neufeldt contends that Thoreau sought to purify the terms of this republican legacy, which he regarded as diluted and debased by those in the mid-19th century who claimed to uphold it but in fact refused to accept its demands. Thus, Thoreau's politics consisted of an attempt to reconcile the *res-publica* with the *res-privata* so that American self-government would operate as the Founding Fathers had envisioned. Neufeldt concludes that "the crisis of republicanism as Thoreau perceived it also gave his life and literary career a form," particularly in the 1850s when, because of its tacit support of slavery, the state of Massachusetts assumed the place Britain had held in Revolutionary ideology. By claiming that people like Thoreau measured the politics of their age against the discourse of Revolutionary republicanism, Neufeldt also challenges us to re-examine other writers of that period to see how they treated this same inheritance. This is a pioneering essay on the relationship between language and culture in Thoreau.

Unfortunately, the same cannot be said for two related pieces. William L. Stull's " 'Action from Principle': Thoreau's Transcendental Economics" (*ELN* 22:58–62), a slight essay in which Stull argues that in his philosophical writings Thoreau's method is the same as in his treatment of nature—that is, that he examines the actual and then formulates the ideal to which the fact should correspond. His conclusion, that Thoreau relates both political actions and natural facts to higher principles, will not surprise many. In "The Revolutionary Origins of Thoreau's Thought: An Examination of Thoreau in Light

of Crèvecoeur's *Letters from an American Farmer*" (*MHLS* 7:29–38),
Doreen Alvarez Saar attempts to show how Thoreau's thought
emerges from the same Republican ideology as Crèvecoeur's. The parallels she draws are interesting, but her essay suffers when compared to the sophisticated treatment offered the subject in Neufeldt's
essay.

The second important piece, Michael West's "Thoreau and the
Language Theories of the French Enlightenment" (ELH 51:747–70)
also concerned language. Continuing his investigations into how
language study shaped Thoreau's style, West presents strong evidence that Thoreau knew and was influenced by 18th-century speculation regarding an ur-language. In particular, he points to Charles
de Brosses, who postulated an organic, primitive language characterized by a close relation between an object and its vocalization,
and whose work might have been known to Thoreau through Hugh
Blair's summary of it in his *Lectures on Rhetorick and Belles Lettres*
(1783); and to Antoine Court de Gebelin, whose works supported the
ideas of de Brosses and whose ideas Thoreau definitely had encountered. West's essay is a valuable reminder, like Neufeldt's, of how we
have overlooked the 18th-century legacy in our study of the American
Renaissance, a lesson which should have been brought home to us
before this by Robert D. Richardson's *Myth and Literature in the
American Renaissance* (1978). It also is intended to challenge my
own emphasis on Charles Kraitsir's influence on Thoreau, as I presented it in *The Wisdom of Words* (1981). Not one to challenge hard
evidence, I welcome this new knowledge about Thoreau's language
study; but I also would point out that Kraitsir, whose ideas about
the "inherent semantic meaning" of "phonemes" were similar to those
of the Frenchmen whom West discusses and were excerpted in
Thoreau's commonplace books, was lecturing on, teaching, and publishing his notions in Boston in the 1840s with the endorsement of
Transcendentalists such as Elizabeth Palmer Peabody, thus making it
very likely that he was the more important influence on *Walden*.

In "Thoreau and Anarchism" (*MQR* 23:360–84) Myron Simon
argues that Thoreau's politics are best explained by reference to his
disgust at the mediocrity of the democratic mass and not necessarily
by opposition to the restrictive policies of the state. Thus, though
modern commentators have considered Thoreau an anarchist, Simon
claims that he is better understood as an egoist and satirist of the
democratic majority. Simon reviews Thoreau's early reputation, from

Emerson's eulogy on, to show how the nature writer became the critic of industrial society, a transformation in large measure initially carried out by Henry Salt in England. To understand Thoreau's political insights, we must see that he frequently conflated society and the state, and thus could not have been an anarchist, who finally respects the latter and does not deny the need for cooperative action to assure respect for everyone's self-interest. Simon concludes by noting that Thoreau was a libertarian Transcendentalist who still had an interest in religious ideas; but by definition an anarchist is rationalistic and secular. The essay is a strong call to deromanticize the image of Thoreau as social radical that resurfaced in the late 1960s.

Another "revisionary" piece, though less weighty, is Thomas L. Altherr's "'Chaplain to the Hunters': Henry David Thoreau's Ambivalence Toward Hunting" (*AL* 56:345–61), which focuses on the many contradictory statements on the topic in Thoreau's published works and *Journal*. Altherr points out that because Thoreau regarded hunting as "an earthly endeavor fraught with spiritual potential," he should not be enshrined as the patron saint of the wildlife preservation clubs. There is no denying that because the astute hunter confirmed man's connection to the wild, Thoreau tended to romanticize this activity, even as he expressed anguish over bloodshed; Altherr has performed a useful service by marshaling the evidence for this fact all in one essay. A comparable effort is Rosalie Murphy Brown's "Thoreau's Concept of the Wild" (*CS* 17:39–44), in which she argues that Thoreau's response to his encounter with the wilderness in Maine, usually pointed to as a revelatory yet frightening experience for him, in fact merely confirmed the way he felt about nature throughout his life, that it could be experienced in differing degrees of intensity. Jeffrey E. Simpson, in "Thoreau 'Dreaming Awake and Asleep'" (*MLS* 14:54–62), notes that Thoreau's attitude toward dreams was different from that of other Romantics. Rather than being a submergence into the unconscious self or a transport to an otherworldly realm, a dream state to him connoted greater self-fulfillment and thus a spiritual awakening. Because such dreaming is an active state, a pursuit of the real rather than an escape from it, dreaming in fact was central to the Transcendentalist vision, a way to appreciate the infinite possibility of this world. This essay is just the right length for what it has to say, and the offering is in fact worth considering when we compare American Romantics. Finally, in "Authorship Without Authority: *Walden,* Kierkegaard, and the Experiment in Points of View" (*Kierkegaard and Literature,* pp. 164–82), Carole Anne Taylor discusses the rhetorical strategies in *Walden* in relation to Kierkegaard's *The Point of View for My Work as an Author.* Both these writers, she argues, aspire to telling the truth, but "without authority," and thus they ground their texts in a richly allusive dialectic. His prose filled with "self-consciously epic gestures that dissolve into ironic exaggerations," Thoreau, like Kierkegaard, teaches us that if any transcendence is possible, it must come from a method that allows the writer to stand "firmly in the realm of the dialectical and the experimental."

There were two essays in *New England Quarterly* that dealt specifically with *Walden.* The stronger of the two, Richard N. Masteller and Jean Carwile's "Rural Architecture in Andrew Jackson Downing and Henry David Thoreau: Pattern Book Parody in *Walden*" (57:483–510), points out that scholars have neglected Thoreau's attack on popular house pattern books of the 1840s and 1850s in his discussion of architectural style; he parodied their key terms and exposed the superficial ways their proponents used them. Architects like Downing wanted their creations to embody "civilized pastoralism," domestic architecture in a natural setting; Thoreau of course sought wildness. "For Downing," the authors write, "nature has become a context for the improvement of civilization." But for Thoreau, "nature remains the locus of all higher values." Masteller and Carwile have tapped an interesting subject, for both Downing and Thoreau, each in a radically different way, clearly argued that one's dwelling does proclaim things about one's life. While Masteller and Carwile seem to have made a fruitful discovery, I am not so sure of Haskell S. Springer in his "The Nautical *Walden*" (57:84–97); he merely traces nautical imagery in the book and argues that it provides "a syntax of figurative expression" for Thoreau. We long have thought about *Walden*'s metaphoric voyages, it seems to me; and even if nautical terms are used to discuss such things as the socioeconomic situation of mid-19th-century America, I cannot see that our understanding of the book changes when we learn this. Like Altherr's essay on Thoreau's response to hunting, this essay seems only an intellectual exercise.

Finally, there were two brief essays that presented new biographical material on Thoreau. In "Thoreau and Michael Flannery" (*CS* 17, iii: 27–33), Bradley P. Dean discusses Thoreau's charitable attitude toward this Irishman who appears in the journal. And Harmon Smith, in "Henry Thoreau and Emerson's 'Noble Youths'" (*CS* 17, iii: 4–12), details Emerson's and Thoreau's relationships with Giles Waldo and William A. Tappan, whom Emerson had met while on a lecture tour and to whom he wanted Thoreau to introduce himself when he went to Staten Island in 1843 to make his way in the literary world. These shallow, romantic youths immediately disappointed Thoreau; and though Emerson had Waldo visit him in Concord after this, he too finally recognized that they did not fulfill the promise he thought he had seen in them.

iv. Minor Transcendentalists

There were surprisingly few studies of others in the Transcendentalist sphere, though the editions of Peabody's and Fuller's letters more than compensate for this fact. In "A Tentative Transcendentalist in the Ohio Valley: Samuel Osgood and the *Western Messenger*" (*SAR*, pp. 79–92), Judith Kent Green notes that Osgood contributed many pieces to the *Messenger* and analyzes the nature of his commitment to transcendentalism by studying them in detail. She finds that he retained allegiance to some Unitarian ideas, as befitted a Harvard graduate of that period, and toyed with some notions from the "New Thought" without fully embracing them. This is a good sketch of a little-studied minister who later re-entered the Unitarian fold as Orville Dewey's replacement at the Church of the Messiah in New York City.

There was at least some interest in Margaret Fuller. In "The Angelic Artistry of Margaret Fuller's *Woman in the Nineteenth Century*" (*ELWIU* 11:293–98), William J. Scheick makes a case for the artistic integrity of Fuller's book. Though most critics find it poorly crafted and organized, and inadequately argued, he claims that in fact she successfully integrates "a Transcendental creed about artists, Swedenborgian dogma about angels, and [her] own belief in the 'Idea of Woman.'" The recurrent angel imagery in the book offers the aesthetic coherence, and Fuller, as acting artist and communicating angel, herself reveals the secrets inherent in the hieroglyph of Woman. This is an ingenious, if finally too brief, reading of a book little studied on such terms.

Two other authors included Fuller in book-length studies of their topics. For Joyce W. Warren in her *American Narcissus*, Fuller is the one who fully realizes the conflict between woman's place and the male-centered individualistic ethic of the day, and who thereupon asked for a comparable independence. But she also finds Fuller sentimental about such "others" as Native Americans and members of the lower classes, as befits someone, so Warren thinks, who imbibed Transcendentalist ideas. Warren includes a predictable discussion of the Fuller-Emerson "affair," in which Emerson's self-centeredness and his purported inability to understand Fuller's needs offer much grist for Warren's mill.

A much more sophisticated understanding of the 19th-century woman's plight comes in chapter 6 of Annette Kolodny's *The Land Before Her*, a model of innovative feminist criticism. "Margaret Fuller: Recovering Our Mother's Garden" deals with *Summer on the Lakes* (1844), specifically with Fuller's discovery that the western Eden promised in contemporary promotional literature was in fact unavailable to women. Kolodny explains Fuller's attraction to the bountiful prairie lands as a reaction to the material and emotional privation she had experienced on her family's farm in Groton, Massachusetts, but she points out as well Fuller's growing recognition that the slovenly cabins that marked midwestern settlement contained women trapped in the same drudgery as their eastern counterparts, an insight that was not lost on her when she wrote *Woman in the Nineteenth Century* shortly after her western trip. Thus, unlike Warren, who views Fuller's sympathy for Native American and lower-class women as sentimental, Kolodny claims that such individuals, subjugated to men's interests even in this paradise, focused her ideas about the extensive enslavement of her sisters. Kolodny's book is rich and in its entirety deserves a wide reading.

University of Colorado

2. Hawthorne

Rita K. Gollin

Many of this year's books and some of the essays make important contributions to scholarship in displaying Hawthorne as an intelligent and open-minded writer who read widely and pondered problems of morality and identity in New England from Puritan times to his own, exercising almost complete creative control over his fictions. Historical criticism dominates, but psychological and textual approaches abound. Few critics are thesis-ridden, most of them write intelligibly, and although many bring old news, only one book and a few essays can be completely dismissed. But assessment of trends and emphases is difficult: for example, the 21 notes and essays in the *Nathaniel Hawthorne Journal 1978* (the eighth and last of the series) were prepared for publication years ago. As one consequence of the demise of the *NHJ*, the *Hawthorne Society Newsletter* now includes not only notes and bibliography but also short articles. There is almost nothing new in primary materials this year, though the Centenary *Letters* are on the verge of publication.

i. Texts, Editions, Bibliography, Biography

In his introduction to the year's only new text, The Scarlet Letter *and Selected Writings* (Modern Library), Stephen Nissenbaum discusses Hawthorne's ouster from the customhouse as it shaped his strategy in "The Custom-House" and *The Scarlet Letter*, and he includes ten letters from Hawthorne to friends and one from Sophia to her mother as well as "The Great Stone Face." Though Hawthorne claimed to be apolitical, he was (like Dimmesdale) an ambitious man who wanted "to keep a valuable office" yet "keep up a public image of innocence and sanctity," and both men made confessions "not intended to be deciphered." Hester is treated as a variant form of the artist, acknowledging guilt and without ambition; curiously, Nissenbaum invents a "male admirer" or "patron" who provides her with luxury items. Discussing Hawthorne's desire for public patronage, he reads "The Great Stone Face" as a paradoxical expression of his desire for fame.

Joel Myerson's "Nathaniel Hawthorne" in *The Transcendentalists* (pp. 328–35) is a succinct and judicious account of Hawthorne's relationships with Transcendentalists as he wrote about them and as biographers and critics have perceived them. Myerson includes M.A. theses and other relatively unfamiliar studies, and indicates which avenues of research remain open. The only other guides to scholarship aside from the *MLA Bibliography* are Buford Jones's regular annotated "Current Hawthorne Bibliography" (*HSN* 10:27–34) and the cumulative index to the *Nathaniel Hawthorne Journal*, included in the 1978 number.

Two books move from biographical to literary analysis. Gloria C. Erlich's *Family Themes and Hawthorne's Fiction: The Tenacious Web* (Rutgers) is a complex and well-argued "thematic study of the continuities between Hawthorne's life and his art, the psychological and experiential sources of his fiction." Erlich provides important information about Hawthorne's many Manning relatives, especially his benevolent yet authoritarian Uncle Robert, who looms behind many of the older men in his fiction; and she examines his relationships with his widowed mother and "light" and "dark" sisters, discusses their transformations in his fiction, and suggests that the public shaming of two 17th-century Manning sisters for incest with their brother was a "scaffold scene" that informed *The Scarlet Letter*. Drawing on Erikson and Daniel Levinson, she argues that his midlife crisis provoked a "creative breakthrough." Philip Young's *Hawthorne's Secret: An Untold Tale* (Godine) is simpler and more sensational, arguing that Hawthorne had *a* secret—obsession with incest, as performed by his 17th-century ancestors and as it affected relations with his sister Elizabeth—which generated the specters of guilt and the incest motif in his fiction. The only support for the hunch that "Something Happened" between Hawthorne and Elizabeth is that "it stretches credulity to think that his nature contained such an area of culpability as a result of nothing more than imagination or longing."

A few notes augment the biographical record. Margaret B. Moore in "Hawthorne's Uncle John Dike" (*SAR 1984*, pp. 325–30) discusses the Salem businessman who married Hawthorne's Aunt Priscilla in 1817. His concern about his nephew and nieces made him a source of "affectionate stability," and his return to prosperity after two business failures proved a good man might survive in a competitive world. My own "Hawthorne Contemplates the Shakers: 1831–1851" (*NHJ 1978*, pp. 57–65) begins with Hawthorne's jocular reports of his visits to the Canterbury Shakers in 1831, accounts for criticisms he levied a few months later in "The Shaker Bridal" and "The Canterbury Pilgrims," then suggests why in 1851 the Hancock Shakers utterly repelled him. James O'Donald Mays in "Hawthorne and the 'Oxford' Photograph" (*NHJ 1978*, pp. 39–45) discusses the group portrait taken in an Oxford garden by the famous British photographer Delamotte (treated more fully in my *Portraits of Nathaniel Hawthorne*, 1983). In " 'Aunt Ebe,' Critic of Books and Their Writers" (*NHJ 1978*, pp. 17–37), Raymona E. Hull demonstrates that Hawthorne's strong-minded sister was a voracious reader who reached shrewd independent judgments. She recorded reminiscences of her brother, but condemned Lathrop's "foolish book"; she praised everything Hawthorne wrote, but criticized Sophia's edition of his notebooks and deplored publication of the unfinished *Septimius Felton*.

ii. General Studies

Two of the year's most important books and many of the essays take historical approaches. Michael J. Colacurcio in *The Province of Piety: Moral History in Hawthorne's Early Tales* (Harvard) presents Hawthorne as "our first intellectual historian," engaged in moral reinterpretation of New England history. His readings of a sketch like "Sir William Phips" or the major historical tales are solidly grounded in history and Hawthornean scholarship; and as Hawthorne meditates seriously but often tentatively and playfully, so Colacurcio. Although some discussion seems protracted and not all his readings are equally persuasive (the rock in "Roger Malvin's Burial" seen as Plymouth Rock, or the kindly gentleman in "My Kinsman, Major Molineux" as a conspiratorial minister), his methodology and evidence bring us closer to Hawthorne and his fiction.

John P. McWilliams, Jr., also takes an empirical historical approach in *Hawthorne, Melville, and the American Character*. Examining Hawthorne's concern with "the development of New England character" from the heroic but flawed first Puritans through generations of spiritual decline in the context of commemorative oratory, Bancroft, Tocqueville, and Cooper (among others), McWilliams includes works that have attracted relatively little attention, such as

Grandfather's Chair and "The Canal Boat," but also offers new readings of familiar passages—e.g., the end of "My Kinsman," and Dimmesdale's Election Sermon. Although it may seem disconcerting to think about *Septimius Felton* right after "My Kinsman," the methodology works. "Alice Doane" becomes increasingly intelligible in the context of the commemorative tradition; Dimmesdale, Goodman Brown, and Doane display the "defensive conformity" and morbid introspection of second- and third-generation Puritans; the broken wire in "Main Street" suggests that "progress seems to depend more on severance than on linkage with the Puritan past." Like Colacurcio, McWilliams takes account of Hawthorne's complexities and uncertainties (and makes only a few minor factual errors, e.g., the date Hawthorne acquired The Wayside).

Just before the presidential election in November, a discussion of Hawthorne's politics appeared in a journal not normally scrutinized for ALS—*The Village Voice*. In "The Scarlet D: Hawthorne and the Troubled Soul of the Democratic Party" (29 [9 Nov.]: 50–55), Paul Berman discusses Hawthorne as a lifelong Democrat, taking account of his political appointments, his loyalty to Franklin Pierce, his emphasis on democracy "as an almost mystical force," the politics of Brook Farm, and the social assumptions of *The House of the Seven Gables,* jauntily saying "his was the kind of career that begins in campus activism, proceeds to radicalism, flirts with socialism, turns to conservatism in middle age, and continues thusly to no good end." With his usual clear-mindedness, Richard Brodhead in "Hawthorne and the Fate of Politics" (*ELWIU* 11:95–103) treats "Citizen Hawthorne's" distrust of, yet commitment to, political engagement as part of his characteristic pattern of self-reversal. "Chiefly About War Matters" ironizes "opinion about the Civil War" and expresses skepticism about any effective social action. The novels make similar reversals: through Hester and Zenobia, Hawthorne advocates change in the treatment of women but says "there is no such thing as disinterested action for public ends" and denies the possibility of adequate reform; yet (as the final turn of political thought) disengagement from social action generates "a sense of loss." According to the scheme Richard Predmore proposes in "The Development of Social Commentary in Nathaniel Hawthorne's Works: 1828–1844" (*CLQ* 20:6–21), from 1828 to 1836 Hawthorne was relatively silent; for the next two years he was essentially a neutral observer although "Endicott and the Red Cross" and "Legends of the Province-House"

experimented with "bringing concrete social relevance to his interpretation of American history"; and from 1842 to 1844 he shifted attention to the modern city, expressing opinions that "closely approximate Jacksonian Democracy," sympathy with the poor and criticism
of corrupt businessmen and America's "mechanistic pragmatism."
But the scheme is flawed. Hawthorne always urged the need for remaining part of the "magnetic chain of humanity": it was not an
evolving position or one he took only or even primarily on social
grounds; his isolatoes are not usually associated with wealth and
power; and increasing interest in social issues does not adequately account for his shift to the novel.

The authors of two important essays discuss different ways critics'
promulgations have affected Hawthorne's reception. Nina Baym in
"Concepts of the Romance in Hawthorne's America" (*NCF* 38:426–
43) demonstrates that "the idea of American romance now controlling
so much American literary study is a recent invention." Hawthorne's
contemporaries sometimes used "novel" and "romance" interchangeably, or drew idiosyncratic distinctions, or used one of two "mainstream" definitions: the novel as modern romance, or the romance as
a highly wrought novel. Hawthorne's distinction was his own, as
contemporary reviewers noted; and neither he nor his contemporaries
thought the romance was particularly American. Using Hawthorne
as her example, Jane Tompkins in "Masterpiece Theater: The Politics
of Hawthorne's Literary Reputation" (*AQ* 36:617–42) asserts that
"there is no ahistorical literary greatness," that "an author's reputation
depends upon the context in which it is read" including critical standards and publishers' strategies. Dependence on Faust and Crowley
for examples of Hawthorne's critical reception leads to a few errors:
Longfellow and other readers of Hawthorne's early anonymous publications *did* distinguish them "from the surrounding mass of magazine fiction" (and she is mistaken about when Hawthorne suggested
that they collaborate). And although contemporaries who admired
Hawthorne also admired Susan Warner, it is not true that "given
their way of seeing, there *was* no difference": Melville among others
praised Hawthorne's depth and darkness; and Margaret Fuller and
Elizabeth Peabody were two of the many men and women who
praised him as "the best writer of the day." Further, although the
literary establishment supported Hawthorne, others with similar support (such as Holmes or Bayard Taylor) are rarely read today. But
clearly, each age "completes" a text differently, and it is important to

reassess the canon and retrieve "the values and interests embodied in other, noncanonical texts."

The remaining general studies take a wide variety of methodological approaches to Hawthorne-in-his-times or -in-his-texts. Allan Gardner Lloyd Smith in *Eve Tempted: Writing and Sexuality in Hawthorne's Fiction* (Barnes & Noble) applies the methodology of Derrida, Iser, and Lacan and the theories of Rousseau, Freud, and Foucault to Hawthorne and his fiction, offering fresh readings admixed with exaggerations and distortions—e.g., Owen and Giovanni each "prefer death to giving himself to the other"; Hepzibah's shop is analogous to her sexuality; Priscilla's veil is a hymeneal image and an anagram for evil. The approach to art and particularly sculpture in *The Marble Faun* is provocative though limited: a sculptor's transformation of matter into life and again into senseless matter is said to recapitulate "the arc of sexual desire in morbid form." The main title is misleading: the book is not about women; copyediting and printing are below standard; and it seems reductive to end by suggesting that anxiety about guilt, as in "Fancy's Show-Box," undoubtedly expresses the "masturbation phobia" evident in 19th-century hygiene books. Nonetheless, such concepts as substitution, trace, and absence do "stimulate a new kind of reading of Hawthorne."

Two critics praise Hawthorne's women characters. In "The Claims of the Other," a chapter in *The American Narcissus* (pp. 189–230), Joyce W. Warren says Hawthorne, unlike most American writers, created "fully drawn women characters," particularly Hester, Zenobia, and Miriam, because he "did not subscribe to the individualism that characterized nineteenth-century America." That last contention can be attacked from several positions, but certainly Hawthorne deplored withdrawal from or violation of the human community, whether by a man or a woman. And although he criticized "unfeminine" women, he deplored women's limited opportunities for self-fulfillment, and Warren says he valued the individuality of his mother, sisters, wife, and daughters. Kristin Herzog also discusses Hawthorne's complex women characters who have a "right to human wholeness" in "Primitive Strength in Hawthorne's Women," in *Women, Ethics, and Exotics* (Rutgers; pp. 3–54), arguing that Georgiana, Beatrice, and the heroines of the four romances variously demonstrate a "primitive power of love and trust." Terminology tends to be equivocal (Maule is an ethnic, Hilda a woman of primitive strength).

But Herzog makes interesting comparisons (Zenobia as exotic Eve, Priscilla as passive Persephone) and discusses Hawthorne's inversion of conventional images; thus, "a passionate tigress like Miriam might save a man's soul."

Tobin Siebers concentrates on Hawthorne in "Witchcraft, the Romance, and Romanticism" in *The Romantic Fantastic* (Cornell; pp. 122–66), which includes with slight modification the essay on "Hawthorne's Appeal and Romanticism" reviewed last year, augmented by discussion of "The Gentle Boy" and other fiction, and by comparisons with Poe. Beginning with "Alice Doane" and stressing (like Colacurcio and McWilliams) that Hawthorne synthesized historical fact and moral perspective, Siebers argues that in the "dynamics of accusation," persecutors like Leonard Doane, the witchcraft judges, or Chillingworth damn themselves. Citing Benjamin and others, he considers allegory as one way Hawthorne supplemented history with ethical interpretation. Though a few readings are questionable (e.g., about Brand's willfulness in laughing or inciting the crowd), most specific readings and general arguments about Hawthorne's indictment of accusation (and thus his anxiety about the accusations leveled in his fictions) are convincing, provoking the hope that Siebers will some day tackle all Hawthorne's "fantastic," from "The Old Woman's Tale" to *The Marble Faun* and the unfinished romances.

A Hawthornean may be attracted by the title of Marion Montgomery's *Why Hawthorne Was Melancholy* (Sherwood Sugden), but nothing beyond. It is a rambling rumination setting against the modern "gnostic and Manichean spirit . . . such prophetic writers as O'Connor, West, Hawthorne, Strauss, Voegelin, Niemeyer; St. Augustine and St. Thomas; Gilson, Maritain, Pieper, and all the others on whom we have ourselves relied to summon the popular spirit back to known forgotten things of the spirit." There are no footnotes, and the bibliography lists (for example) the Dell edition of *The Blithedale Romance* and the Airmont edition of *Twice-Told Tales*.

John Dolis in "Hawthorne's Metonymic Gaze: Image and Object" (*AL* 56:362–78), citing Merleau-Ponty, treats Hawthorne's descriptive techniques as conditions of the consciousness of a spectator who "assumes a spatial relation to the thing in terms of his restricted situation and not the 'ubiquitous' position of optical perspective." Descriptions of the dead Zenobia or Westervelt's grin are treated as instances of metonymic presentation. Selected detail and "syntax" do not imply independent existence: "Nearly all of Hawthorne's signifi-

cant objects are metaphors which *express* the meaning with which
they are invested by the gaze." Similarly, in "Hawthorne's Tactile
Gaze: The Phenomenon of Depth" (*MLQ* 44:267–84), Dolis argues
that in his notebooks and fictions, Hawthorne was not seeking fixed
reality but "the transitory and opaque appearance itself" unfolding
in time, "a lived experience whose numerous aspects discontinuously
surface to the touch of an incarnate gaze." In "Hawthorne's Mor-
phology of Alienation: The Psychosomatic Phenomenon" (*AI* 41:
47–62), Dolis discusses the "ruinous effects of egotism" on Hawthorne's villains and other isolated figures who separate head from
heart and suffer psychosomatic symptoms. The villain experiences a
"void . . . in the center of his being. . . . Whenever the subject isolates
itself from the other, it loses itself as well." Dolis's "Hawthorne's
Letter" (*Notebooks in Cultural Analysis* 1:103–23), a Lacanian/
Derridean disquisition elucidating Hawthorne as the father of his
own text, relates "The Custom-House" "pre-text" to the forest scene—
the novel, the letter A, and Pearl alike as signifying and signified
text with no single acknowledged creator. The essay is often clever
though sometimes merely clever (Hester will not "sign her name in
the Black Man's book" yet "refuses to resign herself to another text"),
expounding what Hawthorne could accept if it was translated into
his own language: "If at its origin the self is always already written
by another, it nevertheless is called upon to inaugurate the manner
and meaning of its significance . . . [;] the self thus authorizes its
emergence into the world." Dolis's use of French critical procedure
is sometimes obtrusive and his metaphors sometimes mixed; the passages from Hawthorne (and others) used in one essay reappear in a
second or even a third; and I question some of his assumptions: e.g.,
although Hawthorne drew distinctions between truths in painting
and in sculpture, he believed the spectator's imagination had to complete both; and he repeatedly asserted belief in some "higher" truth.
But the four essays published in one year constitute a significant
achievement.

I examine Hawthorne as a would-be connoisseur of art in "Hawthorne and the Anxiety of Aesthetic Response" (*CentR* 28:94–104).
Certain that great art must be based on reality but suggest higher
truths, he worried about his own capacity for perception and judgment. Postulating a "receptive faculty" for art (like the mental faculties of Scottish Philosophers) he believed his was unusually limited.
In Italy, he was often "surprised into admiration" yet continued to

question his ability to perceive *any* truth or beauty in art; this ambivalence animates *The Marble Faun.* There is nothing new in Thelma J. Shinn's "A Fearful Power: Hawthorne's Views on Art and the Artist as Expressed in his Sketches and Short Stories" (*NHJ 1978*, pp. 121–35); and as an example of the essay's rambling and question-begging interconnections of "art" and belief, discussion of "The Prophetic Pictures" concludes, "It is hard to believe that Hawthorne saw the artistic ability as evil, even if he might have allowed it to be called witchcraft, when we remember his offense at the Puritans' condemnation of witches and his portrayal of the poet in 'The Great Stone Face.'" R. K. Gupta in "Laughter in Hawthorne's Fiction: A Psycho-Literary Approach" (*NHJ 1978*, pp. 205–17) points out that Hawthorne used a variety of laughs in his fiction (with "expression of the self-mockery of a disordered mind" his "unique contribution"), then says that laughter serves a variety of narrative functions. Alfred Kazin begins "The Ghost Sense: Hawthorne and Poe," in *American Procession* (pp. 81–102), with Hawthorne at the end of his life unable to "separate himself from his symbols" as he tried to complete his last romances, asserting that he always mistrusted himself as a storyteller while turning out guilt-haunted narratives. It is a distortion to call Hawthorne "the surliest . . . of Yankees" with "a Timon-like contempt for his idealistic contemporaries," and there is nothing new in this rambling, autumnal account.

iii. Novels

Danny Robinson in "Rufus Wilmot Griswold and Hawthorne's 'Early Unavowed Romance'" (*RALS* 12:43–48), asks how and when contemporaries learned about Hawthorne's authorship of *Fanshawe* (1828): Griswold referred to an anonymous 1832 romance in an 1851 review article (informed by Goodrich) and Fields had received an evasive answer when he questioned Hawthorne about it. Curtis gave the title and the correct date in an 1864 essay. The puzzle still has gaps, but Annie Fields said in her Hawthorne biography that her husband not only owned a copy of the "disowned" publication but knew of at least five others: his own copy was "put away and jealously guarded, but others have appeared from which the gist of the book has been given to the world."

Mary Gosselink De Jong deals with all four major novels in "The Making of a 'Gentle Reader': Narrator and Reader in Hawthorne's

Romances" (*SNNTS* 16:359–75), analyzing the narrator's use of personal pronouns and possessive adjectives, his modes of address to the reader, and the kinds of information he gives and withholds in fictionalizing his readers, satisfying their desire for "improvement and diversion," and involving them in the search for meaning. De Jong's painstaking approach leads to provocative discriminations—e.g., "The proliferation of pronouns implicating the reader of *The Marble Faun* . . . seems to suggest the author's anxiety about establishing a common ground. . . . [He] approaches familiarity and he snubs the reader who cannot or will not appreciate Hawthornean romance."

As usual, there were more discussions of *The Scarlet Letter* than any other novel. Several are source studies. Sarah I. Davis proposes "new" New England sources for *The Scarlet Letter* in "Another View of Hester and the Antinomians" (*SAF* 12:189–98). She traces Hester back to Hawthorne's biographical sketch of Anne Hutchinson and his comments about her in *Grandfather's Chair*, then traces Dimmesdale back to Cotton Mather's account of John Cotton, and Chillingworth to his discussion of Vane. The essay could use some tightening, but Davis argues convincingly that the Antinomian controversy clarifies the novel's "strategy of atonement": to leave the community is "to risk the loss of meaning." Sargent Bush, Jr., in "Hawthorne's Prison Rose: An English Antecedent in the Salem *Gazette*" (*NEQ* 57:255–63) suggests a source for the wild rosebush beside the prison door in *The Scarlet Letter*: an anonymous English moralized children's tale entitled "Prison Roses," which appeared in the Salem *Gazette* in 1843; the narrator requests permission to pluck a blossom; and the plot concerns a wronged woman who is imprisoned for a time and an innocent young girl who is associated with roses. Mona Scheuermann suggests a different line of ancestry in "The American Novel of Seduction: An Exploration of the Omission of the Sex Act in *The Scarlet Letter*" (*NHJ* 1978, pp. 105–18)—18th-century American seduction novels such as *Charlotte Temple* which stress the psychological effect of illicit sex; but she is on weak ground when she says Hester and Dimmesdale "need nothing from society" and reduces the significance of their relationship to their need to "exist outside the regulations of society."

Lester H. Hunt takes a different approach to moral and social order in "*The Scarlet Letter*: Hawthorne's Theory of Moral Sentiments" (*P&L* 8:75–88) anatomizing Hawthorne's theory of sympathy in the context of Adam Smith's *Theory of Moral Sentiments*, which contends that social order is "mutilated when an artificial order is imposed on it" as by the Puritans, who reduce Hester to the category "adulteress" without bringing her back into the fold. Similarly, morality "reduces" Dimmesdale and ruptures his relationship with the world; and through Pearl, Hawthorne expresses in a different way the belief he shared with Smith that "full sympathy can be had only at the price of self-revelation or 'truth.'" But Smith grounds morality in sympathy while Hawthorne shows them at odds and so cannot "conceive of a utopia of both virtue *and* happiness." David B. Downing in "The Swelling Waves: Visuality, Metaphor, and Bodily Reality in *The Scarlet Letter*" (*SAF* 12:13–28) examines the division between Dimmesdale's (and the Puritans') conventional language and underlying emotions as this contrasts with the interrelationship of mind and body in the central metaphor of "Tongue of Flame" and in Hawthorne's stress on subjective perception. Although some points are obvious (about psychosomatic illness, for example), and a few readings are dubious (e.g., Dimmesdale's "choosing death"), Downing clearly shows the minister's distortion of his emotions in acceptable religious discourse as a loss for him and his society.

Henry J. Lindborg in "Hawthorne's Chillingworth: Alchemist and Physiognomist" (*TWA* 72:8–16) ties Chillingworth's transformation "from a high-minded philosopher to a fiend" to the novel's larger concern with transformation, particularly rebirth after death, including Hawthorne's after his "decapitation" and his characters' in the pages of his romance. Lindborg argues that Hawthorne's "symbolic frames of reference beyond Puritanism" include alchemy and physiognomy: thus Chillingworth propels "the minister toward a rebirth which fits patterns of both alchemical and Christian symbolism," and Hawthorne's suggestion that after death the antipathy of Chillingworth and Dimmesdale was "transmuted into golden love" can be read as "an alchemical analogy." In "'Circle of Acquaintance': Mistress Hibbins and the Hermetic Design of *The Scarlet Letter*" (*ESC* 9[1983]: 294–311), David Ketterer asks why Mistress Hibbins "looms so large in the overall design of the romance" and provides a "characterological geometry" that exaggerates her importance and distorts the book: a pentangle "which may be construed as five A's" within a hermetic circle connects her with the four major characters (linking her with Hester, "an adulterous mistress," and placing her between Chillingworth and Pearl, "who do not make a natural pair" or fuse into each other). Certainly Hawthorne worried that writing fiction was a form of witchcraft, but Mistress Hibbins is not "almost" a symbol of community; and other arguments are spurious, e.g., the novel's "sexual sin . . . might as well be incest" which "like the alphabetical placing of the letter A . . . is simply that which comes before all else." In "Atropine Poisoning in Hawthorne's *The Scarlet Letter*," in the *New England Journal of Medicine* (311[9 Aug.]:414–16)—a note picked up by newspapers across the country—Jemshed A. Khan accounts for Dimmesdale's "bizarre behavior and ultimate demise" by asserting that Chillingworth poisoned him, which is to ignore both Dimmesdale's desire to keep on tormenting the minister and the fact that the alleged symptoms of poisoning appeared before the leech arrived in Boston. (Rebuttals by Philip Young and others including myself appeared a few months later.)

Robert Shulman gives over half his space in "The Artist in the Slammer: Hawthorne, Melville, Poe and the Prison of Their Times" (*MLS* 14:79–88) to *The Scarlet Letter*, treating Hawthorne and Hester as artist-prisoners (by now a critical commonplace). He argues that Hawthorne "tried to disguise matters from a part of himself" by creating a story of the 17th century which was "really" about contemporary social rigidity, that his "twenty years of experience in the marketplace . . . and with his wife and his high-minded friends at the Old Manse" required him to perfect "the skills of symbolic indirection," and that Hester used "a symbolic code to escape the censorship of the authorities"; but he does not adequately distinguish self-evasion from self-expression or communication, and construing societies as prisons is at once too limited and too generalized.

Most discussions of *The House of the Seven Gables* recognize Hawthorne as a moralist, a social observer, and a self-observing craftsman, as Bruce Michelson does in "Hawthorne's House of Three Stories" (*NEQ* 57:163–83) before arguing that his "ghost story" is about the loss of self resulting from excess of reality or imagination and that in the end, the four characters "viewed as part of a whole" can leave the haunted house. I question whether the "right" of romance Hawthorne asserts in his preface is "improvisation" and whether he conceived Hepzibah and Clifford as revenants or the Judge as shapechanger; but the essay is sensible about the novel's demonstrations of the need to balance the worlds of imagination and reality. George Monteiro in "Hawthorne's Fable of the Reformable Man" (*DQR* 14:18–29) takes a more traditional approach to a balanced and balancing Hawthorne by tracing the development of two organizing metaphors (the house as edifice and family, blood as physiological fact and Gothic curse) before (like Michelson) evaluating Holgrave's final role. Monteiro finds the ending "comedic and conciliatory" as the possibility of progress conjoins with "conservation" in Holgrave's final approximation of Hawthorne's belief: a house should be built to last, though the occupants should be free to remodel. Sarah I. Davis in "The Bank and the Old Pyncheon Family" (*SN* 16:150–66) proposes a new context for understanding: the novel, "about aristocracy in the democracy at midcentury, deals with the inheritance from the Bank controversy in New England," in which the aristocratic moneyed class was defeated by egalitarian Democrats. Davis presents the ruined bank president Nicholas Biddle as a source for both Clifford and the Judge, and Hawthorne's quixotic cousin Eben Hathorne as another model for Clifford. Interpreting the novel's conclusion as "a gesture toward the revival of aristocratic grace as well as the redistribution of aristocratic wealth," Davis offers as clarification a principle Edward Everett affirmed in an 1836 review of Tocqueville: "Power is inevitably redistributed with the succession of generations." Kenneth Marc Harris in "'Judge Pyncheon's Brotherhood': Puritan Theories of Hypocrisy and *The House of the Seven Gables*" (*NCF* 39:144–62) treats the Judge as a religious hypocrite, deceiving but also self-deceived, tracing the type back to Puritan theologians such as John Cotton and Samuel Shepard, but also William Cobbett: Pyncheon is goatish as in Cotton's discourse, slothful as in Cobbett's. *The House of the Seven Gables* is "Hawthorne's most narrowly Calvinistic novel in its treatment of the crucial issue of salvation and damnation," Harris believes, and argues that because the Pyncheons are self-deceived, the narrator is necessarily uncertain about their motives. In "Hawthorne's 'Modern Psychology': Madness and Its Method in *The House of the Seven Gables*" (*BuR* 27: 108–31), Marvin Karlow offers not a source but a psychological interpretive scheme: the novel is a psychomachia comprehended through R. D. Laing's differentiation of the true and false self, with Clifford the artist as schizophrenic and Holgrave as his double. The distinction of true vs. false selves applies well to the opposition of the imagination-dominated Clifford and the body-dominated Judge, and many of Laing's observations about the schizophrenic—including voracity as "reality-hunger" and regression as a condition of maturity—are applicable to Clifford. Yet many suggestions appear overingenious, e.g., the history of the house identified with the development of an ontologically insecure person, Clifford as "really" a Maule, or the novel's conclusion as expressing Hawthorne's belief that "art is a stage—and a potentially deadly one—one passes through before becoming an authentic person." J. Gill Holland's "Hawthorne and Photography: *The House of the Seven Gables*" (*NHJ 1978*, pp. 1–10) notes that midcentury daguerreotypes often combined stark realism with intimations of underlying character, as do Holgrave's, and suggests the appropriateness of his role as mesmerist. Finally, John L. Idol, Jr., in "Clifford Pyncheon's Soap Bubbles" (*AN&Q 23*: 39–41), says Clifford's bubble-blowing originates in Dunlap's account of Malbone, the artist Hawthorne identifies as the painter of Clifford's miniature.

Two essayists view *Blithedale* from different perspectives. Charles Swann in "*The Blithedale Romance*—Translation and Transformation: Mime and Mimesis" (*JAmS 18*:237–53) begins with the names Coverdale and Fauntleroy as signifying translation and forgery, then addresses Hawthorne's "ironic deployment of the translator metaphor" through his narrator. The Blithedalers created a pseudoworld despite marketplace realities and Coverdale oscillates between presenting the mime and the enclosing reality, while Hawthorne knows both are fictive. Carol Wershoven treats Priscilla peculiarly in "America's Child Brides: The Price of a Bad Bargain" (*Portraits of Marriage*, pp. 151–57). She is "an envoy of death and disease" who desperately adores a master, a sexless vacuum exploited as "a kind of child prostitute" by the "pimp" Westervelt; she is Hollingsworth's nemesis, a succubus who absorbs his soul. Wershoven sweepingly includes *The Bostonians, The Age of Innocence*, and later fiction as evidence of "a veiled and sanctified emptiness at the heart of American literature," with the child-wife as "the romantic reward at the end of the economic road."

Essays on *The Marble Faun* range enormously in method and merit. Conrad Shumaker in " 'A Daughter of the Puritans': History in Hawthorne's *The Marble Faun*" (*NEQ 57*:65–83) stresses Hawthorne's moral interpretations of New England history as Colacurcio and McWilliams do, and (like Warren and Herzog) focuses on Hawthorne's women. Hilda is taken as "the apotheosis of the American girl as the nineteenth century envisioned her" and Hawthorne's "final commentary on the course he believed American history should take," his "corrective" to *Blithedale*, which showed woman as "victim of the historical movement she was meant to lead." Hilda at the carnival is at a point "full circle from Merry Mount"; but her character is not fully integrated, and the America where she is to function as household saint (Shumaker too sweepingly says) "would never exist." In *"The Marble Faun* as Transformation of Author and Age" (*NHJ 1978*, pp. 67–77), David Kesterson discusses Hawthorne's receptivity to every aspect of his experience in Italy, his "broadened vision of the past mingled with the present" as well as his "awakening to art" and to the efficacy of religion. His characters' transformations—particularly Donatello's paradigmatic loss of innocence—are related to America's movement beyond the romanticism of the Jacksonian period: the book's "sombre tone echoes the growing sobriety of a generation of romantics." Patrick Brancaccio in "Emma Abigail Salomons: Hawthorne's Miriam Identified" (*NHJ 1978*, pp. 95–104) discusses the beautiful young Jewess Hawthorne met at the Lord Mayor's banquet in London in 1856, the wife of the mayor's 60-year-old brother. Emma Salomons's taboo "racial distinctness" and her apparently inappropriate union entered into his conception of Miriam; and portraits validate the notebook description of her haunting beauty, appropriated in the novel to describe Miriam. According to Arnold Goldman in "The Plot of Hawthorne's *The Marble Faun*" (*JAS* 18: 383–404), the novel can be seen "as a contemporary fiction of surveillance, detection and intrigue, set in the topography of an historical police state" and as a recapitulation of "the history of the race." Some interpretations are reductive or overelaborate: Donatello is arrested because Papal authorities want his estate and his surrender is a condition of Hilda's release; the secret Miriam almost tells Kenyon is that she has been protected by the authorities in return for surveillance of Donatello ("We recall that the theme of female treachery to men is central to her art"); Donatello's "return to innocence enacts not merely the Fall but the Redemption." But Goldman gives useful information about Italian politics and the symbolic appropriateness of particular locations. In "Hawthorne: The Fine Edge," which concludes *Problematic Fictions* (pp. 50–119), Judith L. Sutherland argues that art and artists function in *The Marble Faun* as "negative redeemers" displaying a fallen world. Asserting that "the consensus is that the book is a failure," she ignores the many critics who argue otherwise (citing only two articles, one from 1948 and the other from 1953, and a curious footnote says the Centenary edition of the Italian notebooks was "unavailable"). Although Hawthorne solicited the imaginative cooperation of his readers, Sutherland sometimes takes her license too far, as when she says "the figure who links the fragmented elements of the text . . . *is* Christ and the fact of the Christian incarnation," or when she interprets the image of grapevines twisted around trees as "emblematic of the distorted balance between style and content in the work." Yet she offers some interesting interpretations—for example, of Hilda's "Pelagian" innocence. In "Some New Light on Hawthorne's *The Marble Faun*" (*NHJ 1978*, pp. 79–86) Paul A. Lister contends that the novel is an allegory of "Christ's redemption of mankind from Satan. . . . Kenyon represents God, the Father; Donatello represents Christ; Hilda, the Holy Spirit; Miriam, mankind; the model, Satan." This approach both requires and produces stretches and distortions (e.g., Lister says the qualities of Donatello's wine, Sunshine, "bear a strong resemblance to Holy Communion," without coping with the question of why Christ would offer it to God). Harry De Puy's "*The Marble Faun*: Another Portrait of Margaret Fuller?" (*ArQ* 40:163–78) is also riddled with misinterpretations and peculiar attributions: the model *is* James Nathan, Donatello *is* Ossoli, Kenyon and Hilda are the sculptor William Story and his wife; Margaret Fuller is sometimes Hilda (who left Rome to deliver a packet as Margaret to deliver a child), sometimes the obnoxious Miriam over whose fall in Sophia/Hilda's estimation Hawthorne "gloats," and she *is* the Marble Faun—"the title itself contains her initials." As proof that Hawthorne was dealing with Fuller's pregnancy and "how it came about," De Puy quotes Kenyon's perception that Miriam flung herself "on one passion, the object of which, intellectually, seemed far beneath her," then says "note the pun." We do not encounter Fuller, Hawthorne, or his text in this reader's response.

Lisa Hodgens in "Hawthorne's Last Period, or, Death Rattle in a Moonlit Room" (*NHJ 1978*, pp. 231–38) treats evidence of the struggle to bring fictions to life in the manuscripts of the uncompleted romances as "more frenzied versions" of what he had said before: "The Custom-House" adumbrates his later concern with the burden of the past as well as his anxiety about waning creative powers. But Hodgens might easily go back much further, to the Oberon sketches among others.

iv. Short Works

The year's most important treatments of the short stories are in the books of Colacurcio, McWilliams, and Siebers, but several studies are enterprising. Veronica Bassil's "Eros and Pyche in 'The Artist of the Beautiful' " (*ESQ* 30:1–21) argues that there is no irony or ambiguity about Owen's ultimate triumph as exemplary artist. Explaining the life cycle of the butterfly itself, particularly the stages when the caterpillar sheds its skin, she compares Owen's spiritual and artistic development to the caterpillar's; in creating the butterfly, he completes his metamorphosis (though I am not convinced that the caterpillar's "instars" correspond to the problems Owen encounters or that his triumph is complete). Bassil then presents Owen as both the story's dominant figure of Psyche (the seeker of Beauty) and (as lover and creator of the beautiful) an Eros figure. "The destruction of the butterfly may be Hawthorne's most ominous prediction of the future of art and artist in an industrialized society," she suggests; "it represents the death of the symbol as a mode of knowing." In "Hawthorne's 'Gentle Boy': Lost Mediators in Puritan History" (*SSF* 21:363–73), Frederick Newberry discusses patterns of opposition in the story which Hawthorne later developed: Puritans' persecution of non-Puritans, but also "the far more important contest between Puritan absolutism and moderation." After presenting a source for Pearson—a soldier disaffected by Cromwell in Scott's *Woodstock*—Newberry compares his leaving Cromwell's "unholy war" to his estrangement from the American Puritans. He is a "potential mediator trapped between warring factions" and so "lost." As a Quaker, he "wrongly suffers for doing right," though it misrepresents the story to say that Catherine and the old Quaker "rightly suffer for doing wrong." Puritan persecution certainly led to Ilbrahim's death and Pearson's isolation; but even though such severity increased in New England after the period of Hawthorne's story, that does not make its final suggestion of increased Puritan forbearance merely "sporific." Edwin Haviland Miller in "Wounded Love: Nathaniel Hawthorne's 'The Gentle Boy' " (*NHJ* 1978, pp. 47–56) reads the story as "a tender tale of parents and a child confronting loss and rejection." He believes Hawthorne drew on his own agonies to write it, the death of his father and "the seeming desertion of a mother," agonies he confronted again when writing *Dr. Grimshawe's Secret*.

In " 'Why are Those Girls Laughing?' The Unity and Failure of
'Alice Doane's Appeal,' " published last year in *Reconciliations:
Studies in Honor of Richard Harter Fogle* (Univ. of Salzburg; pp.
161–76), Tom H. Towers raises a good question, but to answer that
the laughter expresses relief that Alice is absolved of sin or contempt
for the wizard's curse imposes a false dichotomy. Further, the girls'
tears do not prove "that they like the risen dead of the inner tale or
the condemned witches in Mather's procession, are guilty, even
though they also may not know their crime"; and although the narrator has manipulated the girls' emotions, that does not prove he is
guilt-obsessed and "has called morally oblivious mankind to account."
Certainly Hawthorne worried about the destructive effects of guilt,
but Towers does not adequately recognize the story's ironies or ambiguities or the narrator's concern about his effects.

A few notes contain interesting speculations. In "Roger Malvin's
Grandson" (*SAF* 12:71–77) Ann Ronald says Hawthorne treats the
"sad demise" of the pioneer spirit and the American dream of the
West through the death of Cyrus, a youth of glorious promise.
Though we may question whether the Bournes have no prospect but
"pathetic expiation," or whether in dooming Cyrus to be shot by
Reuben's gun and the "patriarchal Puritan heritage," Hawthorne
"killed off a frontier optimism and the frontier dream," it makes sense
to read the story in the context of the Leatherstocking tales and other
elegiac treatments of the West. In "Names and the Root of Evil in
'Rappaccini's Daughter' " (*NHJ 1978*, pp. 175–80), Kent Bales makes
suggestions about Hawthorne's "linguistic cuing": e.g., Baglioni was
the name of a notorious Renaissance family; Giovanni's last name is
close to "Gascon" and Dante associated Gascons with avarice; and
the name Bearhaven in the preface is an allusion to Rappaccini, since
the Dutch physician Boerhaave had a famous garden and a lovely
daughter courted by fortune hunters.

Some notes are more uneven. Robert Zajkowski in "Renaissance
Psychology and Hawthorne's 'My Kinsman, Major Molineux' " (*NHJ
1978*, pp. 159–70) offers the four humors as a gloss on the story. Some
interpretations seem overly schematized or irrelevant—e.g., the ferry-
man and the innkeeper as phlegmatic, or Robin as developing from
sanguine to choleric to melancholy to phlegmatic, corresponding to
stages of the life cycle; but it is fitting if not essential to see the two-
faced man as a choleric individual who also displays melancholy
black humor. In " 'Young Goodman Brown': Hawthorne's Condem-

nation of Conformity" (*NHJ 1978*, pp. 137–46), Terence J. Matheson argues that Brown's problem was "preserving his public image." Other points are as specious—e.g., if Faith really wanted her husband to stay home, she would have persisted in her urging; or, Brown's resolve about clinging to her skirts indicates that he thought "salvation depended on geographical proximity" to a virtuous person. Herbert Perluck in "The Artist as 'Crafty Nincompoop': Hawthorne's 'Indescribable Obliquity of Gait' in 'Wakefield'" (*NHJ 1978*, pp. 181–96) suggests "Hawthorne is putting himself on" by writing a tale that "undermines its own experience." But there is distortion and inflation in approaching Wakefield as a comically inverted self-portrait and saying the story recreates "the existential grounds of the truly sacred" and undermines "the allegorical genre." Mark Johnston's point in "'The Canterbury Pilgrims': Hawthorne's Typical Story" (*EAS* 12:37–41) is that in this story as in other short narratives, Hawthorne wrote of the vanity of human wishes, using a fixed observer, a fixed vantage point, and a processional sequence; but he assumes the fiction is merely the embodiment of ideas and that Hawthorne's "technique did not permit him, generally, to write subtle fiction." In "Between the Walnut-Tree and the Fountain: Perspective of the Earthly Life in Hawthorne's 'An Old Woman's Tale'" (*ReAL* 11:13–20), Amy Patterson puts too heavy a weight on the tale—e.g., in associating Esther and David with their biblical "counterparts"—though it is true that the story has "the Hawthorne magic" and asserts the importance of living in the present.

In one of two notes on how Hawthorne used his sources, Robert C. Grayson in "Sources of Hawthorne's 'Sir William Pepperell'" (*CLQ* 20:100–06) shows how Hawthorne modified Belknap's *History of New Hampshire* by his focus on two scenes as well as his graphic style, and says his skills in incorporating data from various sources proved useful for his work on *Grandfather's Chair* and *The Magazine of Useful and Entertaining Knowledge*. And in "Hawthorne's 'April Fools': Source and Significance" (*ATQ* 53[1982]:67–72), Danny Lee Robinson presents the text that accompanied an engraving of an April Fool in the *Magazine* as representative of the way Hawthorne dealt with illustrations his editors provided. By contrast with the random list of April Fool pranks in the "source," Hawthorne assembled an ironic list of fools that self-reflexively included a dreamy student, an ambitious author, and (in conclusion) the editor who had composed the catalog.

v. Hawthorne and Others

As usual, critics have traced Hawthorne's influence on writers from his time to ours—on Melville, James, Flannery O'Connor, Fuentes, Paz, and Borges. (For comparisons with Poe, see Siebers and Kazin in section *ii;* for an indebtedness to Lamartine, see Reynolds in section *iii;* for a debt to Scott, see Newberry in section *iv.*) In "The Seashore Sketches in *Twice-told Tales* and Melville" (*ELN* 21:57–63) Rosemary F. Franklin says Melville's reading of Hawthorne's 1842 edition of *Twice-told Tales* in 1851 "probably reinforced rather than altered a number of the techniques, themes, and characters he was developing in *Moby-Dick.*" In support, she examines three Hawthorne sketches with seaside settings—"The Village Uncle," "Chippings with a Chisel," and "Foot-Prints on the Sea-Shore"—considering their use of the first person, their mix of humor and melancholy, parallels of subject and character, and such issues as human mortality and the need for solitude.

Watson Branch is concerned with the influence of "Rappaccini's Daughter" on *Daisy Miller* in "The Deeper Psychology: James's Legacy from Hawthorne" (*ArQ* 40:67–74). The egocentric and shallow Giovanni is a source of Winterbourne, who destroys the innocent Daisy: both are men of strong but repressed sensuality and active imagination (though it exaggerates to say that each "young woman's aura of innocence must be destroyed by the young man because it frustrates his hopes for sexual contest"); both men bear moral responsibility for the heroines' deaths (though I do not agree that they are depicted as evil). James appropriated Hawthorne's interest in moral responsibility and in "the way the human mind really works."

In "George Sand in American Reviews: A Context for Hester" (*HSN* 10:12–14) Nina Baym suggests that "the terms in which Hester gives up her claim to speak for women are . . . clearly derived from the George Sand controversy" in 1840s reviews which condemned her for asserting women's rights to happiness in marriage and insisted that novelists should celebrate only modest, womanly women. When Hester abandons her reformist ambitions, Hawthorne speaks for her; unlike "the vociferous George Sand," she is then a "true" and necessarily fictional woman.

William Rodney Allen in "Mr. Head and Hawthorne: Allusion and Conversion in Flannery O'Connor's 'The Artificial Nigger' " (*SSF* 21:17–23) traces echoes of "The Custom-House" (particularly the passage about moonlight in a familiar room) in the beginning of "The Artificial Nigger." O'Connor makes ironic use of Hawthorne's moonlight, but like him contrasts it with sunlit reality, and in the end the moonlight is magical. Allen argues that Hawthorne's concluding "benediction" marks his artistic conversion, while O'Connor ends with Head's religious conversion, but for both, escape from "provincial" limitations "comes masked as catastrophe."

Information about Hawthorne's influence on South American writers comes from two sources. Lois Parkinson Zamora in " 'A Garden Inclosed': Fuentes' *Aura*, Hawthorne's and Paz's 'Rappaccini's Daughter,' and Uyeda's *Ugetsu Monogatari*" (*RCEH* 8:321–40) concentrates on Fuentes, first comparing his 1962 novella and Hawthorne's story, then suggesting that Paz's 1956 surrealistic poetic drama was the "intermediary." Common to all three is a concern with the relationship of body to spirit, an enclosed realm controlled by a powerful individual, and a young man who enters as suitor of a young woman who is victim and victimizer. "A great writer creates his precursors and perfects them," Jorge Luis Borges said, as "Kafka modifies and refines the reading of Hawthorne." He does so himself in one of *Twenty-four Conversations with Borges* (Housatonic, Mass.: Lascaux; pp. 103–06). Drawing on Hawthorne's fiction, notebooks, and letters, Borges sees Hawthorne as "a creator of fables," though "an aesthetic error led him to append a moral . . . which often weakened them." He was "a true storyteller," beginning with imagined situations and delighting in the game of pretending they were real. Reading "Wakefield" as "an allegory of Hawthorne's reclusion" which "prefigures Kafka," Borges suggests that Hawthorne "turned or tried to turn literature into a function of his conscience." But "what matters is the end result": Hawthorne is "a writer who originates a manner of dreaming and makes us his heirs."

State University College of New York, Geneseo

3. Poe

Kent P. Ljungquist

In 1984 Poe remained a favorite target for applications of Continental theory, probably because his works invite such sharp focus on the interrelationship between the self and language. His tales of terror, with their anxiety-ridden narrators and uncanny atmospherics, present case studies of troubled selves under stress. Under the aegis of French literary theory, critics continued to scrutinize Poe's tales of ratiocination as well as his satiric efforts, both of which disclose his fondness for wordplay and horseplay. The playful texture of many of these tales invites practitioners of Continental theory to unloosen established interpretations. The openness of thematic purpose reflected in Poe's penchant for satiric caprice, his delight in literary hoax, and his fondness for puns add up to a challenge to fixed meanings. In recent years, however, as the novelty of Francophile criticism has worn off, expressions of discontent directed at the proponents of Continental theory have become more common. In a review-essay on John Irwin's *American Hieroglyphics*, "Reading Glyphic Writing: Vor-Textual Strategems" (*SoR* 19[1983]:913–18), Bainard Cowan suggests that many Deconstructionists do not practice what they preach, that is, they monitor recurrent images, rather than investigate a complete text in advance of the process of deconstruction. A more serious flaw in Deconstructionist criticism, according to Cowan, is neglect of historicity, an indifference to the temporal situation in which a literary work is created and transmitted to a readership. Whether Deconstructionists and Historicists will engage in a pitched battle—the Poe of Francophile theory pitted against the Poe of literary history—remains to be seen. The contours of potential conflict nevertheless sharpened in 1984, a year highlighted by the publication of two volumes in the Library of America series as well as by increased attention to Poe's achievements in the detective genre.

i. Editions, Books, Scholarly Tools

The Library of America *Poetry and Tales*, ed. Patrick Quinn, presents essential texts in an accessible and readable one-volume format. It would be a mistake to claim that this volume constitutes a "new edition," since it generally follows Mabbott for the tales (using revised versions from the *Broadway Journal*) and Stovall for the poems (using last revised versions). Heavily revised or retitled versions of the poems appear separately: "Imitation" and "A Dream Within a Dream"; "Introduction" and "Romance"; the two distinct versions of "Fairy-Land"; and "Mysterious Star," later dropped from "Al Aaraaf." All the so-called sketches, including "The Island of the Fay" (a later version rejected to allow for plate accompaniment), "Some Account of Stonehenge," "Byron and Miss Chaworth," and "Morning on the Wissahiccon," also appear. The full text of *Eureka*, based on the painstaking textual work and thorough documentation of Roland Nelson, is a most welcome inclusion. Quinn's clear, concise notes add usefulness to this volume that should serve multiple purposes for scholars, students, and general readers.

Even more welcome is G. R. Thompson's Library of America edition of *Essays and Reviews*. Scholars will no longer have to visit specialized holdings to consult several significant reviews, since Thompson reprints Poe's notices of *An Account of the United States Exploring Expeditions*, Cooper's *History of the Navy of the United States*, and George Jones's *Ancient America*. Contrary to Thompson's claim, however, Poe's review of Cooper's *Wyandotté* did appear in the Harrison edition. Thompson reprints all the primary documents in the "Longfellow War" so that scholars now have easy access to the essentials in one of Poe's most famous literary battles. For most titles, Thompson chooses the first appearance of each review unless it was subsequently expanded. Unsigned reviews receive verification through Poe's correspondence or by recourse to William Doyle Hull's unpublished dissertation, "A Canon of the Critical Works of Edgar Allan Poe." Thus no works of dubious authorship appear. Thompson enhances the usefulness of the volume with terse notes. The index incorrectly identifies a reference to Bryant as William Cullen rather than Jacob (pp. 642–43), and Thompson accepts somewhat casually the theory that the "Outis" of the Longfellow plagiarism controversy was Poe himself. Nevertheless, this edition presents, in an eminently readable and clear format, the widest range of Poe's criticism available in one volume, a canon of reviews called by Paul Zweig one of the "intellectual monuments of the Jacksonian era" (see Zweig, *Walt Whitman: The Making of the Poet* [Basic Books], p. 45). One can lament only that the Library of America, probably because of space considerations, did not choose to include all verified reviews. One must still, for example, consult *Burton's Magazine* (1839) for his notice of Dimitry's *Lecture on the Study of History*, and a variety of sources for other pieces.

Of the two books devoted exclusively to Poe this year, Bettina Knapp's *Edgar Allan Poe*, part of Ungar's Literature and Life series, is a distinct disappointment. The author offers chapters on Poe's life, the poems, and the tales. No separate chapter on the criticism, though Knapp does make brief comments on key essays. The subheads in the section on Poe's fiction—"The Descent," "The Anima," "The Shadow," and "The Mystical Quest"—reflect her reliance on Jungian psychology, but previous scholarship by Barton St. Armand, Martin Bickman, and Steven K. Hoffman is not cited (see *ALS 1983*, p. 55). Although many insights in this book have been anticipated by various critics, no articles on Poe appear in the bibliography, and the most recent book consulted is Burton Pollin's *Discoveries in Poe* (1977). Verbal expression in this study often falters because of jargon—"Lenore went through the depersonalization process when she died as a human being and was reborn as an image" (p. 83)—and mixed metaphors—"As the word is unleashed in the verse, washed of earthly dross, divested of mundane chatter, cut from the world of mundane contingencies, it ascends to collective spheres, endowing the subject, be it beauty or the mourning lover with archetypal force" (p. 99). While Knapp brings knowledge of a range of foreign literatures to bear on her subject, errors become obtrusive: "Eleonora" is misspelled throughout as "Eleanora"; "The City in the Sea" allegedly presents an underwater metropolis; and Knapp even implies that Rowena is killed by lead poisoning (p. 134).

The other book to appear in 1984, Kent Ljungquist's *The Grand and the Fair: Poe's Landscape Aesthetics and Pictorial Techniques* (Scripta Humanistica) deftly argues Poe's knowledge and use of concepts of the sublime and picturesque, along with the linked topics of ruins and daemonism.[1] (See the related discussion of Catherine Rainwater's essay below.) Although Poe was as well-versed in the

---

1. This paragraph and the two following were written by Benjamin Franklin Fisher IV.

modes of landscape writing as his contemporaries, Ljungquist argues that he did not admire, nor did he ape, their overwhelmingly physical descriptions expressed in terms of vapory appreciation. Instead, Poe often used such landscape means toward the end of revealing limits to the vision of humankind. "MS. Found in a Bottle," *Pym*, and "A Descent into the Maelström" form a progression from Poe's early mode of half-humor, half-horror to an altogether noncomic dramatization of sublimity. Unlike most of his contemporaries, Poe did not employ American settings for his best landscape effects. His general method was to move from the pictorial to the abstract. Thus, in "Usher," "Eleonora," and the landscape sketches, Poe subtly leads us from externals into an imaginative world where caprice reigns.

Many cherished notions of "major" and "minor" Poe will sustain shocks because of this book. *Julius Rodman,* for example, emerges here not as cursory hack-writing, but as an unsuccessful attempt to combine 18th-century aesthetic theory with a narrative of travel into the American frontier. "Mellonta Tauta" is interpreted as parody of the sublimity of *Pym*. The landscapes of "A Tale of the Ragged Mountains," induced as they probably are by drugs and mesmerism, imply Poe's skepticism of the entire landscape mode, as do the Arnheim–Island of the Fay pieces. This skepticism also emerges from "Eleonora," wherein madness may inform the plot. In all Poe's "landscaping," he offers implication rather than precision. Thus he reinforces his critical dictum that undercurrents of suggestion inform all works of art.

Ljungquist brings his own theoretical guns to bear upon many warhorse Poe titles, as well as upon some of the less frequently analyzed materials (e.g., *Politian*, "The Elk," and some early poems). His interpretations offer fresh, provocative readings which should stimulate additional analyses.

My discussion of the sea tales can be profitably read in light of the chapter on *Pym* in Judith L. Sutherland's *Problematic Fictions*, a brief monograph that relies intelligently on reader-response theory. According to Sutherland, "problematic texts" like *Pym, The Marble Faun,* and *The Sacred Fount* resist thematic interpretation. For Poe, in particular, thematic analysis does not account for the anxiety his tales induce in the reader, a result of Poe's employment of language to render "an hermeneutical nightmare" (p. 16). As in the case of *Pym,* the reader's questionings end in frustration. After reader attention is expanded by the description of the "shrouded human figure," the

Author's Note deflates such expectations, and the desire for ultimate knowledge becomes frustrated. Presented with a series of collapses, recoveries, and deceptions as the narrative concludes, the reader must hover between surrender and detachment. Within this reader-response framework, Sutherland approaches Pym as a flat character, the unwitting butt of Poe's humor. In the final third of the narrative, the reader, along with the title character, forge on to the South Pole, but ultimately one must realize that "to arrive at a single pole is not to arrive at an answer" (p. 30). This sustained indeterminancy results from Poe's artful manipulation of fictional illusion. Sutherland's lucid, witty, and jargon-free analysis brings a sophisticated theoretical approach to bear on a challenging text, and intelligent comparisons with Poe's contemporaries, most notably Emerson, surface in her footnotes.

Michael Burduck has assembled a helpful scholarly tool, "An Index to *Poe Studies*: Volumes I–XVI" (*PoeS* 17:1–10), a comprehensive index to the journal, including its early numbers as the *Poe Newsletter*.

The full bibliographical apparatus in Ottavio M. Casale's "Edgar Allan Poe," pp. 362–71 in *The Transcendentalists*, enhances the essay's usefulness as a scholarly aid. Casale distinguishes two brands of transcendentalism, the popular fad that Poe abhorred and the ennobling philosophy that attracted him. His satiric barbs directed at the New England Frogpond reflect sectional and aesthetic differences rather than wholehearted distaste for transcendentalism. Casale's discriminating survey of books and articles on Poe and transcendentalism reflects the work of a scholar in full command of his subject.

ii. Sources and Influences

Source and influence study has become much more sophisticated since the days when verbal echoes constituted proof of literary borrowing. In "Recovering Byron: Poe's 'The Assignation' " (*Criticism* 26:211–29), Dennis Pahl uses the writings of Derrida to claim that Poe's early tale presents a meditation on recovering a life through language. Because of concealment, Byron remains an elusive figure colored by subjective interpretation and expanding legend. "The Assignation" suggests Byronic influence, but Poe does not call forth the authentic Byron as much as an interpretive fiction inspired by the Romantic poet.

While Pahl argues that a reclaiming of literary origins necessitates an act of interpretation, Maurice J. Bennett uses a more common-sensical approach in "Edgar Allan Poe and the Tradition of Lunar Speculation" (*SFS* 10:137–47). Like Pahl, Bennett deals with literary precedents, a range of authors (Lucian, Kepler, Godwin, Richard Adams Locke, and George Tucker) who developed the generic conventions of lunar speculation. Fictional explorations of the moon, Bennett notes, present a satirical juxtaposition of lunar and earthly customs. When Poe turns to this genre in "Hans Pfaall," he follows the techniques and assumptions of his predecessors in describing the earth, but his portrayal of the moon deviates from tradition in invoking a romantic landscape of the imagination. "Hans Pfaall" thus presents a unique blend of science and mysticism.

One of several studies that treat the sources of Poe's fiction, Robert Lance Snyder's "A De Quinceyan Source for Poe's 'The Masque of the Red Death'" (*SSF* 21:103–10) calls our attention to an episode in Thomas De Quincey's gothic novel *Klosterheim: or the Masque* (1832), in which an intruder becomes entrapped at a costume ball. Acknowledging that there is no external evidence that Poe read *Klosterheim*, Snyder notes parallels in setting, plot, and incident. In "Insipiens Fortunatas" (*AN&Q* 22[1983]:9–10), Ronald Pepin suggests that the lucky fool in Cicero's *De Amicitia* may have helped to inspire Fortunato in "The Cask of Amontillado." Along similar lines, Stuart Levine, in "Masonry, Impunity, and Revolution" (*PoeS* 17:22–23), suggests that the Latin motto in "Cask," translated as "No one insults me with impunity," may have become known to Poe through commonly known details in Richmond history.

Katrina E. Bachinger provides two tidy notes on the fiction. In "The Obscure Webb(e) and Poe's 'The Man of the Crowd'" (*N&Q* 31:478–79), she suggests that the oceanic imagery and compulsive movement in Cornelius Webb's *Glances at Life in City and Suburb* (1836) may have contributed details to Poe's urban vision. In "Poe's Folio Club: A Pun on Peacock's Folliot" (*N&Q* 31:66), she alerts us to chapter 6 in *Crotchet Castle* in which a Reverend Dr. Folliott presides over a series of discourses by diverse characters attending a dinner. Not primarily a source study, Walter Shear's note on "Poe's Use of an Idea About Perception" (*AN&Q* 21:134–36) cites a common idea on indirect perception that derives from 18th- and early 19th-century optics. Shear then follows Poe's redeployment of a comment on "seeing the obvious" in "Berenice," "Hans Pfaall," and "The Purloined Letter."

While critical analysis of Poe's verse continues to be scant, several brief studies increase our knowledge of his poetic sources and his processes of composition. Burton R. Pollin, in "Traces in 'Annabel Lee' of Cunningham's Poems" (*AN&Q* 22:133–35), adduces evidence that Alan Cunningham's "Lily of Nithsdale," included in Longfellow's *The Waif*, influenced the form and content of Poe's famous ballad. In a related study, "Longfellow and Poe: An Unnoted Hexameter Exchange" (*MissQ* 37:474–82), Pollin makes the small but interesting discovery that a model Greek hexameter in "The Rationale of Verse" was aimed at Longfellow and his friends. Reminding us that no thorough study of the Poe-Longfellow relationship exists, Pollin provides further encouragement for students of Poe and his contemporaries. Calling our attention to a contemporary from across the Atlantic, Guy Woodall, in "Another Source for the 'Misty Mid Region of Weir' " (*AN&Q* 23:8–10), suggests that the 1829 appearance in *Blackwood's* of James Hogg's "A Tale of the Martyrs," and "John Weir, a Ballad" may have inspired an allusion and the ghoulish atmosphere in "Ulalume." This is perhaps the most convenient place to mention another note by Katrina Bachinger, "Poe's 'For Annie' " (*Expl* 43:33–35), which suggests that a reordering of the poem's sequence heightens the comic effect of narration by a dead speaker.

The most substantial study of Poe's verse to appear in 1984 mentions the biographical sources of his poetry only to conclude that they have been overestimated. G. Richard Thompson, in *Circumscribed Eden of Dreams: Dreamvision and Nightmare in Poe's Early Poetry*, is more interested in Poe's refinement of the poetic genre of the apocalyptic dreamscape than in whether Sarah Elmira Royster inspired specific poems. The longest and most ambitious lecture printed by the Baltimore Poe Society and the Enoch Pratt Library, Thompson's study approaches the length of a good-sized monograph. In a revisionist interpretation of the *Tamerlane* volume, Thompson observes "consistent development of tension between visionary experience and circumscription of that experience" (p. 8). Less insistent about Poe's ironic and hoaxical tendencies in this essay than in previous studies, Thompson does note framing devices and the tone of amused Byronic distance in "Tamerlane." The title poem introduces the identifying theme of the volume: a visionary dream overwhelmed by the ill demon of the imagination. Thompson proceeds to survey individual poems in the volume by downplaying biographical readings along the way. A highlight of this penetrating overview is his

appreciative analysis of "The Lake—To," a poem that locates both
terror and delight in the rites of artistic passage.

Two notes deal with Poe's possible influence on 19th-century
authors. In "The Ruins of Romanticism in *The Confidence-Man*"
(*AN&Q* 22[1983]:40–43), Edward Strickland takes up the theory
first advanced by Harrison Hayford that Poe is the crazy beggar in
chapter 36 of Melville's masquerade. Strickland further speculates
that the "rhapsodical tract" mentioned there is "The Poetic Principle," which Poe took on the lecture circuit in 1848–49. Melville's
satire thus plays off Poe, a piece of human wreckage, against the
duplicitous Mark Winsome. In "Poe, Rossetti, and the Doctors
Mauldsley" (*PoeS* 17:22), Jay Jacoby distinguishes Dr. Henry Mauldsley, an ardent Poe defender, from Dr. Henry Carr Mauldsley, who
attended Rossetti before his death.

Articles that connect Poe to French literature deal with questions
of literary inheritance and problems of translation. Mary Ann Caws,
in "Insertion in an Oval Frame: Poe Circumscribed by Baudelaire"
(*FR* 56[1983]:679–87), suggests that translation is an act of framing,
that is, the process of translation gives definition to what is both absorbed and lost in rewriting. Like Caws, Rosemary Lloyd, in "Baudelaire's Creative Criticism" (*FS* 36[1982]:37–44), claims that Baudelaire's fascination with Poe's works served positive ends. Haskell
Block's "Poe, Baudelaire, Mallarmé, and the Problem of the Untranslatable" in *Translation Perspectives* (pp. 104–12) notes the
shaping effects of translation on Mallarmé's career. Further noting
that Baudelaire thought "The Bells" untranslatable and that Mallarmé thought poems were untranslatable as poetry, Block acknowledges the French contribution of *poèmes en prose*, a new genre that
emerged via Poe's influence in the 19th century. In "The Importance
of T. S. Eliot's 'Note sur Mallarmé et Poe'" (*YER* 7[1982]:36–41),
G. V. West translates a review that Eliot published in French in
Nouvelle Revue Française (1926). The example of Poe, West argues,
helped Eliot to distinguish between metaphysical and philosophic
poetry. Implied but not stated in West's essay is a possible Poe influence on "Little Gidding."

West's essay reflects the increased scholarly attention given to
Poe's influence on 20th-century authors. A contemporary writer not
previously analyzed in the light of such influence is John Hawkes,
who receives thorough treatment from Charles Berryman in "Hawkes

and Poe: *Travesty*" (*MFS* 29[1983]:643–54). After noting general affinities—nightmare imagery, foreign settings, and a terrifying atmosphere—Berryman discusses *Travesty* and its treatment of a favorite Poe theme: the relationship of art to death. Hawkes portrays Tara as a Poe-esque female, he delineates quintessentially gothic settings, and he formulates an aesthetic fable that horrifyingly connects creation and destruction.

In "Poe and Fuentes: The Reader's Prerogatives" (*CL* 36:34–53), Susan and Stuart Levine, by citing Poe's influence on Borges, Cortázar, and most notably Carlos Fuentes, remind us that John E. Englekirk's *Poe in Hispanic Literature* (1934) urgently needs updating. Attuned to sophisticated theories of literary influence, the Levines argue that we can and should read Poe differently in the light of the Spanish Modernistas. In the ambitious *Terra Nostra* (1975) the fictional descent into the vortex, the black and white imagery, and the juxtaposition of temporal and spatial situations reflect Fuentes's playful but thorough adaptation of motifs from *Pym*. In his updating of Poe's novel, Fuentes offers both a maritime adventure and a metafictional *tour de force*, dual strains that serve to affirm as well as mock previous literature. In sum, Fuentes infuses *Terra Nostra* with a spirit of "transcendental buffoonery" reminiscent of Poe. Alice Pollin contributes another worthwhile essay on Poe and Spanish literature in "Edgar Allan Poe in the Works of Llanos y Alcaraz" (*Hispano* 79 [1983]:22–37). Calling attention to the first musical/dramatic setting in a foreign language of a Poe tale, she discusses a Spanish version of Poe's comic story, "The System of Doctor Tarr and Professor Fether."

In the realm of Poe studies, literary influence is often a two-way street, as Gerhard Hoffman reminds us in his scholarly study, "Edgar Allan Poe in German Literature," in *American-German Literary Interrelations in the Nineteenth Century*, ed. Christoph Wecker (Munich: Wilhelm Fink [1983]), pp. 52–104. The first part of this systematic study deals with Poe's exposure to German Romantic theory. Even though denying the impact of German literature in his preface to *Tales of the Grotesque and Arabesque*, Poe borrowed elements of the fantastic tale from Tieck, Hoffman, Arnim, and others. Perhaps more valuable because of the novelty of the findings, the second half of Hoffman's essay focuses on Poe's influence on modern and contemporary authors. Poe and Kafka, for example, shared the common medium of fantasy, though Hoffman discerns significant differences: in Poe's fiction, the unnatural invades a natural situation; in Kafka's enigmatic fables, the unnatural or perverse infuses the texture of the entire world. Hoffman turns over the final portion of his survey to an examination of Arno Schmidt's idiosyncratic fictional experiment, *Zettels Traum*. With its playful adaptation of elements from *Pym*, Schmidt's work will undoubtedly repay further attention from other scholars.

iii. Individual Works and Special Concerns

In "The Analytic of the Dash: Poe's *Eureka*" (*Genre* 16[1983]:437–66) Joan Dayan offers a significant new study of Poe's prose poem. By calling attention to an interesting pattern in Poe's punctuation, Dayan claims that he uses the dash consciously to give precision to an indefinite effect. Distinguishing indefiniteness from mere vagueness, Poe's dashes record graphically the stops and starts on the "unutterable journey" toward apprehending the immensity of the universe. Dayan makes an interesting correlation between the "digressions" in *Eureka* and the "rhetoric of inconsequence," the excess verbiage that characterizes his anxious narrators on their tortuous pathway toward disclosure.

While the ingenuity of Dayan's analysis is certainly impressive, some readers will balk at an approach that seems to reduce Poe's artistry to a linguistic *tour de force*. In *Poe: A Phenomenological View (1973)*, not cited by Dayan, David Halliburton commented on Poe's propensity for dashes, but arrived at a much different conclusion. Whatever the implications we draw from practices in punctuation, conclusions should be based on the text that most accurately reflects Poe's intentions. As Roland Nelson pointed out in 1978, "Observations of this sort (i.e., observations on punctuation) are obviously dependent upon the availability of a text representative in every way of what the author actually wrote" (*SAR 1978*, p. 188). Rather than the Price-Hurst-Wakeman copy of *Eureka* extensively corrected in Poe's hand, Dayan cites the Virginia edition, a text that had undergone Harrison's imposition of house styling in matters of punctuation. In addition, one wonders what Dayan would make of Mabbott's observation that the revisions for Poe's *Phantasy-Pieces* reflect his replacement of dashes by commas and semi-colons.

In "The Identity of Berenice, Poe's Idol of the Mind" (*SIR* 23:

491–513), Dayan returns to Poe's manipulation of language and structure. Despite his pronouncements on absolute beauty, he inevitably focuses on material forms: the irradiated particles of matter in *Eureka* and the haunting spectrum of teeth in "Berenice." If the dash serves as a tool of stylistic segmentation in *Eureka*, a succession of sharply delineated segments recurs in "Berenice" with each narrative unit followed by asterisks that mark the fitful processes of memory. By suggesting possible sources in St. Augustine, Catullus, and John Locke, Dayan notes that for Egaeus memory displaces experience itself. As in *Eureka*, the activity of thought materializes on the printed page, a consequence of Egaeus's obsessive hoarding of words and memories. A thoughtful reconsiderer of Poe's quest for "identity," Dayan positions this search in a state of tension between matter and spirit, dispersal and reunification. Her comments on the reader's sense of elevation should be read in the light of Judith Sutherland's discussion in *Problematic Fictions* (see section *i.* above).

Two studies from 1983 deal with psychological implications of individual tales. In "Lacan, Poe, and Narrative Repression" (*MLN* 98 [1983]:983–1005), Robert Con Davis, using Lacan's theory that literary texts contain conscious and unconscious systems in various stages of unity, focuses on "The Tell-Tale Heart," a tale that reflects the pattern of seeing without being seen. Conforming to Lacan's interpretation of the Gaze, this form of voyeurism illustrates aspects of textual repression distinguished by gaps in the narrative. In "The Struggle of the Wills in Poe's 'William Wilson'" (*SAF* 11[1983]:73–79), Valentine Hubbs addresses the title character's perception of Doctor Bransby. Wilson's inability to comprehend paradox in human behavior, which he refers to as "monstrous," reflects his own futile attempt to reconcile warring internal forces. Hubbs's comments on the Jungian concept of the shadow do not advance our knowledge beyond Eric Carlson's psychological reading of the tale (see *ALS 1976*, p. 40).

In "Psychological Crisis and Enclosure in Edgar Allan Poe's 'The Pit and the Pendulum'" (*CEA* 45[1983]:28–31), Leonard Engel suggests that enclosure images reinforce the juxtaposition of conscious and unconscious states. He does not add significantly to his previous discussion of the same motif (see *ALS 1983*, p. 54). In a related essay, "Inside 'The Masque of the Red Death'" (*SubStance* 13:50–53), Martin Roth explores the dialectic between inside and outside in

Poe's tale. In a story in which an external invader arrives at an interior location which is given over to outer display, the concepts of inside and outside become confused and interchangeable. According to William Crisman, in " 'Mere Household Events' in Poe's 'The Black Cat' " (*SAF* 12:87–90), the narrator's comments on homely household events should not be taken comically. Rather, the narrator, whose greatest youthful fear was potential infidelity, sees the cat as a rival for his wife's affections. The tale thus presents a serious fable of jealousy.

Narrators who betray their own inadequacies are found even in Poe's landscape tales, according to Catherine Rainwater ("Poe's Landscape Tales and the 'Picturesque' Tradition," *SLJ* 16:30–43). In "The Domain of Arnheim" and "Landor's Cottage," according to Rainwater, Poe uses the volatile aesthetic category of the picturesque, a choice that reflects his vacillation between formal and affective principles. She provides good background on 18th- and 19th-century aestheticians who aimed to preserve the morally elevating effect of picturesque scenery while maintaining Formalist criteria of artistic appreciation. This distinction, as I note in my related study of Poe's picturesque aesthetics (see section *i.* above), has an analogue in Poe's opposition between "the physique and the morale" of scenery in "Usher." A proper reading of the landscape tales, Rainwater concludes, suggests that the gullible narrators, prone to facile aesthetic categories burlesqued by Poe, are taken in by the complex, deceptive nature of art.

iv. Poe and the Genre of Detective Fiction

With popular forms receiving increased scrutiny, Poe's pioneering contributions in the detective genre have become the object of wider and more varied attention. Scholars are applying all sorts of methodological strategies to Poe's tales of ratiocination—perspectives ranging from those of literary theory and psychoanalytic criticism to those of comparative literature and literary history. The results are mixed. In "The Literary *Histrio* as Detective" (*MSE* 8[1982]:1–8), Susan F. Beegel makes the unoriginal point that Poe's detective stories and "The Philosophy of Composition" derive from the same impulse, the desire to unravel an artfully constructed situation. She does offer an insightful comment on the role language plays in the insoluble riddles posed by these tales, a point previously made by Dennis W. Eddings in his 1982 essay on "Poe, Dupin, and the Reader" (*UMSE* 3:128–35). In "The Detective Story Genre in Poe and Borges" (*LALR* 11[1983]:27–37), Julia Kushigan observes that Borges's "Death and the Compass" follows the linear construction of the detective story. In contrast to Poe, however, Borges presents an almost infinite range of imaginative elements and "solutions." Maurice J. Bennett provided a more subtle analysis of the Poe-Borges relationship in an essay published last year (see *ALS 1983*, p. 49).

Françoise Meltzer begins her discussion of "Laclos' Purloined Letters" (*CritI* 8[1982]:515–29) by mentioning Lacan's identification of the letter as pure signifier, not so much a unit of meaning as an entity that produces certain effects. Using Poe also as a point of departure, she proceeds to an analysis of the epistolary novel with specific focus on Choderlos de Laclos's *Les Liaisons Dangereuses*. In both Poe and Laclos, the fact of the letter assumes greater importance than its meaning, since it carries a powerful force of signaling and manipulation. An essay that also connects Poe to other authors, William Goldhurst's "Misled by a Box: Variations on a Theme from Poe" (*Clues* 3[1982]:31–37) notes parallels among Poe's "The Oblong Box," Doyle's "That Little Square Box," and Eugene O'Neill's "In the Zone."

The year's most substantial and intelligent discussion of Poe's contribution to the detective genre appears in Stefano Tani's *The Doomed Detective: The Contribution of the Detective Novel to Postmodern and Italian Fiction* (So. Ill.), pp. 3–15. Sensitive to the historical roots of the genre, Tani notes that the detective story was an outgrowth of Enlightenment rationalism. The paradox of detective fiction, however, was its incorporation of two strains, the encyclopedic, lucid rationality of the 18th century joined with the nascent interest in madness and irrationality of gothic fiction. The rational, "realistic" strain in this incipient tradition, reflected in rogues' biographies, ultimately merged with elements of popular adventure. Poe's revolutionary achievement, a "fusion of rational and irrational currents" in the first three detective stories, finds expression in the two sides of Dupin's personality, the creative and the resolvent. In a pattern reflecting Poe's love-hate attitude toward his art, the "creative" criminal must be stifled by the forces of reason, a formula that undergoes subtle variation in other tales. In post-Modern fiction, Tani claims, authors like John Gardner, Thomas Pynchon, and Umberto Eco subvert the principle of rationality celebrated by Poe, but the Poe-esque duality continues in a new guise, the polarized relationship between writer and reader. As students of postmodernism suggest that contemporary authors have remade Poe in their own image, Tani thoughtfully monitors the stages of descent from Poe's signal achievements in this unique genre.

Worcester Polytechnic Institute

4. Melville

Brian Higgins

Following last year's excitement over the discovery of the papers in a barn in upstate New York, Melville made headlines again in 1984: the post office issued a commemorative stamp on the 165th anniversary of his birthday, and, causing more of a stir among Melvilleans, his heavily annotated two-volume edition of Milton surfaced briefly at the Phillips Gallery, New York, before disappearing again, after auction, into the hands of an unnamed buyer. The other event of the year was the publication of the latest volume of the Northwestern-Newberry edition—volume 10, *The Confidence-Man*. Otherwise very little was published on Melville that's likely to be of any lasting value. There was no sign in Melville studies of that engagement of literary theory and traditional criticism "in a renovating debate about practice" which my predecessor looked forward to last year.

i. Editions and Lexicons

The "Editorial Appendix" in *The Confidence-Man* follows the usual format of the Northwestern-Newberry edition, with a "Historical Note" by Watson Branch, Hershel Parker, and Harrison Hayford, with Alma A. MacDougall, which gives accounts of the book's place in Melville's literary career, its composition, publication, and reception by American and British reviewers, and its treatment by 20th-century scholars and critics; and a "Textual Record" by the editors, Hayford, Parker, and G. Thomas Tanselle. The appendix also includes a section of related documents, containing reproductions of the book's surviving manuscript fragments and the rejected manuscript passage titled "The River," with genetic transcriptions by Hayford and analysis and commentary by Hayford and MacDougall; a reproduction of "Melville's Indian-Hating Source," chapter 6 of the second volume of James Hall's *Sketches of History, Life, and*

Manners, in the West, accompanied by marginal page and line numbers to indicate the corresponding passages in chapters 26 and 27 of the Northwestern-Newberry edition; and a reprinting of the "Rivers" section in the introduction to the 1828 edition of Timothy Flint's *A Condensed Geography and History of the Western States,* some version of which Melville drew upon in "The River," with a headnote by Hayford. For the great majority of readers, the most useful part of the appendix will undoubtedly be the "Historical Note," particularly the two sections on composition, the most comprehensive account to date of the book's sources; and the section on the book's treatment in the 20th century. Easily the most impressive parts of the appendix, however, are Hayford's genetic transcriptions of the manuscript fragments and Hayford and MacDougall's analysis of the fragments and their relation to each other and to the printed text—painstaking and brilliant contributions to our knowledge of Melville's methods of composition and revision.

Hayford also wrote the note on the texts and notes for the third Melville volume in the Library of America series, published in 1984. This compact and handy volume contains *Pierre, Israel Potter, Piazza Tales, The Confidence-Man,* "Uncollected Prose," and *Billy Budd, Sailor.* In addition to the uncollected tales, including "Fragments from a Writing Desk," the "Uncollected Prose" contains "Authentic Anecdotes of 'Old Zack'" and the five reviews Melville published in the *Literary World.* The texts are those of the Northwestern-Newberry edition, with the exception of *Billy Budd;* the text for the latter is the "reading text" edited by Hayford and Sealts in 1962.

Native speakers of English may find *A Melville Lexicon* (Tokyo: Kaibunsha), compiled by Shigeru Maeno and Kaneaki Inazumi, useful on occasion. The volume gives definitions of "about eight thousand words, compounds, and phrases" used by Melville. The compilers "have tried to collect almost all Melville's Americanisms, all his new words, all his archaisms," and words and phrases difficult for nonnative speakers of English. Definitions are culled from dictionaries published in Melville's lifetime and from 20th-century dictionaries.

ii. General Studies

Only one critical book devoted wholly to Melville appeared in 1984: *Melville: Reassessments,* a collection of essays by British and American critics edited by A. Robert Lee, that "seek[s] to open up a number of fresh avenues into the overall range of his writing." Despite the presence of a number of well-known names in the volume, most of the essays fall short. Lee himself contributed the two best essays, one on *Moby-Dick* and one on *The Confidence-Man*. Individual essays in the collection are discussed in relevant sections below.

The section devoted to Melville in John P. McWilliams, Jr.'s *Hawthorne, Melville, and the American Character* provides a useful survey of Melville's expression of national concerns and portrayal of national characteristics from the years in which he wrote *Redburn* and *White-Jacket* and began *Moby-Dick*—"a time of an almost unqualified national faith" for Melville, when he "treasured the expectation that men of the New World would combine the best qualities of the pioneer, the Christian, the democrat, and the primitive"—through to his increasingly conservative later years, when his "millennial expectations" had proved to be "an unrealizable myth." Much of what McWilliams has to say about individual works has long been familiar, however. Most of his treatment of *Moby-Dick*, for instance, is fairly routine (Melville, for example, "celebrates the size, technological expertise, and heroic courage of American whalemen" but also provides "a convincing critique of the exploitation and waste of American industry"). It is rescued from commonplace by his brief discussion of Ahab in terms of Tocqueville's analysis of the American character and imagination, a discussion that lends weight to the claims of earlier critics that for all his mania Ahab is characteristically American. In places McWilliams's search for "national implications" in the works leads him to oversimplify, as in his account of Pierre's "democratic idealism," which misses the complexity of Pierre's idealism and exaggerates his democratic concerns.

Joyce W. Warren's chapter on Melville in *The American Narcissus* (pp. 115–47) sheds no new light on an old topic, Melville's infrequent and inadequate portrayal of women. Warren argues that Melville "was able to portray women only from a distance or as the unreal, will-less maidens of the courtship period" because "he regarded real women—with their own ideas and personalities—as a threat to the development of the masculine self." Like Emerson, according to Warren, Melville was so concerned with "the preservation and assertion of the self" that he "could not recognize the selfhood of the other, least of all the female other." These notions stem from a facile interpretation (derived from Weaver) of Melville's relation to his male protagonists—all, including Ahab and Pierre, seen simply as projections of Melville's "conception of himself"—and from superficial analyses (influenced by Weaver and Mumford) of Melville's relationship with Hawthorne and with his family. Wilma Garcia's chapter on Melville in *Mothers and Others* (pp. 59–102) gives strained and reductive readings of several of the works, including *Moby-Dick*, in a "search for meaning within the patterns of female imagery in Melville's ironic quests of the hero." According to Garcia, the recurring "ironic conflict" of Melville's works is "the hero's need to be about his quest, and to participate in the fertile act of sexual union, only to feel the painful pull of mother, symbol of origins and safety, drawing him back."

My own chapter on Melville in *The Transcendentalists* (pp. 348–61) surveys research and criticism treating Melville's responses to transcendentalism and Transcendentalists. I conclude that despite the plethora of articles, chapters, and dissertations on this subject large gaps still remain in our knowledge of what Melville actually knew of the Transcendentalists and their writings. Another general study, Michael S. Kearns's "Phantoms of the Mind: Melville's Criticism of Idealistic Psychology" (*ESQ* 30:40–50) claims that Melville's criticism of idealistic psychology was "detailed and insightful" but never establishes, or attempts to establish, what he knew or might have known about that psychology and where his knowledge came from; nor does it lay out clearly which of its tenets he would have been familiar with through his knowledge of Emerson or other idealistic philosophers. As Kearns acknowledges, there is no direct evidence that Melville read the contemporary psychologists. Kearns's claim, moreover, that from *Typee* to *Pierre* Melville dramatizes "the need for a pragmatic rather than an idealistic psychology, for a psychology based on an individual's social nature" makes Melville appear far more programmatic in his interest in psychology than the works themselves seem to warrant.

Hershel Parker touches frequently on Melville throughout his *Flawed Texts and Verbal Icons*. He uses examples from Melville—particularly *White-Jacket*, *Pierre*, and *Billy Budd*—to illustrate the kinds of anomalies writers often introduce into their works as they compose under successive and sometimes contradictory creative impulses, anomalies critics have been all too prone to overlook in their eagerness to celebrate the unity of the finished (or, as in the case of *Billy Budd*, even unfinished) text, or more recently, to deconstruct it.

iii. Biography

Biographical writing about Melville in 1984 was limited to Howard
C. Horsford's modest "Melville in the London Literary World" (*EAS*
13:23–42), which adds minor details to our knowledge of the publishers and literati Melville encountered in London in 1849, and James
C. Wilson's more ambitious "Melville at Arrowhead: A Reevaluation
of Melville's Relations with Hawthorne and with His Family" (*ESQ*
30:232–44), which draws on the cache of letters discovered in upstate New York in 1983 (see Section *v.* below). The new letters Wilson
quotes add fascinating details to what we already know of Melville's
relations with the Hawthornes and with members of his own family
from Jay Leyda's *Melville Log*, Leon Howard's and Eleanor Melville
Metcalf's biographies, and Davis and Gilman's edition of the *Letters*.
But Wilson is not content to discuss the letters in those rather modest
terms; instead he uses them as evidence that "Freudian Melville
scholars" have "distorted" Melville's relationship with Hawthorne
and with his family. The new material he quotes scarcely amounts,
however, to a "restoration" of a previously lacking familial and social
context for Melville's relationship with Hawthorne, as Wilson claims;
rather it confirms impressions already conveyed by documents previously available (in Metcalf's volume, for instance, which Wilson
never mentions) that, in Wilson's words, "the texture of Melville's
life during his first two years in the Berkshires was a complex network
of literary, family, and social relations that involved a wide circle of
friends and acquaintances" and that "the Melville-Hawthorne relationship was not exclusively male or literary, but instead a friendship between families." It is hard to imagine that Freudian Melvilleans will find their view of Melville's relationship with Hawthorne
seriously compromised by the new letters. Freudians—and others—
are likely to find Wilson's commentaries on the letters rather naive.

iv. Influence Studies

Ever since the contemporary reviews of *Mardi* critics have talked
about similarities between Melville and Sir Thomas Browne. Now,
in one of the better essays on Melville to appear in 1984, "Herman
Melville and the Example of Sir Thomas Browne" (*MP* 81:265–77),
Brian Foley shows precisely what the similarities are, listing with
appropriate quotation "distinctive attributes" of Browne's prose style

that have their counterparts in *Mardi* and *Moby-Dick*. This part of
the essay is an effectively detailed demonstration (though rather
vague and impressionistic when discussing the superiority of Melville's use of Browne's devices in *Moby-Dick*). Foley is on boggy
ground when he claims that Browne's and Melville's use of "doublets"
(pairs of words joined by a conjunction) "calls attention to the limitations of language" and "reflects a struggle to 'say in words what
cannot be said in words.'" But in the rest of the essay Foley effectively
shows that throughout the cetological chapters Melville employed,
with various modifications, Browne's method of eliminating "vulgar
errors" in order to "reveal the impenetrable mysteries beyond," often
drawing on the content and methods of organization and argumenta-
tion in *Pseudodoxia Epidemica*.

In "'Vast and Varied Accessions . . . From Abroad': Herman Melville and Edward Young on Originality" (*SAR*, pp. 409–24), Charlene
Avallone points out a number of interesting contrasts between Melville's views on originality in "Hawthorne and His Mosses" and *Pierre*
and Edward Young's in *Conjectures on Original Composition*. There
is no direct evidence, however, that Melville ever read the *Conjectures*
and Avallone produces no verbal similarities that show conclusively
that Melville developed his ideas on originality partly in response to
Young. Avallone's claim that Melville "follows Young in viewing Enceladus as a type of the artist who fails to move out from the influence
of literary sources to the originality that lies beyond" is based on an
eccentric reading of the Enceladus passage in *Pierre*.

In "Melville's Copy of Goethe's Autobiography and Travels"
(*SAR*, pp. 387–407), James McIntosh argues that "in all likelihood"
both volumes of the English edition that Henry A. Murray donated
several years ago to the Berkshire Athenaeum belonged to Melville,
though only volume 2 contains Melville's signature and characteristic
markings. Both volumes contain markings that are uncharacteristic
of Melville, but McIntosh speculates that they may be an "early man-
nerism" Melville "discarded by the time he ceased to be a public
author and became the more scholarly reader responsible for most of
his extant marginalia." (Melville acquired his two-volume set of the
Autobiography in London in December 1849.) Nothing, however,
compellingly links with Melville the markings McIntosh cites from
volume 1, and other evidence proves conclusively that this is not one
of the volumes Melville bought in 1849: in its endpapers, as Harrison

Hayford points out in a forthcoming article, a list of books already available includes works not published till 1850 and 1851. McIntosh's discussion of the markings characteristic of Melville in volume 2 is a more useful contribution toward an understanding of Goethe's impact on Melville's ideas on such matters as artistic form in verse (and perhaps, as McIntosh suggests, on the poem "Naples in the Time of Bomba").

v. Miscellaneous

Leo Miller, who spent half a day examining Melville's newly surfaced copy of Milton at the Phillips Gallery, characterizes the marginalia as "biographically very valuable" and showing "wide reading in ancient and Renaissance classics," while the markings "show a creative author's sensitivity to a striking image, to the apt phrase and the well-chosen word" ("Melville *Milton* Marginalia Discovered," *MiltonQ* 18: 67). According to Miller, the volume also reveals Melville's "sharp eye for the artistic and ideological problems Milton faced in his theological epics, and particularly for his heresies." "Melville's Milton" (*MSEx* 57:7) reprints the description of the volumes in the gallery's press release and reproduces a sample page from *Paradise Regained*.

In "Old Trunk Story" (*ABC* 5:3–10) Donald L. Anderle gives an account of the New York Public Library's acquisition of the trove of Melville family letters and other material, including Melville manuscripts, discovered in a barn in upstate New York in 1983 (see *ALS* 1983, p. 61), and prints Melville's exuberant letter to his brother Allan announcing the birth of his son Malcolm, as well as extracts from the family letters concerning Melville. Susan Davis, Curator of Manuscripts at the library, itemizes the new papers in "More for the NYPL's Long Vaticans" (*MSEx* 57:5–7). One more family letter surfaced in 1984: in "Another Triumph for Maria's Firstborn" (*MSEx* 58:1–3), Henry A. Murray prints a letter of 28 December 1826 from Mrs. Allan (Maria Gansevoort) Melvill to her mother, Mrs. Peter Gansevoort, with a postscript by Allan Melvill. The letter gives an account of the recent public examination of scholars at the high school during which Gansevoort had received the crown for "best speaker" and, as Murray notes, "nicely and unforgettably illustrates a mother's unabashed pride in one of the remarkable performances for which her eldest and favorite son was already notable at the age of ten."

vi. Typee to Moby-Dick

Nothing of great importance was published on the early works this year. Herbie Butterfield's unoriginal " 'New World All Over': Melville's *Typee* and *Omoo*" (*Melville: Reassessments*, pp. 14–27) might serve as a useful introduction for someone who has read neither book. Wai-chee Dimock's "*Typee*: Melville's Critique of Community" (*ESQ* 30:27–39) is perceptive about the communal nature of the Typee's lying and about the characterization of Fayaway and Kory-Kory, which affirms "the sovereignty and integrity of the tribe." But Dimock's argument that it is "Typee as civilized ideal" that Melville "finds most troubling and most dangerous" and that his "critique of Typee implicates America as well" involves a dubious equating of social harmony and unity with cannibalism and a flimsy analysis of Typee as "exemplary counterpart" of America.

John Samson argues in "The Dynamics of History and Fiction in Melville's *Typee*" (*AQ* 36:276–90) that "contradictions" in Melville's narrator, his wavering attitudes toward the Typees, are the result of his "naive reading" of ideologically opposed accounts of the natives by sailors such as David Porter and missionaries such as Charles S. Stewart and William Ellis. From the first, he maintains, Tommo remains "so completely reliant upon the categories in the narratives he has read that he himself becomes both an explorer and a missionary." Samson simply ignores the narrator's statement in chapter 1 that he had "never happened to meet with" Porter's *Journal* and the possibility that Melville did not read the book himself until he provided additional informational chapters at the request of his English publisher, John Murray. The rest of Samson's attempt to dissociate Melville from his narrator is unconvincing. Few readers, I imagine, will be persuaded, for instance, that the narrator's fear of the Typees stems not from his fear of cannibalism but "from a realization, perhaps subconscious, that his preconceived notion of noble savages/ignoble savages is hopelessly muddled, that none of the ideas he has gleaned from the narratives he has read obtain in the real world of the Typees, who are at once innocently benevolent and fiercely cannibalistic." Probably few readers too will revise their opinion of *Omoo* on the basis of Samson's "Profaning the Sacred: Melville's *Omoo* and Missionary Narratives" (*AL* 56:496–509), which argues that *Omoo* is rescued from its seeming inconsequence if we recognize it as a parodic missionary narrative, with Long Ghost and the narrator as parodic missionaries and spiritual leaders.

Melville: Reassessments provides the year's only essays devoted solely to *Mardi* and to *Redburn* and *White-Jacket*. Harold Beaver's slackly written "*Mardi*: A Sum of Inconsistencies" (pp. 28–40) focuses on repetition, circularity, dream, the "coherence of the incoherent" in *Mardi*, and the "splintering of consciousness" as the book's "most constant mode," offering little in the way of fresh insight. James H. Justus's oddly titled "*Redburn* and *White-Jacket*: Society and Sexuality in the Narrators of 1849" (pp. 41–67) argues that the two narrator-protagonists are connected by "an instinctive self-regard that is translated socially into a bias that radiates throughout their often difficult relationships aboard ship, insuring the perpetuation in their lives of a kind of spiritual orphanhood; and their ambivalent attraction to homoerotic sexuality that they must overtly reject." In discussing their "unresolved sexuality," Justus is more persuasive about Redburn than about White-Jacket, who, he claims, is almost too secure in his place in the ship's social hierarchy and almost too complacently moral "to permit self-inquiry into the sexual bases of his little society" in the maintop, while his "springs of action come from a complex of half-disclosed, half-understood, and unadmitted motives."

Two pieces deal with Melville's sources in the early works. R. D. Madison's brief note on "Redburn's Seamanship and Dana's Guide-Book" (*MSEx* 57:13–14) shows that Melville may have drawn on R. H. Dana, Jr.'s *Seaman's Friend* for certain passages in *Redburn* regarding seamanship and shipboard practices. Paul McCarthy's "Facts, Opinions, and Possibilities: Melville's Treatment of Insanity through *White-Jacket*" (*SNNTS* 16:167–81) cites possible sources of Melville's knowledge about insanity, including the article on insanity in the *Penny Cyclopaedia*, and examines his "mad or insane characters" in the light of "contemporary psychological tenets," particularly those concerning "moral insanity." McCarthy concludes that "the understanding of insanity evident in pre-*Moby-Dick* works"—whatever its source or sources—"appears comparable in quality to the best scientific thought in America at that time."

vii. Moby-Dick

In "*Moby-Dick* as Anatomy" (*Melville: Reassessments*, pp. 68–89) A. Robert Lee uses "anatomy" as "a conveniently approximate description aimed at capturing the encyclopaedic impulse and the play of speculative intelligence at work" in the book. According to Lee, *Moby-Dick* is pledged (among other quests) "to explore the competing overlap of classifications and codes . . . whereby mankind has sought to express reality" and testifies "to the way things and 'meanings' operate fictively—mythically—and so resist all final encapsulation." As this might suggest, rather than offering a new perspective on *Moby-Dick*, the essay confirms by now rather established findings (there is some overlap with Lee's own longer essay "*Moby-Dick:* The Tale and the Telling" in Faith Pullin's earlier Anglo-American collection, *New Perspectives on Melville* [*ALS 1978*, p. 51]). But Lee writes with intelligence and verve and cogently illustrates the book's narrative and anatomical strategies, skillfully evoking the complexity of the reading experience it offers "in the balance of these two dynamics."

Most readers will probably be hard pressed to say exactly what Eric Mottram's freewheeling " 'Grown in America': *Moby-Dick* and Melville's Sense of Control" is about (*Melville: Reassessments*, pp. 90–115). Lee might be close when he tells us in his introduction that Mottram "approaches *Moby-Dick* as a Lawrentian fable about the sexual and resonantly mythic origins of power, the ancestral urge to find identity (and manhood) in the subduing of Nature and its dynamic, titular expression in the form of the whale."

None of the remaining pieces on *Moby-Dick* is very enlightening. Zbigniew Lewicki's loosely argued chapter "*Moby-Dick:* Apocalypse as Regeneration" in *The Bang and the Whimper* (pp. 21–32) finds an "overall pattern of the traditional, or optimistic, apocalypse" in the book, with a St. John the Divine–like Ishmael and a Beast of Revelation–like Ahab. John Miles Foley's "The Price of Narrative Fiction: Genre, Myth, and Meaning in *Moby-Dick* and *The Odyssey*" (*Thought* 59:432–48) is a laborious exercise in reader-response criticism, which attempts to explain "what kinds of experience these two texts and the traditions behind them provide for the reader, and how this experience is stimulated by their idiosyncratic encoding of genre, myth, and meaning." Mark R. Patterson in "Democratic Leadership and Narrative Authority in *Moby-Dick*" (*SNNTS* 16:288–303) argues that Ishmael's narrative authority "presents an analogous, but alternative version of Ahab's authority" and that this contrasting narrative authority "can be seen as a keen analysis of the psychological and linguistic sources of authority in a democracy." Patterson has nothing incisive to say about the authority of either character, however, or what he calls their "remarkably similar rhetorical premises." He wants us to believe, among other things, that Ishmael employs Ahab's "oratorical constructions in order to call attention to the common linguistic basis of their authority." Rosemary F. Franklin ("The Seashore Sketches in *Twice-told Tales* and Melville," *ELN* 21:57–63) believes that Melville's reading of Hawthorne's *Twice-told Tales* in early 1851 "probably reinforced" a "number of the techniques, themes, and characters he was developing in *Moby-Dick*," though it's hard to see why from the parts of "The Village Uncle," "Chippings with a Chisel," and "Footprints on the Sea-Shore" she examines.

viii. Pierre

In contrast to 1983, *Pierre* attracted relatively little attention this year. Richard Gray seems unaware of most of what's happened in *Pierre* scholarship and criticism in the last 15 years, including publication of the Northwestern-Newberry edition (he cites the Signet). His mainly unoriginal " 'All's o'er, and ye know him not': A Reading of *Pierre*" (*Melville: Reassessments*, pp. 116–34) focuses on elements of the book that make the reader likely to feel "that he has been caught in a Chinese box of fictions, a book in which everything comments on its own origins, making, and development."

Wai-chee Dimock points out the interesting recurrence of the word "confidence" in *Pierre* ("*Pierre*: Domestic Confidence Game and the Drama of Knowledge," *SNNTS* 16:396–409), but exaggerates the term's importance—and its ambiguity—in an attempt to demonstrate that Melville creates a structure "built on the various senses of the word." By the time Dimock concludes, in the last paragraph, that in *Pierre* all attempts at knowledge (whether psychological or epistemological) "degenerate into an empty confidence game," the term "confidence game" has been drained of all meaning.

Attempting to account for the flawed second half of *Pierre*, Gerald W. Shepherd in "Pierre's Psyche and Melville's Art" (*ESQ* 30:83–98) finds that Melville failed to "sustain his original and primary intention" (a "study of the psyche") primarily because he lacked "an integrated vision of the psyche"; his "deepened recognition" of the elusiveness of "the psyche's enigmas" gained through his earlier analysis of Pierre prompted him in the second half (among other failings) "to skim the burdensome depths of his hero's development" and "to ac-

celerate his unanalyzed progress to approximate Melville's own confused insight." Shepherd's argument is worth attention, but a comprehensive account of the causes of the flaws in the second half of
Pierre needs to pay closer attention than Shepherd does to what is
known about the book's composition, particularly its late enlargement. (Shepherd evidently had not seen the introduction to the
Higgins-Parker collection of essays on *Pierre* [*ALS 1983*, p. 70],
which contains the fullest account of the book's composition and the
circumstances of its enlargement.)

According to James W. Mathews, the discrepancy between the
auburn hair and brown eyes of Guido Reni's supposed portrait of
Beatrice Cenci and the blonde hair and blue eyes of the young woman
in the copy of the portrait Lucy contemplates in book 26 of *Pierre*
derives from Melville's knowledge of Shelley's *The Cenci*, where
Beatrice is depicted as a blonde ("The Enigma of Beatrice Cenci,
Shelley, and Melville, *SoAR* 49:31–41). Mathews argues that Melville "chose Shelley's prototype for a climactic image to expose the
foolish absolutism of Pierre and the pernicious deception of Lucy's
angelic appearance and manner."

ix. Stories, *Israel Potter*

What "is perhaps truly stunning about Melville's accomplishment,"
William Wasserstrom holds, "is the pervasiveness of *contrapposto*,
an Italianate style of antithesis which contorts the figure by twisting
a part of the body in a direction opposite to that of other main parts"
("Melville the Mannerist: Form in the Short Fiction," *Melville: Reassessments*, pp. 135–56). Wasserstrom provocatively links such antithesis and contortion to "the fact of contradiction" he sees at the
heart of the political "scheme of things on this continent" since the
framing of the Constitution. But the rest of the essay, which discusses "Benito Cereno," "The Town-Ho's Story," and *Billy Budd*, is
anticlimax (for all its talk of Melville's forcibly wedding "a theology
of predestination to the First Law of Thermodynamics" in *Billy Budd*).
Despite the essay's title and its author's sense of Melville's "queer
disproportion of form" there is no real analysis of form in any of
these three works.

Werner Senn addresses important questions in "Reading Melville's Mazes: An Aspect of the Short Stories" (*ES* 65:27–35): what
happens when we first become aware of the depths in Melville's

stories and start to explore their "secret recesses" and when and how
does "the deception" Melville practices turn into recognition for the
reader? The rather arbitrary-seeming key in Senn's answer is the recurrent figure of the labyrinth in the stories, a key he uses to open a
whole box of contemporary critical clichés. The labyrinth apparently
functions "as the pivot where deception turns into recognition, where
the deceptive surface discloses not so much the 'real meaning' as a
bewildering multiplicity of meanings encoded in the text. The labyrinth signals, as it were, a turbulence in the hermeneutic process
which the reader is left to straighten out by choosing one particular
possibility over the others, but finding it nearly impossible to do so."
The figure "has less to do with the narrative itself than with its hermeneutic code, apparently mirroring the reading process itself." Senn
gives no indication that any of this is offered as pastiche.

In his approach to "Benito Cereno," "Bartleby," and *Billy Budd*,
Brook Thomas ("The Legal Fictions of Herman Melville and Lemuel
Shaw," *CritI* 11:24–51) focuses on Melville's relation to Judge Shaw,
offering what he describes as "an example of an interdisciplinary historical inquiry combining literary criticism with the relatively new
field of critical legal studies," and arguing "that the ambiguity of
literary texts might better be understood in terms of an era's social
contradictions rather than in terms of the inherent qualities of literary
language or rhetoric." According to Brooks, Bartleby undermines
mid–19th-century contractual ideology, which held that when an
employee consented to employment he entered into "the free contract of a free man"—an ideology buttressed by Judge Shaw's formulation of "the fellow-servant rule." Thomas also discusses the complexity in Melville's situation vis-à-vis Judge Shaw—"one of the
leading spokesmen for the capitalist system which Melville's fiction
evaluates" yet also a source of his financial support—and its bearing
on the story as a parable of the artist. It's not altogether clear from
any of this how the "ambiguity" of "Bartleby" is better understood in
terms of the "era's social contradictions."

"Bartleby" was the subject of several short notes. "The Significance
of Petra in 'Bartleby'" (*MSEx* 57:10–12), according to James C.
Wilson, lies in its reputation for crass materialism, the comparison
between the ancient city and Wall Street forming part of Melville's
"bitter indictment of American capitalism." Wilson claims that Melville could have read about Petra "in any number of popular books
and newspaper articles published in the 1840s and 1850s," though he

cites only one that antedates "Bartleby," William Henry Bartlett's *Forty Days in the Desert*. The connection Richard H. Friedrich seeks to establish in "Asleep with Kings and Counselors: A Source Note on Bartleby in the Tombs" (*MSEx* 58:13–14) between the narrator's response to Bartleby's death in the Tombs and Sir Thomas Browne's *Hydrotaphia* is tenuous at best; and Raymond Benoit's evidence in "*Bleak House* and 'Bartleby, the Scrivener'" (*SSF* 21:272–73) that the "germ" of "Bartleby" can be found in the description of Mr. Vholes and his office in chapter 39 of Dickens's novel is negligible. Michael H. Friedman argues implausibly that the epilogue to "Bartleby" is "a subtle reworking" of "The Bagman's Uncle's Tale" in *Pickwick Papers* ("*Pickwick Papers* as a Source for the Epilogue to Melville's 'Bartleby the Scrivener,'" *SSF* 21:147–51), apparently unaware of closer parallels in contemporary local journalism, such as the article quoted in Hershel Parker's "The 'Sequel' in 'Bartleby'" (see *ALS 1979*, p. 55). As Parker reported in *ALS* more than a decade ago, "evocative articles about dead-letter offices had something of a vogue in the years just before Melville wrote 'Bartleby.'"

"Benito Cereno" continued to attract a good deal of attention, with critics as far away as ever from a consensus on what the story is "about." Marianne Dekoven is scarcely original in finding "a number of veiled suggestions that the institution of slavery" is "the plot's originating evil"; she goes over well-trodden ground and comes up with nothing new in arguing that "the story is most powerful when its suppressed historical-political referent, slavery, is most palpably inscribed in its form, in specific instances of imagery, allusion, and semantic ambiguity that constitute the best, and the best known, moments in the story" ("History as Suppressed Referent in Modernist Fiction," *ELH* 51:137–52). James Rodgers's "Melville's Short Fiction: Many Voices, Many Modes," in *Contemporary Approaches to Narrative*, ed. Anthony Mortimer (Tübingen: Narr; pp. 39–50) also tells us nothing new for the most part about this story, or the other *Piazza Tales*, though it might be original in its odd, unsupported claim that the legal documents in the deposition are "entirely fictitious." According to Rodgers, Melville's "manipulation of narrative is fundamentally subversive in quality," and "the only voice we can trust is the voice that never speaks as narrator, Babo's voice, the voice of the slaves," the "voice of those who never speak historically."

Barbara Baines's evidence in "Ritualized Cannibalism in 'Benito Cereno': Melville's 'Black-Letter' Texts" (*ESQ* 30:163–69) that the

Ashantis had a "reputation" for cannibalism lends some support to suggestions by other critics that Aranda's body was cannibalized, though the evidence amounts to no more than an incident recounted in one book, published in 1841, and repeated in another, published in 1856 (after the initial publication of "Benito Cereno"). Her evidence for thinking that in unwittingly eating "of the body of his best friend" Cereno "participated in a diabolical communion with the Negro," a communion conceived by Babo as "a grotesque parody of the Eucharist," amounts to even less. James H. Kavanagh holds that the problem "at stake" in "Benito Cereno" is "the problem of ideology as figured in Delano" and that "it is *the* mistake" to "read this text for the ambiguous knowledge it gives at any moment of 'events aboard the San Dominick'; one must rather read the text for the unambiguous knowledge it gives at every moment about Delano's ideological construction of, and self-insertion into, that situation." ("'That Hive of Subtlety': 'Benito Cereno' as Critique of Ideology," *BuR* 29:127–57.) At issue in the story "is how, for a man immersed in Delano's ideology, a belief in one's own 'goodness' and 'moral simplicity' is not just 'naiveté,' but a necessary condition for the violent, sometimes vicious, defense of privilege, power, and self-image" we see Delano engage in. The notion that the text "at every moment" gives knowledge of Delano's ideologically controlled responses is typical of the exaggeration in the essay. Kavanagh's strained readings will probably convince few readers that Delano is indeed a victim of megalomania and paranoia, with schizophrenic tendencies.

Allan Moore Emery in "'Benito Cereno' and Manifest Destiny" (*NCF* 39:48–68) sees as Melville's primary concern in the story "the false claims and confidences" of 19th-century American expansionism. Evidence that Melville was "particularly concerned by mid-century arguments for American intervention in Latin America," as Emory claims, is slight, however: Melville might have read a couple of expansionist articles in *Putnam's Monthly* in January 1853 and February 1854 (these two "perhaps the most accessible" to him among "many similar defenses of American expansion"), articles which, like the story, contrast American "energy," "libertarianism," and "efficiency" with Spanish "weakness," "despotism," and "disorderliness." In "Re-envisioning America: Melville's 'Benito Cereno'" (*ESQ* 30:245–59) Sandra A. Zagarell seems intent on making as many grandiose claims for the story as possible: it presents "the extensive cultural discontinuities that prevail under an unstable social order"; it explicates "the multivalent indeterminacy" of conventions whose fixity men like Delano take for granted; it represents "Melville's indirect but powerful effort to destabilize the existing social order by undermining the sort of authority on which it rests"; it shows "racial characteristics as cultural constructs" and "dramatizes gender as a cultural convention," revealing "the literal instability of gender." Still more: Melville suggests "that *all* meaning in his readers' world derives from convention, and that meaning itself is therefore unfixed." Whatever one's skepticism in the face of some of these claims, however, Zagarell is perceptive in her discussion of Babo's "silent communication" and of the ways in which all of the characters are "claustrally restricted by preexisting authority."

Drawing on Judge Shaw's record in connection with the Fugitive Slave laws of 1793 and 1850, Brook Thomas (in "Legal Fictions") argues that "the text's silences and ambiguities can be explained in terms of the historical contradictions which slavery posed to 'enlightened' whites such as Melville and Shaw." I'm not sure, however, that Thomas explains anything about the text in those terms. Babo's silence, for example, is "explained" (on p. 33) in psychological and political terms, but not in terms of the "historical contradictions" slavery posed "enlightened" whites.

David Chacko and Alexander Kulcsar's "Israel Potter: Genesis of a Legend" (*WMQ* 41:365–89) traces the real-life Potter's history, examining and explaining discrepancies in Henry Trumbull's *Life and Remarkable Adventures*, Melville's basic source, and suggesting that Potter may have been a British agent. What "comes to light" from their investigation, as they claim, "is a story far more remarkable than Trumbull revealed or Melville suspected."

x. The Confidence-Man

The most comprehensive of the year's essays on *The Confidence-Man* is A. Robert Lee's "Voices Off, On and Without: Ventriloquy in *The Confidence-Man* (*Melville: Reassessments*, pp. 157–75). Focusing on "layers of voicing in the text"—passenger and avatar voices, the "ostensible authorial voice," and "behind all of these, deafeningly silent and wrily just out of reach and hearing, Melville's own"—Lee succinctly evokes the nature and complexity of the book's "interlinking verbal encounters" and its whole "equivocating din of speech," all designed in Lee's view to illustrate indeterminacy—of meaning,

characters, words, and universe. As in his essay on *Moby-Dick*, Lee
lends eloquent and intelligent support to one of the now fairly established readings of the book, rather than breaking wholly new ground.
David Sewell in "Mercantile Philosophy and the Dialectics of Confidence: Another Perspective on *The Confidence-Man*" (*ESQ* 30:
99–110) makes a convincing case for adding to the list of Melville's
satirical objects in *The Confidence-Man* the popular optimistic mercantile philosophy to be found in the success manuals and mercantile publications of the 1840s and 1850s, though William A. Alcott
(author of *The Young Man's Guide*) and Freeman Hunt (editor of
Hunt's Merchants' Magazine and anthologist of *Worth and Wealth:
A Collection of Maxims, Morals, and Miscellanies, for Merchants and
Men of Business*) were not necessarily Melville's specific targets, as
Sewell at times seems to imply. Hans-Joachim Lang identifies the
"dungeoned Italian" referred to in chapter 21 of *The Confidence-Man*
as "Italy's most famous nineteenth-century prisoner," the revolutionary Silvio Pellico ("Silvio Pellico, Melville's 'Dungeoned Italian,'"
MSEx 58:4–6). References to Pellico by name occur only in Melville's
later works and marginalia, but Lang plausibly suggests that "the
cluster of motifs and images Melville connected with Pellico was
complete by 1856."

John Bryant, in " 'Nowhere a Stranger': Melville and Cosmopoli-
tanism" (*NEQ* 39:275–91), notes that a lengthy review of the memoirs
of one Vincent Nolte, "merchant, financier, caricaturist, medallionist,
and raconteur," in the same issue of *Putnam's Monthly* in which the
third installment of *Israel Potter* was published may well have caught
Melville's eye; it may also, as Bryant argues, have "provided him
with a source for Frank Goodman," though the parallels Bryant
cites are far from conclusive. Christopher S. Durer's "Melville's *The
Confidence-Man* and Jean-Jacques Rousseau" (*CLS* 21:445–62) contains little to support his claim that linguistic and stylistic similarities between parts of *The Confidence-Man* and some of Rousseau's
writings "imply that Melville may have deliberately used these writings for the purpose of puns, double-entendres, and word-games in
general to enrich the texture of his novel." More plausibly, Durer
argues that the book, particularly in chapters 21–25, uses concepts
such as the goodness of man and nature and the corrupting effects of
civilization which may have been taken directly from Rousseau or
the Rousseauistic tradition, with the independent, solitary Pitch embodying positive traits of Rousseauistic philosophy yet at the same

time representing "the forces of reaction" against the Romantic, Transcendentalist, progressive legacy of Rousseau.

In Rebecca J. Kruger Gaudino's "The Riddle of *The Confidence-Man* (*JNT* 14:124–41) *The Confidence-Man* becomes yet another text about the difficulties of reading and writing. The evidence for Melville's concern with "the issue of fiction" is not (as one might expect) the presence of three chapters that discuss fiction, but rather the "abundance" of writing materials, readers, writers, and texts within the book. The texts include "a myriad of written texts" ("placards, slates, Bibles, handbills, pamphlets, books, vouchers, receipts, money, labels, and transfer-books") and, rather predictably, "a multitude of human texts," the latter all problematical texts, naturally, illustrating "the plethora of interpretations possible in any text." At "this point" in his career, Gaudino holds, Melville "seriously questioned" the worth of fiction: "Fiction, man's invention to render life understandable, was just that—an invention, a deception, and as such, futile, even absurd"; and the scenes in the novel present the complicated, and, as Melville saw it, "dismaying processes of writing and reading." Texts are contradictory and unreliable; fiction "cannot tell truth" but instead "further beclouds truth." Oddly enough, for all the talk in the essay of the "pessimistic theories of fiction" Melville held at the time of composing *The Confidence-Man*, the three chapters in the book that discuss fiction—chapters not notably pessimistic—go almost without mention.

xi. Poetry

Andrew Hook's finding of a lack of "general enthusiasm" for Melville's poetry seems valid (*Melville: Reassessments*, pp. 176–97), but his survey of critical responses to the poetry neglects to mention all but one of the books and essays on the subject that have appeared since 1970. His own contribution amounts to little more than a partial summary of the themes of *Battle-Pieces*, *Clarel*, *John Marr*, and *Timoleon*, with occasional judgments on the overall value of the works or the merits of the verse. In Hook's view, *Battle-Pieces* "remains the best and most satisfying" of Melville's volumes of poetry. Warren Rosenberg's claim that Melville could "successfully integrate the erotic theme" and "overcome the guilt and confusion which marred his prose works" only in his poetry, where he was "protected by a defined and cryptic form," is based on a brief and inadequate analysis

of Melville's treatment of the "sexual theme" in *Mardi* and *Pierre*
("'Deeper than Sappho': Melville, Poetry, and the Erotic," *MLS* 14:
70–78).

xii. Billy Budd, Sailor

H. Bruce Franklin's "From Empire to Empire: *Billy Budd, Sailor*"
(*Melville: Reassessments*, pp. 199–216) tries to settle "once and for
all" the "noisy, misleading debate about whether Melville condemns,
approves, or is ambiguous about Vere's killing of the morally innocent
Billy Budd." Franklin holds that Melville's meaning is "fundamentally unambiguous," and he lists 22 points, no less ("just consider
these twenty-two points"), to prove that Melville condemns Captain
Vere. Among the many critics Franklin acknowledges indebtedness
to are Harrison Hayford and Merton Sealts, who "found fresh evidence in the process of Melville's composition" to support his case
against Vere, the evidence he cites being Vere's violation of British
naval code. Franklin ignores Hayford and Sealts's evidence that it
was Melville's late revisions in his manuscript that bring Vere's
behavior into question while "passages composed earlier which are
still retained tend to represent Vere favorably." Franklin settles nothing by ignoring Hayford and Sealts's evidence, in spite of his 22
points. Nor does R. Evan Davis, who sees Billy as representing early
America but devotes most of his essay to this old debate about Melville's attitude toward Vere, arguing that the text, "in tone and in
fact, is neutral" ("An Allegory of America in Melville's *Billy Budd*,"
JNT 14:172–81). S. A. Cowan in "The Naming of Captain Vere in
Melville's *Billy Budd*" (*SSF* 21:41–46) inconclusively revives another
old topic of debate, the significance of Vere's surname, arguing that
Melville derived it from the word "severe" and may have been punning on the nautical sense of "veer," to turn to another course.

Brook Thomas (in "Legal Fictions") notes a number of interesting similarities between Vere's behavior in the trial of Billy Budd and
Judge Shaw's behavior in the murder trial of John White Webster in
1850. The similarities are hardly sufficiently revealing, however (the
dissimilarities are perhaps more striking), to sustain Thomas's claim
that "an important way in which *Billy Budd* is an inside narrative is
that it gives a son-in-law's inside perspective" into the workings of
Shaw's "legal mentality." In Thomas's view, reading *Billy Budd* alongside the Webster case "allows us to see more precisely how the legal

system criticized in 'Benito Cereno' and 'Bartleby' so effectively silences certain voices within society." Lastly, Miriam Quen Cheikin's rather flimsy *"Billy Budd:* Reclaimed by the Nineteenth Century" (*EAS* 13:43–59) for the most part samples reviews of a number of late-19th-century novels and speculates about the ways in which reviewers might have responded to *Billy Budd* had it been published in the 1880s or 1890s.

University of Illinois at Chicago

5. Whitman and Dickinson

Jerome Loving

This was a prodigious year for both Whitman and Dickinson scholarship, producing 14 volumes and approximately 60 articles—more than 5,000 pages of print. One would have thought this unusual quantity the result of the now ubiquitous word processor and its "televised" texts that too often trick the writer out of his sense of economy, but in fact the bulk of the material comes to us in the form of well-edited if not always well-written monographs, editions, and essays. In the way of books on Whitman we received the late Paul Zweig's enthusiastic biography, Edward F. Grier's multivolume edition of the *Notebooks and Unpublished Prose Manuscripts,* and yet another collection of family letters. The life and art of Dickinson are also considerably illuminated by Polly Longsworth's edition of the love letters between Austin Dickinson and Mabel Loomis Todd, Barton Levi St. Armand's *Emily Dickinson and Her Culture,* and Vivian R. Pollak's *Dickinson: The Anxiety of Gender.* In all there were six books on Dickinson, including a descriptive bibliography by Joel Myerson.

i. Whitman

a. **Bibliography, Editing.** William White, indefatigable in his editorial duties on Whitman, continues to provide "A Current Bibliography" in each issue of the newly founded *Walt Whitman Quarterly Review* (still cited as *WWR*). That journal also contains two specialized bibliographies this year. In "Walt Whitman Bibliographies, 1897–1982" (*WWR* 1:38–45) Donald D. Kummings both augments and updates James T. F. Tanner's 1968 chronological checklist. It represents, he maintains, "a complete, or at least reasonably complete," listing of the bibliographies on Whitman's life and work. This bibliographer's bibliography, however, is missing a few important

Preparation of this chapter was facilitated by the research assistance of Susan Roberson.—*J.L.*

items. More reasonably complete and interesting—particularly in
the wake of C. Carroll Hollis's *Language and Style in* Leaves of Grass
(*ALS 1983*, pp. 80–81)—is Sherry G. Southard, "Whitman and Language: An Annotated Bibliography" (*WWR* 2:31–49). The annotations to this primary and secondary bibliography are clear and concise. Probably its only error, if it has one, is the now too-easy
assumption that Whitman wrote all or part of William Swinton's
Rambles Among Words (1859).

The debate over the question of Whitman's authorship of this
dissertation on language began in 1959 with C. Carroll Hollis's article
in *American Literature*. It was rebutted—or at least doubted—in
Floyd Stovall's *The Foreground of* Leaves of Grass (*ALS 1974*, pp.
62–63). The consensus is now shifting back to the Hollis position. In
"Whitman as Ghostwriter: The Case of *Rambles Among Words*"
(*WWR* 2:22–30), James Perrin Warren argues with murky evidence
that Whitman not only contributed one or two chapters to Swinton's
book but that the poet "brought as much to William Swinton [regard-
ing the book's composition] as Swinton did to Whitman." Whitman,
of course, has been accused of ghostwriting a number of books, but
in almost every case the subject has been the poet himself. One can
hardly imagine his motive in concealing his authorship on a subject
that would have perhaps extended his reputation as a man of letters.
Indeed, Swinton's argument is an *apologia* for Whitman's "language
experiment" in *Leaves of Grass*—something the poet attempted himself in his preface. Warren, whose acumen in analyzing the poet's use
of language is recognized below, appears all too ready to add this
book to the Whitman canon in order "to discuss both the poet's
theory of language and the relationship of the theory to his poetic
practice." But he neglects to find a place for that time-consuming
activity in Whitman's biography and glosses over Swinton's statement
that "the whole book was written" in 1853 or 1854 when the author
was teaching in Greensboro, North Carolina. Perhaps we ought to
forget about trying to catch Whitman redhanded again and begin to
consider Swinton as a possible influence on the first or second edition
of *Leaves of Grass*. Swinton came to New York City in 1854 or 1855,
and both he and his brother John (editor of the *New York Times*
during the war) were friends of the poet in the 1850s. Who knows
whether or when Whitman might first have seen William Swinton's
theory of language and been moved by it?

Edward F. Grier might have had this possibility in mind when he decided to include *Rambles Among Words* in his exhaustive six-volume edition of Whitman's *Notebooks and Unpublished Manuscripts* (NYU). This important contribution to the Collected Writings of Walt Whitman edits material from the Whitman collections in the Library of Congress, Yale, Duke, the Huntington, and other libraries. The project was originally begun under the joint editorship of Grier and William White, who was to edit relevant materials from the Feinberg Collection. White finished before Grier and published his own edition under the title of *Daybooks and Notebooks* (*ALS 1978*, pp. 59–60). Grier's edition also includes some 40 pages of manuscript from the Feinberg Collection left out of White's volumes. The edition is equally divided between "Manuscripts" and "Notes," but there is considerable overlap between these sections and their subsections. The problem characterizes the difficulty Grier must have faced in sifting through and classifying what can undeniably be claimed as Whitman's "ramble among words." It covers everything from biographical notes to "Projected Poems," "Poems," and "Politics." We are given new information about one of the most elusive figures in Whitman's biography—the poet's father. We can also speculate with greater assurance now that the first *Leaves*, or some of it, was drafted first in prose and then shifted into free verse. Grier is to be congratulated for sticking to the job over the last 20 years and transforming a veritable wilderness into a scholarly garden of sorts. We might wish for fuller annotation in places and greater consistency in the notes, but on the whole the value of these volumes cannot be overestimated.

b. **Biography.**   Yet another life of the poet was published this year: Paul Zweig's *Walt Whitman: The Making of the Poet* (Basic Books). It will replace neither Gay Wilson Allen nor Justin Kaplan (*ALS 1980*, pp. 70–71) for reliability, but it might for readability. That is to say, this is definitely a "popular" biography which contributes more to the myth than to the life of the poet. From a miserable beginning as the unloved son of a brooding father in a troubled home, Zweig's protagonist develops into a poet who strides "greedily from star to star, prancing like some cosmic Yankee peddler across geological ages and astronomical distances." The thesis is that the poem created the poet in 1855, a proposition not altogether novel except in the way the author executes it. A poet himself, Zweig pays tribute to a greater poet as he recaptures the excitement that Whitman must have felt as he came into his own according to the Emersonian prediction about

the self-reliant individual. Unfortunately, the narrative waxes tauto-
logical in its last hundred pages and is plagued throughout by minor
errors of fact. As I remarked in another review, Zweig's study is
Whitman at 36,000 feet.

Far more dependable, if not as exciting, is *Dear Brother Walt: The
Letters of Thomas Jefferson Whitman* (Kent State), ed. Dennis Berthold and Kenneth M. Price. Most of the 106 letters in this impeccably
edited collection were written to the poet during the Civil War and
afterward when Jefferson Whitman had relocated to St. Louis, Missouri, and directed the construction of that city's water system. Digging into the St. Louis archives, the editors have discovered that their
correspondent was successful not only as Whitman's favorite brother
but also as a civil engineer. With the publication of these letters, most
of the family correspondence has been published. Will the editor of
the mother's letters now come forward with his edition?

There is no substitute for such primary material, but not all of it
can be used equally. That is the point of John C. Broderick, formerly
Chief of the Manuscript Division of the Library of Congress and *de
facto* curator of the Whitman collections there, in "Traubel's Biographical Technique Revisited" (*SAR*, pp. 425–27). Responding to
Tibbie E. Lynch's argument for a reconsideration of Horace Traubel's
With Walt Whitman in Camden volumes (*ALS 1982*, p. 83), Broderick
reminds us that Traubel's dialogues with the aging poet may look
like actual records of conversations but are in fact the product of
transcriptions from rough notes taken by Traubel on the scene. In
the case of volume 1 of *With Walt Whitman*, ten years elapsed between the initial notetaking (in 1888) and its transcription to the
autograph notes on which the 1906 volume is based. Broderick recom-
mends we consult Traubel's manuscripts (available in the LC since
1980) before drawing any firm conclusions about Traubel as Whitman's Boswell. I suspect that such an investigation would reveal a
broad gap between initial notes and their records in Traubel's volumes (at least the first three, which came out during his lifetime).
For Traubel was one of the "hot little prophets" who complained so
bitterly about the first objective biography of Whitman in 1906, Bliss
Perry's contribution to the American Men of Letters series. Traubel
and other members of the Whitman Fellowship formed in the late
1890s believed that Perry had underestimated their poet's greatness.
One can easily guess their reaction had they known what George
Monteiro has recently discovered: that Whitman's late appearance

in the series was because its director from 1881 to 1900, Charles Dudley Warner, did not think Whitman deserved the title of poet ("Whitman, Warner, and the American Men of Letters Series," *WWR* 1: 26–27).

c. Criticism: General. In "Whitman and the Crowd" (*CritI* 10:579–91) Larzer Ziff attempts to show how Whitman moves beyond the "Imperial Self" of Emerson and Poe to the "crowd" or "common consciousness" of the "real Me." The thesis is intriguing, but to make it work Ziff has to focus on "Crossing Brooklyn Ferry" rather than "Song of Myself," where the poet's pluralism is restricted to the One instead of the Many. The subject of pluralism is also taken up by Samuel H. Beer and Irving Howe. The first essay is dull and inaccurate ("Walt Whitman on American Community," *NewRep*, 23 January, pp. 26–30); the second at least displays ingenuity in expressing an old idea ("Toward an Open Culture," *NewRep*, 5 March, pp. 25–29). Another old bottle reopened is the centerpiece of Joseph G. Kronick's Structuralistic analysis of the poet in *American Poetics of History*. Whitman is one of the players in that soap opera known as the Anxiety of Influence. To have him wriggling on the pin of Emerson's ideology, the concept of transcendentalism is turned inside out to depict Emerson as seeking disciples instead of Whole Men. Whitman's writings, too, are released from their chronological context: a quote from an old-age echo is offered as evidence that the bard was plotting to overcome Emerson's influence in the first edition of *Leaves of Grass*. Taken on its own premises and interpretation of primary materials, Kronick's argument is intriguing and witty, but in the context of Emerson and transcendentalism it is wide of the mark.

If critics these days are not deconstructing their texts, they are often busy finding parallels that lead to equally remote analyses. Such is the case with Dennis K. Renner in "Tradition for a Time of Crisis: Whitman's Prophetic Stance" in *Poetic Prophecy* (pp. 119–30). He suggests that *Leaves of Grass* employs biblical prophetic devices to observe a typology between Israel on the brink of exile and America on the brink of civil war: like the Hebrew prophets of the Old Testament, Whitman faced a crisis in which the unity of his nation was threatened. The parallel is shaky at best, the argument becoming so general that it could support just about any thesis. Far more convincing is Harold Aspiz's "Walt Whitman: The Spermatic Imagination" (*AL* 56:379–95). Aspiz extends (and more sharply focuses) the thesis of his book (*ALS 1980*, pp. 71–72) by explaining just exactly how Whitman gets from sex to song in *Leaves of Grass:* "Because the persona's virile physicality is generally pictured as an element of his vatic or bardic powers, Whitman's invention of a spermatic trope seems to have been an inevitable next step." The inspired vocalism, therefore, acts as a surrogate for orgasm. Aspiz also offers the interesting observation that Emerson stopped short of Whitman's method by allowing the idea of a seminal art but denying a phallic art. The contrast, of course, does more for Whitman than it does for Emerson. And after Joel Porte's book on Emerson (*ALS 1979*, pp. 6–7), we cannot dismiss so easily the complexity of Emerson's attitude toward sex.

Whitman is one of five poets considered in Ronald Wallace's *God Be with the Clown* (Missouri). Drawing the dubious distinction between comic poetry and light verse, Wallace sees Whitman's work as a blend of American humor and Aristotelian comedy in which the brag of the backwoods *alazon* underscores life's deadly paradoxes ("Walt Whitman: Stucco'd with Quadrupeds and Birds All Over," pp. 53–75). Needless to say, this exclusive reading of such an expansive poet allows for the misinterpretation of important passages and poems in *Leaves of Grass*. Indeed, the general conclusion is that Whitman celebrates the condition of being *out* of harmony with nature. The argument becomes even more curious in the light of Emerson's essay on "The Comic" (discussed by Wallace), which warns that humor results when the part is out of harmony with its whole. For years critics have asserted (as vaguely) that there is deep humor in *Leaves of Grass*, but I have yet to see the reading that allows Whitman or his persona to become anything more than the straight man in a cosmic comedy. If Whitman was laughing, he no doubt realized by the time of "Calamus" the identity of the Fool. This poem is also seen as the turning point in *Leaves of Grass* from the sensual to the spiritual in James Perrin Warren's "The 'Paths to the House': Cluster Arrangement in *Leaves of Grass*, 1860–1881" (*ESQ* 30:51–70). Whitman's shifting clusters between the 1855–60 and the "definitive" 1882 editions indicate an attempt to create an ensemble or "House" to hold both private and public themes. The argument more properly belongs in an undergraduate survey and not in the published scholarship where the point about Whitman's transition from poet to "speechmaker" has been made several times since Richard Chase in the 1950s.

d. **Criticism: Individual Works.** Warren more than redeems himself, however, in "The 'Real Grammar': Deverbal Style in 'Song of Myself'" (*AL* 56:1–16), a brilliant piece on how Whitman achieves a language that is both elliptic and idiomatic. These are the poet's terms to indicate poetry that is fluid and not fixed by prescriptive grammar. Desiring a rhetoric that evokes the law of organic linguistic change, Whitman employs such deverbal nouns (words that look exactly like their verbal base) such as "urge," "breed," and "merge" to reflect a dynamic instead of a stative language in "Song of Myself." Warren points out that the denominal verb has been the most common type of conversion in most periods of the English language, including that in which *Leaves of Grass* was written. Whitman's practice, therefore, runs directly counter to this particular evolution of the language and thus evokes a vitality that is unmatched in American poetry to that time. Warren is less successful but nevertheless engaging in "'The Free Growth of Metrical Laws': Syntactic Parallelism in 'Song of Myself'" (*Style* 18:27–42). Here he takes issue with Gay Wilson Allen's method of classifying rhythmical devices in *American Prosody* (1935) to produce a taxonomy of his own. Warren is right to argue that Allen stressed sense over syntax in his original thesis on the subject, but he should have consulted Allen's attempt to rectify that mistake in *A Reader's Guide to Walt Whitman* (*ALS 1970*, p. 60) before going forward to correct it.

In a belabored reading of "Song of the Broad-Axe," Dorothy M-T. Gregory finds a fusion of personal and national concerns ("The Celebration of Nativity: 'Broad-Axe Poem,'" *WWR* 2:1–11). The same pluralism—or panorama of the spirit—is uncovered in Whitman's "Sun-Down Poem" by Eugene McNamara in "'Crossing Brooklyn Ferry': The Shaping Imagination" (*WWR* 2:32–35). The article is informed by the author's greater knowledge of the visual arts—as is Peter Conrad's, which finds in Whitman's city a panoramic extension of its inhabitants ("The Epic City" in *The Art of the City: Views and Versions of New York City* [Oxford], pp. 3–21). Less exciting is Paul A. Orlov's solipsistic argument, "On Time and Form in Whitman's 'Crossing Brooklyn Ferry'" (*WWR* 2:12–21). Orlov replays established observations, but the last word on Whitman's 1856 poem belongs to Arthur Geffen this year. In "Silence and Denial: Walt Whitman and the Brooklyn Bridge" (*WWR* 1:1–11) he ponders Whitman's silence over the construction and completion of the Brooklyn

Bridge and concludes that it was due to (1) the poet's love of ferries, (2) his fear that the bridge's completion would pose a threat to the Fulton Ferry Community, and (3) his greater fear that the bridge would render his great poem a period piece!

Perhaps we ought to grant across-the-board tenure and promotion for the next three years in an attempt to silence this free-for-all in recent Whitman scholarship. In a ludicrously wrongheaded reading of Whitman's great elegy for Lincoln, one that completely ignores the poet's vocational catharsis in "Out of the Cradle Endlessly Rocking," Patricia Lee Yongue insists that the author of "Lilacs" is a "fledgling" poet who rebels against his earlier, optimistic self. Also misinformed is Yongue's assertion that Whitman had not seen the real violence of the war, only its aftermath, until the assassination of Lincoln ("Violence in Whitman's 'When Lilacs Last in the Dooryard Bloom'd,'" *WWR* 1:12–20). Sister Monica R. Weis also argues at the expense of the earlier poetry that "The Mystic Trumpeter" deserves to be considered a major poem in Whitman's (later) canon: "What in Whitman's early poetry is quasi-ventriloquist expression of the Self, a belief in the 'valvèd voice' of the Soul, is in 'The Mystic Trumpeter' something more." The extra ingredient is the poem's music, which is seen as an organizing principle and an extension of language itself ("Translating the Untranslatable: A Note on 'The Mystic Trumpeter,'" *WWR* 1:27–30).

Whitman's concept of culture is investigated to some profit by Robert L. Pincus in "A Mediated Vision, a Measured Voice: Culture and Criticism in Whitman's Prose" (*WWR* 2:22–31). Pincus demonstrates through a learned discussion of the essays that eventually combined to produce *Democratic Vistas* (1871) that Whitman's idea of "self-culture" or what the bard called "Personalism" was predicated not on the concept of one class or social aristocracy but on the practical life of working-class America. This in itself is nothing particularly new, but Pincus's merit is in tracing this idea all the way back to the early journalism. Though silenced by the idealism of *Leaves of Grass* in the 1850s (the very decade in which Matthew Arnold invented the word "culture"), Whitman's more rational social ideas resurface in the late 1860s as a result of Thomas Carlyle's attack on democracy in "Shooting Niagara." Pincus sees Whitman's idea of personalism, finally, as a literary and cultural criticism characterized by the contrapuntal movement of idealism and realism.

e. **Affinities and Influences.** In "Whitman on Emerson: New Light on the 1856 Open Letter" (*AL* 56:83–87) Kenneth M. Price focuses on the "internal tensions" in Whitman's famous letter: while he addresses Emerson as "Master," he also criticizes *all* American poets as pedants and eunuchs who are afraid to introduce sex into their writings. Price attributes the inconsistency to Whitman's early attempt to distance himself—as the initiator of a new poetic tradition—from Emerson's artistry. The article also reproduces a previously unpublished manuscript by Whitman which, its editor contends, supports the notion of Whitman's early anxiety of influence. The scholarship, both primary and secondary, on Whitman and Emerson from 1855 to 1982 is briefly discussed by me in *The Transcendentalists*, pp. 375–83.

In "Echoes of Walt Whitman's 'Bare-Bosom'd Night' in Vincent Van Gogh's 'Starry Night' " (*AN&Q* 22:105–09) Lewis M. Layman sees Whitman's apostrophe to night and earth in "Song of Myself" as a primary inspiration. Karl Keller, on the other hand, offers his own apostrophe in "Whitman and the Queening of America" (*AmerP* 1 [1983]:4–26), an extravagant argument which adopts the thesis of Robert K. Martin (*ALS 1979*, p. 64) that Whitman initiated the homosexual tradition in American literature. Keller's screed is long on wit but short on evidence. The poet's alleged homosexuality is also the subject of Alan Helms's "Whitman Revised" (*EA* 37:257–71). Helms argues that the poet spent the last two decades of his life expurgating his book in order to obscure its homosexual theme and thus be accepted as America's national poet. The essay is rigorous in its display of evidence but ultimately reductive in its conclusion that *Leaves of Grass* has its "source in, or [is] importantly conditioned by" a sexual preference known only till Oscar Wilde's era as "sodomy" and "buggery."

Two others that deal with Whitman's influence concern Charlotte Perkins Gilman and William Carlos Williams. In "Charlotte Perkins Gilman and the Whitman Connection" (*WWR* 1:21–25) Joann P. Krieg digs up all sorts of interesting facts in laying the foundation to her argument that the author of "The Yellow Wallpaper" would have agreed with Whitman's view of women. "Like Whitman," Krieg allows, "Gilman had little interest in women's suffrage; indeed, her interest in economics and what is now called sociology was all predicated on her belief that once freed from the confines of the home and made economically independent through their own labor, women

would no longer feel obliged to choose husbands for economic reasons and could engage in selective mating. . . . Though not so cosmic
as Whitman's, it was a vision of perfect motherhood deeply akin to
his." The difference, however, that Krieg may overlook in her well-
researched article is that Whitman celebrated motherhood more than
the mother herself and might have balked at Gilman's portrait in *Her-
land* (1915). Whitman is also an item of considerable interest in
Stephen Tapscott's *American Beauty: William Carlos Williams and
the Modernist Whitman* (Columbia). Tapscott introduced his ideas
on Whitman in *Paterson* a few years ago (*ALS 1981*, p. 83), but in the
larger study it becomes clear that his focus is not on Whitman's influence *per se* but Williams's "invention" of Whitman in his own
pursuit of a Modernist poetic. Williams's deconstruction of Whitman
was conscious, and so is Harry Gershenowitz's as he may commit the
intentional fallacy in "Two Lamarckians: Walt Whitman and Edward Carpenter" (*WWR* 2:35–39).

Source studies are easily forgotten, of course, unless their discoveries cast significant light on the subject at hand. This is clearly
the case in the best article on Whitman this year, C. Carroll Hollis's
"Rhetoric, Elocution, and Voice in *Leaves of Grass*: A Study in Affiliation" (*WWR* 2:1–21). An excellent postscript to his *Language and
Style in* Leaves of Grass (*ALS 1983*, pp. 80–81), the essay explains
and illustrates the nature of the *speaking* persona in Whitman's book.
In a sense, Hollis does for Whitman's dots in the early *Leaves* what
we have tried and failed to do for Dickinson's dashes; that is, he gives
us their rule, which is found in the 19th-century texts and guides to
elocution, rhetorical grammar, and oratory. But more than that, he
shows us that Whitman's familiarity with contemporary grammars of
oratory in the '20s and '30s, as he was "simmering," led to his discovery of a way of "doing democracy" in *Leaves of Grass*. What
Whitman accomplished, as no other American poet before him, was
to involve poetry with the democratizing spirit of the Jacksonian
period; he adopted and adapted oratorical rhetoric in order "to make
or to shape this country's first contribution to world poetry." Hence,
the orator-persona in *Leaves of Grass* between 1855 and 1860; after
that, with the third edition in the hands of a commercial publisher,
Whitman appears to have accepted the printed page as his dominant
means of communication—"with consequent changes in his style
thereafter."

ii. Dickinson

a. **Bibliography, Editing.** William White brings the Dickinson bibliography up to date in "Bibliography of Emily Dickinson Accumulated Annual Checklists into a Master One, 1981–84 Early" (*DicS* 54:3–25); and Sister Regina Siegfried divides her material between critics who see the poet's loss of faith and those who find a more optimistic poet in "Bibliographic Essay: Selected Criticism for Emily Dickinson's Religious Background" (*DicS* 52:32–53). The real bonus this year, however, is Joel Myerson's *Emily Dickinson: A Descriptive Bibliography* (Pittsburgh), a remarkably thorough primary bibliography. His work includes all printings of the poet's poems in separate editions, collections, and serials through 1982. Following the format of his equally comprehensive Emerson bibliography (*ALS 1982*, pp. 3–4), Myerson also provides an index of poems (even more useful in Dickinson's case) which gives succinctly the publishing history for each entry. As if this were not sufficient bibliographical bounty, we also received this year James Woodress's updated survey of Dickinson scholarship in *Fifteen American Authors Before 1900* (pp. 185–229). Woodress provides insightful summaries of the best work since 1970 and correctly places David Porter's second book on Dickinson (*ALS 1981*, pp. 86–87) in the company of those by George Frisbie Whicher, Charles R. Anderson, Albert J. Gelpi, and Richard B. Sewall.

In "New Dickinson Civil War Publications" (*AL* 56:17–27) Porter's former student Karen Dandurand continues to discover poems published during the poet's lifetime (see *ALS 1982*, p. 91). The sum of this welcome contribution is to announce the contemporary publication of two more poems ("These Are the Days When Birds Come Back" [J. 130] and "Flowers—Well—If Anybody" [J. 137]), but we also learn that three others (whose single publication we already knew about) were published in more than one journal. Whereas, for example, it was thought that "Success Is Counted Sweetest" (J. 67) was first published in *A Masque of Poets* (1878), we now know it first appeared in the Brooklyn *Daily Union* of 27 April 1864. (It is tempting here to hope for a Whitman connection since the "disgraceful" bard also published in this newspaper during the war.) Thanks to Dandurand's detective work, we can today count ten poems as published during Dickinson's lifetime. If any criticism can be made here, it is that Dandurand is (at this juncture) a better scholar than she is a critic. Because several of the discovered publications appeared in *Drum Beat*, a journal founded to assist the war effort, Dandurand leaps to the conclusion that Dickinson was not indifferent "to the catastrophic events of the Civil War." Of course, the matter of the poet's indifference to the war as well as to publication itself has been foolishly overstated and oversimplified in the past; but Dandurand's hasty speculations err in the other direction.

b. **Biography.**   In writing his definitive life of Dickinson (*ALS 1974*, pp. 70–71), Richard B. Sewall discovered that the poet's "secret" lay not as much in sources or literary influences as in people—the many correspondences she maintained throughout her life ("In Search of Emily Dickinson," *MQR* 23:514–28). Hence, he began his biography by focusing first on the lives of those who surrounded the elusive poet. The approach turned up a number of new facts, including the interesting information that the poet's brother carried on a long extramarital affair with Mabel Loomis Todd, the wife of one of the Amherst professors and original editor of the poems and letters. Now the entire story of that liaison is told in Polly Longsworth's *Austin and Mabel: The Amherst Affair & Love Letters of Austin Dickinson and Mabel Loomis Todd* (Farrar). As to be expected, most reviewers have pronounced the letters boring, but what should we expect from love letters? What makes this volume valuable to students of Dickinson is not what the two lovers pledged to each other but the nature of their affair and how it redounded upon Amherst and the poet who made the town famous. Longsworth's research and writing for this edition are first-rate. If anything, she ought to have paraphrased the letters and made her edition into a narrative—as her headnotes are far more interesting and readable than the letters they introduce. Be that as it may, the editor has dutifully fleshed out the domestic details of the lives involved in this tryst—the very ones Dickinson surveyed from the second story of her house and mind. Austin and Mabel's love affair—really a *ménage à trois* which included Mabel's husband—was more ardent and sensuous than Sewall had indicated, but Longsworth transcends the scandal to give us revealing portraits of the poet's sister, sister-in-law, and brother— the three individuals closest to the poet, who emerges from this study as the most "normal" Dickinson of the lot.

Also surfacing this year is a letter by the poet's father in Daniel J.

Lombardo, "Edward Dickinson and the Amherst and Belchertown Railroad: A Lost Letter" (*Hist. Jour. of Mass.* 12:36–43). The letter of 28 July 1851 indicates how deeply Edward Dickinson was involved in public affairs, and the editor speculates that it also indicates the first signs that the poet would become a recluse. The validity of this conclusion remains in question, especially in the light of a letter by Austin that suggests an even earlier beginning. The hypothesis probably would not satisfy Joyce Van Dyke, but then no one biography does either, except the one she is possibly writing herself. In "Inventing Emily Dickinson" (*VQR* 60:276–96), she contradicts herself by urging the future biographer, on the one hand, to get back to the flesh-and-blood details of the poet's life and, on the other, to become more "inventive" in his use of these details. In "Reading Emily Dickinson's Letters" (*ESQ* 30:170–92) Suzanne Juhasz looks for those flesh-and-blood details and "invents" a figure who is torn between the demands of womanhood and the desire for recognition as a (male) poet. Finally, Anna Mary Wells defends the actions of Thomas Wentworth Higginson, suggesting that we might not have Dickinson's poetry today without his efforts ("Note on Higginson's Reputation," *DicS* 51:20–21).

c. **Criticism: General.** Higginson's reputation is also salvaged in Barton Levi St. Armand's *Emily Dickinson and Her Culture: The Soul's Society* (Cambridge), but that is merely one of its many feats. This strikingly original and thoroughly researched study is more than the sum of the author's many articles on the poet over the years. Using an "American Studies" approach, St. Armand attempts to "reimmerse Dickinson's texts in the nourishing context of their culture." At times it looks as though his method will render the poet up to her neck in mortuary poetry (e.g., Emmeline Grangerford). Yet this critical portrait stops short of seeing the poet as sentimental and one-dimensional (as she becomes frequently in William H. Shurr's characterization [*ALS 1983*, pp. 87–88]). Dickinson "selected her own society from her culture," St. Armand writes, but she never accepted the facile conclusions the culture fostered in the form of domesticated heavens and loving unions beyond the grave. She took her cue from the culture, but the conclusions she reached were starkly her own. In probably his strongest chapter, St. Armand interprets the poet's nature verse in the new light of contemporary landscape painting. Future biographers will also welcome St. Armand's discovery concerning the finances of Edward and Austin Dickinson with regard to the purchase of the Evergreens.

Another valuable contribution to the study of Dickinson is also the end product of a series of essays, Vivian R. Pollak's *Dickinson: The Anxiety of Gender* (Cornell). Focusing on the poet's relationship with her sister-in-law in the early chapters (models in the use of biography in criticism), Pollak demonstrates the complexity of Dickinson's psychosexual fears concerning men and how this anxiety carried over to her poetry as a kind of "marriage fiction." If the argument falters, it is in the later chapters where the claim for a more conscious feminism may be pressed too far. Suffice to say that *The Anxiety of Gender* probably shows more clearly than previous studies how Dickinson's sense of male sexuality was the catalyst that transformed potentially morose and sentimental poems into profound psychic insights. In doing so, this study avoids the excesses of previous feminist arguments to make the poet's dilemma almost exclusively a question of gender. In that department Barbara Antonina Clarke Mossberg summarizes the thesis of her book (*ALS 1982*, p. 92) in " 'Everyone Else is Prose': Emily Dickinson's Lack of Community Spirit" in *Critical Essays on Emily Dickinson* (Hall), ed. Paul J. Ferlazzo (pp. 223–38).

Lynn Keller and Cristanne Miller mount a similar charge in behalf of the feminist position in "Emily Dickinson, Elizabeth Bishop, and the Rewards of Indirection" (*NEQ* 57:533–53). Had Dickinson not been a woman suppressed by the male world, she might have discovered the poetry of indirection. The question of indirection aside, the essay is yet another example of attributing 20th-century feminist values to 19th-century experiences. This is the central complaint in Jane Donahue Eberwein's not altogether original argument in "Doing Without: Dickinson as Yankee Woman Poet" in *Critical Essays on Emily Dickinson*. She finds Dickinson making "negative decisions" by refusing what she cannot have. Eberwein does not, however, find Dickinson frustrated or particularly deprived as a woman writer in 19th-century America. While her male contemporaries were either out on the lecture circuit or confined to a customhouse in order to make a living, "Dickinson was simply writing." She already had what Virginia Woolf a generation later would say every woman artist craves—"a room of her own."

The main idea in Shira Wolosky's *Emily Dickinson: A Voice of*

War (Yale) can also be found in her article, "Emily Dickinson's War Poetry: The Problem of Theodicy" (*MR* 25:22–41); the rest of the book merely provides a larger metaphysical frame for the idea that Dickinson's themes become less "pathological . . . once the context of war is freely admitted." To this end Wolosky stresses the battle imagery in the poems but does not account for the fact that many of them—including the famous "Success Is Counted Sweetest" (J. 67)— were penned before the war. Wolosky also succumbs to the temptation of using one of the many straw men that people Dickinson criticism: the facile notion that there was little or no relation between the poet's interior reality and external "issues and events." Fortunately, the author does not seek out a literal parallel between the two realms but rather goes on to argue that Dickinson's response to the war mirrored her response to God—with whom she carried on a friendly quarrel in her poems. Because her challenge to the Almighty remained "dialogical," it ended in silence instead of publication. For Christopher E. G. Benfey in a thoughtful analysis of many of the poet's more obscure poems (*Emily Dickinson and the Problem of Others* [Mass.]), Dickinson is not simply a skeptic but a student of skepticism. Her poetry gives "fuller expression to what blocks our efforts to engage the world and other people than it gives to what might grant us access." Not always clearly focused, Benfey's study is nevertheless original—particularly with regard to the concept of privacy in Victorian America.

Dickinson fits the comic paradigm better than Whitman (discussed above) in *God Be with the Clown.* In "A Day! Help! Help! Another Day!" (pp. 77–105), Ronald Wallace joins George Frisbie Whicher in seeing Dickinson as the Downeast Yankee wit whose laconic, self-effacing posture fits Aristotle's definition of the *eiron.* The chapter also contains a few interesting, if not completely original, contrasts between Whitman and Dickinson. One is that whereas Whitman "inflates himself to the size of a god and fathers the universe," Dickinson "deflates herself to the size of a child and asks to be fathered." Certainly "I'm Nobody! Who Are You?" (J. 288) suggests a Jack Downing with a cosmic orientation. Also useful and interesting is Douglas Anderson's essay, "Presence and Place in Emily Dickinson's Poetry" (*NEQ* 57:205–24). He finds in many of the poems a "transcendant presence" in which the scene described in a particular poem serves as a synecdoche for a larger apprehension.

d. **Criticism: Individual Works.** Critics this year were more interested in the general rather than the particular Dickinson, and thus
this category is almost empty. Perhaps the most interesting item is
Jane Donahue Eberwein, "Dickinson's 'I Had Some things That I
Called Mine'" (*Expl* 42:31–33). Using the holograph of J. 116 from
The Manuscript Books (*ALS 1981*, pp. 84–85), Eberwein speculates
that "Shaw" in the poem alludes to Lemuel Shaw, Chief Justice of
Massachusetts, whom the poet says she will retain as her lawyer in a
legal action against God over the question of who owns her garden.
What better counsel in a quarrel with God than the father-in-law of
Herman Melville. In other contributions, George Monteiro connects
the buzzing fly to a folk tale about the flies on the crucified body of
Christ ("Dickinson's 'I Heard a Fly Buzz,'" *Expl* 43:43–45); Darryl
Hattenauer finds Dickinson venting feminist frustrations in her bird
poems ("Feminism in Dickinson's Bird Imagery," *DicS* 52:54–57);
and William H. Galperin reads "Because I Could Not Stop for
Death" as the poet's realization of the sacrifice she has made by be-
coming a poet instead of a wife ("Emily Dickinson's Marriage
Hearse," *DQ* 18:62–73).

e. **Affinities and Influences.** Paul J. Ferlazzo gives a balanced survey of the scholarship on Dickinson's relation to the Transcendentalists in *The Transcendentalists* (pp. 320–27). Where one critic asserts
Emerson's influence, for example, another rejects it. Standing in the
middle, however, may be Robert Luscher in "An Emersonian Context
of [sic] Dickinson's 'The Soul Selects Her Own Society'" (*ESQ* 30:
111–16). In the context of Emerson's essay, her pronouncement is not
a rejection of society outright but a dramatization of the "active
process by which the soul concentrates on, and grows through,
'Society.'"

Emerson's influence was probably as compelling to 19th-century
American poets as Whitman's has been to those in the 20th, but critics
look in all directions for sources for the poet who remained "stock
still" in her room on the second story. In "Beauty-Truth Re-Echoed:
The Keats-Dickinson 'Marriage' Annulled" (*HJ* 38:19–21) Robert F.
Fleissner attributes "I Died for Beauty" not only to Keats's "Ode on a
Grecian Urn," but to Shakespeare's "The Phoenix and the Turtle."
Jonathan Morse speculates rather freely that Dickinson's "Ancestors'
Brocades" remark echoes a line from Royall Tyler's play, *The Contrast*

("Query re 'Ancestors' Brocades' Source," *HJ* 38:18). Frances Bzowski finds a parallel between "the dreamlike entrance into eternity" of the persona in "Because I Could Not Stop for Death" and that of Christian's progress towards the Celestial City in Bunyan ("A Continuation of the Tradition of the Irony of Death," *DicS* 54:33–42). In doing so, she picks up the thread of Monteiro and St. Armand in their interesting monograph on the poet's knowledge of emblem books (*ALS 1981*, pp. 91–92). In another parallel ("Houses Within Houses: Emily Dickinson and Mary Wilkins Freeman's 'A New England Nun,'" *CentR* 28:129–45), Aliki Barnstone is less helpful—though the author's remarks on "After Great Pain, A Formal Feeling Comes" are worth consulting.

A handy summary of the allusions to Greek antiquity can be found in Persephone Tselentis-Apostolidis, " 'And I Will Be Socrates': Greek Elements in the Poetry of Emily Dickinson" (*DicS* 52:3–21). In the other direction we have Betsy Erkkila's "Dickinson and Rich: Toward a Theory of Female Poetic Influence" (*AL* 56:541–59). This latest version of the feminist alternative to the anxiety-of-influence theory might have been titled "Dickinson and *the* Rich," for it suggests how much female poets—particularly Adrienne Rich—owe to Dickinson. The argument also resembles Tapscott's for the Whitman-Williams affiliation (discussed above): Rich finds her feminist voice not in rejecting Dickinson—or killing off the mother—but in accepting and *re-conceiving* her. Whitman and Dickinson remain the central figures of influence in American poetry precisely because their work discourages disciples while encouraging the best of them to become poets in their own right.

Texas A&M University

6. Mark Twain

Louis J. Budd

The beginning of the centennial for *Adventures of Huckleberry Finn* brought so many popular articles, photo-essays, and feature stories directed not only at the novel but also at the author's career and personality that even sampling them would take too much space away from the academic writing. It is proof enough to report that the May issue of *Cobblestone: The History Magazine for Young People* was billed as "The World of Mark Twain." Also, it is pleasant to report that Robert Quackenbush's *Mark Twain? What Kind of Name Is That? A Story of Samuel Langhorne Clemens* (Prentice-Hall), a biography for the "juvenile" audience, has the facts both straight and fairly fresh. The coming generation of Twainians will start out soundly informed.

i. Bibliographies, Editions, and Collections

William M. McBride, *Mark Twain: A Bibliography of the Collections of the Mark Twain Memorial and the Stowe-Day Foundation* (Hartford, Conn.: McBride) announces the "first ever fully illustrated" such venture. Browsers will enjoy the plates, mostly black and white; collectors and book dealers will pick up new points; scholars will appreciate most the excellent layout on the early states of *Huckleberry Finn*, including of course the defaced drawing. Users must remember, however, that McBride, as he warns, confined himself to items available locally. Casting down his bucket thousands of miles from home, Thomas Amherst Perry's *Bibliography of American Literature Translated into Romanian / with Selected Romanian Commentary* (Philos. Lib.) allows us to judge the reception of Twain (and others) in Eastern (or Middle) Europe outside the Soviet Union; his biggest surprise lies in the popularity of some minor sketches such as "An Encounter with an Interviewer."

Reprint houses naturally tooled up for a centennial boom with such volumes as *The Hidden Mark Twain* (Crown). Yet the only important ones came from the Mark Twain Library (Calif.) based upon the editing conducted at the Mark Twain Project in Berkeley. Besides the three earlier volumes we now can assign *The Prince and the Pauper*, ed. Victor Fischer and Michael B. Frank, and *A Connecticut Yankee in King Arthur's Court*, ed. Bernard L. Stein. Our students will get truly authoritative texts, all the original illustrations, and sparing but highly reliable notes. Other publishers will doubtless strain to compete, and if the classic model for capitalism operates properly, the consumer can only benefit. The Library of America has of course its special pattern and goals, which control its second Twain volume containing *The Innocents Abroad* and *Roughing It*. Guy Cardwell again picked the texts and composed the 27 pages of notes. For *The Innocents Abroad* this is now the most reliably useful edition, based in the 1869 printing and sensitized by others' research into its origins and pitfalls.

The most provocative anthology is *The Science Fiction of Mark Twain* (Archon). Though David Ketterer's introduction had in effect appeared earlier (*ALS 1983*, p. 101), he now supplies 40 pages of explanatory notes and a useful bibliography. He argues not simply that Twain was the "first American writer to exploit fully the possibilities for humor" in sci-fi but that Twain earned mainline, lasting significance, guaranteed by *A Connecticut Yankee* as his "best and most influential work" in the rising genre. Critics can question Ketterer's superlatives or his choice of sketches and stories but not his grounding in theories of the genre, which he has already demonstrated elsewhere. Likewise, Charles Neider has already established his intrepidity in handling Twain texts. His *Plymouth Rock and the Pilgrims, and Other Salutary Platform Opinions* reprints 82—or fewer than half—of Twain's speeches after having "regularized" the punctuation and "edited the text for consistency." However, since Harper & Row came up with an attractive format for the texts, often reconstructed from newspapers rather than a manuscript, we may as well welcome Neider's edition as inviting more interest in Twain's public art.

ii. Biography

Currently almost all the writing about Twain's personality follows the lines laid down by his major biographers. At least John R. Cooley,

"Mark Twain's Angel-Fish: Innocence at Home?" (*MissQ* 38:3–19), conflates the sources of evidence so thoroughly as to offer fresh perspectives on the elderly Twain's rapture (pedophilia, a few have hinted) over prepubescent girls. Though Cooley will hear charges of having flinched, he has proceeded without irony or disdain to present that cosseting as a game enjoyed unsuspiciously by just about everybody in sight. M. E. Grenander, " 'Five Blushes, Ten Shudders and a Vomit': Mark Twain on Ambrose Bierce's *Nuggets and Dust*" (*ALR* 17:170–79), continues her digging into Twain's relations with a rival who considered himself as creating "wit," a higher order of literature than Twain's "humor." The facts she has recovered earn her the right to speculate on why Twain and Bierce interacted so unpredictably yet gingerly. Robert Luscher, "Italian Accounts of Mark Twain: An Interview and a Visit from the *Corriere della sera*" (*ALR* 17:216–24), translates two primary documents, the second especially interesting for spectators of the Lyon-Ashcroft quarrel. Unfortunately, Tim Hodgson's six-part "Mark Twain Abroad" (in *Bermudian*) deserves merely a warning that scholars need not try to get it since it uses only the obvious sources available in the United States.

iii. General Interpretations

Of the eight essays—originally lectures—in *Mythologizing of Mark Twain*, the three by John C. Gerber, Alan Gribben, and myself deal from different angles with Twain's career as a popular writer and a personality vivid not just for his times but quite evidently up into the present. Henry Nash Smith's essay—the keynote for a symposium—develops further his thesis that Twain's crucial weapon as well as gift to posterity was his vernacular style. With "Mark Twain and the Myth of the Daring Jest" Stanley Brodwin adds greater depth and impact to his ongoing analysis of Twain's synthesis of humor, agonized idealism, and inversions of Christianity. More than any other article for 1984, Brodwin's deserves the label "Cannot be summarized in less than another article" so read it for yourself and enjoy.

Naturally, Alfred Kazin devoted major space (35 pages) to Twain in *American Procession* without, however, very original results. After deciding that his "world was all personal, disjointed, accidental," Kazin narrows to *The Adventures of Tom Sawyer* and *Huckleberry Finn* and then insists, furthermore, that the later far outclasses the earlier novel in both artistry and insight. For *Exiles at Home* Daniel

Marder runs through the major works but again comes to no newer
conclusion than that Twain felt isolated in his native culture because
he rejected its confidence in the Christian system. Two female critics
also offered a synoptic view. Entitling her relevant chapter "Old
Ladies and Little Girls," Joyce W. Warren, *The American Narcissus*,
joins the consensus that Twain did not present women as individuals
in their own right; though especially awkward with traits of sexuality
he could not create believable children or older women either. Refreshingly, Wilma Garcia's "Initiation into the World of Men," a chapter of her *Mothers and Others*, concedes that her enthusiasm for
Twain as a satirist has pulled against resentment over his portraits of
womankind. While mostly predictable, she extends the standard view
when arguing that Twain attacked Mary Baker Eddy because she
combined the oppression of both organized religion and the mother
forcing sons into Victorian gentility.

Thomas Schirer, *Mark Twain and the Theatre* (Nuremberg: Hans
Carl), tries too hard to tie the playwriting to major books, to *The
Innocents Abroad* and *A Tramp Abroad*, for instance. But he did
thorough research in a badly neglected subject; only a few scholars
have known that Twain began at least 11 plays, got involved in another ten collaborations, and translated three plays from German.
Schirer is particularly rich on the Vienna period of 1897–99, both for
fresh details and his insights. More generally, he demonstrates that,
during a weak period for drama in the United States, Twain earned
both royalties and prestige from his long-nurtured enthusiasm for
the stage and that he was even a sound critic of the plays he attended.

iv. Individual Writings before 1884

Having had his say about *Huckleberry Finn* decades ago, Edgar M.
Branch keeps digging around in the early years with impressive results. "Three New Letters by Samuel Clemens in the *Muscatine
Journal*" (*MTJ* 22,i:2–7) enriches the record of what the journeyman
printer was seeing and thinking in 1854–55; more specifically, these
travel letters prove the surprising tenacity of memory in somebody
often brushed off as an intellectual butterfly. Branch's "Did Sam
Clemens Write 'Learning Grammar'?" (*StAH* ns2:201–05) combs
through a newspaper few of us suspect of having been in the universe at all to uncover a comic letter in 1856 possibly by Twain—not
an important item, but every careful biographer will want to con-

sider it. For a signed sketch of 1864—"Concerning Notaries"—Guy Louis Rocha and Roger Smith, "Mark Twain and the Nevada Notary Stampede" (*Nev. Hist. Soc. Quar.* 26[1983]:83–92), supply the forgotten context through research in archives. With far wider meaning for the western years, Richard H. Cracroft, " 'Ten Wives is All You Need': Artemus Twain and the Mormons—Again" (*WHR* 38:197–211), compares the sketches in which two humorists exploited Brigham Young. After judging, convincingly, that Twain at first "was less inspired, generally dependent on, and often bettered by his mentor," Cracroft avoids charging us with neglect of Artemus Ward; Twain did soon outgrow him to become "enduringly funnier." Robert C. Rosen, "Mark Twain's 'Jim Blaine and His Grandfather's Ram' " (*CollL* 11:191–94), isolates a slightly later yarn in order to explicate its artistry and also its "underlying logic," which demonstrates that "truth is a 'skeptical state of mind.' "

All the books preceding *Huckleberry Finn* evidently drifted toward the background as the centennial loomed. Robert H. Hirst and Brandt Rowles, "William E. James's Stereoscopic Views of the *Quaker City* Excursion" (*MTJ* 22,i:15–33), painstakingly document the source for some of the illustrations in *The Innocents Abroad* while the broader point advances our grasp of both its comic and realistic perspectives. For *Roughing It*, Harold H. Kolb, Jr., "Mark Twain and the Myth of the West" (in *Mythologizing of Mark Twain*), finds that it embodies the "full range" of complex and contradictory attitudes that the settled citizenry held toward the raw territories. Provocative rather than solid, Martin Green, "Twain's *Roughing It*" (pp. 133–50 in his *Great American Adventure*), ultimately must be evaluated within a larger theory about the serious tale of adventure as a vehicle for expansionism, at home as much as abroad. Green has a challenging mind whose own reach expands restlessly.

Allison R. Ensor, " 'Norman Rockwell Sentimentality': The Rockwell Illustrations for *Tom Sawyer* and *Huckleberry Finn*" (in *Mythologizing of Mark Twain*) exhibits a cause of reader-response added long after Twain had chosen a different kind of artist. Forrest G. Robinson, "Social Play and Bad Faith in *The Adventures of Tom Sawyer*" (*NCF* 39:1–24), assumes a tightly cohering narrative persona who intended depth even for secondary characters like Aunt Polly and who made his structural keystone the strength of "bad faith"—those "sublimated deceits that society resorts to in its quest for stability and equanimity." Of course Tom is the "consummate gamesman" who does not simply trick the elders but rather "serves briefly as a kind of high priest in a ritual affirmation of the enabling paradoxes of quotidian social life." Robinson certainly shows that the tide of taking *Huckleberry Finn* with the highest seriousness has overlapped *Tom Sawyer*.

The other major forerunner of *Huckleberry Finn* benefits from James M. Cox's "*Life on the Mississippi* Revisited" (in *Mythologizing of Mark Twain*). Always inventive, Cox teases further subtleties out of the dialectic between Samuel Clemens and Twain while suggesting a heretofore hidden unity within the book. For a Viking Penguin paperback Cox manages to sound original about the much discussed "Old Times" chapters and makes the later chapters as attractive as can be done convincingly. Since he reinserts suppressed—or just discarded—passages and adds six pages of endnotes, he has constructed the best edition of *Life on the Mississippi* until the Mark Twain Library can compete. The book got an incidental boost, meanwhile, from a rising controversy among professors of law. Paul Carrington's "Of Law and the River" (*Jour. of Legal Educ.* 34:222–28), hailing it as the "best book in English about professional training," fleshes out a comparison between a good pilot and as good an attorney. That's pleasant for Twainians, but Carrington was primarily addressing doubts about the fixable meaning and social neutrality of the documents upon which courts base their justice.

v. *Adventures of Huckleberry Finn*

Carl Dolmetsch, "*Huck Finn*'s First Century: A Bibliographical Survey" (*ASInt* 22,ii:79–121), combines a selective bibliography, his own commentary, and a few statistics into a handy guide for anybody setting out to explore Twain's masterpiece, which now would fill P. T. Barnum with envy over how it seems to have something for everybody. *American Heritage* (35,iv:81–85) thought it rated a colorful spread; so did a monthly published for physicians (*M.D.*28,vi:117–33); *Childhood Education* (61:9–12) compared it and *E. T.: The Extra-Terrestrial* as "subtle acts of subversion"; more militantly, an editorial in *Humanist* (44,ii:35–36) praised a still relevant critique of "narrow-minded religious and social structures"; reading it for the first time since boyhood, Norman Mailer was relieved to find it "so up-to-date!" (*NYTBR*, 9 Dec. 1984, pp. 1, 36–37).

Fascinating in several ways, a Russian text (Moscow: Raduga), presenting a classic for study in the schools, clearly imitates the Norton edition though it has to supply further apparatus including a glossary. Incidentally, the edition that John Wallace expurgated for racism (*ALS 1983*, p. 98) is showing up here and there.

Thomas A. Tenney had a fine idea for his *Mark Twain Journal*—a special issue (22,ii) entitled "Black Writers on *Adventures of Huckleberry Finn:* One Hundred Years Later." Surprisingly, of the eight essays (nine, if we count the trenchant preface by guest editor Thadious M. Davis) only Julius Lester's enters an overall verdict that the novel "demeans blacks" and "does not take slavery and, therefore, black people seriously"; he blames Twain's "simplistic" mind, hobbled by a "white male psyche" trapped in "nostalgia for a paradise that never was." In effect, David L. Smith disagrees the most sharply with Lester by holding that Jim bursts through the stereotypes upon which racist discourse depends. Of all the essayists, only Smith discusses the Evasion chapters kindly—because Tom's shallowness makes Jim that much nobler. More broadly, *Huckleberry Finn* "contradicts entirely the overwhelming and optimistic consensus of 1884." Like Smith, Rhett S. Jones keenly analyzes the evolving interplay between Jim and Huck, but he turns stern about the white friend who is always ready to backslide into ruling attitudes and who cooperates as the "ending spirals down to a dispiriting and racist close." Charles H. Nilon, after deciding that the novel essentially concerns the cruel treatment of the freedman during the 1880s, instead grills Jim to reprimand his kowtowing to Tom, who typifies the whites certain that they know what will benefit or else please the blacks. Drawing on formidable scholarship, Arnold Rampersad widens the context to Afro-American fiction which *Huckleberry Finn* anticipated in several ways, especially by unmasking the "moral inversion" at the heart of a society in which legalized oppression violates the natural sense of compassion. Nevertheless, the novel failed on a major count—not so much through its ending as through not allowing Jim or any other black to rise to a spirit of "disruptive alienation."

For differing reasons the other three essayists for the special issue of *MTJ* agree, in Charles H. Nichols's words, that *Huckleberry Finn* qualifies as an "indispensable part of the education of both black and white youth." While patiently weighing pros and cons and protesting

that—by Huck writing "nigger" far more often than dramatic propriety requires—Twain was "legitimizing" the epithet, Kenny J.
Williams concludes that the novel "does suggest—and rightly so—
that the fates and fortunes of the races are so closely intertwined
that one cannot exist without the other." After objectively stating the
case against assigning *Huckleberry Finn* in the schools, Richard C.
Barksdale develops a defense through arguing that it achieves an
"ironic appraisal of the American racial scene circa 1884." Yet Barksdale worries that the portrayal of Jim may traumatize young blacks
today. He would have worried harder if he could have read Frederick
Woodard and Donnarae MacCann's "*Huckleberry Finn* and the Traditions of Blackface Minstrelsy" in *Interracial Books for Children
Bulletin* (15,i–ii:4–13). Twainians should hunt down this periodical
to learn the full force of how minstrel-show clowning shaped Jim.

Though anybody concerned about racism grapples with the ending, it attracts many other approaches, and Dolmetsch found more
than 30 articles on it alone. Of the latest commentaries David W.
Hiscoe, "The 'Abbreviated Ejaculation' in *Huckleberry Finn*" (*StAH*
ns1[1983]:191–97), stays closest to the text in chiding that "our own
love for the sensational and sentimental" blinds us to hints that Miss
Watson had set Jim free; extending the thesis of Pascal Covici's *Mark
Twain's Humor: The Image of a World* (1962), he therefore applauds the Evasion as a "literary hoax by which Twain implicates his
audience in the very attitudes that his readers have lampooned
throughout the story." Both R. J. Fertel, "'Free and Easy'?: Spon-
taneity and the Quest for Maturity in the *Adventures of Huckleberry
Finn*" (*MLQ* 44[1983]:157–77), and John Earl Bassett, "*Huckleberry
Finn*: The End Lies in the Beginning" (*ALR* 17:89–98), find that the
final chapters ominously confirm traits of Huck's character evident
back in St. Petersburg, traits that could lead him to grow up more like
Pap than we care to think. His "moral backsliding" carries a "sad
inevitability" for Fertel because "improvisation, free living, passivity,
and misplaced [i.e., for the King and the Duke] sympathy together
make a pretty sorry pathway to maturity." For Bassett, who keeps
stretching the philosophical frame of his analysis, the Evasion not
only re-exposes Huck's flaws but extols Tom's contrasting ability to
"move between real and fictive worlds." Bassett has furnished a
lasting synthesis of several viewpoints for those readers who can accept ignoring the comedy throughout the novel. Only such readers

can admire the relevant chapter, pp. 88–97, in August J. Nigro, *The Diagonal Line*. Incidentally, Nigro devises two new glosses for the decision to "light out for the Territory ahead of the rest." First, Huck is determined to go it alone; second, the final phrase may modify "Territory," designating it in "Twain's fractured Shakespeare 'the undiscovered country from whose bourne no traveler returns.'"

Only prestigious or else reckless critics dare nowadays to publish an openly judgmental essay on so ennobled a masterpiece. Leslie Fiedler qualifies on either count, of course. "*Huckleberry Finn*: The Book We Love To Hate" (*Proteus* 1,ii:1–8) typically demolishes both its friends and foes before celebrating a "therapeutic release of the repressed elements" of experience; serving the "Devil's party" here, Twain intended a "travesty of High Art quite as much as of conscience and duty and 'sivilization.'" With the candor typical for him, Henry Nash Smith, "The Publication of *Huckleberry Finn*: A Centennial Retrospect" (*BAAAS* 37,v:18–40), decides not to swell the recent "avalanche" of explication; instead he concentrates, rewardingly, on how the novel "was related as a work of art to the literary situation within which it was written." In passing he separates it deftly from local-color fiction. Burton Raffel, distinguished for his criticism on other figures, achieves a gracefully emphatic essay, "Mark Twain's View of *Huckleberry Finn*" (*BSUF* 24, iii[1983]:28–37), which tries to retrace the movement of the author's mind as he began a sequel to *Tom Sawyer* almost lackadaisically and just slowly got involved at the deepest level of his psyche. Eminent in England, John Fraser, who took a breather from his favorite interests with his estimate of *Huckleberry Finn* in 1967, has collected it in *The Name of Action: Critical Essays* (Cambridge). The pages exhibiting Tom as a "false comedian" in Edward L. Galligan's *The Comic Vision in Literature* (Georgia) are essentially reprinted from *Sewanee Review* (see *ALS 1977*, p. 95). Both essays are sophisticated enough to be worth reading again.

Narrowing their focus deliberately, several approaches proved worthwhile if only for their relative freshness. In "Huck Finn and the Slave Narratives: Lighting Out as Design" (*SR* 20,ii:247–64) Lucinda H. MacKethan exploits fully the chance that because Twain doubtless knew some of the escape-accounts, he borrowed from them for "design"—of theme and also of tangential details and even style. Furthermore she proposes that he intended to treat Huck like a run-

away slave after he sided with Jim. Karol Kelley, "*Huckleberry Finn*
as a Popular Novel" (*Proteus* 1,ii:19–26), set out to diagram what
"social values Twain might share or not share with the popular authors of his lifetime." Pushing to the limit an idea explored occasionally, Kevin Murphy, "Illiterate's Progress: The Descent into Literacy
in *Huckleberry Finn*" (*TSLL* 26:363–87), stresses how and why
Huck uses his lately learned ability to read and write; after sensi-
tizing us to passages seldom explicated he builds an intense and "in-
sidious" link "between literacy and dehumanization, between language and repressive social institutions." A welcome change from
portentousness, Leland Krauth, "Mark Twain, Alice Walker, and the
Aesthetics of Joy" (*Proteus* 1,ii:9–14), a running comparison with
The Color Purple, appreciates *Huckleberry Finn* for a "surprising
release of the self from the world of pain." Though Bobby J. Cham-
berlain, "Frontier Humor in *Huckleberry Finn* and Carvalho's *O
Coronel e o Lobisomem*" (*CLS* 21:201–16), is more intriguing than
persuasive when comparing Twain's humor with a supposed Brazilian counterpart, we need challenges to the sense of Huck as
uniquely American. Within a highly specialized, biblical tradition,
John E. Becker's "Twain: The Statements Was Interesting but
Tough," pp. 131–42 in *Poetic Prophecy*, grows darker and darker
about Huck's most vital search, which is for a "much larger sort of
freedom, the possibility of escaping from the mythos of society into
a deeper truth"—a possibility that humankind never fulfills.

Finally, two commentaries from outside the guild of English
draw attention for just that reason. In "Decency and the Good Old
Boy Syndrome" (*SAQ* 83:434–46) a distinguished sociologist, Edgar T. Thompson, crowning Huck as "one of the most delightful
rascals in literature," presents him as following the familiar, time-
less compromise between humane, face-to-face warmth and strict
legality. With "Law and Nature in *The Adventures of Huckleberry
Finn*" (*Proteus* 1,ii:27–35) a political scientist, Catherine H. Zuckert,
sorts out professionally the issues that even the most formalist critics
usually end up judging somehow. She shows that Huck must return
to organized society, if simply for self-protection; with whatever
reluctance, Twain warned that "there is no freedom without law" and
that both "idealization of the return to nature and a confused vision
of an aristocratic past" will undermine democracy. Zuckert poses a
particular challenge to those who assume Huck can and will reach
autonomy out in the Territory.

vi. Individual Writings after 1885

Considering the backlog some periodicals carry and the lead-time in any case, longer than contributors expect, happenstance must partly explain the extreme emphasis on *Huckleberry Finn* during 1984. We heard little more about Hank Morgan than Lawrence I. Berkove's "The Reality of the Dream: Structural and Thematic Unity in *A Connecticut Yankee*" (MTJ 22,i:8–14), which, having assumed a tight design projected through an unreliable and imperceptive narrator, spells out a gloomy purpose based not even in the shortcomings of the late 19th century but in human nature endlessly repeating its mistakes. But can faith in Twain's patient matching of details survive Hershel Parker's "*Pudd'nhead Wilson:* Jack-leg Author, Unreadable Text, and Sense-Making Critics" (pp. 115–45 in his *Flawed Texts*)? This chapter, which expands an article (*ALS 1983*, p. 106), gains force from the overarching thesis of the book and its findings for other major writers. With no larger motive, Nick Karanovich, "A 'Suppressed' Mark Twain Chapter" (*ABC* 5,iv:3,6–11), constructs a definitive history for the passage (on Twain's vital organs) once intended as chapter 51 of *Following the Equator*. Convincing to me anyway, Earl F. Briden and Mary Prescott, "The Lie That I Am I: Paradoxes of Identity in Mark Twain's 'Hadleyburg'" (*SSF* 21:383–91), center on the abstractions controlling Mary and George Richards, who are best explained not from their unique temperament but from Twain's late philosophical essays. Briden and Prescott fortify earlier readings of the story as encouraging mass condemnation, as manipulating the Richardses to exemplify the conflicting determinisms that a moralistic yet money-seeking society exerts.

After adapting the currently orthodox judgment that Hank Morgan is more a destroyer than a light-bringer, Zbigniew Lewicki, pp. 33–46 in *The Bang and the Whimper*, moves on to insightful comparisons among the three manuscripts on that Mysterious Stranger. For example, he points out that while Young Satan blithely rearranges futures in the "Chronicle," No. 44 does not toy with predetermined destinies. Kenneth Cook, "What's So Damn Funny? Grim Humor in *The Mysterious Stranger* and *Cat's Cradle*" (*PMPA* 7[1982]:48–55), arrives at no startling insights though he elaborates a pairing that will especially please undergraduates. Except for Ketterer's claiming some of the "Great Dark" pieces for science fiction, they have not attracted the interest I had predicted. A helpful push could come from M. D. Coburn's "The Enchanted Wilderness: Mark Twain and the Sea" (*Oceans* 17:16–19), a popularizing yet informative essay.

Undoubtedly *Huckleberry Finn* will have dominated the writing about Twain during 1985 also. But explications of it have grown so many-sided that no essay or even book will strike a majority as definitive. For 1984 anyway, I nominate as highlights the two additions to the Mark Twain Library, Stanley Brodwin's bold diagram of Twain's theology, Carl Dolmetsch's bibliography, and the issue of the *Mark Twain Journal* from black critics.

Duke University

7. Henry James

Robert L. Gale

The recession is over. Henry James's stock has never been higher. Books, chapters, articles, and dissertations on James, and reprints of works by him, poured out in 1984. Complete coverage is impossible in a chapter of this length. Selection and brevity become a necessity now.

i. Bibliographies, Biographies, Letters, Collections

Three bibliographical items are notable. "Henry James" (*JML* 11:458–61) lists books (with comments, some acerbic), dissertations, special journal numbers, and articles on James from 1981 to 1983. (Do see the cover photograph of James on his bicycle.) In "James Studies 1982: An Analytic and Biographical Essay" (*HJR* 5:158–86) Richard A. Hocks, this time with coauthor Paul Taylor, offers another of his reviews of Jamesian scholarship. The essay begins with books, then reviews praise of Leon Edel, turns to general articles, and discusses essays on individual writings—with fierce stress on "The Turn of the Screw." Hocks and Taylor locate many out-of-the-way items. Another in the growing number of books reprinting previous scholarship is *Henry James: Washington Square and The Portrait of a Lady: A Casebook* (Macmillan), divided into "Origins and Reception," "Early Criticism," and "Later Criticism."

Five biographical items are noteworthy. Howard M. Feinstein in "A Singular Life: Twinship in the Psychology of William and Henry James," pp. 301–28 in *Blood Brothers: Siblings as Writers* (Int'l. Univ., 1983), ed. Norman Kiell, with stunning brilliance discusses the "symbiotic sibship" of William and Henry James. It was physically difficult and psychologically impossible for the two to be-

Whatever thoroughness this chapter has is owing in large part to *Literary Criticism Register* and the kindness of its admirable editor Sims Kline of Stetson University.—*R.L.G.*

come different, because they suffered common half-attractive ill-
nesses, parental discouragement of healthy separateness, thoughts
of madness, ambivalence concerning work and pleasure, "puritanical"
guilt over spending unearned money, and what Feinstein boldly calls
"incestuous strivings." He shows that "in the fiction of Henry
James ... one finds the twin relationship most thoroughly delineated
and explored." Kiell's introduction sets the James brothers in a context including 11 other pairs of sibling writers. "The Names of the
Action: Henry James in the Early 1870s" (*NCF* 38:467–91) is a pre-
view "of an ongoing work to be called 'The Jameses: A Family Narrative'" by R. W. B. Lewis, who offers here four sections concerning
young James, together with interpolations locating those sections in
his projected book and summarizing omitted parts. Lewis discusses
James's 1869 "descent into Italy," his touring, appreciation of Italian
Renaissance artists, "defining his ideal self" as spectator/creator,
then work in Florence in 1874 on *Roderick Hudson*. Vital to Lewis
here are James's intellectual interactions with family members and
such relatives as Minny Temple. Ann Thwaite in *Edmund Gosse: A
Literary Landscape, 1849–1928* (Secker & Warburg) sheds light on
James as a literary and personal friend of Gosse. Leon Edel begins
his "Walter Berry and the Novelists: Proust, James, and Edith Wharton" (*NCF* 38:514–28) with a sketch of Walter Berry—one of those
"[p]eripheral figures ... that walk into creative lives ... [and] are
often difficult to document." Berry was a lawyer, judge, counselor of
Washington embassies, literary amateur, cosmopolite, Chamber of
Commerce president, orator, Francophile, snob, and friend of James.
Henry James: Interviews and Recollections, ed. Norman Page (St.
Martin's), reprints 62 passages, usually short, from almost as many
friends who described James in letters, diaries, autobiographies, and
reminiscences. The selections are divided into "Impressions," "Places
and People," "Occasions," "Life at Rye," "Conversation," and "The
War and the End."

Two collections of letters are significant. For the fourth and last
volume of his edition of selected letters by James, entitled *Henry
James Letters: 1895–1916* (Belknap), Leon Edel provides two services, mainly admirable. First, his introduction valuably analyzes
"James's psychosexual life." It discusses his relationship with Edith
Wharton, her lover W. Morton Fullerton, and her automobile, and
with Gaillard Lapsley; and generalizes on "[t]he epistolary James ...
in his late letters." Second, Edel excellently introduces each of the

five sections of the volume: "Withdrawal from London, 1895–1900" (about James's turning to dictation, a literary agent, the first of several young male friends; about his only owned home, Lamb House); "The Edwardian Novels, 1900–1904" (his major-phase fecundity, the Boer War, other British miseries); "The American Scene, 1904–1905" (his visit to his native land); "Revisions, 1905–1910" (his New York edition, late plays, last social flings); and "Terminations, 1911–1915" (his Lamb House solitude, consequent London flat, autobiographical dictation, World War I, terminal sickness). For this volume, Edel provides especially valuable annotations and a fine index. And what of James himself as revealed in these majestic letters? I cannot comment in detail here. The letters must be gratefully dipped into, again and again, by those who admire their compassionate, ever-articulate, professional, self-demeaning, loving author. Here James feelingly writes to friends and relatives about his work, travels, loneliness, and aging. He hungers for what he repeatedly calls "participation" in his friends' sorrows. Raymond S. Moore in "A Literary-Gossipy Friendship: Henry James's Letters to Edmund Gosse" (*SoR* 20:570–90) presents 18 letters from James to Gosse, written between 1882 and 1915—all edited supremely well. They concern James's own writings and his difficulties with editors, Gosse's literary criticism, the death of Constance Fenimore Woolson and later that of William James, Gosse's vacation in Italy, the abortive project of reburying Robert Louis Stevenson in England, and James's becoming a British subject. James reveals his joy in wordplay, urges the Gosses to come home from Italy "intoxicated, & reeking of the purple wine, to your poor old attached abstainer," calls Gosse's praise of New York edition volume 1 "chocolate-creams of criticism & homage."

Four reprints deserve mention. Every self-respecting Americanist knows about the Library of America. Now two new James volumes have been added to it: *Literary Criticism: French Writers, Other European Writers, The Prefaces to the New York Edition* and *Literary Criticism: Essays on Literature, American Writers, English Writers*, both edited by Leon Edel and Mark Wilson, and each considerately arranged and with splendid chronology, note on the texts, notes, and index. These are the fullest and most beautiful James books ever published. Comprising almost 300 items, including 100 or so never published before in book form, they clearly reveal James as America's premier literary critic qualitatively and quantitatively. Publishing criticism spanning more than half a century, he wrote about both major and minor authors, usually aiming to reveal the subject's whole achievement. He praises good writers for their intention and accomplishment, and adversely criticizes weak ones for hypocrisy and bungling. He especially reveres the novel for its prodigious possibilities as an art form. He is unusual among American critics for handling French literature masterfully. His prefaces, as we know, discuss subject, origin, place in corpus, autobiographical detail, and self-evaluation. The importance of these two beautiful volumes, totaling 2,892 pages, cannot be overemphasized. The book of the year on James to be most lovingly handled is *Quotations from Henry James, Selected by Louis Auchincloss* (Virginia). In his introduction Auchincloss notes that James was a "mandarin" who "wrote for the pleasure of telling," and whose mere "shards" of prose therefore show glittering, impressionistic embellishment. Auchincloss's choice of more than 200 passages and snippets concerns people (real and fictional), things (including paintings), places, tense scenes and dialogue, and literary criticism. James is brilliant here, partly because Auchincloss is always tactful. Another useful collection is James's *The Art of the Novel* (Northeastern), ed. R. P. Blackmur, here with a fine new foreword by R. W. B. Lewis. Calling James's prefaces "without rival in our language," Lewis discusses New York edition difficulties—with copyright owners, title selections, and the number of volumes—and then mentions elements of prefatory "self-appraisal." Lewis charmingly comments on Blackmur, who was highly influential in Jamesian criticism and is now "passing perceptibly into legend."

Less impressive is the reprinting of a dozen short stories in *Henry James' Shorter Masterpieces*, vols. 1 and 2 (Barnes & Noble), ed. with brief introduction and skimpy notes by Peter Rawlings. Some of the selections are wrongly said to be central or inaccessible.

ii. Sources, Parallels, Influences

Since James was such an extensive reader in his day and has since attracted critics who examine his work closely, this category continues to be statistically of overriding importance in Jamesian criticism.

Elissa Greenwald in "The Ruins of Empire: Reading the Monuments in Hawthorne and James" (*CEA* 46:48–59) explores the idea that characters in the fiction of both Nathaniel Hawthorne and James often "pause to read the inscriptions on European monuments," both

English and Roman. While doing so "they . . . transform meditation on the historical structures to reflection on their own situations," so as "to take full possession of their personal past." In " 'The Eye of Mr. Ruskin': James's Views on Venetian Artists" (*HJR* 5:107–16), W. R. Martin traces stages of James's subservience to and gradual independence of John Ruskin's judgments on Venetian painters, especially Titian and Tintoretto. Martin boldly speculates that James worked free of Ruskin's qualified preference for Tintoretto because in his fiction James tried in his own terms to combine the repose, harmony, dignity, and ceremony of Titian with the motion, conflict, energy, and drama of Tintoretto. Adeline R. Tintner reports in "Abraham Solomon and Henry James's 'The Birthplace' " (*PRR* 4:56–61) that the picture that Morris Gedge mentions near "The Birthplace" ending must be one of a narrative " 'before' and 'after' set" by the Pre-Raphaelite genre painter Abraham Solomon. Peter Buitenhuis in "After the Slam of *A Doll's House* Door: Reverberations in the Works of James, Hardy, Ford and Wells" (*Mosaic* 17:83–96) shows the influence of "Nora's act of leaving husband, children and home" in Henrik Ibsen's 1879 play *A Doll's House* on works by four novelists, including the author of *The Ambassadors*, in which Madame Marie de Vionnet is compared to Ibsen's Nora. Wayne W. Westbrook's "Selah Tarrant à la Daudet" (*HJR* 5:100–106) is a conventional influence essay: for his characterization of Verena Tarrant's father in *The Bostonians* James drew on Alphonse Daudet's characterization of Delobelle in his 1874 novel *Fromont jeune et Risler aîné*. In a short essay long on wisdom, entitled "A Literary Youth and a Little Woman: Henry James Reviews Louisa Alcott," pp. 265–69 in *Critical Essays on Louisa May Alcott*, ed. Madeleine B. Stern (Hall), Adeline Tintner points out that in an 1865 review of an Alcott novel James displays "youthful priggishness," whereas in an 1875 review of a later Alcott novel he more perceptively comments on her "straddling of the two worlds of childhood and adulthood." Tintner in "*False Dawn* and the Irony of Taste-Changes in Art" (*EdWN* 1:1, 3, 8) suggests that James's prematurely adverse opinion of Italian primitives might have contributed to a plot element in Edith Wharton's 1922 novella *False Dawn*. Tintner in "O. Henry and Henry James: The Author of the Four Million Views the Author of the Four Hundred" (*MarkhamR* 13:27–31) identifies six stories in which popular O. Henry alludes seven times to elitist James—more often than to any other author— sometimes in parody, sometimes in admiration. Tintner discusses

Ernest Hemingway's "love-hate relationship with . . . the figure of
James and with his work" in her "Ernest and Henry: Hemingway's
Lover's Quarrel with James," pp. 165–78, in *Ernest Hemingway: The
Writer in Context*, ed. James Nagel (Wisconsin). She summarizes
Hemingway's respect for much of James's writing, his coarsely
phrased dislike of James's alleged "male old wom[a]n" ways, and his
response to James's "obscure hurt" as compared to his own real
wound. Tintner notes the possible influence of James's "The Great
Good Place" on Hemingway's "Big Two-Hearted River." According
to Daniel Mark Fogel in "Imaginative Origins: 'Peter Quince at the
Clavier' and Henry James" (*WSJour* 8:22–27), Wallace Stevens might
have been inspired by James's image of Shakespeare (as composer
improvising at harpsichord or violin) in his 1907 essay on *The Tem-
pest* (see *ALS 1982*, p. 126). A more complex influence essay by Fogel
is his "henryJAMESjoyce: The Succession of the Masters" (*JML* 11:
199–229), in three main parts. First, Fogel shows that Joyce responded to and concealed James in *Ulysses*: James is caricatured in
Joyce's Philip Beaufoy ("Calypso"); James's "The Birthplace" is
cribbed from and is otherwise reflected in Joyce's attitudes concerning Shakespeare's life and writings ("Scylla and Charybdis"); and
James's major-phase style tempts Joyce to parody ("Eumaeus").
Second, Fogel sketches "Joyce's pre-*Ulysses* relations with Henry
James": Joyce read much James starting in 1904, used *The Portrait
of a Lady* as one model for *Stephen Hero*, and was influenced by
James's *The Better Sort* (especially "The Beast in the Jungle" therein)
when composing *Dubliners*. And third, Fogel returns to "the Henry
James trope in *Ulysses*" to allege that part of "Joyce's anxiety of in-
fluence" might have been due to his awareness of James as an an-
tagonist to master or exorcise. John B. Humma's "James and Fowles:
Tradition and Influence" (*UTQ* 54:79–100) shows that John Fowles
parallels aspects of many influential world-class writers, including
James, in the process of writing himself into "a solid moral tradition."
Two influence essays concern the modern writer Margaret Drabble.
In "Margaret Drabble's *The Needle's Eye*: Jamesian Perception of
Self" (*CLAJ* 28:33–45) Mary M. Lay tries to assuage readers of Drabble's 1972 novel who are discontent with its apparently unexciting
conclusion by remarking that "[b]oth James and Drabble describe
life as a stream of incidents . . . where joy is . . . temporary, and the
greatest achievement is perception of self," to gain which characters
must move beyond egocentricity, shed illusions, and devise new

standards. Lay notes parallels between *The Ambassadors* and *The Needle's Eye*. Charles W. Mayer in "Drabble and James: 'A Voyage to Cythera' and 'In the Cage' " (*SSF* 21:57–63) identifies "parallels of theme, character, action, and method" between Drabble's 1967 short story "A Voyage to Cythera" and James's "In the Cage." Both works feature imaginative heroines who live vicariously, central consciousnesses reflecting "all values," and epiphanic scenes.

iii. Criticism: General

It is in this category that critics of James truly excelled in 1984, with six book-length studies, as well as several notable chapters and articles.

At the outset, I recommend to all irrational James buffs William R. Macnaughton's review article, "The Question of Henry James (Revisited)" (*CRevAS* 15:323–35) for its healthy anti-Jamesian common sense. "I will confess that one of my naughty solitary pleasures over the years has been to search out criticism on James which contains passages hostile to the Master." So Macnaughton begins; and he takes off from there by using five recent books on James as stiff springboards, unsafe because perhaps cracked. More serious are the implications in Michael Sprinker's "Historicizing Henry James" (*HJR* 5: 203–07), occasioned by his desire to discount recent work by Mimi Kairschner, Mark Seltzer, and Bruce Robbins (see below). Sprinker concludes more generally and ominously that, "astute" though James now seems, he may not appeal to critics forever.

Jean-Christophe Agnew treats James in "The Consuming Vision of Henry James," pp. 65–100, 221–25, in *The Culture of Consumption: Critical Essays in American History, 1880–1980,* ed. Richard Wightman Fox and T. J. Jackson Lears (Pantheon, 1983), as only seemingly embarrassed by items "of the commodity world: the world of goods, newspapers, and advertisements." In reality "appropriative spectator[s]" such as James himself, with their all-grasping powers of observation and inner vision, are so haunted by "the specter of appropriation" that they convert commodities into symbolic "bundles of attributes," which are acquired not by purchasing them but by pervasively knowing them.

Carron Kaston's *Imagination and Desire in the Novels of Henry James* (Rutgers) is an original analysis of a central concern in James and hence in Jamesian criticism, "the psychology, aesthetics, and metaphysics of renunciation." Kaston's three main chapters concern "loss of self that results from living in parental houses of fiction"; "ambassadorial consciousness as a metaphor for the failures of imagination that result from such a loss of self"; and moving from "parental houses of fiction . . . [to] structures of the self." "[R]enunciation and . . . childhood states" are associated: Christopher Newman's loss of temper and Claire de Cintré's renunciation (*The American*) resemble Alice James's threat of suicide. Dr. Sloper shows half-admirable moral irony when he reacts to his daughter's silence (*Washington Square*). Isabel Archer renounces "material of . . . her life" which James has depicted positively (*The Portrait of a Lady*). Fleda Vetch is "decentered" ambassador between mother and son, and Poynton's fire is both "symbol and consequence" of Fleda's "absence from herself" (*The Spoils of Poynton*). *The Ambassadors* studies "substitutive or second-hand agency." By questioning "its own ambassadorial theme," "In the Cage" anticipates the "alternative to self-transcendence" enacted by Maggie Verver (*The Golden Bowl*), who tries for possession of "both self and world."

In his forceful book *Henry James & the Art of Power* (Cornell), Mark Seltzer seeks to correct the notion that James was not interested in writing about political power. Suggesting that critics have followed James's own critical lead and have analyzed technique and form in James for too long, Seltzer contends that, instead, "art and power are not opposed in the Jamesian text but radically entangled." He finds support in three long works. In *The Princess Casamassima* James's narrative vision and use of point of view "reproduce social modes of surveillance and supervision" (see *ALS 1982*, p. 121). Later James became more subtle. In *The Golden Bowl* "the imperative of organic form guarantees the Jamesian values of love and freedom even as it achieves a virtually 'automatic' regulation of character and narrative." In *The American Scene* James shows "the links between forms of discourse and the structures of power." Seltzer (following Michel Foucault) explains how "recent theories of an intrinsic literary 'difference' [between art and power] ultimately underwrite the very strategies of power those theories are imagined to subvert." See also Seltzer's "James, Pleasure, Power" (*HJR* 5:199–203), which draws on his book to reiterate comments on the "rich entanglement of power, care, and pleasure."

Several general critical essays have varying degrees of merit. In one chapter of his six-chapter *Literary Inheritance* (Mass.) pp. 155–

201, Roger Sale relates James to the thesis that "in recent centuries literary tradition has been made, or unmade, primarily by the relations authors have established with important writers in the immediately preceding generation." James in London in 1876 inherited and was menaced by George Eliot and her shadow, and those of certain other specified authors. Quentin Anderson's "Henry James's Cultural Office" (*Prospects* 8[1983]:197–210) says that James, absorbed and convinced, expressed his widening consciousness, invited readers to participate and possess, and blended our public and private worlds. James teaches us to quit "preying" and become children of light. Anderson makes some curious assertions: James's characters do not renounce (since they do not want); James is not ambiguous (save in "The Turn of the Screw") but simply presents "the great feast of life"; and James was post-Modern (even before European modernism) through being Emersonian via his father. Anderson notes that James pleases us not by immersing us "in a social world" (save in *The Bostonians*) but rather by catering to our Emersonian individualism. In "The Thematics of Interpretation: James's Artist Tales" (*HJR* 5:117–27) Hana Wirth-Nesher suggests that, far from being the limited aesthete or moralist some label him, James "uses the theme of the making of and understanding of art as a metaphor of all human interaction, and he uses stories about human relations . . . to comment on the nature of art." John Gerlach in "Closure in Henry James's Short Fiction" (*JNT* 14:60–67) shows that typically the endings of James's short stories display conventional closure despite not only his anti-Victorian critical theory but also his novelistic practice of illustrating that "scenic presentation without authorial mediation" offers the best fictive ending. While tracing the evolution of American literary "modernism" from Emerson to about 1930, Alfred Kazin in *American Procession* includes a chapter on James (pp. 211–34) full of biographical facts and critical truisms on his loneliness, respect for fiction, and attitudes toward America and Europe. Joyce W. Warren's *The American Narcissus* has the best chapter on James in any book this year devoted to a larger subject. The title of her last chapter, "The Woman Takes Center Stage: Henry James," is a compliment to James, some of whose intriguing female characters, as well as the real-life women closest to him, Warren discusses with a common sense refreshingly different from much recent criticism on the subject: James wrote well about women because of his internationalism, his unassertive personality, his distrust of

"American expansionism and American individualism," and his "un-American awareness of and interest in the other." Nathalia Wright glancingly treats innocent, morally sound Americans in some of James's most popular fiction, as they make contact with aristocratic, corrupt Europeans and Europeanized Americans, in "The American Writer's Search for Identity: Some Reflections" (*SoAR* 49:39–55).

A fine book on James's treatment of women is Virginia C. Fowler's well-reasoned *Henry James's American Girl: The Embroidery on the Canvas* (Wisconsin). Her thesis: since American commercialism is controlled by men, American culture is left to women, who, being thus abandoned, exposed, and betrayed by their men, are psychologically crippled. James's *The American Scene* shows male ruthlessness. Fowler discusses (*à la* "opaque" Jacques Lacan) the separation of the child from "the Other," and the child's consequent confused desire for both reunion and continued uniqueness—but with fear following knowledge. Sentient American women have hard-to-see inner beauty; "unaware" ones are "pretty" but can doom civilization by their ignorant fearlessness. Fowler reductively excoriates Christopher Newman (*The American*), among other American men, for his aggressiveness. Best is Fowler's analysis of Isabel Archer (*The Portrait of a Lady*), her late-acquired fortune, its effects on her notion of "power," her vain hope that marriage need not be a cage, and her ultimate realization of the need to suffer. As for Milly Theale (*The Wings of the Dove*), that poignant heiress's "fatal illness might be viewed as a symbol or metaphor for an inner deficiency created by her situation as an American woman" (see *ALS 1980*, p. 114). Fowler discusses unique Maggie Verver (*The Golden Bowl*)—James's only American girl with father, husband, and child—to demonstrate (*à la* "clinical" R. D. Laing) the dynamics of the changing Verver family, to the end that "Maggie can effect her separation from Adam [her father] only by pretending that she does not want to do so and by concealing from him that she is achieving an identity of her own."

Less effective is *A Woman's Place in the Novels of Henry James* (St. Martin's). In it Elizabeth Allen starts off by discussing women as reductive "sign" (thing, object with particular meaning), analyzes the 19th-century stereotype of womanhood ("piety, purity, submissiveness and domesticity"), and clarifies by discussing Hester Prynne of Hawthorne's *The Scarlet Letter* as "sign in the literary text" even while she is staunchly "resisting subjecthood." All of this semiological feminism, evidently, makes us ready to see that the hero (male) of

James's *The American* is not "sign" whereas Daisy Miller (female) is. With later heroines James goes beyond—to persons, public figures, and more signs—but now with "confusing signification" and yet with even power to interpret and prevail.

John Carlos Rowe explains that his well-named book, *The Theoretical Dimensions of Henry James* (Wisconsin), concerns "the ways . . . modern theories of literature and its interpretation have constructed . . . versions of that literary 'mastery' James has come to typify." Even as different theoretical approaches interpret James, his work evaluates their limitations. Rowe devotes six chapters—each provoking its successor—to "the psychology of literary influence," feminism, Marxism, psychoanalysis, phenomenology, and reader-response criticism. Rowe aims to show that by transgressing repressive criticism he is "socializing" James, a "high-modernist," and is encouraging theorists to address the ways literature in general helps represent and preserve culture. As for Nathaniel Hawthorne's influence, see Rowe's earlier article (*ALS 1983*, pp. 44–45). The discussion of James's "defensive response" to Anthony Trollope's influence is superb. Heroines of *The Bostonians, The Spoils of Poynton,* and "The Aspern Papers" are seen as "James's most prominent treatments of the fate of Woman in her late-nineteenth-century social environment." Rowe targets "The Turn of the Screw" to overdiscuss "the use and abuse of uncertainty," i.e., varyingly acceptable critical responses to Jamesian ambiguity. Rowe offers a Marxist critique of *The Princess Casamassima,* analogous to "[Fredric] Jameson's second horizon of reading [see his *Political Unconscious,* 1981]: the representation of contradictions that belong ultimately to an analysis of the class system"; Rowe resorts to Georg Lukács, who "helps explain the subtler reasons why James is mythologized by Marxists as the exemplar of formalism and originator of a decadent modernism." The topics of the last two chapters ("literary impressionism and the implied reader") are central to "the formalist conception of literature."

Both simpler and more helpful is Edward Wagenknecht's *The Tales of Henry James* (Ungar), a companion volume to his *The Novels of Henry James* (see *ALS 1983*, p. 116). It is a balanced, down-to-earth survey mainly of the short fiction that James, whom Wagenknecht calls "one of the elect among the masters," chose for his New York edition, but also includes brief commentary on those tales either thought unworthy of that edition or written after it was published. For each story, Wagenknecht handles facts of publication, sources (if any), James's opinions on it (if any), plot summary, and critical commentary, incorporating awareness of previous scholarship—revealingly called here that "cloud of sense and nonsense." Especially brilliant is this pepper-and-sage old critic's treatment of "Madame de Mauves," "The Aspern Papers," "The Pupil," "The Altar of the Dead" (Wagenknecht's favorite), "The Great Good Place," and "A Round of Visits." Less happy is occasional prolixity. Wagenknecht reductively handles the ghost stories, especially "The Turn of the Screw," which he sturdily declines to "desupernaturalize." This book is the best introduction in existence to James's short stories.

Hershel Parker in chapter 4 of *Flawed Texts*, which is a contribution to the history of recent literary history, is properly critical of commentators on James's revisions who consult those revisions incompletely. Then Parker in "Henry James 'In the Wood': Sequence and Significance of His Literary Labors, 1905–1907" (*NCF* 38:492–513) exposes critics of James's revisions as New Critics at heart, whether they say so or not, believers that late intentions are identical to original intentions. He then provides a fascinating "literary log of the most difficult phase of James's work on the New York Edition, the period when he was 'retouching' the first three novels . . . in the series." This "log" is letters by James to his agent James B. Pinker and others, and letters from Pinker and others, between 6 June 1905 and 31 December 1907, concerning those revisions and the prefaces for the edition. Parker draws invaluable conclusions about James's rewriting *Roderick Hudson, The American,* and *The Portrait of a Lady* partly together, and his adaptability, dismaying interruptions, brilliant prefaces, and joyful sense of rightness during the whole fierce labor.

iv. Criticism: Individual Novels

Several novels enjoyed or endured brief treatment, with *The Sacred Fount* and the major-phase works receiving the most attention.

Alan Bird in "Suspect Chronology in *The American*" (*N&Q* 31:70) dates the action of *The American* as 1868–71 but notes that Mrs. Tristram could not have sent letters to its hero "in America from a beleaguered Paris" in 1870 nor seen new plays in theaters, then closed because of the Franco-Prussian War. William A. Johnsen in "The Moment of *The American* in *l'Écriture Judéo-Chrétienne*" (*HJR* 5:216–20) believes that René Girard's "general theory of demythification of sacrificial violence" will help us understand elements in *The American*. For me, Johnsen valuably explains only the sterility of international rivalry and the futility of scapegoat sacrifice to quell it.

The fine thesis of Victoria Rosenberg's "*Washington Square:* 'The Only Good Thing . . . Is the Girl' " (*DR* 63[1983]:54–68) is that, *contra* most critics, Catherine Sloper in *Washington Square* has "depth and constancy of . . . emotions." She loves, avoids self-defining, is naively honest, develops only gradually and alone, is logical, and endures.

"London in *The Portrait of a Lady*" (*HJR* 5:96–99) by John Kimmey discusses the "three London scenes, each one marking a crucial stage in Isabel's life." They occur, first, in chapters 15–16, when Miss Archer "survey[s] . . . the world and test[s] . . . her freedom"; second, in chapter 31, which "concerns a . . . stroll and shows her participating in the world and enjoying her new freedom"; and third, in chapter 53, with Mrs. Osmond returning from Italy and "submitting to the strictures of the world and acknowledging the limits, if not the loss, of her independence."

Leo F. O'Connor finds room in his *Religion in the American Novel* to contend that "the all-encompassing motif" of *The Bostonians* "is the increasing spiritual and cultural desperation of New England life, as manifested in the pursuit of the occult and in the rise of charlatans and opportunists who paraded themselves as traditional New England reformers." Better, Janet A. Gabler in "The Narrator's Script: James's Complex Narration in *The Bostonians*" (*JNT* 14:94–109) defends the novel against the charge of disunity. She argues that "James's devices in *The Bostonians* are quite controlled and quite deliberate. Rather than being a struggle toward a refinement of formal style, James's . . . narrative seems a direct response to the novel's evolving theme."

In "Maisie Supposed to Know: Amo(u)ral Analysis" (*HJR* 5:207–16), Dennis Foster theorizes (following Jacques Lacan) that, to be "in a position of mastery," Maisie Farange (*What Maisie Knew*) "need not know dark truths" of the physical and moral world around her. "It is enough that she masters the terminology."

Rhoda B. Nathan in "The Farce That Failed: James's *The Spoils of Poynton*" (*JNT* 14:110–23) reasons that *The Spoils of Poynton* is unique among the novels of James for combining "dramatic tricks in a novelistic frame," thus abandoning "that 'architectural purity' on which he prides himself," and offering instead "a literal conclusion which did not permit a variety of interpretations." Farce is the dramatic trick James uses here; note the emoting and scheming, caricature gestures," violence . . . literalized in . . . horseplay," "intemperate" speech, and indecorous wishful thinking. But when "the center of sentience" shifts from Mrs. Gereth to Fleda Vetch, farce ends and Fleda's renunciation is alleged to be meaningless.

Jean Gooder in "*The Awkward Age:* A Study in Ephemera?" (*CQ* 13:21–38) counters critics (such as Ezra Pound) who dismiss *The Awkward Age* for displaying only ephemeral observation and knowledge, and suggests instead that the novel is intelligent, though subversive, and that it exposes thin, cruel social shabbiness so as to make "moral ugliness" unattractive. Gooder likens James's art to that of Goya, who "neither suppressed nor distorted reality, but 'analysed' it with a keenness verging on cruelty."

Susan Winnett's "*Mise en Crypte:* The Man and the Mask" (*HJR* 5:220–26) uses ideas from Nicolas Abraham's and Maria Torok's 1976 *Cryptonymie* to theorize that James got productively beyond his technical dilemma in *The Sacred Fount* by burying alive the idea of any solution. John Carlos Rowe comments in "After Freud: Henry James and Psychoanalysis" (*HJR* 5:226–32) on Susan Winnett's essay and also those of William A. Johnsen and Dennis Foster (see above): "These three papers share a concern with overcoming both literary and psychoanalytical formalisms by means of strategic intertextuality." Paralleling Winnett to a degree is part of Judith L. Sutherland's *Problematic Fictions.* In it Sutherland discusses *The Narrative of Arthur Gordon Pym, The Marble Faun,* and *The Sacred Fount,* which she ably contends are all "hermeneutical nightmare[s]" and "superb failures" "hover[ing] on the borderline between romance and self-parody" since they show American-mode symbolism approaching "nihilism and the absurd." After *The Sacred Fount,* James drew "on the lessons he learned there," and "returned [in his major-phase fiction] to a more limited, controlled point of view, no doubt realizing, as he emphasized . . . in *The Sacred Fount,* that one always does so at a cost."

And now for that major phase. Kathleen L. Komar argues in "Language and Character Delineation in *The Wings of the Dove*" (*TCL* 29[1983]:471–87) that despite alleged "extensive similarity of tone and thought pattern" in separate works, James subtly "use[s] . . . language . . . to create differences of character and consciousness"— in *The Wings of the Dove.* In his *Money and Fiction* John Vernon

uses "the theme of money . . . as a prism . . . to separate and examine
. . . narrative time, plot, and the representation of material objects,
all of which are formal expressions of the novel's social and economic
context." Pertinent here is Vernon's neat chapter on *The Wings of
the Dove*, which "integrates the sordidness of money into the very
world of beauty and leisure which seems to exclude it."

In her *Seeds of Decadence in the Late Nineteenth-Century
Novel: A Crisis in Values* (St. Martin's, 1983), Suzanne Nalbantian
ill-advisedly discusses *The Ambassadors* in a context of more apt examples of novels that "explore the repercussions of a divestiture of a
tradition of Western moral criteria and of a decline in established
religious, aesthetic and philosophical values of the Western world."
She makes too much of James's allegedly decadent "structures of post-
ponement." Better is Eileen T. Bender's " 'The Question of His Own
French': Dialect and Dialectic in *The Ambassadors*" (*HJR* 5:128–34),
which subtly shows that James characterizes several personages, especially Lambert Strether and Madame de Vionnet, partly by their use
of French. Strether gains proficiency as his "vision and moral sensibility" are expanded. At the last he disengages himself "from grace-
less American cant" and "see[s] through the most charming European
[i.e., here, French] mirage." Best is "The Selfish Eye: Strether's Principles of Psychology" (*AL* 56:396–409), in which Susan M. Griffin
corrects earlier critics for not "analyz[ing] Jamesian visual perception
as a complex physical and psychological process." This failure leads
them to conclude wrongly not only that "observation and experience
are opposed in James" but also that his protagonists are detached,
cerebral observers. Griffin's discussion of Strether neatly proves
otherwise.

Mimi Kairschner in "The Traces of Capitalist Patriarchy in the
Silences of *The Golden Bowl*" (*HJR* 5:187–92) argues (after Pierre
Macheney and Fredric Jameson), first, that texts in general not only
picture and reflect but also distort and conceal "the materials of a
culture" so as to protect "the fundamental structuring elements of
power in the [relevant] society"; and second, that silences in *The
Golden Bowl* "mask . . . domination" by male, rich, acquisitive Adam
Verver. Jean Gooder in *"The Golden Bowl*, or Ideas of Good and
Evil" (*CQ* 13:129–46) suggests that, like the fifth canto of Dante's
Inferno, The Golden Bowl is "directed to the *mystery* of love, . . . preoccupied with its destructive and creative aspects, and [is] perhaps
as clear . . . as to the ultimate distinction between good and evil." *The*

Golden Bowl is an unusual novel because it challenges earlier depic-
tions of remorseless imagination and value-denying. By its midpoint
it has confused good and evil; but the second half, in spite of certain
critics who seek "to nail down the moral," remains ambiguous and
does not end by showing the triumph of good. Maggie may be either
James's last main character to misunderstand reality or his best character for abandoning dread isolation. L. A. Westervelt offers a healthy
reading of Maggie as properly triumphant, in his essay "The Individual and the Form: Maggie Verver's Tactics in *The Golden Bowl*"
(*Renascence* 36:147–59). She wins at last by "us[ing] the language of
. . . worldly society to assert herself against a threat of traditional
values."

v. Criticism: Individual Tales

James's short fiction got short shrift by critics in the year 1984. But
a few essays are notable.

Curtis Dahl begins "Lord Lambeth's America: Architecture in
James's 'An International Episode' " (*HJR* 5:80–95) by calling James
a "master of detailed depiction of the American scene," especially
for "his detailed description of actual buildings and streets, . . . his
recording of the architectural fashions of the time, and . . . his use of
both of these to further his plot and express his ideas." Dahl shows
that "An International Episode" names real places and buildings, describes architectural styles representative of the age, and symbolizes
"national cultural differences" through buildings, streets, and ships.
The proof here is a guided tour of New York, Long Island, and New-
port, complete with 15 charming old illustrations.

In "The Artist and the Man in 'The Author of Beltraffio' " (*PMLA*
63[1983]:102–08) Viola Hopkins Winner calls "imperfect" the linking in "The Author of Beltraffio" of "aesthetic idea" and "moral, psychological conflict," and also Mark Ambient's ideas on art and the
action.

Robert T. Levine in "A Failure of Reading: *The Aspern Papers*
and the Ennobling Force of Literature" (*EAS* 12[1983]:87–98) convincingly contrasts evidently kind, considerate Jeffrey Aspern and the
egocentric, imperceptive, base, cruel narrator of "The Aspern Papers."
The latter, Levine posits, was not ennobled by any reading of Aspern's poetry.

Martha Banta's "Artists, Models, Real Things, and Recognizable

Types" (*SLitI* 16[1983]:7–34) broadly concerns problems that American artists faced a century ago when trying to represent the human form realistically. In the course of concentrating on "the ways certain painters actually used models in their studios, together with the fictional depiction of artists and models," Banta describes the Monarchs in James's "The Real Thing" as willing to "sell . . . themselves directly as images of worth on the open market." But they are only themselves and hence can never "represent that core of identity upon which the artist builds in supplementation of the other data that stimulate his perceptual eye and prompt his mental activity."

"The Turn of the Screw" was given a welcome rest this year. Bruce Robbins does, however, amusingly gripe in "Shooting Off James's Blanks: Theory, Politics and *The Turn of the Screw*" (*HJR* 5:192–99) at modern critics for expressing annoyance at the endlessness of debates between interpreters and theorists over the governess (is she deluded or not?) even as they practice " 'endless' criticism" themselves. Robbins also discusses (with sleazy documentation) the subsurface theme in the story of "love between the classes."

Adeline Tintner rescues a neglected story by James when in " 'The Great Condition': Henry James and Bergsonian Time" (*SSF* 21:111–15) she contrasts loser Bertram Braddle in "The Great Condition" with winners Henry Chilver and Mrs. Damerel. Braddle wrongly rushes and fights against abstractly measured time, whereas the other two have an easy "relation[ship] . . . with [Bergonsian *durée*] time . . . and . . . work well within it."

vi. Criticism: Specific Nonfictional Works

Brief comments on five essays will now bring this discussion of Jamesian scholarship to a close.

Sergio Perosa's *American Theories* has a chapter on James which considers his early thoughts on American materials and incipient realism, his influential essay "The Art of Fiction," his "framing" by identification "with the inner life of the observer" and by use of "limited" point of view and scenic method, and his "idea that the novel 'competes with life.' " Perosa includes an appendix called "Henry James in the Twentieth Century," largely about the prefaces.

Stuart Johnson in "Prelinguistic Consciousness in James's 'Is There a Life After Death?' " (*Criticism* 26:245–57) says that James's 1910 essay on immortality "celebrates a consciousness that he places prior to any articulation or differentiation." Johnson relates his thesis to several fictional works by James, best to "The Altar of the Dead," which "places life after death at the seam between articulated and undifferentiated consciousness."

William E. Buckler's "Rereading Henry James's Rereading Robert Browning: 'The Novel in *The Ring and the Book*'" (*HJR* 5:135–45) is a stupendous essay. Its hypnotic thesis: James, whose intellectual evolution resembles that of Giuseppe Caponsacchi in Browning's poem, worked through from early doubts concerning that poem to faithful acceptance of it on its own terms—all of which means not only agreement with its main point, "that there is no perfect machinery for resolving . . . conflicts," but also the conclusion that Browning's poem "is inexplicably right just as it is." Buckler sees the structure of James's 1912 address on Browning as analogous to a Browning dramatic monologue—with James as monologuist, his audience as Browning's readers, his 15 prose paragraphs as stanzas, and the "one unifying issue" poetic unity itself.

Carol Holly's "Henry James's Autobiographical Fragment: 'The Turning Point of My Life'" (*HLB* 31[1983]:40–51) prints for the first time a three-page fragment in which James barely started to explain how a change in his attitude (in 1910) toward autobiography caused him to re-evaluate his behavior while in law school (in 1862–63).

I nominate as the best essay considered in this chapter on James Paul John Eakin's "Henry James and the Autobiographical Act" (*Prospects* 8[1983]:211–60). Its complex subject is James's reshaping of his past in his *Autobiography* because of his needs (defensive, therapeutic, artistic) as a narrator-autobiographer recalling his small-boy self as dawdling gaper at home and abroad in a "dialectical relationship" (with himself as mature artist) which ultimately "dissolves" opposition of young and old as past and present "interpenetrat[e]." In his first autobiographical volume James limns his juvenile self as free, perceptively "taking in" everything, seemingly of promise only in his own eyes, having fun "listening to himself listening" even as he wonders whether his imagination is admirable, or negative and predatory. Eakin discusses James's Galerie d'Apollon dream as emblematic of his autobiographical text, with its demonstration of creative powers. In his second volume James expresses anew his inferiority, defends again his "formative years abroad" (which William James deplored), discusses more "taking in" of perceptions, and depicts his

gallery of friends mainly as they impinge on his observant self. Eakin
is at his best when he touches on James's attitude toward his father,
then analyzes at length James and the Civil War: the truth and fiction
of his "obscure hurt" (the fiction of that "shining stigma" becomes
truth, since truth is what one experiences), his visiting the wounded,
his law-school days ("a plausible 'cover' for the private exercises of
his imagination"), his emergence as a publishing writer at war's end—
rather like a veteran returning home from war. Eakin discusses much
more and documents everything with great thoroughness.

University of Pittsburgh

8. Pound and Eliot

Hugh Witemeyer

i. Pound

To supplement its *Catalogue of the Poetry Notebooks of Ezra Pound* (1980) the Beinecke Library at Yale University has produced a two-volume, handwritten register of manuscripts and correspondence in the Pound Archive. The register is being computerized, but there is currently no plan to make it available to other libraries.

***a*. Text and Biography.** In 1922 Pound translated two collections of short stories by Paris writer Paul Morand, *Tendres stocks* (1921) and *Ouvert la nuit* (1922). These translations, together with an introduction by Marcel Proust, are now published as *Fancy Goods and Open All Night*, ed. Breon Mitchell (New Directions). One of the nine stories, "Borealis," also appears separately (*ParisR* 91:188–203). The Scandinavian typist in "Borealis" accurately describes the narrator of these precious, sexist portraits of women as "an international pig." In "Pound's Contributions to *L'Art libre* (1920)" (*Paideuma* 13:271–83) Archie Henderson translates two of Pound's French essays about the British literary scene.

Two well-edited volumes of correspondence bracket Pound's career. *Ezra Pound and Dorothy Shakespear: Their Letters, 1909–1914*, ed. Omar Pound and A. Walton Litz (New Directions), contains 235 superbly annotated letters and journal entries. They tell the story of a difficult courtship, reveal the biographical origins of many poems in *Canzoni* and *Ripostes*, and provide a rich introduction to the Georgian literary milieu. *Ezra Pound/John Theobald: Letters*, ed. Donald Pearce and Herbert Schneidau (Redding Ridge, Conn.: Black Swan Books), presents 51 letters exchanged by Pound and a California professor in 1957–58, mainly on the topics of education and religion.

Eleven further studies employ previously unpublished correspondence. In "A Letter by Ezra Pound" (*MissR* 6[1982]:117–35) Timothy Materer reproduces a long and interesting epistle to John Quinn, probably written in 1915. Selections from Pound's correspondence with Hemingway between 1925 and 1957 highlight Jacqueline Tavernier-Courbin's "Ernest Hemingway and Ezra Pound" in *Writer in Context*. Part of a cheery 1956 missive from Hemingway to Pound is given by William French in "Fragment of a Letter" (*Yale Literary Mag.* 150, ii[1983]:54–60). Five of William Carlos Williams's "Letters to Ezra Pound" (*Grand Street* 3,ii:102–09) also belong to the St. Elizabeths period, as do five letters from Pound to Wyndham Lewis, ed. Bryant Knox and Seamus Cooney, in *BLAST 3*, ed. Seamus Cooney (Black Sparrow). *BLAST 3* is a mild-mannered avatar of the original Vorticist magazine.

The Hound and Horn *Letters*, ed. Mitzi Berger Hamovitch (Georgia, 1982), includes a poorly annotated selection of letters from Pound to the editors of a magazine which took its name from his early poem, "The White Stag." In "Seven Letters of Ezra Pound" (*Collections* [Univ. of Delaware] 1:13–27) James J. Gould presents some of Pound's correspondence in 1931–32 with Richard Johns, editor of *Pagany*. Archie Henderson's misleadingly titled " 'Townsman' and Music: Ezra Pound's Letters to Ronald Duncan" (*LCUT* 25:118–35) is more concerned with Pound's contributions to the music section of the *Townsman* than with his letters to the magazine's editor. In " 'I Like to *Get* Letters': Ezra Pound and a Canadian Correspondent" (*Malahat Review* 66[1983]:129–39) R. T. K. Symington surveys the letters Pound wrote to Else Seel between 1946 and 1959, urging her to translate Frobenius into English. Clark Emery's "St. Elizabeths" is a verse memoir of his contacts with Pound between 1951 and 1961; Robert Casillo annotates the poem and describes the "Letters of Ezra Pound to Clark Emery in the University of Miami Library" (*The Carrell* [Journal of the Friends of the Univ. of Miami Library, Coral Gables, Florida] 21[1983]:14–35).

Mary Barnard's *Assault on Mount Helicon: A Literary Memoir* (Calif.) includes a generous selection of the letters she received from Pound between 1933 and 1958. Part of this delightful autobiography appeared last year as "Ezra Pound, Sappho, and My Assault on Mount Helicon" (*Malahat Review* 66[1983]:140–44). In "New Light on Iris Barry" (*Paideuma* 13:285–89) Jeffrey Meyers describes the later career of the woman to whom Pound sent some of his liveliest early letters. Finally, the Pound chapter of Carlos Baker's *The Echoing Green* reviews the biographical backgrounds of the *Pisan Cantos* and offers a memoir of Baker's 1965 meeting with Pound in Venice.

Turning to biography proper, we find all we need to know about the Wabash College debacle of 1907–08 in James J. Wilhelm's "On the Trail of the 'One' Crawfordsville Incident or, the Poet in Hoosierland" (*Paideuma* 13:11–47) and James E. Rader's "The Value of Testimony: Pound at Wabash" (*Paideuma* 13:67–130). Wilhelm makes it clear that Pound was fired not for a single offense but for a series of violations of community decorum. Rader uses more than 50 memoirs of former Crawfordsville residents to illustrate "the stiff Presbyterian conformism and conventional morality of the town" in Pound's day. The Wabash incident led directly to Pound's self-exile, but Doris L. Eder does not illuminate that subject in her superficial study of *Three Writers in Exile: Pound, Eliot & Joyce* (Whitston).

Having used the Freedom of Information Act to gain access to the U. S. Government's legal and medical files on Pound, Stanley I. Kutler in *The American Inquisition: Justice and Injustice in the Cold War* (Hill and Wang, 1982) and E. Fuller Torrey in *The Roots of Treason: Ezra Pound and the Secrets of St. Elizabeths* (McGraw-Hill) reach similar conclusions: that Pound "was not insane in any accepted clinical or legal sense" (Kutler); that Dr. Winfred Overholser, the head of St. Elizabeths, perjured himself and suppressed many diagnoses by the psychiatrists on his own staff each time he testified that Pound was incapable of standing trial; and that Pound regularly sabotaged efforts to gain his release because "he was happy at St. Elizabeths. . . . He had the things he valued most—intellectual stimulation, attention, good food, and sex" (Torrey). Better documented here than in the articles published by Kutler and Torrey last year (see *ALS 1983*) these conclusions merit the serious consideration, if not the full agreement, of future biographers. Of less merit is Torrey's hostile account of Pound's earlier career, which slants its evidence to confirm a moralistic thesis about the poet's "narcissism."

Two memoirs published this year can be read as rebuttals of the Kutler-Torrey thesis. James Laughlin's "For the Record: On New Directions and Others" (*AmerP* 1,iii:47–61) contains, among its reminiscences, a defense of the insanity plea that led to Pound's committal. And Marcella Booth, in "Ezrology: The Class of '57"

(*Paideuma* 13:375–87), asserts that the only special consideration Pound received from Dr. Overholser was protection from drugs and electroshock.

Meanwhile, Lawrence Pitkethly's film, *Ezra Pound: American Odyssey* (New York Center for Visual History) provides an excellent classroom introduction to the poet, skillfully mixing biographical narrative, dramatic readings, recent interviews, and historical footage.

b. **General Studies.** Burton Raffel's *Ezra Pound: The Prime Minister of Poetry* (Archon) is no better than the same author's embarrassing *T. S. Eliot* (see *ALS 1982*). In his chapter on *The Cantos*, for example, Raffel commits several egregious errors, such as attributing the metamorphosis in Canto 2 to the power of Circe, because he refuses to use the *Annotated Index* or the *Companion* or even to list them in his bibliography. A more intelligent, though no less ambivalent, assessment of Pound's life and work may be found in Alfred Kazin's *American Procession.*

Pound figures in two excellent studies of poetic theory this year. In her striking demonstration of continuities between *Victorian and Modern Poetics* (Chicago) Carol T. Christ argues that Pound's array of dramatis personae, theory of the image, and use of myth and history in a long poem all descend "directly from Victorian poetics" and share with them a post-Romantic need to "give objectivity to personal utterance." Michael H. Levenson's *A Genealogy of Modernism: A Study of English Literary Doctrine, 1908–1922* (Cambridge) also emphasizes the tension between the subjectivist and objectivist strains in Modernist poetics. Levenson distinguishes constituent ideas and traces their "incremental changes," arguing that the "early modernism" of Ford, Pound, and Hulme the Imagist "stood against the later orthodoxy" of Eliot and Hulme the Abstractionist.

Several lesser studies also treat the different movements and ideologies through which Pound's early career took him. Neither Walter Baumann's "Ezra Pound's Metamorphosis during His London Years: From Late-Romanticism to Modernism" (*Paideuma* 13:357–73) nor William Pratt's "Imagism and Irony: The Shaping of the International Style" (*SAQ* 83:1–17) has much that is new to say. In *BLAST* 3, ed. Seamus Cooney (Black Sparrow), Reed Way Dasenbrock and Giovanni Cianci disagree sharply about the relationship of English Vorticism to Italian Futurism. In "Vorticism among the Isms" (pp. 40–46)

Dasenbrock sees Vorticist style as a distinctive "synthesis of Cubist form and Futurist movement." In "Pound and Futurism" (pp. 63–67), on the other hand, Cianci emphasizes "the great debt Vorticism owed to Futurism" for "a revolutionary strategy based on *soirées*, manifestos, proclamations, publicity stunts, expeditions [sic] and so on."

Pound's "brief transit through Dadaism in 1921–22" is the subject of Richard Sieburth's "Dada Pound" (*SAQ* 83:44–68). Sieburth suggests that Picabia's use of "metasemiotic" and "intertextual" devices such as "citation, plagiarism, transcription, translation, parody, and pastiche" may have helped Pound to devise the techniques of the Malatesta Cantos and to edit *The Waste Land*. Whereas Sieburth's essay is lucid and informed, Andrew M. Clearfield's *These Fragments I Have Shored: Collage and Montage in Early Modernist Poetry* (UMI Research) is neither. Clearfield's basic distinction between collage and montage, and his claim that Pound is "the montage poet par excellence," are not adequately illustrated.

Four other essays and a book evaluate Pound's politics and economics. The historical origins of his economics are clarified in Leon Surette's excellent discussion of "Ezra Pound and British Radicalism" (*ESC* 9[1983]:435–51). Surette relates Guild Socialism, *The New Age*, and Social Credit to Fabianism and the "Radical Right" of Chesterton and Belloc. In "Ezra Pound, Mussolini, and Fascism" (*Standpunte* 36[1983]:20–30) Anthony Woodward argues that Pound was attracted to Mussolini by his anticapitalism and by "a shared fascination with the creative dynamism of the will." Charles Reznikoff assesses Pound's antisemitism in "Entries for *Encyclopedia Judaica*: Ezra Pound, Louis Zukofsky," written in 1969 but only now published in full in *Charles Reznikoff: Man and Poet*, ed. Milton Hindus (Maine). Eric Mottram's " 'Man under Fortune': Bases for Ezra Pound's Poetry" in *Modern American Poetry*, ed. R. W. (Herbie) Butterfield (Barnes and Noble), criticizes Pound from a left-wing viewpoint for having "no revolutionary sense which would destroy class and caste." Finally, in his uneven but worthwhile study of *Ezra Pound: Politics, Economics, and Writing* (Macmillan), Peter Nicholls sees a "close connection between politics and poetic practice." As Pound's politics evolved toward fascism, according to Nicholls, *The Cantos* moved from openness toward authoritarian closure, so that the Chinese-history and Adams cantos offer "precedents for the fascist regime" and the *Pisan Cantos* are politically unrepentant.

Post-Structuralist critiques of Pound's politics and poetics usually follow one of two predictable lines: either (1) Pound understands the arbitrariness of signs and practices a liberating poetics of indeterminacy, or (2) Pound does not understand the arbitrariness of signs and practices a totalitarian poetics of logocentricity. The first position is that of Joseph G. Kronick in *American Poetics of History*. Kronick's Pound is a full-blown Deconstructionist, who believes that "nature and the past do not exist outside of language," that "self can only have existence in language," and that language necessarily involves "a polysemia which would elude the grasp of man."

The second, and more commonly taken, position may be seen in Philip Kuberski's "Ezra Pound and the Calculations of Interest" (*NOR* 10[1983]:69–74) and Andrew Parker's "Ezra Pound and the 'Economy' of Anti-Semitism" (*Boundary* 11[1982–83]:103–28). Kuberski argues that Pound's "positions on economics, politics, and race" are "consequences of his commitment to the natural sign." Parker likewise finds that Pound's views of language, money, and race are erroneously predicated upon "an originary unity in which sign would be connected 'naturally' to referent." This resembles the position of Lewis Hyde in his chapter on "Ezra Pound and the Fate of Vegetable Money" in *The Gift: Imagination and the Erotic Life of Property* (Random House, 1983). In "Who Built the Temple? or, Thoughts on Pound, *Res*, and *Verba*" (*Paideuma* 13:49–63) Massimo Bacigalupo reiterates his sense that Pound's actual handling of language contradicts his statements of regard for referentiality. In a Lacanian study, "Plastic Demons: The Scapegoating Process in Ezra Pound" (*Criticism* 26:355–82), Robert Casillo relates Pound's antisemitism and antifeminism to his fear of castration and "general cultural undifferentiation." For many post-Structuralist critics, as Ben D. Kimpel and T. C. Duncan Eaves note in "The Intentional-Fallacy Fallacy and Related Contemporary Orthodoxies" (*SAQ* 83:103–13), "Pound is at fault for believing in a fixed world of objects and events, a fixed observer of it (the author), and 'a truth pre-existing language.'" According to Jeffrey S. Walker in "Aristotelian Poetics: Reading Ezra Pound with Michael Riffaterre" (*Style* 18:43–63), "the mimetic dimension of the *Cantos* is meant to be fully as significant as the semiotic."

A concern with poetic language also distinguishes five intelligent studies of Pound's translations. Ronnie Apter breaks new ground in *Digging for the Treasure: Translation after Pound* (Peter Lang), as she compares Pound's theory and practice with those of his Victorian predecessors and his modern followers. Although Apter ignores a number of relevant studies published since 1974, her book should nevertheless be an indispensable point of reference for future discussions of the subject. In "A Language to Translate into: The Pre-Elizabethan Idiom of Pound's Later Cavalcanti Translations" (*Studies in Medievalism* 2 [1982]:9–18) David Anderson explains why Pound adapted a diction from Chaucer and Wyatt for his 1929 renderings of five Cavalcanti sonnets. Mark I. Smith-Soto evaluates "Ezra Pound's 'Map' of Arnaut Daniel" (*Comparatist* 8:14–20), noting that Pound often sacrifices sense to sound when translating his favorite troubadour. In adapting Propertius into English, Pound is equally attentive to "il messagio poetico" and "il segno linguistico," Arturo Cattaneo argues in "Homage to Sextus Propertius come manifesto linguistico e poetico del primo Pound" (*Aevum* 57[1983]:373–95). And in "Cantos, traduction: les mesaventures de l'original" (*Paideuma* 13:445–52) Philippe Mikriammos wryly describes the headaches of translating into French a poem which is in parts an English translation of a French translation of a Chinese original.

Pound's work on Chinese and Japanese originals is treated in six recent studies. The Pound chapter of Sanehide Kodama's *American Poetry and Japanese Culture* (Archon) is more imaginative but less comprehensive than the comparable chapter of Beongcheon Yu's *The Great Circle*. Monika Motsch's *Ezra Pound und China* (Carl Winter, 1976) is a competent but incomplete survey of Chinese elements in Pound's oeuvre. Pound is not the only Westerner to find in the Chinese written character a confirmation of his own "etymopoetics" or "grammatology," Hwa Yol Jung notes in "Misreading the Ideogram: From Fenollosa to Derrida and McLuhan" (*Paideuma* 13:211–27); these interpretations "are not so much wrong as one-sided." As if to confirm Jung's point, John Cayley shows in "Ch'eng, or Sincerity" (*Paideuma* 13:201–20) that Pound's etymology of the *ch'eng* ideogram is idiosyncratic yet not totally mistaken. In a related study of "Ezra Pound: The Gold Thread in the Pattern" (*Agenda* 22,iii–iv:126–33) Cayley reads the four Confucian ideograms at the beginning of *Guide to Kulchur* as an interpretive key to *The Cantos*.

c. **Relation to Other Writers.** Several essays compare Pound to other writers in order to clarify issues of poetic theory. In "Herder, Pound, and the Concept of Expression" (*MLQ* 44[1983]:374–93) Thomas H. Jackson finds in both poets a "thoroughly expressionist" conception of language as constitutive of thought and consciousness. In "An Inheritance of Poetic Referentiality" (*CLS* 20[1983]:329–45) Lois Oppenheim argues that Pound and French poet-critic Jacques Garelli both believe in "the inherently perceptual referentiality of the word." Elsewhere, the implications of sculpture for modern poetic form interest Albert Cook in "Aspects of the Plastic Image: Pound and Arp" (*Dada* 12[1983]:37–47) and Michael Heller in "'Translating Form': Pound, Rilke, Their Sculptors and the Contemporary Poem" (*Ironwood* 12,ii:41–53). Finally, in "Ezra Pound, René Thom, and the Experience of Poetry" (*SubStance* 43,ii:39–49) Strother B. Purdy relates the discontinuous form of Pound's *Cantos* to the "catastrophe theory" of Thom's mathematics.

Turning from theory to other grounds of comparison, we find Peter Faulkner, in "Pound and the Pre-Raphaelites" (*Paideuma* 13:229–44), arguing that the painting of Rossetti and Burne-Jones was important to Pound, whereas "the socially critical ideas of Ruskin and Morris" were not. Faulkner is wrong on the second of these points, as Lorne A. Reznowsky's "The 'Chesterbelloc' and Ezra Pound" (*Paideuma* 13:291–95) implies. Like Leon Surette, Reznowsky stresses the similarities in the Ruskinian social and economic views of Pound, G. K. Chesterton, and Hilaire Belloc. Elsewhere, A. G. Woodward contrasts "Pound and Santayana" (*SAQ* 83:80–90) as types of the active and contemplative mentalities. Pound's London friendship with two Australian expatriates is the subject of Laurie Hergenhan's "Ezra Pound, Frederic Manning, and James Griffyth Fairfax" (*AuLS* 11:395–400). And Kevin Oderman's "Of Vision, Tennis Courts, and Glands" (*Paideuma* 13:253–60) shows how Pound sought in Louis Berman's *The Glands Regulating Personality* (1921) a physiological basis for visionary experience.

Another poet with glandular interests figures in "Stretching and Yawning with Yeats and Pound," a chapter of David R. Clark's *Yeats at Songs and Choruses* (Mass., 1983). In Yeats's poems, Clark observes, stretching and yawning nearly always signify the arousal of sexual desire. This odd association may derive from Pound's translation of a poem by Arnaut Daniel. The ideas of Yeats and Florence Farr influenced Imagist principles of poetic cadence, according to Ronald Schuchard in "'As Regarding Rhythm': Yeats and the Imagists" (*Yeats* 2:209–26).

Four recent studies examine another Irish connection. G. Singh's "Pound as a Critic of Joyce" (*AJES* 7[1982]:108–24) is an honorific survey of the material in Forrest Read's *Pound/Joyce* (1967). Else-where, "The Pound/Joyce Connection" (*AmerP* 1,iii:20–37) presents two more theoretical essays. In " 'Letter, Penstroke, Paperspace': Pound and Joyce as Co-respondents" Marjorie Perloff sees the con-trast between their epistolary styles as a contrast between "construc-tivist" (Pound) and "aesthetic" (Joyce) attitudes toward the art of writing. My own "Zounds of Sounds: Why Pound Disliked *Finnegans Wake*" argues that Pound saw a denial of both political and linguistic referentiality in Joyce's last novel. Finally, Paul Edwards's " 'Clo-doveo' and 'Belcanto': Wyndham Lewis and James Joyce" in *BLAST 3* describes Pound's role in an uneasy literary friendship.

Sagetrieb describes itself as "A Journal Devoted to Poets in the Pound–H. D.–Williams Tradition." This year two of its essays touch directly upon Pound. Douglas Messerli's "A World Detached: The Early Criticism of William Carlos Williams" (*Sagetrieb* 3,ii:89–98) describes "the impact of Pound upon Williams' critical writings" of 1902–13, while Tom Sharp documents Pound's involvement between 1927 and 1935 with "The 'Objectivists' Publications" (*Sagetrieb* 3,iii: 41–47). But M. L. Rosenthal calls into question the very assumption upon which the journal is founded when he asks "Is There a Pound-Williams Tradition?" (*SoR* 20:277–85). Rosenthal argues that Pound and Williams "share an approach to lyrical structure" that is "seldom pursued by the Black Mountain or Beat poets or by younger figures now coming into prominence."

For its part *Paideuma*, the companion journal to *Sagetrieb*, ought to be more selective about what it accepts for publication. In "Frost's Ancient Music" (*Paideuma* 13:415–18) Robert F. Fleissner asserts, without offering a shred of evidence, that Frost's use of the expression "Goddam" in "Lucretius versus the Lake Poets" is indebted to Pound's "Ancient Music."

d. **The Shorter Poems and the Cantos.** In addition to the work on Pound's translations discussed above, five capable studies are de-voted to the shorter poems. In "Self-Concealment and Self-Expression in Eliot's and Pound's Dramatic Monologues" (*VP* 22:217–26) Carol T. Christ aligns Pound's personae with self-expression, arguing that they create "a reflexive play between the poet and his mask." In "Ezra Pound's *Canzoni*: Toward a Poem Including History" (*Paideuma* 13: 389–405) James Longenbach strives bravely but unpersuasively to show that Pound originally intended the contents of *Canzoni* to fol-

low a "chronological table of emotions" modeled upon Victor Hugo's
La Légende des siècles. Timothy Materer's "Ezra Pound and the Alchemy of the Word" (*JML* 11:109–24) notes some striking resem-
blances between Pound's early poem "The Alchemist" and several of
the late cantos which also invoke magic for "poetic synthesis and self-
renewal." In "Mauberley, Logopoeia, and the Language of Modernism" (*SAQ* 83:18–43) Jo Brantley Berryman discusses the opening
"Ode," reiterating the thesis of *Circe's Craft* (see *ALS 1983*, p. 137)
that the poem presents "a consistently ironic portrait of the untrustworthy critic." In "A Marginality of Context: Dobson's Gautier and
Pound's Mauberley" (*AN&Q* 22:141–43) Ian F. A. Bell notes that Austin Dobson, late-Victorian translator of Gautier and author of *Prov-
erbs in Porcelain* (1893), is a marginal poet of precisely Mauberley's
type.

   This was a fine year for studies of *The Cantos*. Volume 2 of *A
Companion to the Cantos of Ezra Pound*, ed. Carroll F. Terrell
(Calif.), covers Cantos 74–117, most of which were omitted from the
Annotated Index (1959). Terrell is the first to acknowledge that his
5649 line-by-line explanatory glosses doubtless contain errors, omissions, and eccentricities. He ought also to acknowledge that the *Companion* is keyed to a faulty text of the poem. Nevertheless, this hercu-
lean labor of devoted and generally accurate scholarship is certain to
be indispensable to future students of *The Cantos*.

   The faulty text of the poem concerns Christine Froula in an uneven but important study, *To Write Paradise: Style and Error in
Pound's Cantos* (Yale). Froula combines a close textual analysis of
one canto with a post-Structuralist interpretation of the entire epic.
She offers a genetic text and variorum edition of Canto 4 as a painstaking model of the type of editing Pound's poem needs. Her hard-
won and original meditation upon textual errors modulates into an
unconvincing account of the poem's subversion of "the traditional
concept of epic authority." From a somewhat different angle of approach, James F. Knapp reaches similar conclusions in "Discontinuous Form in Modern Poetry: Myth and Counter-Myth" (*Boundary*
12[1983]:149–66). Knapp reads Canto 21 "not as a retreat from history . . . but rather as an opening into time."

   Pound's use of historical materials also occupies Philip Furia in
Pound's Cantos Declassified (Penn. State). Furia argues that Pound
made his poem "an archive for texts he feared were threatened by the
historical blackout." Furia's cleanhanded survey of documentary pas-

sages accepts Pound's own evaluation of his materials and does little independent grubbing among primary sources. Similarly dustfree is Margaret Dickie's attempt, in "*The Cantos:* Slow Reading" (*ELH* 51: 819–35), to demonstrate that Pound reads and writes as a philologist. The genre and structure of *The Cantos* continue to attract intelligent critical attention. The most recent statement in the ongoing debate between Michael André Bernstein and Max Nänny over the genre of the poem (modern verse epic or Menippean satire?) is Nänny's "More Menippus than Calliope: A Reply" (*Paideuma* 13: 263–68). In *Fugue and Fresco: Structures in Pound's Cantos* (Maine) Kay Davis offers a lucid analysis of the different kinds of subject-rhyme that organize the poem. These structures range from a simple Eleusinian dark-light progression to more complex patterns of ring composition (*ABCBA*), fugal voicings, and cosmological zonings like those of the Schifanoia frescoes in Ferrara.

The motif of descent and ascent is central to four studies of *The Cantos* this year. In "The Map for the Periplum: Canto 1 as Archetypal Schema" (*AmerP* 1,ii:49–59) Albert Gelpi offers a Jungian reading of the nekuia, arguing that it "confronts Pound-Odysseus with the major archetypes" of anima, shadow, and androgynous wise man that he must face in his "psychological journey." Angela Elliott's "Pound's 'Isis Kuanon': An Ascension Motif in *The Cantos*" (*Paideuma* 13:327–56) describes a composite goddess, drawn from many religious traditions, who pervades the poem as "a mediatrix between her poet devotee and the ineffable glory." In " 'As towards a Bridge over Worlds': The Way of the Soul in *The Cantos*" (*Paideuma* 13: 171–200) Colin McDowell relates the hell-heaven progressions in the poem to Pound's knowledge of Hermetic literature. In "God's Eye Art 'Ou': Eleusis as a Paradigm for Enlightenment in Canto CVI" (*Paideuma* 13:419–32) N. M. Perret seems unaware that many other scholars have anticipated his arguments about Pound's creative adaptations of the Eleusinian rites.

Four studies focus upon the cantos Pound wrote at the end of World War II. In "The Poet at War: Ezra Pound's Suppressed War Cantos" (*SAQ* 83:69–79) Massimo Bacigalupo offers a negative assessment of Cantos 72 and 73, which were published in Italian in 1945 but never included with the rest of the poem. They illustrate, according to Bacigalupo, "the limitations (intellectual, linguistic, moral)" of Pound's approach to "things Italian." Brian Cheadle's "The Rhythm of a Canto: A Reading of Canto 81" (*ESA* 23[1980]:103–16) is an uneventful close reading of the most popular Pisan canto. The famous conclusion of that canto refers not to Pound's vanity but to that of his captors, according to the revisionist reading proposed by William French in "Peacocks in Poundland" (*Paideuma* 13:139–48) and Peter D'Epiro in "Whose Vanity Must Be Pulled Down" (*Paideuma* 13:247–52). The poet himself, French contends, is "totally devoid of penitence."

In "Salta sin barra" (*Paideuma* 13:408–14) Carroll F. Terrell connects a line of Canto 87 with images of bull-vaulting in Goya's etchings and the Minoan frescoes at Knossos.

As our survey comes to an end amidst vanity, peacocks, and bulls, it is chastening to be reminded of Pound's own literary criticism, a service Donald Davie performs in "Ezra Pound" (*SR* 92:421–32). Writing always as the working poet "in his shirt sleeves," Pound "cuts the critic down to size, which is now, in 1984, a pressing need."

ii. Eliot

The *Yeats Eliot Review* is defunct. A *T. S. Eliot Annual*, ed. Shyamal Bagchee (Macmillan), was announced for 1984 but did not appear. Meanwhile, the obstructionist policy of the Eliot estate continues to delay the publication of manuscript material while denying scholars permission to quote from it (see the *TLS* correspondence of 27 Jan.–16 Mar.).

a. **Text, Biography, and Bibliography.** That policy affects several recent studies. For example, Peter Ackroyd was not allowed to quote from the unpublished material he consulted in 20 libraries for his new *T. S. Eliot: A Life* (Hamish Hamilton). Nevertheless, this is the most thorough and balanced account of Eliot's life yet published. It reveals no dramatic secrets, denies that Eliot's friendship with Jean Verdenal was homosexual, and refuses to treat Vivien Haigh-Wood as a destructive monster. Ackroyd's evenhanded account of Eliot's first marriage, some of which appears as "Viv and Tom" (*Vanity Fair* 47,viii: 30–37, 97–98), has much in common with Michael Hastings's biographical play, *Tom and Viv* (see *ALS 1983*, p. 140). To appreciate the depth of Ackroyd's work, one need only compare it with Doris L. Eder's superficial *Three Writers in Exile: Pound, Eliot & Joyce* (Whitston).

Mitzi Berger Hamovitch was likewise denied permission to use

Eliot's correspondence in her edition of *The* Hound and Horn *Letters* (Georgia, 1982). Hamovitch prints eight letters from the magazine's editors to Eliot, but must paraphrase his replies. Alan Bold adopts a similar strategy in his edition of *The Letters of Hugh MacDiarmid* (Hamish Hamilton), reproducing 27 letters from MacDiarmid to Eliot and footnoting excerpts from Eliot's answers.

"Creatures of 'Charm': A New T. S. Eliot Poem" by Jeanne Campbell and John Reesman (*KR* 6,iii:25–33) contains the only Eliot text to appear this year, a four-line cat poem from a 1940 letter to Miss Bertha Rives Skinker. A. L. Rowse's "T. S. Eliot Fifty Years After" (*Yale Literary Mag.* 149[1981]:67–73) preserves some of Eliot's editorial comments on an early Rowse manuscript. A 1919 *Athenaeum* review of Yeats's *The Wild Swans at Coole* is attributed to Eliot by David Spurr in *Conflicts of Consciousness*, discussed below. And the publication history of Eliot's early work is narrated in a derivative chapter of Sally Dennison's *(Alternative) Literary Publishing*.

Robert H. Canary's *T. S. Eliot: The Poet and His Critics* (ALA, 1982) is a major review of Eliot scholarship. Canary devotes nearly 400 pages to summaries and evaluations of material published mainly in the 1960s and 1970s. For both research and reference, this digest will be immensely useful to other scholars.

b. **General Studies.** This year's work focuses upon the conflicts and contradictions in Eliot's art and personality. We may begin with the perennial issue of classicism versus romanticism in his literary theory. In *The Tradition of Return: The Implicit History of Modern Literature* (Princeton) Jeffrey M. Perl seeks to restore Eliot's classicism to intellectual respectability by aligning it with a widely shared post-Renaissance "ideology of history" which envisions a *nostos* or return of the modern world to its spiritual home in ancient Greece. Perl adduces many neoclassical elements in Eliot's work, but stumbles when he maintains that Eliot located his positive social norm "in classical antiquity" rather than the Christian Middle Ages. Like Perl, Michael H. Levenson argues that "modernism returns to classicism" in the work of Eliot. Levenson's *A Genealogy of Modernism: A Study of English Literary Doctrine, 1908–1922* (Cambridge) shows how Eliot gradually altered the fundamentally Romantic doctrines of impressionism, imagism, and vorticism into a "later orthodoxy" quite different in substance and tone.

Several other studies argue that, far from superseding romanticism, Eliot's classicism is a post-Romantic or Symbolist theory despite itself. Thus Eliot figures prominently in Carol T. Christ's demonstration of the continuities between *Victorian and Modern Poetics*. Christ identifies Victorian precedents for Eliot's use of personae, doctrine of the objective correlative, and theory of the mythical method. In "Symbolism and Modernist Poetry" (*BuR* 26[1982]: 97–118) Jon Rosenblatt emphasizes "the dialectical tension between symbolist and discursive modes of writing" in the poetry of Eliot and others. In *The Symbolist Movement in the Literature of European Languages*, ed. Anna Balakian (Budapest: Akadémiai Kiadó, 1982), Ruth Z. Temple raises the question "Eliot: An English Symbolist?" Her answer is a qualified "yes."

The tensions between Eliot's classicism and romanticism are reinterpreted in psychological terms by David Spurr in *Conflicts of Consciousness: T. S. Eliot's Poetry and Criticism* (Illinois). Spurr discerns a "war of intellect and imagination" throughout Eliot's writing, a ceaseless battle between willed impositions of external order and spontaneous uprisings of "Romantic visonary experience." Despite a certain tendency toward reductionism, Spurr's is the best book on Eliot published this year.

Tony Pinkney agrees with Spurr that Eliot's poems are above all "*strategies* . . . against the psychic conflicts that buffet" the poet. "Any Eliotic text has to, needs to, wants to, in one way or another, do a girl in," Pinkney argues in *Women in the Poetry of T. S. Eliot: A Psychoanalytical Approach* (Salem, N. H.: Salem House). He traces in Eliot's work a disturbing pattern of "violence against women," which he explains in terms of "the psychoanalysis of Melanie Klein and D. W. Winnicott." In "The Women of Eliot and Baudelaire: The Boredom, the Horror, and the Glory" (*MLS* 14,iii:31–42) Kerry Weinberg relates Eliot's "scathing criticism of women" not to emotional ambivalence but to a longstanding cultural and literary tradition. In "*The Waste Land* and the Fantasy of Interpretation" (*Representations* 8:134–58) Andrew Ross offers a farfetched Lacanian analysis of exchange, indebtedness, bankruptcy, and castration in Eliot's life and work.

According to Alan Weinblatt in *T. S. Eliot and the Myth of Adequation* (UMI Research) the primary tension in Eliot's poetry, drama, and criticism is between experience and language. "One finds in Eliot recurringly a single, infinitely complex, infinitely rich moment of experience, hovering precariously on the edge of meaning, then slipping back toward the edge of chaos, momentarily accessible to the 'relief of speech,' then lost again through the nets of language." Several other recent studies also stress Eliot's quest for a perfect bond between signifier and signified. "Eliot's Intolerable Wrestle: Speech, Silence, Words and Voices" by A. V. C. Schmidt (*UES* 21 [1983],ii:17–22) emphasizes the poet's preoccupation with the ideal of the Logos, "the word as the ultimate source of the meaning of words." In *Towards a Christian Poetics* (Macmillan) Michael Edwards argues that Eliot writes "a poetry enacting the fall of language" even as he yearns for "a language in process of redemption." Eliot's nostalgia for logocentricity makes him the antagonist of Joseph G. Kronick's Deconstructionist argument in *American Poetics of History*. None of these four studies adequately acknowledges the existence of previous scholarship on the subject of Eliot's concern with language.

We may close this part of our survey by noticing two traditional, belletristic studies, Alfred Kazin's *American Procession* and Hyatt H. Waggoner's "Eliot as Poet" (*SR* 92:432–41). Kazin provides a general assessment of Eliot's life and work, while Waggoner offers a personal selection of the poems he finds "most rewarding."

c. Relation to Other Writers. Several recent studies compare Eliot with other writers in order to clarify his poetic and social theories. In a wide-ranging essay entitled "Igor Stravinsky and T. S. Eliot: A Comparison of Their Modernist Poetics" (*CCrit* 4[1982]:169–91) W. Bronzwaer identifies three points held in common by the artists: the conscious renewal of tradition, an impersonalist conception of the creative process, and an ethical neoclassicism. In "The Case of the Missing Abstraction: Eliot, Frazer, and Modernism" (*MR* 25:539–52) Jewel Spears Brooker compares the method of *The Waste Land* with that of *The Golden Bough*. Both rely, Brooker argues, upon a comprehensive abstraction formulated not in the text but in the minds of author and reader.

Two unsatisfactory studies of Eliot's social views also employ comparative methods. Lucy McDiarmid's *Saving Civilization: Yeats, Eliot and Auden between the Wars* (Cambridge) remains bland and superficial because the critic refuses to discuss "the poets' positions on specific political or social issues." Rajendra Verma's comparisons in *Man and Society in Tagore and Eliot* (Humanities, 1982) are likewise too general and woolly to be illuminating. Eliot's knowledge of

Indian philosophy, religion, and language is the subject of a competent if pedestrian chapter of Beongcheon Yu's *The Great Circle.*
Four essays treat Eliot's relationship to continental European
writers. G. M. Hyde's discussion of "T. S. Eliot's Crime and Punishment" in *F. M. Dostoevsky (1821–1888): A Centenary Collection*, ed.
Leon Burnett (Colchester: Univ. of Essex, 1981), shows how Eliot's
early poetry both imitates and parodies Dostoevsky. Maryanne C.
Ward's "Eliot and Pasternak: Restoring the Waste Land of Lost
Culture and Tradition" (*PCL* 9[1983]:3–11) compares mythical
archetypes in *The Waste Land* and *Doctor Zhivago.* In "The Balking
Staircase and the Transparent Door: Prufrock and Kröger" (*Comparatist* 8:21–32) Robert F. Fleissner suggests that Eliot's "Love Song"
was "directly affected by [Thomas] Mann's similar study of spiritual
debilitation" in "Tonio Kröger" (1903). Finally, Karl Malkoff compares "Eliot and Elytis: Poet of Time, Poet of Space" (*CL* 36:238–
57), focusing upon *Four Quartets* and the Greek poet's *To Axion Esti.*

Six studies examine Eliot's relationships with 19th-century British
writers. Carlos Baker's *The Echoing Green* surveys Eliot's published
views of the Romantic poets. Cory Bieman Davies compares Eliot's
dramatic monologues with those of Browning in " 'Natural Evolution' in 'Dramatic Essences' from Robert Browning to T. S. Eliot"
(*BIS* 11[1983]:23–38). Vincent P. Anderson's "Preserving the Faith:
An Argument between Matthew Arnold and T. S. Eliot" (*Arnoldian*
11:5–15) contrasts their views of Christianity and its role in modern
culture. An impassioned defense of Arnold against the "carping, nig-
gling, slighting remarks" of an ungrateful Eliot may be savored in
Sudhaker Marathe's "Eliot on Arnold: A Reaction" (*Arnoldian* 11:
16–33). Finally, two essays examine Eliot's relationship with Kipling:
Maria-Teresa Gibert's "Honneur à Rudyard Kipling: hommage et
témoinage littéraire de T. S. Eliot" (*CVE* 18[1983]:49–58), and
P. S. Sri's "Thunder in *The Waste Land:* An Echo from *Jungle Book?*"
(*ELN* 21[1983],ii:41–43). Sri suggests that Kipling's description of a
drought in *The Second Jungle Book* (1895) resounds in "What the
Thunder Said."

Other critics hear American echoes in Eliot's work. Despite his
frequent disparagement of Ralph Waldo Emerson, Eliot has much in
common with his New England forebear, according to Ronald Bush
in "T. S. Eliot: Singing the Emerson Blues" in *Emerson: Prospect and
Retrospect*, ed. Joel Porte (Harvard, 1982). Dennis Welland links
Eliot with another New Englander who was also an expatriate and

playwright in " 'Improvised Europeans': Thoughts on an Aspect of Henry James and T. S. Eliot" (*BJRL* 66[1983]:256–77). In "T. S. Eliot: The Reluctant Humanist" (*Southern Partisan*, Fall [1982], pp. 15–19) T. John Jamieson describes Eliot's friendship with Paul Elmer More, making use of their unpublished correspondence. The connection between "Karl Barth and T. S. Eliot" (*Standpunte* 35[1982]:35–42) interests Ian Glenn, who maintains that "Barth's description of the meaning of mystical experience in the Christian tradition" affects the poems and plays Eliot wrote between 1933 and 1942. In "*Invisible Man*: Ralph Ellison's Wasteland" (*CLAJ* 28:150–58) Mary Ellen Williams Walsh argues persuasively that "important scenes, characters, and events" in Ellison's novel are indebted to *The Waste Land*.

d. The Poems and Plays. For the last two years the study of Eliot's early poems has been in the doldrums. Will 1984 be remembered as the year Michael Gillum discovered "Ennui and Alienation in Eliot's Poetry" (*MQ* 25:386–96)? Or as the year Jay Dougherty offered yet another interpretation of "T. S. Eliot's 'The Love Song of J. Alfred Prufrock' and Dante's 'Divine Comedy'" (*Expl* 42,iv:38–40)? Only Carol T. Christ's "Self-Concealment and Self-Expression in Eliot's and Pound's Dramatic Monologues" (*VP* 22:217–26) is at all noteworthy. Christ argues that Eliot's "mask lyrics," like Tennyson's, seek "an ironic objectification of Romantic introspection."

Students of *The Waste Land* continue to identify mythological patterns in the poem. In *Struktur und Funktion der apokalyptischen Elemente in der Lyrik T. S. Eliots* (Peter Lang, 1980) Reinhold Quandt relates the apocalyptic imagery, discontinuous structure, and visionary speaker of Eliot's poem to a tradition of *Revelationsliteratur* descending from the New Testament. For Audrey T. Rogers in " 'He Do the Police in Different Voices': The Design of *The Waste Land*" (*CollL* 10[1983]:279–93) the poem is unified by "the archtypal myth of the eternal return" perceived through the consciousness of Tiresias. Sherlyn Abdoo makes a weak case for "Woman as Grail in T. S. Eliot's *The Waste Land*" (*CentR* 28:48–60), arguing that "the feminine broods in the intertextual" as the unacknowledged goal of the quest for regeneration. In "The Belladonna: Eliot's Female Archetype in *The Waste Land*" (*TCL* 30:420–31) Philip Sicker focuses upon the figure of "the sexually violated yet sterile female." According to S. A. Cowan in "Philomela and Marie: A Note on *The Waste Land*" (*CLAJ*

28:159–63) "most of the women merge in the story of Philomela," to which four of the poem's five sections allude.

As usual, *The Waste Land* attracted a number of brief source studies. The opening lines of "A Game of Chess" are indebted to chapters 40 and 54 of *Dombey and Son*, Patrick Diskin argues in "Eliot, Dickens, and *The Waste Land*" (*N&Q* 31:511). Eliot's description of the Thames in "The Fire Sermon" echoes a description of the Seine by Flaubert, according to Philip Cohen in " 'Oil and Tar': An Allusion to *Madame Bovary* in *The Waste Land*" (*AN&Q* 21: [1983]:75–77). The vague reference to "Shackleton" in Eliot's note to "What the Thunder Said" is pinned down by C. J. Ackerley in "Eliot's *The Waste Land* and Shackleton's *South*" (*N&Q* 31:514–15). In "Dry Bones Can Harm No One: *Ezekiel* XXXVII in *The Waste Land* V and *Ash-Wednesday* II" (*ES* 65:39–47) Marianne Thormählen argues that, whereas Eliot's biblical source carries hints of resurrection, his poems treat them ironically. According to Peter L. Hays in "T. S. Eliot's 'The Waste Land' " (*Expl* 42,iv:36–38) the allusion to Hieronymo in part V is meant to evoke St. Jerome as well as Thomas Kyd's avenger. In "T. S. Eliot's 'The Waste Land' " (*Expl* 43,i:51–53) A. N. Dwivedi maintains that the poem's closing lines connote an "unruffled condition of mind" if we consider their Vedic and Upanishadic sources. Finally, "The Waste Land without Pound" by Louis Auchincloss (*NYRB*, 11 October, p. 46) suggests that the poem would be "more coherent" if some of the passages excised by Pound were restored.

Two essays take "The Hollow Men" as their starting point. Julia M. Reibetanz's "Accentual Forms in Eliot's Poetry from *The Hollow Men* to *Four Quartets*" (*ES* 65:334–49) duplicates the prosodic analysis she published last year (see *ALS 1983*, p. 146). In "T. S. Eliot's 'The Hollow Men' " (*Expl* 42,iv:40–41) Robert F. Fleissner uses J. E. Cirlot's *Dictionary of Symbols* to distinguish the emptiness of Eliot's speakers from nothingness. As we observed in the Pound section above, Fleissner is adept at making something out of nothing.

The *Ariel Poems* attracted four recent studies. A. P. Riemer's "The Poetry of Religious Paradox—T. S. Eliot and the Metaphysicals" (*SSEng* 8[1982–83]:80–88) relates the subject matter, structure, and style of "Journey of the Magi" to those of Donne's "Good Friday 1613, Riding Westward." E. F. Burgess, in "T. S. Eliot's 'The Journey of the Magi' " (*Expl* 42,iv:36), connects several lines of the poem with Persian oral literature and Zoroastrian prophecies. In "T. S. Eliot's

Hugh Witemeyer 151

Animula: A Source for 'Boudin'" (*N&Q* 31:77) Tom Gibbons identifies "Boudin blown to pieces" as Martial Bourdin, the French anarchist whose sensational demise near Greenwich Observatory in 1896 figures in Conrad's *The Secret Agent.* "Animula" may also be indebted to F. Scott Fitzgerald's short story "The Love Boat" (1927), as William Harmon and Susan W. Smock explain in "How T. S. Eliot Probably Borrowed a Sentence from F. Scott Fitzgerald" (*AN&Q* 21 [1983]:110).

Issues of religious faith and poetic language dominate current discussions of *Four Quartets.* In "Poetry and Belief: Notes on an Old Debate" (*KR* 5[1983],ii:3–13) L. C. Knights argues that "believer and unbeliever alike" can give the poem their full assent. Eliot solicits that assent, according to Frank Burch Brown in *Transfiguration: Poetic Metaphor and the Language of Religious Belief* (N. C., 1983), by representing in the poem "the dynamics of the experience of coming-to-faith." For Anthony Libby in *Mythologies of Nothing: Mystical Death in American Poetry, 1940–70* (Illinois) the central dynamic of the poem involves a clash between two kinds of mysticism—"transcendent and immanent." Paul Jay's reading of the poem in *Being in the Text: Self-Representation from Wordsworth to Roland Barthes* (Cornell) deploys the characteristic paradoxes of Deconstruction: "Eliot's poem tends both to leave open the circle it seeks to close and to discover, if not to affirm, the absence of what it is searching for."

Metaphysical or linguistic absence poses no problem for Sister Mary Anthony Weinig, who assumes an orthodox Christian viewpoint and concentrates faithfully upon *Verbal Pattern in Four Quartets: A Close Reading of T. S. Eliot's Poem* (Troy, Mich.: International Book Center, 1982). Sister Mary Anthony analyzes Eliot's logic, rhetoric, syntax, diction, imagery, rhythm, rhyme, and sound patterns, citing no secondary sources published since 1955. Equally out of touch with recent scholarship is Ruth Barton in "T. S. Eliot's Secret Garden" (*N&Q* 31:512–14). Barton is unaware that Leonard Unger called attention in 1982 to Eliot's echoing of *The Secret Garden* by Frances Hodgson Burnett. In "The Senses of Eliot's Salvages" (*EIC* 34:309–18) Eleanor Cook considers the multiple meanings of an Eliot title.

Eliot's development of a "tragicomic vernacular" suited to "satire-drama" interests Barbara Everett in "The New Style of *Sweeney Agonistes*" (*YES* 14:243–64). Among other styles, according to

Everett, *Sweeney* employs a "speech of the Dumb Blonde" adapted
from Ring Lardner and Anita Loos. The Group Theatre's 1934–35
production of *Sweeney Agonistes* is described by its stage designer,
Robert Medley, in *Drawn from the Life: A Memoir* (Faber), which
also reproduces several letters from Eliot to Rupert Doone. Eliot's
characters are forever imprisoned in "social roles defined by language
fixed in time," S. Jaret McKinstry emphasizes in "Mixed Meanings:
Role-Calling in T. S. Eliot's *The Cocktail Party*" (*RaJAH* 2[1982],ii:
87–108). For that matter Eliot himself is "tradicionalmente encasil-
lado en el estereotipo de gravedad y pesimismo," according to María
Teresa Gibert in "Eliot entre los gatos" (*Arbor* 117:93–105). But the
musical *Cats* and the poems upon which it is based should help to
break down that stereotype.

e. **The Criticism.**   Eliot's idea of tradition still provokes lively discussion. In an unusual essay on "The Historical Sense: T. S. Eliot's
Concept of Tradition and Its Relevance to Architecture" (*Architectural Rev.* 176,x:68–70) Colin St. John Wilson argues that some
modern architectural styles, no less than literary ones, use quotation
and allusion to signify their continuities with tradition. According to
Sheldon W. Liebman in "The Turning Point: Eliot's *The Use of
Poetry and the Use of Criticism*" (*Boundary* 9[1981]:197–218) Eliot
completely altered his early conceptions of tradition, objectivity,
"literary esotericism and critical elitism," beginning with his Norton
Lectures of 1932–33. Such a revision of formulated theory is characteristic of Eliot, Victor P. H. Li maintains in "Theory and Therapy:
The Case of T. S. Eliot" (*Criticism* 25[1983]:347–58); theory for
Eliot is never more than an "enabling fiction," subject always to the
"therapy" of "revisionary doubt." Revisions of a textual sort concern
Linda M. Shires in "T. S. Eliot's Early Criticism and the Making of
The Sacred Wood" (*PSt* 5[1982]:229–38). Shires examines the ad-
ditions, deletions, and omissions that Eliot made when he first gathered his London essays for book publication.

Two Marxist analyses challenge Eliot's conception of literary and
social tradition. One is Robert Weimann's *Structure and Society in
Literary History: Studies in the History and Theory of Historical
Criticism*, first published in 1976 and now reissued in an "expanded
edition" (Hopkins). Because Eliot neglects the dialectical processes
of literary genesis and reception, Weimann argues, his theory of
tradition ignores "the world of history" and divorces literature "from

its total social context." Pamela McCallum agrees with Weimann that for Eliot "tradition has the concealed purpose of resisting history." In her Jamesonian study of *Literature and Method: Towards a Critique of I. A. Richards, T. S. Eliot, and F. R. Leavis* (Humanities, 1983) McCallum treats the social and cultural theories of all three critics as symptoms of "the poverty of liberal thought" in a period of historical crisis.

McCallum discerns a greater degree of consensus among her critics than does Bernard Bergonzi in "Leavis and Eliot: The Long Road to Rejection" (*CritQ* 26:21–43). Bergonzi traces the "zig-zag progress" of Leavis's "changing approach to Eliot." To conservative critic George A. Panichas, McCallum's contention that Eliot's social views represent "liberal thought" must seem inexplicable. In his chapter on "T. S. Eliot and the Critique of Liberalism" in *The Courage of Judgment: Essays in Criticism, Culture, and Society* (Tenn., 1982) Panichas contrasts Eliot's beliefs with those of John Dewey, endorses Eliot's condemnation of a society "worm-eaten with Liberalism," and defends Eliot's "Christian anti-Judaism." Panichas concludes that "in his social criticism Eliot has become one of the great modern prophets." Clearly Eliot's criticism can still touch some of its readers where they live.

University of New Mexico

9. Faulkner

Linda W. Wagner-Martin

This was truly a year of international assessment of Faulkner's work and reputation within various countries. Several collections from the University of Mississippi annual Faulkner conference—particularly *Faulkner: International Perspectives*, proceedings from the 1982 meeting, the publication of which was delayed; the special Faulkner issue of *L'Arc*; the continued publication in Japan of *William Faulkner: Materials, Studies, and Criticism*; the existence of the International Colloquium on Faulkner held in Paris in 1980 and 1982 and in Salamanca in 1984; and other scattered essays—such activity suggests that Faulkner's recognition as America's premier Modernist has been greatly extended.

After the extremely heavy production of full-length studies of Faulkner's writing in 1983, this year's publications were more often essays and chapters in books, a perhaps necessary balance to the extensive publications of the previous year.

i. Bibliography, Editions, Manuscripts

The valuable survey of research and criticism relating to Faulkner, under the leadership of Dianne L. Cox, continues in *MissQ* (37:397–426); the "Checklist" of Faulkner materials appears in each issue of the *Faulkner Newsletter & Yoknapatawpha Review*. In addition to such ongoing information, special appendixes to *Faulkner: International Perspectives* provide items of interest on the world scene: Mick Gidley, "Selected Recent British Writing on Faulkner," pp. 319–20; Myriam Díaz-Diocaretz, "Faulkner in Spanish," pp. 320–24, and "Spanish Criticism of Faulkner, 1932–59," p. 324; Monika Brückner, "Faulkner in German," pp. 325–36; M. Thomas Inge, "A Chronology of Faulkner Translations into Russian," pp. 336–38; H. R. Stoneback, "A Checklist of Faulkner Translations into Chinese," p. 338; Kenzaburo Ohashi, "Faulkner in Japanese," pp. 339–42. Many of the volume's essays are also bibliographical by nature, most characterized by candor and thoroughness: Gidley, "Faulkner and the British: Episodes in a Literary Relationship," pp. 74–97; Agostino Lombardo, "Faulkner in Italy," pp. 121–38; Stoneback, "The Hound and the Antelope: Faulkner in China," pp. 236–56; Ohashi, " 'Native Soil' and the World Beyond: William Faulkner and Japanese Novelists," pp. 257–75. In Michel Gresset's "From Vignette to Vision: The 'Old, Fine Name of France' or Faulkner's 'Western Front' from 'Crevasse' to *A Fable*," pp. 97–120, the use Faulkner made of the country of France is discussed; Díaz-Diocaretz comments on variations within Spanish translations of Faulkner's work in "Faulkner's Spanish Voice/s," pp. 30–59; Jorge Edwards compares Faulkner's country with his own location as a novelist in "Yoknapatawpha in Santiago de Chile," pp. 60–73; and three essays assess Faulkner in Russia: Alexandre Vashchenko, "The Perception of William Faulkner in the USSR," pp. 194–211; Sergei Chakovsky, "William Faulkner in Soviet Literary Criticism," pp. 212–35; Inge, "Teaching Faulkner in the Soviet Union," pp. 174–93.

Petra Gallert provided "Dutch and Belgian Translations of Faulkner: A Checklist" (*MissQ* 37:385–88), and three essays speak to publishing and collecting Faulkner: Lawrence H. Schwartz, "Publishing William Faulkner: the 1940's" (*SoQ* 22:70–92); Carl Petersen, "On Collecting Faulkner: A Subjective View" (*WiF* 6:77–88); and Louis Daniel Brodsky, "Il Penseroso and L'Allegro: The Poetics of a Faulkner Collector" (*Faulkner IP*, pp. 276–97). Brodsky continues his reminiscence in the proceedings of the 1983 conference ("On the Road to the Mullen Holdings: A Faulkner Collector's Odyssey," *New Directions*, pp. 254–69).

The second volume of the Brodsky guide series, *The Letters* (Miss.), includes the texts of nearly 500 letters, but only 129 of those were written by Faulkner, and many of those have been previously published (although sometimes excerpted). Well worth the publication, this volume prints many letters from Estelle, Phil and Emily Stone, Saxe and Dorothy Commins, Ruth Ford, and others. Robert W. Hamblin's introduction is an expert summary of the contents, and Brodsky and Hamblin share publication credits.

O. B. Emerson's *Faulkner's Early Literary Reputation in America* (UMI) is also primarily bibliographical. Covering the years 1924 through 1954 (from the publication of *The Marble Faun* through *A*

Fable), Emerson works both thematically and chronologically to provide some understanding of the uneven currents of appreciation (and vituperation) that greeted Faulkner's work at various times in his early career. He devotes chapters to the "cult-of-cruelty" criticism, Marxist response, and "new" Faulkner criticism, placing these chapters within the more helpful overviews of early reaction, "growing maturity" of the criticism, and the Nobel Prize criticism. Faulkner's critical fate in this country is worth a book and while this one is sometimes a bit ponderous, and sometimes stays too long with one essay or critic, it is solid and worth publication.

Other essays of bibliographic interest include Kioyouki Ono's "The Japanese Reception of William Faulkner" (*NMW* 16:13–24), Hans H. Skei's "The Reception and Reputation of William Faulkner in Norway" (*NMW* 16:25–58), and William Boozer's listing of some of the 400 books found in the second-floor storeroom of Faulkner's home ("Rowan Oak Storeroom Holds Treasure in Foreign Editions," *Faulkner Newsletter* 4,i:1,3).

Two important manuscript publications occurred in 1984. The re-issue of Faulkner's *The Sound and the Fury* was greeted with approval mixed with some skepticism: were there enough changes to warrant this publication? Under the editorship of Noel Polk, the new text consisted of correlations among Faulkner's holograph manuscript, the carbon typescript (both in the Faulkner Collection of the Alderman Library at the University of Virginia), and the 1929 Cape and Smith first edition. According to Polk's note that closes the book, choices among variants were made to preserve Faulkner's "final intentions" for the books; unfortunately, since no galley proofs exist, determining those intentions is sometimes difficult. Brief tables of changes follow the closing note. Because most of Faulkner's novels have never been "edited" for any kind of publication, as have many 19th-century works, for example, this process is valuable.

Random House also published Faulkner's *Father Abraham*, a text James B. Meriwether in his introduction calls "the brilliant beginning of a novel which William Faulkner tried repeatedly to write, for a period of almost a decade and a half, during the earlier part of his career—the novel about the Snopes family." Probably written late in 1926, these 24 pages of manuscript introduce Flem Snopes and his family, include the "spotted horses" tale, and chart Mrs. Armstid's pathos. The title describes Flem (whom Faulkner introduces here as

"legendary as Roland," heavily ironic even in 1926), named Father
Abraham in *Flags in the Dust* as a kind of travesty of the fruitful,
courageous biblical founder of Judaism.

As part of a two-book publication, University of Texas Press published Faulkner's early poem sequence, *Vision in Spring*, edited by
Judith L. Sensibar (see section *iii. a.*). The sequence of 14 love poems,
presented as a handbound book in 1921 to Estelle while she was still
married to Cornell Franklin, shows a great deal about Faulkner's
working and writing habits, and it is for this reason that Sensibar insists that the poem sequence was Faulkner's "apprenticeship" for the
novels he soon began writing. She traces the imagery, the techniques
for connecting seemingly disparate poems, and the recurring themes
("sex, love, power, impotence, death, and the powers of the imagination") in her thorough introduction. Such poems as "Love Song,"
"Portrait," and "After the Concert" are important additions to the
published Faulkner.

Volume 3 of Brodsky and Hamblin's guide to the Brodsky Collection reprints *The De Gaulle Story*, Faulkner's film script in several
versions. Written for Warner Brothers during the early 1940s, the film
script went through several versions—titled "Free France"—and only
recently have all the materials been available for collation. (Faulkner
had given some 700 pages of manuscript and other materials related
to the project to his friend A. I. "Buzz" Bezzerides; those have now
been added to the collection.) This is an interesting record of a defunct project: the film was never produced.

Brodsky has written an interesting essay based on manuscripts for
Faulkner's story "Wash" ("The Textual Development of Faulkner's
'Wash': An Examination of Manuscripts in the Brodsky Collection,"
SB 37:248–81). Karl F. Knight speculates on the importance of a de-
leted episode—to the character of Horace Benbow—in "The Joan
Heppleton Episode in Faulkner's *Flags in the Dust*" (*MissQ* 37:391–
95). The Seajay Press has published Faulkner's holograph manuscript
from 1933, *A Sorority Pledge*, with an afterword by Jane Isbell
Haynes. The pledge was written for Virginia McDaniel, roommate of
"Cho Cho" Franklin, on one of her weekend visits to Rowan Oak.

ii. Biography

Joseph Blotner's one-volume, revised (and rewritten) *Faulkner: A
Biography* was the major event in the biographical section this year.

Omitting the family history that had slowed the important two-volume version of this account, Blotner has added much new material, has moved from a somewhat tentative approach to Faulkner's story to a tone of authority and control, and has better integrated his discussion of the fiction into the life.

Ten years have passed since the two-volume study, and during that time much material that Blotner was avoiding has become public (most of Blotner's omissions were out of deference to the family's feelings, and time has also helped that situation). The inclusion of the Meta Carpenter story, for one; the filming of *Intruder in the Dust*; meeting Joan Williams—Blotner brings life to events that had previously been recountings. There is no reason for another Faulkner biography now.

Sherwood Anderson's description of Faulkner has been published in *The Winesburg Eagle* (9:3)—"the story teller doing his story teller's job," and Mac Reed recollects a few Faulkner mannerisms in "Remembering Faulkner" (*Faulkner Newsletter* 4,iv:1,4). George Boswell collects reminiscences of local residents about Faulkner in "Faulkner in Pascagoula" (*MissFR* 18:31–33), and James G. Watson's approach in "New Orleans, *The Double Dealer*, and 'New Orleans'" (*AL* 56:214–26) is partly biographical. Watson shows the ways Faulkner used elements from his visits to New Orleans and other cities— characters, situations, emotional tone—to shape the early vignettes that were published as prose poems, transitional pieces, fragmentary stories. Watson stresses that Faulkner's work shows "it is not so much a place that the city of voices describes as a condition," that of post-Modern and postwar despair and indecision.

iii. Criticism: General

a. **Books.**   Judith L. Sensibar approaches the problem of Faulkner's apprenticeship in *The Origins of Faulkner's Art* (Texas), a psychoanalytic study based heavily on the place in his development of the poem sequence (published as a paired book to *Vision of Spring*). Thoroughly supported with references to all of Faulkner's earlier writing, Sensibar's thesis is that what the young writer learned in working through his 1920 dream-play and the three poem sequences that followed made possible his accomplishments in fiction. Sensibar makes extensive use of manuscript versions, of texts, and of all existing Faulkner criticism to prove her thesis.

Much of the collection *New Directions* can properly be classified as general criticism. Panthea Reid Broughton's "An Amazing Gift: The Early Essays and Faulkner's Apprenticeship in Aesthetics and Criticism" (pp. 322–57) continues the direction of Sensibar's work as it correlates what Faulkner was saying with what he was attempting to do simultaneously. P. V. Palievsky discusses Faulkner's aesthetics more generally in "Faulkner's View of Literature" (pp. 270–82) and Berndt Ostendorf changes directions from aesthetics to "An Anthropological Approach to Yoknapatawpha" (pp. 94–118). Ilse Dusoir Lind approaches Faulkner's writing to determine how he used Jewish characters ("Faulkner's Relationship to Jews: A Beginning," pp. 119–42) and Arthur E. Kinney describes an important thematic interest throughout the fiction in " 'Topmost in the Pattern': Family Structure in Faulkner" (pp. 143–71). One of the more interesting essays in the collection is that by James Hinkle, who did his research listening to hours of tapes of Faulkner himself speaking—in classes, lectures, etc.—to assess his pronunciation of the names he chose for his fiction ("Some Yoknapatawpha Names," pp. 172–201).

Thomas L. McHaney discusses "Faulkner and Modernism: Why Does it Matter?" (pp. 37–60) and concludes that because Faulkner was integral to Modernist writing—his work being both influenced by it, and influencing it—he must be seen in its contexts. McHaney feels that too often critics have used a 19th-century approach to reading Faulkner, looking for "meaning" and moral tags where they might better have looked for intricacies of language and structure that would have changed ostensible meaning. All of his fiction must be studied from that perspective because "Faulkner wrote no manifestoes, what he did was to perform them."

Michael Millgate's masterful "William Faulkner: The Shape of a Career" (pp. 18–36) emphasizes the randomness of Faulkner's "progress"—the fact that his spectacular output during the 1920s and 1930s was the product of his passionate search for "an always elusive experience of final and absolute creative achievement" and not just another building block toward some preconceived end. Millgate's essay takes as its thesis the fundamental paradox that "criticism believes before scholarship demonstrates," and then offers some plausible explanations for the writer's choices in subject, technique, and progression.

André Bleikasten stresses the reading difficulties Faulkner's work occasions, and the changing reader response ("Reading Faulkner," pp. 1–17). He applauds the tendency to read Faulkner as a Modern, not as a 19th-century writer.

James G. Watson ("'But Damn Letters Anyway': Letters and Fictions," pp. 228–53) suggests the relationship between many of Faulkner's actual letters and the ones he creates for his fictions. What seems to be a biographical study, at least in part becomes an important means of determining the significance Faulkner saw in the written word. Watson is particularly good on the epistolary conventions evident in what he calls Faulkner's "master-student relationships and letterly situations from his own fictions."

Wolf Kindermann's *Analyse und Synthese im Werk William Faulkners: Generation und 'community' in der Entwicklung seines Denkens* (AAF 17) concentrates on genealogy and Faulkner's interest in relationships among generations. He locates seven stages in Faulkner's development, as his attitudes change from veneration to a more open acceptance of earlier conventions, arriving eventually at a utopian vision of the South.

Richard H. Brodhead has edited the second collection of Faulkner essays in the Twentieth Century Views series (Prentice-Hall, 1983). Titled *Faulkner: New Perspectives*, the collection includes a good introduction by the editor, excerpts from the work of Cleanth Brooks, Irving Howe, Hugh Kenner, John T. Irwin, David M. Wyatt, David Minter, Calvin Bedient, Donald M. Kartiganer, Susan Willis, and Gary Lee Stonum. Except for the Willis essay, most of the selections are historically sound and useful. (Brodhead makes the point in his introduction that, because 16 years had passed since Robert Penn Warren's first volume appeared, he was attempting to include significant criticism during that time—particularly Brooks and Irwin.) The problem with most of them is that they are excerpts from books that are, for the most part, readily accessible.

The Willis essay, "Aesthetics of the Rural Slum: Contradictions and Dependency in 'The Bear,'" places Faulkner's work in the context of global changes in capitalism, complete with its historical conflicts. She applies André Frank and Immanuel Wallerstein's dependency theory, an economic theory of underdevelopment, to Faulkner's text of "The Bear." Her commentary brings useful information to the relationship among the four parts and to the character of Ike McCaslin (pp. 174–94).

b. **Essays.** One of the most important essays this year, or any of the past several, is Calvin S. Brown's "From Jefferson to the World" (*Faulkner IP*, pp. 3–27). Brown's knowledge of Faulkner's writing from the perspective of Classical and allusive literatures is impressive, and his seemingly effortless essay contains a fund of new insight and facts. His major thesis is that, because Faulkner was self-educated, we are surprised both by what he knew and what he did not know (and there are illustrations aplenty of the former). His tactic is to identify allusions and (particularly helpful here) poems used in the texts: for example, Faulkner's addition of his own verse to two stanzas from the *Rubaiyat*.

Karl F. Zender ("Faulkner and the Power of Sound," *PMLA* 99: 89–107) sets forth a new prolegomenon for reading the fiction based on his premise that Faulkner often created a "sustained meditation on the artist's power." That meditation, however, changed as his career advanced, and his choices of images show the shifts and modulations. Among these, his use of sound, of voice, and his tendency to describe sound as inimical, relate to his sense of diminished ability. Much focus on Quentin Compson.

Ruel E. Foster and Jie Tao contributed essays to *Thalia* (6[1983]: 9–16 and 57–60), both concerned with Faulkner's humor. The former's essay "The Modes and Functions of Humor in Faulkner" was the basis for the latter's comment about the influence of that humor on Chinese writers.

Two other essays from *Faulkner IP* are of interest. Joseph Blotner's "From the World to Jefferson" (pp. 298–318) and Lothar Hönnighausen's "Faulkner's Graphic Work in Historical Context" (pp. 139–73) summarize Faulkner's appeal for international readers and set his drawings and sketches in the broad context of *fin de siècle*, Art Nouveau, Japanese art, as well as Beardsley and calligraphy. The many reproductions of Faulkner's work enhance this essay. Hönnighausen also has written a study of "Faulkner's First Published Poem: 'L'Après-Midi d'un Faune'" (*WiF* 6:1–19).

iv. Criticism: Special Studies

a. **Ideas, Influences, Intellectual Background.** Joseph W. Reed has written what he calls comparative biography in *Three American Originals: John Ford, William Faulkner, & Charles Ives* (Wesleyan). The book provides integrated chronologies of the three unusual

Americans (since America is democratic, unique people are rarer than we might suppose), showing that all three of these artists were aiming to "stretch" their audiences. Faulkner's art was the most personal as he constantly pushed himself past his failure of nerve. His love for the good of community was his central theme, an unconventional concept for his time. Reed assesses all three men, finally, as conservatives: they all dwell on the old tunes, despite what they tried to accomplish in their art.

Darlene Unrue discusses "The Complex Americanism of Henry James and William Faulkner" (*The Origins*, pp. 247–53) while Zuzana Hegedüsová assesses "Faulkner's Contribution to the Contemporary Art of Narration" (pp. 255–59, and scattered references to Faulkner throughout this volume). Other comparative studies this year include Mick Gidley's analysis of Faulkner's later speeches and comments ("Malraux and the Attractions of Rhetoric in Faulkner's Later Public Comments," *WiF* 6:20–35); William Oxley's "The Sick Novel," which compares Faulkner with Camus and Steinbeck (*A Salzburg Miscellany: English and American Studies, 1964–1984*, ed. Wilfried Haslauer, 2:117–29); and Philip Cohen's "Balzac and Faulkner: The Influence of *La Comédie humaine* on *Flags in the Dust* and the Snopes Trilogy" (*MissQ* 37:325–51). Cohen's thesis is that there is a great deal of influence between Balzac's works and Faulkner's *Father Abraham* (Snopes). There are many similarities between *Les Paysans* and *The Hamlet* in both theme and authorial attitudes. Both writers were confronted with startling social transitions, but Faulkner remained the psychological realist rather than the social. Aesthetic considerations often overrode historical and sociological considerations in Faulkner's writing.

Donald Palumbo compares Faulkner with Camus and Dostoyevsky in "Father-Son Ruptures in Modern Existentialist Fiction: Camus, Dostoyevsky, Faulkner" (*CEA* 46:56–63), seeing that the loss of belief in a deity has crippled all father-son relationships in these writers' fictions. He moves toward similar conclusions in two other essays, "Sadomasochism and Modern Existential Fiction" (*WVUPP* 28[1982]:49–61) and in "Convergence of the Left and Right: The Ironies of Political Extremism Viewed through the Existential Perspectives of Dostoyevsky, Faulkner, and Sartre" (*LJHum* 9[1983]: 21–31).

Mick Gidley ("The Later Faulkner, Bergson, and God," *MissQ* 37:377–83) describes Bergson as the center of Faulkner's philosophy.

He shared with Bergson the vision of God as force, activity, the original source of the élan vital common to all creatures, "the centre from which worlds shoot out." Randolph D. Pope discusses the use Faulkner makes of Bergson's concepts of memory ("Benet, Faulkner, and Bergson's Memory" in *Critical Approaches to the Writings of Juan Benet* [New England], ed. Roberta C. Manteiga, David K. Herzberger, Malcolm Alan Compitello, pp. 111–19). The concepts of fluid reality, the nature of time, and the vital energy are illustrated through *As I Lay Dying*. In the same collection, Mary S. Vásquez discusses Benet's debt to Faulkner in "The Creative Task: Existential Self-Invention in 'Una meditacion'" (pp. 64–71). She also points to important differences between Yoknapatawpha and Benet's Region, places both for existential alienation and existential creation.

Steve Glassman considers "The Genesis and Influence of Faulkner's Popeye" (*SCCEA* 25:3–4) and concludes that the character was based on Neal Kerens Pumphrey (nicknamed Popeye), real-life Memphis gangster. Glassman speculates that *Sanctuary* had much to do with the "tough-guy" novels of the 1930s. Francis S. Heck traces Eula Varner to Zola's Nana (*ArQ* 40:293–304), claiming that each is a destructive force of nature, inimical to men.

b. **Style and Structure.** Sonja Bāsić discusses Faulkner's importance to narratology in "Faulkner's Narrative Discourse: Mediation and Mimesis" (*New Directions*, pp. 302–21), paralleling the attention given to Faulkner's writing by Ralph Flores (*The Rhetoric of Doubtful Authority: Deconstructive Readings of Self-Questioning Narratives, St. Augustine to Faulkner* [Cornell]). Bāsić describes work by Gérard Genette, Roland Barthes, and Tzvetan Todorov in suggesting modernism's antimimetic basis, and Faulkner's varied role in it. She sees *The Sound and the Fury* and *Absalom, Absalom!* as opposing narratives, the former relying on "verisimilitude and referentiality," the latter on inventions and constructions which are distorted by the several narrators and consequently "denaturalized" through language. Faulkner's remarkable power as fictionist allows him to create superb novels in two different models. Andrea Dimino's focus in "Narration as Initiation: Myth and History in Faulkner's *Absalom, Absalom!*" falls on Faulkner's mode of narration (*Sigfrido nel nuovo mondo: Studi sulla narrativa d'iniziazione*, ed. Paola Cabibbo, Goliardica, 1983, pp. 257–76), as does Marijke Rijsberman who uses Michael Millgate's critical term "interrupted monologue" to discuss

Faulkner's later work ("Interior Viewpoints and Psychological Realism in Some Faulkner Novels," *Neophil* 68:150–59). When Faulkner changes from interior monologue, which he uses in *The Sound and the Fury*, to interrupted monologue, that spoken to an audience, he is attempting to integrate external reality and inside views of experience "without doing violence to the convention of psychological realism." She too uses *Absalom, Absalom!* as exemplar text.

One of the most important essays of 1984 is Martin Kreiswirth's "Centers, Openings, and Endings: Some Faulknerian Constants" (*AL* 56:38–50). Deriving patterns from what seem to be myriad possibilities within Faulkner's fiction, Kreiswirth opens key fictions to new insight. Judith Bryant Wittenberg's "The Art of Ending" in *New Directions* (pp. 358–79), correlates with Kreiswirth's essay, but she stresses Faulkner's ending for *The Reivers* as entirely different from his customary mode of ending. His intention in that novel is to rehearse a 19th-century convention, that of ending as closure, so as to conclude his writing career.

Roger Fowler chose *The Sound and the Fury* to illustrate Faulkner's juxtaposition of modes of discourse in order to involve readers in the evaluation process ("Studying Literature as Language," *DQR* 14:171–84). Faulkner is able to use the structure of his discourse to take the place of authorial or narrative commentary.

c. Race. Except for commentary in analysis of individual novels such as *Light in August, Go Down, Moses,* and *Absalom, Absalom!,* the criticism on racial issues and Faulkner's use of those issues in his fiction was a single item, published in 1983: Günter Gentsch's *Faulkner zwischen Schwarz und Weiss: Betrachtungen zu Werk und Persönlichkeit des amerikanischen Nobelpreisträgers* (Akademie). Gentsch's approach is to study Faulkner's development through the portraits of his black characters and his reaction to the South's handling of racial problems. Drawing on Faulkner's letters and speeches as well as fiction, this Marxist-Leninist study is somewhat dated.

v. Individual Works to 1929

The Sound and the Fury had a great deal written about it this year, often in studies devoted to more general topics. Richard Pearce's *The Novel in Motion: An Approach to Modern Fiction* (Ohio, 1983) traces the explosion of energy that characterized many Modernist texts, using this novel as example. John J. Conder's *Naturalism in American Fiction* also focuses on this novel (pp. 160–95) as a culmination of the "second line of development" away from determinism in naturalism. Again drawing on Bergson, Conder identifies Quentin Compson as Bergson's shadow self, the social product lacking freedom which is the product of spatialized time. Each of the brothers, in fact, is a variant on Bergson's theories, a progression from "the bedrock human consciousness of Benjy to more developed consciousnesses"—climaxing in Dilsey's ideal selfhood.

James M. Mellard provides a new reading for the novel in "Faulkner's *Commedia:* Synecdoche and Anagogic Symbolism in *The Sound and the Fury*" (*JEGP* 83:534–46). He draws on Frye's anagogic criticism, using "the mode of synecdoche" to trace the image patterns of blood and voice, particularly in the fourth section. Quentin's voice is sacrificial (representing the Fall and ultimate alienation); Jason speaks of the weight of his family responsibilities (the Flesh); Benjy can only "try to say," but in that purpose comes closer to the spiritual, culminating in Reverend Shegog's sermon, which brings the final realization to Dilsey. (Shegog's sermon is also full of blood and voices.) While the novel is not Christian—and is, in fact, much more mythic, with Dilsey mediating between Mrs. Compson (the Terrible Mother) and Caddy (the Virgin Mother), Faulkner's use of Christian symbolism is crucial background, and provides our vision of Dilsey as the synecdochic image of the book as Pietà. She has the vision, she is the Madonna (in her caring for, and holding, Benjy), the emblem of resurrection.

James A. Means alludes to Eubulus and the hymn "Rock of Ages" in his note on this novel ("Faulkner's *The Sound and the Fury*," *Expl* 42:42–43). Joseph R. Urgo sees the Shegog sermon as central to interpretation of the novel in "A Note on Reverend Shegog's Sermon in Faulkner's *The Sound and the Fury*" (*NMAL* 8:Item 4). He compares several things—Shegog's physical size, his unfamiliarity, his purpose by coming to preach—with Faulkner's being tested through his works, having to become a virtuoso of his art.

Sergei Chakovsky's "Word and Idea in *The Sound and the Fury*" (*New Directions*, pp. 283–301) brings real meaning to the notion of "the word" as he defines Faulkner's structure as skewed to emphasize that importance. Because Benjy is unable to talk, our consciousness is alerted to the crucial message of the novel—the differences between word and action. In traditional fiction, the narrator cannot be a character; in this novel, he is, "and his word becomes a factor of the plot" as it becomes an act. "In his turn the narrator struggles with the plot, trying to set the logic of speech against the logic of life": Faulkner wrote an extremely innovative fiction.

In the same collection, Noel Polk's " 'The Dungeon Was Mother Herself': William Faulkner: 1927–1931" (pp. 61–93) analyzes this novel as well as *Sanctuary*, *Light in August*, and *Flags in the Dust* on the basis of Freudian conflicts and imagery related to them. Most of the male protagonists from this period of Faulkner's writing are drawn to, yet repulsed by, women—Quentin, Horace Benbow, Joe Christmas. As Polk describes Horace, for example, "Horace identifies himself completely with Temple, Little Belle, and Popeye: he is at one and the same time male, female, androgynous; the seducer and the seduced; the violater and the violated; the lover and the protector; father, brother, sister; son, lover, destroyer." He insists that we recognize the emotional tone of these works: "Childhood in Faulkner is almost invariably a terrifying experience." Emphasis on the child's relation to the mother (paralleling the man's to the woman) is a constant throughout these seemingly disparate novels (and stories). There is mention also of Freud's 1925 case history, "Wolf Man," with which *Sanctuary* has many similarities.

Sartoris also provoked several interesting essays this year: Nancy Dew Taylor argues ("Moral Housecleaning and Colonel Sartoris's Dream," *MissQ* 37:353–64) that Colonel Sartoris's refusal to carry a gun to meet Redmond was not a moral act but rather a self-serving one. He was, in effect, leaving his son to avenge his death and his dream, and Bayard recognizes the bind his father's act has placed him in when he says "He was wrong." What Bayard does is the real focus of Faulkner's novel. Dexter Westrum deals with the code of honor from another perspective in "Faulkner's Sense of Twins and the Code: Why Young Bayard Died" (*ArQ* 40:365–76). Bayard's suffering results not from jealousy but rather from the intense complementarity that twins experience (as witnessed in Faulkner's portrayal of Buck and Buddy McCaslin). Bayard's feelings for Johnny are complicated, however, by his Sartoris conscience, much like that of Quentin Compson: death becomes the logical answer in this world of convoluted decisions. Hans Beatrice asks some of the same questions in "A Future for Sartorism?" (*ES* 64[1983]:503–06), but concludes that Sartoris men follow a code of "violence, arrogance and rashness" which leads to self-destruction; whereas its women are realistic and hopeful.

Philip Cohen's note on "Ahenobarbus' Vestal: Belle Mitchell and Nero" (*NConL* 14:8–9) discusses Horace's descriptions of Belle in *Flags in the Dust*, and his discussion of Faulkner's trope, borrowed perhaps from James Branch Cabell in *Jurgen*, is useful ("Faulkner's Player and His Pawns: The Source of a Metaphor," *AN&Q* 23:16–19).

The earlier fiction received little comment: Lucas Carpenter's "Faulkner's *Soldiers' Pay:* 'Yaphank' Gilligan" (*NMAL* 8:Item 17) identifies the source for Gilligan's nickname as being the location of Camp Upton, in the middle of Long Island; Philip Castille's "From Pontchartrain to Yoknapatawpha: Faulkner's *Mosquitoes*" (*XUS* 83,iii:40–46) comments on the less-than-effective social criticism achieved as the novel becomes more and more an aesthetic treatise.

vi. Individual Works, 1930–39

Absalom, Absalom! once again received extensive commentary. Elisabeth Muhlenfeld edited *William Faulkner's* Absalom, Absalom! *A Critical Casebook* (Garland), which reprints essays or sections from books by Richard Poirier, Arthur L. Scott, James H. Justus, Floyd C. Waktins, James Guetti, Duncan Aswell, Walter Brylowski, John V. Hagopian, T. H. Adamowski, Carl E. Rollyson, Jr., Elisabeth Muhlenfeld, and François Pitavy. Each essay is provocative, useful, and—in keeping with the editor's rationale for inclusion—somewhat difficult to obtain. The most valuable part of the book is Muhlenfeld's introduction, tracing the composition of the novel from "Evangeline," connecting it with events in Faulkner's personal life, and providing information for the reader who knows little about the writer or this work.

David Krause continues his excellent work with Faulkner's use of letters in "Reading Bon's Letter and Faulkner's *Absalom, Absalom!*" (*PMLA* 99:225–41), using a sophisticated reader-response approach to describe the impact of that letter in this "novel unusually full of and self-reflexive about problematic acts of reading." His focus in this essay is on the scenes of the characters reading the texts; the development of the essay is the myriad uses we as readers make of those scenes, under Faulkner's expert tutelage. Reginald Martin places Bon's character in the matrix of black-white relations ("The Quest for Recognition over Reason: Charles Bon's Death-Journey into Mississippi," *SCB* 43[1983]:117–20), while Lynn Dickerson studies

"Thomas Sutpen: Mountaineer Stereotype in *Absalom, Absalom!* (*AppalJ* 12:73–78) and Michel Bandry discusses him as self-made man ("Et Sutpen crea Sutpen" in *From Rags to Riches: Le mythe du self-made man,* ed. Serge Ricard; Provence; pp. 83–94).

Elizabeth Langland places the novel as social novel, with Quentin's struggles to find a social truth about Sutpen and the South so as to come to terms with his own place in society as primary theme (*Society in the Novel;* N. C.). As she discusses Faulkner with Kafka and Pynchon, who all believe that "society, whether real or imagined, exerts an enormous influence on individuals," Langland stresses the mystery involved with assessment. As *Absalom, Absalom!* shows, knowledge itself is problematic. For Martin Christadler, the novel is of interest because of its historical focus ("William Faulkners *Absalom, Absalom!* (1936): Geschichte, Bewusstsein und Transzendenz: Das Ende des historischen Romans," *A&E* 24:51–65). Cheryl B. Torsney finds "The Vampire Motif in *Absalom, Absalom!*" (*SoR* 20: 562–69) of metaphoric value rather than literal. She compares Thomas Sutpen with Count Dracula in that both desire to transcend history. Sutpen's history embodies such traditional elements of the vampire myth as wrestling, rape, power, and illness. The Sutpen identity, and legend, drains everyone connected with it, including Quentin Compson.

Two items focus on the story that served as precursor for the novel, "Evangeline": Brenda G. Cornell's "Faulkner's 'Evangeline': A Preliminary Stage" (*SoQ* 22:22–41) and Steven T. Ryan's " 'Mistral' and 'Evangeline': The Gothic Derivation of *Absalom, Absalom!* (*KRev* 5[1983]:56–71). The latter argues that Faulkner started with Old World gothicism and then tried "to reshape the gothic tradition for a uniquely American experience." Other brief items include Clarke Owens's "Faulkner's *Absalom, Absalom!*" (*Expl* 42:45–46) in which Quentin's questions about why Rosa Coldfield singled him out to hear the Sutpen story lead to the destruction of linear time, and Virginia O. Bond's "The Twining of Wistaria" (*DeKalb Lit. Arts Jour.* 20:19–23) focuses on flower imagery.

Ikuko Fujihira studies textual revision in the novel, and considers the role of speech in narration compared to that of writing, "in "From Voice to Silence: Writing in *Absalom, Absalom!*" (*SELit,* Eng. no.:75–91).

As I Lay Dying also was the subject of a Garland casebook, this one edited by Dianne L. Cox. Cox's introduction is excellent, and the collection includes two new essays, one by Gail Moore Morrison ("The House That Tull Built," pp. 159–77, discussing the versions of the Bundren story as told by both Vernon and Cora Tull), the other by Catherine Patten ("The Narrative Design of *As I Lay Dying*," pp. 3–29; followed on pp. 30–32 with "The Chronology of *As I Lay Dying*," a day-by-day tracing of events).

Janis P. Stout considers this novel a blend of several types of "journey narratives" in her *The Journey Narrative in American Literature: Patterns and Departures* (Greenwood, 1983). Faulkner's deviation from standard formats shows some ambivalence in his choice of narrative form.

Perhaps the most important work on *As I Lay Dying* this year is Eric J. Sundquist's essay "Death, Grief, Analogues Form: *As I Lay Dying*" in *Philosophical Approaches to Literature: New Essays on Nineteenth- and Twentieth-Century Texts*, ed. William E. Cain (Bucknell, 1983; pp. 165–82). With ease and authority, Sundquist presents a thorough study of Faulkner's narrative method which focuses on the presentation of the self (the various selves) and enlarges earlier comprehension of character interaction in the novel. Also of value are John Tucker, "William Faulkner's *As I Lay Dying*: Working Out the Cubistic Bugs" (*TSLL* 26:388–404) (the various images, especially that of the coffin, are related to cubism and its aesthetics) and Patrick O'Donnell's "The Spectral Road: Metaphors of Transference in Faulkner's *As I Lay Dying*" (*PLL* 28:60–79).

The most important essay on *Sanctuary* this year is that by John T. Matthews, "The Elliptical Nature of *Sanctuary*" (*Novel* 17:246–65) in which Matthews proves that "Temple's story is an elaborate transmogrification of Horace's story, and that the two plots of the story, like the two versions of the novel, are more intimately related than earlier criticism has granted." Subtlety in the narration is achieved through calculated ellipsis, a subtlety that has led readers far from Faulkner's intentions, so far as Temple is concerned. Also of interest are Kathryn Lee Seidel's "From Narcissist to Masochist: A New Look at Temple Drake" (*JEP* 5:27–35) and Terry Heller's "Terror and Empathy in Faulkner's *Sanctuary*" (*ArQ* 40:355–64). The latter relies on reader-response theory, especially that of Wolfgang Iser, to build his argument. Both these essays are less convincing in light of Matthews's work.

Anthony Libby uses *Light in August* in "Conceptual Space: The Politics of Modernism" (*ChiR* 34:11–26) much as he does Richard Wright's *Native Son* to show the reader response as indicative of acceptance of the author's views, however oblique in statement. Of the other two essays dealing with this novel in 1984, Doreen Fowler attempts to avoid oversimplification in "Faulkner's *Light in August:* A Novel in Black and White" (*ArQ* 40:305–24). Although the author's light and dark imagery is complex, generally characters outside community—whether or not that position is desirable—have imagery of darkness connected with them. Society as well designates people who are outsiders as "dark." The ideal of both community and author, Fowler concludes, is to bring all human beings into worthwhile relationship with each other, into community, and into the light of fruition. Maria Gillen's "Joe Christmas as Symbol of Southern Protestant Christianity" (*NDQ* 51[1983]:137–43) relates Christmas and his treatment in *Light in August* to southern Protestantism.

Hollis Cate discusses "*Old Man:* Faulkner's Absurd Comedy" (*CollL* 11:186–90) as a source of genuine comedy, and Richard Godden and Pamela Rhodes comment on "*The Wild Palms:* Faulkner's Hollywood Novel" (*AmSI* 28[1983]:449–66) in relation to his life in Hollywood and California lifestyles, from the perspective of the Frankfurter Schule, Lukács, and intertextuality.

vii. Individual Works, 1940–49

Go Down, Moses continues to intrigue critics, whether considered as a whole or the sum of its various "story" parts. Thomas C. Foster treats the work as a whole in "History, Private Consciousness, and Narrative Form in *Go Down, Moses*" (*CentR* 28:61–76), noting Faulkner's expert syntactical cohesion and the seamless lines between form and content. Kathleen Latimer defends "Comedy as Order in *Go Down, Moses*" (*PCL* 10:1–8); her genre classification is valuable. Richard Pascal does a thematic analysis in "Love, Rapacity, and Community in *Go Down, Moses,*" (*ArielE* 15:63–79).

W. E. Schlepper comments upon "Truth and Justice in *Knight's Gambit*" (*MissQ* 37:365–75), stressing the thematic structure rather than just the development of Stevens's personality. Faulkner is trying to establish believing, knowing, and remembering as three different processes. The momentary attainment of insight and certainty was the point that interested Faulkner. All these stories deal with the question of how—once the extreme of murder is resorted to—people endeavor to gain truth and to approximate justice.

viii. Individual Works, 1950–62

Of Faulkner's later works, only *Requiem for a Nun* received attention, except fragmentarily or as a part of the *oeuvre*. Ikuko Fujihira compared the history of the community and the novel's relationship to legend through a discussion of the role of written language as compared to that spoken ("Beginning Was the Word: The Written/Spoken Word in *Requiem for a Nun*," *WiF* 6:57–76). In the same issue, Jacques Pothier discussed the community as a collective ego, using psychoanalytic theories ("Jefferson, From Settlement to City: The Making of a Collective Subject," pp. 36–56).

ix. The Stories

The importance of Faulkner's stories to a consideration of his writing as a whole seems finally to be recognized. Much about Faulkner's writing process is to be learned from Noel Polk's essay "William Faulkner's 'Carcassonne'" (*SAF* 12:29–44). The protagonist of the story is "one of a long line of Faulkner's failed idealists—a list including Horace Benbow, Quentin Compson, and Gavin Stevens"; and the way Faulkner builds the collection in which the story appears, *These 13*, tells a reader a great deal about his sense of structure. Polk also points to the connections with Eliot's poetry.

James B. Carothers ("Faulkner's Short Stories: 'And Now What's to Do'" in *New Directions*, pp. 202–26) suggests that his five short stories, the two novels sometimes treated as story collections (*The Unvanquished* and *Go Down, Moses*), and his uncollected stories constitute a substantial body of work that bears study, the same kind of study his novels receive. "As a general procedure, we ought to approach individual Faulkner short stories with an openness to the possibility that each of them has a coherent and discoverable narrative structure, a setting in place and time appropriate to the narrative situation, characters who are rendered with sufficient precision, solidity, and depth to stand up on their hind legs and cast shadows, and serious thematic purpose to reward close reading." Carothers then does just that, comparing Hemingway's "The Killers" to several of

Faulkner's "Lugger" stories. He also discusses Faulkner's characteristic ambiguity, and his use of trickster characters.

Among the best treatments of Faulkner's single short stories are
Dennis W. Allen's "Horror and Perverse Delight: Faulkner's 'A Rose
for Emily,'" *MFS* 30:685–96, a psychological approach to the social
stratification and the issues of sexuality the story recounts; Laurence
Jay Dessner's "William Faulkner's 'Dry September': Decadence Domesticated" (*CollL* 11:151–62), with an insistence that the imagery
leads to a meaning not usually found; and Michael Grimwood's
"'Delta Autumn': Stagnation and Sedimentation in Faulkner's Career" (*SLJ* 16:93–106), viewed as autobiographical fiction, stressing
the passivity of the old man as artist, whose central subject is exhaustion. Also useful is Joann Bomze, "Faulkner's 'Mountain Victory': The Triumph of 'The Middle Ground'" (*CEA* 46:9–11).

Michigan State University

10. Fitzgerald and Hemingway

Michael S. Reynolds

In the fall of 1984, when I agreed to do this essay, I took it to be a duty, something one did as a professional obligation. As I was always told in the Navy when assigned another collateral duty, "It's good training for a junior officer." After reading 12 books and 50-odd articles, I agree: it has been a learning experience. I've learned why in our own writing we so often ignore recently printed articles: if one does not read them when they first appear, one finds they are spending a year at the binder's. I've also learned a good deal about the difficulty of controlling my own biases, which you, gentle reader, will discover as you proceed. In vintage terms, it was not a classic year. Château Hemingway produced an almost record number of books and articles of uneven quality. Château Fitzgerald's yield was small but select, each book worth laying down.

i. Bibliography, Texts, and Biography

This year saw an important Fitzgerald bibliography, a major Fitzgerald biography, two significant Hemingway biographies, two other important peripheral biographies, a collection of Hemingway aphorisms on writing, a spate of Hemingway biographical articles of varying quality, and one memoir of minor value.

Jackson Bryer, with his continuing devotion to excellence in scholarship, brought out "Supplement One Through 1981" to his standard work, *The Critical Reputation of F. Scott Fitzgerald* (Archon Books). Since the first volume of his reference work (1967), Bryer has assembled another 542 pages of Fitzgerald bibliography presented in the same format as the original: reviews of Fitzgerald's works, articles, books, dissertations, and reviews of Zelda Fitzgerald's *Save Me the Waltz*. Checklist appendixes update and supplement the first publications of both Fitzgeralds. The beauty of Bryer's bibliography is not only his unflagging accuracy but also his pithy synopses of books and articles. Moreover, his index is a scholar's dream, making the contents completely accessible.

The year's most impressive biography was James Mellow's dual study of Scott and Zelda Fitzgerald: *Invented Lives* (Houghton Mifflin). For the beginner who has not read everything previously published on the subject, Mellow has written a deeply researched, finely honed study with a style and structure that make it a delight to read. Drawing on all primary and secondary sources, Mellow's analysis and use of detail warrants the attention of mature scholars as well. His reconstruction of the Fitzgerald-Hemingway relationship is particularly well wrought. With multiple views and judicious extrapolations, Mellow shows the Fitzgeralds feeding off of each other with Scott consuming a double portion. Skirting all sides of the biographical trap, Mellow manages to use the fiction to flesh out the biography without falling into the trap.

Invented Lives is also a literary biography as it relates life to fiction, fiction to life—a relationship with the Fitzgeralds so intricately interwoven that it is sometimes "impossible to know what is authentic and what is invented." Mellow neatly shows the couple using "their fictional stories to send each other signals, warnings, provide excuses and justifications for their behavior." He deflates the myth while simultaneously underlining Scott's need for myth in his life as well as his talent for appropriating the lives of others for his fiction. What may be the last Fitzgerald biography for a while is also one of the best.

There were two Hemingway biographies, both partial and both useful in different ways. Norberto Fuentes's *Hemingway in Cuba* (Lyle Stuart) is a rich and wonderful survey of Hemingway's last 24 years, the legendary years during which so many false or partial portraits of the artist-hero emerged. Mixing oral history with basic research, Fuentes gives us much new information on Hemingway's years at Finca Vigia.

Fuentes interviewed all the living Cubans and several Russians who were part of Hemingway's life between 1936 and 1960: men and women who will never again be available to American scholars. Using multiple perspectives, shifting point of view, and detailed surfaces, Fuentes paints a complex and contradictory Hemingway, along with a multitude of fresh details. Through long and multiple interviews with Gregorio, captain and cook on the *Pilar*, Fuentes recreates the days of sub-chasing that became *Islands in the Stream*. In the appendixes there is a room-by-room inventory of every item in the house. Even better, Fuentes tells us what was left behind when Mary Hemingway brought the manuscripts and paintings out in 1961. Still at La Vigia are the corrected galleys for *Across the River and Into the Trees*, portions of which Fuentes prints. There are draft fragments from *For Whom the Bell Tolls*; a corrected post-publication copy of "Night before Battle"; Hemingway's corrections to the film script of *The Old Man and the Sea*; and an early, unknown draft of "In Another Country" which includes what we now call "Now I Lay Me." Printed in the text are letters from Ivens Joris, Roman Karmen, and Winston Guest. In his appendixes, Fuentes prints the unpublished "Benchley"; draft dialogue for a nameless story; 33 pages of unpublished letters to the then Mary Welsh (November–December 1944); unpublished letters to family and friends; and incoming letters from Christopher LaFarge and Evan Shipman.

Another partial Hemingway biography was John Raeburn's meticulous and thorough *Fame Became Him: Hemingway as Public Writer* (Indiana) which examines the development of the public mask Hemingway tried out in the '20s, perfected in the '30s, and wore so frequently thereafter that he and the mask became one. Rather convincingly, Raeburn shows how Hemingway's nonfiction of the '30s consciously created the authoritative Papa figure: insider, expert, boxer, sportsman, soldier, hard drinker, "self-congratulatory, oracular, often belligerent, always self-confident" (pp. 97–98). From the hundreds of newspaper and popular magazine articles on Hemingway, we see Hemingway creating "a personal character so successful and so memorable that it bulked larger than his fiction in the public mind."

Two peripheral but important books came out last year which enrich the legendary lives of Fitzgerald and Hemingway. Noel Riley Fitch's *Sylvia Beach and the Lost Generation* (Norton, 1983) is a carefully researched panorama of the Paris literati as they circled about Shakespeare and Company's leading lady. Fitch has more information on Hemingway than on Fitzgerald, but the whole book is solid and substantial. Honoraria Murphy Donnelly, the only surviving Murphy child, wrote the lives of her parents in *Sara and Gerald* (Holt Rinehart) in which both Fitzgerald and Hemingway figure prominently throughout.

As a footnote to literary biography, Diane Darby has edited the journal of her father, Arnold Samuelson, *With Hemingway: A Year*

in Key West and Cuba (Random House). Fifty years ago Arnold
Samuelson entered literary history as the "Maestro" in Hemingway's
Esquire letter "Monologue to the Maestro: A High Seas Letter" (October 1935). In exchange for a year's writing tutorial, Samuelson
performed odd jobs on Hemingway's fishing boat, the *Pilar*, and
helped out around the house in Key West. More interested in his own
reactions than in detached observation, Samuelson says little about
Hemingway that we did not already know. He does, however, let us
inside the house on Whitehead Street to see Pauline, the second wife,
mistressing over the establishment. Unfortunately, Samuelson's journal does not give us any better information on Hemingway the writer.
Samuelson was present during the year Hemingway wrote *Green
Hills of Africa*, but we learn nothing significant about that composition. Nor do we learn anything new about Hemingway's advice to
young writers, for everything Samuelson records has appeared earlier
in other forms.

Larry Phillips's *Ernest Hemingway on Writing* (Scribner's) is a
collection of aphorisms culled from Hemingway's fiction, nonfiction,
and letters. Phillips has cut and re-pasted most of Hemingway's pithy
statements on his métier into generic categories like working habits,
characters, titles. Within each category the quotations are arranged
not in chronological order but according to the editor's sense of unity.
Without an index, finding a specific quotation can be time consuming.
Although Phillips has reproduced Hemingway's key statements from
the so-called nonfiction, he has relied heavily on the *Selected Letters*
to fill the book. His principle of selection is not stated, leaving the
scholar to wonder what was left out.

Anticipating the several new Hemingway biographies waiting in
the wings, scholars were busy adding small details to the broad
canvas. Jacqueline Tavernier-Courbin continued her relentless pursuit of Hemingway's re-creation of his Paris days ("Fact and Fiction
in *A Moveable Feast*," *HemR* 4,i:44–51). Through manuscript study
and meticulous research, she agrees with Hemingway's preface,
which warns the reader that the memoirs may be taken as fiction.
The major facts—the who, what, where, when—she shows to be
basically accurate; the fictional part resides in Hemingway's slanting
of facts, in his innocent and honest narrator, and in his sometimes
malicious intent.

Max Westbrook's "Grace Under Pressure: Hemingway and the
Summer of 1920" (*Writer in Context*, pp. 77–106) was the most im-

portant Hemingway biographical essay of the year. Drawn from the wealth of Hemingway family materials at the University of Texas, this essay gives us the first inkling of the new biographies to come. Westbrook rewrites the book on Hemingway's relations with his family after the Great War. For the first time we see the mother and son conflict without bias and clear of faulty memory. Westbrook then relates this biographical information to the family conflicts of Hemingway's early stories in such a judicious way that it should become a model for scholars.

Into the dark room of Hemingway's relationship with Ezra Pound during the poet's St. Elizabeths confinement, William French has let a bit of light with his clear assessment of the two men's friendship, printing an unpublished and richly humorous Hemingway letter to Pound ("Fragment of a Letter," *Yale Literary Mag.* 150:154–60).

With his full-scale Hemingway biography waiting in the wings, Jeffrey Meyers's four biographical essays printed in 1984 set a new indoor record. We may be reading parts of his biography in advance, or these essays may be material cut from the final draft—Meyers does not indicate which. In a concise and generally fair manner, Meyers first reviewed the numerous memoirs of family and friends ("Memoirs of Hemingway: The Growth of a Legend," *VQR* 60:587–613), concluding that the "scholar concerned with the truth finds himself lost in rumor and half-proved fact, in conflicting statements and pure fantasy." Meyers's next piece of literary history analyzed the publishing history and content of a 1934 essay on Hemingway that was suppressed in part by Hemingway himself ("Lawrence Kubie's Suppressed Essay on Hemingway," *AI* 41:1–18). Meyers also printed Kubie's essay—"Ernest Hemingway: Cyrano and the Matador"—a psychoanalytic exercise emphasizing the oedipal struggle beneath the surface of Hemingway's fiction. In "Chink Dorman-Smith and *Across the River and Into the Trees*" (*CritQ* 25,iv:35–42) Meyers provided the biographical background of Hemingway's close friend from the '20s, suggesting that Col. Cantwell's bitterness in *ARIT* is based on Eric Dorman-Smith's own military experience. In his best and most interesting essay, "Hemingway's Second War: The Greco-Turkish Conflict, 1920–1922" (*MFS* 30:25–36), Meyers clears the murky waters of Hemingway's journalistic involvement in that war, relating the importance of the experience to Hemingway's fiction.

In one of the better biographical essays of the year, Linda P. Miller ("Gerald Murphy and Ernest Hemingway: Part I," *SAF* 12:

129–44) drew on her deep Murphy research for a detailed analysis of the split between the two friends, which, Miller persuasively argues, was the result of Murphy's hero-worship and Hemingway's later guilt for divorcing Hadley—a divorce that he came to believe Murphy had too eagerly supported. As part of Miller's pending biography of Murphy, this essay and its second installment are clearly written, informative, and judgmental without prejudice. The Murphy letters to Hemingway are quoted extensively, four in their entirety.

ii. Influence Studies

Most of the influence studies focused on Hemingway, but Robert Roulston's "Something Borrowed, Something New: A Discussion of Literary Influences on *The Great Gatsby*" (*Critical Essays*, pp. 54–66), while opening no new ground is an admirable survey of all such studies on *Gatsby*. Roulston reviews and evaluates the wildly diverse suggestions that have been made, homing in on the most important ones: Oswald Spengler, T. S. Eliot, H. L. Mencken, Theodore Dreiser, Willa Cather, Henry James, and Joseph Conrad. His suggestions on Cather's influence are particularly interesting. Elizabeth Morgan's "Gatsby in the Garden: Courtly Love and Irony" (*CL* 11:163–77) showed how several traditional motifs worked in *Gatsby:* devotion, generosity, secret trysts, adultery. Morgan's conclusion that Fitzgerald uses courtly love motifs as ironic commentary on the lovers' emptiness is less convincing.

In Hemingway studies, Mark Spilka continued to open new territory with his "Victorian Keys to the Early Hemingway: Captain Marryat" (*Novel* 17:116–40). Noting several curious biographical parallels, Spilka firmly documents Hemingway's interest in Frederick Marryat which began in Oak Park and continued throughout his life. The British author, a martial man turned writer, exemplified the man of both action and letters. In Marryat's work Spilka finds several recurring themes which may have influenced Hemingway, who was drawn to Marryat's "descriptions of warfare and his repeated concern with . . . courage, skill and humanity." In a more narrowly focused note, "A Source for the Macomber 'Accident': Marryat's *Percival Keene*," (*HemR* 3,ii:29–37), Spilka uses solid, detailed parallels to show that cowardice while facing a dangerous animal, a shot in the back of the head, and a hunting accident grounded in hidden motives all have their antecedents in Marryat.

In an effort to specify James Joyce's oft-noted but seldom-detailed influence on Hemingway, Robert E. Gajdusek published a provocative monograph that deserves attention, *Hemingway and Joyce: A Study in Debt and Repayment* (Square Circle). First Gajdusek provides a clean overview of past critical statement and literary biography. Then, drawing on the entire Hemingway canon, Gajdusek finds Joycean themes, motifs, patterns, and techniques rampant in Hemingway. In particular, Gajdusek sees Hemingway using Joycean cyclical structures, crossovers, and rituals in a modified manner. Some will find the monograph too insistent, but long neglect of an obvious literary relationship may require extreme measures. Jeffrey Meyers's "Hemingway and Kipling: The Lesson of the Master" (*AL* 56:88–99) is a thorough and systematic overview of Hemingway's debt to Kipling which locates the themes, attitudes, subject matter, and treatments connecting the two authors.

Kenneth Johnston did two influence studies: "Hemingway and Freud: The Tip of the Iceberg" (*JNT* 14:68–73) and "Hemingway and Cézanne: Doing the Country" (*AL* 56:28–37). In the first, Johnston notes that the popularized triangular chart of the Freudian mind—the conscious, preconscious, and unconscious—is similar to Hemingway's omission theory in which only one eighth of the story was clearly visible, the rest omitted. Like Hemingway's theory, Freud said, "The poet's art consists essentially in covering up." In his Cézanne comparison, Johnston gives clear descriptions of the Cézanne paintings available to Hemingway and then looks at the painter's omission of detail and restructuring of nature. In a clear example, Johnston compares "Up in Michigan," written before Hemingway had absorbed Cézanne, and "Big Two-Hearted River," a post-Cézanne story, to show what Hemingway learned about landscape from the painter.

iii. Criticism

a. **Full-Length Studies.** There were no canonical studies of Fitzgerald this year, and of numerous Hemingway books, only one attempted to explain the entire canon. Gerry Brenner's *Concealments in Hemingway's Works* (Ohio State, 1983) is the most irritating, informative, obsessed, provocative, eclectic, and ultimately important analysis of Hemingway's life work that we have had in some time. Combining New Critical, generic, and psychoanalytic approaches,

Brenner, whether one agrees with him or not, cannot be ignored. Several of his chapters have been reviewed in earlier years, but the pattern of his approach was not obvious on a piecemeal basis.

Every chapter holds some surprise. For example, Brenner finds that Jake Barnes and Frederic Henry are both untrustworthy narrators, that Santiago is a malicious old man, that Frederic Henry's narrative is a long suicide note, that Hemingway was latently homoerotic, that Hemingway's unrequited fixation on his father lies beneath the surface of all the works: suggestions guaranteed to provoke response. Brenner also makes a strong case for the generic models of Hemingway's middle period: Izaak Walton's *Compleat Angler* and *Death in the Afternoon*; the tragedy of blood and *To Have and Have Not* (Harry Morgan doomed from the first day in Havana); the epic and *For Whom the Bell Tolls*; Dante and *Across the River and Into the Trees*.

In a badly printed volume, E. Nageswara Rao's *Ernest Hemingway: A Study of His Rhetoric* (Humanities Press) analyzes Hemingway's rhetorical devices, looking at change over time. Rao reinforces the argument that Hemingway's writing breaks into distinct periods, each with its own rhetorical devices. Rao concludes that the later rhetoric "was less effective and less persuasive" than Hemingway's early work.

In response to early critics and contemporary feminists, Roger Whitlow's *Cassandra's Daughters: The Women in Hemingway* (Greenwood) pushes the thesis that we have misread most, if not all, of Hemingway's female characters. Quite rightly he sees the psychic scars that several heroines bring to their relationships. Whitlow argues that Catherine Barkley, Marie Morgan, Maria, and Renata offer a life-affirming alternative to the mission-oriented men with whom they are involved. Whitlow's emphasis falls on the therapeutic effect of love. In trying to offset the bitchiness of Brett Ashley and Margot Macomber, he is less successful. (Margot had only four seconds to get off her shot, which shows she did not intend to kill her husband.) Whitlow's thesis and arguments are undercut when he ignores much of the critical commentary from the last ten years. By referring to only eight essays written since 1974, he ends up beating a few dead horses no longer worth punishing.

b. **Collections.** The year produced two notable collections of essays, one on each author. First, Scott Donaldson edited *Critical Es-*

says on F. Scott Fitzgerald's The Great Gatsby, an excellent selection of previously published essays and four new essays (see section *iii. d.*). From what could have been a multivolume work had he reprinted all of the *Gatsby* criticism, Donaldson judiciously chose representative essays, primarily from the '60s and '70s, to complement earlier collections. The book is sectioned into overviews, craftsmanship, critical approaches, and "history-myth-meaning." There is also a fine section of letters to and from Fitzgerald which bear on *Gatsby*. This collection provides easy access to mainstream *Gatsby* criticism from the last 20 years, and its new essays point toward the future.

The second collection, Jim Nagel's *Writer in Context* (see section *iii. b.*) is a rare animal: a conference collection with a coherent pattern and flow. The four sections—reminiscences, craft of composition, interpretations biographical and critical, and relationships with other writers—represent the four basic directions of Hemingway scholars and illustrate the change that has taken place in the last ten years of the Hemingway business. Nagel persuaded Charles Scribner, Jr., Patrick Hemingway, and Tom Stoppard to speak of their relationships with Hemingway. More valuable are the two excellent manuscript studies: Robert W. Lewis's "The Making of *Death in the Afternoon*" and Paul Smith's "The Tenth Indian and the Thing Left Out" (see section *iii. d.*). The "Biographical and Critical" section contains the totally unexpected essay by Max Westbrook—"Grace Under Pressure: Hemingway and the Summer of 1920" (see section *i.* above).

c. **General Essays.** The strangest Hemingway item of 1984 was Malcolm Cowley's "Hemingway's Wound—And Its Consequences for American Literature" (*GaR* 38:223–39) which was more about Cowley's conflict with Kenneth Lynn than about Hemingway. Lynn had attacked Cowley's introduction to the Viking *Portable Hemingway* (1944) as a stimulus to anti-American interpretations of our literature. Cowley's amusing counterattack gives his own version of 1930–50 literary history, denying political motivation in his Viking introduction. Cowley also combats Lynn's interpretation of "Big Two-Hearted River" by referring to his correspondence with Hemingway, letters that are now in a private collection. In the following issue (*GaR* 38:668–72), the feud continued with letters from Kenneth Lynn and Philip Young along with Cowley's response to both. The Lynn-Cowley imbroglio remains unsettled on both sides. More may be heard from these two later.

Because of Hemingway's anti-intellectual pose, theorists have not been attracted to his work, but Erik Nakjavani's complexly worded essay ("The Aesthetics of Silence: Hemingway's 'Art of the Short Story,'" *HemR* 3,ii:38–45) begins to reconcile Hemingway's deceptively simple iceberg theory of omission with the whole theory of silence, its background and its aesthetic. Relating Hemingway's idea to phenomenologists and Heidegger, this essay is obviously prefatory to a book-length study of Hemingway's aesthetics.

Responding to feminist attacks on Hemingway's treatment of women, several critics sprang to the defense. In a compassionate review of Hemingway's "marriage group," Charles J. Nolan ("Hemingway's Women's Movement," *HemR* 3, ii:14–22) argued that Hemingway frequently shows great sympathy for the plight of long-suffering women coupled with ego-centered males, who, insensitive to the women's needs, blame their own failures on the women. In what may be the best single essay on Hemingway's female characters, Robert D. Crozier, S. J., in his "The Mask of Death, The Face of Life: Hemingway's Feminique" (*HemR* 4,i:2–13) examined the roles of Maria, Pilar, and Renata, showing in detail the values they represent. Crozier's analysis is systematic, coherent, and valuable. Contrary to mainstream belief, Crozier shows how these Hemingway women possess and share important qualities, without which the male characters would be the less.

d. **Essays on Specific Works: Fitzgerald.** *Tender is the Night* received short but significant shrift in Judith Fetterley's sometimes strident but provocative feminist indictment "Who Killed Dick Diver? The Sexual Politics of *Tender is the Night*" (*Mosaic* 17,i:111–28). Her thesis—that culture, not biology, allows man to impose upon woman her fate—concludes that Fitzgerald blamed the American crackup on the feminization of our culture. Fetterley believes that Fitzgerald's own sanity and career were "purchased at the price of Zelda's." In the novel Fitzgerald reverses the sexual roles: Dick Diver creates the motherly, tender, woman's world and "women respond to him as if he were a woman." Because it is Dick, not Nicole, who is destroyed by love, Fitzgerald, in a self-serving way, blames the vulnerability of the American male on his growing femininity. Sometimes contradictory but always interesting, Fetterley's argument finds a good deal of support in the James Mellow biography above. Robert Wexelblatt's interesting note on allusions that frame the novel—

"Doctor Diver and General Grant in Fitzgerald's *Tender is the Night*"—establishes the parallels between the Union general and Diver (*NMAL* 8: Item 16).

Once again scholars and critics spent more effort on *The Great Gatsby* than on any other Fitzgerald work. The results were mixed but with generally high marks. The most interesting essay was Ross Posnock's " 'A New World, Material Without Being Real': Fitzgerald's Critique of Capitalism in *The Great Gatsby*" (*Critical Essays*, pp. 201–13). Without turning the novel into a polemic, Posnock takes Fitzgerald's avowed Marxism seriously. Drawing on basic ideas from Marx and Georg Lukács, Posnock looks at the effects of corruptive capitalism, effects that are the chaos at the novel's core where money alienates and people become commodities. This corruption touches and taints everyone in the novel; Jay Gatsby and his dream are corrupted by capitalism, but so are the Buchanans and Nick Carraway. Nick's romanticism at the end cannot evade the "reality of exploitation."

The recurring question of Nick Carraway's reliability as narrator got its share of attention. Kent Cartwright found Carraway's narration at crucial moments confused, misleading, or inaccurate; the narrator's view of Gatsby exaggerated, unstable, and self-compromising. In "Nick Carraway as Unreliable Narrator" (*PLL* 20:218–32) Cartwright argues for an open-ended novel, which Carraway's judgments prohibit: it is Nick, not Gatsby, who reduces the dream to ashes; it is Nick's irrelevant detachment that misrepresents the dream. While covering the same ground, Scott Donaldson's "The Trouble With Nick" (*Critical Essays*, pp. 131–39) is a more balanced and more convincing assessment of Carraway's narrative reliability. Donaldson correctly defines Nick's character: his snobbishness; his evasion of emotional commitment; his wit, irony, and sarcasm; his "basic contempt for mankind"; and his romantic inclinations, which run counter to his sense of propriety. For Nick, decorum is more important than his self-proclaimed honesty. Nick's reliability is partial; he is a divided man, the perfect narrator who never understands Jay Gatsby completely.

Alan Margolies surveyed *Gatsby*'s checkered career in other media in "Novel to Play to Film: Four Versions of *The Great Gatsby*" (*Critical Essays*, pp. 187–200), an excellent synopsis of the novel's life on stage and screen. Margolies provides hard-to-find details of the various adaptations and evaluates what went wrong, what got changed.

He concludes that as yet Fitzgerald's balance between satire and the dream has evaded his adaptors. A more important survey was Jackson Bryer's "Style as Meaning in *The Great Gatsby:* Notes Toward a New Approach" (*Critical Essays*, pp. 117–29). With his customary thoroughness, Bryer reviews chronologically the development of major *Gatsby* trends, concluding that much scholarship has been either redundant or too narrowly focused. Finally Bryer suggests and illustrates what should be the next stage: the detailed study of Fitzgerald's style and language. Bryer shows how ambivalent adjectives and evocative verbs do, at points, "encapsulate" the meanings of the novel.

e. **Essays on Specific Works: Hemingway.**   Perhaps because it is so often in the classroom, *The Sun Also Rises* continued to attract more than its share of attention. As the following essays show, we've reached a point of diminishing returns on this novel. The critic who does not draw on primary materials or expand his context runs the danger of self-abusive cleverness.

In "Jake's Odyssey: Catharsis in *The Sun Also Rises*" (*HemR* 4,i:33–36) Wolfgang E. H. Rudat pursues the Circe allusion but is more interested in the psychological implications of the novel's end, which he claims reverses Odysseus's relationship with Circe and exorcises all romantic illusions. In "Robert Cohn, the Fool of Ecclesiastes in *The Sun Also Rises*" (*DR* 63:98–106), S. A. Cowan tries to establish that "Robert Cohn symbolizes the concept of folly in Ecclesiastes." That Cohn is a fool we've long agreed on; that Hemingway modeled him on the biblical wisdom of the prophet, while obvious to Cowan, is not so obvious in the manuscript where there is no indication that Hemingway consulted the Bible for his title until he had finished his first draft. Nevertheless, this essay is a useful delineation of Cohn's foolishness. Nina Schwartz, in her essay "Lovers' Discourse in *The Sun Also Rises:* A Cock and Bull Story" (*Criticism* 26: 49–69), creates a sometimes too clever explanation of "the dialectic of castration and desire." Schwartz combines Derrida and neo-Freudian terminology to argue that "Jake's loss [castration] is thus a magnificent gain" for it enables him to master Brett, "evoking in her a desire he will never fulfill." Schwartz parallels the Jake-Brett relationship in a not altogether convincing way with the Romero-bull relationship, in which Romero's bull ring behavior "sounds suspiciously like that of a woman arousing a lover's desire." This difficult analysis ends up with the dilemma of the bullfight depicting "the symbolic destruction of man by woman." The essay's conclusion fails to bring the two elements of the paper back into clear focus.

Charles J. Nolan's "Shooting the Sergeant—Frederic Henry's Puzzling Action" (*CollL* 11:269–75) tries to make this understated action in *A Farewell to Arms* more understandable. His argument finally rests on Frederic's having acted "properly under military law," which does not really raise Frederic to the heroic level Nolan wants for him. A more complex and interesting article with broad implications is Trevor McNeely's "War Zone Revisited: Hemingway's Aesthetics and *A Farewell to Arms* (*SDR* 22,iv:14–38). McNeely approaches the apparent split between a love story and a war story from the wider perspective of "realism" and "romance," which he takes as the twin poles of Hemingway's world. In a detailed and complex argument, McNeely suggests that "thinking" in Hemingway falsifies reality, which is his touchstone for "truth." Hemingway's characters are ultimately crippled by love, for love is a romantic illusion, equally unfaithful to "truth." As McNeely suggests throughout the article, the implications of his analysis are far-reaching.

Increased interest in Hemingway's so-called failed novels is beginning to offset their state of neglect. Steven T. Ryan's "Prosaic Unity in *To Have And Have Not*" (*HemR* 4,i:27–32) sees Hemingway's experimental novel as a complex structure of oppositions in which the roles of the various women are crucial. As the several women—those who have had "Life" and those who have not—respond to the deaths of loved ones, they complete a complex range of responses. Ryan's analysis is another step in reassessing the importance of Hemingway's female characters.

Hemingway's texts and manuscripts continued to receive attention this year. Until a standard edition eventually restores the inadvertent deletions and corrects the multiple errors, scholars should keep the pressure applied. A sadly neglected Hemingway book received special attention in Robert W. Lewis's densely packed article "The Making of *Death in the Afternoon*" (*Writer in Context*, pp. 31–52). Based on the University of Texas manuscript, Lewis describes in detail the first draft and its multiple revisions, which are characterized as developmental, stylistic, and thematic. Lewis gives clear descriptions of each type with judicious explanations for their occurrence. Included are numerous short quotes from manuscript and a partial list of errors in the published version. This preliminary study underlines the need for more work on *Death in the Afternoon*. In fact, Lewis's article is the blueprint for a book that needs to be written.

A clear example of misprinted text is Christopher Knight's argument ("Ernest Hemingway's 'Under the Ridge': a Textual Note," *NMAL* 7,iii:no.15) that a dropped holograph emendation to this minor piece in fact improves the story. Reproducing Hemingway's paragraph, Knight shows that without the passage the text has an obvious problem in narrative continuity. Neal B. Houston's "Old Lady, Now Here Is Where the 'Wow' Is" (*AN&Q* 22:78–80) compares the unpublished manuscript "There's One in Every Town" with Hemingway's encapsulated story of homosexuality in *Death in the Afternoon*, showing the differences between the two versions. A more substantive article based on manuscript study was Paul Smith's "The Tenth Indian and the Thing Left Out" (Nagel, pp. 53–74). Smith examines the three Kennedy Library drafts of Hemingway's "Ten Indians," finding the neat parallel structure present from the first draft. Dating and comparing the three variant endings, Smith reaches some pertinent conclusions about Hemingway's much-misinterpreted omission theory. He also prints and compares manuscript deletions and changes to good advantage.

Alice Hall Petry's detailed and coherent analysis of Liz Coates's brutal seduction ("Coming of Age in Hortons Bay: Hemingway's 'Up in Michigan,'" *HemR* 3,ii:23–28) emphasizes Hemingway's implicit sympathy with the female condition. Petry argues convincingly that Hemingway's interest resides in the hopes, illusions, responses, and fears of the woman.

Now widely anthologized, "Hills Like White Elephants" received yet more attention, perhaps more than it will bear. Philip Sipiora ("Hemingway's 'Hills Like White Elephants,'" *Expl* 42,iii:50) adds up the pregnant woman's alcoholic intake and concludes that she is legally drunk by the time the train arrives. What appears to be assent to her abortion is only her inebriated condition speaking; nothing has been resolved. *Au contraire* says Thomas M. Gilligan ("Topography in Hemingway's 'Hills Like White Elephants,'" *NMAL* 8: Item 2). Retracing the relationship of train station, river, track, and sun, Gilligan concludes that the debating couple actually do not go to Madrid, but are getting on the Barcelona train, having decided "to allow the pregnancy to continue."

Kenneth G. Johnston (" 'The Snows of Kilimanjaro': An African Purge," *SSF* 21:223–27) gets caught in the biographical trap when he argues that "Snows" may be read "as a report on the artistic and spiritual health of its author." Johnston's correlation between the failed fictional author and Hemingway depends upon Hemingway's slight output of fiction between 1929 and 1936. Johnston notes that during this period Hemingway was prolific in nonfiction, but he had neglected his "serious craft." This judgment, one that Hemingway never made, says that nonfiction is not serious, a debatable conclusion. In "The Songs in Hemingway's 'The Snows' " (*AN&Q* 23:46–48), Johnston shows how the allusions to Mother Goose and Cole Porter lyrics relate meaningfully to the story's conflicts, conjuring up "a world of lost innocence."

Robert Fleming's "Hemingway's 'The Killers': The Map and the Territory" (*HemR* 4,i:40–43) is a first-rate analysis of the faulty signs by which Hemingway underlines his theme: as the signs no longer mean what they once did, neither do the old codes of the previous generation have the same significance. Referring back to the manuscript drafts, Fleming shows Hemingway consciously creating absurdist detail that emphasizes this black comedy of misunderstandings and false impressions. Nick Adams's psychological problems continue to fascinate critics like Howard L. Hannum ("Soldier's Home: Immersion Therapy and Lyric Pattern in 'Big Two-Hearted River,' " *HemR* 3,ii:2–13). While suggestive and in part interesting, Hannum's essay is discursive and erratically organized with too many asides. His main points fail to coalesce in a coherent way. Hannum, like many readers, relies heavily on Nick stories written both before and after "Big Two-Hearted River," turning the sequence into a life story that Hemingway never published.

In what may be the year's most amusing Hemingway note, Paul Smith and Jacqueline Tavernier-Courbin spoof esoteric scholarship with their amusing parody " 'Terza Riruce': Hemingway, Dunning, Italian Poetry" (*HemR* 3,ii:50–51), which is so well done that some may take it seriously. The doctor says: consult the Hemingway MS and add three grains of salt before using.

North Carolina State University

Part II

11. Literature to 1800

William J. Scheick

Colonial American studies this year are characterized by excessively long titles and a tendency to discuss cultural rather than specifically literary features of early American texts. Several of these discussions are very valuable, but the most outstanding works this year are encyclopaedic volumes summarizing in useful detail the current state of historical and literary scholarship in the field. These works form a plateau, as it were, that makes possible an overview of early American studies in a consolidating way which should result in a more informed and vigorous survey of the diverse terrain of early American literature.

i. Puritan Poetry

In "Puritan Poetry: Its Public and Private Strain" (*EAL* 19:107–21) Agnieszka Salska rehearses the obvious in noting that distinct polarities in Puritan verse reveal a division in poetic sensibility; whereas private verse psychologically probes religious anxiety and doubt, public poems didactically confirm Puritan communal ideals. The most popular example of public verse in Puritan times is scrutinized in "'Ladders of Your Own': *The Day of Doom* and the Repudiation of 'Carnal Reason'" (*EAL* 19:42–67), in which Jeffrey A. Hammond argues that Michael Wigglesworth focused on the limits of carnal reason by presenting the saints in his poem as silent witnesses, whereas the damned in the poem use words in an argument of verbal distortion originating from fallen modes of rational thought that ought to have been replaced by faith and silent assent. One of Wigglesworth's contemporaries who worried about her silence—"Whilst I as mute, can warble forth no higher layes"—is the subject of five chapters in Wendy Martin's *An American Triptych: Anne Bradstreet, Emily Dickinson, Adrienne Rich* (N. C.), pp. 14–76. Martin tries to demarcate three stages in Bradstreet's poetry: the first documents the poet's desire to be an accomplished artist by relying on male models; the second, free from male example, defines her human attachments and doubts; the third, when the fatherly deity supplanted earlier male example, records her final concern with heaven. Although some confusion and dubious conclusions mar Martin's discussion—e.g., "she was finally unable to fully accept the Puritan God" (p. 19); "Bradstreet finally managed to believe in God" (p. 76)—and although Martin's feminist slant is somewhat too restrictive and overstated, she is on target in assessing Bradstreet's deference to men as ironic (I would say tongue-in-cheek), the poet's privileging of female experience, and the author's sensitivity to the excommunication of her younger sister.

That Bradstreet's poems, not to mention the prose of her contemporaries, are replete with Classical allusions is a fact one would never guess from reading John C. Shields's "Jerome in Colonial New England: Edward Taylor's Attitude toward Classical Paganism" (SP 81:161–84), which makes much ado about nothing in its enumeration of references to Classical lore in Taylor's verse. Shields claims that in his youth Taylor was enthusiastic about the Classics, later restrained this enthusiasm, and still later again expressed his appreciation of pagan culture and literature. The most Shields can conclude from this pattern is that these allusions add texture to Taylor's work, which the poet did not want to see published by his heirs (Shields seems unaware that this notion was dismissed by scholars long ago) because it revealed his improper attraction to pagan culture and literature. Classical ideas inform as well Catherine Rainwater's "Edward Taylor's Reluctant Revolution: The New Astronomy in the *Preparatory Meditations*" (*AmerP* 1,ii:4–17), an excellent essay maintaining that although Taylor's poems reveal an aesthetic nostalgia for the pleasant order of the crystal spheres, he intellectually tried to accommodate the findings of the new astronomy. In a close reading of verbal nuance in "Meditation 2.21" Rainwater demonstrates Taylor's reluctant effort to let go gradually of the old cosmology and to manage new-astronomy ideas about heliocentricity, planetary motion, and reflected light in order to reconcile them to Puritan doctrine. The specific Puritan doctrine concerning God's delayed just wrath is offered as an explanation of Taylor's use of the expression "Oh Leaden heel'd" in "Taylor's 'Preparatory Meditation 2.1'" (*Expl* 43:22–23) by J. Daniel Patterson.

A contemporary of Taylor figures in "Pictures of New England's

Apocalypse: Benjamin Tompson's Transformation of the British Advice-to-a-Painter Poem" (*EAL* 19:268–78), in which Robert L. Pincus argues that whereas its English prototypes are panegyric and satiric, Tompson's "Marylburyes Fate" is elegiac and castigatory, giving political events a sacred millennial interpretation in the tradition of the jeremiad. Not the advice-to-a-painter poem but English philosophic sublime poetry influenced the generation of poets after Tompson. In "The Religious Sublime and New England Poets of the 1720s" (*EAL* 19:321–48) David S. Shields notes that whereas natural sublime verse delights in the ability of reason to harmonize the features of nature, the religious sublime verse of early 18th-century New England poets dissolved the sense of rationally perceived harmony and appealed to the reader's imagination in order to evoke terror and wonder; in appealing to the imagination these poets were conjoining theology and art.

Not terror and wonder, but death, disaster, and celebration inform the verse collected in *Early American Latin Verse, 1625–1825* (Bolchazy-Carducci), Leo M. Kaiser's anthology of 111 untranslated poems. Although Kaiser's introduction is brief, his biographical information on the known authors of these poems is helpful. The dedications, subscription lists, and illustrations of colonial verse publications are documented in "Poet and Printer in Colonial and Federal America: Some Bibliographic Perspectives" (*PAAS* 92[1982]:265–361) by Roger E. Stoddard.

ii. Puritan Prose

In "John Winthrop Writes His Journal" (*WMQ* 41:185–212) Richard S. Dunn discusses the gradual changes in composition that Winthrop's notebook underwent as its author became more of a historian than a journalist; Winthrop's later entries, no longer written shortly after the events they record, were composed in lengthy sections at one sitting and reveal a greater emphasis on the details of political and theological issues. The degree to which the private writings of a Puritan reflect the larger social issues of his time is also the subject of David D. Hall's "The Mental World of Samuel Sewall" (in *Saints and Revolutionaries: Essays on Early American History* [Norton], ed. David D. Hall, John M. Murrin, and Thad W. Tate, pp. 75–95), which concludes that in its focus on time, history, and catastrophe Sewall's diary records the extensive amount of ritual that informed Puritan behavior. A Puritan mental ritual of sorts, according to Richard VanDerBeets in *The Indian Captivity Narrative: An American Genre* (Univ. Press), seems evident in the pattern of separation ("death"), transformation, and reunion ("rebirth") that characterizes the lives of the protagonists of Indian captivity narratives. VanDerBeets delineates three stages in the development of these narratives: in the 17th and the early 18th century these accounts rely on religious typology and symbolism in designating the captivity as a divine test; in the early and mid-18th century these accounts became less religious in design and more propagandistic concerning Native Americans and the French; in the late 18th century and the early 19th century these stories became stylized, sensationalized, and exaggerated pulp thrillers.

Captivity of another kind, specifically the danger of being taken into captivity by the Old World during the 1680s and 1690s (when England was especially interfering in colonial affairs) concerns Terry Engebretsen in "Joshua Moody's Funeral Sermon for Thomas Daniel as Political Jeremiad" (*CRevAS* 15:369–83). Engebretsen remarks how Moody builds implicit political views into the traditional argument of a sermon in a way that suggests the English political threat to the American colonies and that laments the possible divine punishment in store for a potentially wayward New Israel. Another way in which the traditional form of the sermon was modified interests Teresa Toulouse, whose very instructive " 'The Art of Prophesying': John Cotton and the Rhetoric of Election" (*EAL* 19:279–99) details how Cotton sometimes fragmented and subverted the conventional formulaic structure of the sermon because he aimed his preaching at the elect; in Cotton's opinion, the elect did not need a forward-focused unraveling of a progressive and deductive sermonic argument, but benefited from a digressive manner informed by an imagistic suspension of various possibilities and incomplete meanings.

Certainly not likely to be among this elect group, at least in the opinion of Cotton and his associates, are most of the "wayward" individuals at the center of Philip F. Gura's attention in *A Glimpse of Sion's Glory: Puritan Radicalism in New England, 1620–1660* (Wesleyan), a well-detailed, if repetitious, account of the ideas of separatists, radical spiritists, general and particular baptists, millenarians, and Quakers. Gura convincingly concludes that New England Puritanism developed as it did because of, not in spite of, radicals who criticized nonseparating Congregationalists and that Puritanism was indeed pluralistic, evincing a gradual evolution of ideology that incorporated some of the energy of radical thought. Gura's argument for a gradual evolution of theology would have been aided had he remarked the Protestant notion of a continuing Reformation, which as an underlying idea grants Protestant religions a divinely sanctioned space in which to develop and modify beliefs. One of the most prominent of the radicals in Gura's discussion also appears in Sydney V. James's "Ecclesiastical Authority in the Land of Roger Williams" (*NEQ* 57:323–46), which focuses on the quarrels of Rhode Island settlers concerning integrity of conscience and control of the church. Apparently no such quarrel emerged among the early church members of Cambridge, Massachusetts. In "The Meeting of Elite and Popular Minds at Cambridge, New England, 1638–1645" (*WMQ* 41: 32–48) George Selement studies the conversion narratives collected in Thomas Shepard's *Confessions* and concludes that Shepard's parishioners understood well his teachings and, as a result, that these documents reveal something like a "collective mentality" which can be assessed from a history-of-ideas approach. No "collective mentality" of this kind, however, appeared in the Northampton congregation during Eleazer Mather's ministry. In "Preparing the Way for Stoddard: Eleazer Mather's *Serious Exhortation* to Northampton" (*NEQ* 57:240–54) Philip F. Gura demonstrates the laity's fear of ministerial prerogative on the subject of church membership, a fear also evident later during the ministry of Solomon Stoddard.

Eleazer's brother figures in "Increase Mather's Friends: The Trans-Atlantic Congregational Network of the Seventeenth Century" (*PAAS* 94:59–96), in which Francis J. Bremer traces in detail the web of informal personal contacts between New England and transAtlantic Puritans that helped preserve a sense of ideological conformity in the colonies for three generations. Increase's son, especially his search for ideological conformity, is the subject of Kenneth Silverman's *The Life and Times of Cotton Mather* (Harper). Silverman's Mather is not so much a "national gargoyle" as he is a very human man of conflicts and tensions, someone at once retrospective and forward-looking, ambitious and self-deprecating. Silverman's Mather struggles with self-doubt and religious qualms; he is a man sensitive to others (particularly members of his family) and equally sensitive to slights (even imagined ones). Silverman is little interested in Mather's ideas, but he has given us a useful impression of Mather's humanity.

An excerpt from Cotton Mather's prose appears in *American Colonial Prose: John Smith to Thomas Jefferson* (Cambridge), an eccentric anthology edited by Mary Ann Radzinowicz, whose introduction emphasizes the Englishness of American origins and offers an interesting contrast between Smith and Bradford. Not a single sermon is included in this anthology, which features brief passages by Smith, Bradford, Mather, Mary Rowlandson, Sarah Kemble Knight, William Byrd II, Jonathan Edwards, Benjamin Franklin, and Thomas Jefferson. Similarly eccentric is Stephen Fender's *American Literature in Context, I: 1620–1830* (Methuen, 1983), which is a serviceable guide for students to some of the prose works representative of colonial America. Fender is especially good on the early American tendency to write catalogues, but his work is not at all original and utterly lacks any discussion of the writings of Bradstreet, Taylor, and Wigglesworth, albeit works by Philip Freneau and Joel Barlow are presented.

iii. The South

An inventory of estates, explain Joseph F. Kett and Patricia A. Mc-Clung in "Book Culture in Post-Revolutionary Virginia" (*PAAS* 94: 97–147), reveals that except for the Bible, books were depended upon little for ideas even by wealthy late 18th-century residents in Virginia. More than a century earlier in Virginia, however, George Sandys believed that books were central transmitters of knowledge and that poetry in particular bridged the distance between the divine origin of truth and human comprehension of it. In his translation of *Metamorphoses*, argues Lee T. Pearcy in *The Mediated Muse: English Translations of Ovid, 1560–1700* (Archon; pp. 37–99), Sandys kept in mind that the oblique truths of Ovid's myths could be reconciled to the lucid truths of Scripture; his translation therefore differed from others because Sandys attempted to render features of Ovid's rhetoric into English in order to avoid interfering with the transmission of the truth underlying the myths in *Metamorphoses*.

Just as Sandys recessed his authorial presence and emphasized the poem, so did Ebenezer Cook a generation later in Maryland. In "The Case against Ebenezer Cooke's Sot-Weed Factor" (*AL* 56:251–61) Robert Micklus cautions that we should not associate the views of the narrator in "The Sot-Weed Factor" with Cook's opinions, for the narrator is presented as a cowardly buffoon whose credibility is destroyed by Cook. In contrast, Peter Wagner's " 'The Female Creed': A New Reading of William Byrd's Ribald Parody" (*EAL* 19:122–37) argues that no distinction exists between Byrd and his persona in the use of scatological and obscene language to satirize superstitions, Roman Catholics, and the gentry. In the earliest of his diaries, however, Byrd's narrating voice fails to conform to his image of himself; subsequently, observes Norman S. Grabo in " 'Going Steddy': William Byrd's Literary Masquerade" (*YES* 13[1983]:84–96), in his writings Byrd tries on a series of masks until the explosive self of the early diaries gives way in *The History of the Dividing Line* to a voice speaking as the compassionate, contented man of sense he had initially hoped to be. That the poetic voice of a Maryland contemporary of Byrd ranged beyond the influences of John Milton, John Dryden, and James Thompson is the thesis of " 'At Once the Copy,— and the Original': Richard Lewis's 'A Journey from Patapsco to Annapolis' " (*EAL* 19:138–52), in which Pierre Marambaud claims without success that Lewis's use of New World subjects, his sensitivity to poetic structure, and his transformation of natural description into philosophical musing distinguish his poem from its prototypes.

iv. Edwards and the Great Awakening

Clyde A. Holbrook's "Jonathan Edwards on Self-Identity and Original Sin" (*ECent* 25:45–63) pursues Edwards's attempt to clarify the problematic concept of identity, a concept that eluded precise definition but was for Edwards finally grounded on the fact of God's continuing creative action and the predicament resulting from humanity's share in original sin. Edwards's interest in the sense of identity experienced by the elect is the subject of "The Sociology of 'Holy Indifference': Sarah Edwards' Narrative" (*AL* 56:479–95), in which Julie Ellison cogently notes the difference between Sarah Edwards's account of her religious affections and her husband's later revision of it; whereas the earlier version stresses the Northampton milieu as an important agency of divine grace, the later version exhibits an indifference to society and stresses a more abstract inner, psychological purity of motive for religious ecstasy. This editorial transformation of his wife's account gives important clues to Edwards's thoughts and feelings, clues similar to those underlying his editorial changes in the memoirs of David Brainerd (*The Writings of Jonathan Edwards*, 1975, pp. 106–11); in the instance of his wife's narrative, Edwards's changes reveal his increasing sense of isolation and alienation from the laity of his parish.

Edwards was not the only minister to experience trouble with his parishioners during and after the Great Awakening. As George W. Harper indicates in "Clericalism and Revival: The Great Awakening in Boston as a Pastoral Phenomenon" (*NEQ* 57:554–66) Boston ministers were entangled in controversy as a result in part of the radically divergent pastoral styles of the Old and the New Lights. Among the Old Lights was Ebenezer Gay, whose positions were often unpopular with his parishioners but who was nonetheless well liked by them. In *The Benevolent Deity: Ebenezer Gay and the Rise of Rational Religion in New England, 1696–1787* (Penn.) Robert J. Wilson III reviews Gay's prominent role in the rise of Arminian religion during the 18th century and provides a good discussion that would have been even better had Wilson probed Gay's ideas more deeply. Responding to ideas such as Gay's were Edwards's disciples, the concern of William Breitenbach's "The Consistent Calvinism of the New Divinity" (*WMQ* 41:241–64), which makes a convincing case concerning the effort of the New Divinity to find a middle position between the Old and the New Lights by arguing that each person is accountable for sin and at the same time is depraved and utterly dependent upon God.

If Edwards's disciples tried to reconcile the teachings of the Old and the New Lights, there seemed to be little possible reconciliation between proponents of old-style psalmody and reformers advocating a new style. In "Earwitnesses to Resonance in Space: An Interpretation of Puritan Psalmody in Early Eighteenth-Century New England" (*AmerS* 25:25–47) Eldon Turner concludes that the old style was characterized by space filled with spirit, the immobilization of time, the importance of ceremony, and the prominence of ancestor worship; the new style emphasized an unceremonial (despiritualized, demystified, desymbolized) linear song with brisk tempo and a subordination of linear flow to history (rhythm-time). While psalmody reformers were trying to demystify rustic allegorical consciousness, George Berkeley hoped to demystify poetic diction in *Alciphron*, which William H. McGowan ("George Berkeley's American Declaration of Independence," *SECC* 12[1983]:105–13) thinks should be considered an American text because it was written while its author resided in New England. McGowan simplifies and distorts in his account of

17th-century attitudes toward figurative language, but he does alert us to Berkeley's emphasis in *Alciphron* on the function of poetic diction, especially metaphor, when the imagination is allied with reason.

v. Franklin, Jefferson, and the Revolutionary Period

In "Suppose that Jefferson's Rough Draft of the Declaration of Independence Is a Work of Political Philosophy" (*ECent* 25:25–43) Robert Ginsberg maintains that the earliest version of the Declaration not only conveys a sense of shared ideas during the late 18th century, but also outlines Jefferson's convictions and anticipates his later political activity. According to Douglas L. Wilson ("Sowerby Revisited: The Unfinished Catalogue of Thomas Jefferson's Library," *WMQ* 41:615–28), the range of these ideas is even greater than we have known, for Jefferson's reading and his ownership of books are more extensive than the standard catalogue of his library indicates. Specifically Jefferson's idea of a national university concerns Neil McDowell Shawen, whose "Thomas Jefferson and a 'National' University: The Hidden Agenda for Virginia" (*VMHB* 92:309–35) focuses on Jefferson's clever tactic to divert the attention of his peers toward a state university of national stature to be located in central Virginia.

Ideas of a different sort inform Dickinson W. Adams's edition of *Jefferson's Extracts from the Gospels* (Princeton, 1983), which prints documents by Jefferson that express his personal religious opinions. A new anthology of his works, *Thomas Jefferson: Writings* (Library of America), appeared this year; also useful is Frank Shuffelton's *Thomas Jefferson: a Comprehensive, Annotated Bibliography of Writings about Him (1826–1980)* (Garland, 1983), which contains nearly 3500 entries.

The writings of a tragically ambitious man, whose influence among Republicans Jefferson tried to diminish after losing confidence in the "Lunatick," are published in the two-volume *Political Correspondence and Public Papers of Aaron Burr* (Princeton), ed. Mary-Jo Kline and Joanne Wood Ryan. The writings of another peer, whom Jefferson once described as "the greatest man and ornament of the age and country in which he lived," appear in *The Papers of Benjamin Franklin, Vol. 23: October 27, 1776, through April 30, 1777* (Yale, 1983), ed. William B. Willcox et al. And the work of a naturalist who was strongly supported by Franklin has been reprinted as *The Life and Travels of John Bartram from Lake Ontario to the River St. John* (Florida, 1982), with a detailed account of his busy life by Edmund and Dorothy Smith Berkeley.

The image, rather than the writings, of still another peer of Bartram, Franklin, and Jefferson is the subject of *Cincinnatus: George Washington and the Enlightenment* (Doubleday), in which Garry Wills discusses the changing representations of Washington from his time to today. The earliest expressions of admiration, Wills explains, took the form of biblical comparison, which later yielded to parallels to Cincinnatus, the Roman general who returned to his farm after saving his country. Self-image, as much as public image, concerned John Adams, who in John E. Ferling's " 'Oh That I Was a Soldier': John Adams and the Anguish of War" (*AQ* 36:258–75) is a man profoundly disturbed by his failure to soldier, but who eventually convinces himself that he has made a sacrifice for his country and that his intellectual endeavors are as manly and noble as are the virtues and acts of the soldier hero. Image also interests John L. Brown, whose "Revolution and the Muse: The American War of Independence in Contemporary French Poetry" (*WMQ* 41:592–614) surveys the image of the new American Republic in both popular poetry and pretentious epics written in France.

Image was certainly at stake when Adams called Hamilton "the bastard brat of a Scotch pedlar" and when Jefferson accused him of "dealing out treasury secrets among his friends." In alliance with James Madison and John Jay, Hamilton composed the Federalist Papers, the voice of which conveys an impression of someone who is quietly honest and disinterested. In the succinct, well-written, and clarifying *The Authority of Publius: A Reading of the Federalist Papers* (Cornell) Albert Furtwangler argues that these documents exhibit a rhetorical strategy which closes the distance between author and reader, and which imparts an integrity to the essays. Especially noteworthy is the strategy of candor, which emphasizes positive achievement, an appearance of rigid rationalism, and patience in response to objection—all features of a tone of reasoned agreement or of harmony among different collaborative minds. Furtwangler revises our sense of these documents, which we are now told are not a work of high philosophy and did not influence the adoption of or provide an orthodox reading of the Constitution.

vi. The Early National Period

Wondering in "St. John De Crèvecoeur in the Looking Glass: *Letters from an American Farmer* and the Making of a Man of Letters" (*EAL* 19:173–90) whether during the war Crèvecoeur revised his pre-Revolution notes and memories, Bernard Chevignard speculates that perhaps he was depressed at this time and tried to revive an image of the vanishing past, an image (including the portrait of himself as an ideal farmer) which he came to see as a mirror of the promise of young America. Investigating a similar contrast of moods, the idyllic and darker sides of *Letters*, Robert P. Winston (" 'Strange Order of Things': The Journey to Chaos in *Letters from an American Farmer*," *EAL* 19:249–67) discerns the structure of romance (with patterns of ascent, descent, and reascent) in Crèvecoeur's work, for which the narrator (James) is appropriately fashioned.

Like Crèvecoeur, Noah Webster might have experienced a depression. The apparent darkening cast of his mind, as he began to doubt the possibility of human reform in America, as well as the range of his ideas and career as a writer and an editor are set forth by Richard J. Moss in *Noah Webster* (TUSAS 465). One of Webster's ideals for America is discussed in "Noah Webster's Linguistic Thought and the Idea of an American National Culture" (*JHI* 45:99–114), a very good essay by Vincent P. Bynack, who focuses on Webster's adaptation of Edwardsian theology to construct a belief that individuals and the everyday world were grounded in an absolute divine reality; this change of view after his conversion experience reinforced his hope in a national language for America that would give the country access to truth.

The sort of writing that Webster's fellow editors were publishing ranged from grand epics celebrating the new nation to sensationalist, journalistic accounts celebrating deviant individuals in the new Republic. The former is the topic of John Bidwell's "The Publication of Joel Barlow's 'Columbiad' " (*PAAS* 93[1983]:337–80), which traces the complex history of the publication of Barlow's work in a luxurious edition that sold poorly not because of derision by the poet's enemies, but because it was too expensive. While Barlow was trying to make an elevated contribution to the literature of the new nation, texts of a very different sort were also beginning to define American letters. In "Rogues, Rascals and Scoundrels: The Underworld Literature of

Early America" (*AmerS* 24[1983]:5–19) Daniel E. Williams cogently remarks the American fascination with the criminal, a fascination expressed in three stages: first, the criminal was portrayed by Puritan ministers as the archetypal sinner who accepts punishment and henceforth strives for redemption; second, from about the mid-18th century to the Revolutionary War the criminal is presented as a personality (rather than as a type) who justly defies authority and challenges social limitations; third, after the war the criminal emerges as a hero (as if symbolizing America's successful, roguelike defiance of England) who escapes punishment and whose characterization and story are developed as entertainment. Williams repeats all of this in "Doctor, Preacher, Soldier, Thief: A New World of Possibilities in the Rogue Narrative of Henry Tufts" (*EAL* 19:3–20), which focuses specifically on one typical post-Revolutionary account.

Two groups of early national writers received special attention this year: lawyers and women. In *Law and Letters in American Culture* (Harvard) Robert A. Ferguson notes that for about 50 years after the Revolutionary War lawyers replaced clergymen as the dominant intellectual and literary force in the new nation. In the writings of John Trumbull, Royall Tyler, and Hugh Henry Brackenridge, Ferguson discerns an advocacy of the writer-lawyer who uses humor to instill virtue and reform the public. He also gives careful attention to Jefferson's *Notes on the State of Virginia*, in which Ferguson sees a strategy of order derived from an accumulation of facts, with room for elaboration, that parallels common law legal formulations; this technique is informed by Jefferson's sense of law as providing a solution to the need for stability in America. Ferguson's book is a useful and interesting pioneer study of the role of the lawyer in post-Revolutionary America. Aside from its tendency to wander far from its main concerns, its chief defect, in my judgment, is its avoidance of any deep probe into the antilawyer sentiment so prevalent in early American literature. He remarks Brackenridge's observation, "Down with lawyers has been the language of the human heart since the first institution of society," but does not pursue its implications, especially in Charles Brockden Brown, who Ferguson contends merely had a grudge against the profession. Since for Ferguson, Jefferson is the model of the lawyer-writer, I wonder whether he pondered Jefferson's critical observation in *Notes* that "there are . . . places at which . . . the *laws* have said there shall be towns; but *nature* has said there shall not."

That nature was a feature of the frontier of which post-Revolutionary women were more appreciative than were men is a thesis in Annette Kolodny's *The Land Before Her*. Kolodny sees a sharp contrast between transformative male myths of the frontier that stress destructive mastery and domestic female myths of the frontier that stress appreciative pacification. Women, Kolodny states, seem to be less willing to accept the male urge to transform the land into wealth without regard for its inherent beauty and for the possibility of familial community with cultivated gardens. Before they could express this difference, women used the Indian captivity narrative as an expression of their projected fear of and anger over the male vision. By the mid-18th century, Kolodny writes, female captivity narratives lose the pattern of typological spiritual drama of affliction and redemption, and begin to emphasize the actual experience of women suffering in the wilderness. By the end of the 18th century, as is evident in the "Panther Captivity Narrative" (1787), two images of the frontier competed in the American imagination: the female fantasy of the domestic agrarian ideal and the male fantasy of the isolated anarchic wilderness. Kolodny's book is worth attention, but its chief weaknesses include limiting the garden fantasy to women (although she mentions Jefferson and Crèvecoeur) and failing to assess the fact that the garden fantasy requires (albeit in a different sense than the male fantasy) the destruction of the wilderness.

One woman's hope for the end of the wilderness of slavery in post-Revolutionary America surfaces occasionally in Phillis Wheatley's poetry, which is reprinted in facsimile in *Phillis Wheatley and Her Writings* (Garland); editor William H. Robinson also prints her earlier and later poems, her letters and proposals for printing her book by subscription, variants of her poems and letters, and several unsigned poems possibly written by her, among other contemporary items relating to the poet. The only known satiric treatment of Wheatley during her life was edited by me in "Phillis Wheatley and Oliver Goldsmith: A Fugitive Satire" (*EAL* 19:82–84).

vii. Brown and Contemporaries

In *Law and Letters* (see above) Ferguson interprets Charles Brockden Brown's fictive management of yellow fever as a metaphor for Brown's negative view of American society; Brown particularly exposes the superficiality of conventional conduct and vocations, and

challenges the civic vision of the presumed legal guardians of the
young nation. Ferguson provides an interesting reading of *Memoirs
of Stephen Calvert*, in which he sees the two female protagonists as
embodiments of Brown's vocational dilemma: Louisa Calvert represents the socially acceptable and responsible profession of the lawyer;
Celia Neville represents the socially unacceptable and illicit profession of the creative artist. Brown's position on another challenge to
conventional social attitudes is studied, particularly in relation to his
last works, in Fritz Fleischmann's *A Right View of the Subject: Feminism in the Works of Charles Brockden Brown and John Neal* (Er-
langen, W. Ger.: Palm and Enke, 1983). Women and society, especially in terms of the ideal of family, figure as well in "Charles
Brockden Brown's *Wieland:* A Family Tragedy" (*SAF* 12:1–11), a
limp essay by Roberta F. Weldon, who thinks that *Wieland* is less a
study of individual characters than of the family unit based on a classical model which fails in the new Republic. Weldon particularly
becomes entangled in her efforts to explain away the seemingly joyful note with which the romance ends.

The influence on Brown not of classical models, but of picturesque
tradition in landscape painting informs "Charles Brockden Brown,
Edgar Huntly, and the Origins of the American Picturesque" (*WMQ*
41:62–84), in which Dennis Berthold contends that Brown took hold
of the picturesque as a mode of perception which provided him with
an aesthetic for restraining exaggerated emotions and for framing
his views of rude nature. Brown helped popularize the picturesque
in America as he exploited the loosely defined aesthetic as a fictional
resource, especially in *Edgar Huntly*, where Brown converted European notions of the picturesque into an American variety combining
refined perception and the pragmatics of survival. Attention to landscape has been a mainstay of scholarship on this romance, which has
now been released in an excellent new edition: *Edgar Huntly* (Kent
State). In one of the best introductions to the Bicentennial edition of
Brown's works, Sydney J. Krause reviews Brown's thematic interests
(particularly sleepwalking and Native Americans) and reviews the
scholarship on the romance.

Landscape also figures in Marietta Stafford Patrick's "Romantic
Iconography in *Wieland*" (*SoAR* 49:65–74), which demonstrates
how Brown's management of setting (the temple, Clara's house, the
summer home by the river) reveals a carefully structured work; essentially this structure is a circular movement of withdrawal, inward

journey, and return symbolized through images of transformation that dramatize the theme of self-discovery and identity. Identity is also at issue in "Arthur Mervyn's Revolutions" (*SAF* 12:145–60), in which Robert S. Levine takes an opposite position from Patrick's by arguing that the idea of revolution was important to Brown's challenge to the sensationalist epistemology of John Locke; in *Arthur Mervyn* the protagonist's beliefs are pre-Revolutionary, whereas his actions are post-Revolutionary, and the latter reveal how the Revolution teaches the limits of the rational mind by destabilizing authority, weakening cause-and-effect schematizations, and leaving the mind nearly shattered in a precarious post-Revolutionary world.

A valuable annotated bibliography of writings about Brown was published four years ago by Patricia L. Parker, who is also the compiler of *Early American Fiction: A Reference Guide* (Hall), which I have not seen but which promises to be as useful as its predecessor. And "Elizabeth Graeme Ferguson: A Poet in 'The Athens of North America'" (*PMHB* 108:259–88) prints the writings of a Philadelphia author whose life and thematic interests are outlined by Martha C. Slotten.

viii. Miscellaneous Studies

The highlight of this year in early American studies is the publication of *The Dictionary of Literary Biography, Volume 24: American Colonial Writers, 1606–1734; DLB, Volume 31: American Colonial Writers, 1735–1781;* and *DLB, Volume 37: American Writers of the Early Republic* (Gale), each edited by Emory Elliott. Exemplifying beautiful book production (glossy paper, wide margins, large type, numerous photographs), these works are bibliographically accurate and their entries excellently synthesize current scholarship. They are a valuable research tool not only for students but also for scholars, who will profit from using them before beginning to work on a pertinent project. Also noteworthy is *DLB, Volume 30: American Historians, 1607–1865* (Gale), ed. Clyde N. Wilson.

Another valuable book published this year is *Colonial British America: Essays in the New History of the Early Modern Era* (Hopkins), in which Jack P. Greene and J. R. Pole collect 15 essays by established scholars who present an excellent overview of the last 40 years of historical research in colonial American culture as well as the likely direction of future scholarship in the area. This work is important to literary critics in the field because it emphasizes underlying cultural features, of which these critics are too often inadequately informed. The otherwise impressive comprehensiveness of this book is unfortunately marred by a lack of attention to women, blacks, and Native Americans. Also somewhat useful is *Seventeenth-Century New England* (Boston: Colonial Soc. of Mass.), a collection of ten essays edited by David D. Hall and David Grayson Allen. Particularly pertinent are Lillian B. Miller's "The Puritan Portrait: Its Function in Old and New England" (which does not go far enough in decoding pictorial symbols), David D. Hall's "A World of Wonders: The Mentality of the Supernatural in Seventeenth-Century New England" (which makes a good case for the presence of folkloric, even pagan elements in Puritan popular culture), and Robert St. George's fascinating " 'Heated' Speech and Literacy in Seventeenth-Century New England" (which painstakingly details the extremes of Puritan oral patterns as preserved in court records).

The shipboard experience of the migrating Puritans is emphasized in "The Vast and Furious Ocean: The Passage to Puritan New England" (*NEQ* 57:511–32), in which David Cressy argues that crossing the Atlantic was a liminal event for the Puritans, who thereby participated in a rite of passage and engaged in a binding form of *communitas*. Not the community but the individual concerns William Boelhower, whose "New World Topology and Types in the Novels of Abbot Pietro Chiari" (*EAL* 19:153–72) discusses an Italian author's late 18th-century works presenting didactically prototypical American heroes who bring into focus a contrast between the Old and the New Worlds.

And, finally, of interest is a round of essays (*ECLife* 8[1983]:93–188) on 18th-century American garden design that includes commentary on examples in the South and particularly on Jefferson's vision of the landscape of Monticello.

University of Texas at Austin

12. 19th-Century Literature

David J. Nordloh

A second year at this chapter tempts me to imagine myself fully qualified to offer facile judgments about the comparative quality of one year's "output" against another's. But since scholarship is a continuity of effort and interest, and not a Guinness competition, I'd rather emphasize the surprising amount and variety of productive work I've had the opportunity to review this past year: new critical editions of novels, journals, and letters; solid and sometimes provocative monographs and essays on major and minor authors and topics; several volumes of useful reference material and essay collections. Especially impressive is the number of fine books treating women writers and feminist questions, a healthy sign of the fundamental strength of this area of study.

I'm certainly better qualified now to acknowledge how much important material I failed to report in last year's essay. The current state of bibliographical resources makes comprehensiveness difficult—and journals published six months or a year after their cover dates and books published in disdain of official publication dates don't help much. I'll accept most of the blame for missing things earlier, but not all of it.

i. General Studies

Nina Baym's *Novels, Readers, and Reviewers: Responses to Fiction in Antebellum America* (Cornell) provides a critical foundation that will shape the ongoing redefinition of 19th-century American literature. Baym undertakes an examination of reviews of the novel in 21 periodicals (from the *Atlantic Monthly* to *Godey's Lady's Book*) in circulation before the Civil War, to identify not the judgments being made about individual works but the criteria on which the pertinent judgments were based, dividing the commentary according to specific topics (plot, narration, classes and types of novels). Her effort is thus primarily descriptive rather than evaluative, and the book provides as a result a context from which to study both works and critical programs—for example, the pronouncements of the major novelists of the period can now be seen more clearly as persuasive of an attitude rather than descriptive of a reality. One of the few conclusions Baym draws from her own research is that a concentration on the "Americanness" of writers and works obscures the international variety of the materials American readers were reading and American reviewers reviewing.

A book of a very different sort but with perhaps more obvious potential for influencing the content and contour of the canon is Annette Kolodny's *The Land Before Her*. Continuing the exploration begun in her *The Lay of the Land* (1975), Kolodny traces the development of a female myth of "locating a home and a familial human community within a cultivated garden." In setting out a construct obviously echoing R. W. B. Lewis's American Adam, she follows Eve from *her* paradise and a theological function in captivity narrative through the optimistic sales fictions of promotional literature to the full domestic myth, especially in the midcentury novel. Kolodny draws upon such diverse documents as Lydia Maria Child's fiction *Hobomok* (1824)—in which white and Indian cultures are irreconcilable—and James Everett Seaver's *Narrative of the Life of Mrs. Mary Jemison* (1824)—an account of a real woman who actually did adopt Indian society—as well as unpublished papers in developing her argument. There is no overlooking the feminist perspective insistently at work, but it is wonderfully supported by the range of materials. A provocative, sensitive book. A less satisfactory discussion centered on the same general period and cultural milieu is *The Indian Captivity Narrative: An American Genre* (Univ. Press). Richard VanDerBeets is mostly unconscious of the male orientation of his folkloristic analysis of such texts as the *Narrative . . . of Charles Johnston* (1827) and *An Account of the Captivity of Hugh Gibson* (1837), in which he finds the archetypal patterns of death and rebirth of the hero, as well as separation, transformation, and return. That this slim pamphlet intentionally avoids historical context further reduces its usefulness.

But to another study of literature by and about women. Mary Kelley in *Private Woman, Public Stage: Literary Domesticity in Nineteenth-Century America* (Oxford) studies 12 "literary domestics," women writers who wrote best-sellers about home life and traditional women's issues but who were also aware of the "untraditional, unfeminine fashion" of their status as celebrities. Kelley's look at the likes of Maria Cummins, Mary Jane Holmes, Harriet Beecher Stowe, and Susan Warner becomes jargonish at its general moments, but nonetheless does justice to the variety of intellectual and emotional ways these women reconciled the cultural definition of them as private persons with their public reputations and influence.

Two recent essays address other perspectives on women's questions and domestic fiction. Jane P. Tompkins, "The Other American Renaissance" (*American Renaissance*, pp. 34–57), examines the functions and publications of the American Tract Society, the first mass publisher of religious literature, to identify—like Kolodny—a set of beliefs familiar to and accepted by the women who constituted the major part of the audience for that literature and for fiction. Tompkins suggests that such an audience certainly brought emotional and intellectual preconceptions different from those of modern readers and critics, that within such preconceptions the domestic role was defined as courageous rather than escapist, and that sentimental fiction of the mid-19th century substituted for worldly, male authority "a feminist theology in which the godhead is refashioned into an image of maternal authority." Frances B. Cogan, "Weak Fathers and Other Beasts: An Examination of the American Male in Domestic Novels, 1850–1870" (*AmerS* 25,ii:5–20), implicitly supports Tompkins's generalizations. Cogan proposes that the marked negative treatment of men in the fiction of the most popular of the women writers, Caroline Hentz, Mary Jane Holmes, Augusta Evans, and Elizabeth Stuart Phelps, constituted a way of setting an effective occasion for a revelation of the true woman; male incompetence is thus a justification for female self-sufficiency, ability, physical strength, even late marriage. Cogan is careful to identify such a strategy as a political design and not necessarily as a cultural reality.

A book about the male myths of America might seem stale and belabored by contrast to the toughness and thoroughness of these strongly feminist studies. But Martin Green's *The Great American Adventure: Adventure, Manliness, and Nationalism* (Beacon) has a skill and perceptiveness of its own, imbuing old ideas with a new cultural relevance. Green defines adventure as "the energizing myth of empire," and sees in the texts he discusses much conflict of egalitarianism and aristocracy, much caste and other social distinction. He argues that America, by the historical fact of remaining so long a frontier society, retained and exploited the adventure narrative as a continuing forum for cultural debate rather than settling into the gentlemanly romance for that purpose as other literatures had done. Readings of *The Pioneers, A Tour on the Prairies, Nick of the Woods, Two Years Before the Mast, The Oregon Trail,* and Kit Carson's *Autobiography* support his thesis.

In *History and Myth in American Fiction, 1823–52* (St. Martin's), Robert Clark sets a different sight on the same material. He applies what he refers to as a "materialist premise"—the literary significance of a text, in his construct, "consists in its articulation of the dominant ideological contradictions of its historical moment"—to the general question of the development of American writers and readers and to the distinction between romance and the novel in their relationship to "real" history. Sadly, Clark's American history, if real, is awfully vague, and his emphasis on Cooper, Hawthorne, and Melville doesn't decrease the demand for specificity. He urges that the works of these writers "were so acutely addressed to the political life of the nation that a failure to understand their politics becomes a failure to understand their central literary significance," but can then offer only such weak, conventional judgments as that a virgin land inhabited by an innocent hero, as in Cooper, "is a mythologizing transformation of Jacksonian political belief." The kernels of critical truth here could be less coated with overabstraction, jargon, and presumptive knowingness.

Carl S. Smith's topic is not history and myth, but history, time, and place. *Chicago and the American Literary Imagination* is an introductory exploration of "a major episode in the aesthetic response to the rise of the modern industrial city in America." Citing Howells, Herrick, Garland, Fuller, and Norris, as well as Jane Addams and Louis Sullivan and some now-forgotten popular writers of the period, Smith identifies major thematic and formal patterns arising in the literary uses of Chicago's relentless explosion of growth and wealth and power, from Norris's notion of the businessman as the new artist to the widespread employment of the city's physical features (railroads, skyscrapers, stockyards) as literary tools. The book seems awkward and elementary at times, and some readers may wish for more acknowledgment of earlier work on the topic (for example, Morton and Lucia White's *The Intellectual Versus the City,* 1962). Still, it supplies a clear introduction to the terms of the argument and useful divisions of the issues. Some familiar names and somewhat more conventional perspectives made their contributions to a general view.

Alfred Kazin is content to turn platitudes into quotable lecture hall one-liners in *American Procession*. Kazin skims the peaks of the crests of the surface in describing Stephen Crane as one who "*chose* to be negative about whatever his class took as gospel—especially the Gospels" and Henry Adams as having "a literary imagination so insistent that it was to prove mystifying even to itself." Still, the book is acceptable enough for beginners, and deft at putting writers in their places. The first chapter of Malcolm Bradbury's *The Modern American Novel* (Oxford, 1983), entitled "Naturalism and Impressionism: The 1890s," also very introductory, does place literary movements effectively within the contexts of industrialism and Darwinism, and does fit Mark Twain, Howells, Henry James, Garland, Norris, and Stephen Crane inside the movements. A revised edition of Donald Pizer's *Realism and Naturalism* drops three chapters from the 1966 original and adds six, all thoroughly representative of Pizer's skills in organization, definition, and perception. Those relevant to this chapter are "American Literary Naturalism: An Approach Through Form," "The Problem of Philosophy in the Naturalistic Novel," and "Hamlin Garland's 1891 *Main-Travelled Roads:* Local Color as Art." Most of the essays were originally published elsewhere. Pizer's ideas, as well as those of Charles Child Walcutt, are very prominent in John J. Conder's *Naturalism in American Fiction*. Attempting to say something distinctive, Conder sounds much like Pizer—though on a more abstract and less carefully focused level— in proposing that the evolution of American literary naturalism is "a progressive development that shows, among other things, a paradoxical shift in conceptions of nature and the self." That Conder's perspective is philosophical rather than economic or social is made clear in the book's first chapter, "American Literary Naturalism: From Hobbes to Bergson," and in chapters on Crane (particularly "The Open Boat," "The Blue Hotel," *Maggie*, and *The Red Badge of Courage*) and on Norris's *McTeague* (in which Conder argues *against* discussing *The Octopus*). Another American pioneer in the analysis of naturalism, Richard Lehan, discusses the significance of Zola in "American Literary Naturalism: The French Connection," a contribution to the issue of *Nineteenth-Century Fiction* dedicated to Blake Nevius (38:529–57). The essay says nothing that Lehan hasn't argued more convincingly elsewhere.

Eric J. Sundquist articulates some interesting connections between literature and national politics in "Slavery, Revolution, and the

American Renaissance" (*American Renaissance*, pp. 1–33). Sundquist studies the "conflicting impulses and contradictions" that the
pre–Civil War generation felt in attempting to conceive of slavery
in terms of "the legacy of the Revolution." His examples include
Daniel Webster and Lincoln, William Lloyd Garrison, Thomas Wentworth Higginson, Harriet Beecher Stowe, and Frederick Douglass.
Michael Kreyling's "The Hero in Antebellum Southern Literature"
(*SLJ* 16,ii:3–20) sets out the theoretical premise that literature serves
two important functions: scriptural—"the use of the written word to
forge and defend a people knowable to themselves in their sacred
texts"—and political—organizing the lives of society's members "toward an ideal of behavior that transcends topical propaganda." On
this premise he examines southern fiction, particularly novels by
George Tucker, Beverly Tucker, and William Alexander Caruthers,
and with particular emphasis on the figure of the hero. His conclusion—a response to such critics as W. D. Howells—is that despite
smacking of "Walter Scottisms" this fiction was not merely imitative:
it intended to forge "a sort of foundation myth, a myth which—in
large measure—aimed to supplant history in the Southern imagination as the explanation of the nature of things." But intention alone
doesn't redeem the second-rate.

The reader interested in a survey of the topic will find Leo F.
O'Connor's *Religion in the American Novel* useful enough. The four
chapters—on religion in the New England tradition and in frontier
literature, on literature treating the new religions both native-born
and immigrant, and on religion and reform literature—certainly
range over enough authors (interestingly, Howells is a major com-
ponent of all four), but with analysis that is cursory and simplistic,
however earnest it may be. O'Connor's premise is that "When a
writer emphasizes his commitment to giving a true portrait of society, it argues for the reliability of his fiction as a primary source for
social data," and his conclusion is that these writers searched and
didn't find, just as we do and don't. An essay by Edwin H. Cady, " 'As
Through a Glass Eye, Darkly': The Bible in the Nineteenth-Century
American Novel" (*The Bible in American Arts and Letters*, pp. 33–
56), examines a narrower range—Cooper, Stowe, Howells, Frederic,
Chopin, Cahan, and Crane—and reaches a more provocative conclusion: there is in fact little of "the real thing" of biblical text and
context in the novel, and the novel and the Bible are not "quite com-
patible"—"it may be true that the American imagination works bet-

ter with human and secular than with heroic and sacramental dimensions of life." Also on matters literary and religious, chapter 2 of Ezra
Greenspan's *The Schlemiel Comes to America* (Scarecrow, 1983)
discusses the novels and stories of Abraham Cahan as well as the
antisemitism of Henry Adams and James Russell Lowell.

The year's work included some useful additions to the reference
shelf. *American Historians, 1607–1865* (Gale), edited by Clyde N.
Wilson, is another businesslike addition to the "Dictionary of Literary
Biography" series, lightened as usual by effective illustrations and
weighted with full primary bibliographies and briefer secondary ones.
The authors discussed in individual encyclopaedia entries, each prepared by a specialist, fit a narrower modern conception of history,
so that authors of firsthand accounts, like U. S. Grant in his *Memoirs*,
are excluded. Even so there is a plenty of major 19th-century names
here: George Bancroft, Francis Parkman, James Parton, William
Hickling Prescott, Washington Irving, William Gilmore Simms, and
Mason Locke Weems. Another basic reference is the revised edition
of the bibliographical review, *Fifteen American Authors Before 1900*,
ed. Earl N. Harbert and Robert A. Rees. (The first edition was known
as "Rees and Harbert"; the revision, conveniently, can be "Harbert
and Rees.") The revision provides updated chapters by their original
compilers on most of the authors—Bryant, Cooper, Crane, Holmes,
Longfellow, Lowell, Norris, and Whittier are appropriate to this
chapter—and completely new essays by new contributors, on Howells
(myself) and Irving (James W. Tuttleton). Relentless expansionism
has also meant sacrifice, as pioneers and bibliographers know so well:
the chapters on the literatures of the Old and the New South are
gone. Even so, a sensible starting point for research has been made
more timely.

William Bedford Clark and W. Craig Turner have compiled
Critical Essays on American Humor (Hall), part of the Critical Essays on American Literature series. The volume reprints 16 essays
originally published between 1838 and 1970, and publishes seven
new ones, five of them appropriate to this chapter: Walter Blair, "A
German Connection: Raspe's Baron Munchausen" (pp. 123–39); Milton Rickels, "The Grotesque Body of Southwestern Humor" (pp. 155–
66); David B. Kesterson, "Those *Literary* Comedians" (pp. 167–83);
Sanford Pinsker, "On or About December 1910: When Human Character—and American Humor—Changed" (pp. 184–99); and Emily
Toth, "A Laughter of Their Own: Women's Humor in the United

States" (pp. 199–215). Andrew Hook's *American Literature in Context, III: 1865–1900* (Methuen) sets out survey chapters on single works by Henry George, Howells, Bellamy, Garland, Crane, Frederic, Norris, Chopin, and Veblen; focuses on the relationships of economic and literary life in the period; and begins each chapter with "an extract from the chosen text which serves as a springboard for wider discussion and analysis." In one of the essays in *Literature of Tennessee*, Elmo Howell supplies a rapid, intelligent survey, with selected bibliography, of "The Literature of Tennessee Before 1920." A survey of a lighter sort, but with more pretensions, is Elizabeth McKinsey's "The Honeymoon Trail to Niagara Falls" (*Prospects* 9:169–86), which skims over Caroline Gilman, Cooper, and Howells to demonstrate Niagara's "fitness as a visual metaphor for the passion channeled into marriage, as well as its union of male and female principles, power and life."

ii. Irving, Cooper, and Their Contemporaries

I'll depart from the usual pattern of this section to pay tribute first to a significant publication about a "contemporary." William Cullen Bryant II and Thomas G. Voss continue their edition of *The Letters of William Cullen Bryant* (Fordham) with volume 4:1858–64. Their patient labors are yielding an unpretentiously impressive achievement in primary materials and thorough annotation. This volume, covering the period of Bryant's greatest public influence—because of the closeness of Bryant's New York *Evening Post* to the Lincoln administration during the Civil War—prints 503 of 619 known letters, in six sections introduced by brief surveys of relevant events.

Two new volumes also appeared in "The Complete Works of Washington Irving" (Twayne), a project that moves tantalizingly closer to completion. Michael L. Black and Nancy B. Black have edited in the usual CEAA/CSE style *A History of New York*, and Wayne R. Kime and Andrew B. Myers *Journals and Notebooks, IV: 1826–1829*. Given the complicated history of the *History*, the editors essentially reproduce the Author's Revised Edition (1848), arguing that Irving's revisions of the original version of 1809 in 1812 and 1848 produced distinct works. No doubt that point, and the thoroughness of the analysis of the textual background to the 1848 text, will occasion some discussion. *Journals and Notebooks*, on the other hand, reproduces unique manuscript documents, and concentrates on an-

notation, historical context, and a record of internal manuscript alter-
ations—the last incorporated into the text proper rather than isolated
into lists. Kime, who completed the editing task begun by Myers,
also supplies an introduction surveying Irving's major activities of
the period, especially the writing of six historical works.

The most interesting of three essays about Irving is Jeffrey Rubin-
Dorsky, "*The Alhambra:* Washington Irving's House of Fiction"
(*SAF* 11[1983]:171–88). Rubin-Dorsky discusses the Spanish sketches
in the context of the opposing demands of fiction and reality with
which Irving's writing constantly wrestled, sees the work as having
a real—rather than an entirely romantic—basis in Irving's experience,
and defines the effect on the artistic imagination of sacrificing the
vital persona of Geoffrey Crayon for the sake of "a transcendent
moment in reality." In "Root and Branch: Washington Irving and
American Humor," another essay in the special issue of *NCF* dedicated to Blake Nevius (38:415–25), John Seelye proposes Irving as a
distinctively American humorist, ancestor to Mark Twain and others.
Seelye sees Irving in "The Legend of Sleepy Hollow" hiding his European sources and emphasizing native sentiments and values. That
argument doesn't quite prove Seelye's principal contention, but it
does nicely explain the continuing appeal of Irving's crucial stories
in their thoroughly American attitude. Patricia Lee Yongue, "*The
Professor's House* and 'Rip Van Winkle'" (*WAL* 18:281–97), evaluates the extent and the effect of Cather's drawing upon Irving's other
best-known story in creating "the essential Americanness of her unwilling hero," Godfrey St. Peter, and in using the Rip story in a variety of ways to expand the psychological complexity of her novel.

"The Writings of James Fenimore Cooper," another solidly productive editorial project (SUNY), has produced three titles representative of three different areas of Cooper's creative work: *The Last
of the Mohicans*, ed. James A. Sappenfield and E. N. Feltskog, with
an introduction by the general editor of the series, James F. Beard
(1983); *Gleanings in Europe: France*, ed. Thomas Philbrick and Constance Ayers Denne (1983); and *Lionel Lincoln; or, The Leaguer of
Boston*, ed. Donald A. and the late Lucy B. Ringe. The three volumes
are distinguished by sensible editorial policy, significant commentary
on Cooper's biography and his literature, and handsome bookmaking
echoing traditional design. The carefully chosen illustrations are an
added pleasure.

In a critical work whose physical design also fits its intellectual emphasis, William P. Kelly, *Plotting America's Past: Fenimore Cooper and the Leatherstocking Tales* (So. Ill.), sees the books not as Cooper's efforts to create a myth but as his attempt to "conceptualize rather than transcend America's history." Kelly describes Cooper as gradually reshaping his earlier contradictory notions of his fiction as a "flight from temporal restriction" and embodying "historical continuity" until in *The Deerslayer* he abandons his "reassuring contrivances" and confronts "the limits of history." Kelly's idea is an attempt to see the *Tales* as a whole. At times, though, his plan is too ambitious for him: the book is oppressively overvocabularized, and fraught with abstractions o'erleaping facts.

Thomas Brook's essay, "*The Pioneers*, or the Sources of American Legal History: A Critical Tale" (*AQ* 36:86–111) examines Cooper's relation to history from another angle, comparing the fictional Marmaduke Temple to the real New York jurist James Kent and Temple's and Natty Bumppo's conflict to issues of individual and social justice as Kent and his legal generation perceived them. Brook's conclusion that historically Temple and Natty represent facets of the same individualistic ideology and thus evolution rather than opposition suggests once again how Cooper's greatness lies in enacting national feelings, not in describing national fact. Renata R. Mautner Wasserman, "Re-Inventing the New World: Cooper and Alencar" (*CL* 36:130–45) both describes the debt of the Brazilian to the American, a debt José Martiniano de Alencar attempted to deny, and compares the "implicit ideology of individualism and instinctive right thinking and action" both novelists adopted as a myth. Alencar, she proposes, had to destroy history to maintain the myth: Cooper retreated from it. Joyce W. Warren includes a chapter on "Solitary Man and Superfluous Women: James Fenimore Cooper" in *The American Narcissus*. Warren's conclusions are standard stuff: Cooper's women act for others since to act for oneself would be unfeminine, and he couldn't portray strong women because of the definition of American individualism he accepted. Michael Clark finds "The Oak in Cooper's *The Pioneers*" (*ELN* 22:53–55) suggestive not of a misguided America, as most commentary would have it, but of Indian John.

Lewis Leary provides something of a popular biography—which means, among other things, much quotation, no footnotes, and no guide to the location of the rare sources drawn upon—of the man known primarily as Washington's biographer, in *The Book-Peddling Parson: An Account of the Life and Works of Mason Locke Weems*

(Algonquin). Leary supplements that information with a separate re-printing of Weems's " 'Good News for the Devil': An Early Southern Admonitory Tale" (*SLJ* 17:96–100), a dual-purpose fable against drunkenness and advertisement for his other publications.

Charles S. Watson provides an edition of William Gilmore Simms's *Woodcraft; or, Hawks About the Dovecote* (New College and Univ. Press, 1983), reprinting with corrections and annotation the text from Simms's Collected Works (1854). Astonishingly, this is a new typesetting, not a photofacsimile. And Charmaine Allmon Mosby explores Simms's creation of a cavalier fictional hero who serves as the true protagonist in stories based on historical events in "William Hinkley/Calvert: The Key to *Charlemont* and *Beauchampe*" (*SLJ* 16,ii:21–29).

A thorough and sensitive appreciation of an increasingly neglected work is provided by James M. Cox in "Richard Henry Dana's *Two Years Before the Mast:* Autobiography Completing Life" (*The Dialectic of Discovery*, pp. 159–77). Drawing on the perspective toward Dana's nonfiction taken by D. H. Lawrence in *Classic Studies in American Literature,* Cox argues that the power of idea and event in the narrative lies in the reader's continuing sense of Dana's honesty in keeping himself what he is, not redefining for the sake of dramatic—and thus, fictional or untrue—effect: "The point is that, whatever his refinement censors, Dana is aware of the true middle-class drama of his life. He does not repress that drama in order to show off his experience." *James Kirke Paulding,* by Larry J. Reynolds (TUSAS 464), and *Noah Webster,* by Richard J. Moss (TUSAS 465), add to the usual workmanlike introductory stuff of Twayne's United States Authors Series thorough studies of two writers whose literary productivity was significant and varied. J. Michael Pemberton edits Henry Ruffner's *Judith Bensaddi: A Tale* and *Seclusaval; or the Sequel to the Tale of Judith Bensaddi* (LSU). The texts, taken from their original appearances in the *Southern Literary Messenger,* are modernized, and Pemberton's description of their histories not altogether clear. He adds a biography of Ruffner (1790–1861), Presbyterian minister and sixth president of what is now Washington and Lee University, and explores the background and content of the fictions, southern romances of some interest because they treat the marriage of Jew and Gentile. Paul D. Erickson explores the symbolic use of American history in oratory in "Daniel Webster's Myth of the Pilgrims" (*NEQ* 57:44–64). Donald A. Ringe defines "The Function of

Landscape in Prescott's *The Conquest of Mexico*" (*NEQ* 56[1983]: 569–77), noting the skillful handling of "themes to be found in the works of Bryant, Irving, and Cooper and on the canvases of their artistic contemporaries." Jan Bakker examines the contradiction between approval of slavery and disapproval of inferior status of women in "Another Dilemma of an Intellectual in the Old South: Caroline Gilman, the Peculiar Institution, and Greater Rights for Women in the Rose Magazines" (*SLJ* 17:12–25). Another treatment of contradiction—this time between historical and cultural truth and the demands of romantic form and idea—is Robert P. Winston, "Bird's Bloody Romance: *Nick of the Woods*" (*SoSt* 23:71–90).

iii. Popular Writers of Midcentury

The Transcendentalists, ed. Joel Myerson, is a bigger, more repetitious book than it has to be, combining as it does encyclopaedia and bibliography. But there can be no complaining about thoroughness. The book includes general introductory chapters on transcendentalism, the times, the periodicals, and so on; then *Eight American Authors*–style chapters, surveying research materials, on both the best- and least-known authors, including Thomas Wentworth Higginson (by Howard N. Meyer), Christopher Pearse Cranch (David Robinson), and Sylvester Judd (Francis B. Dedmond); and then a section on "The Contemporary Reaction," offering more such survey chapters, narrowly focused on the subject at hand, dealing with other authors who had views on transcendentalism—they include James Russell Lowell (Thomas Wortham), George William Curtis (W. Gordon Milne), Orestes Brownson (Leonard Gilhooley), and Samuel Johnson (Roger C. Mueller). *And* there is a 119–page bibliography supplying full citations of works referred to in the texts, and an index.

The most ambitious of the few essays dealing with the Fireside Poets is John Seelye, " 'Attic Shape': Dusting Off *Evangeline*" (*VQR* 60:21–44), an effort to explain how and why the poem haunts readers despite its being "an oleaginous balm with a sweet smell, reminiscent of the sickroom or, worse, the schoolroom." In describing Longfellow's mood at the time of writing, as well as his reading (particularly of Homer) and his longing for European experiences, Seelye provides an effective biographical context without answering his original question and without explaining how the West that Longfellow envisions in the poem becomes "an American Alph emblematic of the national imagination and darkly prophetic of the national fate." Alice Hall Petry argues against Dante's "Purgatorio" and for "Methought I saw my late espoused Saint" as a principal poetic influence in "Longfellow's 'The Cross of Snow' and Milton" (*ELWIU* 11:299–304). And Burton R. Pollin offers an unnecessarily complicated history of a two-line poetic comment on Poe made by Longfellow in "Longfellow and Poe: An Unnoted Hexameter Exchange" (*MissQ* 37:475–82).

James Russell Lowell is the subject of two essays, both dealing with *The Biglow Papers*. Emmanuel Gomes supplies a cursory, not entirely connected comparison between that work and Langston Hughes's *Simple Speaks His Mind* in "The Crackerbox Tradition and the Race Problem in Lowell's *The Biglow Papers* and Hughes's *Sketches of Simple*" (*CLAJ* 27:254–69). Gomes's conclusion, that both writers demonstrated how such a lightweight literary tradition could carry a grave theme, is worth a further look. Edward H. Brodie, Jr., in "Lowell's *Biglow Papers: No. 1*" (*Expl* 42,iv:21–23), suggests that "Freedom's airy" is not an area but an eagle's nest, and that critical understanding changes as a result.

Eugene England, "Tuckerman and Tennyson: 'Two Friends . . . on Either Side the Atlantic' " (*NEQ* 57:225–39) assembles full information about an acquaintance, and also illuminates literary work and artistic influence. Tuckerman was the one American successful in drawing Tennyson out about himself and his work; Tuckerman's originality, and especially his antiromanticism, is more understandable in light of Tennyson's influence; and Tuckerman's notes on Tennyson's poems in his own copies are derived from Tennyson's comments to him, and thus establish the truth of allusions various scholars have proposed. The essay is a nice example of the value of modest yet careful scholarship. In "Christopher Pearse Cranch's 'Journal. 1839' " (*SAR 1983*:129–49), Francis B. Dedmond transcribes the text of a document from a crucial period in Cranch's midwestern ministerial career, full of reflection on Emerson and Carlyle. On another midwestern matter, John E. Hallwas, in "John Regan's *Emigrant's Guide*: A Neglected Literary Achievement" (*JISHS* 77:269–94), surveys a life and ideas, and points out how the Scottish-born Regan drew on close description, colloquial speech, and humor to depict western Illinois culture.

iv. Local Color and Literary Regionalism

The amount of work focused on popular women writers seems to increase geometrically. More importantly, the quality of such criticism continues to rise. There were, for example, four significant essays on *Uncle Tom's Cabin* alone. The most ambitious of these—at least in its comprehensive generalizations—is James M. Cox, "Harriet Beecher Stowe: From Sectionalism to Regionalism" (*NCF* 38: 444–66). Cox conceives Stowe's novel as "radically democratic in its universally clear and legible effort to express an essential moral universe in a postsacred era." Cox sets Stowe's domestic universe against the world of public law, and conceives her imaginative creation of a substantial southern evil as the route of escape from abstract New England Puritanism. The essay is least satisfactory in explicating the issues proposed in its title, Stowe's move from national conflict to local color and the unavailability to her in the process of a viable New England attitude. And feminist critics may disagree, Cox knows, with his premise that "there is something in her work and in her imagination that is extremely resistant not only to our sense of literature but to our sense of society." Thomas P. Joswick concentrates on the book that defines a world rather than the world that circumscribes the book in "'The crown without the conflict': Religious Values and Moral Reasoning in *Uncle Tom's Cabin*" (*NCF* 39:253–74). Stowe was articulating in the novel her conviction "not only that human character is at the root of any social system but that moral character, by its pervasive influence, is the real authority in society," and that true social bonds are formed not by law but by feeling. *Uncle Tom's Cabin* attempts, then, to articulate the unspoken, and to set the deep moral truth against the public, and especially the legal, convention of behavior and belief.

Gillian Brown takes another perspective on Stowe ("Getting in the Kitchen with Dinah: Domestic Politics in *Uncle Tom's Cabin*," *AQ* 36:503–23). Dinah's kitchen is disorderly, more like the economic hustle of the outside world than the domestic peace with which women associate the true home. Brown's essay is repetitious and sometimes overwritten but effectively explicates Stowe's strategy of enlisting women against slavery by defining it as a threat, couched in politics and authority, against the home itself. Stephen Railton undertakes yet another explication, seeing the novel not as opposed to public culture or arising out of domestic order but as "split right down

the middle between confirming and condemning Victorian America."
In "Mothers, Husbands, and *Uncle Tom*" (*GaR* 38:129–44), which
includes a useful survey of the book's place in the literary history of
its time and the extent of its popularity, he examines the care with
which Stowe reconfirms the Americanness of motherhood and Christianity while opposing other national institutions.

Ruth K. MacDonald's *Louisa May Alcott* (TUSAS 457), in the
format of the series, is more introductory than exploratory. But in
treating Alcott's adult and her children's literature as both fiction and
echo of biography, MacDonald does incline toward the current notion
of Alcott as using her writing in complicated ways to deal with "the
more troubled aspects of her own personality." Karen Halttunen's
"The Domestic Drama of Louisa May Alcott" (*FSt* 10:233–54) sees
the psychological dilemmas underlying the surface pleasantry of such
books as *Little Women* and *Jo's Boys* and addressed straight on in
stories like "Behind a Mask; or, a Woman's Power" as expressions of
a conscious philosophical program. Alcott was applying in fiction her
father's encouragement that his daughters act out their "childish
fancies" in order to enable the body to reflect the mind, using melodrama to express moral feeling and in turn to "extend Bronson Alcott's
perfectionist cult of domesticity and his creed of self-restraint to a
generation of middle-class Americans." Sarah Elbert, *A Hunger for
Home: Louisa May Alcott and* Little Women (Temple), offers an
Alcott who is a disciple of Margaret Fuller, had a gift for reaching
ordinary women with the feminist program, and tried to write things
personal and true. The whole is more language than idea: "Her childhood reverberated with conflicts between the social pillars of established order and the various outcasts who struggled to shape a new
order."

Alcott scholarship is not particularly well advanced by Madeleine
B. Stern's *Critical Essays on Louisa May Alcott* (Hall), a confusing
arrangement of old and new material. Of the many items in the six
sections of the book, only the 19th-century reviews are dated in the
table of contents; thus the reader has to search carefully through the
source notes on each item to identify the seven essays published for
the first time here (a paragraph late in the introduction referring to
them is not precise). Those new essays, as it happens, are minor
performances anyway: for the record, they are Freda Baum, "The
Scarlet Strand: Reform Motifs in the Writings of Louisa May Alcott"
(pp. 250–55); Martha Saxton, "The Secret Imaginings of Louisa Al-

cott" (pp. 256–60); Joel Myerson, "'Our Children Are Our Best
Works': Bronson and Louisa May Alcott" (pp. 261–64); Adeline R.
Tintner, "A Literary Youth and a Little Woman: Henry James Re-
views Louisa Alcott" (pp. 265–69); Marie Olesen Urbanski, "Thoreau
in the Writing of Louisa May Alcott" (pp. 269–75); Mary Cadogan,
"'Sweet, If Somewhat Tomboyish': The British Response to Louisa
May Alcott" (pp. 275–79); and Alma J. Payne, "Louisa May Alcott:
A Bibliographical Essay on Secondary Sources" (pp. 279–86).

C. Vann Woodward and Elisabeth Muhlenfeld have edited, annotated, and introduced *The Private Mary Chesnut: The Unpublished
War Diaries* (Oxford). The text makes available for the first time the
seven extant diaries of ten Chesnut apparently wrote during the Civil
War period, diaries she drew upon in creating a literary record she
wrote in the 1880s and which is best known by the title of its 1905
republication, *A Diary from Dixie*. Woodward and Muhlenfeld's introduction is especially interesting for its comparison of the private
and public forms. Woodward restates that theme in "Mary Chesnut
in Search of Her Genre" (*IR* 73:199–209).

Sarah Orne Jewett, the subject of much traditional analysis as a
local-colorist and, more recently, as a woman writing about her woman's world, becomes an object lesson in contemporary critical theory
in Louis A. Renza's *"A White Heron" and the Question of Minor
Literature* (Wisconsin). Renza is concerned with identifying the
authentic qualities of a literature which by its exclusion from the
official literary canon is effectually dismissed as insignificant. He
proceeds then to evaluate Jewett's story from a variety of canonical
perspectives—regionalist, feminist, pastoral, and other—only to conclude of each that "A White Heron," attractive to him because its
very impulse denies the usual canonical prejudice in favor of the "intellectual" or the "sensational," is always something more. Like much
of the abstract argument from which it derives, the book is often tiresome and insistent—and finally reaches a conventional conclusion in
an unconventional way. Gwen L. Nagel has edited *Critical Essays on
Sarah Orne Jewett* (Hall), another volume in the Critical Essays
series. The choices are sensible, and the mix of old and new kept
clear: the volume reprints 16 reviews and eight essays, and prints
eight additional essays for the first time: Judith Roman, "A Closer
Look at the Jewett-Fields Relationship" (pp. 119–34); Jean Carwile
Masteller, "The Women Doctors of Howells, Phelps, and Jewett: The
Conflict of Marriage and Career" (pp. 135–47); Barbara A. Johns,

" 'Mateless and Appealing': Growing into Spinsterhood in Sarah Orne Jewett" (pp. 147–65); Elizabeth Ammons, "Jewett's Witches" (pp. 165–84); Rebecca Wall Nail, " 'Where Every Prospect Pleases': Sarah Orne Jewett, South Berwick, and the Importance of Place" (pp. 185–98); Richard Cary, "The Literary Rubrics of Sarah Orne Jewett" (pp. 198–211); Josephine Donovan, "Sarah Orne Jewett's Critical Theory: Notes Toward a Feminine Literary Mode" (pp. 212–25); and Philip B. Eppard, "Two Lost Stories by Sarah Orne Jewett: 'A Player Queen' and 'Three Friends' " (pp. 225–48), which reprints them both. Alice Hall Petry prints "An Unpublished Jewett Letter" (*CLQ* 20,i:51) to someone about tickets for something.

Leah Blatt Glasser examines the ambivalence in a woman's attitude toward being a woman generally and personally in "Mary E. Wilkins Freeman: The Stranger in the Mirror" (*MR* 25:323–39). Aliki Barnstone employs a vague, inspired, insistent voice in "Houses Within Houses: Emily Dickinson and Mary Wilkins Freeman's 'A New England Nun' " (*CentR* 28:129–45). Comparing the house of Louisa Ellis in Freeman's story to Emily Dickinson's more abstracted "house of consciousness," Barnstone argues for a similarity of methods and images but an opposition in attitude: Freeman's character accepts the "spotless white wall of stillness," Dickinson's poetic persona resists it. Among discussions of other women writers, Joann P. Krieg in "Charlotte Perkins Gilman and the Whitman Connection" serves up an inconclusive mishmash of evidence (*WWR* 1,iv:21–35) in an effort to explain why Gilman presented Whitman's views on women at the final meeting of the Walt Whitman Fellowship in 1919. Lawrence Buell and Sandra A. Zagarell have edited Elizabeth Stoddard's *The Morgesons and Other Writings, Published and Unpublished* (Penn.). Besides the novel, the volume includes two pieces of short fiction, selections from Stoddard's column in the *Daily Alta California*, 1854–58, and excerpts from her letters and her 1866 journal. The editing is essentially correction and annotation. The editors add a biographical and critical introduction and a selected bibliography of primary and secondary works about a writer defined as, "next to Melville and Hawthorne, the most strikingly original voice in the mid-nineteenth-century American novel," and as a woman who addressed questions of female power in terms of insistent individualism rather than united sisterhood. Sisterhood and "a stunning use of domestic imagery" are the interest of Thelma Shinn in "Harriet Prescott Spofford: A Reconsideration" (*Turn-of-the-Century Women* 1:36–45),

whose survey of ideas and images is focused especially on the stories
in Spofford's *The Amber Gods*.

Southern and southwestern and western humor and humorists got
their own swarm of attention. Robert Higgs's "Southern Humor: The
Light and the Dark" (*Thalia* 6,ii[1983]:17–27), in a special issue of
that journal devoted to the topic, defines the subgenre as a combination of backwoods humor and the minstrel show. Kimball King
supplies *Augustus Baldwin Longstreet* and Paul Somers, Jr., *Johnson
J. Hooper* in Twayne's United States Authors Series (Twayne).
Both books are competent in introducing humorists who were much
more—the former a lawyer-judge, politician, clergyman, and college
president, the latter a lawyer, editor, and officer in the Provisional
Confederate Congress. Somers is particularly good in sketching the
humorous tradition in America and placing Hooper within it. William C. Hall's "Yazoo Sketches" and other writings are the topic of a
not completely coherent essay by Mark A. Keller, "The Cowardly
'Lion of the (Old South) West': Mike Hooter of Mississippi" (*MissFR*
18:3–18). Joel Chandler Harris's best-known work is the subject of
Hugh T. Keenan's "Twisted Tales: Propaganda in the Tar-Baby
Stories" (*SoQ* 22,ii:54–69). Keenan offers a variety of plausible readings, incorporating both white and black perspectives, all demonstrating that "the inherent qualities of ambivalence, paradox, and
clear conflict" continue to produce a convenient vehicle for contradictory propaganda statements. Harris himself is the concern of W. J.
Rorabaugh, "When Was Joel Chandler Harris Born? Some New Evidence" (*SLJ* 17:92–95). Paul H. Gray examines "Poet as Entertainer:
Will Carleton, James Whitcomb Riley, and the Rise of the Poet-
Performer Movement" (*LPer* 5:1–12). Elaine Gardiner sets out a not
especially well-written picture of "Sut Lovingood: Backwoods Existentialist" (*SoSt* 22[1983]:177–89), and Thomas D. Young rushes
rapidly through George Washington Harris's literary skill and comic
ideas, embodied in Sut, in "A Nat'ral Born Durn'd Fool" (*Thalia*
6,ii[1983]:51–56). James L. Treadway conceives of the American
folk hero as highly dependent on providence—what kind is not entirely clear—in another *Thalia* essay more survey than the critical
analysis it pretends to be, "Johnson Jones Hooper and the American
Picaresque" (6,ii[1983]:33–42). Paula Hathaway Anderson-Green
takes a folkloristic perspective in identifying the themes and motifs
in the little-known *Fisher's River (N.C.) Scenes and Characters by
Skitt who was Raised Thar*, in "Folktales in the Literary Work of

Harden E. Taliaferro: A View of Southern Appalachian Life in the Early Nineteenth Century" (*NCarF* 31[1983]:65–75). *Mississippi Scenes* (1851) and *Leisure Labors* (1858) are the focus of Robert L. Phillips's "Joseph B. Cobb and the Evangelicals in the Old South" (*Thalia* 6,ii[1983]:28–32). Mary Ann Wimsatt, "Baldwin's Patrician Humor" (*Thalia* 6,ii[1983]:43–50), sees *The Flush Times of Alabama and Mississippi* (1853) as reflective of Joseph G. Baldwin's affection for the world he describes and of his patrician Virginia background, so that he is both "critic and celebrant of the boisterous vigor of the Gulf region." In a slim but very handsomely produced and illustrated book, Richard A. Dwyer and Richard E. Lingenfelter offer a narrative—not quite a biography—of James William Emery Townsend, western newspaperman, opportunist, and possible source of Bret Harte's "Truthful James." The most interesting section of their *Lying on an Eastern Slope: James Townsend's Comic Journalism on the Mining Frontier* (Florida) is the account of Townsend's resurrection of a newspaper in a dead town to help in pushing a mining-stock scheme. And last—but best—of the various items dealing with the humorous tradition in regional and local-color writing is John J. Pullen, *Comic Relief: The Life and Laughter of Artemus Ward, 1834–1857* (Archon, 1983), a solid, unpretentious biography emphasizing Ward as a lecturer, full of fact and fine anecdotage.

v. Henry Adams

William Wasserstrom's *The Ironies of Progress: Henry Adams and the American Dream* (So. Ill.) is not so much *about* Adams as it is *around* him. The book sets out to explore certain ambivalences in American culture broadly conceived, and identifies Henry Adams with the most perceptive sense of the depth and variety of them. Adams's concerns—and Wasserstrom's—are social progress and social chaos, providence and doom, organicism and technologism, energy and entropy, defined both as issues of his own personality and as structural premises of his writing. But that conception of Adams only lurks vaguely and indeterminately at the center of Wasserstrom's argument and the pattern of the book, just as Adams lurks obscurely in the *Education*. Even the titles of Wasserstrom's chapters obscure Henry Adams's active place in his argument: "Strangeness of Proportion in America," "The Aboriginal Demon: Irving, Cooper, Hawthorne," "Abandoned in Providence: Harriet Beecher Stowe, Howells, Henry

James," "Hydraulics and Heroics: William James, Stephen Crane," "Notes on Electricity: Henry Adams, Eugene O'Neill," and "The Goad of Guilt: Adams, Scott and Zelda"—this last chapter also mentioning D. H. Lawrence, Gertrude Stein, William Carlos Williams, and Kenneth Burke. Others will no doubt find the book, ponderous in the facility of its high-lecture style and teasing in its definition of the most abstract components of its argument, more accessible than I do.

In an essay intended for the Blake Nevius issue of *NCF* but received too late, Denis Donoghue ("Henry Adams' Novels," *NCF* 39: 186–201) reads *Democracy* and *Esther* as essentially one novel with the same plot—a woman with a vacant life looks for a cause, finds a man, recognizes his selfish terms, and withdraws into greater vacancy—projecting the same process of failure, a process which Donoghue sees as "a constitutional necessity" for Adams "rather than a conclusion imposed by a train of events." Despite the casual structure of his presentation and an unrigorous Aristotelian question-answer methodology, Donoghue supplies exciting readings of the novels and locates them usefully among Adams's whole production. Lois Hughson does an effective job in setting Adams's biographies of Albert Gallatin and John Randolph in the context of his philosophical and historical values in "Power and the Self in Henry Adams's Art of Biography" (*Biography* 7:309–24). Linda A. Westervelt explores yet another dimension of Adams's negative if not pessimistic conception of human effort in "Henry Adams and the Education of his Readers" (*SHR* 18:23–37). Westervelt identifies the contradiction in Adams between the principle of doubling, around which the *Education* is organized, and his claim that "any attempt at ordering must falsify experience," and she praises his vigor in searching for truth and success even as he continued to discover only confusion and failure.

Three recent books include limited discussions of Adams among their larger interests. Joseph G. Kronick sets out a tough essay in intellectual history, including a thorough reading of the process of the *Education*, in "Henry Adams and the Philosophy of History" (*American Poetics of History*, pp. 124–65). "Henry" is one chapter of Paul C. Nagel's *Descent from Glory: Four Generations of the John Adams Family* (Oxford, 1983); though the treatment is mostly biographical, it effectively identifies Adams within the social activities and other personalities of the clan, and defines his literature as a response to family—the *Education*, for instance, is "an indictment of his family for having behaved as if it had hope, despite its private pessimism."

And Jerome Hamilton Buckley offers five summary pages (pp. 108–13) on Adams as the only American included in *The Turning Key: Autobiography and the Subjective Impulse Since 1800* (Harvard).

Of lesser importance are Lynn Bryce's description of the influences of Saint-Gaudens and Buddhism on Adams's artistic ideas in "Silent Confluence: Eastern and Western Themes in Adams' Monument at Rock Creek Cemetery" (*NDQ* 51,ii[1983]:84–93); the text of an address by Ernest Samuels, "Henry Adams and Bernard Berenson: Two Boston Exiles" (*PMHS* 95[1983]:100–113); and Arline Boucher Tehan's *Henry Adams in Love: The Pursuit of Elizabeth Sherman Cameron* (Universe, 1983), an overload of quotation as well as an annoyingly speculative journalistic rehash.

vi. Realism and the Age of Howells

In *The Circle of Eros: Sexuality in the Work of William Dean Howells* (Duke, 1983) Elizabeth Stevens Prioleau defines by close analysis of significant texts five progressively more complex but also more affirmative stages in the development of Howells's ideas of sexuality, from youthful neurosis to mature adult love ethic. Prioleau's confident Freudianism ignores some crucial works in its sweep, and plays down Howells's family relationships; on the other hand, it constitutes a significant contribution to the conception of Howells as a moral thinker who, despite reticence and fastidiousness, explored modern problems deeply.

The Old Northwest, perhaps capitalizing on its success in the same effort several years ago, offered another special issue devoted to Howells (vol. 10, Spring) with six mostly satisfactory essays. Thomas Wortham's " 'The Real Diary of a Boy': Howells in Ohio, 1852–1853" (pp. 3–40) offers an introduced, annotated, and excerpted text not of a Howells diary, but of a Howells essay about the diary. In "Winifred Howells and the Economy of Pain" (pp. 41–75), John W. Crowley writes a life of Howells's elder daughter and an interpretation of her illness and Howells's implication in and response to it. Crowley uses Winifred's own writings very effectively, praises Howells for having an "exaggerated sense of responsibility" for her death, and blames him for his "unconscious complicity in the neuroses of his wife and daughters, by whom in turn he had felt psychologically manipulated." William Wasserstrom applies his premise—the correlation of "a disquiet of family life with the dilapidation of houses, both urban and rural, very much as if a mismade object itself served to signify a mismatch of home and homeland"—briefly to Stowe's *Uncle Tom's Cabin* and then more thoroughly to *The Rise of Silas Lapham*. His essay, "Howells and the High Cost of Junk" (pp. 77–90), concludes that the novel's failure to hold together was a "triumph of misalignment," an archetypal tale which in both structure and idea embodies "the high cost and utility of junk." Kenneth E. Eble supplies an affectionate introductory look, adapted from his forthcoming book, on "Howells and Twain: Being and Staying Friends" (pp. 91–106). Glen A. Love is a bit murky and allusive in explicating "*The Landlord at Lion's Head:* Howells and 'the Riddle of the Painful Earth'" (pp. 107–25); even so, he does demonstrate that the novel conveys Howells's sense of the dislocation of his world by focusing on Darwinian evolution and the absence from art and life of "coherent messages." And in "The Ohio World of William Dean Howells—Ever Distant, Ever Near" (pp. 127–37), Alma J. Payne notes that Howells retained Ohio values and influences after he left.

Several essays address Howells and the matter of realism. Michael Davitt Bell's "The Sin of Art and the Problem of American Realism: William Dean Howells" (*Prospects* 9:115–42) examines Howells's pronouncements on the topic not as pure theory but as a reflection of the artist's *need* for such a label. Defining oneself as a Realist, says Bell (echoing elements of Alfred Habegger's *Gender, Fantasy and Realism in American Literature* [1982]), constituted a way of responding to society's notion of the artist as not a "real" man by "obscuring the distinction between 'a thing . . . said' and 'a thing . . . done.'" And thus, says Bell, Howells, who in the 1850s "was troubled by his ambiguous social and sexual identity," made himself real by making art real and by associating his literature with real—i.e., "nonartistic"—people. Bell applies his argument to Frank Norris and John Gardner as well. The assertions are provocative but would have been more convincing if they acknowledged the historical and cultural milieu of which realism was a part and if they had set Realists against Romanticists or Idealists. Patrick K. Dooley's "Moral Purpose in Howells' Realism" (*AmerS* 25,ii:75–77) discovers a review of *The Rise of Silas Lapham* by Horace Scudder and describes Scudder's views of and associations with Howells; but he misses Scudder's help in the writing of *A Modern Instance* and the fact that the review in question was cited in the *Lapham* volume in "A Selected Edition of W. D. Howells" some years ago. George C. Carrington, Jr., explores a special dimension of Howells's art, but one he proves is nonetheless at the center of the traditional sense of Howells as both serious and socially and intellectually alive, in "Howells and the Dramatic Essay" (*ALR* 17:44–66). Howells liked the dramatic essay, says Carrington, because it was "a mode of continuous personal action, Howells's way of dealing with—that is, making sense of—events and situations as they occurred and as best he could."

Dale E. Peterson serves up a modest comparatist statement in "From Russia with Love: Turgenev's Maidens and Howells's Heroines" (*CSP* 26:24–34). Though Howells expressed his interest in Turgenev as a craftsman, it is clear he also felt a "temperamental and cultural affinity": "As literary types and as cultural embodiments, Howells's early heroines emerged from under the petticoats of Turgenev's strong Russian women." Another literary relationship is Elsa Nettels's topic. "Howells and Hardy" (*CLQ* 20:107–22), which repeats much already known, discusses friends who shared both themes and artistic principles.

Responding to the current interest in environmental matters, the University of Wisconsin Press has issued two books dealing with John Muir. *John Muir: Summering in the Sierra*, ed. Robert E. Engberg, reprints 15 essays by Muir from the San Francisco *Daily Evening Bulletin*, 1874–75. Engberg supplies a general introduction on Muir's "wilderness journalism" (which he intended to "free his countrymen from their myopic and 'arithmetical' judgments, to bring mankind and mountain together"), as well as detailed individual statements relating the essays to Muir's other writings, interests, and travels. The only flaw here is a failure to specify whether these represent *all* of Muir's *Evening Bulletin* contributions. The other book, Michael P. Cohen's *The Pathless Way: John Muir and American Wilderness*, is a very personalized, sometimes uncritical act of criticism, a biography focused on Muir's "spiritual journey" into the environment and environmental politics. Cohen is especially good on Muir's involvement in the plans for Yosemite National Park, on the history of the American environmental movement, and popular and political sentiment about ecological questions during Muir's lifetime. Together the books are substantial additions to Wisconsin's program of books by and about Muir.

A number of authors were treated in single essays. Earl F. Bargainnier, in "*Red Rock*: A Reappraisal" (*SoQ* 22,ii:44–53), examines the contradictory impulses in Thomas Nelson Page's best-selling novel of the 1890s, the most significant novel by a southerner published in that decade. Bargainnier sees Page attempting "not just a defense but a glorification of antebellum Southern life" as well as a spiritual reconciliation of North and South, goals sufficiently opposed to each other that Page had to resort to stereotypes and unrealistic renditions of northern personalities to bring them off. The result is not a great novel but a vital cultural document. Bruce A. Lohof's subject is a document of another sort, "*Helen Ford:* Horatio Alger Jr.'s Book for Girls" (*JPC* 17,iv:97–105). The conclusion, after a thorough outline of theme and structure: for Alger, "as his book for girls makes clear, American morality—whose essence was virtue, charity in particular—was unisexual." Gary Scharnhorst provides a biographical sketch of "W. R. Alger: Forgotten Man of Letters" (*ATQ* 53[1982]: 5–23), Horatio's cousin, well known in his time for scholarly publications and opposition to slavery, who died and was forgotten. Kate H. Winter's *Marietta Holley: Life with "Josiah Allen's Wife"* (Syracuse), is the very competent literary biography of the rustic humorist, literary comedian, writer of domestic fiction, and spokesperson on women's issues, most famous for Samantha, "Josiah Allen's Wife." Holley's writing forms an interesting mixture of feminism and realistic depiction of 19th-century rural New York farm life. Gloria Shaw Duclos sees "Thomas Wentworth Higginson's Sappho" (*NEQ* 56: 403–11) as "less a poet of supreme lyric gift than an intellectual bluestocking, more a Margaret Fuller than an Emily Dickinson," a figure appropriate to Higginson's interest in women who "embodied *his* highest ideal for womanhood . . . emancipated, intellectual, creative." Lee Scott Theisen surveys the writing, publication, adaptations, and popularity of "one of the most durable and significant literary properties in American literary history, in " 'My God, Did I set all of this in Motion?' General Lew Wallace and *Ben Hur*" (*JPC* 18,ii:33–41). Bruce A. White, "The Liberal Stances of Joaquin Miller" (*Rendezvous* 19,i[1983]:86–94), describes how Miller became identified as a liberal despite also being known as a literary *poseur*—his pioneering muckraking *Destruction of Gotham* (1881), his defense of Walt Whitman, his speaking on behalf of the Japanese, the Chinese, and the American Indian. White's closing hymn of praise oversteps, however. Louis J. Budd prints a rare piece of praise from a writer not known for being kind, in "Gertrude Atherton on Mark Twain" (*MTJ* 21,iii[1983]:18). Thomas S. Gladsky, "John Esten Cook's *My Lady Pokahontas:* The Popular Novel in History" (*SoSt* 23:299–305), explores Cooke's strategy in his 1885 novel to restore a sense of truth to the Pokahontas "legend." Gladsky's theoretical discussion of "fictional history" is vague, his account of Cooke's skill in defending John Smith more specific.

In matters strictly bibliographical, James Stronks supplies "Supplements to the Standard Bibliographies of Ade, Bierce, Crane, Frederic, Fuller, Garland, Norris, and Twain" (*ALR* 16[1983]:272–77), mostly items from the pages of the Chicago journal *The Echo*.

vii. Fin-de-Siècle America: Stephen Crane and the 1890s

James B. Colvert provides a direct, uncluttered biography in the Twayne pattern in his *Stephen Crane* (Harcourt), one in a series of "album biographies." The "album" is filled with pictures, of Crane from the age of two until shortly before his death in 1900, of pages of his manuscripts, even of his gravestone. The clear factuality of the biography is refreshing, and the pictorial material presents the physical man who remains the intellectual mystery.

Maggie received more attention than any of Crane's other work. Sydney J. Krause, "The Surrealism of Crane's Naturalism in *Maggie*" (*ALR* 16[1983]:253–61), is not particularly convincing in defining in the abstract how naturalism when "pushed to deformity" becomes surrealism, but does make a solid point about the operation of this work of fiction: Maggie's final expulsion, Krause notes, centers on the question of her "respectability," "the chief social target of an essentially surrealist viewpoint, regardless of era or métier. . . . This is the point on which Crane's naturalism and surealism consistently meet: the sense that nothing matters, that virtuousness has no relation to the needs of the psyche, that our social being is finally devoid of reality." In an examination of the story in the tradition of literature dealing with prostitution, Lawrence E. Hussman, Jr., "The Fate of the Fallen Woman in *Maggie* and *Sister Carrie*" (*The Image of the Prostitute*, pp. 91–100), concludes that Crane was "indulging his moral prejudices instead of breaking new ground with a realistic presentation of the prostitute's plight." The story "moves only a quarter step forward, replacing death before dishonor with death immediately after dishonor." Dreiser, says Hussman, was truer to life. Such conclusions must follow inevitably upon such premises; but if the premises—that Crane was a realist, that he wanted, like Dreiser, to describe how a prostitute really thought—aren't true? And Alice H.

Petry, in "*Gin Lane* in the Bowery: Crane's *Maggie* and William
Hogarth" (*AL* 56:417–26), exhausts the parallels between the story
and the 1751 engraving on which Crane could have drawn: intem-
perance, slum life, breakdown of the family, uselessness of the
Church, chaotic social environment.

In "The Common Man's *Iliad*" (*CLS* 21:270–81), N. E. Dunn joins
the debate about Crane's ironic intent in *The Red Badge of Courage*.
The novel, says Dunn, is in the mode of a literary allegory, not "the
complex allegorical mode . . . which emphasizes a general theological
frame of reference, but the relatively simple device of sustaining
parallels with an earlier literary work to help him say efficiently what
he has to say." That earlier work is the *Iliad*, which Crane's story,
with its 24 chapters paralleling 24 books, draws upon for satire and
irony. Working in the novel as the modern form of the epic, he thus
inverted it to produce a mock epic. Of less ambition, but more precision, is Rudolph F. Dietze, "Crane's *The Red Badge of Courage*"
(*Expl* 42,iii:36–38), correcting critics who attribute to Henry Fleming actions that the novel clearly assigns to others.

George Monteiro perceives yet other influences for yet another
Crane story in "Text and Picture in 'The Open Boat'" (*JML* 11:307–
11). Crane not only quotes from Mrs. Caroline E. S. Norton's "Bingen
on the Rhine," but interpolates into his description of the scene
created by that poem details from an 1883 illustrated version of it.
He also employs elements of religious parable and "demythologized"
shipwreck stories from grade school textbooks. In a piece of safer
fact, Paul Sorrentino, "A Reminiscence of Stephen Crane" (*Courier*
19:111–14), reprints a brief statement by Samuel Ripps, an Army
captain stationed in Virginia when Crane was brought back from
Cuba, bearing on the matter of Crane's being fired by the New York
World for accusing the 71st New York of cowardice. Sorrentino also
discusses "Stephen Crane's Sale of 'An Episode of War' to *The
Youth's Companion*" (*SB* 37:243–48), pointing out that Crane did
indeed sell the story to the magazine in 1896 as he said, but that the
magazine didn't print it until 20 years later. Sorrentino discusses the
textual relationship of this version to the one printed in the Virginia
edition, and supplies a list of variants. The Virginia edition is also
featured in a chapter on Stephen Crane in Hershel Parker's *Flawed
Texts*, primarily a play-by-play account of Parker and his colleagues
vs. the Establishment on textual issues, though with some explanation of the purely intellectual basis for the argument. To be used with

caution, since Parker's friends naturally write "tough, eloquent" paragraphs and the opposition "complain" and resort to intimidation.

Just as the midcentury women writers receive of late substantially more attention than the men, so Kate Chopin overwhelms her 1890s competition with a dozen essays, six of them focused on *The Awakening* (four in a special issue of *Southern Studies*). Robert White's "Inner and Outer Space in *The Awakening*" (*Mosaic* 17:97–109) describes the pattern of the novel as "built upon the armature of polarities expressed in the gender mapping of 'man's world, woman's place,'" and employing conceptual imagery very similar to Erik Erikson's notions of male "outer space" and female "inner space." Edna moves outward, intent only on going, not on arriving, and the whole of the novel, White proposes, is thus similar in idea to Chopin's earliest known story, "Emancipation: A Life Fable." In another exciting explication, Rosemary F. Franklin (*"The Awakening* and the Failure of Psyche," *AL* 56:510–26), argues that the core of Chopin's narrative is the myth of Psyche, with emphasis on "Psyche's struggle with unconscious power." That myth illuminates action, character, and symbol, and conclusion: "The paradigm of Psyche reveals Edna's exploit as heroic, but it also shows where she fails to finish her task and is dragged down by fear of a long and lonely period of change." Edna's final feeling of success is ironic: "She goes down to darkness, absorbed in a regressive allusion—that she is wading into the bluegrass meadow of her childhood." Kathleen Margaret Lant, "The Siren of Grand Isle: Adele's Role in *The Awakening*" (*SoSt* 23:167–75), studies the "mother-woman" who first awakens Edna to the "female life of sensuousness and physical fulfillment," but who, in giving birth, also awakens her "to the horrible knowledge that she can never, because she is female, be her own person." What Lant does not discuss is the special uniqueness of Edna Pontellier in responding with sadness to what Adele accepts in joy. In an essay that clothes some sensible explication in some tawdry theory, Robert Collins, "The Dismantling of Edna Pontellier: Garment Imagery in Kate Chopin's *The Awakening*" (*SoSt* 23:176–90), suggests that the garment metaphors so prominent in the novel reveal that its very structure is "an unveiling, a disrobing, a dismantling, a kind of striptease, especially since we know, because the story is narrated in the past tense, that the narrator is aware throughout of what Edna's fate will be." Marina L. Roscher, "The Suicide of Edna Pontellier: An Ambiguous Ending?" (*SoSt* 23:289–98), employs passionate assertion rather than reasoned criticism in answering her own question: the ending is ambiguous in containing multiple meanings rather than in seeming not to have a clear one. More useful and coherent is Joyce Coyne Dyer's comparison of "Lafcadio Hearn's *Chita* and Kate Chopin's *The Awakening*" (*SoSt* 23:412–26). The essay says much about both Hearn and Chopin, and about alternative kinds of naturalism as well as local-color materials.

Dyer is author of two other Chopin essays. In "Epiphanies Through Nature in the Stories of Kate Chopin" (*UDR* 16,iii[Winter 1983–84]:75–81), analyzing "Loka," "The Story of an Hour," "The Unexpected," and "A Morning Walk," as well as *The Awakening*, she concludes that Chopin's recurrent use of the same narrative pattern involving persons and nature emphasizes "the central place of the instincts and the desire for freedom" in human life. In "A Note on Kate Chopin's 'The White Eagle'" (*ArQ* 40:189–92), Dyer insists that unlike the mostly banal fiction after *The Awakening*, this story—published in May 1900—offers "an image that recalls the symbolic ambiguity and density of Edna Pontellier's ocean." Gina M. Burchard, "Kate Chopin's Problematical Womanliness: The Frontier of American Feminism" (*JASAT* 15:35–45) praises the honesty of Chopin's portrayal of the "arbitrariness and intensity of female passion," notes Chopin's disapproval of aggressive feminism, but mistakenly equates Chopin with her characters (a typical problem: Per Seyersted, Burchard's major source, does the same). Dorys Crow Grover, "Kate Chopin and the Bayou Country" (*JASAT* 15:29–34) provides slight evidence for the assertion that Chopin "was convinced . . . that the Southern philosophy of class, caste, and race rested on a false base." Sam B. Girgus reviews Cynthia Griffin Wolf's Laingian study of Edna, "Thanatos and Eros: Kate Chopin's *The Awakening*" (1973), in "R. D. Laing and Literature: Readings of Poe, Hawthorne, and Kate Chopin" (*Psychological Perspectives*, pp. 181–97). And Barbara C. Gannon, "Kate Chopin: A Secondary Bibliography" (*ALR* 17: 124–29), brings the record up to 1981.

Ambrose Bierce is advanced as a writer much before his time in Cathy N. Davidson's *The Experimental Fictions of Ambrose Bierce: Structuring the Ineffable* (Nebraska). Addressing herself to the strategies of the fiction and the role of the reader, Davidson identifies Bierce as an "impressionistic, surrealistic, philosophical, postmodernist fictionalizer" who combines realism and impressionism, naturalism and surrealism, and who had "surprisingly modern views on the nature of language and the interrelationships between language, perception, and fictional forms." Davidson takes her esthetic vocabulary from C. S. Peirce rather than the Moderns, to be truer to the milieu, but she accepts the assumptions of contemporary literary theory. Four of the six chapters include "perception" in the title, the fifth bears the subtitle of the book, and an afterword—in some ways the most interesting because the least repetitious—discusses Jorge Luis Borges's debt to Bierce. Davidson also supplies a foreword to a companion volume from the same publisher, a facsimile reprint of Ernest Jerome Hopkins's 1970 edition of *The Complete Short Stories of Ambrose Bierce*. "Complete" here really means "collected," as neither Hopkins nor Davidson bothers to make clear. George Cheatham and Judy Cheatham, "Bierce's *An Occurrence at Owl Creek Bridge*" (*Expl* 43,i:45–47), point out the irony of Peyton Farquhar's name, irony appropriate to the Romantic view of things embraced by this "patrician" who is so "manly or brave."

The other Realists and Naturalists of the Crane-Chopin-Bierce generation receive less attention. Robert C. Leitz III and Joseph R. McElrath, Jr., in "A New Short Story by Frank Norris" (*ALR* 17:1–11), print "As Long as Ye Both Shall Live," first published in the San Francisco *Examiner* in 1899, and add a critical afterword setting Norris's work against popular romantic fiction of the period and his own *Blix*. David L. Deratzian does a thorough onomastic study of a Harold Frederic novel in "The Meaning and Significance of Names in *The Damnation of Theron Ware*" (*LOS* 11:51–76). John C. Hirsh, "The Frederic Papers, the McGlynn Affair, and *The Damnation of Theron Ware*" (*ALR* 17:12–23), demonstrates the value of the Frederic materials in the Library of Congress for illuminating crucial structural and thematic elements. Frederic may have modeled his Father Forbes partly on the real Father Edward McGlynn, but comparison distinguishes the intellectual from the intellectual-activist.

Adeline R. Tintner locates and explicates a total of seven allusions to Henry James by O. Henry in "O. Henry and Henry James: The Author of the Four Million Views the Author of the Four Hundred" (*MarkhamR* 13:27–31). M. H. Dunlop, "Unfinished Business: Hamlin Garland and Edward MacDowell" (*ON* 10:175–85), offers an interesting account of Garland's dabbling in psychic phenomena and his attempt, after MacDowell's death, to reach his friend through a medium in order to complete a musical composition. Dunlop sensibly concludes that Garland himself was really the medium in the experience. While we argue whether an author born in England who came to the United States at the age of 16 and who died an American citizen belongs in TEAS or TUSAS, Phyllis Bixler's *Frances Hodgson Burnett* has appeared in the English series (TEAS 373). Fortunately, Bixler doesn't fret the national issue, and provides a sensible study emphasizing the versatility of the writer too many people recognize only for *Little Lord Fauntleroy.*

It seems right to end a chapter in which matters of women's literature are so dominant by noting the auspicious beginnings of *Legacy: A Newsletter of Nineteenth-Century American Women Writers*, published at the University of Massachusetts. The first two semi-annual issues offer a rewarding variety of articles on significant writers and genres, syllabi for courses in women's literature, reviews, and even a scholar's index. The newsletter becomes a full-scale journal in Fall 1985.

Indiana University

13. Fiction: 1900 to the 1930s

John J. Murphy

The harvest of books and essays on the writers of this period was particularly fruitful in 1984. The year's scholarship on Cather alone warrants chapter-length consideration in this volume, and most of the other major writers generated one or more book-length studies as well as numerous articles. In addition there seems to be a continual regleaning of the field for neglected or minor writers.

i. Willa Cather

Besides more than a dozen articles scattered through several journals, three journals devoted special numbers to Cather: Margaret Anne O'Connor edited a collection for *Women's Studies*, theoretically reflecting "a consciousness of the femaleness of the novelist" (11,iii); *Great Plains Quarterly* (4,iv) offered a variety of essays under the title "Willa Cather Today"; and *Western American Literature* (18,iv) devoted its essays to *The Professor's House*. The year's two book-length studies on Cather were Marilyn Arnold's *Willa Cather's Short Fiction* (Ohio), giving overdue attention to this neglected area, and my own *Critical Essays on Willa Cather* (Hall), which contains five lengthy original essays on Cather and her fiction and departs from the usual format of this series by including a group of reviews and essays on each major work as well as a general essay section.

The introduction to *Critical Essays*, "The Recognition of Willa Cather's Art" (pp. 1–28), by Kevin A. Synnott and myself, thoroughly reviews Cather's career chronologically, clearly reflecting the ups and downs of her literary reception, and then defines trends in the criticism since Cather's death in 1947. A briefer survey of Cather's critical reputation, David Stineback's "The Case of Willa Cather" (*CRevAS* 15:385–95), expresses righteous indignation at Cather's treatment by amateur psychoanalysts among American critics who have dismissed her as limited by locale and defeated by nostalgia and insincerity because she was a lesbian. In actuality, argues Stineback, the character relationships she explored were ingeniously "intuitive," and among our novelists, she had "by far the most acute sense of social change as a subliminal fact of life in America." Recent scholarship on *My Ántonia* and *The Professor's House* is assessed by James E. Miller, Jr., in "Willa Cather Today" (*GPQ* 4:270–77). Admittedly biased, Miller sees certain recent feminist, sociological, and psycho-analytical approaches as distorted and distorting, and he asks critics to explore the beatific ambiguities in the latter novel and the concepts of adult and child and of self and desire in both novels. The issue of lesbianism is attacked squarely by Sharon O'Brien, the most respon-sible of the Cather scholars focusing on this issue. In " 'The Thing Not Named': Willa Cather as a Lesbian Writer" (*Signs* 9:576–99) O'Brien provides a definition of lesbianism to include women "who never consciously experienced or acted on sexual desire for another woman," and then traces the history of female friendship through the turn of the century when deviance became a factor. In her letters to Louise Pound at Duke, key documents in "establishing Cather's sexual identity," Cather "challenges the ideological yoking of same-sex friendships with deviance . . . , while . . . agreeing . . . with its ac-curacy." O'Brien goes beyond Cather's masquerading her lesbianism and explores how Cather's sexual identity contributed to her modern-ism and the richness of her fiction. Blanche H. Gelfant in " 'Lives' of Women Writers: Cather, Austin, Porter / and Willa, Mary, Katherine Anne" (*Women Writing in America*, pp. 225–48) speculates on dis-tinctions made between the lives of men and women writers by plac-ing Cather with Austin and Porter against Hemingway. Refusing to espouse in her lifetime the feminist ideals she now represents, Cather is unfortunate in her latest biographer (Phyllis Robinson in *Willa* [1983]), whose qualifications "seem . . . ignorance and nostalgia." Gel-fant significantly observes that the "friends" Robinson sees as objects of Cather's lesbian passion contributed to her "clear-headed intention to create a design for living which would allow her solitude in which to write and yet not leave her isolated and lonely." The lesbian issue has become such a factor in Cather critical circles that James Wood-ress, a veteran critic ordinarily concerned with other issues, attempts to set the factual record straight in "Cather and Her Friends" (*Critical Essays*, pp. 81–95). Although he believes the lesbian image of Cather largely in the eye of the beholder, he admits that if we use Lillian Faderman's embracing definition of lesbianism as emotional attach-

ment not necessarily involving sexual contact, then Cather's relationship with Isabelle McClung was "certainly . . . a lesbian relationship,
and her long association with Edith Lewis also may have been." As
Cather's biographer, Woodress also reflects on her friendships with
Elizabeth Sergeant, Dorothy Canfield Fisher, and Zoe Akins.

Perhaps the most significant, certainly most embracing, essay in
Critical Essays is David Stouck's "Willa Cather and the Impressionist
Novel" (pp. 48–66), an exhaustive survey of the French writers
Cather was indebted to for her literary credo and her Symbolist-
Impressionist method. Through detailed paralleling of specific works,
Stouck sees Cather resembling Mérimée in formal structure, Daudet
in sensory appeal, Flaubert in image and scene, while Maupassant
and Mallarmé anticipate her *roman démeublé* principles. Also focusing on Cather's impressionism is my "Nebraska Naturalism in Jamesian Frames" (*GPQ* 4:231–37), which groups the youthful Cather
with Norris, London, Crane, and Dreiser as a Naturalist and proceeds to show how in her major work, after her "Jamesian phase" of
artists and drawing rooms, she employed versions of the Jamesian
consciousness as filters for the naturalistic contents of her prairie
novels. The essay analyzes Cather's impressionism in *My Ántonia,*
comparing it to James's and declaring that her achievement is a successful fusion of the close-to-nature and highly-civilized.

Cather's most popular novel is also the subject of Patrick W.
Shaw's "*My Ántonia:* Emergence and Authorial Revelation" (*AL* 56:
527–40). Shaw addresses Jim Burden's supposedly perplexing supposed lack of development as an element of a submergence-emergence
theme, equating Jim's final illumination by Ántonia as emergence.
The essay then turns to the popular theory that Cather failed to separate her male and female personas through Jim and Ántonia, and that
she glorified childhood and the past because they were less touched
by sexual dogma. Neither part of this Janus-faced analysis is original.
Local Nebraska history is the subject of Beth Bohling in "The Husband of My Ántonia" (*WAL* 19:29–39), which uses the obituary of
John Pavelka, the husband of Annie Sadilek Pavelka (prototype of
Ántonia), and interviews with the Pavelkas to ascertain the extent
to which Ántonia's husband, Anton Cuzak, and Anton Rosicky of
"Neighbour Rosicky" were indebted to the real man. Bohling discovers "few discrepancies between John in his late forties and Anton
Cuzak, or between John in later life and Anton Rosicky." *My Ántonia*
is also treated in "The Image of the Hired Girl in Literature: The

Great Plains, 1860–World War I" (*GPQ* 4:166–76) by Sylvia Lea
Sallquist, who uses memoirs and histories to compare the demo-
graphic characteristics of domestic servants in fact and fiction.
Cather's portraits of hired girls in *My Ántonia* are generally true to
fact regarding age and marital status, less so regarding sexual devi-
ancy, and least so regarding education and immigrant status. Cather's
other notable prairie novel is the subject of my "A Comprehensive
View of *O Pioneers!*" (*Critical Essays*, pp. 113–27), an examination
of the novel's biblical dimensions, its social satire (anticipating Sinclair Lewis), the Keatsian and Dantean dimensions of the love element, and Cather's debt to Whitman's "Song of Myself" and "The
Sleepers." I see the agricultural and tragic love stories as integrated
yet representing a tension within heroine Alexandra Bergson:
"Cather's passionate romance . . . thus dramatizes the natural law,
while the story of Alexandra framing it celebrates the law of restraint. The same kind of sympathetic dualism is evident throughout
The Scarlet Letter."

One of several of the year's articles on *The Professor's House*,
Doris Grumbach's "A Study of the Small Room in *The Professor's
House*" (*WS* 11:327–45) begins as a survey of Cather's literary renditions of her upstairs bedroom in the Red Cloud childhood home and
her study in the McClung house in Pittsburgh, and then, through
crafty use of the text, attempts a "new" reading of the novel in which
Tom Outland has replaced Lillian St. Peter as the professor's love.
Grumbach's conclusion about this conclusion, while not new or unexpected, needs to be aired: Professor St. Peter's letting go of Tom
represents Cather's rejection of happiness outside of heterosexual and
family love. Margaret Doane concentrates on the abandoned wife in
"In Defense of Lillian St. Peter: Men's Perceptions of Women in *The
Professor's House*" (*WAL* 18:299–302), a listing of numerous incidents of male bias in the novel to support the conclusion that "Cather
. . . established an anti-female bias as a dominant aspect of the book
. . . which is a study in point of view . . . of a man with a strong bias
against women." "*The Professor's House* and 'Rip Van Winkle'" by
Patricia Lee Yongue (*WAL* 18:281–97) is an intriguing view of this
problem novel. Without undue stretching, Yongue considers several
similarities between the Cather and Irving works: dramatic landscape descriptions, structural and thematic functions of Rip's dream
and Tom Outland's dreamlike story, and the role of Tom and the out-
landish stranger in leading the protagonists into their dreams. Con-

trasts include Tom's Washington adventure as an inversion of Rip's mountain one, and the muted conclusions of the professor's and Tom's stories against the happiness of Rip's. Also attempting to establish this novel firmly within the American tradition is Richard Dillman's "Tom Outland: Emerson's American Scholar in *The Professor's House*" (*MQ* 25:375–85), which comes close to truth in pushing a comparison between Emerson's ideal American and Cather's hero but misses the mark in concluding that the failure of Emersonian ideals and of Tom's is the fault of our materialistic century. Paul Comeau's "*The Professor's House* and Anatole France" (*Critical Essays*, pp. 217–27) is an extended analysis of a literary debt merely noted previously. Cather's references to the protagonist of *Le Mannequin d'osier* and the Dreyfus controversy emphasize and give perspective to the theme of betrayal and alienation central to her novel. James F. Maxfield takes issue with Edel's biographical reading of Cather's novel in "Strategies of Self-Deception in Willa Cather's *Professor's House*" (*SNNTS* 16:72–86), citing obvious personal deficiencies as reasons for St. Peter's despair and placing Cather closer to Tom's and seamstress Augusta's wisdom than to the confusion of the protagonist. "Willa Cather's 1916 Mesa Verde Essay: The Genesis of *The Professor's House*" (*PrS* 58,iv:81–92) reprints the "lost" 1916 Cather piece from the *Denver Times* with commentary by Susan J. Rosowski with the late Bernice Slote. Cather's article sheds light on her creative process, the refining that occurred during the nine years between the article's and novel's publications; it also suggests a positive resolution to a novel usually considered to conclude pessimistically. It is difficult to classify James C. Work's "Cather's Confounded Conundrums in *The Professor's House*" (*WAL* 18:303–12), an occasionally humorous complaint against Cather's use of allusions and symbols. While mocking Cather's method and perhaps critics who exaggerate its convolutions, Work comes close to "cracking" several riddles, including Professor St. Peter's tableau involving King Richard and the Saladin, and its connection to the *S. S. Berengaria*.

Cather's 1922 Pulitzer Prize–winning novel is the subject of two studies. Frederick T. Griffiths's "The Woman Warrior: Willa Cather and *One of Ours*" (*WS* 11:260–85) is a confusing mixture of several positive insights in defense of Cather's maligned war novel. Some of these (Cather's reversal of the "myths" of Joan of Arc, Semele-Zeus-Dionysius, Adam and Eve, Orpheus, Hippolytus, etc.) would prove significant if developed. Griffiths does give more than fleeting atten-

tion to the role of hero Claude's mother, Evangeline, as wise and
bitter oracle who "recognizes in him all of the redemptive illusions
he had always suspected in her." Jean Schwind's "The 'Beautiful' War
in *One of Ours*" (*MFS* 30:53–71) relates hero Claude's failure to his
inability to develop the indigenous art demanded by the modern
world; this is a crippling failure because he then depends for sight
on the conventional pastoral tradition which obscures the reality
both of women and war. While there are some sound insights on
Cather's use of fine art devices, the contributions of Stanley Cooper-
man and more recent critics of this novel might provide Schwind
with sharper focus.

A Lost Lady is the subject of two essays in the *Women's Studies*
issue. Nancy Morrow's "Willa Cather's *A Lost Lady* and the Nineteenth Century Novel of Adultery" (pp. 287–303) is a clear, well-
structured essay placing the novel within its tradition. Morrow views
Cather as clinging to the patterns of other novels, particularly *Anna
Karenina* and *Madame Bovary*, while evaluating her heroine aesthetically rather than morally. Morrow's conclusion that Cather rejects
the traditional moral precepts that would condemn her heroine makes
Cather more radical than she would want to be, although the insight
that she radically altered her sources is definitely on target. Diane
Cousineau's application of the Freudian "family romance" structure
in "Division and Difference in *A Lost Lady*" (pp. 305–22) puts Cather
definitely on the side of patriarchal culture and committed to denying Marian Forrester identity on her own terms, which explains why
Cather views her from the vantage point of a male.

Cather's neglected last two novels, *Lucy Gayheart* and *Sapphira
and the Slave Girl*, received significant attention. Susan J. Rosowski
in "Willa Cather's American Gothic: *Sapphira and the Slave Girl*"
(*GPQ* 4:220–30) argues convincingly that the ultimate irresolution
of the Virginia novel's dualities combined with elements of plot,
characters, and setting define the novel as a gothic romance. Particularly insightful are Rosowski's viewing the change from evil and
dissension to community and harmony in relation to the Eucharist
and her handling of the first-person epilogue, which links the dark
contradictory forces to our world, the world on the eve of World War
II. Eugénie Lambert Hamner examines Cather's use of first-person
narration in the epilogue of *Sapphira and the Slave Girl* in "The
Unknown, Well-Known Child in Cather's Last Novel" (*WS* 11:347–
57). The five-year-old narrator is the most direct of Cather's many

versions of herself and as such constitutes a foreshadowing of the "re-fined sense of detail" and "tenacious memory" employed successfully throughout Cather's long career in fiction. Hamner concludes with the interest this child betrays in stories of displaced women—but this seems tacked on to fit the feminist angle of the *Women's Studies* collection. In a major if overdone consideration of a minor novel, "Movement and Melody: the Disembodiment of Lucy Gayheart" (*Women Writing in America*, pp. 117–43), Blanche H. Gelfant sees this unappreciated novel much as she had *My Ántonia* in an earlier essay as holding "in constant tension opposite and irreconcilable views." In futile and dangerous flight-and-pursuit patterns Cather's lovers seek fulfillment from each other's inner selves while the novelist herself questions the power of words to communicate life. "As Lucy transfers her desire from human lover to 'Life itself' [which eludes words], she is transformed from a stereotypical small-town girl . . . into a personification of a powerful though mysterious Energy." And the novel, concludes Gelfant, is transformed from pulp romance to an allegory of the Romantic imagination. Susan J. Rosowski emphasizes the same novel in "Willa Cather's Female Landscapes: *The Song of the Lark* and *Lucy Gayheart*" (*WS* 11:233–46), which evaluates both novels as celebrations of "the closeness of the relationship between gender and consciousness." The landscape in *Song* contains metaphors of generation and outward movement from the confining womb, while those in *Lucy* focus on inward movement, engulfment, dependency. Of particular interest is Rosowski's consideration of the 1911 short story "The Joy of Nelly Deane" as anticipating in its "external trappings of a female world" the "internal landscape" of *Lucy Gayheart*. *The Song of the Lark* also is given brief attention in "Willa Cather's Artist Heroines" (*WS* 11:223–32) by Linda Pannill, who sees the control of Cather's writing as a result of her discovery of identity as a writer, a discovery dramatized by Thea Kronborg in the Panther Canyon episode. In *Chicago and the American Literary Imagination* (pp. 53–56) Carl S. Smith notes that in *The Song of the Lark* the city is a necessary evil, needed by the artist for the opportunities it offers, but also "an irredeemably hostile, restrictive, and commonplace world." Smith reminds us that to Cather art was an end in itself, not a means to social reform, although it can deeply enhance the lives of others. L. Brent Bohlke supplies some background information on Cather's masterpiece in "Willa Cather's Nebraska Priests and *Death Comes for the Archbishop*" (*GPQ* 4:264–69), which convinces that the Episcopal faith and its pioneer churchmen, Bishop George Allen Beecher and Rector John Mallory Bates, contributed as much to the novel as did Catholicism and its missionaries.

Undoubtedly the year's significant contribution on Cather's short fiction is Arnold's *Willa Cather's Short Fiction*, a volume of careful and intelligent criticism which begins to fill a glaring gap in Cather studies. Arnold's commentaries on point of view are superlative, and her insights on Cather's use of language only slightly less so. This volume contains the best discussions available on the three stories in *Obscure Destinies* and some of the best discussions of the three stories in *The Old Beauty and Others*. The book does well where Cather provides stories capable of standing on their own, without the crutches of better-known novels, and would be a better book if Arnold had refrained from frequent and lengthy comparisons of stories to novels. In general, the study mirrors the inconsistent quality of the subject matter addressed. In "Cather's Last Three Stories: A Testament of Life and Endurance" (*GPQ* 4:238–44) Arnold attempts to rescue Cather's posthumous *The Old Beauty and Others* from dismissal as a surrender to nostalgia by viewing it as the resolution of two conflicting Catherian tendencies: to escape from the painful present, and to survive and prevail (in the Faulknerian sense). The title story represents Cather's rejection of unadaptability, while the last, "Before Breakfast," celebrates the durability of humanity; between these, "The Best Years" establishes change and death as "natural and acceptable." In "Coming, Willa Cather!" (*WS* 11:247–60), Arnold calls attention to the 1920 story "Coming, Aphrodite!" ("Coming, Eden Bower!" in an altered version) as "Cather at her best, in control . . . yet wonderfully flexible" in chronicling the loss of Eden by elemental man and woman and in "insist [ing] that human aspirations toward art and self-realization are circumscribed by . . . primeval drives." In "The American Short Story: 1900–1920" (*The American Short Story* pp. 51–59) Ellen Kimbel briefly treats *The Troll Garden* and *Youth and the Bright Medusa* collections. She sees "The Sculptor's Funeral" as the reverse of "A Death in the Desert" in Cather's theme of the demands of art, and "Paul's Case" as an exploration of the tragic otherness of the artistic temperament. Kimbel considers these early stories superior to those in the latter collection, including "Coming, Aphrodite!" (!) simply because Cather as a sophisticated New Yorker was closer to her material and cynical about her artistic subjects. Finally on the short stories, my "Willa Cather's Children of Grace" (*WCPM*

Newsl. 28:13–15) evaluates the protagonists of "Jack-a-Boy," "The Joy of Nelly Deane" and "The Best Years" as manifestations "of God's grace . . . bringing people together in family," and examines the religious imagery in each of these stories.

Miscellaneous items on Cather include photographer Lucia Woods's "Light and Shadow in the Cather World: A Personal Essay" (*GPQ* 4:245–63), a reflection on the insights she has gained from a decade or more of attempting to photograph the "journey of Cather's life and work": the need to address the darkness of evil (in *Archbishop*), the dark mystery of earth (in the prairie novels), and human darkness (in *Sapphira*). Cather, Woods concludes, challenges the artist to be free from literalness, while being specific. In "Willa Cather and the Swedes" (*GPQ* 4:213–19) Mona Pers comments on the growth of Cather's reputation in Sweden. In personal reflections on reading Cather, "From the Tree House" (*WS* 11:359–68), Ned Ryerson makes the observation that beyond bitterness and materialism Cather found loneliness and enduring struggle, and that what she sought was "the endurance in others to meet that loneliness."

ii. Edith Wharton, Ellen Glasgow, Elizabeth Madox Roberts

Several fine articles appeared in the growing body of criticism on Wharton. The best of these, Judith Fryer's "Edith Wharton's 'Tact of Omission': Harmony and Proportion in *A Backward Glance*" (*Biography* 6[1983]:148–69), analyzes the novelist's construction of a perfect self to introduce her life's work. Fryer sees Wharton's childhood fantasizing and the sexual passion surfacing in the "Beatrice Palmato" fragment as indicative of a fascination with disorder, a disorder controlled or omitted in *A Backward Glance* to allow for the depiction of the graceful descendant of old New York Wharton wanted her readers to perceive. Duality is also the controlling concept in Wendy Gimbel's *Edith Wharton: Orphancy and Survival* (Praeger Women's Studies Series), a treatment of four novels as searches for houses of selfhood. In *The House of Mirth* Lily Bart is defeated in her search for a house in marriage within New York society, finally rejecting that "house of mirth" in her decision to burn the letters but incapable of constructing her own structure. Gimbel contends that in *Ethan Frome* homeless Mattie Silver extends Lily's search but into perpetual death-in-life with Ethan as crippled child of mother Zeena. Charity Royall's similar search in *Summer* takes her to the brink of independence, but she regresses by returning to the house of the father in a relationship with sinister incestuous overtones. Ellen Olenska in *The Age of Innocence* is the successful female, escaping a patriarchal marriage and a profane love triangle to construct her sacred space in Paris. Many penetrating insights in this study encourage a rich experience with the fiction, but they are pushed too far: Lawyer Royall as a fisher king, Ellen on Boston Common as Christ in Gethsemane, brownstone New York as nightmare landscape, etc. One wonders why Gimbel omitted *The Custom of the Country* and skirted the benefits of Elizabeth Ammons's *Edith Wharton's Argument with America* (*ALS 1980*, p. 252).

The novels Gimbel does include are the subjects of other essays. Bruce Michelson divides *The House of Mirth* into dramatic acts in "Edith Wharton's House Divided" (*SAF* 12:199–215) and shows how Wharton uses dramatic clichés (letters, mistaken identity, coincidence) while maintaining Ibsenian moral silence. He sees the novel's real world as suffused by stage trickery and Lily and Selden unsteady, complex performers, their "dilemma [as] of 'reality' itself, the problem of finding a way through all the pretenses of modern living, of finding a way even to the essential self." Marred by distortion and shrill feminism is Carolyn L. Karcher's "Male Vision and Female Revision in James's *The Wings of the Dove* and Wharton's *The House of Mirth*" (*WS* 10:227–44), which says that Wharton's novel responds to James's redemption in his of his male observer by making Densher/Selden into a hypocrite with an oedipal fixation on his mother and by combining angel Milly and monster Kate in Lily Bart. Feminist criticism is better served by Barbara A. White's "Edith Wharton's *Summer* and Woman's Fiction" (*ELWIU* 11:223–35), a comprehensive view of Wharton's fusion of seduction novel plot conventions and those of "the single tale" of the orphan. While building toward the conclusion that such fusion explains disparities between optimistic and pessimistic readings of *Summer*, White surveys nature (including sexual) imagery and Charity's revision of negative illusions regarding Lawyer Royall. Citing an obituary in a Pittsfield, Massachusetts, newspaper supporting her contention that Wharton was aware of the danger of sitting at the front of a sled, Jean Frantz Blackall argues in "The Sledding Accident in *Ethan Frome*" (*SSF* 21:145–46) that Ethan's wanting to sit ahead of Mattie in the sled is protective, not a symptom of regressive behavior. Nancy Morrow's

"Games and Conflict in Edith Wharton's *The Custom of the Country*" (*ALR* 14:32–39) begins as a comparison of game metaphors in Wharton's novel and James's *The American* and then concentrates on competitive Undine Spragg's three major contests, her imitation of others, and her final bewilderment.

Catherine M. Rae's treatment of the Whitman dimension of *The Spark* and her observation that Wharton's nostalgia for her native city is directed more toward "appurtenances and trappings of society, and extends only tangentially to its customs and values," are perhaps the most interesting things in her brief study of Wharton's *Old New York* novellas, *Edith Wharton's New York Quartet* (Univ. Press). Rae sees *The Old Maid* as a possible compromise between the maverick and the confining society, *False Dawn* as a "serious study of how human relationships are affected by the world in which they exist," and *New Year's Day* as Wharton's "enshrinement of marriage." These generally sensible comments are marred somewhat by Rae's insistent paralleling of the fiction with Wharton's life, so that every evil mother or father (!) becomes Wharton's mother, Civil War involvement masks the author's in World War I, and Lizzie Hazeldean's conversion to Catholicism in the last story might hint at Wharton's similar interest, etc., etc. R. W. B. Lewis contributes a graceful foreword to the slim volume, commenting on Wharton's deceptively lucid narrative surfaces, suggesting contrast with the lively obscurity of Faulkner's, and distinguishing her "historian" of her native city. The thesis of Rae's related article on *The Old Maid*, "Edith Wharton's Avenging Angel in the House" (*DQ* 18,iv:119–25), is that in old New York the women behind the scenes, not the men who thought they were in charge, actually ran the show; but her subject is instead the feuding cousins and Wharton's manipulation of sound and language in preparing for their "scene." The analysis is sound.

Four representative short stories are surveyed by Ellen Kimbel in Stevick's *The American Short Story* (pp. 41–51) to emphasize Wharton's seriousness as a writer of short fiction: "The Eyes," for the Hawthorne theme of head over heart; "Souls Belated," "The Other Two," and "Autre Temps," for the questioning of marriage and divorce in a world swiftly moving from narrow-mindedness to moral chaos. Judith E. Funston views the subject of " 'Xingu': Edith Wharton's Velvet Gauntlet" (*SAF* 12:227–34) as Wharton's retaliation for James's tactless criticism of her work. Response to the fiction of novelist Osric Dane in Wharton's story reflects Wharton's disapproval of aspects of James's fiction: lifeless characters, scientific narrative strategies, and rigid designs.

Finally, three articles explore Wharton's relationships with her contemporaries. Ellen Phillips Dupree quotes from eight recently discovered Wharton letters in "Wharton, Lewis and the Nobel Prize Address" (*AL* 56:262–70). Written between 1922 and 1925 to Sinclair Lewis, these and a ninth letter (reproduced by Dupree) protesting an attack on Howells in Lewis's Stockholm address trace the cooling of a friendship. In this last letter Wharton evaluates Lewis's later fiction and indicates preference for *The Man Who Knew Coolidge* because she felt Lewis indebted to her and to Howells in his portrait of Lowell Schmaltz. "Wharton's Forgotten Preface to Vivienne de Watteville's *Speak to the Earth*: A Link with Hemingway's 'The Snows of Kilimanjaro'" (*NMAL* 8:Item 10) by Adeline Tintner speculates on Hemingway's indebtedness to Wharton for sending him de Watteville's volume, which he closely followed in parts of his story; Tintner quotes generously from Wharton's 500-word introduction to *Earth*. Leon Edel examines Wharton's friendship with Walter Berry in "Walter Berry and the Novelists: Proust, James, and Edith Wharton" (*NCF* 38:514–28) and includes an interesting account of his own visits with Wharton while researching Berry's life. Edel concludes that Berry gave Wharton confidence and authority and that associating with her and the other novelists gave Berry a semblance of the imagination he lacked: "She was in love, a little like Isabel Archer, with an image in the mirror of herself, disguised as a man. Some flaw in his self-esteem perhaps found itself mended by the trust and confidence of this gifted woman."

The year's work on Glasgow is significant in quality if not quantity, taking us beyond the narrow confines of defensive feminism. J. E. Bunselmeyer offers the most embracing treatment of Glasgow in "Ellen Glasgow's 'Flexible' Style" (*CentR* 28:112–28), a fascinating analysis of the novelist's combining of ironic syntactic balancing in introducing characters, right-branching structures in realistic descriptions, and explicit repetition of syntax patterns (especially question clusters) to express thought processes. All three styles blend in distancing the reader while resulting in a conflict of tones. Bunselmeyer argues that this method was appropriate for a novelist whose "theme is the lack of value systems—the hollowness of the old conventions and the self-interest of the new." In "Ellen Glasgow and the

Southern Agrarians" (*AL* 56:203–13) Ellen M. Caldwell notes in *Barren Ground* Glasgow's "dramatic break with [her] previous fifteen novels" in depicting characters "struggling to recover a regional identity." Caldwell sees the Southern Agrarian movement, particularly Glasgow's contact with Allen Tate, as refining her view of the past and tradition in her major fiction. On the strength of *Barren Ground*, *The Sheltered Life*, and *Vein of Iron* Tate's view of her work changed dramatically, from labeling her "one of the worst novelists in the world" for ridiculing the foibles of the South to a novelist capable of depth and universality. A similar about-face toward Glasgow is recorded in the correspondence between Glasgow and H. L. Mencken assembled with comments by Ritchie D. Watson, Jr. (*EGN* 20:[6–17]). Through the efforts of writer Sara Haardt (the future Mrs. Mencken), an avid Glasgow fan, Mencken moved from grouping "La Glasgow" among bad novelists in the early '20s to enthusiastically endorsing the 1933 Old Dominion edition of her works for their "blistering realism." The more than 50 exchanges indicate Glasgow's growing friendship for Mencken, which was reciprocated with a somewhat distant warmth. Thomas Gullason briefly treats Glasgow in "The Question of Regionalism: Limitation and Transcendence" (*The American Short Story*, pp. 164–67), although his emphasis is not on her regionalism but on her ghost stories, which he judges conventional but carefully crafted. He feels "Whispering Leaves" better than "The Shadowy Third"; among non–ghost stories he favors "The Difference." He speculates that Glasgow devoted the short story form to her interest in mysticism and idealist philosophy. Of interest in this connection is the reprinting of "Ellen Glasgow's Credo" in the *Ellen Glasgow Newsletter* (21:6–12); in this 1938 apology the novelist describes herself as inheriting a tragic conflict of types—her father's forbidding Calvinism and her mother's beneficent Episcopalianism— and traces the development of her faith, from her childhood belief "in Santa Claus and in Original Sin" to belief in Good, blessedness, the challenging mind, "the unreconciled heart, and in the will toward perfection." We lapse into narrower views in Lynette Carpenter's "The Daring Gift in Ellen Glasgow's 'Dare's Gift' " (*SSF* 21:95–102), where the daring gift seems to be a woman's destruction of her lawyer husband's career due to her female moral superiority and his romantic stereotyping of women.

A more absorbing feminism marks the most significant study in *The Southern Review*'s very welcome special section of papers read at the 1981 Elizabeth Madox Roberts Centenary Conference at St. Catherine College, Springfield, Kentucky. Lewis P. Simpson's "The Sexuality of History" (20:785–802) seems at times to stray from Roberts but successfully emphasizes her unique universality. Using heroines to represent different aspects of consciousness in the conflict between the self and the restraints of history (the southern inward sense of history), Roberts depicts the defeat of the poetic sensibility in *The Time of Man*, the identification of sexuality with history (and the reversal of masculine and feminine creative power) in *My Heart and My Flesh*, the emergence of woman as shaper of history in *The Great Meadow*, and transcendence to super-life in *He Sent Forth a Raven*. Simpson feels that "in her struggle with history Roberts is the peer of William Faulkner, Allen Tate, and Robert Penn Warren." In "Through Language to Self: Ellen's Journey in *The Time of Man*" (pp. 774–84), Victor A. Kramer tries to clarify the complexity of Roberts's linguistic achievement by examining passages demonstrating the value and limitations of words in Ellen Chesser's journey of self-awareness. The challenge facing Roberts was to express in words the always passing "no time" of man, which is beyond language. Language helps Ellen find and sustain the rhythm of life: when her consciousness becomes imprisoned or hardened into words, language returns her to the ongoing rhythm beyond language. Pearl Andelson Sherry notes in "Symbolism in the Letters of Elizabeth Madox Roberts" (pp. 824–28) that Roberts's objective in *He Sent Forth a Raven* and *Black Is My Truelove's Hair* "is to use symbolism to delineate what happens against a background of what is known from myth and legend and religion—from the great writing and rumor of the past." Roberts's settings in these novels provide "a reality through which the symbolic characters move in their multiple natures." Sherry links various characters to biblical and mythological figures and concludes by quoting from a letter Roberts wrote to her about the relationship between reality and the ideal. William H. Slavick laments the lack of a biography of Roberts in "Taken with a Long-Handled Spoon: The Roberts Papers and Letters" (pp. 752–73) and presents a potpourri from her private papers and correspondence to literary friends (dipped into surreptitiously with such a spoon) to serve in the meantime. These reveal her attempts in *The Time of Man* "to achieve a form in which the uses of poetry and prose are identical." Her unfinished fiction indicates her readiness to experiment—she had read Joyce and felt *Ulysses* the form toward which prose "has been moving for ten years or more." She believed her function as a writer was the ordering of chaos, a belief in form as sensed by the artist and lowly folk. Janet Lewis's "Elizabeth Madox Roberts: A Memoir" (pp. 803–16) is a moving tribute to a friendship of 20 years, dating from student days at Chicago. Lewis tells of Roberts's introduction to Florentine art, her dedication to Kentucky as her subject, and her fondness for the quote from Virgil in Cather's *My Ántonia* about bringing the muse into one's province. Lewis offers delightful passages from Roberts's letters to her from rural Kentucky in "Letters from the Little Country: The Summers of 1919 and 1920" (pp. 829–35). With wit and poetry the novelist describes a library "book shower," a country fair, a Farmer's Chatauqua, a visit to a Catholic church, etc. Finally, the late Maurice Lesemann (the man—20 years her junior—believed to have been loved by Roberts) contributes in "Elizabeth Madox Roberts: A Reminiscence" (pp. 817–20) firsthand information on her working method: her helter-skelter note-taking, her use of envelopes as files for each chapter, her composing on the typewriter. Roberts's copying the typed manuscript of *The Time of Man* in longhand has led to erroneous conclusions about her fluent method of composition.

iii. Theodore Dreiser and Jack London

Michael Spindler situates Dreiser on a broad social canvas in "The Rise of the Entrepreneur in the Work of Howells, Norris and Dreiser" in *American Literature and Social Change* (pp. 48–73). Spindler sees the significance of the Cowperwood trilogy as a development beyond Howells's agrarian mentality in *The Rise of Silas Lapham* and Norris's sympathy for and knowledge of American business in *The Pit*. Dreiser's portrayal of a ruthless superman rejects traditional American values while reflecting aspects of both Franklin's and Emerson's principles of success. A related chapter, "The Condition of the Poor in the Work of Howells, Dreiser and Sinclair" (pp. 74–93), places Dreiser within the tradition of *A Hazard of New Fortunes* and *The Jungle*, noting that Dreiser had firsthand experience that took him beyond Howells in depicting poverty. Spindler convinces that the careers of Carrie, Drouet, and Hurstwood in *Sister Carrie* dramatize the decline of Puritan conscience to social convention and then the violation of convention by desire for success. In "Class and the Consumption Ethic: Dreiser's *An American Tragedy*" (pp. 135–

49) Spindler examines the changing social and ideological forces operating in the novel. Clyde is seen as wavering between the Protestant ethic of hard work and virtue and the hedonism of a society based on appearances and consumerism, between family and peer pressure, and between privileged and working classes. Carl S. Smith gives attention to the Cowperwood trilogy and *Sister Carrie* in *Chicago and the American Literary Imagination* (pp. 70–78, 115–20); he evaluates the city as art object offering a challenge to Cowperwood, the financier/artist, and Carrie's entrance into Chicago by train as a period piece and a moral tale, noting Dreiser's debt to Hamlin Garland's *Rose of Dutcher's Coolly*. Social issues also concern Thomas P. Riggio in "Theodore Dreiser: Hidden Ethic" (*MELUS* 11:53–63), which first enumerates literary and social reasons why Dreiser remained a "hidden" ethnic writer, and then explores clues in *Sister Carrie* establishing it as an ethnic novel. " 'The Feast of Belshazzar' and *Sister Carrie*" (*ALR* 17:40–43) by William J. Burling takes a hint from the title of the 23rd chapter to make Ames a Daniel from Indianapolis, a seer exposing to Carrie the empty materialism of Babylon. In "Flux Metaphors in *Sister Carrie*" (*DrN* 15,i:1–9) John J. McAleer finds textual evidence in the novel and *A Book About Myself* that Dreiser envisioned Carrie as a wandering sea bird and that corresponding flight and tidal as well as rocking chair allusions support his idea of constant flux.

Donald Pizer devotes two chapters to Dreiser in his revised edition of *Realism and Naturalism*. "American Literary Naturalism: The Example of Dreiser" (pp. 41–58) successfully defends the integrity of American naturalism by showing how in *Jennie Gerhardt* the deterministic "philosophy" is inseparable from the temperaments of the various characters dramatizing it; also, Pizer argues that our response to book 1 of *An American Tragedy* is "not as [to] an exercise in determinism but as [to] a subtle dramatization of the ways in which a distinctive temperament [Clyde's] . . . interacts with a distinctive social setting." In his final chapter, "Theodore Dreiser's 'Nigger Jeff': The Development of an Aesthetic" (pp. 180–93), Pizer tries to trace the development of Dreiser's beliefs about the nature of art through a comparison of three versions (*c.* 1895, 1901, and 1908) of the frequently anthologized story. Somewhat similar to Pizer's are Lois Hughson's concerns about the artistic source of Dreiser's impact as a novelist in "Dreiser's Cowperwood and the Dynamics of Naturalism" (*SNNTS* 16:52–71). The accomplishment of *The Financier* is

Dreiser's ability to view life from within the natural energy process as well as from outside it: "The perspective that sees Cowperwood only as an agent is overlaid with a perspective that makes any separation between energy and agent, game and player, a falsification." Yet this duality implies differences between Dreiser's naturalism and Emerson's transcendentalism, in which primal energy subsumes the self. More pointedly a defense of Dreiser's art, Paul A. Orlov's "Technique as Theme in *An American Tragedy*" (*JNT* 14:75–93) is a convincing and thorough argument that the novel's effective dramatization of the ironic theme of Clyde's losing himself in the struggle to find himself according to Horatio Alger values depends upon its structural parallels, manipulation of point of view, and symbolic commentary on the plot.

Among miscellaneous Dreiseriana are Eugene L. Huddleston's argument in "What a Difference Thirty Years Make: *A Place in the Sun* Today" (*DrN* 15,ii:1–12) that the 1951 film version of *An American Tragedy* is outdated and flawed because producer-director George Stevens emphasized the love story at the expense of Dreiser's social criticism and removed the ambiguity from the drowning incident, making Clyde's conviction and execution implausible to later audiences. Frederic E. Rusch's "Lycurgus and Dreiser's *An American Tragedy*" (*NMAL* 8:Item 18) fails to make a convincing connection between the Lycurguses of myth and history and Dreiser's choice of a name for the New York "classical belt" setting of his novel. Ellen Kimbel appreciates Dreiser's counterpoising of human cruelty and natural beauty in "Nigger Jeff" and of the prosaic and lyrical in "The Lost Phoebe" in *The American Short Story* (pp. 59–61). A slightly belabored effort on a much lesser short story achievement than either of these is Joseph Griffin's " 'Butcher Rogaum's Door': Dreiser's Early Tale of New York" (*ALR* 17:24–31), which seems successful in proving Dreiser's intention to write a Bowery fairy tale rather than a short story. Finally, there are two biographical pieces. Richard W. Dowell quotes liberally from correspondence in the Lilly Library at Indiana in "Dreiser's Courtship Letters: Portents of a Doomed Marriage" (*DrN* 15,i:14–20), revealing Dreiser's success anxiety and doubts about his love for "Jug" and implying her uneasiness. James L. W. West III adds to the saga of Dreiserian publishing lore in "Dreiser and Random House" (*DrN* 15,ii:13–17), a speculation on why Bennett Cerf overcame and then yielded to his aversion to Dreiser by having a letter written inviting him to publish with Random House and then never sending it. The letter, signed by Cerf's partner, Donald S. Klopfer, is included in the essay.

The year's single book-length study of London, Carolyn Johnston's *Jack London—An American Radical?*, one of Greenwood Press's "Contributions in Political Science," avowedly is not a literary consideration. Claiming to be the first account of London's radicalism drawing on all his personal papers (the collections of which are listed in a generous bibliographical section), Johnston concludes that her subject was a rebel rather than a radical, a contradictory thinker corrupted by the bourgeois life he rebelled against. Her portrait is of a man constantly betwixt and between, in conflict with conservative New York socialists yet in despair at the inevitable bloodshed he envisioned, and in sympathy with yet disdainful of the proletariat. Johnston attributes the power of *The Iron Heel* to this dichotomy, its ability to instill fear of struggle and defeat among both the sympathizers and opponents of socialism. While this study offers few literary insights, it does provide a clear survey of London's confused but representative political views. Gorman Beauchamp's reader's guide, *Jack London* (Starmont House), is, without indicating so, an introduction to London's science fiction; also, because partially taken from a 1980 essay, the bibliography lists no scholarship beyond the '70s. However, bearing these limitations in mind, the brief work offers a useful view of an aspect of London's fiction. A chapter is devoted to seven science fiction stories—three others, "The Strength of the Strong," "Goliah," and "The Red One" are treated in other chapters in relation to novels. Novels considered under the science fiction rubric include *Before Adam*, *The Scarlet Plague*, and *The Iron Heel*. Respectively, these are said to anticipate Jung's ideas on the collective unconscious, Walter M. Miller's *A Canticle for Leibowitz*, and Orwell's *1984*.

Several essays try to be comprehensive. Stoddard Martin's chapter on London in *California Writers* (Macmillan [1983], pp. 17–66) surveys London's career from his early dismay at the hopeless social conditions of cockney underdogs in *The Sea Wolf* and *The People of The Abyss* to his attempt to get under the skin of the oligarchs in *The Little Lady of the Big House*. Martin condenses his treatment of the social contradictions in *The Iron Heel* to concentrate on London's anticipation of *Finnegans Wake* in exploring dream-space while recapitulating history in *The Star Rover*, and on his romantic notions of the primitive and civilizing influences of woman in *A Daughter of the Snows, Adventure, The Valley of the Moon,* and *The Little Lady of the Big House.* The last of these is singled out as anticipating California tycoons Hearst and Hughes, Fitzgerald's *The Great Gatsby,* and, in its interior monologues, the dramas of Eugene O'Neill. Donald Pizer includes among new essays in *Realism and Naturalism* (pp. 166–79) his convincing "Jack London: The Problem of Form" from the 1983 American Realism issue of *Studies in the Literary Imagination.* In "Jack London's Biographical Legend" (*ALR* 17:67–88) David H. Stanley depicts the author as a victim of his own legend, as relying on the popular image he created through fictional techniques as well as autobiographical subjects: "London's continuing search for himself becomes evident in the multiple selves which he imagined himself to be in his works." In *The Sea-Wolf* London is both Humphrey Van Weyden and Wolf Larsen; he is also Martin Eden, self-made man and alienated artist; *John Barleycorn* is confessional literature, and so on. David A. Moreland reveals intriguing contradictions in "Violence in the South Sea Fiction of Jack London" (*JLN* 16[1983]: 1–35). After establishing London's penchant for violence and his belief in white supremacy, Moreland reviews "Mauki," "Yah! Yah! Yah!," and "The Inevitable White Man" as unduly violent but critical of white ferocity, and then "The Seed of McCoy," "The House of Pride," "Koolau the Leper," and "The Chinago" as exhibiting control in descriptions of violence while critical of white exploitation. Some of London's phobias are treated in Alan Kaufman's "'We're Saxons . . . and Not Dagoes': The Role of Racism in Jack London's Late Novels" (*JLT* 16:96–103). *The Valley of the Moon* records a flight to the soil and the nation's Anglo-Saxon past, and *The Mutiny of the Elsinore* depicts in miniature early 20th-century America and expresses fears of Aryan doom.

Kim Moreland contributes a feminist polemic in "The Attack on the Nineteenth-Century Heroine Reconsidered: Women in Jack London's *Martin Eden*" (*MarkhamR* 13:16–20), which contains valid insights on the title character's ambivalence toward Ruth Morse, to whom he is attracted and repulsed by her genteel limitations, but makes some logical leaps in applying his treatment of Ruth to all women. Finally, Charles N. Watson, Jr., provides a much-needed index for Charmian London's two-volume 1921 biography of her husband in "An Index to *The Book of Jack London*" (*JLN* 16:47–95).

iv. Sherwood Anderson and Gertrude Stein

An edition of letters and a special annual number of *Midwestern Miscellany* (12) highlight work on Anderson. Two essays from the latter try to link Anderson to future writers. David Stouck's *"Many Marriages* as a Postmodern Novel"* (*MMisc* 12:15–22) clearly defines postmodernism, shows how it is "a logical extension" of Anderson's and Stein's experimentation, and indicates where this "not . . . good" Anderson novel illustrates a departure from mimetic realism and an interest in the plastic function of words. In "Sherwood Anderson's Grotesques and Modern American Fiction" (pp. 53–65) David D. Anderson tries to make Saul Bellow a latter-day Anderson by showing how *Dangling Man's* protagonist in seeking identity away from his society of grotesques reflects "an age that denies community and love," while George Willard in *Winesburg, Ohio* reflects late-19th-century values in seeking self in his community of grotesques. Not very convincing is Jim Elledge's "Dante's Lovers in Sherwood Anderson's 'Hands' " (*SSF* 21:11–15), which tries to parallel Wing Biddlebaum in the *Winesburg* story and Paolo and Francesca in Canto V of *Hell*, and Willard and Dante as questioning pilgrims. The innocent Biddlebaum, says Elledge, "devours the crumbs of a wasted life in an act of penance, suffering decade after decade in his self-created hell."

A quarter-century of letters from 24 libraries and private collections are made available in Charles E. Modlin's edition of *Sherwood Anderson, Selected Letters* (Tenn.). Carefully edited with annotations identifying correspondents, references, and locations of the originals, the letters reveal a man of wit, deep feeling, and love of life. Anderson's correspondents range from his mother-in-law, Laura Copenhaver, to Ernest Hemingway. To Georgia O'Keeffe he describes Nevada desert mountains; he apologizes to his son John for not being a better provider; commenting on a writers' conference at Boulder, Colorado, he laments to Thomas Wolfe, "Why do decent people want to write. That should be left to us bastards." The letters also contain vignettes later used in his published writings. Excerpts from Eleanor Anderson's journal of her husband's 1934 trip to northern Ohio are made available in Hilbert H. Campbell's "Sherwood Anderson's Sentimental Journey" (*RALS* 12:64–66). Of artistic and biographical interest is the reprinting of Anderson's 1928 piece "The Young Writer" for a Washington and Lee University publication (*WE*

9,ii:1–2); in it he warns against striving for cheap effects and financial success and compares one's relationship to one's art to human relationships: "If you cheapen your relations with people, your whole life becomes cheap."

In " 'I Want to Know Why' as Biography and Fiction" (*MMisc* 12:7–14) Walter B. Rideout speculates on how Anderson's experiences at Kentucky racetracks and his befriending of blacks during the 1919 racial strife in Chicago inform this story, and on how later writers—from Hemingway to Alice Walker—are indebted to him for a voice that frees our literature from formality, for the theme of sensitivity against ugliness, and for allowing meaning to mold structure. George C. Matthews questions the value of Anderson's depiction of blacks in "Ohio's *Beulah Land* or Plantation Blacks in the Fiction of Sherwood Anderson" (*CLAJ* 25[1982]:405–13). While recognizing Anderson's sympathy for blacks, Matthews concludes that "I'm a Fool," "Out of Nowhere into Nothing," "I Want to Know Why," and even *Dark Laughter* depict stereotypes that reflect Anderson's "impression that the essence of black life was summed up and could be discovered in its 'dance' and 'song.' " Karyn Riedell charges Anderson with similar stereotyping of another "minority" in "Kit Brandon: Androgynous Heroine" (*WE* 10,i:1–5), which concludes that Anderson's title character and her friend Agnes assume masculine roles only because men have become emasculated with the machine age, and that while Anderson "can sympathize with [women] in their desire for dominance and freedom, . . . he also argues that if men were as they should be, then women would find their natural role as man's helpmate."

Anderson's working methods occupy Ray Lewis White in three pieces. "The Revisions in *Windy McPherson's Son*, Sherwood Anderson's First Novel" (*MMisc* 12:23–52) compares the 1916 and 1922 versions and establishes that more than the ending was revised, noting several textual improvements probably by a zealous proofreader. Then White compares the two versions of the endings and concludes that the revised one is more realistic and muted. "*Winesburg, Ohio:* The Story Titles" (*WE* 10,i:6–7) offers a chart of the progressive developments of story titles, from manuscript original through periodical and book publications, to direct study toward the genesis and evolution of the work. In "*Winesburg, Ohio:* The Table of Contents" (*NMAL* 8:Item 8) White traces the arrangement of the work through five stages, noting additions and repositionings of certain stories.

Carl S. Smith views *Windy McPherson's Son* in *Chicago and the American Literary Imagination* (pp. 78–90) within the context of Norris's and Dreiser's fiction for its portrayal of a more sensitive businessman/artist and as combining several recurring formulas involving the provincial in Chicago writing: entrance into the city, triumph in the city, and turning from the city in search for truth.

Finally, Ellen Kimbel, Thomas A. Gullason, and James G. Watson contribute views on Anderson stories in various parts of *The American Short Story* (pp. 62–69, 76–78, 123–24), briefly commenting on selected stories as well as generalizing about Anderson changing the course of American short fiction by revealing the dark side of national life in moments of epiphany.

The year's three book-length studies of Stein exhibit the care and reasonableness that have come to characterize Stein scholarship. Jayne L. Walker's *The Making of a Modernist: Gertrude Stein from Three Lives to Tender Buttons* (Mass.) traces the progress of Stein's struggle with realism during the years between these major works, "a critical episode in the history of representation." Walker devotes a chapter each to *Three Lives, The Making of Americans,* the "portraits," *Two* and transitional works, and *Tender Buttons.* Painstakingly she explains Stein's attempts to create a narrative idiom approximating speech and thought patterns (similar to the patterning of Cézanne's brushstrokes) and then follows Stein's shift away from types toward comprehensive studies of the individual. Stein subsequently distanced herself from analytical thought until in *Tender Buttons* she paralleled Picasso's Cubist experiments in representing "specific random actions, 'pieces of anyday.'" This is a thorough analysis of the early phase of Stein's career with ample notes to each of the six chapters, although no bibliography. In *The Structure of Obscurity: Gertrude Stein, Language, and Cubism* (Illinois) Randa Dubnick takes us further into the career. Addressed to the serious reader rather than Stein specialist, Dubnick's work becomes, nevertheless, as deeply analytical as Walker's as she distinguishes between Stein's obscure prose and obscure poetry styles and examines appropriate works to show how the latter style led to the abandoning of syntax. Attention is given to the merging of the two styles in *The Geographical History of America.* Dubnick's concluding chapter is an excellent introduction to Stein and her critical reception and might be read first. The third study, *Gertrude Stein's Theatre of the Absolute* (UMI Research Press) by Betsy Alayne Ryan, surveys in detail, first, Stein's general aesthetic—to achieve stillness in writing—and then her playwriting aesthetic—to achieve movement within stillness. "Essence of What Happened," landscape and narrative plays divide Stein's dramatic career into periods, and Ryan analyzes representative works against conventional aspects of drama "to help delineate [Stein's] general approach by their sheer opposition to it." A chapter is devoted to the theatrical legacy, Ryan concluding that Stein's theater "was so far ahead of its time that we can only now begin to perceive what she attempted in the medium." A bibliography of production reviews and appendixes listing plays chronologically, play traits (by form, subject, concern), and productions conclude this very complete study of the subject.

Stein, like Anderson, is taken to task in depicting blacks in Milton A. Cohen's "Black Brutes and Mulatto Saints: The Racial Hierarchy of Stein's 'Melanctha'" (*BALF* 18:119–21), which contributes a graph in trying to determine if Stein's racial hierarchy (degrees of blackness and whiteness) reflected her typing of individuals. This and the other two stories in the early collection are Beverly Hume's concern in "Prolonged Banality: Time and Stein's *Three Lives*" (*NMAL* 8: Item 13), which distinguishes between prolonged, or temporal, and continuing "presents" in the work, making it a study of character extremes involving dogma and dream. The Stein-Toklas relationship occupies Catharine R. Stimpson in "Gertrice Altrude: Stein, Toklas, and the Paradox of the Happy Marriage" in *Mothering the Mind* (pp. 122–39). Stimpson introduces the separate then combined biographies, stressing Alice Toklas's independence, especially during the two decades she survived Stein. Stimpson notes the irony of Stein's political conservatism and dependence on men, her playing the baby to Toklas's adult, and her use of their experiences as a couple in her "fictions." The late Virgil Thomson offers a sometimes touching reminiscence in "Remembering Gertrude" (*CLC* 31 [1982],ii:3–17), describing a typical day in the life of the post-1926 writer he knew, revealing her dependence on Toklas and blaming Toklas for terminating Stein's friendships with brother Leo, Mabel Dodge, Hemingway, and French poet Georges Hugnet. Finally, Ray Lewis White intends his exhaustive, annotated *Gertrude Stein and Alice B. Toklas: A Reference Guide* (Hall) of 1,920 entries chronologically arranged to give "to Toklas for the first time the literary recognition that she deserved but did not court until after Stein's death and late in her own life."

v. John Dos Passos, Sinclair Lewis, Upton Sinclair

The year's *big* work on Dos Passos—almost 600 pages of text—is Virginia Spencer Carr's *Dos Passos: A Life* (Doubleday), an exhaustive rather than critical biography which traces the crescent of Dos Passos's career from his boyhood insecurities as the unacknowledged son of a colorful father to his final days as sage of Spence's Point, Virginia. Between these are other poles—his early pacifism and radicalism, his disagreement with Hemingway over the Spanish cause, his friendship with William F. Buckley. Despite the wealth of facts and details she has assembled, Carr manages a readable style, presents rather than editorializes, and avoids intruding as biographer. There are three generous photo sections depicting the young man, the mature writer with literary friends, and the last years. Sweeping views of a more analytical nature concern Michael Spindler in "Undemocratic Vistas: Dos Passos, Mass Society and Monopoly Capital" (*American Literature and Social Change*, pp. 183–201), which notes the native sources of Dos Passos's radicalism—Whitman, Veblen, Goldman, Eastman, and the I.W.W.—and his intention to reflect the currents of history in contemporary events. Considering *Three Soldiers* and *Manhattan Transfer* as well as *U.S.A.*, Spindler contends that Dos Passos's final pessimism in the trilogy "was not entirely justified by historical events." In "Mr. Dos Passos' War" (*MFS* 30:37–52), John Rohrkemper examines Dos Passos's developing view of World War I, the greatest event in his life, from the perspective of his four books on it: *One Man's Initiation, Three Soldiers, 1919,* and *Mr. Wilson's War*. The war is seen first as evil and destructive of humanity, and then the military becomes a microcosm of modern life; modern society is exposed next as spawning and profiting from war; finally, war is condemned as midwife to the leviathan federal government. Robert James Butler sees the trilogy as dramatizing through motion the freedom, independence, instability, and incoherence of American life in "The American Quest for Pure Movement in Dos Passos' *U.S.A.*" (*TCL* 30:30–99). The pessimistic stasis of *The Big Money* is counterpoised by successful questing in its biographies and Camera Eye sections. Also, the vignette of the wanderer Vag which encloses the trilogy has echoes of Deerslayer, Ishmael, and Huckleberry Finn. "Media and Newsreels in Dos Passos' *U.S.A.*" (*JNT* 14:182–91) by David

Seed is a fine analysis of the novelist's technique. The Newsreels are examined as literature, as rich sources of subliminal association in which style becomes information. Finally, David J. Viera's comparative study, "Wastelands and Backlands: John Dos Passos' *Manhattan Transfer* and Graciliano Ramos' *Angústia*" (*Hispania* 67:377–82), illustrates similarities in themes, motivation, main characters, ideologies, imagery, and symbols, but differences in technique, point of view, and use of time. The Brazilian's novel is said to be more definite in affirming the proletariat cause.

Sinclair Lewis is afforded a complete chapter in Spindler's *American Literature and Social Change* ("Satire and Sentiment: Sinclair Lewis and the Middle Class," pp. 168–82) acknowledging the sociological accuracy of his portrayals in both *Main Street* and *Babbitt*. However, Spindler finds disappointing Lewis's sustaining of the small town myth and middle-class conformity he sets out to undermine. With an eye toward consistency rather than dichotomy, Christopher P. Wilson in "Sinclair Lewis and the Passing of Capitalism" (*AmerS* 24,ii:95–108) stresses Lewis's attempts to scale down the Naturalists' romanticized scenario of American capitalism. Lewis's hope that Fabian socialism and late Victorian "New Thought" would ennoble American business was dashed when business became entrapment in a world of lies. Wilson explores *The Job*'s debt to H. G. Wells and sees the "Lancelot Todd" stories as anticipating *Babbitt* in their "twist[ing] the inflated rhetoric of naturalism into a tone of mockery." The sources of Lewis's success concern Edward A. Martin in "The Mimic as Artist: Sinclair Lewis" (*H. L. Mencken and the Debunkers* [Georgia], pp. 115–38). Lewis derived his fictions from other novelists—*Main Street* from Wharton and Dreiser, and the satire in *Elmer Gantry* from the irony of Frederic in *The Damnation of Theron Ware*. He also espoused H. L. Mencken's theories of mimetic realism and imitated Mencken's cultural criticism and debunking attitudes. Lewis's best works "penetrated deeply into the American consciousness, not just because they ridiculed provincial life and manners but also because they portrayed through imitation and mimicry aspects of the twentieth-century American's perception of self." In "The Question of Regionalism: Limitation and Transcendence" (*The American Short Story*, pp. 167–70), Mary Rohrberger gives short shrift to Lewis's short story efforts. After brief comment on "Let's Play King" and "Moths in the Arc Light," she concludes:

"Beyond surface irony, there is little to a Lewis story. . . . He was not a self-conscious stylist and apparently never considered complex substructures of any kind important in fiction."

The year's most interesting essay on Sinclair, Timothy Cook's "Upton Sinclair's *The Jungle* and Orwell's *Animal Farm:* A Relationship Explored" (*MFS* 30:696–702), makes a convincing argument that the English fable owes more to the popular American novel than to any other work. Sinclair's description of the pork-making process perhaps influenced Orwell's choice of pigs to lead his revolution; Sinclair's Jurgis and Marija are human prototypes for the carthorses Boxer and Clover, and Boxer's refrain, "I will work harder," is lifted verbatim from the text of *The Jungle*. While Sinclair exposes the myth of a capitalist Zion, Orwell attacks a socialist one. In "The Condition of the Poor in the Work of Howells, Dreiser and Sinclair" (*American Literature and Social Change*, pp. 88–93), Spindler sees *The Jungle* as improving upon Howells's treatment of immigrant workers in *A Hazard of New Fortunes* by moving them to center stage and showing the erosion of their community and morality as American workers. He credits Sinclair with the ability to avoid sentimentality while demonstrating compassion in depicting the exploited, and groups him with Norris and Dreiser in documentary method, although occupied with change as much as depiction. The *Upton Sinclair Quarterly* offers more than its usual amount of Sinclairiana in an "Epic Anniversary Issue" (8,iii:3–19), which includes a report of interviews being conducted among surviving participants in the 1934 California gubernatorial campaign, when Sinclair ran on the EPIC (End Poverty in California) ticket, and also lists the highlights of the campaign. Sinclair's experimental 1909 play " 'John D.': An Adventure" is reprinted with commentary in the previous issue (8,i–ii:5–17).

vi. H. L. Mencken and Some Others

Charles Scruggs presents a fascinating aspect of Mencken in *The Sage in Harlem: H. L. Mencken and the Black Writers of the 1920s* (Johns Hopkins). Through Scruggs's reading of unpublished letters and articles in black periodicals, Mencken emerges as an important factor in the Harlem Renaissance, useful to blacks in challenging them directly to produce good fiction and indirectly by ridiculing WASP values and lifestyle. Admitting Mencken capable of racist views, especially in his early career, Scruggs sees him as jolting blacks out of their watermelon darkie image and toward realistic portrayals exposing the strengths and shortcomings of their race. Blacks, Mencken believed, could contribute unique perspectives on the nation's life. Mencken placed hope for black writers in the fiction of Walter White and for black political sanity in the satire of George Schuyler. Limited by his prejudices, however, Mencken refused to see beyond a mimetic and pragmatic realism, refused to understand modernism. Scruggs is uncertain if Mencken would applaud the fiction of a Toni Morrison but is certain that such fiction gives "the privileged view of black life which Mencken had so clearly seen belonged to the Negro novelist alone." Mencken is viewed as a crucial figure in a group of writers committed to mocking the banality of the American middle class and mass culture in Martin's *H. L. Mencken and the Debunkers.* Included in the group are Sinclair Lewis, Ring Lardner, Don Marquis, Frank Sullivan, E. B. White, and Nathanael West, to each of whom Martin assigns full or partial chapters. There is an attempt here to get behind the façade of these writers, especially Mencken, who is the subject of four of the 11 chapters in the book. While Martin delineates the provinciality, hypocritical conformity, and sterile puritanism that infuriated Mencken, he stresses the anguish behind the brag, the bruised humanist and progressive idealist. Language is the key to understanding these debunkers; abuse of language (propaganda, advertising, distortions, etc.) amounted to moral disarray. Their response was to mock such language, to become performing artists of words. "Behind the mockery there was an unshakable anguish and the puritanical sense that such a response was not entirely suitable." Both the Martin and Scruggs studies succeed in providing insights into Mencken's complexity.

Other writers represented by book-length studies this year included Owen Wister, Ole Edvart Rölvaag, and Booth Tarkington. Wister and Rölvaag were each a subject of a Twayne's United States Authors Series volume. In his study of Wister (TUSAS 475), John L. Cobbs devotes a chapter to each of Wister's major contributions, gives intriguing analysis of the "masturbatory-self-satisfying climax" of *The Virginian,* comments on the depth of characterization in the late *When West Was West,* and concludes that Wister's instincts prevented him from successfully rendering the West in literature. Einar Haugen brings considerable critical skills to his volume on

Rölvaag (TUSAS 455), about a third of which is an introduction to
the trilogy including *Giants in the Earth*. Although an even more
extensive discussion is needed, what is here blends the narrative art
well with history and myth. James Woodress provides an informative introduction to *My Amiable Uncle: Recollections about Booth
Tarkington* (Purdue) by Susanah Mayberry, the great-niece of the
subject. Woodress's framework for this charming reminiscence highlights the two-time Pulitzer Prize winner's dedication to Howells,
his achievements in the Howellsian mode (*Penrod* is a realistic
alternative to *Tom Sawyer*—the "escapades are the sort of stuff that
boy life is really made of"), and the worthiness of his masterpiece
The Magnificent Ambersons, "an appropriate companion for novels
by Sherwood Anderson, Edith Wharton, Willa Cather."

Brigham Young University

14. Fiction: The 1930s to the 1950s

Louis Owens

i. "Art for Humanity's Sake"—Proletarians

a. **James Agee, Edmund Wilson, and Others.** As background for this period in American fiction, Harvey Klehr's *The Heyday of American Communism* (Basic Books) is invaluable for its insights into such writers as Edmund Wilson, John Dos Passos, Michael Gold, Malcolm Cowley, and John Steinbeck. An excellent study of the era. Further glimpses of the period are found in excerpts from Malcolm Cowley's memoirs appearing in several journals this year. In "Echoes from Moscow: 1937–1938" (*SoR* 20:1–11) Cowley recalls the civil war in Spain and, particularly, the Moscow trials, offering his "abject apologies to the dead in Russia" for his confessed misunderstanding of the falseness of the trials. In "A Time of Resignation" (*YR* 74:1–14), Cowley discusses the enormous impact on the American left of the Russo-German Nonaggression Pact of 1939 and provides a remembrance of exiles past. "Lament For The Abraham Lincoln Battalion" (*SR* 92,iii:331–47) offers Cowley's close reporting of the American volunteers' battles in Spain, an experience Cowley terms "a long record of heroism and victimage." James Kempf provides a more detached perspective of Cowley in "Encountering the Avant-Garde: Malcolm Cowley in France, 1921–1922" (*SoR* 20:12–28), noting in particular the ambiguity of Cowley's response to "Lost Generation" Europe and underscoring Cowley's distrust of "Rosicrucianism" or "the fear of Being Understood." Cowley's beatnik connection comes further to light in Adam Gussow's "Bohemia Revisited: Malcolm Cowley, Jack Kerouac, and *On the Road*" (*GaR* 38:291–311), an essay stressing Cowley's vital role in editing and publishing Kerouac's novel. Of additional interest for Cowley followers may be Susan Shephard's "Talking with Malcolm Cowley" (*BForum* 7,i:11–12), while an outstanding biography received too late for review last year gives us still another perspective on this period, this time through the life of Josephine Herbst. In *Josephine Herbst* (Little, Brown) Elinor Langer confesses to a close identification with her subject and goes on to write a thorough and compassionate analysis of Herbst and her literary generation. Langer's is a well-written biography that continues the steady flow of fine biographies in this period during the last several years. A second female voice from the '30s to receive attention this year is Tillie Olsen, the subject of Abigail Martin's monograph *Tillie Olsen* (WWS 65). In a loosely structured 42 pages, Martin dwells upon Olsen's feminist instincts and difficulties, being content with quick précis and comparison rather than critical analysis while noting parallels between Olsen and such writers as Steinbeck, Cather, Upton Sinclair, and Ruth Suckow. Martin gets off to a wobbly start by declaring that Olsen is not "in the popular sense of the term" a western writer because "she does not write of man against the elements on the frontier. . . . There are no cowboys or Indians in her work." In "After Long Silence: Tillie Olsen's 'Requa' " (*SAF* 12:61–69), Blanche H. Gelfant looks at the long silences of Olsen's career and declares that in "Requa" Olsen "reclaims once more a power of speech that has proved at times extremely difficult to exercise." Olsen also gets a chapter in *Women Writers of the West Coast*, a volume compiled primarily from public dialogues that took place at Stanford University in 1960. Unfortunately Olsen gets little opportunity to speak in her chapter, the writer's voice nearly disappearing beneath Marilyn Yalom's own summary of Olsen's life and work. Laurence Bergreen's *James Agee: A Life* (Dutton), equals Langer's Josephine Herbst biography in the thoroughness of its research, particularly in the author's use of previously unpublished materials. Bergreen probes his subject intimately, taking advantage of Agee's own writing to give us as objective a view of Agee as possible. Agee is also the subject of Victor A. Kramer's chapter in *Literature of Tennessee* (pp. 133–47). Like most of the essays in this volume Kramer's is a valuable introduction. Steven Aulicino's "James Agee: Secondary Sources, 1935–1981" (*BB* 41:64–72) adds further to bibliographic information available on Agee. Additional biography from this period constitutes a large portion of David Castronovo's *Edmund Wilson* (Ungar). As is usual in Ungar's Literature and Life series, Castronovo's book offers a quick overview, structured here according to Wilson's diverse roles: reporter, critic, novelist, etc. Castronovo's work is clear and concise, a solid introduction to Edmund Wilson. The violence of this period from still another approach is central to Trudier Harris's "Ritual Violence and the Formation of an Aesthetic: Richard Wright," in Harris's book-length study, *Exorcising Blackness*. In a chapter on Wright (pp. 95–128), Harris argues that "Richard Wright uses the lynching and burning ritual, and historical and social connotations surrounding it, to shape the basis of his aesthetic vision of the world." This critic sketches a particularly vivid account of the background of racial violence against which Wright's fiction is set. Wright is also the subject of critical commentary in Sylvia Wallace Holton's *Down Home and Uptown: The Representation of Black Speech in American Fiction* (Fairleigh Dickinson). In a study aimed more directly at linguists than scholars in general, Holton calls Wright "the most outstanding Afro-American writer of the Depression era" and goes on to present a careful analysis of Wright's use of dialect in *Uncle Tom's Children* and *Native Son*, stressing the influence of Gertrude Stein's "Melanctha" on the latter. Holton comments also upon the fiction of Zora Neale Hurston in this study, declaring that *Their Eyes Were Watching God* "represents a coherent integration of folklore and fiction" as well as "a contemporary statement about the attainment of feminine autonomy and individuality." Less satisfying is Henry Louis Gates, Jr.'s discussion of Hurston in *Black Literature and Literary Theory* (Methuen). In a chapter entitled "The Blackness of Blackness: a Critique of the Sign and the Signifying Monkey" (pp. 285–321), Gates brings Hurston's fiction under the close magnification of Structuralist/post-Structuralist theory, a process that at times causes the criticism to wilt under the weight of its rhetorical burden. Each of the essays in Gates's volume was published previously during the last half-decade. Much more impressive is Sam B. Girgus's *The New Covenant: Jewish Writers and the American Idea* (N. C.), a work arguing that "the history of the Jews in America is to a considerable extent the history of an idea." The idea is the American idea/myth. In "A Portrait of the Artist as a Young Luther" (pp. 95–107), Girgus examines Henry Roth's *Call It Sleep*, declaring in opposition to Roth's own explanations of the novel that it is "a novel of regeneration." In these few pages, Girgus supports his reading by a psychoanalytical approach to the character of David Schearl, a reading heavily indebted to Norman Brown's Freudian study of Martin Luther. The only limitation in this interesting discussion is the chapter's brevity. Worthy of brief note this year is Matthew J. Bruccoli's *James Gould Cozzens, Selected Notebooks 1960–1967*

(Bruccoli Clark). This follow-up to Bruccoli's 1983 biography of Cozzens contains material to fascinate the Cozzens reader, particularly in Cozzens's comments upon fellow writers and public figures such as the author's remark that Hemingway "could write, all right; but apparently he could not think." For a broad view of the novel during this period it would be difficult to top Malcolm Bradbury's "Realism and Surrealism: the 1930s" and "Liberal and Existential Imaginations: the 1940s and 1950s" in his *The Modern American Novel* (Oxford, 1983). In his chapter on the '30s, Bradbury touches upon such novelists as Michael Gold, John Dos Passos, Waldo Frank, Edward Dahlberg, Jack Convoy, and Henry Roth before devoting the greater portion of the chapter to Richard Wright, James T. Farrell, John Steinbeck, Thomas Wolfe, Henry Miller, and Nathanael West. Bradbury's chapter on the '40s and '50s gives a concise overview of the work of such figures as Mary McCarthy, Saul Bellow, Isaac Bashevis Singer, Bernard Malamud, J. D. Salinger, John Updike, Norman Mailer, William Burroughs, Jack Kerouac, Vladimir Nabokov, and others.

b. **John Steinbeck and John Dos Passos.** Without a doubt the most important Steinbeck publication in the past decade is Jackson J. Benson's lengthy biography, *True Adventures of John Steinbeck, Writer* (Viking), a 1984 publication reviewed in last year's *ALS*. Two other book-length studies fall drastically short of Benson's work in significance. Stoddard Martin's *California Writers* devotes a chapter to Steinbeck's fiction (pp. 67–122), a discussion that reverberates with intelligence and admirable prose but in the end offers nothing new for Steinbeck readers. While claiming to differ with previous Steinbeck critics, Martin rehashes prior scholarship and at times simply misses the point, as when he accuses Steinbeck of racism in "Johnny Bear" and "The Murder." The result is that the reader feels cheated by a poor critical discussion offered by an obviously talented critic. *Steinbeck: The Good Companion* (Portola Valley, Calif.: American Lives Endowment, 1983) is by Steinbeck's lifelong friend, Carlton A. Sheffield. A poorly printed volume, this work should nonetheless be of interest to Steinbeck critics because of the insight it provides regarding Steinbeck and his relationship with "Dook" Sheffield. Another important Steinbeck publication this year is Robert DeMott's *Steinbeck's Reading: A Catalogue of Books Owned and Borrowed* (Garland). DeMott has divided the volume into four sections: (1) an excellent introduction; (2) a listing of 900 books owned, borrowed, etc. by Steinbeck; (3) 53 pages of notes; and (4) a comprehensive bibliography. For critics interested in the impressive breadth of Steinbeck's reading, DeMott's book will be invaluable. *Cannery Row: A Time To Remember* (Orenda), by Tom Weber, is a monograph-length paperback filled with photographic reminiscence of Cannery Row, the street in Monterey, California, that provided the setting for the novel. Definitely the most impressive essay on Steinbeck this year is Jackson Benson's "Through a Political Glass, Darkly: The Example of John Steinbeck" (*SAF* 12: 45–59). Benson reviews Steinbeck criticism from the '30s to the present, illuminating the abuse Steinbeck received from the political critics of both left and right, from Mary McCarthy's "gratuitous nastiness" in her attack on *In Dubious Battle* to James Thurber's resentment because *The Moon Is Down* was soft on Nazis. Benson is very good at pointing out the narrowness of political criticism and snobbish elitism aimed at Steinbeck from the intellectual left. The *Steinbeck Quarterly* again this year contained a mixture of critical writing and Steinbeck Society miscellany. In *StQ* 17,i–ii, two critical essays share space with Tetsumaro Hayashi's interview series with Steinbeck critics: "Interview with Joseph Fontenrose" (pp. 35–39) and "Interview with Warren French" (pp. 39–44). In the first essay, "Steinbeck's 'The Murder': Illusions of Chivalry" (pp. 10–14), I focus briefly on the illusion of the "tremendous stone castle" in the story's opening paragraphs, arguing that a dominant theme in the story is to be found in Jim Moore's dangerous illusion of chivalric values. In "Steinbeck and World War II: The Moon Goes Down" (pp. 14–34) Roy S. Simmonds provides a much more substantial study in his thorough, rather dry, illumination of Steinbeck's role during the war as both author and correspondent, touching upon *Cannery Row* and the dispatches collected in *Once There Was a War* before focusing on *The Moon Is Down*. The one critical study in *StQ* 17,iii–iv is Stanley Renner's "Sexual Idealism and Violence in 'The White Quail'" (pp. 76–87). Renner wonders aloud here at the different critical receptions given to Steinbeck's "The Chrysanthemums" and "The White Quail," the first and second stories in *The Long Valley*, and then goes on to insist, at length, that "The White Quail" is about "the pernicious effects on marriage of the idealization of women." Superfluous here are Renner's concluding reflections on Steinbeck's own questionable relations with women. Of incidental

interest in this number of *StQ* is Preston Beyer's "The Current Status
of the John Steinbeck Book Collection" (pp. 87–97) and Edwin F.
Schmitz's "On Collecting Steinbeck" (pp. 104–07). Robert DeMott
adds to this number his "Steinbeck's Reading: First Supplement"
(pp. 97–103). One of the few pieces on Steinbeck appearing this year
outside of *StQ* is Carroll Britch and Cliff Lewis's "Shadow of the
Indian in the Fiction of John Steinbeck" (*MELUS* 11,ii:39–58). The
authors look at several Steinbeck works including *The Pearl*, *The
Red Pony*, "Flight," and *Viva Zapata!*, concluding that "Steinbeck's
Indians are doomed when they attempt to fulfill the inner callings of
their racial blood" and lauding Steinbeck's sensitivity to "both the
nobility of their [Indians'] actions and to our need to admire." Britch
and Lewis make an admirable effort here to deal with an issue in
Steinbeck's writing that strikes a sensitive chord among American
Indian and even Hispanic readers. On a related note, Hiroyuki Miya-
gaua looks at Steinbeck's paisanos and use of the Arthurian legend
in "On Steinbeck's *Tortilla Flat*" (*SALit* 20:88–100). "Steinbeck and
Nature's Self: *The Grapes of Wrath*" (pp. 142–59), a chapter in
John J. Conder's *Naturalism in American Fiction,* is another important Steinbeck essay this year. Conder follows discussions of Dreiser
and Dos Passos with this chapter on Steinbeck, arguing that Steinbeck "escapes the tentacles of determinism that hold Dreiser's men
and women in thrall because he does not unravel the Hobbesian
dilemma. . . . He makes consciousness in the service of man's instinct the center of man's freedom." Steinbeck's fiction, Conder declares, is "a logical and satisfying conclusion to naturalism prior to
Dos Passos." In a second excellent chapter, "Dos Passos and Society's
Self: *Manhattan Transfer*" (pp. 118–41), Conder approaches Dos
Passos's novel from the point of view of Sartre's "statistical determinism," claiming that Dos Passos "creates a harmony between freedom
and determinism that is specious because freedom of choice becomes
thoroughly meaningless" in the context of *Manhattan Transfer*. The
stream of biographies from this period continues this year with Virginia Spencer Carr's *Dos Passos: A Life* (Doubleday), a work as
direct and readable as its title. In the kind of book that cheers an
ALS reviewer, Carr brings Dos Passos and his milieu to convincing
life while wisely refraining from more than minimal critical interpretation of Dos Passos's fiction. In "The American Quest for Pure
Movement in Dos Passos' *U.S.A.*" (*TCL* 30:80–99), Robert James
Butler suggests that "one of the most distinctive drives in American

culture is a quest for pure motion, movement which is not directed toward any particular end point." Butler focuses on Dos Passos's ambivalence toward "pure motion" in *U.S.A.*, but stresses, nonetheless, the vitality of such motion in the novel and declares in persuasive contrast to previous darker readings of the trilogy that it "provides a sharply qualified but nevertheless hopeful vision of American life."

ii. Expatriates and Emigrés

a. **Vladimir Nabokov.** The Vladimir Nabokov critical industry continues to thrive this year, led by Phyllis A. Roth's *Critical Essays on Vladimir Nabokov* (Hall), a volume that accurately claims to be "the most comprehensive collection of criticism ever published" on Nabokov and one that is important even in the face of the more than 20 book-length studies of Nabokov in the last two decades. What makes Roth's collection a major event is its breadth, from Mikhail Osorgin's 1926 review of V. Sirin's *Mary* to "reactions" by such contemporary writers as Joyce Carol Oates and John Updike, and what this volume teaches is that as early as 1926 a critic saw Nabokov's genius while as late as Oates's "Postscript" in 1983 Nabokov inspired wary respect. Contained here are four critical reactions to V. Sirin and more than a dozen essays on V. Nabokov, including fine ones by Claude Mouchard, Carl Eichelberger, D. Barton Johnson, and others. In this volume, one can study the metamorphosis of Vladimir Nabokov as well as the increasingly Kinbote-like role of the critical voice in response to Nabokov's Shade. In *Vladimir Nabokov: A Critical Study of the Novels* (Cambridge) David Rampton takes a non-Barthesian route to a critical understanding of Nabokov's fiction, insisting upon the content beyond the form. In a solid introduction, Rampton uses Nabokov's own critical commentary upon such writers as Dickens to prepare the groundwork for Rampton's content-oriented critical analysis of *Invitation to a Beheading, Bend Sinister, The Gift, Lolita, Ada, Pale Fire, Transparent Things,* and *Look at the Harlequins!* Rampton goes beyond the usual quest for pattern and allusion to discuss with admirable clarity what the novels are "about." A second backlash Nabokov study this year is Laurie Clancy's *The Novels of Vladimir Nabokov* (Macmillan). Clancy complains that "if one tries to suggest that the novels are 'about' genuine moral concerns and that these concerns are complex and of significance to all of us one is

made to feel an oaf." He goes on to trace, from the early *Mary*
through the rest of Nabokov's longer fiction, the "way in which
Nabokov's art strove to affirm the power of the imagination as the
supreme source of reality." In a consistently intelligent reading,
Clancy finds "radical failures of execution" in *Pale Fire*, declares
Ada to be "a celebration of the sufficiency of 'this our sufficient
world,' " and finds *Lolita* "moving testimony to the inextricable involvement of the artistic and the human."

More entertaining and much less critically ambitious is Alan
Levy's *Vladimir Nabokov: The Velvet Butterfly*, with photographs
by Horst Tappe (Permanent Press). Levy's original profile which
appeared in the *New York Times Magazine* has been stretched to
book length by a mosaic of biography, interview, quotable quotes,
commentary upon Nabokov's writing and Nabokov critics, bibliography, and chronology. Weighed against the mass of Nabokov criticism, Levy's is a delightfully light attempt, one probably most useful for undergraduates or readers completely new to Nabokov's work.

The monumental stature Nabokov is beginning to attain in American letters is indicated in still another book-length collection to appear this year, *The Achievements of Vladimir Nabokov: Essays,
Studies, Reminiscences, and Stories*, ed. George Gibian and Stephen
Jan Parker (Center for International Studies, Cornell). This gathering of materials from the five-month-long Nabokov "multi-media
festival" held at Cornell University in the winter and spring of 1983
provides just what its title promises. In "Nabokov: Beyond Parody"
(pp. 5–27) Edmund White insists that Nabokov "has kept the romantic novel alive by introducing into it a new tension—the struggle
between obsessive or demented characters and a seraphic rhetoric."
Remembrance and biography constitute the essence of James Mc-
Conkey's "Nabokov and 'The Windows of the Mint' " (pp. 45–59),
Brian Boyd's "Nabokov at Cornell" (pp. 119–45), and a section entitled "Remembering Nabokov" (pp. 215–37). Less a remembrance
of Nabokov than a fascinating study of Borges is the interview with
Jorge Luis Borges printed here as "Conversation with an Audience"
(pp. 61–78), in which Borges says almost nothing about Nabokov but
a good deal about the gamesmanship of fiction. More dryly critical is
Stephen Jan Parker's "Nabokov Studies: The State of the Art" (pp.
81–97), a survey of Nabokov criticism in which Parker comes to the
conclusion that "Nabokov scholarship is in its infancy" and that there
is a crying need for greater access to Nabokov materials, especially

biographical, and for a comprehensive bibliography. "Official and Unofficial Responses to Nabokov in the Soviet Union" (pp. 99–117), by Slava Paperno and John V. Hagopian, brings to this collection an interesting political dimension, characterizing Soviet responses in the pre-Stalinist, Stalinist, and post-Stalinist eras as "aggressive silence, total silence, and cautious silence." In one of the only attempts at critical reading in this volume, "Nabokov's *Lolita* and Pushkin's *Onegin*: McAdam, McEve and McFate" (pp. 179–211), Priscilla Meyer declares that "*Lolita* represents a translation through space and time of a Russian literary movement of the 1820s into an American one of the 1950s." Finally in this volume, Dmitri Nabokov documents his struggles with translation and with such a critic as Sir Charles Johnston, offering extensive commentary in passing upon his father, Vladimir Nabokov.

D. Barton Johnson makes another foray into Nabokov scholarship this year with his "Inverted Reality in Nabokov's *Look at the Harlequins!*" (*StTCL* 8:293–309), another very solid essay arguing this time that *Look at the Harlequins!* is one more Nabokov novel with a schizoid narrator. "Dementia," says Johnson, is "the leading lady" in the novel. Following *The Eye* (1930), *Despair* (1936), and *Pale Fire* (1962), this novel is, according to Johnson, "the culmination of a series of Nabokov novels in which a schizoid narrator creates his own fantasy world and superimposes it upon the 'real' world inhabited by other characters." Nabokov's *bête noire* turns up in J. P. Shute's "Nabokov and Freud: The Play of Power" (*MFS* 30: 637–50). In a clever untangling of Freudian obsession in Nabokov's fiction, Shute declares, "Nabokov denies the authority not only of the decipherer but of decipherment itself; the text declares itself invulnerable." Shute's is a good discussion of Nabokov's "preemptive strategies" against Freudians, particularly in *Pale Fire* and *Lolita*. A more exotic coupling takes place in Michael Long's *Marvell, Nabokov: Childhood and Arcadia* (Clarendon). Long insists that both Marvell and Nabokov "have some important concerns about which to write" and attempts to illuminate these concerns. The result, however, is a book that seems to flit nervously from 17th-century poet to 20th-century novelist in alternating, for the most part frustratingly brief, chapters.

Nabokov's early career and friendship with Edmund Wilson, combined with the difficulties in getting *Lolita* published, are the subjects of "Vladimir Nabokov: The Work of Art as a Dirty Book" (pp. 159–89), a chapter in Sally Dennison's *(Alternative) Literary Publishing*, a well-written study, while Stanley Kubrick's film adaptation of *Lolita* concerns Dan T. Burns's brief essay, "Pistols and Cherry Pies: Lolita From Page to Screen" (*LFQ* 12:245–50). Kubrick's movie, Burns contends, succeeds by means of "dramatic compression." *The Nabokovian* this year contains the usual newsletter materials such as abstracts, updates on foreign scholarship, and notes. Most useful in *Nabokovian* number 13 is Stephen Jan Parker's "1983 Nabokov Bibliography" (pp. 45–59), while number 12 offers one piece of substance in Gene Barabtarlo's "Calendar in *Pnin*" (pp. 44–50), a survey of the "surface chronology" of the novel. In number 14 of this year's *Nabokovian* (pp. 10–14), Dmitri Nabokov makes an effort to correct typos and what he sees as errors and distortions in Herbert Gold's "A Slight Case of Poshlost" published in *The Achievements of Vladimir Nabokov* (see above).

b. **Anaïs Nin, Henry Miller, Ayn Rand.**   Nin is the subject of Nancy Scholar's excellent, but standard, introductory volume, *Anaïs Nin* (Twayne), as well as the most impressive chapter in Dennison's *(Alternative) Literary Publishing*, "Anaïs Nin . . . the Book as a Work of Art" (pp. 119–55). In a volume that deals with a surprising assortment of "alternatively" published authors (T. S. Eliot, Virginia Woolf, James Joyce, V. Nabokov, and Nin), Dennison does a fine job of detailing in quick, succinct prose Nin's struggles to get her early writing published and her doubly futile attempts to establish a press to print her own work and that of such friends as Henry Miller. Though Dennison spends somewhat too much time on biography and not quite enough on the actual process of self-publishing here, her discussions of Nin's publication of *Winter of Artifice* and *Under a Glass Bell* are very good. In "Discourse and Intercourse, Design and Desire in the Erotica of Anaïs Nin" (*JML* 11:143–58), Smaro Kamboureli distinguishes between the "dialectics of desire" in erotica and the "minimal context" of sexuality in pornography, distinctions that make *Delta of Venus* and *Little Birds* "more pornographic than erotic" according to Kamboureli. This critic's intentions are to demonstrate that Nin is "innovative within the genre of pornography" and that the prefaces to *Delta* and *Birds* should be read as "apologias and disguised manifestos about pornography," intentions realized with little impact in this essay. A more practical contribution to Nin scholarship is *Under the Sign of Pisces: Anaïs Nin And Her Circle: An Index, 1970–1981* (Ohio State), by Penelope Pearson and Sandra Kerka. Finally, *Anaïs: An International Journal* has become, with 1984's volume 2, one of the more impressively presented American journals. Bearing still the quality of a newsletter in the miscellaneous nature of its contents, this year's journal offers an excerpt from Nin's unpublished *Diary, Book No. 29* (pp. 3–19), with vintage Nin ("I cry as I write with solitude and excessive responsiveness and unfulfilled desires"), along with an Otto Rank preface to the early diary (pp. 20–23), and assorted correspondence and remembrance by and about such figures as Caresse Crosby, Selden Rodman, Harry T. Moore, and Lawrence Durrell. Of greatest substance in this issue are Philip K. Jason's "The Gemor Press" (pp. 24–39), and Beatrice Formentelli's "The Difficulty of the Real" (pp. 77–94). Jason's essay serves as a valuable complement to Dennison's *(Alternative) Literary Publishing* while going into much greater detail concerning the history of Nin's Gemor Press, which he terms "the story of creative networking." Less profitable is Formentelli's rather turgid "Forum" piece dwelling upon Nin's multiple selves, the *"chingada"* and *"chingon,"* and concluding that "Anaïs Nin was twice exiled from reality—as 'actress' and as writer—and above all she was a reluctant accomplice in this exile." Also of special interest in this issue is Suzette A. Henke's "Lillian Beye's Labyrinth: A Freudian Exploration of *Cities of the Interior*" (pp. 113–26). According to Henke, it can be argued that Nin "structured her fictional representation of women in *Cities of the Interior* around the three principal Freudian categories of the self—ego, id, and super-ego." In Freudian terms, Henke suggests, "Lillian embodies the developing ego in its quest for independent self-realization."

An enjoyable change of critical pace this year is the major Henry Miller event, *From Your Capricorn Friend: Henry Miller and the Stroker, 1978–1980* (New Directions). Irving Stettner's foreword, "Henrysan and the Stroker" (pp. ix–xix), lays out the background for this collection of letters and prose pieces which first appeared in *The Stroker.*

Heavier fare dominates essays in *The Philosophical Thought of Ayn Rand,* ed. Douglas J. Den Uyl and Douglas B. Rasmussen (Illinois), a work that bears only mention here because of its exclusive focus on Rand's nonfiction writings. More comprehensive is *The*

Ayn Rand Companion, by Mimi Gladstein (Greenwood). Gladstein avoids polemics and provides a useful introduction to Rand's life and writing. A surface glance at Rand, this work is hampered at times by a disconcertingly wooden style.

iii. Southerners

a. **Robert Penn Warren and the Agrarians.** One of the finest products in Ungar's Literature and Life series is this year's *Robert Penn Warren* by Katherine Snipes (Ungar). Snipes economically and very effectively introduces the reader to Warren's biography and writing, not being afraid to pass her own careful judgments now and then, as when she declares *Night Rider* to be "one of Warren's best novels because of its relatively uncluttered impact as tragedy" or when she wonders aloud about Warren's antipathy toward Emerson and about the southern bias of Warren's *John Brown*. Warren is also the subject of *A Southern Renascence Man: Views of Robert Penn Warren*, ed. Walter B. Edgar (LSU), a collection of papers presented at the University of South Carolina 1982 Warren program. In the first essay in this volume, "Robert Penn Warren as Historian" (pp. 1–17), Thomas L. Connelly focuses on the "historical experience" in Warren's writing, what Connelly calls "the bonding of reality and ideal, past and present," concentrating at some length on the influence of Warren's grandfather. Of greater interest is Louis D. Rubin, Jr.'s contribution, "Robert Penn Warren: Critic" (pp. 19–37). Rubin takes this opportunity to defend Warren's brand of New Criticism against the assault of structuralism, poststructuralism, and deconstructionism. Characteristic of this piece is Rubin's remark that Terence Hawkes's structuralism "is the literary Marxism of the 1930s dressed up in semiotics." In "Robert Penn Warren as Novelist" (pp. 39–57), Madison Jones provides a quick survey of Warren's novels, noting the critical squabbling that has accompanied them. Warren fails in such novels as *All the King's Men*, says Jones, because of his "determinism to extend meaning beyond the limits that his material demands." In suggesting that *All the King's Men* fails in contrast to the success of *The Cave*, Jones strains. Warren's poetry is the subject of Harold Bloom's "Sunset Hawk: Warren's Poetry" (pp. 59–79) and of James Dickey's "Warren's Poetry: A Reading and Commentary" (pp. 81–93), while Warren's connection with Vanderbilt and the

Fugitives and especially John Crowe Ransom is the dominant subject in Thomas L. Connelly's "Of Bookish Men and the Fugitives: A Conversation with Robert Penn Warren" (pp. 95–110). Warren and Cleanth Brooks are discussed together in Mark Royden Winchell's "Cleanth Brooks and Robert Penn Warren" essay (pp. 89–113) in *Literature of Tennessee*. After a brief introduction commenting upon the two writers' collaborations, Winchell divides his essay neatly into two parts, the second dealing with Warren. Winchell devotes most of his attention to Warren's poetry, claiming that while his poetry "has become more original, more stylistically accomplished . . . the same cannot be said of his fiction." Warren's earlier fiction is his best, according to Winchell, while the path from *Night Rider* to *A Place to Come To* "is one of cumulative . . . decline." Lloyd Davis fills in background material for Warren and the Fugitives in a concise essay also in this volume, "The Southern Renascence and the Writers of Tennessee" (pp. 21–36). Davis focuses on the background and formation of the so-called Southern Renaissance and the places of such figures as Ransom, Allen Tate, Andrew Lytle, and Warren. Warren's milieu is further explored in *Parnassus on the Mississippi: The Southern Review and the Baton Rouge Literary Community, 1935–1942*, by Thomas W. Cutrer (LSU), a book that gives special attention to Warren and provides an excellent bibliography. *All the King's Men* comes in for additional attention in two essays deserving of notice here. " 'Making Good Out of Bad' in *All the King's Men*" is the fifth chapter in John D. Barbour's *Tragedy as a Critique of Virtue: The Novel and Ethical Reflection* (Scholars Press). In a study that deals with Henry James, Melville, and Conrad as well as Warren, Barbour's central thesis in highly simplified form is that "tragedy involves a critique of virtue." Barbour states that "two styles of moral virtue conflict in . . . *All the King's Men:* the ideal of 'being good,' or personal integrity, and Willie Stark's goal of 'making good out of bad' at the cost of 'dirty hands.' " Barbour's discussion focuses on the "tragic conflict" in the novel between these two styles of virtue and looks at the historical/cultural reality behind the real Huey Long and Louisiana.

Warren joins strange company in still another book-length study this year, August J. Nigro's *The Diagonal Line*, a work that brings together Poe, Hawthorne, Melville, Twain, Henry James, Fitzgerald, Faulkner, Dickinson, T. S. Eliot, Wallace Stevens, and Warren. In a chapter on Warren and Ellison, "So We Beat On: *All the King's Men* and *Invisible Man*" (pp. 147–59), Nigro suggests that the "tension between solitude and society, individuality and community—a vital tension in the symbolic pattern of separation and reparation in classic American literature" gives "meaning and shape" to these two novels. Jack Burden, Nigro argues, illustrates Warren's directive in the novel that "the only way to live meaningfully in the modern world is to accept one's separateness as a condition of identity, but also to acknowledge that one is not entirely separate." Place and identity are also central to Mary Louise Weaks's "The Search for a 'Terra' in *A Place to Come To*" (*MissQ* 37:455–67), an essay focusing on the development of Jed Tewksbury. Several other pieces this year are of less substance, beginning with "On Native Soil: A Talk with Robert Penn Warren" (*MissQ* 37:179–86). Additional essays include Robert Siegle's "Species vs. Genus in the Romantic Novel: Warren's *World Enough and Time*" (*KR* 5,ii:46–62), which discusses this work as a romantic novel; and Randolf Runyon's "The Beech, the Hearth, and the Hidden Name in *World Enough and Time*" (*SLJ* 17,i:68–81), focusing on the symbol of the beech tree in the novel.

Another Southern Renaissance figure getting attention again this year is Andrew Lytle, in Charles C. Clark's "Andrew Lytle" (pp. 115–31) in *Literature of Tennessee*. Clark's real subject here is the controlling influence of place in Lytle's work as Clark provides biographical background and quick glances at both nonfiction and novels before looking most closely at what this critic calls Lytle's masterpiece, *The Velvet Horn*. This Lytle novel also receives close attention in Anne Foata's fine essay, "Andrew Lytle's *The Velvet Horn*: A Hermeneutic Approach" (*MissQ* 37:429–53). Foata argues in a thorough analysis of narrative structure that this novel "can be taken as a long hermeneutic sequence liable as such to the deciphering devised by Barthes' *hermeneutic code*." Still another often overlooked writer of this place and time gets attention in "Hugh Holman: From Goldville to Clinton," by James L. Skinner (*SCR* 16,ii:35–49). Skinner's essay is a tribute to Holman, sketching the author's early academic career with brief discussion of Holman's criticism and mystery novels of the '40s: *Death Like Thunder, Trout in the Milk, Slay the Murderer, Up This Crooked Way*, and *Another Man's Poison*. Skinner offers little depth in his criticism, being satisfied primarily to laud Holman's "realistic Southern milieu."

b. **Eudora Welty and Flannery O'Connor.** The major Welty publication this year is Welty's own *One Writer's Beginnings* (Harvard), an extraordinary self-portrait of an author's development, offering a less coy picture than one discovers in the frequent Welty interviews. This publication of Eudora Welty's 1983 Harvard lectures culminates in the fine lines, "A sheltered life can be a daring life as well. For all serious daring comes from within." A critic competing for attention with Welty herself has a difficult task, as *Conversations with Eudora Welty*, ed. Peggy Whitman Prenshaw (Miss.) makes clear. This collection of interviews over a 40-year period also makes it obvious that Welty is in no danger of suffering from neglect. Here the reader listens in on the author being by turns evasive and candid and sometimes profoundly moving as she discusses herself, her writing, the South, and literature in general with such figures as William F. Buckley, Jr., Alice Walker, Reynolds Price, and more than 20 others. Highlights here come in a response to Alice Walker's question "Do you have a 'Philosophy of Life'?" Welty: "No. I have work in place of it." And in Welty's admission on Buckley's "Firing Line" (in conversation with Walker Percy) that she uses anything "that comes in handy" in her fiction. Of more practical use, perhaps, will be Bethany C. Swearingen's *Eudora Welty: A Critical Bibliography, 1936–1958* (Miss.). More interesting yet is Patricia S. Yaeger's " 'Because a Fire was in My Head': Eudora Welty and the Dialogic Imagination" (*PMLA* 99:955–73), in which Yaeger argues that in *The Golden Apples* Welty exploits images and themes from several Yeats poems in her development of central female characters. Yaeger begins by citing French feminists such as Hélène Cixous, Marguerite Duras, and Luce Irigaray as well as Mikhail Bakhtin's *Dialogic Imagination.* Yaeger's source is Bakhtin's insistence upon the dialogic nature of language, "the dialectical interaction between worlds," a fact that leads Yaeger to weight down a very good essay with somewhat excessive Bakhtin summary. Yaeger's strong point here is her extension of Bakhtin's dialogue between Marxist and neo-Formalist criticism to include feminist criticism, adding gender to Bakhtin's categories. Particularly convincing is this critic's discussion of the importance of both "Song of the Wandering Aengus" and "Leda and the Swan" in the stories. According to Yaeger, Welty quarrels "with Yeats' mythology of gender" and "recontextualizes his diction," with the result that Yeats's mythology is both temporalized and satirized and a transference of power from male poet to female fictionalist takes place. Welty and the feminine is also the subject of Lorraine Liscio's "The Female Voice of Poetry in 'The Bride of Innisfallen'" (*SSF* 21:357–62). "Given the terms in which the male and female point of view are cast," says Liscio, "it seems that the female, poetic perspective is more highly valued." In "The Making of *Losing Battles:* Jack Renfro's Evolution" (*MissQ* 37:469–74), Suzanne Marrs examines Jack's decision to become Judge Moody's savior rather than his tormentor and studies the evolution of Jack's motivation through three early drafts of the novel.

The *Eudora Welty Newsletter* provides useful newsletter fare again this year, with *EuWN* 8:i containing "Works by Welty: A Continuing Checklist," by W. U. McDonald, Jr. (pp. 8–9); "Welty's 'A Sketching Trip' in America and England" (pp. 3–8), also by McDonald and dealing with textual variants; and "Sending Schedule for the Stories in *The Golden Apples*" (pp. 1–3), by Noel Polk. *EuWN* 8:ii adds "A Checklist of Welty Scholarship, 1983–1984," by O. B. Emerson (pp. 10–13), and assorted miscellaneous Welty material.

One of the most original treatments of Flannery O'Connor in some time comes this year in Jefferson Humphries's *The Otherness Within: Gnostic Readings in Marcel Proust, Flannery O'Connor, and François Villon* (LSU, 1983). Humphries defines his approach as "an eclectic application of some of the most recent critical strategies" and goes on to consider in turn Proust, O'Connor, and Villon, honoring Freud and Jung among others in passing. "O'Connor shares Proust's belief in a spirit occulted in the flesh," he states before considering the "terrible violence with which the Holy finally and inevitably erupts into their [O'Connor's characters'] willfully profane lives." "What Proust represents psychically, O'Connor represents physically," Humphries declares as he extrapolates on the "ontological violence" in the work of both writers. In *The Language of Grace: Flannery O'Connor, Walker Percy, and Iris Murdoch* (Cowley, 1983) Peter S. Hawkins claims early in his discussion of O'Connor that "she saw that she had to confront the reader with the experience of God," and that "Unlike the writer in an age of faith, she needed not only to create a believable fictive world, but to develop as well the sense of a creator working behind, within, and beyond it." Hawkins is particularly good on the "gap" between reader and writer, the difficulty a contemporary Christian writer faces when confronting an unbelieving audience. A different kind of grace is the subject of another, less impressive piece this year, William Rodney Allen's

"Mr. Head and Hawthorne: Allusion and Conversion in Flannery O'Connor's 'The Artificial Nigger'" (*SSF* 21:17–23). Here, Allen argues that "The Artificial Nigger" owes more to Hawthorne's "The Custom-House" than to *The Divine Comedy*, suggesting that Mr. Head's conversion in O'Connor's story parallels Hawthorne's own "transformation from a bored Surveyor of Customs . . . into the author of three major novels in less than three years." Also of limited importance is "Flannery O'Connor's Names," by A. R. Coulthard (*SHR* 28:97–105), an inventory with rather unenlightening commentary upon O'Connor's clever use of names in her fiction. Much more useful for O'Connor readers is Jane Marston's "Epistemology and the Solipsistic Consciousness in Flannery O'Connor's 'Greenleaf'" (*SSF* 21:375–82), in which Marston writes that "the solipsism of characters like Mrs. May [in "Greenleaf"] creates certain epistemological problems that bear upon one of O'Connor's recurrent subjects: the relationship between nature and divine revelation." Marston finds the reason for the ambiguity of the story's ending to be the "untrustworthiness of the senses." A more mechanical study is Sura Prasad Rath's "Comic Polarities in Flannery O'Connor's *Wise Blood*" (*SSF* 21:251–58). This essay sums up recent critical writing on comic effect in O'Connor's fiction and then takes a generic approach, examining *Wise Blood* as "an archetypal comic novel," an approach heavily indebted to Northrop Frye's delineation of *eiron* and *alazon*. In a brief discussion, "O'Connor's 'The Comforts of Home'" (*Expl* 43,i:57–60), Anthony S. Magistrale gives this story an oedipal reading: "In shooting his mother, Thomas disentangles his Oedipal confusions by unconsciously rejecting the bond with his opposite-sex parent, finally identifying with his father." The editors of *Explicator* apparently liked this unusually substantial note so much that they printed it twice, in *Expl* 42,iv:52–54 as well as volume 43 noted here. A valuable bit of information concerning Joy-Hulga of "Good Country People" comes to light in Ruth M. Holsen's "O'Connor's 'Good Country People'" (*Expl* 42,iii:59). Holsen traces the name "Hulga" to Norwegian "Helga" and Norse "heilagr," meaning "holy" or "the holy one."

c. **Thomas Wolfe and Others.** The key Wolfe publication this year is Elizabeth Evans's *Thomas Wolfe* (Ungar), another in Ungar's Literature and Life series. A useful introduction, Evans's study deftly weaves biography and slight critical commentary as the author follows Wolfe's life and work. Cautious in her praise, Evans cites Wolfe's strengths as creator of memorable characters and writer of "hauntingly beautiful lyric passages." Evans concludes that, along with most other writers, he was both a "failed artist" and "a man of great talent." In "The Narrator in *Look Homeward, Angel*" (*SHR* 28:1–9), Hugh M. Ruppersburg argues that, like Proust and Joyce, Wolfe in this novel "relied on narrative point of view to maintain a critical, objective distance from [his] text." Ruppersburg defends Wolfe against the common criticism of the author's "narcissistic inability to remain separate from his story," a defense weakened somewhat by the critic's attempt to gloss over structural problems in point of view in the novel. The *Thomas Wolfe Newsletter* this year contains much useful miscellany and some critical speculation. *TWN* 8:i offers "Thomas Wolfe: A Critical Revisit" (pp. 43–52), Kenneth Brown's summary of the author's treatment in criticism; "Thomas Westfall and His Son William: Major Thomas Casey Westfall" (pp. 1–10), biography and discussion by Richard Walser; and "Thomas Wolfe's *Welcome to Our City:* An Angry Young Man Looks Back" (pp. 20–26), a discussion of Wolfe's attitudes toward the South and related elements, by Phyllis H. Lewis. *TWN* 8:ii continues this interest in Wolfe and the South with "Thomas Wolfe's 1937 Visits South: You Can Go Home Again" (pp. 36–48) by Elizabeth Evans. A different relationship is taken up in another piece here, "Thomas Wolfe and the Metier of French Writers" (pp. 27–34), by John L. Idol, Jr.; and John S. Philippson contributes more conventional newsletter material in "Quotable Thomas Wolfe" (pp. 11–13).

Erskine Caldwell surfaces in his own voice twice this year in "Portrait of an American Primitive: A Conversation with Erskine Caldwell," by D. G. Kehl (*SAQ* 83:396–404), and "Fifty Years Since *Tobacco Road:* An Interview with Erskine Caldwell," by Richard Kelly and Marcia Pankake (*SWR* 69,i:33–47). Particularly interesting in the Kehl interview is Caldwell's ability to deflate questions that might have led to posturing by a less self-assured writer. In their article, Kelly and Pankake have edited the results of a public interview with Caldwell at the Wilson Library celebration of the 50th anniversary of the publication of *Tobacco Road*. Caldwell's responses deal primarily with being rejected and with writing habits and methods. Caldwell is also a subject of critical discussion in *The American Short Story*. In "The American Short Story: 1930–1945" in this volume (pp. 103–46), James G. Watson declares that of the short story writers of the 1930–45 period, only Faulkner and Katherine Anne Porter still "are recognized as masters of the form," and that "Caldwell mastered the subject matter of the new movement but not the technique." Saroyan, Watson adds, "really never mastered either one." Watson goes on to survey a wide swath of writers from this period, from Sherwood Anderson and Hemingway to Farrell and Richard Wright, touching upon Kay Boyle, William Carlos Williams, Thomas Wolfe, Flannery O'Connor, and Eudora Welty. In another chapter of this volume, "The Question of Regionalism: Limitation and Transcendence" (pp. 147–82), Mary Rohrberger first intelligently questions the critical concept of regionalism and then examines Caldwell and such other authors as Ruth Suckow, Jesse Stuart, Langston Hughes, Jean Toomer, Ellen Glasgow, James T. Farrell, Sinclair Lewis, John O'Hara, and John Steinbeck within the category of regionalism. Of Steinbeck, Rohrberger declares, "As a novelist he is competent; as a short story writer, he can be superb."

One of the most monumental efforts this year is H. Edward Richardson's *Jesse: The Biography of an American Writer* (McGraw-Hill). From dozens of interviews and an apparent mountain of research materials, Richardson has put together an exhaustive, at times tedious, account of Stuart's life, dwelling fondly upon the backwoods boyhood and Lincolnesque qualities of Stuart's foray into college and intellectual life. Jesse Stuart as American Archetype seems to be what most interests Richardson. Complementing the biography is the release of Stuart's *Clearing in the Sky and Other Stories* (Kentucky), with a foreword by Ruel E. Foster. Foster is appropriately modest in his foreword's claims for this collection, claiming only a place "near the top" for Stuart in the history of the American short story, and citing Stuart's "talismanic sense of place." Another piece on Stuart this year is H. Edward Richardson's reminiscence, "Jesse Stuart Remembered" (*ArQ* 40:101–21).

Another southerner often relegated to the category of "popular" writer is the subject of Leonard J. Leff's "David Selznick's *Gone With the Wind*: 'The Negro Problem'" (*GaR* 38:146–64). In examining the translation of Margaret Mitchell's best-seller to the screen, Leff focuses on the social position of black Americans during this period and race-relations involved in and evolving through the film's production. Leff's is a thoroughly researched and well-written essay. Finally, George Bixby does important McCullers work in "Carson McCullers: A Bibliographical Checklist" (*ABC* 5,i:38–43), and

Minrose Gwin contributes an unusual essay in "Mentioning the Tamales: Food and Drink in Katherine Anne Porter's *Flowering Judas and Other Stories*" (*MissQ* 38:49–57), in which Gwin suggests that the eating and drinking in the stories "seems to become the physical, external manifestation of human complexity and indefinability."

iv. Detectives and Iconoclasts

Detective fiction attracted an impressive volume of critical attention this year, with several book-length studies and a number of articles. One of the most entertaining and readable studies is Ernest Mandel's *Delightful Murder: A Social History of the Crime Story* (Pluto Press). In a heavily Marxist argument, Mandel contends that "the history of the crime story is a social history," supporting that reading with an impressive understanding of the genre and the social evolution paralleling the rise of crime fiction. In a discussion ranging from Poe to TV's "Kojak" and including Raymond Chandler, Dashiell Hammett, Rex Stout, and even Umberto Eco, Mandel concludes that the detective story is "quintessentially bourgeois," and that Chandler and Hammett were the two dominant figures in "the first great revolution in the crime novel," a revolution characterized by an abrupt break with the "gentility of the classical detective story."

A second book-length study is *Los Angeles in Fiction*, a grouping of essays not limited to detective fiction but gathering in its scope a fascinating collection of writers who have focused on southern California, from authors of the '30s and '40s to such contemporaries as Joan Didion, Thomas Sanchez, and Oscar Zeta Acosta. In his introduction, Fine points out that the writers of the '20s and '30s—James M. Cain, Nathanael West, Aldous Huxley, F. Scott Fitzgerald, Horace McCoy, Chandler—gave Los Angeles "its metaphoric shape," suggesting that Los Angeles fiction "is the work of the outsider," of men and women who came from somewhere else and never lost the "estrangement and sense of dislocation" that colors this writing. In "Los Angeles and the Idea of the West" (pp. 29–41), the first essay in this volume, Richard Lehan examines the very familiar westering impulse underlying the creation of this country and this city, noting in writing about Los Angeles a movement "from a sense of promise to a sense of the grotesque." Lehan's discussion effectively brings together Fitzgerald's *The Last Tycoon*, West's

Day of the Locust, Horace McCoy's *They Shoot Horses, Don't They?*, Chandler's *The Big Sleep*, John Gregory Dunne's *True Confessions*, and Thomas Pynchon's *The Crying of Lot 49*. David Fine concentrates on only two of these figures in "Beginning in the Thirties: The Los Angeles Fiction of James M. Cain and Horace McCoy" (pp. 43–66). According to Fine, Cain's *The Postman Always Rings Twice* (1934) and McCoy's *They Shoot Horses, Don't They?* (1935) "mark the real starting place of the Los Angeles novel." For these two writers, Fine declares, "southern California was not the place of new beginnings but of disastrous finishes." Like nearly all of the contributors to this collection of essays, Fine underscores the contradictory myths of violence and redemption in the creation of America and particularly of California with its "betrayed promise of the West." Gerald Locklin's "The Day of the Painter; the Death of the Cock: Nathanael West's Hollywood Novel" (pp. 67–82), is an attempt to defend West against past criticism of structural faults in *The Day of the Locust*. Locklin's premise is that in this novel West is working in the style of his protagonist (painting) rather than following his experience with cinemagraphic techniques. The novel, Locklin contends, "is consistent in form with both the art of its painter-protagonist and the apparent shapelessness of the region." The essay concludes, somewhat limply, that *The Day of the Locust* "is not a purely objective depiction of Los Angeles." The American myth of new beginnings is also central to Paul Skenazy's excellent essay here, "Behind the Territory Ahead" (pp. 85–107). Detective fiction, Skenazy suggests, has "transcribed the shadow side of American life," particularly Los Angeles life. Skenazy's essay provides an overview of the emergent tough-guy novels of the '20s leading to a brief discussion of Hammett's fiction beginning with *Red Harvest* and a quick look at Paul Cain's *Fast One*. In "Raymond Chandler's City of Lies" (pp. 109–31), Liahna K. Babener again delves into the "illusory promise" of southern California, examining the "geography of sham" in such works as *The Big Sleep; Farewell, My Lovely; The High Window; The Long Goodbye; The Little Sister;* and *The Lady in the Lake*.

Chandler and Hammett are both among the authors discussed in *Art in Crime Writing: Essays on Detective Fiction*, ed. Bernard Benstock (St. Martin's, 1983). In "A Knock at the Backdoor of Art: The Entrance of Raymond Chandler" (pp. 73–96), Leon Arden notes the "quiet poetry" of Chandler's prose but devotes most of his time to synopsis and biography. James Naremore's "Dashiell Hammett and the Poetics of Hard-Boiled Detection" (pp. 49–72) comes to the conclusion that Hammett's fiction is "a rare combination of light entertainment and radical intelligence." Hammett, Naremore claims, "challenges the easy distinctions between popular and high art." Unfortunately, Naremore fails to offer much insight into the poetics of Hammett's art. Stoddard Martin's *California Writers* also offers a discussion of James M. Cain, Hammett, and Chandler in a chapter entitled "Tough Guys." Martin provides no new perspectives on these three writers, failing particularly to shed significant light on the "California quality" of the three.

More impressive is *"The Glass Key:* The Original and Two Copies" (*LFQ* 12:147–59), in which Saul N. Scher identifies Hammett as "the major revisionist" of modern detective fiction and declares *The Glass Key* to be an "attempt to break away from the conventions of detective fiction." Scher discusses the novel and the film versions by Frank Tuttle (1935) and Stuart Heisler (1942). Heisler's film Scher labels "interim noir." The familiar chivalric quest element in Chandler's fiction is the focus of Ernest Fontana's "Chivalry and Modernity in Raymond Chandler's *The Big Sleep*" (*WAL* 19:179–86). The novel, says Fontana, is "an ironic or failed romance." Hammett and Chandler receive additional attention this year in *Clues*, with Dominick A. Labianca and William Reeves, Jr.'s "Dashiell Hammett and Raymond Chandler: Down on Drugs" (*Clues* 5,ii: 66–71), and E. R. Hagemann's "Dashiell Hammett and Others in Context: In the Marketplace, 1929–1934; A Chronology" (*Clues* 5,ii: 131–54). In *"The Maltese Falcon* and My Alligator, Academically Considered" (*Clues* 5,i:147–56), Michael Fanning provides a more substantial essay in his study of narrative structure. James M. Cain gets further attention in *"Double Indemnity:* Billy Wilder's Crime and Punishment" (*LFQ* 12:3), a note declaring Wilder's film version of the novel to be a major film "as a picture of its era, and a glimpse at the darker side of America." Interest in Cain should be spurred by the publication of Cain's *Cloud Nine* (Mysterious Press), with an afterword by Roy Hoopes. Wisely leaving critical evaluation of this work up to the reader, Hoopes summarizes with a sharp eye the waning years of Cain's life. *Cloud Nine*, Hoopes says, is "quintessential Cain" and at the same time "different from the classic Cain tale" in its narrator and the absence of the expected Cain terror.

Mickey Spillane receives his own book-length study this year in

One Lonely Knight: Mickey Spillane's Mike Hammer, by Max Allan Collins and James L. Taylor (Bowling Green). This study of the best-selling mystery writer of all time treads the familiar ground of detective as knight-errant (Hammer is "a lone knight of the underworld") and devotes most attention to synopses of Spillane's novels without attempting a serious argument for the literary merit of his work. The authors claim that Spillane is a peer of Chandler and Hammett but fail to support that claim with critical evidence. Spillane comes in for attention again in *Murder in the Millions: Erle Stanley Gardner, Mickey Spillane, Ian Fleming*, by J. Kenneth Van Dover (Ungar). The first third of this book is a tour through Gardner's incredible outpouring of fiction, from the stories and novellas of the '20s through the flood of Perry Mason novels. Of the three writers studied here, only Gardner "acknowledges the more mundane responsibilities of adult life" says Van Dover. While, according to this critic, Gardner is "the novelist of the New Deal," Harry Truman and Ike Eisenhower "found a rather unlikely laureate in Mickey Spillane." Perry Mason, Van Dover states, "reassured his readers that a man might make an endangered system work; Mike Hammer assures his readers that a triumphant system need not overwhelm a man."

Even Rex Stout merits a book this year, with Ungar's publication of David R. Anderson's solid introduction, *Rex Stout*. Among the so-called iconoclasts, Salinger is the subject of Jack R. Sublette's *J. D. Salinger: An Annotated Bibliography, 1938–1981* (Garland). Sublette provides a chronology, primary and secondary lists including short fiction, and sections dealing with letters, the novel, reviews, translations, reference works, dissertations, and theses. The only problem with this thorough and well-organized work is the printing itself, which drifts into the whiteness of the page in a sometimes riddling blankness. Salinger receives brief attention in Mike Tierce's note, "Salinger's 'For Esme With Love and Squalor'" (*Expl* 42,iii: 56–58) and more intense study in Dennis L. O'Connor's look at Taoism and Buddhism in "J. D. Salinger's Religious Pluralism: The Example of 'Raise High the Roof Beam, Carpenter'" (*SoR* 20:316–32). Nathanael West gets additional attention this year in "West, Pynchon, Mailer, and the Jeremiad Tradition," by Donald Weber (*SAQ* 83:259–68). Weber is concerned with the "colonial legacy" to these three writers as exemplified by *The Day of the Locust, The Crying of Lot 49*, and *The Armies of the Night*, works that "reveal a metaphysical obsession with the meaning of America and explore . . .

the long tradition of American Jeremiahs." *Locust*, according to Weber, is "a textbook example of the anti-jeremiad," because for West "the idea of a redemptive America is a lie."

v. Westerners and Others

The resurgence of interest in Saroyan continues with another book this year, Lawrence Lee and Barry Gifford's *Saroyan: A Biography* (Harper & Row), an impressively written and handsomely published work. The final words in this volume are those of Saroyan's very devoted daughter Lucy: "He was better than Santa Claus. As good as God." These words are the right counterbalance to a story of early success and deeply bitter and lengthy disappointment. Lee and Gifford maintain exactly the right distance from their subject, allowing many of Saroyan's friends and family members to tell their stories as part of Saroyan's. Edward Halsy Foster begins his monograph *William Saroyan* (WWS 61) with the rhetorical question, "What is there still to say about William Saroyan?" Foster then goes on to respond to this question with 50 pages of sometimes fragmented and too often shrilly defensive commentary on Saroyan and Saroyan's work. Occasionally Foster is insightful, as when he focuses on "problems of identity" in Saroyan's fiction and when he makes short shrift of Edmund Wilson's provincial remarks in *The Boys in the Back Room*, but the monograph is troubled by a rambling style which lends itself too easily to tangents and painfully general pronouncements upon literature. A much more effective monograph is Helen Winter Stauffer's *Mari Sandoz* (WWS 63). In these 50 pages, Stauffer displays her impressive knowledge of Sandoz's life and writing, providing a concise introduction to both. Reserving her praise almost exclusively for Sandoz's longer nonfiction, Stauffer nonetheless gives synopses of the novels and shorter writing as well, offering faint praise for such antifascist allegories as *Slogum House*, *Capital City*, and *The Tom-Walker*. Most of Stauffer's attention focuses on *Old Jules*, *Crazy Horse*, and *Cheyenne Autumn*. A late claimant to the title "westerner" is the subject of one of the finest of several biographies this year, Lois P. Rudnick's *Mabel Dodge Luhan: New Woman, New Worlds* (N. Mex.), an impressively researched and well-written book that successfully demolishes the myth of Luhan as merely "another rich and restless woman, a footnote in the cultural history of Bohemia." For Rudnick, and for the reader, Luhan emerges as a powerful creative force in her own right, sublimating that force, however, by "allowing the powerful men she collected to draw upon her feminine essence."

A very impressive collection received too late for review last year is *Walter Van Tilburg Clark: Critiques*, ed. Charlton Laird (Nevada, 1983). This collection of evaluations, commentaries, reminiscences, and original material taken from Clark's writing is at times uneven but nonetheless an important publication. Excellent biographical information is provided in the preface and chapters by Laird, Herbert Wilner, James W. Hulse, and Clark's son Robert M. Clark. The importance of place in Clark's fiction also attracts attention here, most effectively in a chapter by Wallace Stegner, "Walter Clark's Frontier" (pp. 53–70), an essay that allows Stegner another opportunity to reflect not only upon Clark's status as a "western" writer, but upon Stegner's and others' positions as well. Writers of the West, Stegner suggests in response to what he sees as a continued misreading of Clark, "are a little like the old folks in the Beckett play, continually rising up out of the garbarge cans to say something, and continually having the lids crammed down upon them again." The most effective essay in this volume is Robert B. Heilman's "Clark's Western Incident: From Stereotype to Model" (pp. 79–104), in which Heilman examines the "millennial impulse" underlying Clark's understanding of the West, a reading that perceptively establishes Clark's genius as an interpreter not of the West but of the dominant archetypal American impulse. Max Westbrook glances briefly at Clark's short fiction in "To Escape the Tiger: The Short Stories" (pp. 105–18) and Arthur Boardman evokes an atmosphere of graduate thesis in "The Shape of Feeling: Unity of Emotion and Rhetoric in the Work of Walter Clark" (pp. 230–47), with his "integrative" and "disintegrative" rhetoric. This is a volume that should stir renewed interest in the author of *The Track of the Cat*, leading, one can hope, to a new critical book on Clark.

James Thurber, an "other" in this section, does receive book-length attention this year in Catherine McGhee Kenney's *Thurber's Anatomy of Confusion* (Archon). Kenney divides her book into four areas: the *corpus mundi*; *Homo loquens*; *corpus mentis*; and time and death. In arguing for Thurber's importance, Kenney begins on the defensive: "Why a serious book about James Thurber?"—a question that unfortunately establishes the tone under which the author labors throughout this study. While inventorying Thurber's comic subjects and devices, Kenney too often seems to belabor the obvious: "The distinguishing characteristic of this special world is a pervasive use of the confusion motif." An additional brief Thurber piece worthy of note this year is Ruth A. Maharg's "The Modern Fable: James Thurber's Social Criticisms" (*CLAQ* 9,ii:72–73). Another "other" in this section this year is the writer of science fiction, who figures in *Women of the Future: The Female Main Character in Science Fiction* (Scarecrow) by Betty King. King documents her subject from the 1930s to the 1980s, with a chapter devoted to each decade and a first chapter offering a historical overview. The approach here is surprisingly dry, with each chapter listing works alphabetically and providing brief synopses for each. A distinctly feminist approach to Shirley Jackson this year comes in Lynette Carpenter's "The Establishment and Preservation of Female Power in Shirley Jackson's *We Have Always Lived in the Castle*" (*Frontiers* 8,i:32–38), in which Carpenter declares, "Female self-sufficiency, Jackson suggests, specifically women's forceful establishment of power over their own lives, threatens a society in which men hold primary power and leads inevitably to confrontation."

University of New Mexico

15. Fiction: The 1950s to the Present

Jerome Klinkowitz

Since 1981, the steady accrual of years has made this chapter the historically broadest among those devoted to 20th-century fiction. The need for some organizational control has become evident not just to this reviewer, but to contemporary scholars and even to current novelists themselves, for the bulk of 1984's work on the past three and one-half decades' fiction has been addressed to sorting out these years as a period, whether it be by theme, metaphor, symbol, informing theory, or by the novelists' own retrospective comments.

i. General Studies

In contrast to 1983's broad attempt to synthesize the present, which included a substantial number of books by both novice and established critics, 1984 closed with no one wishing to play Big Brother as did John W. Aldridge, Frederick R. Karl, Malcolm Bradbury, and their colleagues of the previous year. Rather than fashioning an airtight literary history, scholars are now proposing theories based on the better-known and less ambiguous work of linguistic philosophers as a way of organizing contemporary fiction into articulated modes.

Allen Thiher's *Words in Reflection: Modern Language Theory and Postmodern Fiction* (Chicago) and my own *The Self-Apparent Word: Fiction as Language / Language as Fiction* (So. Ill.) share the premise that instead of simply leading to the traditional realist's despair, "the belief in language's autonomy can also give rise to an often joyous affirmation of fiction's power, as language, to define the world and hence reality." Unlike fictive modernism, which makes the creative act a form of thematic representation, post-Modern fiction writers such as Ronald Sukenick and Raymond Federman reject this

I wish to acknowledge the substantial contribution of my research assistant, Fumiyo Oka.—J.K.

metaphysical and theological sense of authority for their works, choosing instead a strategy of self-representation which grounds their fiction in language as language. Thiher uses the work of Jacques Derrida as his conduit from Heidegger, Saussure, and Wittgenstein to the work of Sukenick, Federman, John Barth, Frederick Tuten, and Donald Barthelme, employing a sense of irony to explain how "the jubilant energy of postmodern fiction arises, in a nearly dialectical fashion, when the postmodern accepts this contradiction as a challenge, and pursuing his alienation, hyperbolically assumes the otherness of language, its schizoid structures, and its pop dementia." Intertextuality as its own history replaces the need for an externally historical response, and in true Saussurean fashion the novel becomes its own grammatical system.

I use Derrida, Julia Kristeva, and Roland Barthes less as interpreters of modern language theory and more as indicators of the shift from speaking to writing, from the monological to the dialogical, and from the death of the book (as authority) to the birth of performance, which helps explain how fiction has made a 180-degree turn in its methods and goals. For me, Sukenick and Federman represent the extreme of experimentation, establishing how far one can carry the nonrepresentational aspects of language without becoming unreadable. From their achievements a new generation of writers, notably Walter Abish, Stephen Dixon, and Kenneth Gangemi have devised a style of "experimental realism" in which the formerly transparent conventions of representation now become opaque materials in themselves, allowing stories to be generated without recourse to a signified reality beyond their text. That such options have always been available is shown by contrasting the "self-effacing" use of signs as indicators in Philip Roth's "Goodbye, Columbus" with Kurt Vonnegut's "self-apparent" use of signs as themselves in "The Hyannis Port Story."

Because critics have been slow to acknowledge such developments in fiction, the writers themselves have emerged as spokesmen for their new style. This year has seen major collections of such essays reaching back to the 1950s by novelists Gilbert Sorrentino, John Barth, John Gardner, and Charles Newman, with similar books by Ronald Sukenick, William H. Gass, and Michael Stephens on the way. Sorrentino has long advocated the recanonization of American letters, away from the *New Yorker*-style fiction of John O'Hara and John Updike, which depends upon the thematics of social signals. In

Something Said (North Point) he constructs a counter-tradition reaching from William Carlos Williams's novels, through Hubert Selby's, to writers as disparate as John Hawkes, Coleman Dowell, and Ross Macdonald; in common, they trust form and exercise language within its limits, as opposed to the moralist John Gardner whose gestures outreach his texts, remanding him to "the puppeteer school of novelists" who suffer from a tin ear for language. Sorrentino's critical position accommodates Thiher's and my view of fictive language, as does Sorrentino's fiction itself. Not surprisingly, John Barth's *The Friday Book* (Putnam's) and John Gardner's *The Art of Fiction* (Knopf) closely reflect their authors' own styles of fictive art. But unlike Sorrentino, whose tastes for innovations accommodated work with methods other than his own, Barth and Gardner are severely limited by their sometimes polemical aesthetics. Sorrentino's prejudice is simply against writing that presumes to place "a held idea into a waiting form," and is for writing that is "the act itself." Barth demands a more Modernist or even Classicist grounding, by which the act of writing involves the construction of a personal myth—in this case, of the storyteller watching himself tell stories of a storyteller watching himself. Such Aristotelian representation of the imitation of an imitation of an action is diametrically opposed to the self-apparent language Sorrentino feels is necessary for fiction to be something other than a secondhand report. For his part, Gardner stacks the deck against self-apparency by misreading it as metafiction. In his view Barth's substitution of artistic commentary on art for novel writing, which is indeed metafictional, defines the work of Barthelme ("formalist irrealism"), Stanley Elkin ("jazzing around" with the imagination), Gass ("fictional pointillism"), Hawkes ("surrealist dreaming"), Jerzy Kosinski (simple surrealism), and Sukenick ("fascination with untrustworthy characters"), all of which Gardner feels is simply fiction exploring fiction making, rather than an attempt (as Sorrentino sees in some of these writers) to return American fiction to the "true Americanism" of employing a neutral, antisymbolistic, solidly opaque surface on which to celebrate the "featureless, fragmented, incongruous American experience."

Even Gardner's polemics, however, pale before the bitter anger that Charles Newman unleashes in *The Postmodern Aura: The Act of Fiction in an Age of Inflation* (*Salmagundi* 63–64:3–199, reprinted by Northwestern). In the tradition of Gardner's own *On Moral Fiction*, which in *ALS 1978* Michael J. Hoffman described as "strikingly antimodernist and sometimes almost hysterical in tone" (p. 431), Newman's corrective admonition to the current state of affairs is based upon the failure of his own fiction to find strong success with either the critical or academic establishment, both of which he claims have had their authority eroded by "climax inflation," which is "the incessant changing of hands and intrinsic devaluation of all received ideas." Although many of Newman's readings are quite pertinent, his argument suffers because he makes his winning points only on the level of metaphor: that the present American age is turn-of-the-century Vienna, and that literary values are exploited just like inflationary currency (and with the same results). Newman's analysis of mass marketing's effect on what the publishing trade calls "manufactured fiction" (such as the Harold Robbins blockbuster quickly turned into a television miniseries) is true but obvious, while the same arguments hardly apply to the more limited world of serious novels and story collections. His belief that the United States has never had an avant-garde, nor even had the need for one, is contradicted by Ishmael Reed's multicultural, nativistic resistance to the Eurocentric colonialism in American letters. And his wish for "a new theory of Authority" leaves the language theories of Saussure, Wittgenstein, Derrida, and Kristeva unread. And again like Gardner, he willfully misidentifies all innovative fiction as the more easily dismissible metafiction, claiming that Laurence Sterne's intrusive author did anything the metafictionists can do two centuries ago (a strategy that disregards the anti-Aristotelian basis of contemporary fiction). There is a fatalism to anticipated inflation, but innovative fiction is hardly an investments game. By calling Federman and Gass "formalists" and by describing Barthelme's achievement simply as being "essentially unparodyable," Newman practices a reductiveness unworthy of the major critic he cites most often, Walter Benjamin, whose pessimism in the face of European modernity was based on firmer grounds than a metaphorical dissatisfaction with the tone of contemporary life.

Turning back to the critics, 1984 finds a wealth of structures, techniques, philosophies, and metaphors by which to organize contemporary fiction. In *Metafiction* (Methuen) Patricia Waugh makes the distinctions Gardner and Newman failed to employ in their own analyses of styles. For her, metafiction is most properly applied to writers who demand no realistic motivation for their texts, and she is careful to distinguish just what motivations Robert Coover, Ronald

Sukenick, E. L. Doctorow, John Barth, Donald Barthelme, Richard Brautigan, Gilbert Sorrentino, and Raymond Federman require; as does Allen Thiher at the end of *Words in Reflection,* Waugh concludes that only a Continental writer can achieve such formal perfection (for Thiher it was Claude Simon, for Waugh it is the Paris-based British novelist and critic Christine Brooke-Rose). Kathryn Hume makes a more conventional analysis in *Fantasy and Mimesis: Responses to Reality in Western Literature* (Methuen), but her familiar categories shed new light on Brautigan (whose *In Watermelon Sugar* is structured by "a mysterious underlying emotional logic") and on Vonnegut (whose *Player Piano* introduces positive standards through a negative framework). Reviewing Deconstruction as a philosophy of reading, Christopher Butler pauses in *Interpretation, Deconstruction, and Ideology* (Clarendon / Oxford) to note that it is "hardly coincidental" that Coover, Federman, Barthelme, and Abish "deliberately embrace contradiction and aporia—usually those of literary convention itself," since their strategies avoid "any consistent mimetic commitment and thus allow the reader to play amongst the deliberately revealed techniques of the creative writer. . . . The text deconstructs itself by involving the reader in incompatible strategies of comprehension." For Stefano Tani Deconstruction is one stage in the reinvention of fiction, a process which he focuses on within a familiar subgenre. In *The Doomed Detective: The Contribution of the Detective Novel to Postmodern American and Italian Fiction* (So. Ill.) John Gardner's *The Sunlight Dialogues* is seen inverting the traditions of certainty and detachment much as does Umberto Eco's *The Name of the Rose;* in *Gravity's Rainbow* and *Falling Angel,* Thomas Pynchon and William Hjortsberg invite the deconstructive readings Christopher Butler describes by suspending solutions and overloading the structure with clues; but like Thiher and Waugh, Tani betrays his Eurocentric bias by finding only Continental writers at the climax of this process, which is the metafictional parody practiced by Italo Calvino and Vladimir Nabokov.

Among the more traditional approaches to fiction, absurdity, game-playing, and the notion of reality still yield good results. Robert A. Hipkiss's *The American Absurd: Pynchon, Vonnegut, and Barth* (Associated Faculty Press) examines a topic previously treated by the "black humor" critics two decades ago and summarized by Raymond Olderman and Charles B. Harris (*ALS 1972,* pp. 268–69). But whereas these earlier studies intuited a return to romance, Hip-

kiss sees more clearly that matters are far less sanguine than Olderman and Harris, with their cheery prescriptions for a diet of caring
and love, had presumed. Vonnegut is especially noteworthy for advocating "basic human sympathy in place of more ideal, stalwart
values," and all three writers, as Absurdists, substitute "sympathy
and decency for love as the beneficent values of human cohesion." A
common emphasis of nonrational means of knowing distinguishes
them from the European Existentialists with whom they have been
too hastily compared, and their outright rejections of a spiritually
guided (and hence "innately moral") America, of Americans as a
new race free of history, of the individual conscience as inviolable,
and of "the ultimate necessity and triumph of self-reliance" set them a
world apart from 19th-century romanticism. Pynchon does seek some
assurance of spiritual transcendence, but in "a world in which there
is far more evidence of damnation"; only "moments of interface"
between historical trends give him hope, and these he exploits for
his finest fiction. Vonnegut's work is a well-meaning "epilogue to the
failure of American idealism" built upon a critique of "the hallowed
myth of American rugged individualism." Barth sees the world's
forces behaving in a dialectical fashion which frustrates man's ability
to reconcile his own divided self. With great acuity Hipkiss notes
that this division corresponds to Barth's most characteristic literary
aesthetic: "Epistemologically, the 'I' is always ultimately regressive
in its contemplation of self, for the contemplating 'I,' once mentally
conceived, shifts from subject to object." *The American Absurd*
combines philosophical depth with broad understanding of these
writers' full works, organizing the contemporary in an eminently
useful fashion. One major fault, however, is the author's practice of
dating books: not from their year of publication, but from the first
year in which any of their subsequent components was copyrighted,
making *V.* a 1961 publication (when some pages in progress were
excerpted for a magazine) instead of 1963, and most glaringly describing *Welcome to the Monkey House* as coming out in 1950 (when
Vonnegut published his first short story) rather than in 1968 (when
the last of several stories throughout the 1960s was written and the
collection finally issued).

Various metaphors for theme and form distinguish a healthy array of books and articles. "Desperate Gambits: Game Theory in
Modern American Literature" (*SCR* 17,i:96–108) by R. E. Foust
shows how meaning is improvised from an otherwise Absurdist life,

as Robert Coover uses ritual as the generative energy for history in *The Universal Baseball Association*, as Joan Didion uses golf as a metaphor for male and female aggressions, and as Pynchon, Gardner, and Barthelme exploit "the creative feature of free recreative participation of the reader that is emphasized by a theory of literary games" and which parody-oriented critics overlook. Roger Sale's *Literary Inheritance* (Mass.) rejects Harold Bloom's metaphor of the anxiety of influence, claiming that the difference between modernist and contemporary work is the latter's choice not to struggle with tradition but blithesomely to ignore it; Heller's *Catch-22*, Roth's *Portnoy's Complaint*, Saul Bellow's *Herzog* and *Humboldt's Gift*, and Updike's *Rabbit is Rich* are works "put in the service of something less in need of votive candles for illumination, more in need of a sense of impulsive exploration." In *The Realist Fantasy: Fiction and Reality Since Clarissa* (St. Martin's) Paul Coates offers a chapter on "Post-Modernism" (pp. 180–222) which contrasts Coover's *The Public Burning* with E. L. Doctorow's *The Book of Daniel* (praising the former for its brash, frontal assault on presumed reality which reveals history as naturalized myth-making) and faults Pynchon's *Gravity's Rainbow* for its failure to create a totalizing vision (as was achieved in *The Crying of Lot 49* by a scrupulously critiqued tension between fact and fiction). F. K. Stanzel's *A Theory of Narrative* (Cambridge) brings an eminently Austrian sense of language theory and narratology to bear on a pleasing range of American works, from the predictable *Herzog* to the surprisingly revealing fiction of Kenneth Gangemi. Stanzel's theory of mediacy (*Mittelbarkeit*) emphasizes the shifting relationship between the story and how it is told. He finds that as broad a range of Americans as Bellow, William S. Burroughs, Pynchon, and Vonnegut practice an "extreme deviation from all norms and conventions of narrative literature" which has not been followed by their British colleagues. Even in as traditional a novel as Saul Bellow's *Herzog* Stanzel notes a curious alternation between first- and third-person pronominal references which "alters the fictional reality of what he is narrating." Vonnegut's *Breakfast of Champions* uses the same technique, just as the author's choice to go against the grain of accepted practices of narration in *Slaughterhouse-Five* denies the world any finality in the realistic sense. When Gangemi uses the language and form of the filmscript as a narrative mode in *The Interceptor Pilot*, he unifies the temporal system of *histoire* with the pronominal system of *discours*.

Sexuality provides Peter Schwenger's and Larry McCaffery's favorite metaphors this year. In *Phallic Critiques: Masculinity and Twentieth-Century Literature* (Routledge), Schwenger notes that each age is characterized by its discovery of one part of the sexual anatomy. For the Victorians it was the bosom, and our age (from *Playgirl* magazine to James Dickey's *Deliverance*) has embraced the phallus. Dickey and Robert F. Jones (*Bloodsport*) devise phallic rituals, while Norman Mailer identifies the male body with action writing, advertising how he writes within the physiological mechanics of time and space. In *An American Dream* and *Why Are We in Vietnam?* Mailer uses words as "a species of manly action." Larry McCaffery's choice of a younger group of writers in "And Still They Smooch: Erotic Visions and Re-Visions in Postmodern American Fiction" (*RFEA* 20:275–87) yields a more exuberant, participatory view of sex for author and reader alike. As post-Modernists search for new fictional forms, they also explore new ways to express love and sexuality, from Raymond Federman's "delirious, improvisational flights of erotic fancy" to Kathy Acker's frank and often brutalized accounts which grow out of the punk sensibility. Gass and Coover use sex for larger, formal issues of artistic creation in *Willie Masters' Lonesome Wife* and *Spanking the Maid*, whereas Steve Katz's *Moving Parts* "creates bizarre situations which somehow produce mysterious resonances that illuminate events in our own lives." Exploring various incarnations of love provides a form for Alexander Theroux's *Darconville's Cat*, while Ted Mooney's *Easy Travel to Other Planets* responds to the overstimulation of life by creating a science fiction counterpart protected from "information sickness." As post-Modernists, these writers are less interested in the product of new variations and positions than in finding ways "to present *the process* of love's in's-and-out's within structures and language that do more than just realistically depict love's sweaty embrace."

Wandering Jews, lawyers, and Jeremiah-like prophets interest another group of critics. Harold Frisch looks at Bellow's protagonists and at Bernard Malamud's hero in *The Fixer* and finds that the former seek myths for meaning, but that only the latter is given vindication; these are two ways to write beyond the simple Wandering Jew / Ahasuerus model which Frisch traces through *Remembered Future: A Study in Literary Mythology* (Indiana), which concludes with an appreciation of how John Barth directly negates the myths of history in *Lost in the Funhouse*. Richard H. Weisberg finds that in Saul Bellow's work "a vitalism and true ethical perspective point the way to a reintegration of language and values," as opposed to the blurring of fact and fiction in Truman Capote's and E. L. Doctorow's novels, a problem he sees as endemic to our age in *The Failure of the Word: The Protagonist as Lawyer in Modern Fiction* (Yale). "West, Pynchon, Mailer, and the Jeremiad Tradition" (*SAQ* 83:259–68) presents Donald Weber's argument that these writers share the colonial legacy of an optimistic illusion that Americans are a chosen people. West inverts this tradition into an antijeremiad which destroys the promised land, but Pynchon cannot abandon the dream despite all skeptical evidence to the contrary. Mailer "catalogues the sins of the nation but cannot abandon the covenant," like Pynchon refusing to cross the threshold into West's abject despair.

The Vietnam War continues to provide a focus for investigations into the shape of current fiction. Kathleen M. Puhr discusses work by John Briley, James Webb, Charles Durden, Gustav Hasford, and John C. Pratt in "Four Fictional Faces of the Vietnam War" (*MFS* 30:99–117), finding that radically different styles can convey the same theme of how a character changes his attitude toward the conflict; Pratt's formal experimentation and thematic choice of dramatizing the air war are advantages in capitalizing on the war's depersonalization. In "Diving Into the Wreck: Sense Making in *The 13th Valley*" (MFS 30:119–34) Thomas Myers shows how John Del Vecchio's novel builds on both the early documentary-style novels and the later, more imaginatively explorative approaches to produce a Melvillean tension "between man and nature, knowledge and innocence, and history and language." Unwilling to make reductive recreations of the war, Del Vecchio shows how no single appraisal can be complete. Eric J. Schroeder's "Two Interviews: Talks with Tim O'Brien and Robert Stone" (*MFS* 30:135–64) contrasts the two authors' divergent trends toward autobiography and invention. *Going After Cacciato* stresses how memory and imagination interpenetrate, determining a course of action. For Stone, the horror of Vietnam in *The Dog Soldiers* is that it follows his protagonist back to the United States, a transformation that Stone feels is better handled by fiction than by journalism. A descriptive but virtually exhaustive guide to the subject is made available by Peter C. Rollins in "The Vietnam War: Perceptions Through Literature, Film, and Television" (*AQ* 36:419–32).

One understated attempt at literary history may be found in Charles Ruas's *Conversations with American Writers* (Knopf), in which he appropriately asks the writers themselves about how and why they write. From his talks with Susan Sontag, Paul Theroux, Capote, Stone, Mailer, Burroughs, Doctorow, and Heller there emerges a credible organization of the period: from the postwar expectations of a great American novel, through a middle-period experimentation with form, to a present enjoyment in making personal, even idiosyncratic slices of life—a new Jamesian style best characterized by Doctorow's *Ragtime*. Changes in cultural attitudes toward the novel parallel these transitions, about which Ruas's subjects are articulate and perceptive. Noteworthy are Stone's personal attitudes which inform his novels, Burroughs's appraisal of the censorship issue (in a roundtable discussion with publisher Maurice Girodias, agent James Grauerholz, and Allen Ginsberg), Mailer's analysis of ex-convict Jack Abbott's role in his own writing and of the open, all-debatable form of Egyptology, and Heller's revelation of how his own wartime experiences were personally beneficial and of how his recent novel, *God Knows*, came to be. Fascinating looks at how conditions of publishing and employment shape fiction are taken by Kenneth C. Davis in *Two-Bit Culture: The Paperbacking of America* (Houghton Mifflin) and by Rust Hills in "How Writers Live Today" (*Esquire* 84,ii:37–39). For example, Kurt Vonnegut's career as a novelist didn't get underway until his story editor at *Collier's*, Knox Burger, was lured to Dell when the "Paperback Revolution" began in the late 1950s; Burger took his best authors with him, and kept his stable intact when Fawcett hired him away two years later with the promise of even more paperback originals. Rust Hills worries about the M.F.A. Creative Writing Program market and its effect on literature. "There can scarcely be an American writer in his [or her] thirties who hasn't been involved in a university writing program somewhere, some time," Hills observes, adding that "it is what is chosen to be taught in these classes that determines a living writer's chances of entering the canon" and becoming a teacher of other candidates for canonization. Hills's regrets are well-taken when one encounters the pallid, academic style of "M.F.A. Modern" which dominates most writing programs and has begun to fill the pages of literary magazines; not much fiction of innovation or substance has come from the workshop so far.

ii. Saul Bellow, Philip Roth, Other Jewish-Americans

Bellow and, this year, Roth commanded the most attention, but in several ways interest has broadened. Most significant is Raymond Federman's argument that the Holocaust both created the role of "Jewish writer" and provided the challenge of a subject matter beyond words. In "Displaced Person: The Jew / The Wanderer / The Writer" (*DQ* 19,i:85–100) he notes that the central technique in his own fiction is the erasure of unimaginable events: "If fiction communicates anything, it can only do so by a slippage, a displacement—by a verbal continuum which may someday reach the right destination, the right aggregate, but not by looking backward to the beginning, but by looking to the process in the present." In a companion piece, "The Necessity and Impossibility of Being a Jewish Writer" (*FictI* 15,i:190–96) Federman adds that Jewish-American writing, like all forms of fiction, must shift its energy from content to form, since the powers of imagination and not the accuracy of memory are the key.

That such an innovator's role has been rejected by more conservative Jewish-American writers is apparent from William E. H. Myer, Jr.'s "Jewish Literature in America: Impossible Assimilation under the 'Tyrannous Eye'" (*WHR* 38:303–13), which argues that Malamud's *The Assistant* and Bellow's *Herzog* and *Henderson the Rain King* resist the Puritan and Emersonian charge to see Nature in the Present; unlike the "eyewitness travelers to many coasts," Malamud and Bellow retain "the Jewish consciousness" which "still believes that God speaks to man in some form of address" and that such texts must be read. This textual proclivity is praised by Stephen J. Whitfield in *Voices of Jacob, Hands of Esau: Jews in American Life and Thought* (Archon), from Woody Allen's sensitivity to language as a vehicle of truth (the anxieties of which are handled like a good Talmudist) to Roth's lightening of the mythic load with realistically comic language (a technique Malamud might well have profited from in *The Natural*); an ideal combination of vibrant myth and lively language is found in Jerome Charyn's *The Seventh Babe*, in which baseball is a metaphor for nothing but itself, a product of its own systematic language. David G. Roskies also finds textuality central to the Jew's role in history. His *Against the Apocalypse: Responses to Catastrophe in Modern Jewish Culture* (Harvard) finds that fiction's reportorial accuracy allowed Russian-Jewish writers to speak freely yet avoid censors, and that in making order out of chaos by imposing a single, schematic plot, the pogrom novel set the structure for later Jewish-American works; Isaac Bashevis Singer's "The Last Demon" shows this power of language to sustain a creature whose demonhood cuts him off from all effective content. Sam B. Girgus assimilates the work of Malamud, Roth, and Mailer by using the jeremiad sense of mission as a text that bridges the gap to American Puritanism; *The New Covenant: Jewish Writers and the American Idea* (N. C.) sees Malamud's *A New Life* as criticizing society for its failure to live up to its vision of itself in a promised land. Roth embraces the writer's role as rendering the American reality beyond its redskin and paleface polarities, while Mailer synthesizes literature with American history and life. Mailer himself plays an active textual role in Hershel Parker's *Flawed Texts*. In a coda added to his study of Mailer's revisions in *An American Dream* (*ALS 1982*, p. 277), Parker campaigns for more scholarly attention to artistic creativity by detailing his own experience with Mailer and with the press, including Mailer's thoughts about restoring his text and Jonathan Yardley's resistance to scholarly influence. The author of *Why Are We in Vietnam?* dominates Martin Green's *Great American Adventure*. As opposed to British fiction, the American novel remains powerful and expansive because the adventure story authenticates and aestheticizes our sense of national adventure, and as a Jewish-American writer Mailer can effectively parody the WASP tradition alien to his own ambitions. Mailer's prejudices reflect this national purpose: anti-Christian, antifeminist, nationalistic, masculine, and typologically stratified, the author's manners inhibit the expansion of self common to adventure stories when they are not burdened with such epic meaning.

The preceding general studies of Jewish-American writers describe a range of purpose and sense of direction which is unfortunately lacking in *Twentieth-Century Jewish-American Writers* (Gale), volume 28 of the *DLB* edited by Daniel Walden. Here an encyclopedic sense of publishing expediency has organized this subfield with little sense of scholarly direction. Too many of the contributions are blandly reductive, and many authors have been included simply by accident of birth. Doris G. Bargen's chapter on Stanley Elkin (pp. 47–50) admits that his protagonists are not always Jews but are "always intellectuals" and therefore share the Jewish vision, which reads like racial slander. The collection's ablest authority, Keith Opdahl, admits in his own fine essay (pp. 8–25) that Bellow feels and reads much more like an American than a hyphenated person. The volume as a whole suffers from the faulty editorial assumption that naming a category and locating a writer within it allows plot and career summaries to be substituted for analysis, much as movie stills are used to illustrate the critical text. The book's ultimate disservice to scholarship is its manner of exclusion: while any number of realistic writers are included no matter how tenuous their connection and slight their fame (Jay Neugeboren, Gerald Greene), the entire group of Jewish-American innovators, some of whom wrote in Israel before emigrating and all of whom use Jewish themes, are ignored in this otherwise overly generous assemblage: Raymond Federman, Ronald Sukenick, Steve Katz, Walter Abish, and Max Apple, to name just a few.

In *Saul Bellow: Vision and Revision* (Duke) Daniel Fuchs reaches into Bellow's manuscripts and letters to consider his craftsmanship with theme and character, but the real value of his research is in the support it provides for his two major interpretive theses: that Bellow's politics of civility in the service of a culture worth preserving makes him the "missing middle" between Norman Mailer's extremes of violence and romantic idealism, and that the effect of his fiction has been to replace Mark Twain with Dostoevsky as a major source for modern American literature. Fuchs does a superb job of countering those critics who feel Bellow's ideas overwhelm his fiction by showing how the author's engagement with his works in progress shows a continual tendency away from discursiveness and toward fable. Bellow's occasional practice of dictation achieves a quality of voice rather than of philosophy. An important clarification of the Dostoevsky influence is found in Allan Chavkin's "The Problem of Suffering in the Fiction of Saul Bellow" (*CLS* 21:161–74); it is not the only source for Bellow's sense of suffering, since his complex reaction to English romanticism, Jewish comedy, and antimodernism must be considered along with the more familiar use of Dostoevskian humanism. To the intense psychological turmoil of his characters, Bellow adds a measure of secular humanism derived from Wordsworth and especially Keats. The symbolic adventures experienced in *Henderson the Rain King* show that *Moby-Dick* was on Bellow's mind, according to Karl F. Knight in "Bellow's Henderson and Melville's Ishmael: Their Mingled Worlds" (*SAF* 12:91–98).

His unhappiness with the quality of intellectual life in America has been growing since *Herzog*, Mark Christhilf claims in "Saul Bellow and the American Intellectual Community" (*ModA* 28:55–67); the intellectuals' insensitivity to social issues is seen in "Mosby's Memoirs," and their failure as an adversary culture is condemned in *Humboldt's Gift*. "Publicity intellectuals" are scorned in *Mr. Sammler's Planet*, and in *The Dean's December* Bellow challenges the assumption of liberal theory that human nature is naturally good—it may be, but such blanket assumptions insure that any contrary evidence will be ignored; Dean Corde's willingness to forego popularity and give voice to an unpleasant reality is a metaphor for Bellow's own "estrangement from his readers" through his compulsion for truth.

　　Saul Bellow Journal remains an essential repository of first-class scholarship. Two broadly synthetic essays deserve special attention beyond an interest in Bellow's work itself: Don D. Elgin's "Order Out of Chaos: Bellow's Use of the Picaresque in *Herzog*" (3,ii:13–22), which shows how this fictional technique allows positive statement in the face of much negativism, and Ted R. Spivey's "Death, Love, and the Rebirth of Language in Bellow's Fiction" (4,i:5–18), which cites William Barrett's *The Illusion of Technique* to explain Bellow's belief that when the individual is renewed, the social order's language as a whole ultimately benefits. Bellow himself is a remarkable spokesman for his own work and for American letters in general, and two recent interviews plus a striking memoir deserve note for his assessments of American materialism (with its energistic vitalism) as opposed to European malaise: Matthew C. Roudané's "An Interview with Saul Bellow" (*ConL* 25:265–80), which also treats his interest in intellectuals, scientists, and art; Rockwell Gray, Harry White, and Gerald Nemanic's "Interview with Saul Bellow" (*TriQ* 60:12–34), in which Bellow also talks candidly about his own responses to literary theory; and Bellow's own "Old Paris" (*Granta* 10:163–73), which describes it as the "heavenly city of secularists" which he thought at one time could harbor his vision, but which now has faded in favor of the business and technological reality of Chicago in particular and America in general—"where all the action is," as he says in *TriQ*.

　　Also in the *TriQ* interview may be found Bellow's amazement that Philip Roth finds writing to be so much pain and trouble—writing should be done for the joy of it, Bellow exclaims. But a look at the second edition of Bernard F. Rodgers, Jr.'s *Philip Roth: A Bibliography* (Scarecrow) shows how Roth and his reputation have been slowly but steadily adding up: Rodgers finds that twice as many primary sources and four times as many secondary materials have collected in the past ten years. The depth of Roth's achievement is also the subject of this year's best essays: W. Clark Hendley's "An Old Form Revitalized: Philip Roth's *The Ghost Writer* and the *Bildungsroman*" (*SNNTS* 16:87–100), which explains that by asking significant questions about art in the contemporary world Roth makes the novel more Nathan's story than Amy's; Barbara Koenig Quart's "The Rapacity of One Nearly Buried Alive" (*MR* 24[1983]:590–608), which shows how from first to last Roth's protagonists must struggle to exist maturely outside the smothering effects of their families; and Barry Gross's "American Fiction, Jewish Writers, and Black Characters: The Return of 'The Human Negro' in Philip Roth" (*MELUS* 11,ii:5–22), which supports Ralph Ellison's belief that black characters are used more positively by Jewish-American writers, specifically by Roth in "Goodbye, Columbus," than by other white American novelists (despite exceptions to the rule by Bellow, Malamud, and Mailer). Hermione Lee, whose fine study of Roth appears in the Methuen Contemporary Writers series (*ALS 1982*, pp. 276–77), conducts an exemplary interview for "The Art of Fiction, LXXXIV" (*ParisR* 93:214–47), covering not just his writing habits and attitudes toward themes but also critical issues such as Nathan Zuckerman's achievement as an impersonation and the role of autobiography in the novelist's own impersonation of life. Especially valuable is Roth's extended consideration of women in his novels and of how feminist critics have reacted.

John S. Friedman elicits similarly important statements from Elie Wiesel in "The Art of Fiction, LXXIX" (*ParisR* 91:130–78). Wiesel explains why his New York residency has not yet appeared in his fiction: he has yet to exhaust the materials of his childhood, which continue to speak to present-day issues with great immediacy (everything he writes is such a response, dictated by social, political, and moral need). That writers can master the interview form is shown in David Neal Miller's "Isaac Bashevis Singer: The Interview as Fictional Genre" (*ConL* 25:187–204). For Singer, being interviewed permits him a role-reversal, turning presumed fact into future fiction. His "plurisignificant texts," which is what his interviews are, may

mean different things at different times; because of their strong intertextuality, Singer's interviews are better viewed as literary productions rather than as biographical documents; his own persona is one
created "on the margin of fictiveness." A similar point is made by
Anita Susan Grossman in "The Hidden Isaac Bashevis Singer: *Lost
in America* and the Problem of Veracity" (*TCL* 30:30–45); his supposed autobiography uses a background of truth for what is actually
fiction, so that the "sharp outline of photographic reality" may be
blurred in a way that allows formal shaping.

iii. Flannery O'Connor, William Styron, Walker Percy, Other Southerners

As a resource for essay-length scholarship, O'Connor seemed mined
out. Individual treatments of her work now tend to be found mostly
in *Notes on Contemporary Literature* and *Explicator,* and are easily
described by their titles. On the other hand, the presence of her work
provides a frequent reference point for scholars who have larger matters to explore. Andrew V. Ettin looks at "A Circle in the Fire" as
O'Connor's "more complex and less immediately recognizable modal
version of the pastoral" which in *Literature and the Pastoral* (Yale)
he aligns with Walt Whitman's natural as opposed to societal pastoral qualities; inevitably citing the violence and grotesque in O'Connor's work, he discusses "urbanization as a form of vengeance against
the pastoral world." Elizabeth Langland's *Society in the Novel* finds
that O'Connor has precluded society by establishing a transcendent
realm in which her characters' fates are evaluated; these conflicting
realities are responsible for what others have seen as a gothic emphasis on the violent and decadent.

    Sophie's Choice gets critical attention not simply because it is
William Styron's most recent novel, but because it leads to a reinter-
pretation of his entire canon. William Heath lodges an objection in
"I, Stingo: The Problem of Egotism in *Sophie's Choice*" (*SoR* 20:528–
45), claiming that Styron forgets that the novel's "central story" is
Sophie's tragedy, not Stingo's voyage of discovery. He objects to the
excessive documentation of Stingo's sexual yearnings, but Carolyn
A. Durham provides a better explanation of this feature in "William
Styron's *Sophie's Choice:* The Structure of Oppression" (*TCL* 30:
448–64), noting that "virtually every chapter . . . contains the same

consistent structural elements: a system of organized oppression, a particular example of sexism, and a commentary on language or literature, thus creating a structural paradigm in which *sexism* illuminates both the *systems* that oppress society and the *literature* that can lead toward an understanding of how they function." Michael Kreyling is another critic ready to accept what others see as Styron's excesses, for in "Speakable and Unspeakable in Styron's *Sophie's Choice*" (*SoR* 20:546–61) he shows how George Steiner's belief that "silence is the answer" pales before Stingo's success with sexual vocabulary in articulating the otherwise unspoken; without the "color, movement, and vitality" of words, mankind will atrophy. John Kenny Crane uses *Sophie's Choice* to reinterpret the entire Styron canon, finding in *The Root of All Evil: The Thematic Unity of William Styron's Fiction* (S. C.) that this latest novel's major theme is an investigation of Styron's own authorship. Crane shows that the major choices are Stingo's and not Sophie's, for the former's need to gain moral awareness and sensitivity (as opposed to being just a "wordsmith") reflects Styron's judgment of his novels preceding *The Confessions of Nat Turner*. The solution, however, is technical and not just thematic: whereas his earlier works have two or three time levels, *Sophie's Choice* operates on four, including the "Transcendent Present."

A fine introduction to Walker Percy's literary history, philosophy, and fictive technique is provided by Jay Tolson in "The Education of Walker Percy" (*WQ* 8,iii:156–66), which stresses Percy's appreciation of the past's hold on characters and how they face the danger of yielding to ready explanations, all of which threatens to add up to a death in life. How Percy's character Max Gottlieb in *Love in the Ruins* extends a swing away from the ideal scientist of *Arrowsmith* is described by Mary G. Land in "Three Max Gottleib's: Lewis's, Dreiser's and Walker Percy's View of the Mechanist-Vitalist Controversy" (*SNNTS* 15[1983]:314–31). The author himself explains his use of temporal modes in *The Moviegoer* and considers his comments on homosexuality, heterosexuality, and the female gender (together with more specific points of linguistics from *Lost in the Cosmos*) in Joe Culledge's "The Reentry Option: An Interview with Walker Percy" (*SoR* 20:92–115).

In previous years the triad of O'Connor, Styron, and Percy all but dominated interest among southern fiction writers, but in 1984

four newer contemporaries have merited attention. David K. Jeffrey
and Donald R. Noble use the format of "Barry Hannah: An Interview" (*QW* 19:102–21) to establish how the author of *Geronimo Rex*
finds syntactic form in music and why he is drawn by violence
("there's no lying in it" and it speaks of "an underside that all of us
have"). Honest humanity is often revealed in embarrassing situations, and hence his work courts them. Plot is less interesting than
the achievement of a cleverly funny, word-conscious voice in the
tradition of Faulkner and Joyce but also with a nod toward Henry
Miller. Paul Ruffin conducts an equally successful "Interview with
George Garrett" (*SCR* 16,ii:25–33), establishing how this historical
novelist is more concerned with recording voices than creating them.
The most controversial of the younger southerners remains Harry
Crews, on whom David K. Jeffrey has prepared a valuable collection
of new critical explorations by various hands titled *A Grit's Triumph:
Essays on the Works of Harry Crews* (Associated Faculty Press).
Of the ten essays and by-now obligatory interview, most helpful to
an understanding of the major issues and techniques in Crews's
fiction are Jeffrey's own "Crews's Freaks" (pp. 67–78), Jack Moore's
"The Land and the Ethics in Crews's Work" (pp. 46–66), and Patricia Beatty's "Crews's Women" (pp. 112–23). Perceived boundaries
in life are illusory, Crews believes, and so he uses freaks and de-
formities to break them down and establish identity with the viewer,
a process that takes the perceiver's energy of rejection and transforms
it into self-knowledge. As for his characters' ethics, these can be
found in their seeking out substitutes for God, a process that the
quality of landscape in Crews's fiction enhances. Women come off
poorly in his work, thematically because they are used simply as
agents of aggression and artistically because Crews sacrifices them
as real characters in order for them to mythically support his real
story, which is about men. A quite different but no less interesting
writer is treated completely but with great concision by Frank W.
Shelton in "The Necessary Balance: Distance and Sympathy in the
Novels of Anne Tyler" (*SoR* 20:851–60). Tyler's constant theme is
"the vexing relationship between distance and sympathy" and is un-
resolvable because she knows that personal freedom and closeness
to others is difficult to balance. Her most complex attempts are in
Searching for Caleb and *Dinner at the Homesick Restaurant*, where
the ramifications of detachment versus involvement are explored by
her protagonists themselves.

iv. The Mannerists: John Updike and John Cheever

Two major Updike scholars offer books this year, with Robert Detweiler revising his 1972 Twayne study by giving more attention to the way American manners and values have been reflected in his stories and novels. The lasting value of Detweiler's *John Updike* (TUSAS 481) is that Updike's sense of metaphor is given full treatment as well. When a character's own creative sense of metaphor fails, as does Jerry's in *Marry Me*, all the accurate descriptions in the world will not save Updike's novel. His Rabbit and Bech sequels are more successful because metaphoric image and literal action are blended more successfully. As he did 12 years ago, Detweiler concludes that Updike's most pervasive mood has been one of nostalgia, which places him in a mainstream tradition "at least as old as Hawthorne"; but a formal interest in exploring sexuality puts him in the company of such post-Modernists as Barth and Coover, reminding us that post-Modern theory must be enlarged to accommodate as expansive a writer.

Donald J. Greiner's *John Updike's Novels* (Ohio) complements his earlier successful study of the materials most other critics overlook, *The Other John Updike* (*ALS 1981*, pp. 288–89). In Updike's shorter works Greiner found that desire and memory prompted the author to favor rhythm, mood, and meditation over character, action, and plot. Turning to Updike's novels, where such traditional factors might be more necessary to hold things together, Greiner finds that too much previous interpretation is thesis-bound. Against this trend he reads Updike's novels closely but openly, learning that a subtle interrelationship of methods and goals makes these works cohere as a creditable *oeuvre*. Both Updike and his protagonists are concerned with the stability of the past; lest it elude memory, the artist must fix it in his work. As a master of "created landscapes," Updike can stabilize the future as well, for purposes of art, as witness such anomalous successes as *The Poorhouse Fair* and *The Coup*. The *Rabbit* trilogy considers the contrary claims of society and self—"inner needs may propel him, but there is no place to go"—and the artistic resolution to this quest is given mythic and personally creative dimensions by what Greiner calls the "home" novels, *The Centaur* and *Of the Farm*. In similar manner *Couples, A Month of Sundays,* and *Marry Me* reveal Updike's care with sexual mores—not just as manners for fictive investigation, but for their ritualization of the times and their correspondence to the problems of writing fiction itself. With his protagonist Henry Bech, Updike is able to take a critical look at how the writer's role can swallow up both the writer himself and his work. Yet even here can be found the fiction of performance, as Bech sustains himself before eager audiences on the strength of earlier texts. Greiner's method encompasses Updike's broad presence as a writer. What makes Greiner a most illuminating and reliable interpreter is the way he locates his perspective inside the writer's texts.

The very real places of southeastern Pennsylvania which locate Updike's *Rabbit* novels, *The Centaur*, and his *Olinger Stories* qualify him as a regionalist, claims Miriam Youngerman Miller in "A Land Too Ripe for Enigma: John Updike as Regionalist" (*ArQ* 40:197–218). From specific childhood memories Updike's statements on "the universal human condition" make him more than a local-colorist, but clues that he may have consulted an architectural study titled *Gritty Cities* indicates the importance of "realistic regional descriptions" to the "metaphoric meanings" he wishes to explore. His several revisions of *Rabbit, Run* are examined for authorial intention by Randall H. Waldron in "Rabbit Revised" (*AL* 56:51–67), and Updike himself ponders the actions of his characters in *The Witches of Eastwick* for Mary Cantwell in "Updike's Witchy Women" (*Vogue*, May, pp. 338–39, 405).

In recent years the trend among John Cheever's critics has been to clarify the experimental impulse that emerged in his last published works. A major document for its critical as well as biographical information is his daughter Susan Cheever's memoir, *Home Before Dark* (Houghton Mifflin). An accomplished writer herself, she is primarily investigating her father's impression on her own life—his death, for example, is repeated perhaps a dozen times as Ms. Cheever abandons a simple chronology in favor of a meditation on John Cheever, his family life, his consistent writerly ambitions, and his evolving techniques and themes. At each stage of his life she emphasizes his love for storytelling as a vehicle for personal myth, but also his feeling that life "was either unbearable or transcendent," a volatility that led to a close appreciation of texture in the language needed to describe it. Cheever left an extensive journal, from which his daughter quotes liberally, and she is especially sensitive to his trials in writing and placing material (the *New Yorker's* failure to publish his more innovative work shames that journal's reputation). Especially helpful is Susan Cheever's clarification of her father's interest in High Church Anglicanism—not for its social status, as so many have presumed, but because of the sense of ecstasy triumphant over grief in *The Book of Common Prayer.*

Susan Cheever's literary criticism draws heavily on her father's notebook drafts for his novels and stories, but her conclusions square with two more detached studies by Robert G. Collins, "Beyond Argument: Post-Marital Man in John Cheever's Later Fiction" (*Mosaic* 17:261–79) and "Fugitive Time: Dissolving Experience in the Later Fiction of John Cheever" (*SAF* 12:175–88). In his first essay Collins explains how Cheever's major theme became "the breakdown of a pattern of mutual mating and the emergence of a new sexual definition for the individual," a topic Susan Cheever treats biographically. Looking beyond heterosexuality involves a "reversing of the traditional view of the individual as polluted to one in which society itself is befouled," and the climax to Cheever's new characterization is the "post-marital man" who has outgrown what he sees as the "female myth." In his second piece Collins finds that Cheever's early fiction stressed nostalgia, his middle work took new concern with "an exploded present moment," and his later novels and stories hung suspended "between a tragic pessimism and a raptured expectancy." Time has reality only in human terms, and when a character loses ability to structure it, events run out of control as they do in *Oh What a Paradise It Seems* (which is only superficially like Cheever's earlier fiction). A Cheever classic is studied for its sense of structure by Hal Blythe and Charlie Sweet in "Ironic Nature Imagery in 'The Swimmer'" (*NMAL* 8:Item 1). References to nature, to all four seasons, to the time of day, and to changes in the weather emphasize the protagonist's actuality as opposed to his "self-deceived vision," and his decline is measured by the increasing irony of these references which direct attention to the reality of old age that he refuses to face in his "fruitless quest" for youth.

v. Realists Old and New

a. **William Buckley, Truman Capote, Joyce Carol Oates.** That the traditions of literary realism no longer interest scholars of contemporary fiction is evident from 1984's approach to these three mainstream artists. Mark Royden Winchell's insightful and comprehensive *William F. Buckley* (TUSAS 452) finds less to study in the author's fictive art than in the ideas that inform it. The key to Buck-

ley's novels is the role political conservatism has taken over the past
several decades. His work draws artistic energy from the alternating
balance of liberal and conservative ideals, and especially from changing national attitudes toward each side. Winchell concludes, however, that Buckley is more a man of letters than a political analyst,
for in the latter role his penchant toward the memoir leads to writing
as good as in his novels.

In "Capote's *Handcarved Coffins* and the Nonfiction Novel" (*ConL*
25:437–51) Robert Siegle resolves a dichotomy among Truman Capote's critics by showing how an investigation of the author's "strategy
of differentiation" between historical and artistic approaches leads
to the same result: whether seen as using fiction to get at the truth,
or truth to uncover the essentially fictive nature of life, Capote concludes with a sense that the methods reinforce each other on their
way to the same answer.

Work on Joyce Carol Oates has been winding down to minor but
interesting notes and explications. Michael J. Coulon finds that references to Schopenhauer's philosophy in *Unholy Loves* enhance
Oates's familiar thematics, especially how an independent woman
can turn Schopenhauer's doctrine of feminine dependency around,
even though male characters will forever cast doubts by citing the
same sources ("Does Brigit Stott Need a Lord and Master?" *NConL*
14,ii:2–3). Larry Rubin's "Oates' 'Where Are You Going, Where
Have You Been?'" (*Expl* 42,iv:57–59) argues that Connie's episode
with Arnold Friend is a dream, emphasizing the "absurd emptiness
and falseness of sexual fulfillment" and the nature of the threat to
Connie's personhood.

b. **John Gardner.**   Realism interests today's scholars when it breeds
controversy, and earlier objections to Gardner's work have spawned
any number of affirmative, supportive studies which by themselves
are among the most curious in the field. Indeed, much reaction to
Gardner himself is puzzling, from the full-page advertisement in
which his publishers memorialized his motorcycle death with a line
from his second novel—"Poor Grendel's had an accident. *So may you
all*"—to the mythologizing of his life by Domenic Stansberry in "John
Gardner: The Return Home" (*Ploughshares* 10,ii–iii:95–123). The
irony is that an appreciation of what in Gardner's hands could be
fair literary art leads to unconscionably bad writing by his critics.
Consider Stansberry's characterization of the falling out between

Gardner and his wife Joan: "Heartbroken, he thought, that's what she was." Or the painfully unreal attitude toward how books are published: "Gardner responded [to a Morris Dickstein review] by dusting off another manuscript and publishing that." (The novel in question is *Nickel Mountain*.)

A similar inclination to forego any deeply probing criticism and simply memorialize the man and his work detracts from the valid points that Gregory L. Morris does make in *A World of Order and Light: The Fiction of John Gardner* (Georgia). Morris's title betrays his bias, which is toward the blandly humanistic affirmations that critics have drawn more from Gardner's criticism and public posturing than from his actual fiction, and that has in turn pervaded the M.F.A. programs in creative writing taught by his students, many of whom are happier as acolytes than teacher/critics. Morris identifies a "humanistic aesthetic" in Gardner's work which, like Romantic music, celebrates art's reality of eye and heart. Gardner's magical landscapes transcend the apparently real. *Shadows* becomes the key summation of his work, but deciding whether the ambivalent inner novel of *October Light* is trickery or essence becomes the key to Gardner as an artist. Unfortunately, this brilliant question is not fully answered in Morris's study, for his investigation stops short. Throughout *A World of Order and Light* he makes large claims for Gardner's importance without considering objections lodged by the innovationists Gardner so fulsomely attacked. Gardner's own pronouncements on "moral fiction" are not weighed against his more experimentally inclined comments to interviewer Joe David Bellamy as published in 1974, nor does Morris investigate the nearly schizophrenic division of Gardner's artistic personality and how it manifested itself in his fiction (the unanswered question of *October Light*). In the mid-1970s, as Gardner's reputation boomed, reviewers Morris Dickstein and Tom H. Towers worried that Gardner might be squandering his talents. Had Morris given this question some unbiased critical thought, and had he looked into Gardner's increasing fascination with other literary forms, his study would be a definitive outline of Gardner's career, rather than the uncritical endorsement of Gardner's "humanistic aesthetic."

More commendable is Robert Merrill's method in "John Gardner's *Grendel* and the Interpretation of Modern Fables" (*AL* 56: 162–80). Critics have misread the novel as an affirmation of Grendel's existentialism, failing to understand the "abrupt introduction" after

150 pages of Beowulf, "who represents the author's ultimate values." Barth, Heller, and Vonnegut also employ this new method of fabulation, which solves the dilemma of honest appraisal of life versus allowing hope for mankind.

c. **James Dickey, E. L. Doctorow, and Others.** Dickey and Doctorow are academic favorites: easily accessible yet with teachably fine points of structure and style, their technical experiments are always in the service of a readily articulated theme, making any of their works an easy run-through for classroom or essay. John E. Loftis demonstrates the latter in "*Deliverance* and *Treasure Island*" (*NConL* 14,iv:11–12), lining up similarities and concluding that in each the crucial act is by reflex rather than by plan—yet the novel does not decide between a "heart of darkness" or a *Treasure Island* ethic. Michael K. Glenday picks up this question in "*Deliverance* and the Aesthetics of Survival" (*AL* 56:149–61), noting that accepting Dickey's assertion that Ed Gentry survives by virtue of his skills of trade (graphic design) calls for a revision of critical emphasis: the thematic momentum would now favor the triumph and continuation of civilized values, not their irrelevance (as an American *Lord of the Flies* as others have presumed).

A familiar interpretation is given new depth, again by an academic run-through method, by Stephen L. Tanner in "Rage and Order in Doctorow's *Welcome to Hard Times*" (*SDR* 22,iii:79–85). Long considered an anti-Western, the novel is now examined for its substitution of patterns, principally those of "modern psychoanalysis and nihilistic philosophy" for the traditional values of this subgenre. That the Oedipal triangle and the death wish are clichés themselves fits Doctorow's purpose in mocking any sense of affirmation that we might expect from a literary form the author believes is bankrupt.

Thomas Berger has more fun with Westerns, Edward L. Galligan shows in *The Comic Vision in Literature* (Georgia). In *Little Big Man* his hero is less a fool than a prankster, who survives to become the narrator of his own tale. Jay Ruud finds a similar sanguinity in "Thomas Berger's *Arthur Rex*: Galahad and Earthly Power" (*Crit* 25:92–100). Berger does not question or revise Arthurian values any more than other writers in the tradition; instead, he emphasizes their universal meaning and appeal. Truth does exist, for example, "somewhere beyond perception." Ruud's clarification of perspective as both a mediaeval and modern concern complements Galligan's understanding of Jack Crabb's talents in *Little Big Man*, where "analogical thinking" lets him see both white and Cheyenne (linear and circular) points of view as "ways of thinking and living." Similarities within them lead Crabb to accept the two as reflective structures, but as a narrator he understands that the linear perspective will finally win out: because it promises, like a story, that "something might happen tomorrow."

Some realists grapple with their material to good effect, says Thomas Maher Gilligan in "Myth and Reality in Jim Harrison's *Warlock*" (*Crit* 25:147–53). Stories often run beyond their credible bounds, but unlike the contemporary readers of Fielding and Austen, who were not trained by a long tradition of realism and so never thought to suspend disbelief, audiences today become emotionally involved in stories, the reality of which they can then dismiss when finished. Harrison enhances this effect by letting his realistically inclined readers see some of his artwork in progress so that they can be as aware of the mechanics that create realism as they are swept away by the realism itself. Kerry Ahearn finds a similarly productive tension in "Pursuing the Self: Maureen Howard's *Facts of Life* and *Before My Time*" (*Crit* 25:171–79), in which the problem of perceiving a "true self" without bias is experienced just as crucially in memoir writing as in fiction. Howard distrusts apparent candor, because the self may well become merely "the sum of its rejections." That American writers still turn to the sea for a sense of "ultimate reality" is shown by Bert Bender in "*Far Tortuga* and American Sea Fiction Since *Moby-Dick*" (*AL* 56:227–48). In Peter Matthiessen's novel the voyager to knowledge must come to terms with death, which is the traditional course, right to the affirmative conclusion in which the survivor wins "a renewed and sustaining sense of his place in the universe."

d. Ann Beattie, Stanley Elkin, and Others.

A fine series of interviews sheds light on the newest crop of realists. Larry McCaffery who with Tom LeClair developed the interview into a scholarly tool in *Anything Can Happen* (*ALS 1983*, p. 292), now works with Sinda Gregory on revealing conversations with Ann Beattie (*LitR* 27:165–77) and William Kennedy (*FictI* 15,i:157–79). Beattie is concerned with how characters can remain trapped in unfavorable situations; since their own analyses fail to help them, Beattie feels it presump-

318 Fiction: The 1950s to the Present

tuous to provide her own resolution, nor does she admit to having a clear overview of the world she lives in or creates. Focusing on moments without psychological resolutions is her strength, not a weakness. Quite to the contrary is William Kennedy, who finds in his home locale of Albany, New York, an "inexhaustible context for the fictional universe he inhabits in his imagination." Family members serve as a cast of characters, and local history provides "the sense of a specific world that is definable," making the "intuitive leaps" to a character's psychology easier and allowing myth to grow naturally from the real.

Richard B. Sale's "An Interview with Stanley Elkin in St. Louis" (*SNNTS* 16:314–25) reveals that Elkin is not a humorist. "Funny things happen along the way," Elkin admits, "but they only happen because someone else is at a disadvantage." His characters dream that they can control reality, and are of course thwarted. Language and not event are the grounds for Elkin's liberties. More limited but nevertheless interesting talks are had with Nicholas Delbanco by Gregory L. Morris (*ConL* 25:387–98), concentrating on biography, and with Gordon Weaver by Thomas E. Kennedy (*WHR* 38:363–71), who probes Weaver for data on his working methods.

vi. Early Innovators: Jack Kerouac, William S. Burroughs, Paul Bowles

Tom Clark's *Jack Kerouac* (Harcourt) reflects both the strengths and weaknesses of the series in which it appears, the HBJ Album Biographies edited by Matthew J. Bruccoli. The narrative is light, almost breezy, blowing among the more substantial signs of Bruccoli bookmaking: photographs of paperbacks and dustjackets, publicity releases, and blurred snapshots of Kerouac and friends. The danger, of course, lies in turning the author into an amalgam of his reputations. But there is also fair attention to Kerouac's work with language; given Clark's experience as a poet, one wishes there had been more. Kerouac's own obsession with his public role as an anti-Establishment writer diluted his own canon, mixing innovation with pure junk. Scholarship still awaits a canonical approach to his work.

Adam Gussow offers some harder information in "Bohemia Revisited: Malcolm Cowley, Jack Kerouac, and *On the Road*" (*GaR* 38: 291–311). At issue is Cowley's editing of this novel for Viking, which Gussow traces through the publisher's file of editorial correspondence. Unlike any other editor, Cowley understood *On the Road* because of his own "road narrative" about his own "rebellious, 'lost' generation," *Exile's Return*. The impatience of a young man "in love with life and language" unites not just the two books but also the two writers and their generations. A common attention to the texture of language which binds each generation into a community made Cowley and Kerouac natural allies, even though previous biographers (without access to Cowley's side of the story) have reported more animosity than sympathy. During the years he worked on Kerouac's fiction Cowley was also decrying the "academic temper" of the age, calling for a new fiction much like Kerouac was then writing. It was after Kerouac's work passed into the hands of other editors and after his reputation was turned into publicity material that the value of his writing declined.

An exhaustive and up-to-date appraisal of William S. Burroughs fills the pages of the first number of volume 4 of the *Review of Contemporary Fiction*. As for other contemporary subjects who are articulate about their own works and—as in Burroughs's case—who have maintained a strong documentary sense of their own material, scholarship draws profitably upon interviews. Burroughs's "Last European Interview" (pp. 12–18) conducted in 1974 with Philippe Mikriammos (a leading French translator of innovative American fiction) and Nicholas Zurbrugg's talk with agent James Grauerholz (pp. 19–32) are valuable reports on biographical, bibliographical, and interpretive matters. Central to Burroughs criticism is Jennie Skerl's "Freedom Through Fantasy in the Recent Novels of William S. Burroughs" (pp. 124–30), showing how the author extends his career by creating a virtual second mythology; as always, he "creates powerful imaginary worlds that critique present reality and that show the reader how to alter his consciousness and thus his world," but a return to narrative in his later works places a new emphasis on the power of storytelling. The transition in Burroughs's earlier work, from the observer stance of *Junky* to the feeling of being a trapped participant in *Naked Lunch*, is described in psychological terms by Allan Johnston in "The Burroughs Biopathy: William S. Burroughs' *Junky* and *Naked Lunch* and Reichian Theory" (pp. 107–20), while Gregory Stephenson turns to metaphysics in "The Gnostic Vision of William S. Burroughs" (pp. 40–49), showing how his fiction exorcises negative elements and replaces them with a new cosmology much as did the mythological systems of the Gnostics in transforming knowledge, self, and status. Burroughs's importance to literary theory is shown by Nicholas Zurbrugg in "Burroughs, Barthes, and the Limits of Intertextuality" (pp. 86–107), as the author's "grain of voice" defies all attempts to expunge its presence from *Naked Lunch*, a technique amplified by Michael Leddy in " 'Departed Have Left No Address': Revelation/Concealment Presence/Absence in *Naked Lunch*" (pp. 33–40). John O'Brien's editorship has made this journal the leading repository for sound scholarship on essentially contemporary work, and readers would do well to study all the contributions to this Burroughs number, which includes discussions of *The Third Mind* by Regina Weinreich, *Cities of the Red Night* by Steven Shaviro, and other works as well.

" 'Sinister Overtones,' 'Terrible Phrases': Poe's Influence on the Writings of Paul Bowles" (*ELWIU* 11:253–66) is Catherine Rainwater's account of how the author's imagination was transformed by his mother's readings of Poe. Landscapes become spatial metaphors for "suffocated states of being," and the human psyche divided against itself offers Bowles both theme and structure in his work, all attributable to Poe's influence. But while "Poe's myth locates the self within earthly settings serving as pathways" to the Infinite, "Bowles's myth locates the self in a possibly hostile, probably indifferent geography where it dwindles to nothingness."

vii. Innovative Fiction

a. **Ken Kesey, Joseph Heller, Kurt Vonnegut, Richard Brautigan.** The appearance of a major essay on Richard Brautigan in *American Literature* signals the maturity scholarship has achieved within this once-undisciplined field, but unfortunately its publication comes in the year of its subject's death. But Kesey, Heller, and Vonnegut happily remain among us, and Kesey's return to the active scene is signaled by his appearance, with a new story, in the special number of *Esquire* (Aug., pp. 86–92) devoted to contemporary American fiction. Work on Heller and Vonnegut continues at its high level, much of it amplifying or correcting earlier scholarship now that serious critical reaction to these authors has entered its second decade.

The method behind Joseph Heller's apparent thematic and technical madness in *Catch-22* is explored in Galligan's *The Comic Vision in Literature*. Yossarian is a "hero who learns his foolishness in time of war"; he must struggle to master the fool's role which comes naturally to Orr, whose final disposition is Yossarian's closing call to action. Lindsey Tucker takes an approach more common to Thomas Pynchon's work in "Entropy and Information Theory in Heller's *Something Happened*" (*ConL* 25:323–40), finding that the decay of communications skills provides not just a theme but also a closed, entropic system within which the novel functions. Slocum as narrator plays the role of Maxwell's demon, struggling hopelessly against the tide of events. In the end he achieves peace only by turning himself into a machine, banishing human communication with its attendant disorder.

Vonnegut as an heir of Hemingway? In a broadly informative essay titled "Stalking Papa's Ghost: Hemingway's Presence in Contemporary American Writing" (pp. 193–211) collected by editor A. Robert Lee in *Ernest Hemingway: New Critical Essays* (Barnes and Noble, 1983), Frank McConnell notes that "hating and fearing history has always been a salient American disease" and a particular one that Hemingway and Vonnegut share. *Slaughterhouse-Five* is "an extraordinary recreation of the *spirit* of Hemingway's response to war"; Hemingway's reductiveness is matched by Vonnegut's chosen frivolity, each of them moral statements to the extent that any conventional articulation "is foredoomed to trivialize the enormity of horror by its very pretence to 'explaining.'" A counterrevolution against the machine can work its way from the fringe to the center, claims Susan Reid in "Kurt Vonnegut and American Culture: Mechanization and Loneliness in *Player Piano*" (*JASAT* 15:46–51), a strategy Leonard Lutwack finds repeated in *Slaughterhouse-Five* and *Slapstick*. Studying what he calls *The Role of Place in Literature* (Syracuse), Lutwack cautions that apocalypse is rarely portrayed because it is not easily imaginable in its totality; hence Vonnegut's war novel dramatizes this difficulty by making the whole book a series of evasions on the part of its chief survivor, Billy Pilgrim. With *Slapstick* Vonnegut adopts a style of gradualism, treating creeping destruction by means of anomalies of scene. The textual movement that Reid and Lutwack describe is noted as an embodiment of the author's own evolving attitude to both the horrors of war and the composition of his novel by T. J. Matheson in " 'This Lousy Little Book': The Genesis and Development of *Slaughterhouse-Five* as revealed in Chapter One" (*SNNTS* 16:228–40), a strategy that prevents the reader from leaving the book with previous moral assumptions intact. How Vonnegut uses laughter rather than comedy is explained by R. B. Gill in "Bargaining in Good Faith: The Laughter

of Vonnegut, Grass, and Kundera" (*Crit* 25:77–91). Comedy demands change, whereas laughter implies adjustment to the "absurdi-
ties and incongruities of modern life" which is the pattern in *Slapstick*
and *Jailbird*. Happy endings of traditional comedy are to be dis-
trusted because they do not affirm individual meaningfulness as does
a good belly laugh. Little games, rituals, and acts of thoughtfulness
are Vonnegut's prescription for coping, rather than dramatizing the
impossibility of coping as do many comic authors who are satisfied
only with a complete satiric revision of what bothers them.

The pertinence of Richard Brautigan to the American literary
tradition is explored by William L. Stull in "Richard Brautigan's
Trout Fishing in America: Notes of a Native Son" (*AL* 56:68–80).
The novel is rich with direct and indirect references to Melville,
Hemingway, Twain, Thoreau, and Nathanael West, adapting their
words to a new purpose. What begins as parody concludes as the construction of a new cultural code, much as *The Waste Land* and
Ulysses draw on the literary and mythic past to construct a new set
of values for the present.

b. **John Barth, Thomas Pynchon, John Hawkes.** Max F. Schulz
undertakes a great amount of work in "The Thalian Design of Barth's
Lost in the Funhouse" (*ConL* 25:397–410), attempting to prove that
instead of a "dead-end" admission of fiction's exhaustion the collection represents Barth's reinvention of storytelling art by grafting
"local realism to postmodernist metafiction using Greek mythology
as the common transplant." The internal structure and editorial po-
sitioning of "Petition" is the key to the volume's progression, which
makes its most notable advance from "Lost in the Funhouse" (sexual
innocence) to "Water-Message" (sophistication as a threat), with
Thalia of "Petition" standing in between as a servant to either the
spirit or the body. Schulz's structural analysis is sound, but whether
one agrees that it makes Barth a great artist depends on whether one
accepts Schulz's undemonstrated belief that Barth's "Literature of
Exhaustion" and "Literature of Replenishment" essays do as much as
"Dryden, Johnson, and Eliot for their respective ages." A much more
justified conclusion is reached by Marilyn Edelstein in "The Function of Self-Consciousness in John Barth's *Chimera*" (*SAF* 12:99–
107), where rather than berate an author's emphasis on process as
nihilistic she praises it for serving a purpose similar to fictions that

celebrate the human self: "The creation of a fiction resembles the creation of a self, real or imaginary."

In 1984 Thomas Pynchon has emerged as his own critic, offering a substantial introduction (pp. 3–23) to his collected early stories, *Slow Learner* (Little, Brown). That Pynchon has a sensitive ear for voice and dialogue is evident from his embarrassment with the lack of it in a story here; but he also notes a precociousness with respect to class and structure, which of course develops masterfully in his mature work. Toward a critical biography Pynchon offers bits and pieces of his glancing acquaintance with the Beats, prompted largely by his own fears of claustrophobia within the university. The character Dennis in "Low Lands" is defined in terms of Pynchon's own youth orientation and male-gender ideals of the times, aspects now seen as detractive. Most important are Pynchon's thoughts on entropy as they figure in his story of that name, which is more socially oriented and less a matter of physics than critics have presumed, except for the nicely complementary reading provided by Joseph Tabbi in "Pynchon's 'Entropy'" (*Expl* 43,i:61–63), where the term is read Romantically as a reconciliation of internal passions to the point that no further generation of action is possible.

Although *V.* and *The Crying of Lot 49* received passing attention in notes and often figure as reference points in larger studies (such as in Langland's *Society in the Novel* where the latter novel is seen as using society as a medium for characters' actions and fates in a world which is otherwise unreal), *Gravity's Rainbow* has remained a prime target for the biggest Pynchon guns. No. 14 of *Pynchon Notes* is given over to a special issue, guest-edited by Bernhard Duyfhuizen, titled "Deconstructing *Gravity's Rainbow*." An awareness of ordering systems pervades this novel, and so Duyfhuizen feels it is appropriate to launch critical investigations using the same method, which when described philosophically becomes "deconstruction." Looking at the text Deconstructively, Steven Weisenburger sees a circle keyed off an imbedded chronology ("The Chronology of Episodes in *Gravity's Rainbow*," pp. 50–64). Terry Caesar sees simply waste, which in its attempt to be excreted from the text becomes the text itself (" 'Trapped inside Their frame with your wastes piling up': Mindless Pleasures in *Gravity's Rainbow*," pp. 39–48). In "Textual Orbits/Orbiting Criticism: Deconstructing *Gravity's Rainbow*" (pp. 65–74) Stephen P. Schuber claims that no one structure of reading fits the novel because none has been privileged by the text, adamant as it has been to displace any authorial authority. But, so ironic for the editor's group of synchronically inclined scholars, history turns out to be the most compelling structure: either as an attempt to overcome a Puritan tradition as explained by Louis Mackey in "Thomas Pynchon and the American Dream" (pp. 7–22), or as a self-doomed effort at transcendence by means of cultural fictions, as Joel D. Black argues in "Pynchon's Eve of Destruction" (pp. 23–38).

Destruction fits Pynchon's masterpiece as nicely as does Deconstruction, and in "Singing Back the Silence: *Gravity's Rainbow* and the War Novel" (*MFS* 30:5–23) John M. Muste reports that it is "a kind of consummation of this century's war fiction" because it emphasizes the machine themes of World War I novels and the social-cause attitudes prevalent in fictions written out of the Second World War experience. In Pynchon's hands, peace can be as Edenic as in World War I (with its Georgian memories), and the causes for its destruction can be as paranoiac as the corporate "Them" that figures in much literature from the second war. Paranoia may have expanded to make survival a worse horror than destruction itself, but the very existence of art that can report it promises hope. René Girard's notion of the "monster" as a form of access to the irreconcilable informs Terry P. Caesar's " 'Beasts Vaulting Among the Earthworks': Monstrosity in *Gravity's Rainbow*" (*Novel* 7:158–70); what cannot be controlled escapes attempts at structuring, becoming "the sacred" and as such an important dimension of experience.

John Hawkes joins Thomas Pynchon in offering readers some first materials of a critical autobiography, adding 11 brief introductions to his stories and novels excerpted in *Humors of Blood & Skin: A John Hawkes Reader* (New Directions). The self-portrait that emerges reveals that the author's experiences, from an asthmatic childhood through ambulance service in the war to the surroundings in which he has written, have provided not so much thematic materials as they have shaped his fiction's formal concerns: that "design always emerges from debris" and that "the beauty of the nightmare is that it inevitably shows forth some unattainable ideal." Of particular note is how the context in which Hawkes writes influences the text he creates. Location and ambiance are sought to rectify particular problems, and a theme that emerges is the author's compulsive attraction to life in southern France. His fiction has taken on a European style of intellect pondering its way through sensuality, which by the end of *Humors of Blood & Skin* becomes almost oppressive. *Virginie* is produced at Venasque, with Sade's château nearby, at "the end of the line in a long search for vineyards, rude beams, red tiles, Picasso's dancing goats, literary voluptuousness." Whether the lyric poet will remain content in his identification with the pornographer, as Hawkes describes it here, will not be seen until he has completed his return to native material (including his Alaskan childhood) in his novel now underway (which is introduced and excerpted in this volume).

Chief among Hawkes's critics this year is William H. Gass, whose introduction (pp. ix–xvi) to the above volume details the writer's brilliance with special combinations of language. Hawkes's sentences add up to a narrative, but along the way their features are always coalescing into a face one can appreciate and even love. In "The 'Crisis of Comedy' as a Problem of the Sign: The Example of Hawkes's *Second Skin*" (*TSLL* 26:425–54) Mary F. Robertson agrees that "language itself is perhaps the primary hero" of Hawkes's fiction and adds that "the problem of signs [is] his most important subject." *Second Skin* demonstrates "semiotic intractability," producing a tension between the innocent voice of story and the aesthetically hermetic tone of jaded sophistication which results once the story opens out. Hawkes does not simply wonder at the limits of language, but asks his readers to analyze, judge, and discriminate among those limits to create an ongoing narrative. There is a certain perverse will to living within language, Jeffrey Laing points out in "Multi-Dimensional Parody in John Hawkes's *Travesty*" (*NConL* 15,i:7–8), which finds room for being by parodying both forms and subjects. That Hawkes's early interests have been indulged again in one of his mature novels is demonstrated by John Kucich in "*The Passion Artist:* John Hawkes's Erotic World" (*TCL* 30:432–47). Unlike his more lyrical novels of the time, *The Passion Artist* projects the erotic into a nonhuman landscape, and just as in *The Cannibal* and *The Lime Twig* this circumstance releases "any legitimate, worldly constraints on eroticism." Indeed, this movement from repression to release characterizes all three works.

c. Donald Barthelme, Robert Coover, William Gaddis, William Eastlake, William H. Gass. Robert A. Morace shows how a major innovationist breaks ranks and embraces popular culture in "Donald Barthelme's *Snow White:* The Novel, The Critics, and the Culture"

(*Crit* 26:1–10). The novel is not a sign of an ethically bankrupt age, but is rather a critique of it fashioned from its own materials. The form of Barthelme's jokes constitutes his critique, an inability to discriminate either words or values; rather than solve problems, language deflects them, and from this texture of evasions Barthelme finds a system for his own fiction. Barthelme also has made a critical statement by establishing a canonical list of what he considers his major, representative short fiction, and in "Failed Artists in Donald Barthelme's *Sixty Stories*" (*Crit* 26:11–17) Lee Upton examines how his recurrent artist figures are haunted by absent forms from the past. There is always a Romantic sublime, just beyond reach, which is part of a "friction between romance and the limitations of common sense, between intuition and the limitations of our creative actions" which enlivens Barthelme's work.

Robert Coover is an author who loves history not for its facts but for its ambiguities. These polar interests are treated by two strong essays, Richard Anderson's "Robert Coover's Dissident Works" (*Mid-AmerR* 4,i:105–13), and Jerry A. Varsava's "Another Exemplary Fiction: Ambiguity in Robert Coover's *Spanking the Maid*" (*SSF* 21: 235–41). Anderson shows how *The Public Burning*, "The Cat in the Hat for President," and "Whatever Happened to Gloomy Gus of the Chicago Bears?" expose the underpinnings of history as myth and serve as ironic commentaries of fictions being formulated into truth. Whereas history once offered a sense of unity and purpose, now the entertainment and advertising media must make do, and as a result culture has been replaced by mind control. Especially valuable are Anderson's integration of the Cat in the Hat novella with Coover's longer work, since the author says the two developed from the same original project. People are too comfortable with letting others make their myths for them, Coover believes, and so he shocks readers into action by challenging their beliefs. How Coover perfects this method is Varsava's subject; by interweaving any number of fictive possibilities, the author frustrates the reader's attempt "to harmonize these various plots into a unified, unambiguous reading of the text." By disallowing generic or paradigmatic conventions, Coover effectively creates his readers just as he creates his text.

Three original contributions distinguish *In Recognition of William Gaddis* (Syracuse) as edited by John Kuehl and Steven Moore. For "The Writing of *The Recognitions*" (pp. 20–31) David Koenig has examined Gaddis's revisions, learning that Wyatt becomes more shadowy in each draft, reducing his visible means of salvation and making the reader's identification with him more symbolic of loss. The Boschean fairy tale aspects of this novel are examined by John Seelye in "Dryad in a Dead Oak Tree: The Incognito in *The Recognitions*" (pp. 70–80), a trait that establishes kinship with Melville's *The Confidence Man.* An exceptionally fine contribution comes from Stephen Matanle, whose "Love and Strife in William Gaddis's *JR*" (pp. 106–18) describes separations in the narrative that show human communication generating disorders, while dialogues reveal that all discourse merely authorizes the self.

For William Eastlake and William H. Gass, we must turn to the authors themselves. Of the many authors given carte-blanche to write their critical autobiographies for Dedria Bryfonski's first volume in the *Contemporary Authors: Autobiography Series* (Gale), Eastlake is one of the few who foregoes self-aggrandizement and a settling of old scores to fruitfully examine the interrelationship of his life and work. "Once upon a time on a dark and stormy night, my mother met my father, both fresh from England," he begins, in a parody of the lesser contributions that mar this volume. Eastlake then continues to evaluate how his army experiences influenced his writing career, how the first step in writing fiction is to develop an ear for listening. Since then he has been drawn to what he calls "Indian country," whether in Vietnam or in America's Southwest, where one form of warfare or another (usually broadly cultural) remains central to his work.

The ever-articulate William H. Gass meets his critical match in Arthur M. Saltzman, whose "An Interview with William Gass" (*ConL* 25:121–35) explores the eroticism of language and the innate self-referentiality of the literary text. Language apprehends reality via inference, and Gass's new novel, *The Tunnel,* will attempt to get "outside of language" so that its referentiality can be escaped.

d. John Irving and Max Apple. Austria appears in each of John Irving's novels through *The Hotel New Hampshire,* and although it is often used as material for fictionalizing, Edward C. Reilly has found that one central historical event has been left intact. "The *Anschluss* and the World According to Irving" (*RS* 51:98–110) tells how that event provides a framework for the author's literary and moral vision. Germany's annexation of Austria not only set a precedent for the brutality and chaos of World War II, but established a tone of random and irrational violence which characterizes Irving's world even to the peaceful shores of Maine and New Hampshire, where children and adults alike fear "the Under Toad" of faceless yet persistent danger. The Anschluss, moreover, led to the degeneration, destruction, and decay of Vienna, which remains an evocative setting for Irving's moral statements. In "A Note About Two Toads" (*NConL* 14,iii:7–8) Reilly shows how Irving's "Under Toad" goes beyond D. H. Lawrence's symbology in *The Virgin and the Gypsy* to represent "everything from bad weather to rapes and murders."

Max Apple is another writer who is willing and able to elucidate his fiction, and for Larry McCaffery and Sinda Gregory's "An Interview with Max Apple" (*MissRev* 37–38:9–32) he provides a complete account of his work and its influences. His emphasis on the cultural play of language may be traced to a deliberate choice to write in English rather than in Yiddish; once this choice was made, he explains, "I saw that I belonged in the real world of Michigan in 1950 rather than in the world of my grandmother's imagination, the Lithuania of 1910." His grandmother, however, remained as a storytelling influence, as did his family's experience in business.

The richness of Apple's intertextuality is studied by Wayne Glausser in "Spots of Meaning: Literary Allusions in Max Apple's 'Vegetable Love'" (*SSF* 20[1983]:255–63). There is such an extensive "network of included fictions" in Apple's work that any simple reading is frustrated by the author's deliberate "overdetermination." The story "Vegetable Love" offers several allusions to introspection, but like the major one—to Melville's Bartleby—it concludes as a narrative about indeterminacy itself.

viii. Women Writers and Women in Fiction

In *Psyche as Hero: Female Heroism and Fictional Form* (Wesleyan) Lee R. Edwards takes a step beyond the pioneering work of Gilbert and Gubar. Women heroes do not merely make "covert reappraisals," Edwards insists, but also make "overt and radical attacks." Maxine Hong Kingston's *The Woman Warrior*, for instance, uses artistic aspiration to evoke the potential of female heroism, by which "the imagination replaces the womb as the structure's central icon." Harriet Arnow's *The Dollmaker* shows how active hope can survive deprivation and disappointment; isolated within her own community, the protagonist voyages out only to find another, deeper loneliness.

But "in learning to distinguish Kentucky from Eden, Gertie redefines her strength and becomes the architect of a world [Detroit] that seems harsher than Kentucky's only because it is not idealized."

Alix Kates Shulman's "Living Our Life" (pp. 1–13) distinguishes editors Carl Ascher, Louise DeSalvo, and Sara Ruddick's collection, *Between Women*. Emma Goldman's influence on Shulman encouraged her to cease hiding among writing not considered "serious" and emerge as a significant novelist, the breadth of Goldman's concerns giving Shulman "a greatly expanded context in which to analyze the gender relations around which my social awareness had flowered." Although a comic novel, *Memoirs of an Ex–Prom Queen* draws upon Goldman's insights into the social expectations placed upon women. Shulman's second novel, *Burning Questions*, began with a study of Goldman's own autobiography as a revolutionary woman. *On the Stroll* uses the same third-person narration as Goldman's work to deal with society's outcasts.

In *Tillie Olsen* (WWS 65) Abigail Martin emphasizes the social aspects of this writer's work, from background sources and biography to the themes in her fiction. Stylistically, Olson is credited with an "intensity of expression" which makes her work more startling than those with whom she's often compared, Ruth Suckow and Willa Cather. "Language, for her, is a shining tool" by which readers can be convinced, and because of her strong convictions her writing occasionally suffers from excess. Blanche H. Gelfant is more forgiving in "After Long Silence: Tillie Olsen's 'Requa'" (*SAF* 12:62–69), which is collected (pp. 59–70) in her *Women Writing in America*. Gelfant finds that in Olsen's hands love and concern can restore people just as effectively as broken parts from a junkyard can be repaired. Like its junkyard setting, Olsen's text is broken visibly into fragments, a discontinuous form which challenges its resurrection theme. When achieved, the character's renewed will to live becomes inseparable from the artist's recovered power to write. Other contemporary subjects treated in Gelfant's book include Grace Paley (pp. 11–29) and Ann Beattie (pp. 31–43). Paley is praised for integrating her life with her work, so that rather than having to overcome the obstacles that hamper women writers she has turned them into form-generating materials as well as used them for themes. Beattie's combination of "verve and depletion" is seen as characterizing a generation, which Gelfant admits is a common cliché: that the violent end to 1960s counterculture left a generation to

mature in a state of inertia. Perhaps too uncritically Gelfant decides
Beattie is a significant writer because her workshop talents allow
this feeling of blankness to be aesthetically expressed.

"If Sylvia Plath could have gotten through the next year or two,"
Grace Paley ponders in her conversation with Blanche Gelfant, her
work might have grown as her life became less taxing. Unfortunately,
all that scholars have to work with for new material are her stories
published posthumously as *Johnny Panic and the Bible of Dreams*.
The two significant original contributions to Linda W. Wagner's
edition, *Critical Essays on Sylvia Plath* (Hall), make use of these
short fictions. Melody Zajdel's "Apprenticed in a Bible of Dreams:
Sylvia Plath's Short Stories" (pp. 182–93) reads them as a testing
ground for *The Bell Jar*, from suicide scenes to sexual politics. Sandra
M. Gilbert's "In Yeats' House: The Death and Resurrection of Sylvia
Plath" (pp. 202–22) shows how "Johnny Panic" revises D. H. Lawrence's fiction of female sacrifice, also leading to *The Bell Jar;* yet
Plath's heroines are still ensnared by a ferociously male alphabet, so
that the author must finally turn from Joyce to Woolf—and to Yeats's
awe of female power. How Plath did create language appropriate to
her commanding sense of thematics is described by Susan Coyle in
"Images of Madness and Retrieval: An Exploration of Metaphor in
The Bell Jar" (*SAF* 12:161–74).

Simply because more than half of the essays are original rather
than reprints, editor Ellen G. Friedman's *Joan Didion: Essays and
Conversations* (Ontario) would demand attention. But a notable
feeling for Didion's art informs this book, making it an essential resource for scholars. Of the nine original contributions, the most helpful are Friedman's own "The Didion Sensibility: An Analysis" (pp.
81–90), Cynthia Griffin Wolff's "*Play It As It Lays:* Didion and the
New American Heroine" (pp. 124–37), and John Hollowell's "Against
Interpretation: Narrative Strategy in *A Book of Common Prayer*"
(pp. 164–76). Read together as they are meant to be, these essays
present a portrait of a writer especially concerned with devising narrative strategies to express her special feelings about past events and
present times. Despairing of a faith in systems, Didion must nevertheless create her own so that events can unfold; we tell ourselves
stories to live, and the efforts of her characters to create them mirrors
her own attempts at writing. Image patterns inevitably reflect a distortion of values, rather than an enhancement, and often her heroines
live only so that they can tell their unhappy tales. But they conclude

that causality explains nothing, and it is finally this "anti-interpretive stance" that best characterizes Didion's work. In a fine separately published essay, "Didion's Disorder: An American Romancer's Art" (*Crit* 25:160–70), Samuel Coale discovers the wealth of Manichean conflicts that paralyze Didion's heroines. They ritualize the emptiness of their lives, often using film as a model to codify their obsessions.

With few exceptions, single-author studies have been the best scholarship on the subject of women writers and women in fiction. When other topics are used to organize investigations, reductiveness and a suspension of critical responsibility too often results. Such is the case with editor Peggy Whitman Prenshaw's *Women Writers of the Contemporary South* (Miss.), in which an unquestioned allegiance to gender and to region allows what might have been an interesting project to go awry. The collection was to have had a focus— that the younger generation of southern women writers has not been limited by the older traditions of race and gender—but nearly every essay that follows rates its subject's achievement by just such means of comparison. The pieces are mostly manufactured criticism, consisting of a house-proud listing of the author's canon (as if each succeeding book were another *Pride and Prejudice*) followed by impressionistic reactions which often lack taste as well as acuity ("And only a black person, it seemed to me, could get inside the head of Roxie Stoner, the simple-minded protagonist and narrator."). At one point a character who murders her child born of her white husband while favoring the child of her black lover is praised for asserting the "woman-identified" side of her being; in the same essay the author is celebrated in a hagiography of books and memberships, virtual page-long annals of eager joinings and rabid resignations. *Women Writers of the Contemporary South* should be a warning of how a reductive subject matter can lead to a suspension of critical judgment and taste.

An emphasis on text instead of simply gender makes Natalie M. Rosinsky's *Feminist Futures: Contemporary Women's Speculative Fiction* (UMI) a more substantial contribution. Her thesis is that nonsexist invention makes a significant impact on social science fiction in the 1960–80 period. Through the polar range from sexual equality to feminine superiority, Rosinsky shows how the reader is empowered through a deconstruction of textual meaning to see each author's intelligence at work. June Arnold's *Applesauce*, for example, revises the role of metamorphosis, while Marge Piercy's *Woman on the Edge of Time* employs a battle-of-the-sexes motif, but each is a politically deconstructive reading. Ursula Le Guin's message-oriented speculation is seen as less effective than the innovations of Mary Staton in *From the Legends of Biel* because Biel has a more apparent sense of fictive artifice (which Deconstructionists prefer).

The subgenre of women's romance, a perennial topic, is given exhaustive treatment in four major studies. Kay Mussell's *Fantasy and Reconciliation: Contemporary Formulas of Women's Romance Fiction* (Greenwood) finds a double standard which was prevalent until about 1970: antiromances which explored the consequences of uncontrolled female sexuality, and pure romances which celebrated the values of virginity and domesticity. After 1970, however, with the success of Kathleen Woodiwiss and Rosemary Rogers, the double standard yields to new, more complete endings. Madonne M. Miner's *Insatiable Appetites: Twentieth-Century American Women's Bestsellers* (Greenwood) uses Grace Metalious's *Peyton Place* as an index to the debilitating liabilities of formula fantasy. In *The Valley of the Dolls* we see Jacqueline Susann entertaining feminist problems but without voicing any complaint, just as the characters of Judith Krantz's *Scruples* surrender to shopping as an act of participatory engagement, consumption alone becoming the work's structure. Tanya Modelski's *Loving with a Vengeance: Mass-Produced Fantasies for Women* (Methuen) studies Harlequin Romances, gothics, and soap operas to conclude that each responds to real (and not invented) needs of women, yet employs textual strategies to undermine or at least neutralize these needs lest they become subversive of the system exploiting them. Harlequins induce the hysteria that they reflect so well, while gothics probe the subconscious in a way that allows a writer with feminist concerns more range for expression. But soap operas, by integrating their structure with the workplace nature of the housewife, reinforces housewifely status while sublimating ambition in collective fantasy. Janice A. Radway's *Reading the Romance: Women, Patriarchy, and Popular Literature* (N. C.) finds manipulation and force to be the key to these works, from the way they are written (a study of technique) through the way they are marketed (including the strategy of B. Dalton stores to create multiple encounters via floor dumps and table displays, prompting impulse buying, and changing rack angles to force a confrontation) to the way they are read (a detailed survey of a controlled reading

group). In the "ideal romance" a woman voices her will only to
have that voice silenced by a man; characters are often symbolic
representations of the immature female psyche which must be developed by the male. Under these conditions, Kathleen Woodiwiss
triumphs by allowing utopian fantasies to come through intact; all
else is rationalized away. The standard conclusion to such romances
legitimizes the woman's psychological commitment to marriage and
to motherhood. Woodiwiss may be a "woman's writer," and Rosemary Rogers may be read as a "man's," but the structures of their
romances are identical.

ix. Science Fiction, Crime and Suspense, Native American and Chicano Fiction, the American West

The inauguration of Robert Scholes's new series, Studies in Speculative Fiction (UMI Research Press) promises to upgrade the level
of scholarship in this often uneven field. As in Rosinsky's *Feminist
Futures*, a Scholes selection reviewed above, the general editor's
familiarity with new literary theory is quite evident, and his authors'
skills at deconstruction, reader-response criticism, and other current
talents do much to make science fiction criticism more worthwhile.
A fine example is Frank Sadler's *The Unified Ring: Narrative Art and
the Science Fiction Novel* (UMI Research Press) which proposes a
wholistic theory of the science fiction novel based on notions of relativity, uncertainty, and probability. Samuel R. Delany's *The Einstein
Intersection* (UMI Research Press) employs relativity in its invented
worlds of mathematical physics and fiction. By "wholistic" Sadler
means structured not by metaphors of time but by models of it, and
his most convincing example is Kurt Vonnegut's *Slaughterhouse-
Five*, where not time itself but the narrator's perception of the universe and its reality determines our own apprehension of it. Reader-
response criticism is evident in William F. Toupence's *Ray Bradbury
and the Poetics of Reverie* (UMI Research Press), showing that tax-
onomies of genre are less important than how meaning is produced
by the reader's anticipation, frustration, retrospection, and reconstruction (techniques of which Bradbury is a master). In *Approaches
to the Fiction of Ursula K. Le Guin* (UMI Research Press) James W.
Bittner finds that complementarity provides both the theme and
structuring device for her work; the principle that informs modern

science also prompts her toward a synthesis of romance form, as realism complements fantasy by marrying history and art, myth and science, and ultimately the materials of pulp fiction with anthropology.

Ursula Le Guin figures prominently in Ann Swinfen's *In Defense of Fantasy: A Study of the Genre in English and American Literature Since 1945* (Routledge). As a religious and political iconoclast, Le Guin "re-evaluates the whole basis of religion, science and belief." Her creation of a secondary world in *The Earthsea Trilogy* allows natural law to operate differently, with magic as an accepted part of daily life, resulting in a new philosophical basis for mankind's relationship to the "eternal verities" which now cannot be assumed but must be defined (in contrast to the more common didacticism of C. S. Lewis). Two other major figures are given short but substantial treatment in Seth McEvoy's *Samuel R. Delany* (Ungar) and Edgar L. Chapman's *The Magic Labyrinth of Philip José Farmer* (Borgo). Delany's progress has been toward a notion of human freedom, and along the way he has found it necessary to use innovative techniques to free his own writing from the limits of tradition. McEvoy is candid about Delany's personal background, suggesting that early bouts with madness were cured by a healthy homosexuality which also prompted him toward new themes and structures in his science fiction. Because of the massive suspension of disbelief operative in science fiction, Delany has been able to experiment with themes and techniques which mainstream readers might not accept. Chapman finds Farmer to be an explorer in the man of letters tradition, inventing worlds to fill the geographical void of new possibilities. A man of broad talents, he can satirize the present as easily as he might project utopias of the future, but the common thread to his work concerns mature earthly hopes rather than mystical, transcendent realms. Above all, he reminds readers that he is playing a game; hence in his pornography, never disavowed, he makes men victims of circumstances which in the common porno formula usually take place at the expense of women. McEvoy's and Chapman's studies are good reminders that innovative fiction can be found on the science-fiction bookshelf, and that thoughtful analysis will pay dividends for such writers.

The critical importance of a major mystery writer is firmly established by the essays commissioned by Ralph B. Sipper for his *Inward Journey: Ross Macdonald* (Cordelia). Unlike the *Women Writers of the Contemporary South* reviewed in section *viii.* above, Sipper's volume rejects the idea of manufactured criticism in favor of encouraging more thoughtful responses to Macdonald's art in which the critic is fully honest about his or her own enthusiasms and prejudices (whereas in the other volume such writerly facets were hidden behind a facade of academic methodology, only to emerge as lapses in judgment and taste). The majority of Sipper's 26 contributors are novelists themselves, but their critical analyses are insightful and acute. Gilbert Sorrentino admired Macdonald's successes within the strict, virtually imprisoning form of his chosen subgenre; to consider him beyond those limits, Sorrentino cautions, is to demean his worth as a craftsman. Jerome Charyn considers the texture and tonality of the crime experience and how the example of Macdonald's work helped him solve stylistic problems with his own. Hugh Kenner remembers reading one of Macdonald's novels in French translation and discovering how much of his effect depended upon the American language. Other contributors probe his biography and consider the importance of his *oeuvre*, making *Inward Journey* an essential volume for both Macdonald studies and for investigation of crime writing in general.

Less successful is Douglas E. Winter's *Stephen King: the Art of Darkness* (NAL). Much like James Egan in "Apocalypticism in the Fiction of Stephen King" (*Extrapolation* 25:214–28), Winter finds a tension between good and evil, but whereas Egan sees King using the presumed decadence of contemporary society as a catalyst for self-destruction, Winter reads the author as pure mayhem, the witches without Macbeth. Religion and materialism, which for other writers might foil horror, become in King's hands another counterpart—a device that Winter praises for its invention rather than questioning for its leaden effect. Too much of Winter's book is given to a retelling of plots which are celebrated for their presumed interest; in this case the critic has surrendered to audience popularity without considering the structure of effect. More helpful analyses of thrillers are found in Seymour Rudin's "The Urban Gothic: From Transylvania to the South Bronx" (*Extrapolation* 25:115–26), which establishes a new landscape for werewolves and monsters; Joe Sanders's "The Fantastic and Non-Fantastic: Richard Condon's Waking Nightmares" (*Extrapolation* 25:127–37), which determines just where this writer's work crosses over from borderline science fiction into outright fantasy; and Donald J. Greiner's "Robert B. Parker and the Jock of Main

Street" (*Crit* 26: 36–44), which considers the author's assumption of the "hard-boiled" mantle and his ingenious variations played against that style.

A great deal of fictive technique blends with autobiography in Gretchen M. Bataille and Kathleen Mullen Sands's *American Indian Women: Telling Their Lives* (Nebraska). Leslie Marmon Silko uses autobiographical fragments as a structuring device in her mixed-media work, most of which qualifies as personal narrative because of its storytelling characteristics. Paula Gunn Allen's novel, *The Woman Who Owned the Shadows,* experiments with legends and lore to blend the significant events witnessed by the narrator with an internal point of view. A full chapter on "Traditional Values in Modern Context: The Narratives to Come" (pp. 127–41) explains how fiction and autobiography have blended to produce a new style of writing.

Assimilationism is a theme considered in John R. Chávez's *The Lost Land: The Chicano Image of the Southwest* (N. Mex.) and in Antonio C. Marquez's "Richard Rodriguez's *Hunger of Memory* and the Poetics of Experience" (*ArQ* 40:130–41). Chávez notes how just as Chicano literature was emerging, elements of Mexican culture were losing their strength as both writers and common citizens began to express the sentiment of José A. Villareal's novel *Pocho:* "If we live in this country, we must live like Americans." But the international example of other displaced groups, notably the Palestinians, brought a new sense of economic and artistic self-identity. Rodriguez's book is best read as a "poetics of experience" with attention to its imaginative elements, since rather than a simple recapitulation of events (which might be decried as assimilationist) it is "a deliberate search for a literary style with which to project his experiences." This "quest for a metaphor of self" leads to a choice of literature over social propriety, going against the Chicano traditions of family and personal privacy in favor of the imaginative resources of language and literature.

A good structure for studying Western writers is provided by Russell Martin in the introduction (pp. ix–xx) to his and Marc Barasch's anthology, *Writers of the Purple Sage* (Viking). The first wave of Westerns from Owen Wister and Zane Grey provided formulaic, hard-riding excitement. In the postwar 1940s and '50s a second wave—Wallace Stegner, A. B. Guthrie, Jr., and Paul Horgan among them—sought to recreate a historical West as palpably believable, yet they wound up writing about "the dusk-lit worlds of Westerners who lived before them." Only with today's contemporaries is the current period treated with any sense of comprehensiveness, now that "the historical West had been *correctly* divined and defined in fiction." Since the late 1960s authors such as Thomas McGuane and Edward Abbey have established a trend away from stories unfolding in earlier eras and "pay artistic attention to the lives and land . . . around them." These writers of the "interior West" reject the utopias of their California cousins and seek instead "safe homes and harbors from the drab disillusionment that surrounds them."

Robert Murray Davis raises this same point, and says that far from being monolithic the Western has shifted from myth to history, from characters in roles to persons suffering a problematic existence, and from a highly wrought, intensive form to a looser, more extensive style of narration, all as evidenced by "Oakley Hall's Westerns: A Sense of Period" (*SWR* 69:444–61). That criticism can respond to such complexities is shown by Stephen Tatum in the field's most important model essay in years, "Closing and Opening Western American Fiction: The Reader in *The Brave Cowboy*" (*WAL* 19: 187–203). Tatum considers reader response important, for how the novel's strategic oppositions are presented establishes a particular interpretation. Abbey's "technique of enumeration" demands a "strong reading" in response, and as the text is alternately opened and closed to such readings initial assumptions are redirected. The prose texture both affirms and denies the factual world, depending upon its strategies of reading, and when details are allowed to take significant shape the reader experiences a similar role in dealing with constraints.

In *Will Henry / Clay Fisher (Henry W. Allen)* (TUSAS 466) Robert L. Gale shows how under each of his pseudonyms Allen was able to temper both the sentimentality and the cynicism that are the bipolar modes of lesser western fiction. His Indians are more than stick figures, a credit to his understanding of cultural diversity, yet Allen's emphasis remains on the white male hero, with history embellished either to inflate or deflate his character according to the story line Allen requires. A vastly different style of writer is described with great care and insight by the poet Peter Wild in *Barry Lopez* (WWS 64). Lopez's sensitivity to environmental issues is seen as instrumental in his development through various phases of romanticism and sentimentality to the balance his present writing has achieved. As both poet and reporter Lopez tempers romantic cultural prejudices with a stable appreciation of the natural world. His achievement is in blending history and folklore; unlike "the European mind [which] tends to keep fact and fiction separate," Lopez combines the two so that readers doubt their previously assumed realities and are opened up to unexpected possibilities.

A critical edition of Jack Schaefer's *Shane* (Nebraska) has been edited by James C. Work, with a foreword by Marc Simmons and several critical pieces, three of them original. Simmons (pp. vii–xii) praises the novel for its grasp of an age in transition, attributable to its control of unconscious symbols. Work (pp. xiii–xvi) provides an interesting list of editorial revisions. Chuck Rankin's "Clash of Frontiers: A Historical Parallel to Jack Schaefer's *Shane*" (pp. 3–15) recounts the history of a Wyoming range war in which one figure, resisting the changing times, persisted like "a blackened tree trunk in the midst of plowed fields, a mute reminder of a bygone era," which is an image Schaefer uses in his novel. The cinematic success of *Shane* is detailed by Michael T. Marsden in "The Making of *Shane*: A Story for All Media" (pp. 338–53) with an eye toward its larger cultural impact, and screenwriter A. B. Guthrie, Jr., contributes a note (p. 358) on the manner in which he approached Schaefer's novel.

The source and final home of all subgenres is Hollywood, a fact that emerges from the essays collected in editor David Fine's *Los Angeles in Fiction*. Detective thrillers, apocalyptic science fictions, and an invigorating mix of different cultures all define Los Angeles as a seat of literary influence. In "Beyond the Territory Ahead" (pp. 85–107) Paul Skenazy tells how the detective novel changed when its writers were drawn from the East Coast to the West by film work, and Jerry Speir's "The Ultimate Seacoast: Ross Macdonald's California" (pp. 133–44) analyzes how the special openness of West Coast life provides a metaphoric extension of the subgenre's familiar themes. Norman Mailer's *The Deer Park* and Joan Didion's *Play It as It Lays* are shown as growing from a specific tradition dating back to Nathanael West's *The Day of the Locust* and F. Scott Fitzgerald's *The Last Tycoon* in Mark Royden Winchell's "Fantasy Seen: Hollywood Fiction Since West" (pp. 147–68). Especially noteworthy is Raymund A. Paredes's "Los Angeles from the Barrio: Oscar Zeta Acosta's *The Revolt of the Cockroach People*" (pp. 209–22). Acosta uses Hunter S. Thompson's fictive blend of "gonzo journalism" to express the special "floating" sense of Mexican heritage with which Los Angeles has never been at ease. Much more a novel than traditional reportage, the book's method shows a special affinity for the temper of Los Angeles life, ranging from anger and alienation to an energetic activism. Acosta's own sudden disappearance shortly after the publication of this politically controversial book is seen as a great loss to Chicano literature and to American writing in general.

University of Northern Iowa

16. Poetry: 1900 to the 1940s

James K. Guimond

It has not been a year of superlatives or strong directions in criticism for the poets in chapter 16—a fair number of well-done, intelligent studies, but no major ones. A wide variety of critical approaches was applied to these poets, from Marxism and Deconstruction to basic biography, but there was no dominant critical method. Rather significantly, two of the most important books in this chapter are collections of criticism mostly written in the past and dealing with poets whose reputations are rather problematical.

i. Bogan, Cummings

During Louise Bogan's lifetime, many poets and critics found it relatively easy to praise and admire her, but until quite recently they seem to have found it considerably more difficult to write about her poetry at any length. Now, 14 years after her death, *Critical Essays on Louise Bogan* (Hall), the first collection of reviews and scholarly articles about her, has been published. It is significant that many of the articles included in this book are laudatory but very brief reviews and that several of the best and longest essays were written especially for it. Nevertheless, the overall quality of this collection is good, and it functions as a belated but useful introduction to Bogan and her poetry. The editor, Martha Collins, has made a good presentation of the available scholarship and criticism, and her own introduction is a serviceable survey of Bogan's career, of the reasons why she has been relatively neglected, and of the critical issues that are related to her poetry. Some of the reviews Collins has selected contain good insights: Yvor Winters, Ford Madox Ford, and Ruth Lechlitner make interesting comparisons between Bogan's poetry and the works of such 17th-century English poets as Herbert and Donne (pp. 31–34, 43–45, 45–49). Morton Dauwen Zabel and Babette Deutsch praise her craftsmanship, and Marianne Moore commented on the "Compactness Compacted" of her poetry (pp. 34–36, 59–61, 61–63). More eccentric insights are contained in W. H. Auden's review of *Poems and New Poems* and Harold Bloom's jacket notes for a recording of Bogan reading her own poetry: Auden's review is mostly an eloquent diatribe against popular culture which says very little about the poet (pp. 54–58), and Bloom advances the idea, mentioned by no one else, that Bogan was really a Romantic poet (pp. 84–87). This collection also includes four longer essays, published late in Bogan's career or shortly after her death, which are more comprehensive studies of her poetry. Theodore Roethke's 1961 "The Poetry of Louise Bogan" is a vivid and intelligent appreciation of a number of her best poems (pp. 87–96). Though Roethke admitted modestly that his critical approach was a "rather simple method of 'pointing out,'" he uses this method so eloquently and conveys so many insights into Bogan's poetic virtues that his essay is one of the best in this group. Paul Ramsey's 1970 "Louise Bogan" (pp. 119–28) also deals primarily with individual poems with an emphasis on Bogan's qualities as a lyric poet. Though he often seems mystified by the subjects of the poems, Ramsey comments intelligently on their metrics, rhythms, and structures. Elder Olson's more systematic "Louise Bogan and Léonie Adams" (1954) is a careful comparison of the two poets which emphasizes Bogan's craftsmanship, her typical subjects and images, and the great differences between her love poetry and Millay's (pp. 71–84). William Jay Smith's 1970 memorial essay is mainly a personal reminiscence—which contains too many long prose quotations—but Smith also included some revealing anecdotes about Bogan's personality and her preferences in poetry (pp. 101–18).

The last six essays were written recently and for this collection. They all deal in various ways with the renewed interest in Bogan created by the women's movement. This is not a totally new approach to her poetry; the first review that Bogan received, by Llewellyn Jones in 1925 (which is in this collection), noted that her poems dealt with the "limitations imposed and self-imposed on women" (pp. 27–29), and Kenneth Rexroth's 1937 review of *The Sleeping Fury* (which is also included) had some shrewd remarks on the relevance of her work to an era when "disabilities and exploitations still existed in the relations of men and women even in literary circles . . . where the linen was so tastefully embroidered with mottoes like Liberty, Equality, and Fraternity" (pp. 40–41). Of the six recent essays containing a variety of feminist perspectives, Ruth Limmer's "Circumspections" is the most disappointing (pp. 166–74). It begins with a promising analysis of a poem that Bogan herself did not publish, "Portrait of the Artist as a Young Woman," presumably because it was too revealing or too self-pitying; but it then turns into a series of speculations about Bogan's personality which contains few insights into her poetry. Deborah Pope's "Music in the Granite Hill: The Poetry of Louise Bogan" is a more successful biographical essay which emphasizes how the technical strategies, imagery, and dominant themes of the poems in Bogan's first book, *Body of This Death*, were influenced by her childhood and sexual experiences; Pope's readings of "Statue and Birds," "Betrothed," and "Last Hill in a Vista" are particularly sensitive and intelligent (pp. 149–66). Another essentially biographical essay, Sandra Cookson's " 'The Repressed Becomes the Poem': Landscape and Quest in Two Poems by Louise Bogan," is a psychoanalytical reading of poems that can be interpreted as related to two of Bogan's chief "obsessions"—her childhood and her miserable second marriage (pp. 194–203). Cookson's main emphasis is on poems containing archetypal sea voyages and desolate or hellish landscapes, primarily "Putting to Sea" and "The Psychiatrist's Song." Carol Moldaw's "Form, Feeling, and Nature: Aspects of Harmony in the Poetry of Louise Bogan" (pp. 180–94) also contains some psychoanalytical interpretations of Bogan's imagery, but Moldaw is concerned more with the poet's techniques than with her biography. Diane Wood Middlebrook's "The Problem of the Woman Artist" deals primarily with "The Alchemist" and a few other poems which she claims constitute Bogan's "private mythology" about her own creativity (pp. 174–80). In these poems, Middlebrook argues, the poet portrays her own creative aspirations in terms of polarities whose positive elements ("breath," "passion wholly of the mind") have been considered "masculine" attainments in our culture, whereas their negative elements ("flesh," "instinct," "mortality") have been regarded as "feminine." Finally, Elizabeth Frank's "A Doll's Heart: The Girl in the Poetry of Edna St. Vincent Millay and Louise Bogan" is a witty, vivid, intelligent comparison of the two poets' respective portrayals of the "liberated" Jazz Age Girl of the 1920s (pp. 128–49). Though Frank tries to be fair to Millay and to acknowledge the virtues of her verse, she considers her poetry to be essentially clever, vulgar, and theatrical—despite Millay's efforts to make it emotionally and technically sophisticated. In contrast, Frank emphasizes that when Bogan dealt with the same themes, she did so in a deeper and subtler way in her poetry of the 1920s. Moreover, Millay was never able to mature past the "persona of the Girl . . . [who] never stopped believing in the rejuvenating power of romance and passion," whereas Bogan was able to change emotionally and psychically in her later poetry so that she could speak in the personas of the Woman and the Child. An excellent essay which also deals shrewdly, though implicitly, with the cultural situation that confronted women poets in the 1920s.

Reading Guy Rotella's *Critical Essays on E. E. Cummings* (Hall) in the context created by Frank's essay on Bogan and Millay, I found it difficult to avoid the idea that if Millay was the liberated Jazz Age Girl, then Cummings was the liberated Boy of the same era. (Girls had to stay in Greenwich Village and follow the traditional lyric conventions; boys could go to Paris and experiment with typography.) One of the frequent charges against Cummings was that he never changed or developed as a poet in a significant way; to some extent this complaint can be applied to a good deal of Cummings criticism, since both his negative and his positive critics sometimes seem to be repeating or paraphrasing the same attacks and defenses over and over. Both Cummings's attackers and his admirers, for example, often seem to take it for granted that his poems are the simple, direct expression of the poet's personality or his attitudes toward life which they then deplore or admire for reasons that do not seem to change very much—the admirers find the personality charming and lovable and the attitudes delightful, whereas the detractors find the personality immature and the attitudes superficial or repellent. This repetitiousness cannot, I think, be blamed on any lack of quality or sensitivity on the part of Cummings's critics; for, as Rotella's book shows, his works have been reviewed and analyzed by many of the best and most sensitive American poets and critics—from Edmund Wilson, Kenneth Burke, and R. P. Blackmur in the 1920s and the 1930s to Helen Vendler and Malcolm Cowley in the 1970s. In other words, there is something about Cummings or his poetry that often blights the growth—though not the quality—of our critical discourse about him.

Rotella seems to be aware of this difficulty and has tried to overcome it in this collection. In his introduction (pp. 5–21), he lists and categorizes in considerable detail the various critical approaches that have been applied to Cummings accompanying them with brief com-

ments which enable them to function as a useful, annotated bibliography and to show that it is possible to find new ways to discuss
the poet. In his selection of reviews and essays, Rotella has included
generous samples of materials representing the positive and negative viewpoints of Cummings, as well as essays representing some
new approaches.

The negatives are well and fairly represented by R. P. Blackmur's
magisterial 1931 essay and by reviews by Edmund Wilson, Randall
Jarrell, Carl Bode, Edward M. Hood, and Helen Vendler. Wilson
(pp. 43–46) and Hood (pp. 92–95) argue that underneath the surface "unconventionality" which "assures the reader of the difficulty,
the tough-witted modernity, the complexity" he has been taught to
find in Modern poetry, Cummings's poems are filled with attitudes
expressing simple platitudes and clichés. Jarrell emphasizes Cummings's lack of tragic awareness (pp. 78–81) with a series of comparisons—beginning with Rilke and ending with Hardy, Yeats,
Proust, and Chekhov—that do not seem very fair. Carl Bode (pp. 81–
85) analyzes his intellectual limitations with dry humor and precision, and Helen Vendler's 1973 review of the *Complete Poems* (pp.
99–105) is the most eloquent summary of all of Cummings's limitations and of the personal qualities in his poetry that are not only an-
noying but disturbing—that "for all his sonnets on sensitive love, he
had a hankering after the know-nothing, the gross, and the violent."
In his essay, "Notes on E. E. Cummings's Language" (pp. 107–25),
Blackmur makes what has been one of the most important statements about Cummings's typographical peculiarities: that their repeated use would eventually make them so familiar that they would
become just another "set of well-ordered conventions susceptible of
general use," which is what they did become for Cummings himself.
He then presents a devastating series of analyses of Cummings's use
of language, his sentimentality, his anti-intellectualism, and his
pretentiousness.

Cummings's admirers and defenders are equally well represented
by Peter DeVries's and John Logan's reviews and by essays by John
Peale Bishop, Robert E. Maurer, and Norman Friedman. DeVries
(pp. 72–76) admires Cummings's attitudes, particularly his "celebration of the individual human identity"; and Logan (pp. 86–90)
praises his "purity" and "compassion." Logan skillfully transforms
some of the critics' negative attacks into positive insights—e.g., he
considers Cummings's anti-intellectualism an "affirmation of the mys-

tery of things"—and he makes some sensitive comments on his typographical and linguistic techniques. Bishop explains and praises Cummings's "romanticism" on the basis of his experiences in World War I
in his 1938 "The Poems and Prose of E. E. Cummings" (pp. 125–35).
Maurer's "Latter-Day Notes on E. E. Cummings's Language" (pp.
136–53) is a careful attempt to refute Blackmur's charges through a
systematic analysis of Cummings's linguistic techniques. Friedman's
1960 essay, "E. E. Cummings and the Modernist Movement" (pp.
160–75) is a fairly successful effort to redefine modernism so Cummings can be considered a genuine Modernist and not a superficial
one who decorated his "conventional" attitudes with Modernist techniques; unfortunately, Friedman then goes on to make a rather
strained attempt to discredit more pessimistic Modernists by claiming that their attitudes are really "faddish," "flattering," and "sentimental"—thus implying that it was more "difficult" for Cummings to
write his overtly affirmative, naive, and sentimental poems. Finally,
Malcolm Cowley's "Cummings: One Man Alone" (pp. 215–32) is
perhaps the best "balanced" essay on Cummings. Essentially a brisk,
biographical survey of Cummings's life and works, it is filled with
intelligent acknowledgments of his limitations and generous appre-
ciations of his virtues.

Essays in this collection that may be considered new approaches
to Cummings and his works include those by Rushworth M. Kidder
and Patrick Mullen, Rotella's own essay, and Friedman's 1979 biographical essay, "Cummings Posthumous" (pp. 259–83). In this essay Friedman relies chiefly on Cummings's *Selected Letters*, published after his death, to show that many of the affirmations and
rages that he expressed (or even flaunted) in his poems were com-
pensations for personal losses, failures, disappointments, and deso-
lations. Having portrayed this darker side of Cummings's life and
personality, Friedman then analyzes the 73 *Poems* to show how they
express ambiguity about existence and an awareness "of pain, loss,
and emptiness, and a correspondingly greater sense of the difficulty
of transcendence." Rushworth Kidder, in his " 'Twin Obsessions':
The Poetry and Paintings of E. E. Cummings" (pp. 242–58), does
not rate Cummings's paintings very highly; but he shows that they
do give insights into his "aesthetic" and his poetic compositions by
analyzing the parallels between three paintings and three poems. Another essay emphasizing parallels, but with the "low" rather than the
visual arts, is Patrick B. Mullen's brisk "E. E. Cummings and Popular

Culture" (pp. 202–14). In his 1950 review, Jarrell had the lovely insight that Cummings's poems were "the popular songs of American intellectuals," and Mullen points out that Cummings not only wrote essays on various kinds of mass culture in the 1920s and the 1930s but that his poetry was also influenced by burlesque, circus, amusement parks like Coney Island, comic strips, and movies. Rotella's essay, "Nature, Time, and Transcendence in Cummings' Later Poems" (pp. 283–303), begins with an interesting comparison and contrast of Cummings with Stevens and Frost as latter-day New England Transcendentalists. He takes issue with the claim that Cummings never "developed" by admitting that, though all of his books contain "weak-minded and weak-spirited" poems, Cummings nevertheless changed and developed to become a more religious and philosophical poet beginning with his 1931 *ViVa*. Rotella acknowledges that even in some of his later poems Cummings still fell back on easy affirmations and reductive dualisms, but argues that he also wrote enough other poems showing a "darker and more inclusive vision" of time and the natural processes to refute the "legend" of the Cummings who was only a "naive singer" of spring and love.

ii. Harriet Monroe, Amy Lowell, Robinson, Sandburg

Articles on these three poets and Monroe's work as an anthology editor dealt with the subject of the relationship between poets and the "general public" (as it would have been called) in the early days of modernism. Craig S. Abbott's "Harriet Monroe's Anthology" (*JML* 11:89–108) is an analysis of the editorial principles Monroe followed and a survey of the poets whom she published in the three editions of her anthology, *The New Poetry*, in 1917, 1923, and 1932. As the popularity of anthologies like Monroe's indicates, there was a significant general readership for poetry in the late 1910s and the 1920s; but poets, critics, and editors—including Monroe—found it difficult to define or to agree on what was "good" or even what was "new" poetry. Abbott discusses Monroe's editorial principles in detail—she was eclectic and democratic and included many minor poets—but he also makes some brief, interesting comments on her main competitors, including Louis Untermeyer and Amy Lowell. This article would have been better if Abbott had illustrated Monroe's tastes by quoting a few of the poems by minor poets whom she included. Obscure even in Monroe's time, poets like Gladys Crom-

well, Hazel Hall, and Glenn Ward Dresbach have now become so
totally unknown that it means very little merely to list their names.
Amy Lowell and Edwin Arlington Robinson were the subjects
of articles on poetry "wars" which they carried on with local critics
who felt the poets had defamed, respectively, Charleston, South Carolina, and Gardiner, Maine. In his "The 'Little Controversy' over
Magenta: Amy Lowell and the South Carolinians" (*ELN* 22:62–66)
Tom Brown gives a brief account of a dispute, which reached the
pages of *Poetry* in the 1920s, when Lowell used the word "magenta"
in her 1922 "Magnolia Gardens" to describe a disappointing magnolia garden in Charleston. When Harriet Monroe printed a letter
claiming that Lowell had been inaccurate, Lowell insisted that another letter, defending her, be printed; Brown argues that she did
this not out of wounded vanity but because accurate observation was
so important to her theory of imagism. Leon Satterfield's "Bubble-
Work in Gardiner, Maine: The Poetry War of 1924" (*NEQ* 57:25–
43) deals with a more extensive dispute between Robinson and certain citizens of his hometown—which he had left years before—who
believed that his sonnet "New England" was critical of life in their
town and region. Robinson's critics attacked him in mediocre prose
and bad verse in the *Gardiner Journal,* and eventually Robinson himself joined the fray with a not very convincing letter to the editor
claiming that his intention had been to make his sonnet an "oblique
attack" on New England's detractors, not the region itself. He also
made a number of minor changes in the next published version of the
poem to make this interpretation more plausible. After analyzing the
sonnet and reviewing the critical interpretations of it by non-Gardiner
critics, Satterfield concludes that it really does criticize New England
life, that Robinson's townspeople were right, and that Robinson himself was wrong, at least in the *Gardiner Journal.*

Unlike some of his contemporaries, Sandburg had no difficulty
writing for the general public. In his "The *Day Book* Poems of Carl
Sandburg" (*ON* 9:205–18) Robert L. Reid has published four poems
which originally appeared in *The Day Book,* a small experimental
Chicago newspaper, but which were not included in any of the collections of Sandburg's poems. Written in 1915, 1916, and 1917, when
Sandburg was a reporter for the newspaper, the poems are heavily
topical and related to preparations for World War I and current Chicago news—qualities that made them poor candidates for reprinting.

iii. H. D., Crane, Tate, MacLeish

Adalaide Morris's "The Concept of Projection: H.D.'s Visionary Powers" (*ConL* 25:411–36) is a forceful, vivid overview of H.D.'s development as a visionary poet. Beginning with H.D.'s major visionary experience, which took place at Corfu in 1920, Morris shows how her belief in visionary "projection" was related to the Imagists' poetic theories and to H.D.'s own Imagist poems which—unlike the other Imagists—she considered "bridges to the sacred." Morris reviews the assorted spiritualist and scientific theories that the poet used to explain her visions and relates them to the cinema in the 1920s; she then shows how H.D.'s fascination with her own visionary powers influenced both her experience as Freud's analysand in the 1930s and *Trilogy*, her major long poems of the 1940s. She concludes with an analysis of how those poems can be read in the context of their alchemical symbolism and H.D.'s theories.

Paul Smith's "H.D.'s Identity" (*WS* 10:321–37) is a psychoanalytical study of H.D.'s relationships with two of the male figures who most influenced her creativity, Pound and Freud. Smith demonstrates how she identified Pound with her own father but considered Freud an "ideal father" who would give her an understanding of symbols. H.D. expressed her ambivalence toward both of these "fathers" in a mixture of submission and resistance, Smith says, and in her writings this resistance took the form—not of a single "transcendent identity" which would be feminine and natural and thus a negation of patriarchy and culture—but of a "series of overlapping and unified identities" which she "unfolded" metonymically, particularly in *Trilogy*.

The Bridge was the subject of two good articles about its basic themes and Crane's intentions. Stephanie A. Tingley's "Hart Crane's 'Quaker Hill': A Plea for a Proper Perspective" (*ELN* 22:55–62) is a careful reinterpretation of a section of the poem which has been dismissed by many critics, starting with Winters, as "cynical," "vague," and "chaotic." Tingley argues that though Crane's epigraphs from Dickinson and Isadora Duncan seem to be cynical about ideals, they can also be interpreted—in their original contexts—as indicating a need to re-evaluate ideals, and that although "Quaker Hill" does contain social satire it also hints that the poet may give his nation new ideals and values. This interpretation is justified, Tingley claims,

by the epigraph from William Blake's "Morning" which Crane used
to link "Quaker Hill" to "The Tunnel," since Blake's is such an affirmative, positive poem. Tom Chaffin's "Toward a Poetics of Technology:
Hart Crane and the American Sublime" (*SoR* 20:68–91) is an intelligent and wide-ranging study of *The Bridge* as being not a "failed
epic" but a sublime "poem of praise." Developing ideas about *The
Bridge* suggested by Sherman Paul and Josephine Miles, Chaffin discusses its relationship to the sublime as described by Edmund Burke
and expressed by Whitman and a number of American painters who
were his contemporaries. He claims that the conception of the sublime
that Crane inherited from Whitman enabled him to write vividly and
powerfully about natural subjects, but he became more hesitant and
ambivalent when he wrote about technology, in "Cape Hatteras,"
because he could not possess Whitman's naive poetic faith in America, technology, and the future.

As its title indicates, "The Cemeteries of Allen Tate and Paul Valéry: The Ghosts of Aeneas and Narcissus" (*SoR* 20:54–67) by Jefferson Humphries deals with very different kinds of poetic myths
and origins—the European background of Tate's "Ode to the Confederate Dead." From France and Europe, Humphries says, Tate
derived the myth of the European Renaissance which was based on
a "ubiquitous imagery of disinterment, resurrection, and renascence."
This imagery is present in Valéry's "*Le Cimetière Marin*," which
Tate had probably read, and therefore it can be considered the precursor of his "Ode." Humphries discusses the similarities in imagery
between the two poems in detail and the mutual indebtedness of the
two poets to Poe. He also analyzes Tate's translations of Baudelaire
to show how Tate "alchemized . . . an English voice" from his works
and Valéry's in the process of becoming an American "strong poet."

Lauriat Lane, Jr., has written two analyses of MacLeish's ambitious 1926 poem, "Einstein." In "Spatial Form in Literature: Mac-
Leish's 'Einstein' " (*ArielE* 15:35–47) he deals with it primarily from
the perspective of Joseph Frank's concept, though he also considers
it in terms of a number of other categories taken from Northrop
Frye's and Joseph Campbell's formulations of the quest pattern. Lane
discusses the poem in the context of Bachelard's *Poetics* in his other
essay, " 'Intimate Immensity': On the Poetics of Space in MacLeish's
Einstein" (*CRevAS* 14:19–29); but he also shows how it is related
to the writings of such American students of the universe as Emerson, Thoreau, and Whitman. His analysis emphasizes how the poet

established a dialectical, ironic interplay between the immense "Not-Me" of space in nature and the subjective spaces of Einstein's personal experiences.

iv. Moore

Twentieth Century Literature has a special issue on Moore with several interesting articles. Margaret Holly's "The Model Stanza: The Organic Origin of Moore's Syllabic Verse" (*TCL* 30:181–91) is a brief but useful analysis of how the poet's 1932–36 syllabic poems were constructed upon the forms established by certain "model" stanzas in which the syllable counts and line breaks follow the syntax of verbal phrases. These poems have to be reconstructed to be read properly because Moore often altered or omitted these key stanzas in her revisions—which makes the poems seem more formally arbitrary than they were originally. Holly also analyzes the significance of this practice to show how it creates a tension between organic and mechanical forms and how it produces interpenetrations of voice and text which implicitly "demythologize" poetry. Patricia C. Willis's "The Rose to Paradise: First Notes on Marianne Moore's 'An Octopus'" (*TCL* 30:242–72) is a detailed account of Moore's poem about Mt. Rainier. (A glacier on that mountain does resemble an "octopus of ice," hence Moore's title.) Willis gives the biographical background of Moore's trips to the Northwest when she climbed the mountain, she analyzes the allusions to the Greek conceptions of paradise in the poem and their relationships to Milton's *Paradise Lost*, and she has included "A Late Manuscript Version of an 'An Octopus.'" (This issue of *TCL* is also illustrated with a photograph of the "octopus" part of the mountain and a picture of Moore and her fellow climbers on the glacier.)

In his introduction to the issue, Andrew J. Kappel (*TCL* 30:v–xxx) gives a long summary, with illustrative anecdotes, of Moore's personal qualities and their relationship to her writing. He attempts to show how these qualities were related to her Presbyterian faith, and he points out differences between her work and personality and those of Stevens, Eliot, and Williams. Bonnie Costello's article on "Marianne Moore and Elizabeth Bishop: Friendship and Influence" (*TCL* 30:130–49) does not contain a great deal of commentary on the two poets' works, but it instead shows how they complemented one another personally. In her "Private Exchanges and Public Re-

views: Marianne Moore's Criticism of William Carlos Williams"
(*TCL* 30:160–75), Celeste Goodridge deals with the more complicated relationship between Williams and Moore, who often seemed
poetic allies in public even though Moore had her private doubts
about Williams and his poetic subject matter. Goodridge shows that
the open "break" between the two poets, which came in 1951 when
Moore criticized *Paterson IV*, was preceded by an earlier ambivalence
(on Moore's part) which actually started in the 1920s and which she
carefully masked by seeming to defer to other poets' criticisms of
Williams and by passing up opportunities to review his books.

Taffy Martin's "Portrait of a Writing Master: Beyond the Myth
of Marianne Moore" (*TCL* 30:192–209) contrasts the critical stereotype of the poet with Moore's own comments on her writing, and
gives readings of "The Steeple-Jack" and "The Pangolin" that emphasize the tensions and "dangers" in Moore's works, which Martin
considers essentially autobiographical.

Lisa M. Steinman and John Slatin analyze Moore's critical and
poetic relationship to American culture. Steinman comments on her
attitudes toward the America of the 1920s in relation to such topics
as industrialism, commercialism, and science in "America, Modernism, and Moore" (*TCL* 30:210–30). She concludes that the poet had
an essentially positive attitude toward America and thought that
these things might be creative rather than negative on the basis of
her readings of "The Student" and Moore's use of writers like Dewey
and Berenson.

John M. Slatin reaches a slightly different conclusion in his " 'Advancing Backward in a Circle': Marianne Moore as (Natural) Historian" (*TCL* 30:273–326). In a long, heavily documented study
of Moore's poems written in 1935–36, he analyzes her allusions to
Wordsworth and Keats and her portrayals of Virginia and American
history in those works to argue that Moore finds imitation—symbolized by the mockingbird—to be a characteristic quality of American
culture. A much lighter but clever reading of a Moore poem is Emeka
Okeke-Ezigbo's comparison of "Moore's 'To a Snail' and Gunn's 'Considering the Snail' " (*Expl* 42,ii:17–18) in which Okeke-Ezigbo analyzes how Moore's wit transforms the snail's limitations into virtues
which are lessons to mankind. The snail, like Moore's poetry, has no
"feet," yet it moves by contriving a balance between the delights of
free verse and the "demands of conventional versification."

v. William Carlos Williams

Critics and scholars who have believed that Williams's poetry constitutes one of the more significant breaks with the 19th-century poetic past may be surprised to learn from Carl Rapp's *William Carlos Williams and Romantic Idealism* (New England) that Williams was essentially a chip off the Emersonian block whose prose and poetry represent an extension of, not a break with, 19th-century literature. Other critics, notably Miller, Breslin, Macksey, and Riddel, have interpreted Williams's early poem "The Wanderer," for example, as being a rejection of Keats, romanticism, and the poetic past; but Rapp claims that it is really a continuation of Keats's "Hyperion." Except for a discussion of Williams's late poems in the final chapter of his book, Rapp has relatively little to say about Williams's actual poetry. What he does instead is to quote extensively from essays by Emerson and lectures by Hegel which are filled with generalities about idealism and art, quote some equally generalized passages from Williams's prose, and then paraphrase these passages until they support his theory that Williams was a Romantic idealist. He also claims in chapter 2 of his book and in an essay, "William Carlos Williams and the Modern Myth of the Fall" (*SoR* 20:82–90), that Williams's assorted complaints about Modern poets and poetry, including his own, can be interpreted as a critique of modernism, that Williams's "notorious iconoclasm is, above all, conservative," and that James Joyce's writing is also "fundamentally conservative." Rapp's own critical method is appropriately idealistic, since he never discusses Williams's biography or personality, nor does he mention his cultural situation and his relationships with other Modern writers in any detail. Instead, Rapp creates a kind of philosopher-poet whose writings can be understood from his theories. Since these theories— as interpreted by Rapp—sometimes do sound like Emerson's, he is able to claim that Williams had more in common with the 19th-century than earlier critics had suspected; however, Rapp does not deal with the important question of why Williams's poems sound and look so drastically different from 19th-century poetry, including Emerson's.

Stephen Tapscott's *American Beauty: William Carlos Williams and the Modernist Whitman* (Columbia) is a lively and intelligent analysis of the ways in which Williams adopted Whitman as an inspiration for his own poetic development. As Tapscott shows in a convincing series of comparisons, Whitman was used by many Modernist poets to justify their rebellions against traditional poetic forms and to explore new ways of relating themselves to their cultures and historical situations. Besides analyzing the effect of Whitman upon Pound, Crane, Stevens, and Lawrence he also has some excellent comments on how Whitman influenced Lorca, Neruda, and Mayakovsky. As for Williams, Tapscott argues that he "invented" a series of Whitmans who corresponded to various stages of his development as a poet. First, there was the relatively simple Whitman that Williams used as a "model" (along with Keats) in "The Wanderer"; then Whitman became the "native modernist" who helped Williams to justify his own form of modernism during the brilliant period between *Sour Grapes* (1920) and *In the American Grain* (1925). In the 1930s Williams created another Whitman to inspire his formal experimentation as an Objectivist, he was inspired by Whitman's ambition when he wrote *Paterson*, and in the mid-1950s he formulated his own concept of a Whitman "tradition" of endless American poetic innovation derived from "a forefather who is both useful and flawed." (Or, though Tapscott does not stress this point, Whitman was useful *because* he was flawed and therefore needed to be completed by Williams and later generations.) Tapscott illustrates how Williams adapted the poetic practices he learned from these various Whitmans in a number of his shorter poems—"St. Francis Einstein," "Danse Russe," and "To a Solitary Disciple"—but his main emphasis is on *Paterson*. An excellent book with good insights into both modernism and Williams.

Tony Baker analyzes the significance of the assorted correct and incorrect spellings of the title "Della Primavera Transportata Al Morale" in his "The Comedian as the Letter 'N': Sight and Sound in the Poetry of William Carlos Williams" (*JAmS* 18:89–104) in various editions of Williams's works. Though this would seem to be precisely the kind of title that printers or Williams himself might misspell, Baker argues that it is possible that the poet might have let a mistake (a missing "n") stand deliberately. To bolster his case, Baker analyzes the various versions of the poem's title and Williams's theories of poetry to claim that he wanted his poems to be seen primarily as visual objects, and therefore he might have preserved a misprint to force readers to be more alert and to see the poem as a changeable "live thing."

Williams's literary relationships with two of his most talented contemporaries were discussed by Celeste Goodridge (see section *iv.*, above) and by Martha Helen Strom in her "The Uneasy Friendship of William Carlos Williams and Wallace Stevens" (*JML* 11:291–98). Strom describes the two poets as being sibling rivals and competitors who both respected and resented one another. She points out that though there may have been some differences between them in the 1920s, their rivalry flowered after Stevens described Williams's subject matter as "anti-poetic" in his introduction to the *Collected Poems, 1921–1931*. After that Williams and Stevens continued to treat each other's work with respect; but their antagonism was revealed by Stevens in his reference to Williams in private letters and by Williams in the backhanded compliments he included in his tributes to Stevens. Strom also shows that, to some extent, the poets saw and criticized in one another the poetic qualities that they disliked in themselves and that their "lifelong argument" had stimulated each of them to "evolve his own unique form of realism."

The relationship between Williams and Stevens is also discussed by Paul Mariani in one chapter (pp. 95–104) of the Williams section of his *A Usable Past*. Though he mentions a few of their poems, Mariani's approach is basically biographical and anecdotal as he concentrates on the two poets' opinions of one another's personalities as revealed in remarks and letters. In other chapters in this collection (essays originally published elsewhere in 1980 and the mid-1970s) Mariani deals with a number of topics related to Williams's ideas and poems when he was working to complete *Paterson*. In "The Poem as a Field of Action" (pp. 37–58) he gives a rather loose survey of Williams's critical speculations about the "line" and "new forms" when he was writing *Paterson*, then relates these speculations to various parts of the poem; and he discusses three poems Williams wrote between 1946 and 1948 ("The Birth of Venus," "The Hard Core of Beauty," "All That Is Perfect in Woman") in the context of his well-known interest in women and the erotic in "The Hard Core of Beauty" (pp. 74–95). The best and most imaginative of these essays is "The Eighth Day of Creation: Rethinking *Paterson*" (pp. 59–73) in which Mariani analyzes the effect of Bosch's *Garden of Delights* upon Williams's conception of *Paterson*: it enabled him to begin *Paterson V* as an "apocalyptic" poem in which time is annihilated; the poet looks at the world from the perspective of the "River of Heaven" and sees "the pattern of his whole life as something accomplished."

The *William Carlos Williams Review* published three short essays in "A Symposium: Teaching (and Being Taught By) *Spring and All*" (10,ii:1–24). Thomas Whitaker's article (pp. 1–6) contains a quick survey of earlier critical comments on that book and suggests a series of dialectical oppositions which can be used to group the poems, such as visual vs. auditory. Lisa Steinman's (pp. 7–12) emphasizes that *Spring and All* itself may have been intended as a work "about the nature of literary education in America" in which Williams tried to implement some of John Dewey's educational ideas by turning the creative imagination loose on routines and conventions. Henry Sayre's "Avant-Garde Dispositions: Placing *Spring and All* in Context" (pp. 13–24) is not really a pedagogical essay, but an analysis of how Williams may have been influenced by Modern European artistic movements of the period, particularly Dadaism and collage. Sayre points out that Williams knew these movements quite well not just because of his own interest in Modern art but also because of his friendship with Marsden Hartley; and Sayre makes a convincing case that Williams may have been influenced by a specific painting, Charles Demuth's 1921 *Spring*, when he was composing his book. This issue of the *Review* also contains a "Descriptive List," ed. Peter Schmidt, of books, manuscripts, and periodicals from Williams's own library which are now housed in Fairleigh Dickinson University in Rutherford, New Jersey (10,ii:30–53). As this list reveals, Williams was an omnivorous reader, and besides a great deal of poetry his library contained all kinds of fascinating items which might be studied by future Williams scholars, ranging from Peter Abraham's *Tell Freedom* to Hans Zinsser's *Rats, Lice, and History*.

vi. Frost

William Pritchard's *Frost: A Literary Life Reconsidered* (Oxford) is a well-written book which may appeal to the poet's admirers who were disturbed by Lawrance Thompson's massive biography. In their dogged, relentless way, Thompson's books raised some difficult and even painful questions about the relationship of creativity to evil and the true status of Frost's literary reputation. Pritchard's "reconsideration" deals with some of the same issues, but it does so in a more graceful, subtle, and merciful way. To use Frost's own terminology, he was the kind of person who loved to dispense justice and receive mercy. No matter how nasty, intolerant, and selfish he might have been to his family and the persons Frost considered his "enemies" and competitors, he was always eager to charm and cajole his friends so that they would be charitable, tolerant, and generous to him. Thompson dealt with Frost as the poet so often dealt with others: by "justly" recording every fault and wrongdoing and ascribing the worst possible motives to Frost's bad behavior. Pritchard's book is much friendlier.

He shows, for example, that Frost was hypocritical and inconsistent in his public and private literary evaluations of contemporaries such as Amy Lowell, but he points out that these inconsistencies "were extraordinarily rich pieces of expression . . . which have in them the essential surprise of poetry." Or he acknowledges that Frost often lied about people, but he seems to accept Frost's own excuse— when he was cornered by one of his friends—that he was only trying to be "amusing." What Pritchard creates, in effect, is a certain amount of aesthetic distance between himself and Frost, enabling him to see his subject's lesser faults as creative performances by which he could be judged on aesthetic rather than ethical standards.

As for the major problems with Frost's character and his current literary status, Pritchard deals with them in a moderately satisfactory way. He shows his disapproval of some of Frost's nastier behavior— which could verge on the pathological—but he does not dwell on it as Thompson often did, and he is careful to quote Frost's own words of contrition to show that the poet was sometimes aware of and disturbed by some of his own behavior. He does not, however, solve the problem of how a poet who has been considered such a fount of "wisdom" could have been so unwise and so selfish, particularly in his family relationships. Pritchard confronts the charge that Frost, as a poet, reached his peak with *North of Boston*, wrote a few more fine poems in *Mountain Interval* and *New Hampshire*, and then spent the rest of his career declining creatively even though—with a little help from his friends—his poetic reputation continued to rise and prosper. He argues the merits of the good poems that appeared in books like *New Hampshire* and *A Witness Tree* in a convincing way, and he admits that the works in *A Further Range* are best appreciated as "expert performances in a mode which approaches light verse." But Pritchard also relies too often on the old tactic of bolstering the poet's reputation by implying that many of the negative criticisms of Frost's "limitations" were inspired by the envy or political biases of the critics; and he does not deal with the difficult question of whether the nation's most popular 20th-century poet was also a major poet. Instead he often relies on a technique that might be described as reputation-by-association in which he briskly compares one of Frost's books or poems with works by Stevens, Williams, Yeats, Pope, or Dryden; but in several cases these comparisons also should have involved some significant contrasts which Pritchard does not make. Pritchard is particularly effective, however, in his descriptions of many of Frost's public readings and "performances" in the latter stages of his career, and his book will be useful to younger scholars and critics who never attended a Frost reading and who may—after reading Thompson's biography—wonder how such an unpleasant man became such a popular literary celebrity.

Three of Frost's best-known poems were the subjects of articles. Peter B. Clarke's appropriately brief "Mending Wall" (*Expl* 43,i:48–50) is an extension of George Monteiro's earlier idea that the neighbor's reverence for walls may be based on ancient religious rituals. Clark has found additional Roman and Hebrew laws, rituals, and curses about laws which give additional ancient reasons for making "good fences." Thomas Elwood Hart's "Frost's 'The Road Not Taken': Text, Structures and Poetic Theory" (*Lang&S* 17:3–43) is a long and laborious effort to prove that the poem contains an assortment of coded references to the poet Edward Thomas, who was Frost's friend at the time. To demonstrate this point, Hart argues that Frost was a very conscious craftsman who "tinkered" with his poems, he points out that Frost himself gave some vague clues that the poem contained "hints" about its meaning, and he makes an extremely long and detailed analysis of every linguistic and formal aspect of the poem that can be used to buttress his case—though he also acknowledges that when Frost sent the poem to Edward Thomas, even Thomas himself did not notice any of these "clues" and "hints." Laurence Perrine's "Robert Frost's 'Provide, Provide'" (*NMAL* 8:Item 5) is a carefully reasoned analysis of whether the poet recommended ironic idealism or cynical expediency in the poem. After comparing the merits of the two interpretations as advanced by earlier critics, Perrine decides that Frost was advising idealism in a rather oblique way.

vii. Stevens

The two best studies of Stevens were relatively unconventional ones which relied heavily on Marxism and biography—critical approaches that are not frequently applied to a poet who was a most successful capitalist and an extremely reticent person about his personal existence. Helen Vendler's *Wallace Stevens: Words Chosen Out of Desire* (Tenn.)—originally given as the Hodges Lectures—is a sensitive and successful attempt to introduce readers to a rather rare Wallace Stevens: one who is a human being instead of the exotic producer of poetic ideas that inhabits so much Stevens scholarship. Vendler believes that the poems "concern the general emotional experiences common to us all," and to substantiate that claim she analyzes four of Stevens's more important topics (desire, the loss of feeling, concealment, and magnitude) in four eloquent but brief chapters. Her intention has been to demolish, or at least diminish, the force of the clichés that he is an excessively "cold," "cerebral," or "remote" poet. To do this, she demonstrates that it is possible to penetrate the elegant carapaces of his poetry, to recreate his feelings imaginatively, to show that he expressed them in his poems, and then to analyze variations of these feelings in other works. Vendler has excellent insights into a number of specific poems, particularly "Chaos in Motion and Not in Motion," "Domination of Black," "A Postcard from the Volcano," and "The Apostrophe to Vincentine"; however, I expect that her book will be most valuable not to Stevens experts but to persons who teach poetry to undergraduates. In particular, in the first pages of chapter 3 she outlines a method for reading Stevens which should be pedagogically foolproof.

Fredric Jameson's "Wallace Stevens" (*NOR* 11:10–19) is a very different but equally important essay on Stevens. Whereas Vendler insists, in a personal and sympathetic way, that despite his "secrecy" Stevens's poetry does possess a great deal of emotional content, Jameson makes a Marxist analysis of that "secrecy" as a system which he considers symptomatic of the state of American culture and poetry as they were received by the 1960s when Stevens's reputation was at its peak (after his death in 1956). For Jameson the basic paradox of the poetry is the way in which it combines an amazing linguistic richness with "an impoverishment or hollowness of content." To explain this paradox, he makes an impressive series of comparisons between Stevens's works and certain aspects of Flaubert, 1920s tourism, and the *pensée sauvage* described by Lévi-Strauss—the last comparison is a particularly interesting one. He then analyzes how the functioning of this system generates Stevens's "strong ideology" (his existentialism, which bores Jameson) at the same time that its internal

contradictions impel it toward postmodernism (Stevens's identification of the theory of poetry with the "life of poetry"—a process that
Jameson considers very significant). Though Jameson describes this
essay as a draft from one chapter of a work-in-progress, it is a promising and provocative piece of criticism in its own right.

Among the other, more conventional articles and essays on Stevens, Gabriella Bedetti's "Prosody and 'The Emperor of Ice Cream':
The Elegiac in the Modern Lyric" (*WSJour* 7:96–101) and Roger G.
Salomon's "Wallace Stevens' 'Comedian' and the Quest for Genre"
(*Genre* 17:297–309) are well-reasoned applications of generic analysis to that much-explicated Emperor and to "The Comedian." Bedetti discusses the alliterative meter of "The Emperor" and contrasts
the relationship of the mock-heroic imperatives of its speaker's voice
with the harsh facts of its imagery. She considers the poem an elegiac
lyric which reveals the Modern poet's "nostalgia for the purity of the
lyric voice" and an implicit criticism of the speaker's "absurd assertions." Salomon acknowledges that Stevens considered most traditional literary genres, including comedy and tragedy, as being among
the "many waltzes [which] have ended," but he proposes that a
special exception should be made for the mock heroic, as being a
genre that may give us special insight into "The Comedian." He
points out Stevens's comments on Cervantes in *The Necessary Angel*
and applies them to "The Comedian" as a parodic or imitation quest,
and he also makes some shrewd distinctions between the mock heroic
and the satiric—which he considers a much cruder genre. He argues
that the poem may also be related to *Don Quixote* in that the relationship between Crispin (the "greenhorn") and Stevens's tone ("the
mature realist") may be analogous to the relationship that exists
between Quixote and Sancho Panza, and he concludes with a perceptive hint that Crispin may also have something in common with a
number of other modern mock-heroic questers—Stephen Dedalus,
Mr. Paterson, Herzog, and some of Nabokov's characters.

An essay that perhaps should have been written from a mock-
heroic or ironic viewpoint but was instead presented all too earnestly
is Alan Filreis's "Wallace Stevens and the Crisis of Authority" (*AL*
56:560–78), a biographical study of Stevens's decision to enter law
school in the fall of 1901 after he left Harvard in the spring of that
year. The "crisis," as defined by Filreis, was a conflict between the
values represented by Santayana at Harvard and Stevens's father,
Garrett Stevens, who persuaded his son that he should "earn a living"

instead of devoting his life to poetry. Filreis says very little about Santayana and a great deal about Garrett Stevens as he tries to show that the poet did not follow his advice strictly for pragmatic reasons, but because he shared some of his father's middle-class provincial values. He does this primarily by discussing their correspondence and comparing some of the elder Stevens's literary efforts, which were printed in the *Reading Times*, with Stevens's early prose in the *Harvard Advocate*. From these materials one might easily deduce that Stevens later reacted *against* his father and his platitudes, but Filreis claims that there were similarities between their viewpoints.

In his *Advance on Chaos: The Sanctifying Imagination of Wallace Stevens* (New England)—which was published in 1983 but did not arrive in time to be reviewed last year—David M. LaGuardia proposes that Emerson and William James were Stevens's spiritual American fathers. Like Carl Rapp whose book on Williams was published by the same press (see section *v.*, above), and though he uses this approach in a more sensitive way than does Rapp, LaGuardia has the same predilection for reading 20th-century poems as illustrations for 19th-century ideas. In this case, the idea is American pragmatism which—as defined by LaGuardia—sounds similar to the well-known "American Optimism" which has been produced so often by Americanists as an antidote for "European pessimism": Nietzsche vs. Emerson, Eliot and Spengler vs. the innumerable political and literary editorials that insist that the modern world is a splendid place to be if one lives on the western side of the Atlantic Ocean. "Old truths" may need to be relinquished, but they will be replaced by new, "pluralistic" ones; the gods may disappear, but they will be replaced by the "perceiving self"—that ever-eager candidate for the Highest Office in the Universe—which will make its "own truth." Like Emerson, LaGuardia tends to be systematically optimistic; and where other critics have found pain, misery, and an awareness of limitations in some of Stevens's poems, he usually finds "affirmations"—that may be convincing if one believes in the "heritage of the American self extending directly from Emerson through Thoreau and Whitman to [Stevens] himself," which considers self-reliance an adequate shield against age and death.

Stevens's activities as a constructor of poetic theories and a deconstructor of his own poems have become perennial topics of scholarship. In 1984 the poet in his Deconstructive mode was analyzed competently by Thomas A. Fink in his "Affirmative Play/Playful Affirmation: Stevens's 'An Ordinary Evening in New Haven' " (*WSJour* 7:87–95). Fink reads that poem as a joyous, Nietzschean "affirmation of the play of the world" and its signs. He emphasizes the play of sight in the "Evening," Professor Eucalyptus's quest, and the interdependence of the concepts of stasis and progress. John Fisher's "Wallace Stevens and the Idea of a Central Poetry" (*Criticism* 26: 259–72) is a well-organized, systematic treatment of some of the ideas about poetry and belief that Stevens constructed, particularly in the 1940s. In his efforts to define what Stevens meant by "a central poetry"—a multiform fiction which would replace traditional religious beliefs with an infinite number of simultaneous truths—Fisher first discusses his conception of the kind of language that would be needed to create such a poetry and compares those ideas with Emerson's. Fisher also analyzes a few late poems—primarily "The Hermitage at the Center"—to show how Stevens tried to enact this concept in his poetry. Finally, Stevens the poetic meditator on death and Last Things is presented by Dinnah Pladott in her "The One of the Fictive Music: A Reading of 'Esthetique du Mal' " (*WSJour* 7:67–78). Pladott is primarily concerned with the structure of the poem which she considers "an essentially musical organization" in terms of its repetitions and major motifs about pain, life, and death which are constructed like chords in music.

Rider College

17. Poetry: The 1940s to the Present

Lee Bartlett

James E. B. Breslin, Alan Williamson, and Charles Altieri each offered a book-length study of postwar American poetry this year, and these volumes are certain to remain of use for a good time to come. Breslin's *From Modern to Contemporary* (Chicago) is both a historical study of five "major dissident movements" in our poetry between 1945 and 1965 and a close reading of five representative poets: Ginsberg, Lowell, Levertov, Wright, and O'Hara. Breslin counters Roy Harvey Pearce's sense of "continuity," arguing that instead American poetry is formed through "a series of disruptions, eruptions of creative energy that suddenly alienate poetry from what had come to seem its essential and permanent nature." His first three chapters carefully analyze the radical transformation that took place in the late '50s, marked by the appearances of *Howl*, *Life Studies*, and the *New American Poetry* anthology—all disruptions that renewed American verse once again as "modern," dismantling the rigidified Modernist "orthodoxy." Breslin's next five chapters are devoted to a poet each: Ginsberg's prophetic vision, social protest, and spontaneous prosody; Lowell's alienation from his early success, ending in a renunciation of "rhetorical sublimity and religious myth in a quest to enter a demystified present"; Levertov's numinous, "colloquial, literalistic language" claiming a new "world of fact and movement"; Wright's repudiation of traditional forms in favor of the "deep image" and imaginative "leaping"; and finally, O'Hara's "multiplicity of styles" in which the self paradoxically becomes "at once transparent *and* opaque." Breslin closes his study with a series of fascinating observations on poetry and criticism of our moment, and on the formation of our current canon. A thoroughly satisfying example of historical criticism, *From Modern to Contemporary* is one of the signal volumes in our area this year.

Probably the most interesting question facing us currently is the notion of "voice" and "emotion" in poetry, and this is generally the subject preoccupying both Altieri and Williamson. Altieri's animated *Self and Sensibility in Contemporary American Poetry* (Cambridge) sees the current dominant mode (Galway Kinnell, Charles Wright, and Brad Leithauser are examples) of Romantic "scenic lyricism" to be far too limited as a poetic strategy, arguing that instead poets must offer "possible selves rather than express given ones." In his study Altieri aims both to analyze this mode as well as to "establish shareable criteria for determining who might be our strongest poets" (Creeley, Ashbery, and Rich are in the running here); the chapter on Rich is particularly rewarding. In his *Introspection and Contemporary Poetry* (Harvard), on the other hand, Williamson argues for the dominant mode, sensing that "confessional" work is in fact "the thoroughgoing yet critical self-absorption that finally allows one to stand a little apart from the self." Each of Williamson's chapters examines either a poet's or group of poets' stance toward the "self," most importantly Lowell, Plath, Snyder, Bidart, Kinnell, Wright, Merwin, Strand, and Wakoski. I am finally more drawn to Altieri's call for a shift in attention than to Williamson's analysis of the way things, at least in part, are; perhaps this is due to Altieri's head-on analysis of his "other camp," over against Williamson's mysterious neglect of any number of poets who might challenge his thesis (there is no mention of Oppen or Zukofsky, for example, or Palmer, Silliman, Coolidge, or other "language-centered" writers). In any case, taken together these three new studies provide a significant chart through the mainstream poetic territory in America over the last three decades.

Williamson published a kind of coda to his study this year in "The Values of Contemporary European Poetry" (*APR* 13,i:28–36), wherein he argues that "recent European poetry seems" to him "wiser, more adequate to experience" than much American work, though he cites few contemporary writers (either European or American) and once again seems oblivious to innovative work. Two other poets picking up aspects of Williamson's inquiry in *APR* are Tess Gallagher and Stephen Tapscott. Gallagher's "The Poem As a Reservoir for Grief" (13,iv:7–11) senses, again focusing on the self, that "poems restore our need to *become*," allowing "strictly private access to the grief-handling process." In "The Poem of Trauma" (13,vi:38–47) Tapscott addresses the lyric poem, this time "a short, intensely lyrical, compact, almost seamless poem of memory, a poem that scrupulously depicts a single scene . . . with little overt meditation or mediation or interpretation of that single image." Poems written, that is, currently by Jorie Graham and Stephen Dobyns which have more in common with Marianne Moore and Thomas Hardy than Ezra Pound.

At the conclusion of his *A Usable Past* Paul Mariani gathers nine occasional essays on contemporary poets including Robert Penn Warren, Robert Creeley, John Berryman, Robert Pack, and Thomas Merton. Of these, the pieces on Creeley (reprinted from *Boundary 2's* special Creeley issue) and Berryman (a reading of "Eleven Addresses to the Lord") are the most fully realized, though Mariani is always a sensitive reader and each essay has something to offer. Gilbert Sorrentino's *Something Said* (North Point) collects his essays, notes, and reviews of the past two decades on Jack Spicer, Louis Zukofsky, Kenneth Rexroth, Ron Loewinsohn, Paul Blackburn, George Oppen, and others. Highly recommended. Also recommended is Richard Jones's *Poetry and Politics* (Morrow), a collection of 28 engaged essays on social issues by poets ranging from W. H. Auden, T. S. Eliot, and Muriel Rukeyser to Galway Kinnell, Adrienne Rich, and June Jordan.

Two British collections are also of interest this year. R. W. Butterfield edited *Modern American Poetry* (Vision Press), a gathering of essays on poets ranging from Whitman and Dickinson to the present. Five pieces of note are Andrew Crozier's "Inaugural and Valedictory: The Early Poetry of George Oppen" (pp. 142—57), Graham Clarke's "The Poet as Archaeologist: Charles Olson's Letters of Origin" (pp. 158–72), "J. V. Cunningham's Roman Voices" by Jack Hill, Gabriel Pearson's "*For Lizzie and Harriet:* Robert Lowell's Domestic Apocalypse" (pp. 187–203), and Clive Meachen's "Robert Duncan: 'To Complete his Mind'" (pp. 204–17). Donald Wesling is the only American contributor to the book, and his "The Poetry of Edward Dorn" (pp. 218–34) is a good introductory essay, covering theory, politics, voice, *Slinger*, and recent work. Dorn is also a subject of a chapter in David Trotter's *The Making of the Reader* (Macmillan), along with John Ashbery and Frank O'Hara, as "Les blancs debarquent." Both books are worth uncovering, for their well-developed readings as well as the British perspective.

The *Chicago Review* (34,ii) offers four essays on "Some Things to Think About Poetry and Politics," all of which will be of interest to readers of this chapter: Anthony Libby, "Conceptual Space: The Politics of Modernism" (pp. 11–26); Gerald L. Bruns, "Language and Power" (pp. 27–43); Hugh Kenner, "The Making of the Modernist Canon" (pp. 49–61); and Marjorie Perloff, "Violence and Precision:

The Manifesto as Art Form" (pp. 62–74). Further, in "Dispersions and Freedom: The Situation of Contemporary Poetry" in (*VQR* 60: 645–60), Robert Schultz remarks flatly that "the current *impossibility* of an avant-garde is one of the most interesting characteristics of our moment" in that "there is no current dogma or force of fashion against which it might define itself," an assertion that both Altieri and Williamson might well find rather charming.

Albert Cook attempts to revitalize the discussion of surrealism in his "Surrealism and Surrealisms" (*APR* 13,iv:29–39) this year, as he traces the various possibilities of definition and the ways in which they have been transformed through the last decades. Good discussion of Lowell, Wright, René Char, and the Surrealist image.

As Breslin points out, Donald Allen's anthology *The New American Poetry*, published in 1960, was of no small importance to the development of our poetry over the last two decades, and in "A History of American Poetry Anthologies" (*Canons*, ed. Robert Von Hallberg; Chicago), Alan Golding provides a much-needed and fascinating guide to the poetics and politics of anthology-making. He is especially good in his discussion of *The Norton Anthology of Poetry*, whose "surface diversity hides a deeper homogeneity" necessary to maintain its "teachability." Two anthologies of note appearing this year are Philip Dow's *19 New American Poets of the Golden Gate* (Harcourt) and *That's What She Said: Contemporary Poetry and Fiction by Native American Women* (Indiana), ed. Rayna Green. Dow's book is a good value, with almost 500 pages of poetry and commentary by poets ranging from Jack Gilbert to Gary Soto, though a few of these poets are hardly "new," while others can be identified only tangentially with the Bay Area. Green's volume provides a service in that it makes easily available work by such poets as Paula Gunn Allen, Linda Hogan, Joy Harjo, and Carol Lee Sanchez, though it seems to me that generally much of the work collected here is a bit predictable.

Prose writings and interviews by poets themselves continue to offer some of our best commentary. Joe David Bellamy's *American Poetry Observed: Poets on Their Work* (Illinois) collects 26 interviews by various hands published more or less within the last decade, out of the nearly 250 interviews he read through, which he considers classic. Most of the figures included here would fit Williamson's paradigm rather than Altieri's (Marvin Bell, Elizabeth Bishop, Galway Kinnell, William Stafford and James Wright, for example);

women poets are well represented, with seven entries. My only quarrels would be with the paucity of the West Coast representation, and more importantly the exclusion of any poets considered even vaguely "experimental" beyond John Ashbery. The same two charges might be leveled at *Epoch's* symposium, "Ecstatic Occasions, Expedient Forms" (33:31–97), introduced by David Lehman, in which 28 poets contribute brief statements meant to both elucidate their particular practice and further the discussion of form.

"Experimental" work and its attendant complexities are the focus, however, of *Writing/Talks* (So. Ill.), an exciting volume of 16 talks given in the Bay Area between 1980 and 1983 by many of those writers we have come to call "language poets." Of particular interest are Charles Bernstein on "Characterization" (pp. 7–30), Rae Armantrout on "Poetic Silence" (pp. 31–47), Barrett Watten on "Olson in Language: Part II" (pp. 157–65), Ron Silliman on "Spicer's Language" (pp. 166–91), Michael Palmer on "Autobiography, Memory, and Mechanisms of Concealment" (pp. 207–29), and Lyn Hejinian on "The Rejection of Closure" (pp. 270–91). While a number of these pieces are perhaps not as closely developed as they might be were they written rather than spoken, at every turn they are engaging. Further, Barrett Watten's "The Politics of Poetry: L-A-N-G-U-A-G-E and Method" (*AmerP* 2,i:69–77) discusses (though at times rather obliquely) the strategies of the "language project." Certainly, a number of these writers have been knocking on our collective critical door for some time now, and their rapping is growing each year more difficult to ignore.

The Collected Prose of Carl Rakosi (Orono, Me.: National Poetry Foundation) draws together Rakosi's seven prose pieces, followed by Burton Hatlen's afterword, "Carl Rakosi and the Re-Invention of the Epigram" (pp. 125–44), which usefully discusses the poet's relationship to other Objectivists as well as the dominance of the epigram in his work. Two important volumes I missed last year are James Dickey's *Night Hurdling* (Bruccoli Clark) and John Logan's *A Ballet for the Ear* (Michigan). The Dickey volume contains essays, conversations, and addresses, as well as a few new poems, and must be regarded (with the inclusion of his difficult-to-obtain piece on Pound and his "Firing Line" interview) an important collection. Logan's interviews, essays, and reviews are uniformly insightful and entertaining, another first-rate volume in Donald Hall's Poets on Poetry series.

Two other substantial volumes appearing in the series this year are Donald Justice's *Platonic Scripts* and Robert Hayden's *Collected Prose* (ed. Frederick Glaysher, with a foreword by William Meredith). Finally Robert Hass collects his various "prose on poetry" in *Twentieth Century Pleasures* (Ecco). Writing on poets ranging from Lowell and Wright to Rilke, Hass has in fact, it appears, been writing these occasional pieces to a larger purpose, working out "the difficult and specific human possibilities of the lyric poem."

In "Lyric Narration: The Chameleon Poet" (*HudR* 37:54–70), Robert Pack addresses the notion of persona, re-emphasizing that "the only criterion that matters in artistic choices is what convinces the reader," over against what "really happened." Gary Snyder's "Notes on the Beat Generation" and "The New Wind" (*AmerP* 2,i: 44–51) print in English two pieces previously published in Japanese in 1960 in order to, according to Snyder, "introduce the poetry and cultural phenomena of the beat generation to the Japanese intelligentsia." I recorded and edited two talks by James Laughlin into "For the Record: On New Directions & Others" (*AmerP* 1,iii:47–61), which includes reminiscences of Delmore Schwartz, Kenneth Rexroth, and Denise Levertov.

Brad Morrow's *Conjunctions* (No. 6) runs a special symposium called "Toward a Human Poetics," a selection "from the presentations made at a three-day gathering in March 1983" at the University of Southern California which attempted "to take the discussion of ethnopoetics beyond its earlier, restricted definitions." Jerome Rothenberg's "Ethnopoetics & (Human) Poetics" (pp. 232–40); Hugh Kenner's "The Invention of the 'Other'" (pp. 241–45); Barbara Tedlock's "The Beautiful and the Dangerous Zuni Ritual and Cosmology as an Aesthetic System" (pp. 246–65); Nathaniel Tarn's important discussion of the relationship between anthropology and poetry, "Dr. Jekyll, the Anthropologist, Emerges and Marches into the Notebook of Mr. Hyde, the Poet" (pp. 266–81); James Clifford's "Interrupting the Whole" (pp. 282–95); Nathaniel Mackey's "On Edge" (pp. 296–300); and Edmund Jabes's "From the Book of Books to the Books of the Book" (pp. 301–03) should be of interest to anyone interested in literary studies, and serve as fine additions to facets of the art bypassed by Breslin, Altieri, and Williamson in their studies.

Finally, I must of course note the publication of the revised edition of Hyatt H. Waggoner's classic *American Poets: From the Puritans to the Present* (LSU). The seventh section of Waggoner's historical study, "After Modernism," includes much new material on many important figures, including Theodore Roethke, Robert Duncan, James Dickey, Galway Kinnell, Robert Bly, Denise Levertov, and John Ashbery. Interestingly, of all the contemporary poets he covers, Waggoner ends with a "postscript" suggesting that Levertov, Dickey, and Stanley Kunitz will emerge as very major figures of our time.

i. The Middle Generation

a. **Elizabeth Bishop.** Last year Elizabeth Bishop's *Complete Poems* appeared to much regard, and this year, perhaps because of that volume, she comes close to outstripping her contemporaries in the garnering of attention. *The Collected Prose* (Farrar), ed. Robert Giroux, draws together the poet's autobiographical essays and stories; her publisher Giroux provides a mix of biography and bibliography in his introduction, setting the context. Anne M. Greenhalgh's 900-plus-page *A Concordance to Elizabeth Bishop's Poetry* (Garland) takes as its base the *Complete Poems*, omitting only translations; a useful volume, though at over a hundred dollars probably destined solely for library shelves.

A special Bishop symposium in *Field* (31:7–45) draws together eight short essays on her work, mostly explications of single poems, by Sandra McPherson, Elizabeth Spires, Marianne Boruch, Sherod Santos, David Walker, Alberta Turner, J. D. McClatchy, and Jean Valentine. In "Elizabeth Bishop: Poet Without Myth" (*VQR* 60: 255–75), Nathan A. Scott sees the poet's primary strength as the absence of any particular metaphysical hobby-horse, but rather the writing of a poetry of "expedition" without "sentimental pastoralism." In David Bromwich's "Elizabeth Bishop's Dream Houses" (*Raritan* 6,i:77–94), Bishop finds a home, and that home is "art." Bromwich reads a number of the poems rather closely, remarking interestingly that "sexuality is the most elusive feature of Bishop's temperament." Mutlu Konuk Blasing's " '*Mont D'Espoir* or Mount Despair': The Re-Verses of Elizabeth Bishop" (*ConL* 25:341–53) concludes that Bishop reverses the strategy of other post-Modernists—here, "it is not art that is reduced to experience, but experience that tends to be reduced to art." Finally, Charles Sanders discusses "Arrival at Santos" in "Elizabeth Bishop's 'Finger Play' " in *Brazil* (*NMAL* 8:Item 3).

By far the most important Bishop criticism to appear this year, though, and in fact probably the most useful single volume on her life and work to date, is *Elizabeth Bishop and Her Art*, ed. Lloyd Schwartz and Sybil P. Estess, a collection in Michigan's new Under Discussion series. Perhaps at some risk I'll admit that I've never been much of a Bishop fan, though if I were this book certainly would hold a secure place alongside her poems and prose on my shelf. Besides a brief foreword by Harold Bloom, the volume collects substantial essays (some previously published, some new) by Helen Vendler, David Kalstone, Robert Pinsky, David Lehman, Penelope Laurans, Alan Williamson, Bonnie Costello, Lloyd Schwartz, and Willard Spiegelman; next are 30 selections from reviews and interviews, as well as poems and jacket blurbs, by writers ranging from Lowell and Jarrell to Mark Strand and Mary McCarthy; finally, a generous gathering of Bishop's own notes, reviews, statements, and interviews rounds out the book, which closes with a concise primary and secondary bibliography.

b. **Robert Lowell, John Berryman, Louise Bogan, Randall Jarrell, Theodore Roethke, Karl Shapiro.** Norman Procopiow's *Robert Lowell: The Poet and His Critics* (ALA) is, like other volumes in the Poet and His Critics series, a book-length study of the mass of criticism that has appeared on Lowell's work over the last 40 years. Procopiow has scrupulously read through what must be yards of writing to synthesize a book-by-book evaluation of critical reaction. Without doubt, a central source for any subsequent studies.

In "'I fish until the Clouds turn blue': Robert Lowell's Late Poetry" (*PLL* 20:312–25), John Paul Russo sees Lowell's final decade as dividing into two phases—the first (*Notebook*) of a "relatively open idiom," the second (*Day By Day*) a return "to the condensed forms of much earlier verse . . . with an energy and license of tone," though both phases "suggest close and serial inspection, not grand perspectives."

In *The Stock of Available Reality* (Bucknell) James D. Bloom examines the relationship between R. P. Blackmur and John Berryman, the poet who "provides the most striking example of the power exerted by the criticism of Blackmur." A thorough and fascinating study using an approach not often taken currently, this volume, especially in its extended treatment of Blackmur's influence on *The Dream Songs*, must stand beside John Haffenden and Joel Conarroe's good groundwork on the poet. Ronald Wallace's *God Be With the*

Clown devotes a chapter to "John Berryman: Me, Wag." (pp. 171–201), in which he argues that Berryman's long poem is "a kind of parody of 'Song of Myself.'" John Pikoulis briefly draws attention to Berryman's uncollected "Elegy, For Alun Lewis" in *AL* (56:100–01). In "John Berryman: The Poetics of Martyrdom" (*APR* 13,ii:7–12), Michael Heffernan deals with the nagging question of "order, unity, wholeness" in *The Dream Songs;* he suggests that the poem represents "an open paradigm of grief and loss, fragmentation, and spiritual collapse" which Berryman "was obliged to transcend both as a person and a poet." Mary Lynn Broe also turns to Berryman this year in "White Man in the Woodpile: John Berryman's Burnt Cork Poetic" (*AmerP* 1,ii:35–48), an essay that attempts to de-emphasize the poet's "confessionalism" in favor of Henry's "*participatory* model of reality," with particular reference to humor and blackface.

The same issue of *AmerP* continues with Robert Miklitsch's "The Critic as Poet, Poet as Critic: Randall Jarrell, Deconstruction, and 'Dirty Silence'" (pp. 35–48), which sets the poet's "persuasively" humane criticism against contemporary Derridean theory in an examination of Stanley Plumly's sense of "Dirty Silence." In "Randall Jarrell: The Paintings in the Poems" (*SoR* 20:300–315), Jeffrey Meyers argues that following the example of Auden, Jarrell "was preeminent among his contemporaries in his use of aesthetic analogies . . . an intensely visual poet." According to Meyers, Jarrell was particularly attracted to northern European painters, and this essay looks at the influence of work by Albrecht Dürer, Georges de la Tour, and Hugo van der Goes. Richard J. Calhoun gives over an issue of *South Carolina Review* (17,i) to a "Seventieth Birthday Tribute" to Randall Jarrell. Following the editor's brief introduction (pp. 50–51) in which he remembers three meetings with the poet, George S. Lensing discusses Jarrell's modernism (pp. 52–60), concentrating primarily on the early poetry; Ronald Moran's "Randall Jarrell as Critic of Criticism" (pp. 60–65) traces the poet's insistence on the "reader/critic," while in "Randall Jarrell and Angels" (pp. 65–71) Sister Bernetta Quinn, O.S.F., reads through a number of poems looking at the poet's "search for immortality"; Suzanne Ferguson's "Narrative and Narrators in the Poetry of Randall Jarrell" (pp. 72–82) argues that the narrative has been central to the poet's project from the start, while poet David Bottoms closes with "The Messy Humanity of Randall Jarrell: His Poetry in the Eighties" (pp. 82–95) in which he usefully discusses his own relationship to the Jarrell corpus, and elicits comments from Dave Smith, Richard Tillinghast, Diane Ackerman, Leon Stokesbury, Edward Hirsch, David St. John, and Robert Hass.

Martha Collins's *Critical Essays on Louise Bogan* (Hall) brings together 34 essays and reviews (most previously published, a few written especially for this volume) by such critics and poets as Yvor Winters, Kenneth Rexroth, Malcolm Cowley, Theodore Roethke, and Diane Wood Middlebrook. Collins introduces her collection with a solid essay tracing the course of Bogan criticism from her first book, published in 1923, arguing convincingly that while the poet has never drawn a wide general readership, other writers have always found much of value in her "concentrated" craft.

Work on Roethke was limited this year to a few essays. Thomas Gardner's " 'North American Sequence': Theodore Roethke and the Contemporary American Long Poem" (*ELWIU* 11:237–55) argues that the poem is, like Duncan's *Passages*, Kinnell's *Book of Nightmares*, Lowell's *History*, and other American long poems, a "self-portrait," in that like each of these poems it attempts to represent "the poet's fluid inner world." In this sense, "North American Sequence" takes "Song of Myself" as a direct model.

Finally, Karl Shapiro publishes two excerpts from his in-progress "Scratchings: a Study of the Making of a Poet" (*TriQ* 60:61–82); the second, dealing with events of 1950, is a fascinating reminiscence of Shapiro's editing of *Poetry*.

ii. A Kind of Field

a. **George Oppen, Charles Reznikoff, Louis Zukofsky.** George Oppen died 7 July, after a long life of political compassion and dedicated art. As if a kind of memorial, a number of essays appeared on this still greatly undervalued poet this year. *Sagetrieb* (3,i:113–28) collects four tributes to Oppen in "A Sheaf for George Oppen, at 75," all given at a special San Francisco gathering in honor of the poet in 1983, by Rachel Blau DuPlessis, Burton Hatlen, Jerome Rothenberg, and David McAleavey. The same issue gives us Kevin Oderman's attempt to bring Oppen's achievement into focus with "Earth and Awe: The One Poetry of George Oppen" (pp. 63–73), a discussion of his "disjunctive poetics."

Elanor Berry's interesting linguistic analysis, "Language Made Fluid: The Grammetrics of George Oppen's Recent Poetry" (*ConL*

25:305–22) sees the characteristics of the poet's newer work to include use of fragments, absence of conventional punctuation, and enjambment, as the poems "cease in the seventies to be palpable as made objects." In "The Psalmic Poetics of George Oppen" (*Poesis* 6,i:40–50), John Martone suggests that Oppen "stands alone in his consciously hymnic and creational concept of poetic language," a language that has its origins in ancient Hebraic poetry. Elanor Berry again examines Oppen this year, this time outlining the "Williams-Oppen Connection" (*Sagetrieb* 3,ii:99–116). In her clearly written piece she finds similarities in theme, versification, and language in the work of both poets.

Milton Hindus has done much to make Charles Reznikoff's texts available, and here he continues at the very high standard of the National Poetry Foundation's Man and Poet series with *Charles Reznikoff*. The point of the series, with volumes on Zukofsky, Bunting, Oppen, Sarton, and Williams, is, as Hindus notes in his preface, to bring "to wider attention a limited number of *real* American poets in our century" who have been critically neglected. Like the other volumes, this book is far too rich a resource to do justice to here. The volume collects 34 essays, memoirs, and interviews on various aspects of Reznikoff's poetry and prose—its "modernity," its "tradition," objectivism, Reznikoff's relation to the Holocaust, his sources, his sense of the epic, *The Manner Music*, juvenilia, and so on—by such writers and critics as Mary Oppen, David Ignatow, Paul Auster, Allen Ginsberg, Michael Heller, L. S. Dembo, Linda W. Wagner, Eric Honberger, Hindus, and Reznikoff himself. Linda Simon's "An Annotated Bibliography of Works About Charles Reznikoff: 1920–1983" and a detailed index close this superb collection, which along with Hindus's early monograph on Reznikoff are fine tributes to a life's work.

"The small and common words that build Reznikoff's tremendous poems will be with me, I think, in my last moments," Oppen wrote in 1979 of his close friend. In *Sagetrieb* 3,iii, Kathryn Shevelow assembles a portfolio of work by and about the two poets from holdings of the University of California, San Diego's Archive for New Poetry. Work includes Reinhold Schiffer's interview with Oppen conducted in 1975, Oppen's "statement on poetics," a "memorial broadcast" for Reznikoff with Oppen and his wife, Mary, and a transcript of comments on his poetry by Reznikoff during a 1974 reading at SUNY Buffalo. Tom Sharp closes the sheaf with "The Objectivists' Publications," a detailed bibliographic history.

In his important "Art And/As Labor: Some Dialectical Patterns in 'A'–1 Through 'A'–10" (*ConL* 25:205–34), Burton Hatlen attempts to expand upon Barry Ahearn's sense of the dialectical patterns that appear throughout Zukofsky's long poem. Specifically, Hatlen argues that the first ten sections of *A* represent "a sustained effort to write, within a poetic mode that derives from Pound, a democratic and socialist response" to Pound's elitist writing of the '30s, "within an explicitly Marxist conception of labor." Cid Corman also looks at *A* in "'A'–2: Getting On With It" (*Sagetrieb* 3,iii:107–14) as "an argument of what poetry is."

b. **Charles Olson, Robert Creeley, Denise Levertov, Muriel Rukeyser.** Olson scholarship went into a bit of a holding pattern this year. In *Sulfur* (11:141–57), George Butterick presents "The Collected Poems of Charles Olson: 1940–49," all previously unpublished. In the same issue, Butterick's fine "Editing Postmodern Texts" (pp. 113–40) draws on his substantial experience working with the Olson materials to describe the myriad problems facing any contemporary editing enterprise. Robert Hogg's "Okeanos Rages" (*Sagetrieb* 3,i:89–104) offers a wonderfully close reading of "*Maximus, at the Harbor*," the "culmination of the process on individuation which began in 'Maximus, From Dogtown—I.'" Shelly Wong's "Unfinished Business: The Work of 'Tyrian Businesses'" (*Sagetrieb* 3,iii:91–106) also looks at Olson's *Maximus*, arguing that the poet's primary compositional concern is the search for a resolution to the dichotomy between the private and the public.

Robert Creeley is well served by yet another of Orono's good projects this year. All sorts of topics are covered in *Robert Creeley: The Poet's Workshop* (Nat. Poetry Foundation), ed. Carroll F. Terrell: Robert Basil's "Creeley Teaches in Buffalo," Pancho Savery's "'The Character of the Speech': 56 Things for Robert Creeley," an interview by Terrell, Brian Conniff's "The Lyricism of This World," William Sylvester's discussion of Marisol and *Presences*, a "Year by Year Bibliography of Robert Creeley" by Timothy Murray and Stephen Boardway, and other features mark this advance in Creeley scholarship.

Dirk Stratton's "If To Is: Robert Creeley's 'If You'" (*Sagetrieb* 3,i:105–109) argues that this poem discovers for Creeley what the poet "can no longer do": "separate his entry from the actual world, or use it to create another world." In "Exploring the Human Community: The Poetry of Denise Levertov and Muriel Rukeyser" (*Sagetrieb* 3, iii:51–61), Harry Martin reads these two poets as attempting to explore in their work the necessity "of the relation I:world."

c. Nathaniel Tarn, Theodore Enslin, Robert Kelly, Clayton Eshleman. Nathaniel Tarn, Theodore Enslin, Robert Kelly, and Clayton Eshleman are often regarded as "outsiders," fitting really into no particular "movement" or "school." However, it seems to me that they can be discussed with a certain amount of comfort in this section. Though born in Paris and educated in England, Tarn considers himself an American, and certainly an American writer, a subject he discusses at length in "Child as Father to Man in the American Universe" (*AmerP* 1, ii:67–85). In this major piece, an intellectual biography of sorts, the poet ranges in his discussion from influences to the nature of the post-Modern, always coming back to what it means to be an American writer. In "America as Desire(d): Nathaniel Tarn's Poetry of the Outsider as Insider" (*AmerP* 2,i:13–35), Doris Sommer discusses the poet's escape from the anxiety of influence, as he moves from a private to more public poetry, and an acceptance of "the beautiful contradictions" in both his life and his art.

Like Tarn, Theodore Enslin is another poet who has been working quietly for many years (he has published over 50 books and chapbooks and at least three major long poems), continually drawing the high regard of other poets, though mysteriously (like Tarn and Robert Kelly) little commentary save for the special issue of *Truck* (No. 20) which in 1978 was devoted to his work. In "Chapters" (*AmerP* 2,i:78–89), Enslin discusses his background and influences, with particular attention given to music, *Origin,* and his nonpolitical stance.

A large part of *Credences* 3,i is devoted to Robert Kelly this year. Jed Rasula's "The Library Record: Robert Kelly: A Checklist" (pp. 91–124) provides a much-needed bibliography for the poet through 1984; while not descriptive, some facts concerning publication of primary works are given, as well as a list of 249 periodical contributions. Rasula follows with "Ten Different Fruits on One Different Tree: Reading Robert Kelly" (pp. 127–75), a wealth of information on the tangled publication history of Kelly's work. For the new reader, Rasula argues against "a retroactive reading based on recent titles" in favor of examination of Kelly's long poem *The Loom;* further, Rasula provides a detailed outline of the writer's "poetics of sequence." April Hublinger's "Robert Kelly's 'The Sound': Notes To-

ward a Reading" (pp. 176–88) treats the poem as a "work which
concerns itself primarily with the nature and process of definition . . .
communication."

Poet, translator, and editor, Clayton Eshleman has been as prolific as Enslin, and in the first essay in her Neglected Poets series
(*AmerP* 1,iii:38–46), "The Attempt to Break an Old Mold—Visionary
Poetry of Clayton Eshleman," Diane Wakoski takes the poet's *Coils*
to "ground" his work in the tradition of Whitman, dominated by a
Jungian vision "speaking of the taboo which is our animal origin." In
the same issue, Eshleman comments on his sense of "Translations as
Transformational Reading" (pp. 68–84), drawing on his experience
working with texts by Cesar Vallejo, Aimé Césaire, and Antonin
Artaud.

iii. The Autochthonic Spirit

a. **Allen Ginsberg.**   Obviously, the most important event for this
section this year, and perhaps the most important event in our area
as a whole, is the appearance of Allen Ginsberg's *Collected Poems,
1947–1980* (Harper), over 800 pages showing the full range of Ginsberg's great strengths and his glaring weaknesses. Following a brief
preface by the poet, the volume presents all of Ginsberg's previously
published books and chapbooks (and some previously unpublished
work) arranged "in straight chronological order to compose an autobiography." The book closes with a wealth of interesting material,
including extensive notes and William Carlos Williams's introductions to *Empty Mirror* and *Howl*. Whether or not Ginsberg finally
survives as the major poet of our age, his great artistic and cultural
influence over the last three decades cannot be denied, and here in
one book we have it *all*.

As a kind of companion volume to the *Collected Poems*, Donald
Hall's new Under Discussion series offers *On the Poetry of Allen Ginsberg* (Michigan), ed. Lewis Hyde. This compendium of close to a
hundred reviews, letters, essays, and documents is extremely well
chosen from the vast quantity of available material. Every major
book gets attention (both *Howl* and *Kaddish* rate extended commentary from Richard Eberhart, M. L. Rosenthal, Kenneth Rexroth, Robert Bly, Louis Simpson, and many others), and in his
introduction Hyde interestingly points out the gaps in Ginsberg
scholarship. A first-rate collection.

Paul Portuges, who is currently writing Ginsberg's biography, continues to work out his sense of the poet's visionary stance in "Allen Ginsberg's Visions and the Growth of His Poetics of Prophecy" (*Poetic Prophecy*). Here Portuges summarizes Ginsberg's various "visitations," commenting on the role of the Bible and Christopher Smart in the writing of *Howl*. John H. Johnston pairs Ginsberg with W. H. Auden, arguing that "perhaps no other two poets of the mid-twentieth century represent so curious or so radical an opposition, or one so indicative of the basic alternatives that confront the writer at a time when the modern metropolis seems to have reached a critical point in its growth cycle," in *The Poet and the City: A Study of Urban Perspectives* (Georgia).

b. **Kenneth Rexroth, Gary Snyder, Robert Duncan, William Everson, Kenneth Patchen, Michael McClure.** Donald Guttierrez offers a reading of Kenneth Rexroth's "Falling Leaves and Early Snows" in "Keeping an Eye on Nature" (*AmerP* 1,ii:60–64), finding in it the de-emphasis of "human importance." Immediately following, I present a two-page "Selected Bibliography of Poetics/Modern (1947)," a reading list Rexroth compiled for one of his Portreo Hill discussion groups, which was discovered among uncatalogued William Everson papers at the Clark Memorial Library.

Thomas Parkinson's "The Poetry of Gary Snyder" (*Sagetrieb* 3, i:49–61) is a clearly written exposition of Snyder's major themes and stylistic structures from *Riprap* to *Regarding Wave*. In "Gary Snyder Riprapping in Yosemite, 1955" (*AmerP* 2,i:52–59), David Robertson quotes from an unpublished interview with the poet centering on his experiences in the High Sierra and in Yosemite toward an examination of Snyder's first collection. Patrick D. Murphy's "Two Different Paths in the Quest for Place: Gary Snyder and Wendell Berry" (*AmerP* 2,i:60–68) argues for the distinction between these two poets—while both "write in strident opposition to modern civilization's misuse of the earth," they differ radically in their conceptions of the Fall.

In "The True Epithalamium" (*Sagetrieb* 3, i:77–88) Michael Heller reads Robert Duncan's "A Poem Beginning with a Line from Pindar" as a "mosaic" of myth and reality "enfolded." Good analysis of both Duncan's sources and his punning. Diane Wakoski's second piece in her Neglected Poets series focuses on "William Everson & 'Bad Taste'" (*AmerP* 2,i:36–43); here she argues for Everson's place in the central American tradition of the Whitmanic "rejoicing in the self," with emphasis on the poet's later verse.

Kenneth Patchen is another of our poets who consistently suffers from critical neglect. Raymond Nelson's *Kenneth Patchen and American Mysticism* (N.C.) may bring more critics to the poet's work, as it attempts to outline a sense of an American mysticism, placing Patchen squarely in that line. According to Nelson, our poetic mysticism emphasizes innocence, the hero, "personalism," open form, and sexual frankness, all characteristics of Patchen's work, as other commentators have noticed. Here, Nelson deals with the Patchen corpus in terms of three phases: "illumination (or conversion), purgation, and union." Further, the study covers Patchen's sense of "antiliterature," his movement toward "organicism," and his political conscience. A modest, concise, and useful examination.

Last, *Line* (4:4–43), published in Burnaby, B.C., presents a selection from the McClure archive at Simon Fraser University, including "Pocket Notebook Poems" drawn by Barry Maxwell from the poet's notebooks kept between 1969 and 1979, as well as selections from two other longer poems.

iv. Dream of a Common Language

Estella Lauter's *Women as Mythmakers: Poetry and Visual Art by Twentieth-Century Women* (Indiana) devotes chapters to Anne Sexton, Diane Wakoski, and a more general discussion of the relationship of Susan Griffin's *Woman and Nature* to contemporary women's poetry. In the first part of her study, Lauter examines a number of individual myths, seeing Sexton's "radical discontent" as produced by a sense of her "exile from God" which might be bridged only through an archetypal act of "soul-making," Wakoski as an intensely nature-oriented (as opposed to confessional) poet, one who "while eschewing the politics of feminism, nonetheless gives access to processes that may enable a collective re-visioning of relationships between women and nature." In the second section of the volume, Lauter concludes that for women poets and artists of the past decade "the mythic issue is no longer the nature of self or the relationship of self and nature, but the female's responsibility to culture." A well-argued study, especially interesting as a corrective to the focus of Alan Williamson's book.

In *A Separate Vision: Isolation in Contemporary Women's Poetry* (LSU), Deborah Pope also looks at the self, narrowing the focus to four representative women poets: Louise Bogan, Maxine Kumin, Denise Levertov, and Adrienne Rich, devoting a chapter to each. This examination is of less interest than Lauter's (or Altieri's or Breslin's) in that Pope seems to have no underlying theme linking her four poets, save that each suffers from isolation, a fact probably true of most artists. Further, while her opening sentence announces both that one of the most important facets of our literature is the expression of a "female consciousness" and that "women's literature is perhaps the major force in the contemporary period" (two observations which, it seems to me, ring more than partially true) her argument outlining four strategies—victimization, personalization, split-self, and validation—somehow doesn't seem to provide a shared context. Still, the individual readings are an interesting mix of criticism and biography, and the chapters on Bogan and Kumin (two rather neglected figures) can be recommended.

In "What Are Patterns For?: Anger and Polarization in Women's Poetry" (*FSt* 10:485–503) Alicia Ostriker examines a similar question. She discusses Margaret Atwood's *Power Politics*, Diane Wakoski's *George Washington Poems*, and Anne Sexton's "The Jesus Papers" in an attempt to "suggest that anger is both necessary to the woman poet and inadequate as a solution to her predicament." Each sequence, she argues, sees "the use of the sexes as a power struggle insusceptible of resolution," the "authority" of the poet "employed as a weapon" and thus self-defeating, and surrealism as indicative of "psychic pain."

Another of Michigan's Under Discussion collections this year is devoted to Adrienne Rich. In *Reading Adrienne Rich: Reviews and Re-Visions, 1951–81*, editor Jane Roberta Cooper opens with a series of essays by Judith McDaniel, Claire Keyes, Marianne Whelchel, Adrian Oktenberg, Joanne Feit Diehl, Jane Vanderbosch, Gertrude Reif Hughes, Wendy Martin, and Susan Stanford Friedman on the poetry, followed by a number of reviews of the verse and the prose, and closing with a thorough primary and secondary bibliography. Like the Ginsberg and Bishop volumes in the series, a benchmark (though here the editor's seemingly unrelenting stress on Rich's feminism seems rather unnecessarily restrictive). In "The Friction of the Mind: The Early Poetry of Adrienne Rich" (*MassR* 25:142–60)

Mary Slowik reads Rich as a "feminist poet who has persistently explored her own anger with a sensitivity and discipline" that molds it "into a creative rather than destructive emotion." In "Dickinson and Rich: Toward a Theory of Female Poetic Influence" (*AL* 56:541–59), Betsy Erkkila argues that the relationship between these two poets "provides a suggestive model of the pattern of separation, return, and renewal" which seems endemic to American women poets. An important essay both on Rich and the more general notion of influence.

A good 1983 study, *Plath's Incarnations: Women and the Creative Process* (Michigan), by Lynda K. Bundtzen, arrived too late to be included in last year's chapter. Here, Bundtzen continues the more general ongoing project of rescuing Sylvia Plath from her role as tortured suicide in favor of an expanded sense of her achievement. Bundtzen is informed by Sandra Gilbert and Susan Gubar's "reformation of the Bloomian poetics," though rather than regarding the poet as a "madwoman in the attic," throughout her argument she chooses instead to see Plath's tension "replaced by the earth mother and Lady Lazarus . . . her early and late archetypes for feminine creativity." A good mix of close reading of both the poetry and the prose, biography, and psychological awareness, *Plath's Incarnations* convinces that "rather than a confessional stance, we confront in Plath's poetry a world shaped by a principle of malign immanence, complicated by ambivalence, and filtered through a distinctly feminine sensibility."

Linda W. Wagner's useful *Critical Essays by Sylvia Plath* (Hall) opens with the editor's clear analysis of the course of criticism over the last few decades on a poet she ventures "changed the direction of contemporary poetry." Wagner collects 19 reviews of individual volumes by such critics as M. L. Rosenthal and William H. Pritchard, followed by 11 essays on numerous aspects of Plath's craft. Essays appearing for the first time include Melody Zajdel's "Apprenticed in a Bible of Dreams: Sylvia Plath's Short Stories" (pp. 182–93); Roberta Mazzenti's "Plath in Italy" (pp. 193–204), a discussion of the poet's Italian translations and her critical reputation there; and Sandra Gilbert's "In Yeats' House: The Death and Resurrection of Sylvia Plath" (pp. 204–22), a fascinating discussion both of the poet's internal dialogue and the implications of her "historical awareness." Marjorie Perloff discusses "The Two Ariels: The (Re)making of the Sylvia Plath Canon" (*APR* 13,vi:10–18) tracing the critical controversy surrounding Ted Hughes's editing of *Ariel* and *The Collected Poems*. This closely argued piece, which examines major shifts of emphasis between "Ariel 1" and "Ariel 2," is an important contribution to Plath studies.

Perloff gives us a second interesting piece in "The Case of Amy Clampitt: A Reading of 'Imago'" (*Sulfur* 10:169–78), an essay that criticizes a much-praised recent poem as an example of the "neo–New Critical" yearning "for a logocentric universe." In "The Journal as Source and Method for Feminist Art: The Example of Kathleen Fraser" (*Frontiers* 8,i:16–20), Suzanne Juhasz examines Fraser's bringing of the "private moment" into the "public world" of her poetry, using the journal (a device with which women have "a traditional affinity") as paradigm.

Source is also of interest to Mary Carruthers this year, as in "Adrienne Rich's 'Sources'" (*River Styx* 15:69–74) she explores that poem as an example of Rich's "naming and definition," and a "pilgrimage." In "Before the Body" (*Seneca Review* 14,ii:60–73) Judith Kitchen reads work by Katha Pollitt, Sylvia Plath, Lisel Muller, and Louise Glück in an interesting discussion of "the urge to go back to a time before the body asserted itself." Finally, in "In the Upper Air" (*Seneca Review* 14,ii:74–84), David Weiss takes Ellen Bryant Voight's task to be mythic—"to redeem the near dead and the dying back to life."

v. A Complex of Occasions

The Imagination as Glory (Illinois), ed. Bruce Weigle and T. R. Hummer, collects a dozen essays on James Dickey's poetry. Following an introduction by the editors which explains their motivation—to "present a history of critical response and the continuing critical exegesis of the unfolding of Dickey's canon"—Howard Nemerov, Robert Duncan, Ralph Mills, Lawrence Liberman, Joyce Carol Oates, Dave Smith, and others discuss the poet's "mysterious universe." Further, *The James Dickey Newsletter* (Dunwoody, Ga.) debuted this year. Volume 1, number 1 included Jane Bowers-Hill's " 'With Eyes More Than Human': Dickey's Misunderstood Monster" (pp. 2–8), Robert S. Lowrance, Jr.'s "James Dickey, Hurdler, and I" (pp. 8–9), and Robert C. Cove's updated bibliography (pp. 15–27). A good start to an interesting project.

Two further volumes in Michigan's first-rate Under Discussion series should be noted here. Joyce Peseroff's *Robert Bly: When Sleepers Awake* divides into two parts. The first reprints 13 of the best essays to appear on the poet in the last 15 years by William Matthews, William Heyen, Richard Howard, Anthony Libby, James F. Mersmann, Ekbert Faas, Charles Altieri, Charles Molesworth, Ralph J. Mills, Jr., Victoria Harris, Wayne Dodd, Donald Wesling, and William V. Davis on subjects ranging from immanence to female consciousness; the second gathers 14 selections from reviews, interviews, memoirs, and poems. Wendy Salinger's *Richard Wilbur's Creation* more or less reverses this ordering, opening with selections from 25 reviews of volumes from *The Beautiful Changes* to *Responses*, followed by essays by Robert F. Sayre, Raymond Benoit, Donald L. Hill, Charles F. Duffy, John P. Farrell, Joseph Brodsky, Raymond Oliver, Charles R. Woodard, Howard Nemerov, Enjer J. Jensen, Bruce Michelson, Brad Leithauser. Additionally, Peseroff's volume includes a fine bibliography of both primary and secondary material.

James Wright continues to command our attention this year, also. In "James Wright: The Garden and the Grime" (*KR* 6,ii:76–91), Peter Stitt (who interviewed the poet for the *Paris Review* in 1975) discusses Wright as a "questing poet," with primary concentration on his last volume, and particular reference to Ohio as a "blighted" and "murderous" landscape. Randall Stiffler's "The Reconciled Vision of James Wright" (*LitR* 28,i:77–92) reads Wright's work as a movement toward "a reconciliation of the possibility of epiphany with the reality of despair," one that intensified as his poetry matured. In "A Redefinition of the Poetic Self: James Wright's *Amenities of Stone*" (*OhR* 33:9–28), Kevin Stein sees the withdrawal of the volume (completed in 1960) as the clue to Wright's transition from formalism (*Saint Judas*) to open verse (*Branch*), in the poet's rejection of "a subject-object dichotomy" in favor of an Emersonian intuition and sympathy.

Sara McAulay's brief " 'Getting There' and Going Beyond: David Wagoner's Journey Without Regret" (*LitR* 28,i:93–98) examines the poet's "animistic acceptance of and reverence for the natural world in all its forms and forces," including death. In "Gerald Stern: The Poetry of Nostalgia" (*LitR* 28,i:99–104) Jane Somerville briefly discusses Stern's sense of nostalgia as "a version of the tragic vision." "Louis Simpson and American Dreams" (*ArQ* 40:147–62) by Bruce Bawer argues that like Whitman, Simpson has made "America" his life-long subject, though much of the poet's work is a critique of Whitman's project.

Bawer also regards James Merrill in "A Summoning of Spirits:

James Merrill and *Sandover*" (*NewC* 2,x:35–42). Here he discusses Merrill's "principal work of poetry . . . the Atomic Age's Answer to Dante." Following a brief analysis of each of the three books, Bawer argues for reading the poem as poem, that "Merrill is not Moses and *Sandover* is not the Pentateuch," and sees it marred finally by Merrill's yoking of "Godhead with homosexuality."

John Tranter interviews David Shapiro (*Meanjin* 43:550–58) on the "New York School": a chatty piece with much information on Frank O'Hara in particular. In "Critical Reflections: Poetry and Art Criticism in Ashbery's 'Self-Portrait in a Convex Mirror'" (*NLH* 15:607–30), Richard Stamelman senses that Ashbery's poem is meant to serve as "an ekphrastic re-presentation of Parmigiano's self-portrait, and at the same time a radical criticism of the illusions and deceptions inherent in forms of traditional representation that insist on the ideal, essential, and totalized nature of the copied images they portray." A detailed and convincing analysis of a difficult poem.

Charles Wright is the subject of Michael McFee's "Wright's Pilgrimage" (*Seneca Review* 14,ii:85–97), an article that sees Wright's journey as "ironic" in the sense that he has returned to the South, keeping always a "bedrock regionalism" as the base of his work. Lorrie Goldsohn's "Approaching Home Ground: Galway Kinnell's *Mortal Acts, Mortal Words*" (*MassR* 35:303–16) examines the poet's most recent volume, finding in his language "an insistence on the ordinary object as the right carrier for meaning."

A number of interviews with poets appear in journals this year: Nina Zivancevic's discussion with Charles Bernstein and Douglas Messerli (*Sagetrieb* 3,iii:63–78); Edwin Frank and Andrew McCord's interview with Robert Fitzgerald on the "Art of Translation" (*ParisR* 94:39–65); Brad Leiter's interview with Howard Moss (*APR* 13,v:27–31); Adam J. Sorkin's conversation with Robert Pinsky (*ConL* 25:1–14); Howard Norman's interview with Philip Levine (*Ploughshares* 10,iv:11–22); Joseph Bruchac's talk with Wendy Rose (*Greenfield Review* 12,i–ii:43–62); Jan Castro and David Hadas's discussion with Carolyn Forché (*River Styx* 15:39–54); David Weiss's interview with Stephen Dunn (*Seneca Review* 14,ii:16–26); Mark Hillringhouse's interview with Gerald Stern (*APR* 13,ii:26–30); Joseph Bruchac's discussion with Luci Tapahonso (*MELUS* 11,iv:85–91).

University of New Mexico

18. Drama

Walter J. Meserve

Each year recently there have been 30–40 books published that deal with or touch upon some aspect of American drama and theater. A few prove to be valuable sources for scholars, although there are bound to be disappointments, but there are an increasing number of competent researchers and writers. There is an obvious need to establish and maintain exemplary scholarship in an area that has been suspect in the past. It is therefore discouraging to find series editors—Bruce and Adele King—whose ignorance of the field and lack of good judgment leads them to select, as the author of *American Dramatists, 1918–1945* (Grove), Bernard Dukore, whose area of expertise is obviously not American drama. Good graduate students with an introductory knowledge of English composition and American theater should be irritated by poor writing—such sentences as "By 1900 New York City was the hub of American theatre, but its plays were naive and provincial"; and by outright errors (Edward Sheldon did not write *The Easiest Way*, nor was the play written in the year indicated). On numerous occasions Dukore tries to ease his discussion of American drama onto more familiar English ground, but his pretentiousness and lack of thought-provoking knowledge of American drama doom that maneuver. Ruby Cohn's book in the same series, on American dramatists from 1960 to 1980, is an excellent resource, but Dukore's volume lacks accuracy and authority.

One of the most intelligent and perceptive critics of American drama is Gerald Weales, whose yearly "theatre watch" provides an excellent insight into the work of contemporary playwrights. "American Theatre Watch" (*GaR* 38:594–606) suggests a lean year except for Mamet's *Glengarry Glen Ross* and Joanna McClelland Glass's *Play Memory*. Weales dispatches with curt words the abundance of musicals and English imports that crowd the New York stages, shows his enthusiasm for the works of Arthur Kopit, and encourages theaters to revive good American plays. Herbert Blau's "The Impossible

Theatre Takes a Little Time" (*PerfAJ* 8,ii:29–42), with its rambling
emptiness interspersed with sparkling phrases and images that create
pleasant effects, is a perfect example of how not to write. His point
in this essay is old and boring, but he cannot always be so easily dismissed. Robert Corrigan pushes a worn-out image to tiresome distrac-
tion in "The Search for New Endings: The Theatre in Search of a
Fix, Part III" (*TJ* 36:153–63). He says that he is promoting a "new
poetics of theatre," but after a great many clichés about the progress
of American theater, he wanders to a halt, having tried, he states, to
distinguish "Postmodern Performance" from "the Modernist Theatre."

The term *"post-Modern"* is being touted as the new password
for the study of contemporary drama. Rodney Simard exploits it
in *Postmodern Drama, Contemporary Playwrights in America and
Britain* (Univ. Press), hailing Harold Pinter and Edward Albee (pp.
25–47) as the first post-Moderns after Beckett successfully brought
the Modern period to a close. "Sam Shepard, Emotional Renegade"
(pp. 75–97) is "the first totally postmodern voice in America." With
a firm belief in his thesis, Simard makes some astute observations and
comparisons in his comments on Shepard, but like all who search
more for categorizing terms than insight into individual achievement,
his objective is more limiting than enlightening.

i. Reference Works

The largest and most expensive reference work this year is the *Mc-
Graw-Hill Encyclopedia of World Drama* (McGraw-Hill), second
edition, published in five volumes. It is a massive undertaking, volu-
minously if not always tastefully illustrated, with a substantial glossary of terms. As far as American drama is concerned, it is essentially
the product of New York scholars. The long major essay on American drama was written by Vera Roberts (origins to 1930), others by
Felecia N. Frank (the 1930s) and Glen Loney (since 1940)—all
from the City University of New York. The individual essays were
written mainly by Gautam Dasgupta, an editor of the *Performing
Arts Journal*, whose reputation as a scholar in American drama is
insignificant. In volume 1 (A–C), for example, of the 42 entries on
American dramatists, 39 were written by Dasgupta and the others
by Terry Miller from the Meridian Gay Theatre in New York. Their
work suggests a competent journeyman effort—mainly plots and
basic information—lacking the insight of good scholarship. As might

be expected, the emphasis is upon modern American dramatists—no Charles Hoyt, no Jessie Lynch Williams, no Charles Rann Kennedy. Edward Sheldon is included, but Booth Tarkington's novels are emphasized over his plays. Howard Teichmann's work is briefly described; there is a sympathetic and substantial entry for Ronald Tavel, and Louis Coxe is noted for his single play. This reference work is, of course, most valuable for librarians, but with a more intelligent selection of entrants and researchers the work on individual American dramatists could have been much better.

Among other reference books, *American Literary and Drama Reviews* (Hall), an index to late-19th-century periodicals by Patricia Marks, will be a valuable tool although limited by its New York orientation and the dozen or so periodicals indexed. The domestic productions of 1801 American and foreign plays includes an astounding number of reviews—15 for *Hazel Kirke*, for example. Richard Peterson's *Who's Who in One Hundred Fifty Modern Plays* (Drama Book Publishers) is a "character catalogue" in which plays are listed by title, author, production date, and publication date and described in about 30 words. Each character in the play is then described in 25–30 words. *Contemporary Theatre, Films and Television: A Biographical Guide Featuring Performers, Directors, Writers, Producers, Designers, Managers, Choreographers, Technicians, Composers, Executives, Dancers, and Critics in the United States and Great Britain* (Gale) is a continuation of *Who's Who in the Theatre*.

James A. Levernier and Douglas R. Wilmes edited *American Writers Before 1800* (Greenwood, 1983), which features entries on 786 writers by some 250 scholars who provided lists of works, biographical information, and suggested readings along with critical appraisals. As a "biographical and critical dictionary" it includes a surprising number of playwrights. "The principal aim" of *Major Modern Dramatists* (Ungar), comp. and ed. Rita Stein and Friedhelm Rickert, is "to give an overview of the critical reception of the dramatist from the beginning of his career up to the present by presenting excerpts of reviews, articles and books" (pp. vii–viii). The American dramatists included are Albee, Hellman, Miller, Odets, O'Neill, Wilder, and Williams, but without some explanatory comment these stark, eclectically selected excerpts—27 for Williams, for example, filling 20 pages in this book—seem to be of negligible value for any reader or scholar.

It is impossible to determine the number of dramatists now writing in America, although the Dramatist Guild lists more than 7000 members. Getting a new play produced, therefore, is a major problem for most playwrights as well as for the hundreds of theaters across America that accept new plays. To assist these playwrights *The Playwrights' Companion* (Nashville, Ind.: Feedback Services), an annual publication compiled by Mollie Ann Meserve, provides comprehensive submission information in clear chart form for more than 400 theaters and over 90 play contests. The *Dramatists Sourcebook* (TCG), another annual publication, provides comparable data on its own TCG theaters, numerous contests, and other market sources of support for playwrights.

At last the Papers and Proceedings of the Conference on the Musical Theatre in America, *Musical Theatre in America* (Greenwood), have been edited by Glen Loney. Well illustrated and carefully revised, these essays by scholars and practitioners provide a rich source of information and opinion.

ii. Anthologies

It is an interesting aberration of the publishing business that the publishing of new and unknown plays appears to be more lucrative than satisfying the complaint of teachers that there are no good anthologies of pre-O'Neill American drama in print. The Theatre Communications Group continues its series with *New Plays USA 2*, edited by James Leverett and introduced by Richard Gilman. *Buck* by Ronald Ribman is among the five plays presented. Richard Nelson's *An American Comedy and Other Plays* (Performing Arts), another continuing series, includes the title play plus *The Return of Pinnochio*, 1982; *Bal*, 1979; and *Conjuring an Event*, 1976.

iii. Works of General Interest

The influence of foreign cultures upon American dramatists is generally traced across the Atlantic rather than the Pacific, with the notable exception of O'Neill and Wilder. Both are treated once again with a certain insight by Hazel B. Durnell in *Japanese Cultural Influences on American Poetry and Drama* (Hokuseido, 1983). There is also a good chapter on the influence of classical Japanese poetry and Noh on the works of T. S. Eliot, Wallace Stevens, Kenneth Rexroth, and James Schevill, as well as an historical commentary on scholars who have brought and taught Japanese Noh and Kabuki to Americans.

One of the strangest approaches to a study of theater and drama is a book entitled *Western Theatre: Revolution and Revival* (Macmillan) by Patti P. Gillespie and Kenneth M. Cameron. Using Thomas S. Kuhn's concept of the paradigm—the perception of the nature of nature—the authors find three paradigms in Western theater prior to the 20th century and proceed to follow their theories in an odd if not chaotically organized argument. Charts provide basic information but the choppy discussions do not encourage readers. In this atmosphere American drama and theater do not fare well as American performers are confused with English performers, wrong information is provided, and broad generalizations do damage to a balanced understanding.

In the areas of theater history in America, Gerald Kahan's *George Alexander Stevens and the Lecture on Heads* (Georgia) provides a scholarly commentary on the popular 18th-century one-man show. *Henry L. Brunk and Brunk's Comedians* (Bowling Green State University Popular Press) by Jerry L. Martin is an interesting and well-documented picture of the "tent Repertoire Empire of the Southwest" as represented by the seven Brunk brothers. With pictures, abundant interviews, and evidence of archival research, it is a good resource for students of the Toby character. George W. Shuttler's "William Gillette: Marathon Actor and Playwright" (*JPC* 17,iii [1983]:115–29) shows good primary research but is poorly organized and written. Equally outstanding in research and well written is Karen R. Gray and Sarah R. Yeates's accounting of the interaction between politics and burlesque in the career of Louisville's Boss John H. Wallen—"The Louisville Burlesque War: Empire Circuit Company vs. Columbia Amusement" (*ThS* 25:25–42). John O'Neal explores another use of theater in "Theatre and History: Experiences from the Southern Civil Rights Movement" (*Southern Exposure* 12, vi:103–04), a brief comment on the difficulty of making choices that will encourage social reform.

Spanish-American or Mexican theater and drama will be increasingly important in the United States as time passes. Nicolás Kanellos's *Mexican Theatre: Then and Now* (Arte Público, 1983) appeared also in *Revista Chicano-Riqueña* (21,i,1983). Created for a touring exhibit of "Two Centuries of Hispanic Theatre in the Southwest," the publication contains a well-illustrated review of the subject (pp.

19–40) by Kanellos, an essay on a Spanish-speaking comedian by
Tomás y barra-Frausto ("La Chata Molesca: Figura Del Donaire,"
pp. 41–51), a discussion of the Spanish woman's role in the theater
of California's Bay Area (pp. 78–94), an interview with Luis Valdez
(pp. 112–20), and Jorge Huerta's essay on "The Influence of Latin
American Theater on Teatro Chicano" (pp. 68–77). Huerta's essay
on "Labor Theatre, Street Theatre and Community Theatre in the
Barrios, 1965–1983" (pp. 62–70) appeared in *Hispanic Theatre in
the United States* (Arte Público), ed. Kanellos.

In " 'The Mystery of Things': the Varieties of Religious Experience
in Modern American Drama," printed in *Drama and Religion* (Cambridge, 1983, pp. 139–57), Thomas D. Adler discusses a number of
American dramas in terms of four common motifs such as the Old
Testament God versus the New Testament God and the reconciliation
of an evil world with a loving God. He agrees with English critics that
American theater has little to do with "mature philosophical analysis"
but concentrates upon the "energy one finds in animals or children."
Continuing his Anglophile bias against American drama, Adler concludes that any "thinking" drama in America is religious drama but
never distinguishes philosophy from religion or America's childlike
simplicity from mature English sophistication.

iv. 18th- and 19th-Century Drama

In a good, clearly argued case for "Determining the Date of Robert
Hunter's *Androbrous*" (*ThS* 25:95–97), Peter A. Davis uses the secular calendar to establish the year as 1715 rather than 1714. He is not
as successful explaining the date on the manuscript, however. Penelope M. Leavitt and James S. Moy sifted through newspapers from
New Orleans, Natchez, Memphis, and Cairo to provide a description
of the architecture of "Spaulding and Roger's Floating Palace" (*ThS*
25:15–27). In "American Theatrical Taste as Class Warfare" (*SDR*
22,i:6–15) Warren Kliewer harangues contemporary society for its
false presumption and neglect of the good theater that has historically entertained the middle class.

There are three books on American actors and acting in America
that deserve some comment. Benjamin McArthur's *Actors and American Culture, 1880–1920* (Temple) is a serious attempt to explain the
actor's role in developing American culture. Although clearly mistaken in his assumption that the cult of celebrity had its beginning

during these years, he provides "an occupational history of actors"—
who they were, how they lived, what they did to promote their profession and their status in society prior to their show of organizational strength in the 1919 actors' strike. McArthur provides a good
bibliography and a few pictures, makes mistakes, as we all do—John
Brougham was not a tragedian—but develops an argument in a manner that is enjoyable to read. Claudia P. Johnson, *American Actress:
Perspective on the Nineteenth Century* (Nelson-Hall) presses her
thesis too hard and presents an unbalanced view, first, of the actress
as harlot and then as a worker whose efforts, as distinct from other
women in the late 19th century, placed her on an equal basis with
men in the theater. Johnson then traces the activity of seven actresses,
but as women rather than actresses. This well-illustrated work is
clearly biased, but there is truth in its argument. Another book
about actresses, ed. Eric Salmon, *Bernhardt and the Theatre of Her
Time* (Greenwood), includes essays by Alan Woods on Mademoi-
selle Rhea's tours in America (pp. 183–201) and by Marvin Carlson
on "Ristori in America" (pp. 203–23). The fact that neither actress
apparently acted in American plays suggests the general attitude of
foreign actors toward the work of American playwrights.

Three books also treated the works of particular American dramatists. Of these, Oliver H. Evans's *George Henry Boker* (TUSAS 476)
is the least effective. Evans, in fact, is not enthusiastic about Boker's
work, never attempts to place Boker in the developing American
drama and shows no understanding or interest in a play as a work
to be produced in a theater. Limited to a discussion of theme, character, and language, Evans seems almost contemptuous of Boker
and his playwriting efforts. In heavy-handed and involved sentences,
Evans's unbalanced and unfair study deserves to be quickly forgotten. In distinct contrast, Don Wilmeth and Rosemary Cullen have
provided a scholarly and shrewd assessment of Daly's contributions
to American theater in *Plays of Augustin Daly* (Cambridge). Reprinting *A Flash of Lightning, Horizon,* and *Love on Crutches,* the
editors, in addition to an appreciation of Daly as manager, innovator,
and entrepreneur, give an excellent discussion of the relationship
between Joseph and Augustin Daly. The book is also well illustrated.

Ronald J. Davis makes an excellent case for *Augustus Thomas*
(TUSAS 478) as an American dramatist who mirrored America with
his plays and worked diligently in his craft. Among the Twayne books
this is one of the most distinguished on American dramatists. With

a good command of background material, Davis carefully analyzes Thomas's work, always attempting to suggest the influences of the times and the plays of other American dramatists. He is particularly effective in describing Thomas as one who helped shape American drama after 1891.

v. The Contribution of Eugene O'Neill

Attention to O'Neill this year is largely confined to two books of essays and the varied contents of the *Eugene O'Neill Newsletter*. *Eugene O'Neill's Critics: Voices From Abroad* (So. Ill.), ed. Horst Frenz and Susan Tuck, is a diverse collection of essays written mainly over a 60-year period (1922–80) by critics from 17 different countries. The idea for this volume is sound and the essays carefully selected, although the translators of foreign-language essays are frequently not identified. Some essays are old favorites, such as St. John Ervine's "Counsels of Despair"; three brief items were written by Sean O'Casey, although most critics are represented by a single essay. Only two of the essays were written specifically for this publication: An Min Hsia's "Cycle of Return: O'Neill and the Tao" (pp. 169–73) comments on the idea of "return" in *Marco Millions* and *Lazarus Laughed*; Tino Tuisanen's "O'Neill and Wuolijoki: A Counter-Sketch to Electra" (pp. 174–81) compares *Justina* to *Mourning Becomes Electra*. The book also contains a list of O'Neill's plays in translation and a list of productions in 32 foreign countries.

James J. Martine's *Critical Essays on Eugene O'Neill* (Hall) collects original essays from 14 writers, only two of whom—Jackson Bryer and Peter Egri—have significant reputations. Martine's introduction begins, "If one were to climb the beanstalk of American drama, what would be discovered at the very top is a giant." His prose does not improve as he writes, and the book is generally a collection of undistinguished essays. Frank Cunningham comments on the "Romantic Elements in Early Eugene O'Neill" (pp. 65–72); Peter Egri provides an extremely thorough analysis of alienation and dramatic form in *The Hairy Ape* (pp. 77–111); Ellen Kimbel's "Eugene O'Neill as Social Historian: Manners and Morals in *Ah, Wilderness!*" (pp. 137–45) is sensible and readable but stresses the obvious.

Thomas B. Gilmore used the principles of Alcoholics Anonymous in "*The Iceman Cometh* and the Anatomy of Alcoholism" (*CompD* 18:335–47) to show that Hickey's ideas and practices present a parody of AA recommendations, although one might observe that this would be indifferent news for O'Neill. The varied menu of the *Eugene O'Neill Newsletter* added Steven F. Bloom's "The Role of Drinking and Alcoholism in O'Neill's Late Plays" (8,i:22–27). Dana S. McDermott found new information among the Macgowan papers at the University of California, Los Angeles, to write about "Robert Edmund Jones and Eugene O'Neill: Two American Visionaries" (8, i:3–10), and Bert Cardullo argued briefly that Simon Hartford was a symbol of truth in *A Touch of the Poet* who became the incarnation of illusion in *More Stately Mansions* (8,i:27–28). In the second number of volume 8 Louis Schaffer recorded—and corrected—more biographical errors. Number 3 included brief comments by Travis Bogard on music in *Anna Christie* (pp. 12–13) and by Robert Perrion on teaching O'Neill's plays (pp. 13–14), plus some pictures and comments on O'Neill's homes by Winifred Frazer (pp. 15–21). In the same issue Shelly Regenbaum made an unconvincing comparison of Jacob and Esau to Robert and Andrew Mayo in "Wrestling With God: Old Testament Themes in O'Neill's *Beyond the Horizons*" (pp. 2–8). In a rather confused manner Marcellini Krafchick argued that Erie in O'Neill's *Hughie* resembles Josie in *Moon for the Misbegotten* as well as Jamie in *Long Day's Journey* (pp. 8–11). The most interesting item in this issue was Frederic J. Carpenter's excellent response to Albert Kalson's superficial criticism of *Strange Interlude*—and to all such criticism (pp. 22–24).

vi. American Drama from 1920 to 1940

The Drama Review published two essays on original productions of plays by Clifford Odets and Paul Green. Lort Stewart and David Barbour wrote about *Waiting for Lefty* (*TDR* 28,iv:38–48), and Richard E. Kramer discussed "The Group Theatre's *Johnny Johnson*" (*TDR* 28,iv:49–60). Each essay became almost a documentary account based on contemporary reaction and later observations by participants. Elmer Rice's *The Adding Machine* is discussed in the German work by Walter Riedel, "Variationen der Wandlung: Gabrielle Roys Roman *Alexandre Cheneveri* und die dramen Georg Kaisers *Von Morgens bis Mitternachts* und Elmer Rices *The Adding Machine*" (*CRCL* 11,ii:205–15).

George S. Kaufman and His Collaborators (Performing Arts) is part of a continuing series of American plays and includes *June Moon,*

Bravo, and *The Late George Appley*. It is introduced by Anne Kaufman Schneider, who wrote, "I think my father was like a chameleon taking on all the coloration of his collaborators while keeping his own identity all the way through each work." David Stephen Calonne's *William Saroyan: My Real Work is Being* (N.C., 1983) is one of a half-dozen studies in progress and still does not take advantage of the "scores of plays" Saroyan left behind him. The constant question in Saroyan's plays, according to Calonne, is this: "How might we best live in order to fulfill our most profound potential as human beings?" Always stressing the relationship between reality and imagination, as Saroyan searches for "true being," Calonne discusses Saroyan's "World and Theater" and his "Allegories for the Stage," commenting that Saroyan's plays are his greatest contribution to American literature. Linda W. Wagner's "The Outrage of *Many Loves*" (*Sagetrieb* 3,ii:63–70) barely fits into the 1920–40 time frame, but in a delightful discussion of W. C. Williams's plays, she uncovers the outrageous "events" of women and their sexuality and explores Williams's best ideas about art, particularly the drama.

vii. Two Major Dramatists: Miller and Williams

a. **Arthur Miller.**   In spite of his inability to write successful plays for the American theater in recent years, Miller continues to attract scholarship and admirers in other parts of the world. One indication of this popularity is the 1983 production of *Death of a Salesman* in the People's Republic of China and his own diary of that event which he called *Salesman in Beijing* (Viking). It was obviously a great experience for Miller, who explains, in rather too much detail and with far too many unnecessary personal observations, the difficulties of producing an American play for a people whose culture is vastly different from that depicted in the original work. Another kind of appreciation of Miller's contributions to world drama may be found in the Japanese publication of Masanori Sata, *Arthur Miller: Gekisakka eno Michi* (Tokyo: Kenkyusha) and Antonio Rodriguez Celada's comparison of Miller's treatment of the common man as tragic hero in *A View from the Bridge* and *The Crucible* to the work of Vallejo Buero in "Buero, Miller y el 'common man'" (*Estrano* 10,i:25–28).

Steven R. Centola's "'The Will to Live': An Interview with Arthur Miller" (*MD* 27:345–60) is an excellent illustration of one way an interview should *not* be conducted. From the outset Centola controls the interview with a series of statements for which he asks Miller's agreement. Intruding constantly, Centola drags the conversation in different directions and points the answers he wants: "Would you say that. . . ?" Miller's tired contributions are limited to "Right," "Absolutely," "Yeah," "Sure," and "That's a good way to put it." One should question the editorial policy of a magazine that would publish such a piece as well as Miller's frame of mind in tolerating the abuse. Dale Maxwell's self-indulgent conversation with himself as he, a practicing psychiatrist, prepares to direct *A View from the Bridge* achieves absolutely nothing—"The Fall of Eddie Carbone: An Internal Dialogue" (*ThSw* 11,iii:14–15).

b. **Tennessee Williams.** Although he has seldom lacked the enthusiastic support and interest of writers in popular and academic journals, Williams's unexpected death set the scholarly mills grinding at a more frantic pace than would normally be expected. A memorable tribute appears in *Tennessee Williams,* the *DLB* Documentary Series, volume 4 (Gale), ed. Margaret A. Van Antwerp and Sally Johns. It is, indeed, an impressive illustrated biography composed of reviews, criticism, letters, interviews, obituaries, several articles by Williams himself, and tributes by John Simon and Louis Auchincloss. In "Late Tennessee Williams" (*MD* 27:336–44) Ruby Cohn discusses *The Two Character Play, Vieux Carré,* and *Clothes for a Summer Hotel,* seeing no decline in Williams's work and suggesting that *The Two Character Play* may be his masterpiece.

Among other articles focusing on Williams this year Jack E. Wallace provided an impressive analysis of the growth of *Orpheus Descending* from *Battle of Angels* with an emphasis upon Williams's use of the confectionery as a "true sign of theater" and the controlling image of the play in "The Image of Theater in Tennessee Williams's *Orpheus Descending*" (*MD* 27:324–35). W. Kenneth Holditch's "Tennessee Williams: Poet as Playwright" (*XUS* 3,xi[1983]21–27) takes an excessively long time to say that Williams is a poet. In "The Role of the Baby in *A Streetcar Named Desire*" (*NConL* 14,ii:4–5) Bert Cardullo argues that Stella's child will be her retreat and that it marks the end of Stanley's benign dominance of her life. Catherine Georgoudaki provides brief analyses of Greek productions of ten plays by Tennessee Williams, the "poet of crushed dreams," in "The Plays of Tennessee Williams in Greece, 1946–1983" (*NMW* 16,i–ii: 59–93).

viii. Since 1960

Among the dramatists writing during the past 25 years, Edward
Albee sustained scholarly interest for a generation. The current idol
of the critics, however, is overwhelmingly Sam Shepard, whose talented creations seem to have emerged from cult adoration to a position of status with critics in other parts of the world. Even the
trend-hunting critics in black drama and women's drama have appeared to reassess their objectives, as critics have had to think more
deeply about directions that black drama should assume as well as
attempt to balance art with feminism.

As Edward Albee has lately become more lecturer than dramatist,
fewer critics have concerned themselves with his plays. In *IJAS* (14,
ii:67–72) Prashant Sinha considers *Who's Afraid of Virginia Woolf?*
and *Zoo Story* as he applies the theories of Erich Fromm and Karen
Horney to "The Disoriented Self and the Oppressive Society: A Study
of Some Major American Plays of the 1950's and Early 1960's." Two
other articles on dramatists of the past dozen years treat A. R. Gurney
and Beth Henley. Attempting to define "The Tragic Vision of Beth
Henley's Drama" (*SoQ* 22,iv:54–70) Nancy D. Hargrove sees Henley's work as thought-provoking, often depressing and negative, but
ultimately cheering and sustaining. Showing "both the despicable
and the admirable elements of human nature," Henley's vision apparently thwarted Hargrove's attempt to classify it. Karl Levett has
provided some excellent background material on the career of "A. R.
Gurney, Jr., American Original" (*Drama* 149[1983]:6–7), discussing
him as one who, as a playwright, exploited his own upper-middle-
class heritage and his admiration for the work of Philip Barry.

As for Shepard, *Inner Landscapes: The Theater of Sam Shepard*
(Missouri) by Ron Mottram provides a detailed study of Shepard's
plays, from which the author attempts to extract the psyche of their
creator. With tremendous enthusiasm, Mottram celebrates Shepard's
lack of inhibition, his ego, and his mystique until he persuades the
reader that Shepard is truly the iconoclastic cult dramatist that Mottram wants to deny. Mottram appears to believe that everything
Shepard does or says is worth knowing, and one feels that Shepard
should plead with Oscar Wilde, who, as he once addressed an audience of Harvard undergraduates dressed in that flamboyant fashion
that was Wilde's customary attire, asked to be defended from his

"followers." Like many other critics, however, Mottram places Shepard "among America's great writers."

"If the drama in the text, as we are always told, is to be realized on the stage, even on the stage there is something unrealized in American drama." So begins Herbert Blau in "The American Dream in American Gothic: The Plays of Sam Shepard and Adrienne Kennedy" (*MD* 27:520–39). With occasional spurts of coherent and impressive thought, Blau praises Shepard as well as Kennedy—whose "obsessional narratives" move in and out of focus like Blau's own prose—in an essay that has nothing to do with either his topic or his beginning sentence. In "Mythic Levels in Shepard's *True West*" (*MD* 27:506–19) Tucker Orbison shows that the persistent analyst can find myths anywhere, and Shepard clearly provides great opportunities. Bert Cardullo, a master of the brief note, argues that "Wesley's Role in Sam Shepard's *Curse of the Starving Class*" (*NMAL* 8:Item 6) is that of the spirit of the playwright whose perception must be understood by an audience that wishes to experience the play perfectly.

Rejecting the opinions of scholars who contend that American blacks have no distinct culture, Isaac Sequeira uses the plays of Bullins and Hansberry to illustrate the images of black culture that he finds distinctive—images of music, humor, and black mothers holding the family together. These "Images of Black Culture in Modern American Drama" (*JAC* 7,i–ii:45–48), however, are vaguely and unconvincingly argued. Myles Raymond Hurd explains how Bullins distorts Amanda's character and attacks Tennessee Williams's sexual preference in "Bullins's *The Gentleman Caller*: Source and Satire" (*NConL* 14,iii:11–12). Explaining that he "experienced genius" when he learned to understand J. Rufus Caleb's *Benny's Place*, Houston A. Baker, Jr., tries to build a public image in "A Yea and an Announcement: Notice of a New Black Playwright and His Work" (*BALF* 18, iii:113–16).

"Feminism as Theme in Twentieth Century American Women's Drama" (*AS* 25:69–89) is a common approach for some writers today. In this essay Sharon Friedman selects her evidence with such prejudicial and preconceived limitations that her efforts—vaguely related to her theme at best—have little value. Stretching back into another generation of women writers, Betsy Alayne Ryan writes of *Gertrude Stein's Theatre of the Absolute* (UMI Research Press).

With reference to some 77 plays, Ryan presents a comprehensive study of this forerunner of post–World War II avant-garde. Susan L. Carlson uses *The Women* and *Uncommon Women and Others* to discuss the progress of women in a society of women. Intelligently written and intellectually appealing, "Comic Textures and Female Communities, 1937 and 1977: Clare Booth and Wendy Wasserstein" (*MD* 27:564–73) explores Booth's bitterness and Wendy Wasserstein's laughter to show change in the playwright's use of dramatic form and in the societies represented by their audiences. Much less compelling is Kathleen Gregory Klein's essay on "Language and Meaning in Megan Terry's 1970s Musicals" (*MD* 27:574–83). Part of the problem lies with the writer's robot absorption with Terry's form of creativity and her naive discovery that, as she states, Terry refuses to allow meaninglessness to mask the uses of language. Klein then examines four plays, including *American King's English for Queens*, to show that Terry's language does communicate something.

At a time when Lillian Hellman—alive and dead—has been riding the crest of popular adoration, Hilton Kramer writes a bitter indictment of her as a vengeful Stalinist and "shameless liar" in "The Life and Death of Lillian Hellman" (*The New Criterion* 3,ii:1–6). Condemning her determination "in typical Stalinist fashion" to silence her critics, Kramer accuses Hellman of poisonous dishonesty and castigates her for "the falsehoods that formed the very fabric of Hellman's autobiographical writings."

ix. Criticism

Contemporary theater artists would surely argue, but the essential element of great drama, or any drama, is the playwright. Rabindranath Tagore, the Indian poet, philosopher, actor, teacher, playwright, and recipient of the Nobel Prize for Literature, explained this point clearly in an essay entitled "The Stage" (1920). Acting, he wrote, "has forlornly to await the coming of the drama; since only in its company can it display its charms. . . . The attitude of the drama should be: 'If I can be acted, well and good; if not, so much the worse for acting.'" To encourage playwrights, to inform them concerning the demands and pleasures of audiences, perhaps to discourage them or, at least, to point out ways in which the superior intellect would effect change, God created critics. Whether or not God was satisfied with this creation, the world of drama and theater has endured them ever since as an affliction or pleasure while scholars and theater enthusiasts have enjoyed almost unlimited opportunity to express their opinions.

The value of the critic—presumably for the encouragement of the playwright or the enlightenment of the audience—clearly depends upon the source of the criticism, and there are neither rules nor fees for participants. One of the better professional critics, Stanley Kaufmann, published *Theatre Criticisms* (Performing Arts, 1983), asserting his basic and honest concern for American dramatists and American drama. Yet how sympathetic he appears to be toward British playwrights and how devastating are his comments on "America's spurious 'great' dramatists." His observations follow a pattern of drama criticism in America that became prominent in the antagonistic views of American drama expressed by national and Anglophile critics during the Age of Jackson. Both then and now prejudices can be exposed—at home and abroad. *Das amerikanische Drama* (Bern: Francke), ed. Gerhard Hoffmann, contains essays on verse drama, social criticism in the drama, and dramatic theory in America. In an admirable study entitled *Theories of the Theatre* (Cornell) Marvin Carlson presents a clear and logical analysis of dramatic theory. He is particularly effective, and most concerned in his discussion, with modern theories and with Americans who profess them. His province is the theater in which plays are produced rather than the drama as it is created by playwrights, but the essence of his discussion relates to both of those inextricable parts which together produce enjoyment and stimulation in the theater.

Some of the best criticism on American drama and the art of the dramatist occasionally comes from dramatists. For example, Robert Anderson, James Kirkwood, A. R. Gurney, Jr., Marsha Norman, and Peter Stone have shared their shrewdest observations in "Five Dramatists Discuss the Value of Criticism" (*Dramatists' Guild Quarterly* 21,i:11–25). The guild has also initiated a program "to inform dramatists, to put forward useful and reassuring role models and to encourage through enlightenment and example." One part of this program consists of "conversations" with distinguished dramatists such as Marsha Norman—"Conversations with Marsha Norman" (*Dramatists' Guild Quarterly* 21,iii:9–21)—who revealed to Robert Brustein a great deal about herself, her way of working, her ideas and reactions, as well as excellent advice for playwrights. "Conversations with Sidney Kingsley" (*Dramatists' Guild Quarterly* 21,iii:21–31), stimulated by John Guare, provided a delightful and informative commentary for playwrights or anyone interested in American drama since Kingsley started writing for the theater more than 50 years ago. Opinions, evaluations, criticisms—all are valuable to the scholar and historian of American drama.

Indiana University

19. Black Literature

John M. Reilly

This was a year of consolidation in the study of black literature. Scholars continued to produce the bibliographies and reference works necessary for definition of the field, while the well-established journals—*BALF* and *Callaloo*—proceeded to suggest areas for investigation by their usual careful selection of articles and presentation of special topics. To be sure the year's output includes innovative work, but what impresses one most is the bulk of publication, preponderantly articles addressing their subjects in the sound but traditional ways of textual interpretation or survey. Many of the contributors are new entrants in this report and some of the publications introduce new writers to the canon, both facts indicating that at least one sector of academia is abuzz with talk of black literature.

i. Bibliography, Reference Works

Besides this continuing series of bibliographical essays begun for *ALS* in 1975, there have been two additional attempts to provide annual guides for the study of Afro-American literature. Charles H. Rowell produced an annotated listing of studies in *Obsidian* from 1974 through 1976, and several scholars at Howard University compiled listings of primary and secondary works for *CLAJ* in 1975 and 1976. Describing "Studies in Afro-American Literature: An Annual Annotated Bibliography, 1983" (*Callaloo* 7,iii:104–39) as a continuation of the previous series in *Obsidian* and *CLAJ*, Marcellus Blount presents the first installment of his new project complementary to *ALS*. In an introduction conceived as prescriptive, Blount singles out seven of his 153 entries for exposition as models of the increasingly rigorous work characterizing the mature criticism of black writing. Each of those works of criticism and bibliography is indisputably first-rate, as are the pithy annotations Blount gives his entries. Including dissertations, which are routinely omitted from *ALS*, and promising to enter primary works in future installments, Blount's bibliography should become a resource as necessary as *ALS*.

Since scholars of black literature rarely adopt an entirely belletristic approach to their subject, they often find themselves needing such general guides as Richard Newman's *Black Access: A Bibliography of Afro-American Bibliographies* (Greenwood). Newman, who earlier compiled *Black Index* (see *ALS 1982*, p. 383), presents in his newest volume a single alphabetical listing of more than 3,000 separately published bibliographies. Though the work excludes a great deal of material by omitting publications dealing strictly with the Civil War, the Caribbean, Latin America, and Africa, the daunting bulk of the remaining items makes users completely dependent upon two indexes: a chronological index indicating inclusive dates of selected publications and a topic index including both very broad and highly specific references. The explanatory preface must be read first.

Turning to bibliographies focused on literature, scholars will find themselves on surer ground, especially when using Russell C. Brignano's revised and expanded edition of *Black Americans in Autobiography: An Annotated Bibliography of Autobiographies and Autobiographical Books Written Since the Civil War* (Duke). The first edition, published in 1974, provided annotations and data for authors, editions, reprints, and library locations for 291 autobiographies (works covering significant spans of a life) and 125 autobiographical books, such as diaries, letters, or other accounts of briefer periods in a life. The new edition, which Brignano terms a replacement for the old, enters 424 autobiographies and 229 autobiographical books. In addition he has expanded the listing of locations and added indexes of organizations and first publication years to the previous indexes of occupations, titles, and geographic locations. Taken all in all the new edition is an indispensable aid for the study of a major genre in black literature.

For notices of bibliographies on individual writers I must first reach back a year to comment that the entry on Zora Neale Hurston written by Daryl C. Dance for *American Women Writers: Bibliographical Essays* (Greenwood, 1983) constitutes a solid representation of the currents of scholarship and criticism up to 1980. Indicative of the history Dance presents is her division of the section of her essay on biography into writing before and after Robert Hemenway's work, which Dance terms definitive despite Hemenway's own disclaimers. Three of the five bibliographies produced on contemporary writers during 1984 appeared in *BALF*. Michael W. Peplow and Robert S. Bravard, who compiled a primary and secondary bibliography on their author for Hall in 1980, write "Through a Glass Darkly: Bibliographing Samuel R. Delany" (18:69–75), commenting on the problems of their earlier work and correcting prevalent errors. In "A Selective Primary and Secondary Bibliography, 1979–1983" (18:75–77) they list new fiction, reprints, nonfiction by Delany, interviews, reviews, and general commentary. One ground rule for the compilation is evident in the title; selectivity is all that might be hoped for from one generation of scholars, the authors say. The other ground rule is exclusion of ghost entries, items they have not themselves seen. For the same issue of *BALF*, one devoted to science fiction writers, the journal's editor Joe Weixlmann contributes "An Octavia E. Butler Bibliography" (18:88–89) compiled with his usual care to avoid ghosts and errors and listing chronologically the novels in their various editions, separately published works, interviews, and concluding with an alphabetical list of criticism for each novel. Susan Kirschner's "Alice Walker's Nonfictional Prose: A Checklist, 1966–1984" (18:162–63) lists chronologically the first publications of essays, reviews, and miscellaneous writings and interviews indicating those items republished in Walker's recent *In Search of Our Mother's Gardens* along with changes in titles. For "A Gayl Jones Bibliography" (*Callaloo* 7,i:119–31) Joe Weixlmann produces a record of the author's output and reputation through expansion of his preferred organization to include chronological listings of fiction, including translations and paperback editions; individual stories; poetry in books and individually published; and other works; together with a record of reviews for each work, criticism, and interviews. The fifth compilation for a recent author is Xavier Nicholas's "Robert Hayden: A Bibliography" (*Obsidian* 8,i[1981]:207–10) part of the long-delayed publication of that journal's tribute to Hayden. The listings by Nicholas supplement the 18-page bibliography noted in *ALS 1981* with additional listings of individual poems, anthology reprints, and commentary on Hayden, exclusive of the special tribute issue.

While the Harlem Renaissance is more an invention of critics and promoters of the 1920s than it was a phenomenon that can bear the scrutiny of historical study, Bruce Kellner's *The Harlem Renaissance: A Historical Dictionary for the Era* (Greenwood) will prove a profitable source for those who consult its nearly 800 entries on writers, composers, personalities and politicians, institutions, and notable works of fiction, drama, and musical performance. Prepared for his task by previous work on Carl Van Vechten, white "Negrotarian" and promoter of the image of a renaissance, and drawing upon research collections and a range of standard sources, Kellner has prepared fully two-thirds of the entries himself, with the remainder contributed by seven associates. The result is an absorbing creation of milieu provided by succinct yet substantial entries with ample cross-referencing. Appendixes range from a listing of titles for "A Harlem Renaissance Library," suitable for beginners, to listings of plays and musicals and newspapers that practiced scholars will use. One needs to resist the temptation to feel that the mass of information provided by the volume, and Kellner's reasonable introduction to it all, answer the questions associated with the definition of a literary period, but provided one does so, the bibliographical apparatus laying bare the construction of the book and the helpful index to entries will provide the way to learn more about the epiphenomena of Harlem in the 1920s.

Volume 33 of Gale's *Dictionary of Literary Biography* is given over to *Afro-American Fiction Writers After 1955*. Edited by Thadious M. Davis and Trudier Harris, the volume naturally employs a repetitive formula that calls for essays to interlace biographical information with exposition of the major works and their reviews in a sequential order leading up to the present stage of each writer's career with concluding remarks on promise for the future. Nevertheless the framework is decidedly useful when applied to writers nearly invisible to academic critics; thus, R. Baxter Miller on Ronald L. Fair, Carol P. Marsh on Frank Hercules, Johanna L. Grimes on Leon Forrest, Sondra O'Neale on Kristin Hunter, Maryemma Graham on Charles R. Johnson, Frank E. Moorer on John A. McCluskey, Jr., and William J. Harris on Al Young, among others, should generate interest. In all there are 49 signed entries, each including a bibliography of primary works and a selected list of secondary items. Besides the value the book offers for writers who have not received adequate criticism, the team of editors and critics have produced a uniformly high level of reference essays. Readers familiar with the *DLB* will know that the production of the book, with photographs of the writers, occasional pages of typescript, and other matter make the new volume 33 a visual pleasure. A more specialized compilation is *Black Women Writers (1950–1980): A Critical Evaluation*, ed.

Mari Evans (Doubleday). For each of 15 writers Evans presents two critical essays, the response to a questionnaire when the subject was willing, a biographical note, and a single listing of publications that provides only year of appearance. In her preface discussing the preparation of entries, Evans makes no suggestion that she prescribed a format for essays but hints at a lack of cooperation by some potential subjects and reluctance to contribute on the part of some critics. Though the structure of the book suggests a reference work, what it provides is a collection of essays largely representative of standard critical approaches and varying in quality. These essays are noted in appropriate sections of this report.

To the substantial shelf of recent books on black drama can now be added Allen Woll's *Dictionary of the Black Theatre: Broadway, Off-Broadway, and Selected Harlem Theatre* (Greenwood, 1983). Taking as his subject Douglas Turner Ward's definition of black theater "by, about, with, for and related to blacks" from 1898 to 1981, Woll enters approximately 300 shows in his dictionary. The first part, arranged alphabetically by title, provides the name of the theater for first production, date, number of performances, the creative personnel, cast, songs, a sketch of the reviews, and plot summary. In the second part, Woll confirms his book's orientation toward history of theatrical production rather than texts by presenting brief sketches of the lives of major performers, writers, directors, and histories of theatrical organizations. For each of the major figures these entries also include a list of credits, and all entries, whether by Woll himself or signed by other contributors, include a listing of reference sources. Adding to the value of the excellent notes in these two parts of the book is apparatus that includes a chronology of the black theater; a discography; a selected bibliography including published versions of shows, books, articles, and dissertations; and indexes to proper names, plays and films, and songs. Greenwood is on the mark in touting the book as an important tool.

ii. General Studies, Literary History

Directly addressing a major problem in definition of the so-called Harlem Renaissance, namely, the lack of evident connection between the small group of writers termed Renaissance artists and the life of the masses in the Harlem community, Tony Martin's *Literary Garveyism: Garvey, Black Arts and the Harlem Renaissance* (Majority

Press, 1983) argues that the Garvey movement in general, and the weekly *Negro World* in particular, "played a role in providing a potential infrastructure for the Harlem Renaissance." Martin likens the Garvey aesthetic of racial advancement and the active promotion of poetry for the people through reviews and contests in the weekly publication, and by participation in clubs and lecture series, to the Black Arts movement of the 1960s. Successful in showing that the popularly rooted Garveyites displayed as much zeal for literature as did the now better-known NAACP and Urban League, Martin's book serves as a corrective work, indicating that the nationalists created a mechanism to foster deliberate and self-conscious black culture that might have affected a mass audience; yet, as Martin acknowledges, the effort failed as the United Negro Improvement Association became preoccupied with the legal struggles that ended with Marcus Garvey's deportation in 1927.

Trudier Harris is also concerned to bring the record of history to bear upon our understanding of literature. Her *Exorcising Blackness* readily demonstrates through historical accounts and citation of the analyses of E. Franklin Frazer and other authorities that black writers do not exaggerate in their repeated representations of the brutality of lynching and the instrumental functions they assume for transference of guilt and sexual repression. Having established the obligatory presence of lynching in black writing, especially that of males, Harris also explains the centrality of lynching to the aesthetic of authors such as Richard Wright and discusses John Wideman's attempt at imagining black lynching of whites. Finally, however, it is not only the historical reality of lynching as dreadful fate that Harris documents; it is also the process by which such a fate creates a literary convention in black literature that is her subject, and from this perspective her interpretations of Toni Morrison's *Tar Baby*, undercutting the suppositions on which lynching rituals are based, and David Bradley's *Chaneysville Incident*, as a novel that exorcises the obsession with lynching, become models of reading texts in terms of their own tradition.

Considering the remarks I have made suggesting the invalidity of the usual ways for designating the Harlem Renaissance as a literary period, it is heartening to cite Michael G. Cooke for providing this year an example of a laudable approach to period formation. *Afro-American Literature in the Twentieth Century: The Achievement of Intimacy* (Yale) posits the development of this century's

black writing out of a matrix of signifying and blues into successive
conditions of self-veiling, solitude, kinship, and intimacy, the antithesis of alienation. Illustrations of the first stage, occurring when
Afro-American literature seeks acceptance in an ambient majority
culture, Cooke finds in James Weldon Johnson's *Autobiography of an
Ex-Colored Man* and the tales of Chesnutt's Uncle Julius. The environment threatened annihilation, so the inner self was veiled and
character invested in a material facade. Cooke admits that some
readers will say they find the subtlety of signifying in these works,
but in response argues that that uniquely black practice requires an
audience to have access to the truth so that the self-possession of
consciousness implied in signifying will be validated. Zora Neale
Hurston's Janie Crawford disavows a material facade but ends in
solitude. Richard Wright's Bigger Thomas, facing the significance of
his killings, moves from self-cancellation to self-avowal, the basis for
the fuller developments of kinship, which Cooke identifies in the
poetry of Michael Harper. The still underdeveloped quality of intimacy he locates as a goal in the verse of Robert Hayden. As a matter
of fact, though, intimacy is elusive of definition even as a chapter on
the ironic denial of it in Toomer's *Cane* offers an illuminating discussion of the consciousness of such characters as Paul and Kabnis.
Despite the inconclusiveness of the sections of Cooke's book that
carry his scheme to conclusion, except for comments on what Robert
B. Stepto terms immersion fiction (a ritualized return to the symbolic South), the project is both provocative and exemplary. Provocative because of the readings it offers in terms of Afro-American
linguistic practices, exemplary because it seeks development of forms
and periods in the intrinsic qualities of the literature as it is shaped
in history.

In two pieces published during 1984 R. Baxter Miller testifies to
the tradition of black literary criticism. In the first, "The Wasteland
and the Flower: Through Blyden Jackson—A Revised Theory for
Black Southern Literature" (*SLJ* 17:3–11) he extrapolates from Jackson's practical criticism the dedication to mimetic fiction, an ideal of
racial advancement through recognition of the quality of black writing that critics can generate in a broad public, and the interest in
entering the mainstream that marks the work of the distinguished
author of *The Waiting Years* (1976). The second piece by Miller,
titled "Who Knows But, that on the Equal Frequencies, We Speak
for Ourselves?" (*MELUS* 11,i:75–79), describing the resistance of

critics like himself to suggestions that Afro-American literary studies should form a part of a multi-ethnic discipline, shows one way in which he departs from Jackson. Charging ethnic studies with pseudo-objectivity, he asserts that accepting shelter within its framework would be self-denial. Two critics resisting self-denial are Gloria T. Hull and Erlene Stetson, whose contributions to *Between Women* explain the personal satisfaction of research. Hull's "Alice Dunbar-Nelson: A Personal and Literary Perspective" (pp. 105–11) states that principles she found through her study of Dunbar-Nelson, such as a resolution to tell all and the sense of engagement that followed upon her identification with her subject, have social along with personal importance. Stetson agrees about unity of motives in "Silence: Access and Aspiration" (pp. 237–51) where she explains that she was led to recovering the history of Georgia Douglas Johnson's poetic career by the anger she felt toward the patronizing attitude of such gatekeepers of literary reputation as Walter F. White.

Convinced of the practical necessity to challenge the fixed canon of American writing first of all in the classroom, Richard Yarborough writes "In the Realm of the Imagination: Afro-American Literature and the American Canon" (*ADE Bulletin* 78:35–42) in a manner Blyden Jackson would approve. Literature has a place, he says, in the documented history of cultural conflict in America, and, if we are to enlarge the concept of American culture to include a study of conflict, we must begin by introducing black writing into mainstream courses in the curriculum. For those who need support in undertaking the job, the article carries with it a "Selected Bibliography of Afro-American Literature" compiled by Jerry W. Ward, Jr., including basic bibliographical sources, anthologies, selected books of criticism, and periodicals.

As Miller and Yarborough clearly show, the consciousness of a political dimension to black literature and criticism remains high. But there is further evidence too. The novelist Charles Johnson, introducing this year's special issue of *Callaloo* on fiction with "Whole Sight: Notes on New Black Fiction" (7,iii:1–6), warns against the danger of being easily satisfied by the popular reception of select black novelists when the aim ought to be to change perceptions of the body of black writing. On a different tack, still political, Calvin Hernton's "The Sexual Mountain and Black Women Writers" (*BALF* 18:139–45) frankly discusses the hostile responses of some male critics to the vibrant work of black feminists. Claiming that superstar black male writers with the exception of James Baldwin have not portrayed women as full persons, that black women have been disregarded in literary history, and that the Black Arts movement established a macho hegemony, Hernton, speaking as one male critic to others, declares that they must recognize the historical justification of black feminism and cease resorting to distracting charges that it is counter-productive or a betrayal.

iii. Fiction

a. **Harper, Chesnutt, Du Bois.** Variations on the convention of the mulatto character are the subject of Vashti Lewis in "The Near-White Female in Frances Ellen Harper's *Iola Leroy*" (*Phylon* 45: 314–22), an essay that argues that despite an implied Caucasian standard of beauty a writer's decision to use a near-white character was a defensible choice for the dual audience of the 19th century, especially in the case of Harper's narrative which shows Iola reared in a nuclear family amidst other mulatto characters performing the vital roles assumed by black women.

Such rhetorical analyses of texts as Lewis's work only so long as they treat conventions and other broad patterns. When, as in the case of "Allegory in Chesnutt's *The Marrow of Tradition*" by James R. Giles and Thomas P. Lally (*JGE* 35:257–69), the analysis converts the text into tendentious argument, interpretation becomes simplistic. Reworking previous studies of the novel, Giles and Lally contend that rather than revealing a conflict between literary conception and reality, the novel presents intentional allegory of the triumph of malevolence in white society. By this reasoning the despairing and unsatisfactory conclusion of the novel becomes a position of black separatism tempered by humanism. A striking contrast to such heavy-handed treatment of Chesnutt is found in Robert B. Stepto's carefully researched and subtle essay " 'The Simple but Intensely Human Inner Life of Slavery': Storytelling, Fiction and the Revision of History in Charles W. Chesnutt's 'Uncle Julius Stories' " (*History and Tradition*, pp. 29–55). By taking into account all of the Uncle Julius stories, not only those published in *Conjure Woman*, Stepto is able to recount Chesnutt's reworking of the basic tripartite narrative structure of departure-return-revenge motifs and to trace the evolution of the frame structure of the stories. The course of this evolution leads from the initial representation of casually uttered folk tales to their formal presentation on the piazza where the audience of Annie and John become reliable listeners or collaborators rather than foils, that is, auditors capable of revoicing in literary English what they have heard of the intensely human inner life of slavery. Part of a forthcoming book on storytelling in the Afro-American narrative, Stepto's essay uncovering a complexity in Chesnutt overlooked even in the recent work of Michael Cooke, noted earlier, should force critical reconsideration. In the meanwhile it can provide informative background to readers of Nancy Ann Gidden's analysis of the wavering balance among story elements in " 'The Gray Wolf's Hant': Charles W. Chesnutt's Instructive Failure" (*CLAJ* 27:406–10).

"Psychic Duality of Afro-Americans in the Novels of W. E. B. Du Bois" by James B. Stewart (*Phylon* 44,ii[1983]:93–107) distills from unpublished and published romances the character types Du Bois created as composite psychological profiles for use in his investigation of double consciousness in the arena of history. The key to characters' resistance to psychic instability is a positive view of black experience that grants them insight into the larger society and a view of racial identity as "transcendental rather than phenotypical in nature." In addition to the merit of its consideration of the three unpublished works, "Scorn," "Bethesda A.M.E.," and "Wings of Atlanta," Stewart's essay claims attention because it exposes a theoretical framework for the narratives Du Bois said he wrote in order to interpret historical fact.

b. **Fauset, Toomer, Hurston.** In "Bad Blood in Jersey: Jessie Fauset's *The Chinaberry Tree*" (*CLAJ* 27:383–92) Mary Jane Lupton takes up William S. Braithwaite's statement in 1934 that Fauset was the potential Jane Austen of black literature. The restrictions of room, house, and yard operating on Austen's characters similarly constrain Fauset's; even so the narrative of female lives presents an authentic perspective on race through the consideration of "bad blood," which to females connotes moral deficiency. On this basis Lupton makes a reasonable case that the commonplace criticism of Fauset as implausibly romantic or prim arose because male critics failed to appreciate female culture.

Surely, for its approach and its conclusions Nellie Y. McKay's *Jean Toomer, Artist: A Study of His Literary Life and Work, 1894–1936* (N. C.) is one of the most provocative critical works of the year. Limiting herself to study of the period from childhood to publication of Toomer's last major work, 31 years before his death, McKay describes her work as an interpretive study rather than a critical biography, though she depends heavily on the autobiographies for an account of Toomer's intellectual life. The discussion of the first fruits of Toomer's artistry, *Balo* and *Natalie Mann*, identifies his kinship with the predominantly white avant-garde, while the heart of the book is an extended reading of *Cane*. The premise of the reading, and of the study as a whole, is that *Cane* signifies two journeys. The first journey, an exploration of artistic means to render black identity, ended successfully in the text that has established Toomer's reputation. Works after *Cane* reveal for McKay, as for other critics, a conflict between the needs of a doctrinaire man and his craft. Where others find partial resolution of that conflict in "Monrovia" and "Blue Meridian," McKay considers only the latter notable. As for the second journey—Toomer's effort to establish personal connection between himself and southern black folk culture—McKay joins her colleagues in noting its failure, but for reasons that depend in her analysis upon speculative interpretation of the writer's life. Toomer, McKay says, identified black folk culture as female, and though he recognized both female and male dimensions of himself, the narratives of *Cane* show the artist "cannot partake of [the culture's] nurturing qualities . . . and it refuses to be controlled by male Jean Toomer, representative of the dominant white culture of art and literature." Like the best of criticism, McKay's is bold. The reviews will show whether scholars of Afro-American literature are prepared to engage a work that anatomizes Toomer with the same concern for characteristics of gender that is shown when the subject is female.

Pursuing interpretation through analysis of Toomer's aesthetics rather than his subjective psychology, Heiner Bus in "Jean Toomer and the Black Heritage" (*History and Tradition*, pp. 56–83) arrives at a description of the writer's failure to realize his identity in the black South that is complementary to McKay's in its conclusion but vastly different in method. The burden of Bus's essay describes, in part 1 of *Cane*, the use of spirituals and blues as structural devices to introduce readers to the Afro-American past the protagonist wishes to possess; and the possibility of reading part 2 as urban blues. The conclusion of *Cane* shows Toomer, like Kabnis, insistent upon distancing himself from the black South. For the fictional protagonist this is the result of a fragmented sensibility, while his creator's detachment derives from his conception of the artist preserving a separation between biography and art, even though the inner logic of his text cries out for redemptive immersion in the South. Can one entertain both the possibility of using autobiographical writing to reveal Toomer's artistic self as does McKay, and Bus's idea that Toomer meant to sustain a separation between the intimate features of the self and his art? Yes indeed, for Bus adduces evidence of his contention from biography itself. One can have it both ways and gratefully so, since Bus's tightly focused argument suggests a contradiction that can lend itself to further application.

In the only original contribution to *Black Literature and Literary Theory*, ed. Henry Louis Gates, Jr. (Methuen), an essay entitled "Metaphor, Metonymy and Voice in *Their Eyes Were Watching God*" (pp. 205–19), Barbara Johnson draws upon Roman Jakobson's seminal "Two Aspects of Language and Two Types of Aphasic Disturbance" to construct a striking Deconstructive analysis of Zora Neale Hurston dramatizing the predicament of Janie, and the black female novelist caught between the urge to universalize and knowledge that only the near and alive can properly be named. Concentrating on the figurative structure of a passage following a crucial argument between Janie and Joe, Johnson demonstrates that Janie gains the power of voice when she can clarify the differences between her inner feelings and the outer environment in which she has lived in the role of wife; thus, Johnson argues, identity for Janie lies not in undifferentiated wholeness of self but in articulation of the different realms of her life. To underline the significance of this analysis as a politics of narrative, Johnson relates the double voicedness of Janie to the double heritage of blacks and then the compounded duality experienced by black women.

c. Wright, Ellison, Baldwin. Overlooked in last year's survey but deserving notice for its illustrative presentation of buried stories is "Richard Wright's Inside Narratives" by A. Robert Lee (*American Fiction: New Readings*, ed. Richard Gray; Barnes & Noble, 1983, pp. 200–221). Lee's description of "ancestral resonances" from within racial history in "Big Boy Leaves Home," for example, and the fantasy of revenge that story shares with "The Man Who Lived Underground" furthers the cause of freeing Wright from confinement in the school of naturalism. But while Wright's work encloses inner narratives derived from imagination working on racial experience, the vehicle for imagination is remarkably powerful realism. It is the task of William Howard in "Richard Wright's Flood Stories and the Great Mississippi River Flood of 1927: Social and Historical Backgrounds" (*SLJ* 16,ii:44–62) to demonstrate the correspondence between Wright's representation of the isolating effect upon characters in *Uncle Tom's Children* of an oppressive society's response to natural catastrophe and contemporary reports from the black press and the Colored Advisory Commission. Further investigation of the richness of Wright's realism in early fiction appears in "Bitches, Whores, and Woman Haters: Archetypes and Typologies in the Art of Richard Wright" by Maria K. Mootry, one of two original contributions to the Twentieth Century Views volume (*Richard Wright*, pp. 117–27). Mootry's chief exhibit is *Lawd Today* where Jake's quest for manhood encounters a serious obstacle in a woman who manifests in the face of the narcissism of the street man a stifling love he violently resists. Citing the authority of William Grier and Price Cobbs whose *Black Rage* diagnoses the effects of suffering on love and referring to Wright's autobiography, which records his own sense of female threat, Mootry convincingly establishes the ambiguities of love and death as a fundamental fantasy in Wright's work, including, of course, *Native Son*.

The imagery in Wright's deeply felt story of Bigger forms the subject of two interesting essays. Ross Pudaloff's "Celebrity as Identity: Richard Wright, *Native Son*, and Mass Culture" (*SAF* 11[1983]:3–18), another work overlooked in last year's survey, generates out of recognition that Bigger is framed in every scene with images provided by mass culture an argument that he is a protagonist deliberately created without depth greater than the self presented him by that culture. A suggestive implication for interpretation is that Bigger mimics the 1930s tough guy as can be seen in the hard-boiled exterior he presents at the conclusion of the novel, but Pudaloff's purpose reaches beyond the immediate text to make, first, the point that while Wright's interest in popular culture is well known, the fact that he eagerly absorbed it into serious art is crucial to understanding his aesthetic, and second, to assert that in employing popular culture to characterize Bigger, Wright prefigures externalized protagonists in the work of Thomas Pynchon and Ishmael Reed. Certainly both matters, but particularly the latter, belong on the agenda for further consideration, because the prevalent view of Bigger as a character moving to fuller consciousness informs most criticism, including "Bigger's Great Leap to the Figurative" by Kathleen Gallagher (*CLAJ*

27:293–314). Gallagher finds the metaphor of potential criminality, enforced by racial stereotypes, haunting Wright's work; thus, Bigger's progress carries him from subjection to images of murderer, through a period of fluctuation when he uses the stereotypes for his own ends, to a point where he supplants secondhand imagery with the self-created metaphor of his own life. Pudaloff's and Gallagher's observations on derivative imagery seem irreconcilable. Their point of contention—the presence or absence of authentic consciousness—necessarily depends upon how the ending of the novel is read. That has been at issue since the novel was published, though perhaps now the dispute has been refined.

Robert J. Butler, whose comparative studies have been noted in previous years, contributes for discussion "Wright's *Native Son* and Two Novels by Zola: A Comparative Study" (*BALF* 18:100–05). An atmosphere of fear, a fascination with violence in characters, and typologically similar imagery are the points of similarity between Wright's book and *Thérèse Racquin* and *La Bête humaine*. As always Butler's intelligent appraisal of textual kinship is welcome because he does not make one novel the clone of another but instead links congruent details to an outlook shared by the authors.

Horace A. Porter's "The Horror and the Glory: Richard Wright's Portrait of the Artist in *Black Boy* and *American Hunger*," the second original piece in Twentieth Century Views (*Richard Wright*, pp. 55–67), cites passages showing Wright assuming power through an ability to interpret words, articulating the relationship to his parents, and adopting literature as a means to free himself in order to show that language is a central autobiographical theme. Though the theme is predictable, Porter usefully collects the evidence.

The year's two essays on Wright's second novel have the common purpose of distinguishing author from protagonist. Chidi Maduka in "Irony and Vision in Richard Wright's *The Outsider*" (*WHR* 38:161–69) claims that the ironic mode of the narrative detaches Wright from Cross Damon, while Amritjit Singh in "Richard Wright's *The Outsider*: Existentialist Exemplar or Critique" (*CLAJ* 27:357–70) says the book is a mechanical effort to rehearse before possible adoption a stance toward the dilemma of the individual in society.

In *The Bang and the Whimper* Zbigniew Lewicki uses Ralph Ellison's *Invisible Man* to illustrate in writing on the black experience inclusion of the tradition of apocalyptic fiction originating with 17th-century Puritans. For Lewicki, Ellison's novel is important both because it reintroduces the apocalyptic mode into 20th-century writing, with evident debts to Twain and Melville as predecessors, and because the black version of the mode renders apocalypse cyclically without the rebirth promised in the religious sources of the tradition. Of course, it is the narrator's continued hibernation that enforces Lewicki's pessimistic reading of the novel. Thorpe Butler's "What Is to Be Done?—Illusion, Identity, and Action in Ralph Ellison's *Invisible Man*" (*CLAJ* 27:315–31) re-examines the problem of Ellison's reluctance to allow his protagonist to surface and endorse direct political action and proposes the explanation that action, like identity in the world Ellison creates, depends upon illusion: therefore, authentic action or self-creation can be accomplished only through the control allowed in the creation of narrative. Given the epistemology of the novel the argument makes good sense.

The rich allusiveness of *Invisible Man* naturally stimulates research, and to accompany Lewicki's proposed source there are several other efforts to uncover the lineage of Ellison's art. Rudolph F. Dietze draws upon propositions earlier advanced in a monograph (see *ALS 1982*, p. 488) to write "Ralph Ellison and the Literary Tradition" (*History and Tradition*, pp. 118–29) which opens by charging that recent studies unduly minimize the nonblack traditions for Ellison's writing and then argues for the significance of André Malraux's *Psychology of Art* along with works by T. S. Eliot and James Joyce as literary ancestors. Since Ellison has made the point for himself, not much is gained by repeating it. Dietze is also responsible for "Crainway and Son: Ralph Ellison's *Invisible Man* as Seen Through the Perspective of Twain, Crane, and Hemingway" (*DeltaES* 18:25–46), which pursues the allusion in a passage on the death of Tod Clifton to "The Short Happy Life of Francis Macomber" and thence to *The Red Badge of Courage* and *Huckleberry Finn*, works both Ellison and Hemingway acknowledge as ancestral. Dietze thus infers a dialogue with literary tradition that finds the quartet of writers sharing a view of life as civil war. The conception of dynamic intertextual relations is what makes this essay effective. Robert J. Butler also has something to say about Ellison. "Dante's *Inferno* and Ellison's *Invisible Man*: A Study in Literary Continuity" (*CLAJ* 28:57–77) builds on an earlier study of circular structure (see *ALS 1980*, p. 447) for an essay about a plausible model for functional images of circularity. "*Invisible Man*: Ralph Ellison's Wasteland" by Mary Ellen Williams Walsh (*CLAJ* 28:150–58) carries the suggestion of textual similarities as far as her ingenuity permits, in the process dissolving a profound book into a collage of encoded references and thereby reminding us of the dangers of source hunting. Phillipe Whyte's "*Invisible Man* as a Trickster Tale" (*DeltaES* 18:47–67) is more successful because it identifies traits of the narrative that may be confirmed in black culture and because it relates the practice of the trickster as a means of survival in the absurd universe of the novel. Similarly, Jerome de Romanet's "Musical Elements in *Invisible Man* with Special Reference to the Blues" (*DeltaES* 18:105–18), though its treatment of motifs is underdeveloped, provides some help because it confines discussion to black musical allusions in the landscape of the novel.

Criticism attending to the dynamics of the text includes a stimulating consideration of the framing of the story by Simone Vauthier in " 'Not Quite on the Beat': An Academic Interpretation of the Narrative Stances in Ralph Ellison's *Invisible Man*" (*DeltaES* 18:69–88). Distinguishing the narrated time of the story from the narrating time of the prologue and epilogue, Vauthier comments on the double contract of novel/memoir and audience. Kimberley W. Benston looks to the order of the hero's experience in "Controlling the Dialectical Deacon: The Critique of Historicism in *Invisible Man*" (*DeltaES* 18:89–103) to explain how the section of the novel on the Brotherhood explodes the Hegelian-Marxian theory of progress through linear development. Images of manipulation and depersonalization lead the narrator to an epiphany in which he recognizes the blindness of those who would raise the agency of History above individual will. Michel Fabre's " 'Looking at the Naked Blonde—Closely' (or Scrutinizing Ellison's Writing)" (*DeltaES* 18:119–31) microscopically examines the rhetorical patterning, intertextual references, and lexical-semantic connotations in the prose of the smoker scene and draws from it evidence of Ellison's careful structure of binary patterns and subliminal references to racism. Finally, it is gratifying to note that the short list of criticism on Ellison's works besides his famous novel is lengthened by Jan Nordby Gretlund's "Protest and Affirmation in Ralph Ellison's 'And Hickman Arrives' " (*DeltaES* 18:15–23). The first of seven fragments of a novel-in-progress published between 1960 and 1977, the Hickman story of mixed racial heritage in a time of segregation provides Gretlund the chance to explicate the historical content of its symbols.

"Love, Race and Sex in the Novels of James Baldwin" by Lorelei Cederstrom (*Mosaic* 17:175–88) depends upon comprehension of the similarity of dominance and subordination in racial and sexual politics; the resulting essay is a detailed analysis of the variations in sexual relations Baldwin presents in his major novels that should help critics understand at last that it is equality in androgyny rather than a more limited sexual preference that Baldwin posits as redemptive. Peter Bruck's "Dungeon and Salvation: Biblical Rhetoric in James Baldwin's *Just Above My Head*" (*History and Tradition*, pp. 130–46) elucidates the contradiction between the gospel songs proclaiming the joy of salvation performed by Arthur Montana and the instances of existential suffering in the novel to show that with the setbacks marked by the death of Martin Luther King, Jr., Baldwin has extended his interest in *homo interior* to the point where for the first time he creates characters whose pain is more individual than racial. However accurate may be Bruck's attribution of cause for the framing of the novel, his analysis of a tension between Old Testament and New Testament elements is illuminating. Richard N. Albert evidently has reflected upon the received opinions of Baldwin's best-known short story to write "The Jazz-Blues Motif in Baldwin's 'Sonny's Blues'" (*CollL* 11:178–85). If the story concerns the black heritage established in music, Albert asks, why then is the leader of the group Sonny plays with Creole, a person who does not share the background of slavery? And why do they play "Am I Blue?" a song written by whites that lacks the classic 12-bar, 3-lined form of blues? Albert's response is in the form of another question: Is Baldwin seeking an image of amalgamation and change as well as heritage? I have a nagging feeling the questions aren't nit picking.

d. **Williams, Gaines, Goines, Reed, Delany, Butler.** The Twayne editors' requirement that volumes in their series chart career development effectively serves Gilbert H. Muller, whose *John A. Williams* (TUSAS 472) delineates three distinct phases in the progression of Williams's novels. The first, including the sensitive presentation of interracial relationships within the special milieu of advanced musicians in *Night Song* and the revision of myths about the black family in *Sissie*, is marked by cautious optimism about American society. The radical historical consciousness of *The Man Who Cried I Am* and the demystification of military history in *Captain Blackman*, along with the prophetic fantasy that book and *Sons of Darkness, Sons of Light* project, show Williams's hopes vanishing before a vision of violence in the second phase. The impasse apparent in *Mothersill*

and the Foxes appears to be surmounted with *!Click Song,* so that the
most recent phase suggests a new affirmation. The scheme gains its
plausibility from Muller's conception of Williams as an author whose
varied modes of writing and varied subjects derives from continuing
interest in re-viewing history under the aspect of contemporary experience. This thesis supports the contention that Williams's nonfiction must be included in discussions of his work and gives occasion
and purpose to Muller's able explanations of structure and theme in
the novels.

John Callahan is one of the critics whose recent work, like that of
Robert B. Stepto, Henry Louis Gates, and Houston A. Baker, investigates the prominent strain of storytelling in the Afro-American tradition in order to mark the transformation of oral folk tale into
literature. This year Callahan contributes to the project "Hearing is
Believing: The Landscape of Voice in Ernest Gaines' *Bloodline*" (*Callaloo* 7,i:86–112). On an immediate level Gaines's provision of characters who are tale tellers and his representation of their idiom com-
pels belief, but the readings of the stories in *Bloodline* offered by
Callahan show that in adapting the continuous present of the oral
tradition so that event and perception occur at once, idiom becomes
narrative voice bridging the inner and outer worlds and showing that
though the old social order seems impervious, it is crumbling. Limiting itself to "A Long Day in November" and "The Sky is Gray," John
W. Roberts's "The Individual and the Community in Two Short
Stories by Ernest J. Gaines" (*BALF* 18:110–13) also addresses the
place of folk culture in *Bloodline.* The theme Roberts identifies concerns the dilemma of characters who find traditional folk values inadequate to the personal needs that arise in a time of historical
change. Roberts presents the dilemma as it is related through a
privileged consciousness that filters events of the narratives; thus, his
essay supplements Callahan's. The particularized history that Gaines
has staked out as his subject is explored by Thadious Davis in "Head-
lands and Quarters: Louisiana in *Catherine Carmier*" (*Callaloo* 7,ii:
1–13). Through exhaustive description of the elements of the narrative Davis portrays the patterns of encounter and change in the
microcosm upon which Gaines founds the psychological drama of his
novel. Informed by sensitivity as well as research, the article is an
example of what is meant by such a term of praise as "a sound study."
Dissent from the usual high opinion of Gaines's fiction can be found
in "History and Fiction in Alice Walker's *The Third Life of Grange*

Copeland and Ernest Gaines' *The Autobiography of Miss Jane Pitt-man*" (*History and Tradition*, pp. 147–63) by Klaus Ensslen. The essence of the argument on Walker appeared in an earlier version (see *ALS 1982*, p. 395), but the new section on Gaines charges that the fictional text covering a phase culminating in the Civil Rights movement obscures rather than articulates historical experience. Despite the effort to have Jane and her speech typify popular experience, Ensslen finds her narrative emptied of the social perceptions and aggressive strategies that must have contributed to historical movement.

Quite a different world than Gaines's Louisiana emerges in Greg Goode's "From *Dopefiend* to *Kenyatta's Last Hit:* The Angry Black Crime Novels of Donald Goines" (*MELUS* 11,iii:41–48). The author of 16 paperback originals that sold over 5 million copies in the mass market, Goines (who also wrote as Al C. Clark) is the foremost exemplar of ghetto crime fiction. Goode, who has established himself as an important critic of crime fiction with an ethnic slant, gives readers an overview of Goines and an introduction to his narrative genre.

A special issue of the *Review of Contemporary Fiction* gives us this year eight essays on Ishmael Reed. "*The Free-Lance Pallbearers*, or: No More Proscenium Arch" by Franco La Polla (4:188–95) identifies the communication system of mass culture as the tool Reed deliberately uses to revise the novel genre and discusses the collage effect which levels all elements that contribute to the shape of traditional texts. Jerry H. Bryant's estimate of Reed in "Old Gods and New Demons—Ishmael Reed and His Fiction" (4:195–202) centers upon the use of caricature to cut the novel's links with realism and naturalism. Deeper and fuller analysis of models, techniques, and their meanings occurs in "From Krazy Kat to Hoodoo: Aesthetic Discourse in the Fiction of Ishmael Reed" by James R. Lindroth (4:227–33). Observing that Reed focuses, as did George Herriman, the artist of Krazy Kat, on language and the art-act, Lindroth describes parallels between *Yellow Back Radio Broke Down* and a Krazy Kat sequence in which discourse is organized around the opposition of realistic mimesis and playful artistic improvisation. Peter Nazareth in "Heading Them Off at the Pass: The Fiction of Ishmael Reed" (4:208–26) ably reads the satire of several novels including *Flight to Canada* and *Yellow Back Radio Broke Down*, while Joe Weixlmann in "Ishmael Reed's Raven" (4:205–08) explains the relationship between Raven Quickskill in *Flight to Canada* and a Tlingit Indian legend's trickster character (a figure known to Reed) as well as an allusion to Poe in the novel. These expositions of satire share purpose with Jack Byrne's "White Men with Three Names (or) If Sam has Kidnapped Checkers, then Who is in the John?—Reed's Journey from Scat to Scatology" (4:237–44), which challenges the obsession of reviewers with the epigraphical references to excrement in *Free-Lance Pallbearers* by a summary of themes and characters that are objects of satire. On the other hand, Geoffrey Green's "Reality as Art: *The Last Days of Louisiana Red*" (4:233–37) expresses impatience with the attention many critics give to Reed's satiric commentary on popular culture and calls for recognition that the social material in the novels is presented to reflect the mythic dimension of reality. As a matter of fact all of the essays noted here do acknowledge that Reed presents the stuff of history as a veil over myth, particularly that mythic system he develops as Neo-HooDoo. Perhaps, though, Green would be more satisfied with W. C. Barnberger's contribution to the special Reed issue, for his "The Waxing and Waning of Cab Calloway" (4:202–04) discusses "Cab Calloway Stands in for the Moon" in terms of its fusion of language and story line with the Neo-HooDoo universe, contending that the story is more successful than the development of its motif in the novel *Mumbo Jumbo*. For a highly useful explication of Neo-HooDoo as a system drawn from folk roots, one can turn to "Blacking the Zero: Toward a Semiotics of Neo-Hoodoo" by Robert Elliot Fox (*BALF* 18:95–99). Fox's essay inquires into the significance of a sign used by Reed which originates as a representation of a loa. Signifying two different realities, it lends itself for Reed to use in relating such doubles as textuality and orality and the interplay of black and white.

The skillful handling of complex systems in the essay on Reed appears also in the article Fox contributes to the special issue of *BALF* on black science fiction authors. "The Politics of Desire in Delany's *Triton* and *The Tides of Lust*" (18:49–56) pairs the treatment of sexuality in Delany's better-known work with its appearance in his pornographic novel to produce a meditation on the trope of love as absence and the artifice and schemes of the texts. Sandra Y. Govan, who produced the piece on Delany for the new *DLB* volume, contributes to the discussion of him in *BALF* with "The Insistent Presence of Black Folk in the Novels of Samuel R. Delany" (18:43–48), which shows that being black or otherwise non-Caucasian in the worlds Delany creates in future fiction matters in ways different from the ways it matters now. Besides exposition Govan's intent is to propose that the variety of Delany's ethnic characters represents his method of grappling with his own position as a black American writer. Mary Kay Bray's "Rites of Reversal: Double Consciousness in Delany's *Dhalgren*" (18:57–61) contends that blackness, as it appears in DuBois's formulation of double consciousness, presents itself ironically in a parodic quest story that has its protagonist diminish in consciousness and control. "The Science Fiction of Samuel R. Delany and the Limits of Technology" by Charles Nilon (18:62–68) examines Delany's treatment of difference and change in texts that show technology to be an agency of change, if properly integrated, but limited in what it can do to humanize experience. Upon this field, then, Nilon sets the figures and ideas that sum up Delany's sociology. The result is an excellent guide through the works, an exemplary demonstration that they are products of the experience of a black person who rejects the notion that otherness is to be contemned, and a proposition that critical method must allow that blackness may shape any sort of text, however subtly or indirectly.

Octavia E. Butler is the other author providing the occasion for the *BALF* special issue on science fiction. Ruth Salvaggio's "Octavia Butler and the Black Science-Fiction Heroine" (18:78–81) seeks the interplay of race and sex in the issues revealed by the protagonists of the Patternist series as Butler's unique black signature upon her genre. Sandra Y. Govan's "Connections, Links, and Extended Networks: Patterns in Octavia Butler's Science Fiction" (18:82–87) amplifies the issue of female power by specifying the connections among the conflicts of will in the Patternist novels.

e. M. Walker, Marshall, Brooks, Morrison, A. Walker, Jones, Bambara.

The most casual reader of these annual reports will have noted the expanding discussion of black women writers. This year it is possible to have an entire section of the fiction report devoted to that discussion. Fortuitously the section begins with Eleanor Traylor's excellent "Music as Theme: The Blues Mode in the Works of Margaret Walker" (*Black Women Writers*, pp. 511–25). Traylor, whose work-in-progress concerns the folk roots of literature, applies in this essay the thesis that music is the significant referent for Afro-American narrative. Reading the account of Vyry's movement through time in Walker's *Jubilee*, Traylor identifies within it the story of a merger of self and community founded upon the wisdom of the blues mode where the "I" has no meaning without the implicit "we."

A similar concern with the self in community marks criticism of Paule Marshall, especially since publication of *Praisesong for the Widow*. With that novel it became possible to see a distinct development, and so Eugenia Collier in "The Closing of the Circle: Movement from Division to Wholeness in Paule Marshall's Fiction" (*Black Women Writers*, pp. 295–315) studies the element of ritual dance in the most recent novel and indicates how it has marked entry into community life and self-integration, however fleeting, in all of Marshall's writing. "And Called Every Generation Blessed: Theme, Setting, and Ritual in the Works of Paule Marshall" by John McCluskey, Jr. (*Black Women Writers*, pp. 316–34) manifests the same attention to assimilation of individual into community and a similar concern with ritual, but in its well-detailed account of characters stresses the significance of the past, first as a barrier to individual sensual expression in early work and then as a source of support in the later. Rosalie Riegle Troester writes "Turbulence and Tenderness: Mothers, Daughters, and 'Othermothers' in Paule Marshall's *Brown Girl, Brownstones*" (*Sage* 1,ii:13–16) to explain the function of Selina Boyce's alternative role models in helping her achieve autonomy and eventually the ability to accept her biological mother as a woman.

Increased attention to women's writing also accounts for the second article in two years on Gwendolyn Brooks's novel published in 1953. "Vision in Gwendolyn Brooks's *Maud Martha*" by Patricia H. Lattin and Vernon E. Lattin (*Crit* 25:180–88) reads the work as a comedy of the commonplace in which the protagonist's ability to see beauty in ugliness moderates her observations of racism. The Lattins warn against approaching the small compass of this novel as though it were the same as, say, *Native Son*, but interestingly they find it helpful to contrast Maud Martha to Bigger throughout their essay.

Toni Morrison's individual novels have been given so many interpretive readings that to gain a hearing now critics must focus their work very tightly on elements of style or address modal patterns still insufficiently studied. "The 'Sweet Life' in Toni Morrison's Fiction" by Elizabeth B. House (*AL* 56:181–202) seeks the expression of conflict between idyllic values and the values of competitive success in food imagery. Natural, simple foods are linked to the Bottom in *Sula* and to Son in *Tar Baby*; sweets are associated, of course, with Valerian Street, and exotic foods with Jadine. This version of a cooked-raw binary structure sounds simpler in summary than it is in exposition, where House follows the implications of the scheme into analysis of characters' conflict. Image studies such as this gain sanction from Morrison's remarking in discussions of her work that she seeks the right metaphor to get her writing going. Peter B. Erickson's "Images of Nurturance in Toni Morrison's *Tar Baby*" (*CLAJ* 28:11–32) explains his topic as a key focus for Morrison's consideration of identity. Jadine who cuts herself off from tradition and cross-generational sustenance also rejects a maternal role, the maternal care of Odine, and the reproductive function of sex. The support of the maternity theme found in the plot of the relationship of the absent child to Margaret and Valerian, along with Son's positive attitude toward reproduction, Erickson adduces as evidence of Morrison's strong differentiation of gender and her insistent heterosexuality. Eleanor W. Traylor's "The Fabulous World of Toni Morrison's *Tar Baby*" (*Confirmation: An Anthology of African American Women*, ed. Amiri Baraka and Amina Baraka; Morrow, 1983, pp. 333–52) skillfully classifies the novel as a fable about disconnection, a disease manifest in the character of Jadine but rooted in the American disposition since Colonial times to slaughter the reality of black cultural presence. C. Lynn Munro's "The Tattooed Heart and the Serpentine Eye: Morrison's Choice of an Epigraph for *Sula*" (*BALF* 18:150–54) accepts the suggestion to compare the novel with Tennessee Williams's *The Rose Tattoo*. Karen F. Stein in "Toni Morrison's *Sula*: A Black Woman's Epic" (*BALF* 18:146–50) intelligently comments on the ironic structuring that repeatedly confronts expectation with mundane events and on the character pairing that leads Nel Wright to learn her own capacity for evil from her second self, Sula Peace. Irony is also the subject for Robert J. Butler's "Open Movement and Selfhood in Toni Morrison's *Song of Solomon*" (*CentR* 28–29:58–75) in the sense that oppositions, such as that between Milkman's limited consciousness and the narrator's mind, give ironic perspective to his journey toward self-discovery.

The critical work of 1984 also gives us three comprehensive treatments of Morrison's canon. One is the contribution by Susan L. Blake to the *DLB* volume noted earlier. The other two appear in *Black Women Writers*. Darwin T. Turner's evaluative essay "Theme, Characterization, and Style in the Works of Toni Morrison" (pp. 361–69) has value for its consideration of a persistent thread of lyricism and the vivid narration of grotesquerie that conquers disbelief, as well as for a provocative examination of themes including the expanded vision of white oppression in *Song of Solomon* and the theme of fail-

ure in heterosexual love that seems apparent in the fact that the only
successful relationships in the novels are single sex or between parents and children. "The Quest for Self: Triumph and Failure in the
Works of Toni Morrison" (pp. 346–60) by Dorothy H. Lee describes
Pecola's quest in *The Bluest Eye* as a heightened enactment of the
views of her parents and community, characterizes the rebirth of
Milkman in *Song of Solomon* as the consequence of his abandoning
ego, and contrasts the goals of Jade and Son in *Tar Baby*. Each case
develops Morrison's broader theme of the effect of community acceptance or rejection on her characters.

The year's work on Alice Walker's fiction includes praise and
second thought. "Alice Walker: The Black Woman Artist as Wayward" by Barbara Christian (*Black Women Writers*, pp. 457–77)
describes the contrariness that leads Walker to challenge fashionable
beliefs in all of her work. The famous story "Everyday Use" might
come to anyone's mind as an illustration of re-examining fashion, but
Christian explains also that *The Third Life of Grange Copeland* expresses anger at attribution of total causality for all ills to white oppression, *Meridian* scrutinizes myths of the black woman, the protagonists of *In Love and Trouble* defy rigid conventions of sexism,
and so forth. No doubt much of the effect of this fine essay lies in its
specification of the radical individuality of waywardness as a mode of
self-knowledge of special use to black women in their historical and
contemporary circumstances. Bettye J. Parker-Smith mixes praise with
caution in "Alice Walker's Women: In Search of Some Peace of Mind"
(*Black Women Writers*, pp. 478–93) which finds Walker's female
characters mirroring the allegation that their condition results from
guilt and inherent weakness, because they serve as repositories for
black male rage and encourage their own victimization, that is, they
do until *The Color Purple*, which elevates women to sovereignty.
Nevertheless, Walker's women are "a disturbing bunch indeed," operating haphazardly as they do, and it is yet to be seen if change will be
permanent. What bothers Trudier Harris in her essay "On *The Color
Purple*, Stereotypes, and Silence" (*BALF* 18:155–61) is the silence
of critics before a work in which the wonderful use of voice cannot
veil the validation it offers to racist notions of black male pathology,
the unrealistic portrayals of character in the assumed time period,
and the fairy tale projected as plot.

Melvin Dixon's "Singing a Deep Song: Language as Evidence in
the Novels of Gayl Jones" (*Black Women Writers*, pp. 236–48) un-

dertakes the dual task of showing how the rhythm and structure of spoken speech in Jones are brought into ritualized dialogue and how language displays the capacity for regeneration that the extreme behavior of plot might seem to place beyond reach. For the contrasting fiction of Toni Cade Bambara there is a contrasting sense of language, according to Ruth Elizabeth Burke in "From Baptism to Resurrection: Toni Cade Bambara and the Incongruity of Language" (*Black Women Writers*, pp. 48–57). Despite the impression of pleasure in speech created by *Gorilla, My Love*, words are barriers to communication or revelation of alienation, and sometimes as in *The Salt Eaters* dialogue is nearly absent, because for Bambara only the innate spirituality of wordless relationship draws people together. Ending this section as it began with an essay by Eleanor Traylor, this one titled "Music as Theme: The Jazz Mode in the Works of Toni Cade Bambara" (*Black Women Writers*, pp. 58–70), allows for notice of a structural analysis that makes clear for once what it means to suggest that a literary composition can be an analogue to jazz. Building her study on a definition of jazz performance as summing up past significance of a theme, extraction of its lasting qualities, and recreation, Traylor analyzes *The Salt Eaters* as a modern story of creation.

f. **General Criticism of Fiction.** The commonest strain of theory in the study of black fiction holds that fictitious characters in imagined narratives mirror history in their experiences. Such a conviction on the part of Gloria Wade-Gayles accounts for the substance and method of her analysis of 12 selected novels from the period 1946 to 1976 in *No Crystal Stair: Visions of Race and Sex in Black Women's Fiction* (Pilgrim Press). Against the background of a chapter of historical overview, which presents statistics and cultural signs documenting such changes as appear in the emergence of a women's movement, the Civil Rights struggle, and the rise of black feminism, Wade-Gayles, through readings of novels she judges to be the most dependable guides to the core of black women's humanity, considers such topics as the tension between motherhood and black experience, the condition of domestic and menial workers, and the challenges to sexism advanced by the fictional characters of Sula Mae Peace and Meridian Hill. Presiding over the discussions, which display a sound foundation in works of social research and feminist analysis, are Wade-Gayles's metaphors of the narrow space of race and the dark enclosure of sex which express her view of the dominant theme of double jeopardy. Despite the lucidity of the book's presentation it is susceptible to criticism on at least two counts. First, though Wade-Gayles declares her book is a literary study, not a theoretical work, it obviously does depend upon a reflection theory that assumes literature documents social experience in an unmediated fashion. Second, Wade-Gayles does not explain her selection of the representative texts from among the 26 major novels she claims were written during her time period and thus leaves the reader suspecting that evaluative literary criteria have a larger role than the idea of literature as documentation allows. A similarly unreflective method coupled with engaging exposition appears in Wade-Gayles's article "The Truths of our Mothers' Lives: Mother-Daughter Relationships in Black Women's Fiction" (*Sage* 1,ii:8–12) which laments the paucity of sociological data on the dynamics of black mother-daughter relationships, but offers fiction as an available substitute. The analyses of fiction are shrewd, as is the concluding observation that, contrary to the contention of white feminists about behavior of mothers in a patriarchy, black women in these novels do not condition their daughters to be passive or irrational. It is precisely because Wade-Gayles offers such findings as this indication of a distinctively black vision of maternity in the literary tradition that one feels it necessary to challenge her methodological assumptions. Scholarship this good owes itself a sounder theoretical base.

In "Culture Clash, Survival, and Transformation: A Study of Some Innovative Afro-American Novels of Detection" (*MissQ* 38:21–31) Joe Weixlmann enlarges upon his study of innovative fiction (see *ALS 1983*, pp. 403–04) by treating the experiments of Ishmael Reed, Toni Morrison, and Clarence Major upon one of the most fixed and redundant forms of narrative. *Mumbo Jumbo*'s parody of detective fiction confronts Western rationality with the uncertainty of multiplicity of answers; *Song of Solomon* defies the convention of closure in the quest narrative; *Reflex and Bone Structure* undermines the central expectations of the whodunit by relating an investigation that widens the possibility of answers to the detection problem. Skillfully argued, the article implicitly advances an idea of a characteristically black way of handling the Afro-American dual heritage.

Toni Morrison brings the authority of a novelist to bear upon discrete phases of the literary process in "Memory, Creation, and Writing" (*Thought* 59:385–90). Describing memory as a form of willed creation that evokes a galaxy of emotions and uncovers their forgotten stimuli, Morrison says that she, for one, seeks a reader's active participation in the non-narrative experience of the text she assembles from memory. This is to say that she views narrative as an access to knowledge of reality, black narrative as means of relating a knowledge discredited in the West and, therefore, requiring use of black art techniques like antiphony and improvisation to map it truly. For illustration Morrison tells how memory led to motif, structure, and theme in *Tar Baby*.

iv. Poetry

a. **Wheatley, Hughes, Cullen, Tolson, Brooks, Walker, Hayden.** To the bio-bibliography (1981) and the compilation of critical essays (1982) with which he established himself as the most active scholar on Wheatley, William H. Robinson now adds the omnibus volume *Phillis Wheatley and Her Writings* (Garland). The opening section, titled "On Phillis Wheatley and Her Boston," recreates the contemporary scene as the poet "would have seen it" and amplifies biography through discussion of Mrs. Susanna Wheatley's role as patron and "editor," the circumstances of Phillis's manumission, and details recorded in an early "life." The general characteristics of the verse are the subject of "On Phillis Wheatley's Poetry" which relates the characteristic ways she employed conventional figurative devices, the imagery, and the references that can defend her against the charge that her writings express too little of an African self. The volume also serves as a complete collection of the works by printing early poems extant in manuscript and newspapers, a facsimile of *Poems on Various Occasions* with extended notes, eight later poems, 25 letters (many of them to her lifelong black friend Obour Tanner), Wheatley's listing of poems in proposals for volumes never published, and variant poems and letters. As if this were not enough Robinson includes in nine appendixes such items as biblical and Latin originals for poems, probable but unsigned poems by Wheatley, contemporary letters about her, and two 19th-century biographical accounts. The volume is amply indexed and a selective bibliography lists sources. Providing everything the critic needs to begin work, the book is an essential source on Wheatley and a model for other projects in early black writing.

Of the year's three essays on the poetry of Langston Hughes the most helpful is "Langston Hughes: Rhetoric and Protest" by Mar-

garet A. Reid (*LHRev* 3:13–20) which observes strategies of contrast
between romantic setting and imagery of violence in "Mulatto" and
offers a consideration of protest in "Junior Addict." Edward O. Ako's
"Langston Hughes and the Négritude Movement: A Study in Literary
Influence" (*CLAJ* 28:46–56) carefully distinguishes between affinity,
which is a matter of similarity in texts; and influence, which requires
demonstrable proof that a source aided in bringing work into existence. The principle certainly seems rigorous enough, but in Ako's
consideration of Hughes's influence on African writers we find that his
evidence is journals that encouraged Africans to read black Americans and a speech by Leopold Senghor attesting to his conscious acceptance of Hughes. Lacking any treatment of poetic form or texts,
we are left merely with reiteration of the familiar idea that Afro-
American writers were congenial to Africans. Ako's distinction between affinity and influence remains viable, however, for application
to "The Blues and the Son: Reflections of Black Self Assertion in the
Poetry of Langston Hughes and Nicolas Guillen" by Eloise Y. Spicer
(*LHRev* 3:1–12). The *son*, a popular dance, serves the Cuban poet
in *Motivas de Son* as formal model much as blues serve Hughes.
Spicer—taking issue with Cuban critics who deny a relationship between Hughes and Guillen—argues that narrative voice, tone, and
the question-response patterns evident in the poets' adaptations show
a similarity of form and African source. The evidence affirms affinity,
but not influence.

A salutary contribution of Alan R. Shucard's *Countee Cullen*
(TUSAS 470) is to set aside much of the promotional talk that surrounded Cullen's career. Attempting to avoid contributing to the
campaign to advance Cullen's reputation, which his preface notes is
difficult when the poet's second wife makes her appeals to a critic,
Shucard focuses squarely on the question of whether the poetry can
be classed as black. The conclusion is that in mass and theme the
verse shows that racial consciousness and pride welled up in Cullen
even as he tried to suppress it and to deny designation as a Negro
poet. On the other hand, the writing devoted to themes such as death
and love that Cullen considered universally poetic are marked by a
high degree of control and a darkness of vision that Shucard speculates might be associated with unresolved sexual identity. Be that as
it may, there is laudable clearsightedness in the summary appraisal
of Cullen as a stunted poet whose affinity for a past that he imagined
was a period of greater grace and beauty made it impossible for him

to respond to the poetic developments of his own time or to develop his facile technique beyond a mannered style.

In "Three Artists in Melvin B. Tolson's *Harlem Gallery*" William H. Hansell (*BALF* 18:122–27) joins the discussion initiated by Mariann Russell's full-length study of *Harlem Gallery* in 1980 and continued by Patricia Schroeder last year to explain at length how the characters of the painter John Laugart, the poet Hidcho Heights, and the composer Mister Starks create the kinds of works that illustrate the new art announced by Tolson's poem.

Gwendolyn Brooks has been well served this year by two critics who feel strong sympathy for the outlook she has developed in the second portion of her career. Addison Gayle, Jr., writing "Gwendolyn Brooks: Poet of the Whirlwind" (*Black Women Writers*, pp. 79–87), attends to the change her poetry exhibited after the declaration of comradeship she made to younger militant writers. New metaphors of creation and intensification of a search for commonality are the signs of growth Gayle finds. On the other hand, the late George Kent's essay "Gwendolyn Brooks' Poetic Realism: A Developmental Survey" (*Black Women Writers*, pp. 88–105) seeks the racial consciousness underlying the entire Brooks canon.

"Fields Watered with Blood: Myth and Ritual in the Poetry of Margaret Walker" by Eugenia Collier (*Black Women Writers*, pp. 499–510) is an exposition of Walker's use of collective black experience for motifs of the South as ancestral home, adaptations of folklore, and primary symbols.

The special issue of *Obsidian*, guest edited by Michael S. Harper (8,i[1981]), includes 32 personal testimonies about Robert Hayden, many of them specially prepared for the purpose of supplying an anecdotal record that suggests raw materials for a narrative of the poet's creative life. Among the contributions serving as criticism also are "Hayden's Portrait of the Poet" by Norma R. Jones (pp. 89–93) who identifies in the poet's self-conception a sometimes comic, often ironic, and nearly fool-like picture rooted in a loner's feeling of vulnerability; Marcellus Blount's "A Dialogue of Poets: The Syndesis of W. B. Yeats and Robert Hayden" (pp. 27–41) that pursues intertextual relationships between "Sailing to Byzantium" and "For a Young Artist" showing an effort to transcend the limitations of language; and "'Mean to Be Free': The Illuminative Voice of Robert Hayden" by John F. Callahan (pp. 156–74) who explains that illumination occurs as Hayden's climactic repetitions arrest time and "hold

past and present suspended in the continuing moment of the poem."
In addition he analyzes the functional rhythm of "Runagate" and the
oratorical form and voice of "Frederick Douglass."

b. **Harper, Evans, Giovanni, Rodgers, Sanchez, Lorde, Clifton.**
Günther H. Lenz in "Black Poetry and Black Music: History and
Tradition: Michael Harper and John Coltrane" (*History and Tradition*, pp. 277–326) undertakes a thorough exploration of the models
for performance and analogue available to poets in the music that
Larry Neal's famous statement of Black Aesthetics, "And Shine Swam
On," identified as the key to survival and culture. Extensive citation
in the first section of the essay makes it clear that it is John Coltrane
more than anyone else who has been the spiritual leader for poets of
the past two decades who attempt to match music's expression of
black life and struggle. In the latter part of his essay Lenz argues that
the inspiration of new jazz goes beyond provision of references, and
works his way through each of Michael Harper's books to elucidate
technique that condenses images and rhythms from music, themes
elaborating on the creative transformation of tradition, and, finally,
verse that gives Coltrane a first-person poetic voice. Outstanding for
its investigation of the difficult matter of the translation of music into
verbal form, the essay brings depth and subtlety to the issue of
influence.

Contributions on Mari Evans to the volume she compiled on wom-
en writers were selected by an editor at Doubleday with the result
that we have David Dorsey in "The Art of Mari Evans" (*Black Wom-
en Writers*, pp. 170–89) characterizing her politically oriented writing as positively didactic in a manner he maintains is required by
black art, and Solomon Edwards's "Affirmation in the Works of Mari
Evans" (*Black Women Writers*, pp. 190–200) describing a central
theme of the recalcitrant black woman.

The difficult job of appraising a poet dependent on the public persona she reveals in performance faces William J. Harris in "Sweet
Soft Essence of Possibility: The Poetry of Nikki Giovanni" (*Black
Women Writers*, pp. 218–28). Harris does the job commendably,
stating delight in egotism of the lusty, comic persona and acknowledging the dross resulting from its overuse. Harris also identifies three
stages in Giovanni's writing, each of them concluding in frustration
for the poet he terms, in contrast to the example of Rod McKuen, "a

good popular poet." Paula Giddings is likewise concerned with evident stages in "Nikki Giovanni: Taking a Chance on Feeling" (*Black Women Writers*, pp. 211–17), which explains that, as the theme of growth to womanhood has supplanted the interest in militant violence seen in Giovanni's early work, the poem of personal feeling remains her formal preference, even as execution of the form shows no development of craft.

Bettye J. Parker-Smith's survey essay "Running Wild in Her Soul: The Poetry of Carolyn Rodgers" (*Black Women Writers*, pp. 393–410) founds her careful study of poetic expression upon biographical analysis of Rodgers's struggle against her mother's values and the feeling of contradiction associated for Rodgers with the attempt to define a black self by the standards of a white social system. By this means Parker-Smith's essay confirms the sense of the poet's engagement with her project and explains the sources of the change from militant to "religious loyalist." "Imagery in the Women Poems: The Art of Carolyn Rodgers" by Angelene Jamison (*Black Women Writers*, pp. 377–91) usefully amplifies biographical criticism with examination of poems representing women's situation as mothers, daughters, wives, and lovers and by remarking the artist's turmoil in "Breakthrough."

While Giovanni and Rodgers can no longer be classed among the politically revolutionary poets, this is not the case with Sonia Sanchez any more than it is with Mari Evans. Haki Madhubuti writing "Sonia Sanchez: The Bringer of Memories" (*Black Women Writers*, pp. 419–32) heaps praise upon Sanchez for her refusal to compromise and with excessive partisanship classes her "among the giants of world literature." More useful is David Williams, whose "The Poetry of Sonia Sanchez" (*Black Women Writers*, pp. 433–48) points out the ironic phrasing of black speech and the imagery characterizing Sanchez's craft.

By now it should be perfectly evident that many of the selections from *Black Women Writers* are basic survey essays, noted in this report as much for the fact that they treat neglected writers as for the insight they display. Such is Joan Martin's "The Unicorn in Black: Audre Lorde in Retrospect" (pp. 277–91), which covers the poems categorically and concludes that they show a progression to security. "In the Name of the Father: The Poetry of Audre Lorde" by Jerome Brooks (pp. 269–76) shows one of the more effective additions to the survey is a biographical theme, as I noted in the Parker-Smith essay.

Brooks identifies such motifs in Lorde as preoccupation with the male principle and the quest for love as the result of conflicts arising from the loss of her father and the effort to become her father's daughter in her writing. Lest this seem entirely a conventional explanation of the avowed lesbianism Lorde's work exhibits, it should be added that his comments on *The Cancer Journals* and the self-conflicts of the verse appear empathetic.

Lucille Clifton is one of the poets for whom the survey essay is a necessity. As a writer composing largely for younger readers, she is unlikely to receive more specialized treatment; thus, "Tell the Good News: A View of the Works of Lucille Clifton" by Audrey T. Mc-Cluskey (*Black Women Writers*, pp. 139–49) with its consideration of Clifton's Christian optimism becomes a fundamental source of information. Haki Madhubuti's "Lucille Clifton: Warm Water, Greased Legs, and Dangerous Poetry" (*Black Women Writers*, pp. 159–60) approves the didacticism in Clifton and applies Madhubuti's considerable ability as a prescriptive poet to consideration of formal structure.

c. General Criticism of Poetry. Allan Flint's "Black Response to Colonel Shaw" (*Phylon* 45,iii:210–19) adds something to our understanding of the black literary perspective in its analysis of the four memorial poems written by black authors on the martyred leader of the Massachusetts 54th Regiment. One poem, written by a man who served with Shaw, is a song for marching; Henrietta Cordelia Ray's sonnet is optimistic; Benjamin Brawley's "My Hero" treats its subject sentimentally and without mention of slavery; so in contrast Paul Laurence Dunbar's sonnet stands out because it declares that Shaw died in vain. The poems by Ray and Brawley are indistinguishable from the 36 poems written by white authors on Shaw, while Dunbar's evident awareness of the bearing of the Klan and lynching on the meaning of Shaw's death gives his poem a decidedly black and modern cast.

"Worksong and Toast: Two Dead Genres" by Bruce Jackson (*History and Tradition*, pp. 244–55) examines the patterns of uniquely Afro-American forms of folk poetry associated with poor black men, indicating their provenance and showing by discussion of changed social conditions the fragility of verse dependent upon immediate function.

v. Drama

a. **Dodson, Ward, Childress, Hansberry.** In his "Introduction to Owen Dodson's 'Freedom, The Banner'" James V. Hatch (*Callaloo* 7,ii:57–58) explains that the openly agit-prop play was written for trainees at Camp Robert Smalls of the Great Lakes Training Center in 1943. The text, taken from the Hatch-Billops Collection, is published in the same issue (pp. 59–71). "Theodore Ward's *Our Lan':* From the Slavery of Melodrama to the Freedom of Tragedy" by Owen E. Brady (*Callaloo* 7,ii:40–56) leads readers through the three drafts of the landmark play of 1947 to show how Ward rewrote to curtail the personal pathos of the historical subject of Freedman's resistance to the reclamation of lands they had been given by General Sherman. Brady also describes staging of the play in 1947, pointing out that in the second production other hands added spectacle. The preferred version is that published by Darwin T. Turner in *Black Drama in America.* John O. Killens chides Alice Childress in "The Literary Genius of Alice Childress" (*Black Women Writers*, pp. 129–33) for failing to delineate clearly the hand of the oppressor in some of her fiction and for deviating from relevance in *Wedding Band,* though he allows that other works are responsible. "Alice Childress's Dramatic Structure" by Samuel A. Hay (*Black Women Writers*, pp. 117–28),on the other hand, addresses the playwright's traditional structures in which he discerns that episodes are designed for theme rather than for character and concludes that her dramatic forms do not reflect the contemporary theater.

The inescapable and unresolved duality consequent to birth in an upper-middle-class black family provides organization for Anne Cheney's study *Lorraine Hansberry* (TUSAS 430). Raised in a family of entrepreneurs, whose experience in purchasing a house provided the inspiration for *Raisin in the Sun,* Hansberry became a political radical and a playwright whose corpus includes two works on "white" intellectual issues, three on black challenges. The book adequately surveys the published and unpublished writings with an eye to theme and the fact that Hansberry saw no difference between art and propaganda. It should be noted that besides the inevitable help of Robert Nemiroff, who in addition to interviews and correspondence also provided bibliographical aid, Cheney's sources include Hansberry's sister, Mamie Hansberry Mitchell, one of several leads Cheney mentions for a full-scale critical biography which this book is meant to encourage.

b. **Baraka, Kennedy, Shange, Caleb.**   In an article from 1982, W. D. E. Andrews began a study of Baraka's schematized dramas (see *ALS 1982*, p. 402). This year's "The Marxist Theater of Amiri Baraka" (*CompD* 18:137–61) considers the presentation of dialectical materialism in *The Motion of History* and *S-1*, plays in which Baraka seeks to dramatize the entry into history by characters converted to revolution by the observation of events as they are displayed to the theater audience. Using exposition of the plays as his evidence, Andrews concludes that they do not fuse revolutionary theory with dramatic situation or image. Herbert Blau's "The American Dream in American Gothic: The Plays of Sam Shepard and Adrienne Kennedy" (*MD* 27:520–39) is devoted to justification of the judgment that his subjects are the most original writers of their generation. The discussion of Kennedy relates her obsessional topics of powerlessness and death to the politics of race existent in the unconscious and emergent in emblem and symbol.

Carolyn Mitchell uses the ideas of Paul Tillich on the inclusive environment of the city as framework for analysis in " 'A Laying on of Hands': Transcending the City in Ntozake Shange's *For Colored Girls . . .*" (*Women Writers and the City*, pp. 230–48). At first the environment imparts fear of diversity, but, as the play shows, a gradually visible circle of women heals. "Yea and an Announcement: Notice of a New Black Playwright and his Work" by Houston A. Baker, Jr. (*BALF* 18:113–16) means to draw attention to J. Rufus Caleb, author of *Benny's Place* produced on ABC Television in May of 1982. For Baker the merit of this work, and a later one also discussed, lies in vernacular orientation, that is, fidelity to lives of ordinary existence.

c. **General Studies of Theater.**   Errol Hill brings the knowledge of an experienced performer to his study *Shakespeare in Sable: A History of Black Shakespearean Actors* (Mass.). This story of great obstacles mines black newspapers for information about early companies of black actors and for the 20th century focuses upon major professional productions. Hill gives high praise to Joseph Papp's New York Shakespeare Festival for performing with multiracial casts so that blacks, ordinarily limited to the four characters Shakespeare made black, have had a chance at new roles. Performances and performers are also the subject of Edward G. Smith in "Black Theatre" (*Ethnic Theatre in the United States,* ed. Maxine Schwartz Seller; Greenwood, 1983; pp. 37–66). Smith outlines his history with attention to minstrelsy, black musicals, the Harlem Renaissance, plays of racial awareness, as well as major playwrights and institutions such as the Federal Theatre and the American Negro Theatre. Citing authorities throughout, Smith's essay becomes a survey of scholarship as well as a basic source for the history of black theater in relation to the so-called mainstream.

vi. Slave Narratives and Autobiography

James Olney's " 'I Was Born' Slave Narratives" (*Callaloo* 7,i:46–73) reaches the startling conclusion that the fugitive slave narratives are neither really autobiography, nor, except for the illustrious example of Frederick Douglass, literature. The inception of Olney's convincing study is the observation of the cumulative and invariant nature of the narratives. The cause of this he lays to the suppression of memory in the fixed form and preferred style of the abolitionist narratives. By his definition of autobiography it is memory that creates significance and emplots the narrative. Because the former slaves were charged with the task of describing slavery, not their own growth, they present only events readily acceptable as "the facts." Olney enforces his argument with a master outline that might represent most narratives and with discussion of the influences of white sponsors on the diction and rhetoric of the narratives. Though Olney demotes the slave narratives from the level of literature, he asserts that the Afro-American literary tradition takes its start through these writings and presents Richard Wright's *Black Boy,* a work free to employ creative memory, as the example of the transformation of the earlier narrative mode into imaginative literature. In her "Language in Slavery: Frederick Douglass's *Narrative*" (*Prospects* [1983], pp. 163–82) Ann Kibbey takes the exception to Olney's rule to explore the linguistic significance of bondage. Douglass, she says, portrays his progress to freedom through sensitive understanding of language usage. The wealth of consequence Kibbey finds includes Douglass's self-image as a social product, his narrative's comprehension of the reified meaning of the designation as slave, and the deep concern on Douglass's part to avoid obscuring bondage with spiritual or symbolic meaning.

" 'For a Moment I Wondered': Theory and Symbolic Form in the Autobiographies of Langston Hughes" by R. Baxter Miller (*LHRev* 3:1–6) locates within the historical narratives of Hughes's wanderings lyric passages that freeze the narrative order so that the moment, for example, of meeting a fellow artist stands out from the passage of time as a figurative instant of interpretation. This suggestive reading is applied to *The Big Sea* and *I Wonder as I Wander*.

Selwyn R. Cudjoe in "Maya Angelou and the Autobiographical Statement" (*Black Women Writers*, pp. 6–24) reads the several volumes of Angelou's ongoing autobiography as works within the quintessentially Afro-American genre that he denominates as personal, yet not subjective or egotistic. By extension of the point each Angelou volume is a story representative of typified experience. Sondra O'Neale in "Reconstruction of the Composite Self: New Images of Black Women in Maya Angelou's Continuing Autobiography" (*Black Women Writers*, pp. 25–36) makes much the same point but with some greater attention to techniques that parallel fiction in their way of presenting the self as archetypal.

State University of New York at Albany

20. Themes, Topics, Criticism

Michael J. Hoffman

After many years of doing this chapter in one format, I am changing the order of things a bit. Many critical works about American literature fit more neatly into other categories, such as those on women's studies, the theory of fiction, or modernism. As a result, I am opening with a section on American literature that consists of books that mostly emphasize literary history. Other sections appear in the following order, each of them with books discussed primarily alphabetically by author: women's studies, modernism, literature and society, theory of fiction, literary theory. This order more nearly reflects the increasing tendency of recent criticism to deal theoretically with material independent of national boundaries.

i. American Literature

I begin with brief mention of Peter Conrad's *The Art of the City: Views and Versions of New York* (Oxford), which traces the artistic rendering of New York City since the mid-19th-century, emphasizing in roughly equal proportions literature, photography, painting, and film. The key early figures who become Conrad's models are Walt Whitman and Henry James, but there are also lengthy treatments of such artists as Stieglitz, Steichen, Hopper, and Wharton. An Englishman who has obviously spent much time in this country, Conrad sees New York City with the acute, critical eye of an outsider but with love and deep cultural insight.

One of the best recent books on American literature and culture is *Law & Letters in American Culture* (Harvard) by Robert A. Ferguson. With degrees in both law and American civilization, Ferguson has a rich understanding of the interlocking relationship of law and ideology in American history. Following the lead of Perry Miller's final book, *The Life of the Mind in America* (1965), Ferguson has studied a "now-forgotten configuration of law and letters that dominated American literary aspirations from the Revolution until the fourth decade of the nineteenth century" (p. 5). He examines not only "the nexus between law and literature in the early republic"— particularly in the context of major writers—but also "the rhetoric within republican writings and . . . reassess[es] its place in American literary culture" (pp. 6–7). Major figures include John Trumbull, Thomas Jefferson, Charles Brockden Brown, Washington Irving, both Danas, and Abraham Lincoln, all of them trained as attorneys, along with many writers who were not trained as attorneys but nonetheless engaged in the national debate over law and ideology.

Ferguson discusses the role of judicial review as well as "the importance of general learning in early American law." The high level of literacy among early practitioners developed because they "lacked court records, case reports, codified statutes, and effective commentaries" (p. 66). Without these tools the practitioners had to depend on the mastery of a few essential texts along with general learning. The age of the specialist was still a long way off. Furthermore, these circumstances contributed to the close relationship between the idea of the law and the idea of America.

It was with the Age of Jackson that the debate over the role of law heightened and the rhetoric changed. In a long chapter on the Richard Henry Danas, Ferguson explores this change. From this point the culture of the American Renaissance "excludes the legal mind from literary enterprise. Hawthorne can describe the possibilities in a moonlit room, and Melville can tell Hawthorne that 'truth is ever incoherent,' but in the law reality is always otherwise. . . . Since 1850 the best American writers have aimed for an original show of consciousness. Lawyers have thought ever more consciously of standards, norms, and rules" (pp. 271–72). This fine book really opens up for the first time the rich role played by the law in American literary culture.

Sam B. Girgus's *New Covenant* examines Jewish-American writers according to their interaction with and promulgation of the "American Idea." The author defines the American idea as "the set of values, beliefs, and traditions of freedom, democracy, equality, and republicanism that are known as the American Way and that give America a unique identity in history. For the Jews this idea included the concept of emancipation . . . [which] meant that Jews could expect to be treated as individuals on a basis of equality with all other individuals" (p. 3). Girgus uses myth extensively, defining three ways in which the myth of America can be discussed: "The first involves a basic espousal of the myth as an ideal and vision of America. The second . . . is in terms of an antimyth, which constitutes an attack on the culture because of the failure to live up to the myth. . . . The third . . . involves a deeper form of alienation through ideological disavowal and psychological rejection of the myth of America" (pp. 13–14). He applies the theory to a series of writers who are associated with the development of these cultural attitudes, including Bernard Malamud, Louis Brandeis and Sidney Hillman, Abraham Cahan, Anzia Yezierska, Henry and Philip Roth, Norman Mailer, and E. L. Doctorow. In a fine chapter on Philip Roth, Girgus says that "Roth, in effect, claims for Jewish writers the kind of linguistic initiative and leadership that characterizes the writers of the New Covenant. In Roth, one finds justification for the argument that the Jewish writer and thinker is a linguistic innovator who develops the rhetorical and narrative structure of the myth and ideology of America while maintaining the role of the modern Jewish hero of thought" (pp. 118–119). Aside from the author's tendency to overestimate the value of certain writers who fit his thesis, this is a rewarding book.

Another lively overview of American literature is Martin Green, *Great American Adventure*, which posits the adventure story as a quintessential American form, one "that seemed to transcend class in America and to bring all the conflicting interests of Americans into harmony" (p. 18). Green's Marxist orientation suggests that "the kind of reading appropriate to the adventure tale is dialectical . . . a way to put as much specific assent and dissent together in as stable a compound as possible" (p. ix). Green follows the tradition of the adventure story in this country from Cooper's *The Pioneers* to Mailer's *Why Are We in Vietnam?* (1967), stopping on the way to examine Irving's *A Tour on the Prairies* (1832), Bird's *Nick of the Woods* (1837), Dana's *Two Years Before the Mast* (1840), Melville's *Typee* (1846), Parkman's *The Oregon Trail* (1849), Carson's *Autobiography* (1856), Twain's *Roughing It* (1872), Roosevelt's *Autobiography* (1913), Hemingway's *The Green Hills of Africa* (1935), and Faulkner's "The Bear" (1942). He is full of generalizations about American manhood, the antifeminism of the adventure story, the adventure story as an apology for imperialism. Green sees contradictions between the conventions of romance and those of adventure, stating that "adventure is more democratic than romance—it pays tribute to the virtues of the people—whereas romance always has a genteel (usually an aristocratic) hero and heroine" (p. 53). Green sees the full emergence of the adventure novel as a genre of serious literature in the 1950s and 1960s, primarily because of Faulkner and Hemingway. A stringent critic of American culture, the author sometimes lets his penchant for the sweeping point get in the way of fact and logic, but this book makes a serious contribution to defining an important part of American character and tradition.

Other *ALS 1984* reviewers will no doubt have much to say about many parts of Alfred Kazin's *American Procession*, but I should like to give a paragraph to what Kazin clearly intends as a magisterial summation of his long, distinguished career. *American Procession* represents all the strengths and weaknesses of Kazin's work. Well written and full of passionate personal commitment, the book is also relentlessly old-fashioned, as it focuses on the concept of the self and the nature of identity in American writers from Emerson to Fitzgerald, the periods in which Kazin has always been most at home. He mixes biography liberally with analysis, but he is most at home with ideas. As a result, it is no wonder that the book leaves the impression that Emerson and Henry Adams are the key figures among all the great authors Kazin parades before us. I found it most pleasant to review these well-known careers with the author, beginning the book with every intention of skimming it but finding myself unable to do so. I hung on every word, but when I reached the end I felt that I had read a survey that followed certain themes but finally had no organizing thesis. A good review of familiar ground.

Zbigniew Lewicki's *The Bang and the Whimper* is a Polish scholar's interpretation of two major streams in American literature. Lewicki relates apocalypse and entropy because—even though they are in many ways opposite—they are both about the end of things. With entropy the end comes through inexorable decline, while apocalypse brings about sudden destruction in the service of regeneration. Lewicki begins tracing his themes with early American texts, finding apocalypse in Jonathan Edwards. He discovers entropy for the first time in Melville's *Bartleby* but apocalypse in *Moby-Dick*. Because this collection of essays is built on a set of theses rather than an extended discussion of a single thesis, it seems disorganized. Among the other writers Lewicki treats are Mark Twain (apocalypse), Robert Coover (apocalypse), Thomas Pynchon (apocalypse), Ralph Ellison ("cyclic apocalypse"), and William Gaddis, Susan Sontag, John

Updike (all entropy). A good book is nestling in all this material, but the idea needs a more thoughtful, detailed treatment.

A more solidly organized work is Leonard Lutwack's *The Role of Place in Literature* (Syracuse). While not ostensibly about American literature, it is so heavily concerned with American themes and texts that it belongs in this section. Not a theoretical work, it is descriptive and taxonomic, discussing the various ways place is used in poetry, drama, fiction, and nonfiction. Lutwack defines "place" as "inhabitable space," distinguishing it from "setting," which "denotes a place of action in both narrative as well as drama . . . , but *setting* is not adequate to describe the use of places unrelated to action, such as metaphors or evocations of places in the speeches or consciousness of characters" (p. 28). In the many pages devoted to American literature, Lutwack defines "the garden," "Eldorado," and "the wilderness" as key elements in any study of American culture. "The relation of the American to his land is a history of the conflict of these concepts" (p. 145). He devotes long chapters to Melville and to "The American and His Land," concluding with a discussion of "Placelessness," which he defines as a key "concern of Twentieth-Century Literature." "The disappearance of familiar places and the proliferation of a more and more limited set of uniform places have caused a peculiarly modern malaise called *placelessness*" (p. 183). His discussion of this phenomenon is full of interesting insights, but the writing is somewhat pedestrian. I think the book will be most useful as a reference work.

I have included Thomas R. Nevin's *Irving Babbitt: An Intellectual Study* (N. C.) here rather than with the literary criticism because the book is primarily a study of the humanistic movement of which Babbitt and his good friend Paul Elmer More were the leading representatives. Not a biography, this is "a history of Babbitt's mind, his allegiances, the courses of his values and his language, and their part in his highly polemical assault upon his era and indeed upon the direction of twentieth-century society" (p. ix). Nevin studies the intellectual positions Babbitt takes with regard to politics, literature, culture, and ethics, placing them with the history of American culture and higher education. He does a good job of showing the tension between Babbitt's humanism and antihumanitarianism, because for Babbitt the "modern humanist was 'interested in the perfecting of the individual rather than in schemes for the elevation of mankind as a whole.' This 'perfecting' was actually nothing more than a cultivated sense of proportion" (p. 15). Nevin shows how Babbitt's thought developed from the conventions of transcendentalism and the examples of both Matthew Arnold and Charles Eliot Norton, both of them "worthy exemplar[s] of the classically critical temper." But it is through the extensive analysis (primarily through their correspondence) of the intellectual relationship of Babbitt and More that Nevin examines the most crucial tension in Babbitt, between his belief in absolute values and his nonbelief in any organized religion. While the book is useful, the writing is a little flat: something like Babbitt's but without his passionate energy.

A much livelier book is Hershel Parker's *Flawed Texts*, a polemical study of the authority of texts, not as givens but as established by strict though flexible scholarship and editorial methods. Parker makes his point of view clear at all times: "All valid meaning," he says, "is authorial meaning, but in standard literary texts authorial meaning may be mixed in with non-sense, skewed meanings, and wholly adventitious readings which result from tampering with the text, by the author or someone else" (p. ix). He is very hard on critics who care too little about the validity of the actual printed text but who write criticism that expounds a transcendental notion of a "text" that may in physical and historical fact be flawed. Parker nonetheless makes clear that while "all authority in literature comes from the author, . . . that authority can be blurred or wholly lost and, paradoxically, it can persist even when the author thinks it has been removed" (p. 16). While a lot of the book seems written in anger (the author settles old scores with antagonists such as Fredson Bowers and Donald Pizer), the author does make the best case I have read for a flexible, non-ideological practice of how to establish textual authority. In order to be a good textual editor, one must, after all, know a great deal about the biography of the author, contemporary readerly conventions, and the conventions of the publisher and the practice of particular publishing houses, as well as the strength of an author's will vis-à-vis his or her editor's or spouse's. The texts Parker examines closely to illuminate their textual problems are Henry James's New York edition, Twain's *Pudd'nhead Wilson*, Crane's *Red Badge of Courage*, and the progress of Mailer's *An American Dream* from serial publication in *Esquire* to its appearance as a book.

Donald Pizer has brought out a revised edition of his now classic text, *Realism and Naturalism*, which omits three of the original essays and adds six others, including one of the better statements I know on naturalism: "American Literary Naturalism: An Approach Through Form." Pizer's approach is more descriptive than theoretical, but as most readers know, his writing is solid, informative, and comprehensive. The book contains chapters on most writers that one associates with the period, with the exception of Twain; I can think of no better work to use when preparing a course in the fiction of that period.

One of the most erudite 1984 texts to have been sent me is Meyer Reinhold, *Classica Americana: The Greek and Roman Heritage in the United States* (Wayne State), a study of the attitudes toward and the uses made of Greek and Roman classics and the Classical tradition in America. Primarily a study of the 19th century, its topics include architecture, ethics, and writing. The theme Reinhold follows throughout all these essays is that of the tension between a new country's attempts to break all ties with the past in its revolutionary fervor and the veneration of classical antiquity that expressed itself in public architecture and in much rhetoric of our 18th-century American *philosophes* and 19th-century forebears. A few chapter titles will give the flavor of this remarkable piece of scholarship: "The Cult of Antiquity in America," "Opponents of Classical Learning in America during the Revolutionary Period," "The Silver Age of Classical Studies in America, 1790–1830," "Vergil in the American Experience from Colonial Times to 1882." The scholarship is so thorough that the book seems at times excessively footnoted, but the writing is surprisingly graceful.

Brief mention goes to *The 60s Without Apology* (Minnesota), ed. Sohnya Sayres, Anders Stephanson, Stanley Aronowitz, and Fredric Jameson, a collection that "corresponds to a special double issue of *Social Text* (volume 3, no. 3 and volume 4, no. 1, Spring–Summer 1984)." In this collection, the '60s are reviewed from a primarily Marxist orientation, the successes as well as failures, with most of the authors trying to take a nonromantic view. The long first section contains a number of stimulating analyses of topics and events germane to the decade. Especially interesting are Stanley Aronowitz's "When the New Left Was New," Simon Firth's "Rock and the Politics of Memory," Ellen Willis's "Radical Feminism and Feminist Radicalism," and especially Fredric Jameson's "Periodizing the 60s." The latter portions of the book contain too many snippets from books or talks. Here the note of nostalgia often creeps in too heavily. There are some good photographs, and for those of us who remember the '60s well, the trip back there will be pleasant even when the analysis is disappointing.

Something Said: Essays by Gilbert Sorrentino (North Point) collects the occasional essays and reviews of the well-known novelist and poet. These are mostly brief essays, important primarily for the reader of Sorrentino's other work, since, as he claims, "I have never had any desire to be creative in my criticism, and it does not yearn, so to speak, for the status of literature" (p. vii). There are many pieces on American authors written during the past 25 years, from an interesting long one on William Carlos Williams to shorter ones on writers both well known and somewhat obscure, such as Charles Olson, Jack Spicer, Jonathan Williams, George Oppen, Dan Rice, John Gardner, and Mort Lucks. To the student of recent American letters Sorrentino's reflections on other writers are always of value, and the essays are better than Sorrentino's modesty would suggest. As usual, North Point has produced an attractive book.

There have been only a few adequate economic readings of American literature since F. O. Matthiessen, but one of the better recent ones is *American Literature and Social Change* by Michael Spindler. Using Marx's theory of the "determining base and the determined superstructure," Spindler divides American economic history since the Civil War into two phases, each one dominated by an ideology: (1) a production-oriented phase, dominated by entrepreneurs like Cowperwood, and (2) a consumption-oriented phase, which began in earnest after the First World War "in the early 1920s, was retarded by the severe recession of the 1930s, and reached full spate after the end of the Second World War." The latter phase is dominated by the consumer, who ranges from the heroic failure of Jay Gatsby to the more pathetic one of Willy Loman. Spindler examines how each phase gave rise to works of fiction or drama that reflected the ideologies and the changing points of view represented in the fiction. Along the way are excellent readings of Howells, Dreiser, Fitzgerald, Lewis, and Arthur Miller. Dreiser is a pivotal figure, whose Cowperwood represents the entrepreneur of the first stage and whose Clyde Griffiths is the consumer of the second one. Spindler claims that "George F. Babbitt is, perhaps, the first fully documented Consumer Man in American fiction," (p. 182), a claim with which I cannot disagree; but I am not as comfortable with his stating that "it was not until Dos Passos' *USA* trilogy (1930–7) with its fragmented, collage structure that the multifariousness of American economic and social experience found an adequate literary form" (p. 47). Dos Passos's technique is more derivative than innovative; his form accommodates comprehensiveness more than profundity. I'm not sure we have ever had a better "consumer" novel than *The Great Gatsby* for both form and social complexity, even though it came early in that phase of American experience. But this is a minor quibble with a very interesting book.

A useful thematic study appears in Janis P. Stout, *The Journey Narrative in American Literature: Patterns and Departures* (Greenwood), which defines the genre of the journey narrative and applies its various aspects to American history and culture. "American literature," she writes, "is indeed characterized by journeys, even obsessed with journeys, possibly to an even greater degree than has been supposed" (p. ix). The author divides the types of journeys as follows: "American history begins with voyages of exploration, escape, and home founding" (p. 30). To these she adds the return to Europe, the quest, and—particularly for rootless Modernists—the phase of "lost and wandering." All these aspects are treated in a descriptive chapter and then given more detailed coverage in chapters that deal with individual works or poets. Getting full treatment are Melville's *Clarel*, Faulkner's *As I Lay Dying*, Bellow's *Henderson the Rain King*, and Roth's *The Great American Novel;* the poets are Hart Crane and Wallace Stevens. Stout's technique is more descriptive than theoretical, her scholarship solid, her writing clear and uncomplicated. There are occasional strong insights, as in the following: "Whatever else the Great American Novel may be, it has been, throughout its history, a fiction zestfully committed to motion and to the free, transcendent individual. Its context has not characteristically been the complex realities of an enclosed, highly structured society, but abundant, beckoning space" (p. 247).

The most brilliant book I have read on an American topic this year is surely Tzvetan Todorov's *The Conquest of America: The Question of the Other* (Harper), first published in French in 1982 and now translated by Richard Howard. Todorov defines his subject as "the discovery *self* makes of the *other*" (p. 3), and his analysis attempts to define the perceptual and linguistic confrontation that occurred when the Spanish explorers came upon the natives of Meso-America in the 16th century, a confrontation that resulted in what the author calls "the greatest genocide in human history." This disturbing book— whose essence I can only begin to suggest—posits a series of explanations that emanate from cultural, linguistic, and psychological predispositions. Todorov's method is speculative and empirical, moving through a series of examinations of both actions and documents about which he asks questions and poses hypotheses, all the time closing more tightly the inevitable conclusion that arises from the way he looks at his materials.

The author divides the book into four sections ("Discovery," "Conquest," "Love," and "Knowledge") in addition to an epilogue, and while each section moves the narrative through a series of historic dimensions, it also moves Todorov through his argument, which begins with an examination of how Columbus's sense of his own discovery was governed by his culturally defined perceptual apparatus. It was, for instance, his obsession with proper names as a way of delineating the world that caused Columbus to view the Indians as "culturally virgin, a blank page awaiting the Spanish and Christian inscription" (p. 36). This limitation caused Columbus either to conceive "the Indians . . . as human beings altogether, having the same rights as himself; but then he sees them not only as equals but also as identical, and this behavior leads to assimilationism, the projection of his own values on the others. Or else he starts from the difference, but the latter is immediately translated into terms of superiority and inferiority (in his case, obviously, it is the Indians who are inferior)" (p. 42). Because Columbus was so locked into his perceptions, the encounter between the two cultures was moved inevitably in one direction.

By not integrating with the world, by defining themselves only as conquerors far from their home culture, the Spanish conquistadores lost all moral moorings and became guilty of massacring the "inferior" peoples subjugated by them: "Massacre is thus intimately linked to colonial wars waged far from the metropolitan country. The more remote and alien the victims, the better: they are exterminated without remorse, more or less identified with animals" (p. 144). Without ever becoming explicit, through such analyses Todorov points us toward a greater understanding of our own barbarous century. Space does not permit me to go on, but this is a wonderful book, imaginatively conceived, vividly written even in translation, full of the most succinct examples.

A book whose authors are discussed in other chapters, *God Be With the Clown*, by Ronald Wallace, is an attempt to establish a theory of humor in American poetry. While referring to the work of Constance Rourke, Wallace is mostly influenced by Northrop Frye's theory of humor as developed in *Anatomy of Criticism*. The terms *eiron* and *alazon* figure prominently in the text, and he follows these figures from the mid-19th-century (Whitman and Dickinson) to the present time. The other poets to whom Wallace devotes chapters are Frost, Stevens, and Berryman, but he also includes shorter discussions of such humorists as W. H. Auden, Woody Allen, and W. C. Fields. There are drawings of each of the poets by David Levine.

I shall close this section with brief mention of a book by Beong-cheon Yu, *The Great Circle*, a chapter-by-chapter study of a series of American authors beginning with Emerson and going through Pound, with an epilogue that considers J. D. Salinger, Jack Kerouac, and Gary Snyder. The treatment of materials is conventional; the book updates earlier treatments of similar subjects done by such scholars as Arthur Christy, Earl Miner, and Frederick Carpenter. Yu's prologue presents a straightforward, unquestioning history of European Orientalism. All parts of the Orient are lumped together, as if there were no real difference between the Near and Far East. After Edward Said's analysis of the ideology of Orientalism in his book of that name, it is difficult to imagine how any writer could so unblushingly treat the subject without at least some irony, but Said's name never appears in this book. The treatment of the authors is descriptive, and it is on that level that the book can be useful to scholars. Setting aside the theoretical problems, nonspecialist *ALS* readers can profit from referring to the chapters on individual authors, most of which will give them the information they need on this topic.

ii. Women's Studies

This section covers books on topics related to the role of women in literature and American culture and to the works written by women as contributions to that literature and culture. They are all distinguished by an interest in the role of gender in understanding writing and culture, but they use many approaches in dealing with that large topic, from theoretical works to those limited to ethnic literatures, to works that are primarily historical in their concerns. There are more books in this section than there would have been even a year ago, a fact that suggests what a growing field women's studies has become, in both sophistication and extent.

In *Women and Death: Linkages in Western Thought and Literature* (Greenwood) Beth Ann Bassein has written a study of the ways women have been portrayed in literature primarily in images of sexuality interlinked with images of death. She points out, for instance, the Renaissance connection between "to die" and "to copulate," often the great source of puns for poets of that time. The early chapters are fairly general, setting the thematic stage and defining terms that Bassein uses later in discussing individual authors. This is a solid, descriptive, historical-cultural study, the kind one associates with the Greenwood Press; it delimits an area of study rather than establishes its theoretical underpinnings. Bassein focuses primarily on 19th-century heroines in a chapter entitled "Adultery and Death: Clarissa, Emma, Maggie, Anna, Tess, Edna," following this with one on "Twentieth-Century Fiction: D. H. Lawrence, Doris Lessing, Margaret Drabble, E. L. Doctorow, Joseph Heller." She concludes with a short chapter on Adrienne Rich in which she tries to show how Rich writes positively about the image of women in an effort to "dislodge the inseparable linkage of women, sex, and death and to free them from an automatic fusion." There is a useful appendix that gives brief bits of evidence of the ways various societies have treated women's lives with minimal respect, thereby adding impetus to their association of women and death.

Gretchen M. Bataille and Kathleen Mullen Sands, in *American Indian Women: Telling Their Lives* (Nebraska), study the lives of American Indian women as they have told them themselves. The tradition begins with the oral telling of tales, some of them passed down by that tradition, others transcribed; both form the basis of a tradition within which contemporary American Indian women write their own lives in autobiography and novel. These documents are usually treated by anthropologists, but in this case Bataille and Sands examine them as literature, discussing the tradition and the various conventions that have evolved within it. They make the case for a number of writers—all of them, alas, unfamiliar to me, including Maria Chona, Anna Shaw, and Maria Campbell. The book is a useful, well-written introduction and demonstrates the developing maturity of a branch of ethnic literary studies.

Also from Nebraska is a book about a leader of the new French feminism: *Hélène Cixous: Writing the Feminine,* by Verena Andermatt Conley. Along with Julia Kristeva and Luce Irigaray, Cixous has been a major name in French feminist theory. A protean figure, Cixous is active as a writer of fiction, autobiography, and literary criticism. I first came upon her when reading her extraordinary study *The Exile of James Joyce* (1967). Influenced by many of the most important figures behind the new intellectual tradition in France, including Freud, Heidegger, Lacan, and Derrida, Cixous has produced a number of the most stimulating and enigmatic writings yet on the matter of sexual difference and gender, such as the frequently anthologized "Laugh of the Medusa." While it is good to have Conley's book, it would be even better if more of Cixous's work were to be translated; this book would thereby be that much more useful.

Although many works treated in Lee R. Edwards's *Psyche as Hero: Female Heroism and Fictional Form* (Wesleyan) are not American, I want to bring this book to the attention of *ALS* readers because the topic it treats is persuasively argued. Edwards's premise is that there are female as well as male heroes, and that furthermore these women heroes are particularly feminine heroes—not just women in men's armor—for they have a specifically female heroic character. Edwards makes her case by treating 18th- and 19th-century novels, such as *Clarissa*, *The Scarlet Letter*, *Middlemarch*, and *Portrait of a Lady*, then moves into the 20th century to write primarily about recent works by such writers as Doris Lessing, Toni Morrison, and Maxine Hong Kingston. While the book could have made its point more briefly, it traces the female hero from someone who had to operate from within the context of family and society to someone who can now transcend that society as a lone survivor. Edwards sees herself as presenting an active counterpoise to the subversive activities that Sandra Gilbert and Susan Gubar propose as the prime activities of victimized women in *The Madwoman in the Attic*.

Women Writing in America brings together a series of essays by Blanche H. Gelfant on 20th-century American writers. While the book is not written to a thesis, it does follow out a number of themes related to the concerns of women writers of fiction, such as "female patterns of development, mother-daughter relationships, romance and marriage, conflicts between caring for others and the self, response to a demand for passivity, and (disguised) forms of rebellion" (p. 4). A brief introduction presents other themes, including the violence inherent in many of the writings about disillusioned women, subversion, and the role of cities. (Gelfant has also written a book on *The American City Novel*.) Some of the authors covered in the current volume are Grace Paley, Meridel Le Sueur (the only poet), and

Willa Cather; there is also an excellent essay on *"Gone With the Wind and The Impossibilities of Fiction."*

One of the most delightful books I have read is *The Light of the Home: An Intimate View of the Lives of Women in Victorian America* (Pantheon), by Harvey Green with the assistance of Mary-Ellen Perry. This was originally the catalogue for an exhibition at the Margaret Woodbury Strong Museum in Rochester, New York, and it is an excellent survey of the situation of women—particularly home-makers—during this period of heavy Victorian domesticity. The many black-and-white reproductions include items of women's clothing, house furniture, home machinery such as sewing machines, carpet sweepers, irons, and cooking ranges. The writing is both scholarly and vivid, and one comes away from this book with a richer sense of the physical situation of women at that time than any single novel can convey.

A very different kind of book is a collection of essays by Florence Howe, *Myths of Coeducation: Selected Essays, 1964–1983* (Indiana), all of them on topics related to women and education. Howe, as most readers know, is a founder of the women's studies movement and former president of the Modern Language Association. Many of these essays were speeches given on official occasions and have that tone of high seriousness. But they are the work of an educational leader, not a polemicist, and they reflect the historical development of the movement from its early years to the point where it became deeply established within the American university system. A sampling of titles will give the reader some sense of the topics dealt with in this book: "Identity and Expression: A Writing Course for Women," "Feminism, Fiction, and the Classroom," "The Future of Women's Colleges," "Feminism and the Study of Literature," "American Literature and Women's Lives." The essays are persuasive and scholarly, and although any collection such as this tends to be repetitive, it is the power and success of Howe's commitment that one remembers.

The University of Chicago Press has instituted a new series on Women in Culture and Society, ed. Catharine R. Stimpson. The first volume of that series is *Women, History & Theory: The Essays of Joan Kelly*, written by a late professor of history at the City College of New York. Kelly was a Marxist and feminist, and what I find most interesting in these pieces is her ability to blend the two points of view. The essays are mostly about older periods of history, but they have a relevance for us because of their sophisticated methodology.

I found most interesting the following essays: "The Social Relation of the Sexes: Methodological Implications of Women's History" and "The Doubled Vision of Feminist Theory," along with one essay that is much referred to by other feminist scholars, "Did Women Have a Renaissance?"

The stated purpose of Annette Kolodny's *The Land Before Her* is "to chart women's private responses to the successive American frontiers and to trace a tradition of women's public statements about the west" (p. xi). Kolodny claims to be writing "neither social history nor literary history, but the sequence of fantasies through which generations of women came to know and act upon the westward-moving frontier" (p. xii), but the book is in fact both a social and literary history that focuses on the ways fantasies and myths intertwine. The male myth of the frontier is of a wilderness, for instance, while the dominant myth of women writers domesticates that wilderness into a garden, thus bringing the codes of society to the frontier, as if they could ever be escaped.

While the book does follow a thesis, it is not really a theoretical work. Kolodny explores this development of a female frontier vision through three centuries of a variety of writings, from captivity narratives to promotional materials to sentimental novels, covering such writers as Mary Rowlandson, Rebecca Bryan Boone, Margaret Fuller, Caroline Kirkland, Mrs. E. D. E. N. Southworth, and Maria Susanna Cummins. Kolodny's insights are often very good, as in her suggestion that the sentimental novel may well have been a political tool for women writers "otherwise disenfranchised. Indeed, in some respects, mid-nineteenth-century sentimental fiction may be seen as *the* political strategy of the disenfranchised, moving its readers to tears in hopes that the sight of those tears might then move husbands and fathers, sons and brothers, to more public forms of responsiveness" (p. 163). "The problem facing the domestic fictionists . . . was that the terrain was already imaginatively appropriated by 'the most significant, most emotionally compelling myth-hero' of American culture, the isolate American Adam" (p. 224). While well written, the book tends to go on at great, and sometimes repetitive, length, making the same points more than once about writings that do not always hold our interest outside a particular thesis. Still, the book does convincingly establish a tradition of female writings about the American frontier, and it brings forward in a fresh way a number of writers whose names we know but have not always found a way of reading well. Another volume exploring the next stage of the tradition seems to be in the works.

Brief mention goes to an interesting collection of essays by Estella Lauter, *Women as Mythmakers: Poetry and Visual Art by Twentieth-Century Women* (Indiana), an interdisciplinary study that treats both poets and artists including Anne Sexton, Käthe Kollwitz, Margaret Atwood, Remedios Varo, Diane Wakoski, and Lenor Fini. The introduction, "Steps toward a Feminist Archetypal Theory of Mythmaking," meditates on how cultures develop myths of selves, gender, and history, a theme that is picked up with variations in the discussions of each poet and artist. Although the various women are treated in discrete chapters, the connections between chapters are made well, and the book seems like an organic whole. The concluding section contains three chapters on more general themes. There are a number of good black-and-white reproductions of works of art.

One of the most unusual books in this section is *Reading the Romance: Women, Patriarchy, and Popular Literature* (N. C.), by Janice A. Radway, a study of how American women read romances. Radway uses survey techniques, including extensive interviews of many women readers of romances, and she bases her interpretations on a rich knowledge of the marketing techniques of the American publishing industry and an understanding of female development based heavily on the work of Nancy Chodorow. She wishes to offer "a comprehensive explanation of why the women I interviewed find romance reading not only practically feasible and generally enjoyable but also emotionally necessary as well." Radway is never patronizing about such fiction. She tries to get at the root of why some women respond so powerfully to it and how the publishing industry has managed through marketing and sales techniques to make such an extraordinary commercial success of mass-producing such books.

Bringing reader-response theory to bear on the developmental perspective gained from Chodorow, Radway concludes that "romances can be termed compensatory fiction because the act of reading them fulfills certain basic psychological needs for women that have been induced by the culture and its social structures but that often remain unmet in day-to-day existence as the result of concomitant restrictions of female activity" (pp. 112–13). The simple language of the romance also makes it easier for the reader to "contribute to the production of the story." But Radway will not draw easy conclusions about the repressiveness of such fiction, because she does not feel she has the evidence to do so. There is a great deal more that I cannot cover in my summary, but this is a very rich study, based on much empirical evidence, carefully marshaled and well conceived.

A work of cultural history that will be of interest to students of American literature is by Ellen K. Rothman, *Hands and Hearts: A History of Courtship in America* (Basic Books). Using documents such as letters, diaries, autobiographies, and manuals for personal behavior, Rothman has painted a warm, ironical, and scholarly picture of the mores surrounding courtship, marriage, and sexual behavior between the Revolutionary period and World War I. Many sexual and marital norms have changed in the past two centuries, but some have also stayed the same. One continuity is the fact that young American men and women have always been given a good bit of freedom of choice about whom to choose as a marital partner. Changes in sexual behavior often have resulted from contraceptive aids, or the bicycle or automobile because they granted freedom of travel and privacy to courting couples. The book is handsomely produced and well written.

Brief mention goes to a book edited by Susan Merrill Squier, *Women Writers and the City*, a collection of essays relating to the experience of women writers vis-à-vis cities. The experience of writers and the city has long been a theme in literary studies, but the specific experiences of women writers and the city has only now become an important subfield in women's studies. This collection has a good introduction that situates the essays and sets an overall theme for the book. Continental, British, and North American writers are all covered, with good pieces on such American writers as Cather and Rich. The editor has contributed a useful bibliography in "Literature and the City: A Checklist of Relevant Secondary Works."

The only reason I shall not write at length about Joyce W. Warren's *The American Narcissus* is that all the material in this book will be covered elsewhere in *ALS 1984*. But I wish to speak briefly about its contribution to women's studies as part of the Douglass Series on Women's Lives and the Meaning of Gender. The basic theory of this well-written book is that the lack of strong women characters in 19th-century literature until Henry James (with the exception of Hester Prynne) was due to the cult of individualism that was so strong a part of the American tradition from its earliest years and was amplified by transcendentalism. Women were defined as "other" in American culture, and "persons regarded as outside the American experience . . . were not seen as individuals. Women, blacks, Indians, and other 'others' had no place in the drama of American individualism. Like the legendary Narcissus, the American individualist focused on his own image to such an extent that he could grant little reality to others" (p. 4). Warren follows out this thesis in a series of early general chapters, then continues by examining the works of Cooper, Melville, Twain, Hawthorne, and James. This book contributes to both feminist studies and the study of American fiction.

iii. Modernism

The growing interest in modernism is reflected in a number of books published in 1984, some of them memoirs of the great age of Modernist innovation, the others theoretical works trying to explain what was going on during that age. The most theoretical of those works is Peter Bürger's *Theory of the Avant-Garde* (Minnesota), translated from the German by Michael Shaw, with a lengthy foreword by Jochen Schulte-Sasse; volume 4 of the Theory and History of Literature series. This difficult, closely argued work is one of the best intellectual studies of the problem of the avant-garde yet written. Quite different from the classic study of that subject by Renato Poggioli, it is much more abstract and dialectical, relying on the German tradition of Marxist hermeneutics. The lengthy foreword is almost like a counterproposal to the theory of Bürger and probably should be read afterwards, but it does have many interesting things to say, and together with the Bürger essay it constitutes the best recent set of theses about the nature of modernism and the avant-garde. The book has been a big success in Germany.

The foreword states that "according to Bürger the development leading to Symbolism and Aestheticism can be best described as a transformation of form into content. As art becomes problematic to itself, form becomes the preferred content of the works" (p. xiii). It is Bürger's main thesis that avant-garde art wages war against the institution of art, substituting form for content; not developing a style of its own, but rather using the styles of the past in any way it wishes. It is therefore important at all times to distinguish between the "institution of art" and the content of individual works of art. One should look back from the avant-garde development to understand previous bourgeois art forms; "it is an error to proceed inversely, by approaching the avant-garde via the earlier phases of art" (p. 19). For Bürger the great Modernist form is the collage, which in the process of attempting to destroy the entire Renaissance tradition of fixed-point perspective, also comments on "reality" by using bits of it in its very attack on the bourgeois institution of art. This is not a book for skimming, but it is one that the student of modernism will want to read slowly more than once.

A somewhat less ambitious but still impressive work is N. Katherine Hayles, *The Cosmic Web: Scientific Field Models and Literary Strategies in the Twentieth Century* (Cornell), which attempts to demonstrate the metaphorical connection between scientific field theories and the worlds portrayed in key Modernist and post-Modernist works. Field theories stress "interconnectedness": "A field view of reality pictures objects, events, and observer as belonging inextricably to the same field" (p. 10). Related to this idea is "the notion of the *self-referentiality* of language. . . . When the field is seen to be inseparable from language, the situation becomes even more complex, for then every statement potentially refers to every other statement, including itself" (p. 10). Hayles defines the metaphor of the "cosmic web" as "a created object whose artificiality corresponds to the conceptualization of the field models it signifies. . . . The prey the cosmic web is designed to entrap is the dynamic, holistic reality implied by the field concept. . . . What is captured by the cosmic web is thus not the elusive whole, but the observer who would speak that whole" (p. 21). The author then relates theory, with its concern for "exploring the relation between the observer and the observed system" to the novel's concern with "exploring the relation between the teller and the tale" (p. 41). Hayles carries out this explanation through excellent analyses of D. H. Lawrence, Jorge Luis Borges, Vladimir Nabokov's *Ada*, Robert Pirsig's *Zen and the Art of Motorcycle Maintenance*, and Thomas Pynchon's *Gravity's Rainbow*.

Michael H. Levenson's *A Genealogy of Modernism: A Study of English Literary Doctrine, 1908–1922* (Cambridge) is a more traditional work of literary historical scholarship, which studies the ideology of modernism as it developed from T. E. Hulme through Ezra Pound and Wyndham Lewis to T. S. Eliot. Levenson studies the statements, criticism, polemics, and letters of various figures, showing how the varying stages of ideology were manifested in the poetry of the age. For Levenson, Modernist ideology falls largely into two stages, one of individualistic revolt and one of conservatism, or consolidation.

Between them occurred a polemical period. The author shows how strongly based in tradition was English literature at the turn of the century, stemming as it did from Arnold, Huxley, and Pater. There is a continuity here, not merely the often claimed breach with the past. Levenson writes well about Hulme's role, and about his Bergsonism and antiromanticism, expanding on the varying roles both Pound and Eliot played in the polemical wars, and concluding with a reading of *The Waste Land* as the culminating document of the Modernist ideology, a conservative ideological resolution within a fiercely individualistic formal structure. This is the best study I know of the ideological history of modernism.

Students of modernism will be pleased that North Point Press has brought out a new edition of *Being Geniuses Together*, originally written and published by Robert McAlmon in 1938 and revised with chapters added by Kay Boyle in 1968. Boyle has written an afterword for the new edition. There are 13 chapters by McAlmon and 12 by Boyle, which appear alternately, thereby adding new perspectives on similar material and deepening the presentation. McAlmon's chapters are incisive and even nasty; he tries to settle a lot of scores. Boyle's are more expansive and sympathetic. Most of the well-known Paris figures appear in these pages, including Joyce and Stein, and one wonders how, with all the parties, any of them got any writing done. This is one of the best memoirs of that period; it is handsomely produced and there are many good black-and-white photographs.

Jeffrey M. Perl's *The Tradition of Return: The Implicit History of Modern Literature* (Princeton) suggests another kind of controlling ideology, this one not so much of polemic as of an implicit assumption about history, which the author calls "the ideology of return." Perl posits a model based on the *nostos* of the *Odyssey*, a return after years of wandering to a stage that pre-existed the cause of the travels. He comments on the fact that in the 19th century "the *Odyssey* surpassed the *Iliad* as the most popular poem of Homer and the most beloved literary work of Europe," suggesting thereby that the pattern of return in that work became embedded in the modern consciousness and found its expression in most of the key works of this century. He further uses both Freud and Nietzsche to reach the following observation: "Ideologists of return share the assumption that man possesses a unified sensibility, and the historical divisions they posit tend to correspond with supposed dissociations or reassociations in the cultural psyche" (p. 25). As one might expect, Perl discusses *Ulysses* at great length, because it so blatantly uses the *nostos* structure, but he also discusses the theme of return as manifested in Eliot, Lawrence, Tolstoy, and James, to name but a few of the authors referred to in this stimulating book.

Another work of interest to students of modernism is the reprinting of an autobiography by Harold Stearns, *Confessions of a Harvard Man: Paris & New York in the 1920s & 1930s* (Paget), originally published in 1935 as *The Street I Know*. Stearns is known to readers today for two reasons: as the editor of *Civilization in the United States* (1921) and as the model for the drunken Harvey Stone who appears early in *The Sun Also Rises* to insult Robert Cohn. Stearns was an interesting minor figure who, aside from his bibulous achievements, wrote a horseracing column for the Paris *Tribune* as Peter Pickem and, after returning to the states in the '30s to dry out, wrote an autobiography and two reappraisals of the United States: *Rediscovering America* (1934) and *America, A Reappraisal* (1937). He also edited another symposium, *America Now* (1938). While *Confessions of a Harvard Man* is not one of the great autobiographies, it is written with a certain dignity and honesty that does not sentimentalize Stearns's weaknesses. I found the most interesting passages to be the early sections that cover the pre–World War I years when Stearns worked in publishing and as a journalist. He is less vivid about Paris in the '20s, perhaps because he spent so much of that time drunk, although he still conveys a good flavor of the city and the times. I was most disappointed with his account of how *Civilization in the United States* was produced. This was something of a Bible for disaffected intellectuals, and it remains Stearns's best-known work. I should say that the current edition comes from another small California press and is part of the Paget Modernist Series, ed. Hugh Ford, which will continue to reproduce books like this one. Students of literature can only be thankful that such presses exist, interested in bringing quality books back into print without regard for the best-seller list.

iv. Literature and Society

The works in this section are concerned with how literature and society are interrelated. Most of the books are Marxist, and a few could also be discussed in other sections such as the one on literary theory.

Perry Anderson's *In the Tracks of Historical Materialism* (Chicago) was originally given as the Wellek Library Lectures at the University of California, Irvine. Introduced by Frank Lentricchia, it retains the lecture format. Anderson, who is best known for *Considerations on Western Marxism* (1976), believes that the quality of Marxist thought has declined in Latin countries, such as France and Italy, where Marxism has always been traditionally strong. It has maintained a strong tradition in Germany (as in the work of Jürgen Habermas), and has begun, in England and the United States, to develop an intellectual seriousness not previously apparent. Anderson shrewdly reviews recent French critical thought from Lévi-Strauss and the Structuralists to Lacan and Derrida, showing how these strong theorists have actually mounted a successful challenge to Marxism. He wonders whether there is in fact a conflict between Marxism as a theory and socialism as a political and economic program. The final chapter presents a blueprint for the development of Marxist thought in the rest of the 1980s. While Anderson is little concerned with literature, he does discuss many theorists with whom literary critics are involved.

I discuss Chris Baldick's *The Social Mission of English Criticism 1848–1932* (Oxford) because it suggests that a similar study might be done of American criticism and literary study. In examining the sociohistorical bases beneath the critical study of English in England, Baldick studies the evolution of literary studies from the time of Arnold, through Pater, Walter Raleigh, and Leavis, focusing on both class backgrounds and the role of the universities. I know of no book quite like it on American literary studies, even though a book by William Cain, which I shall discuss in a few pages, does some of the same things. I recall Howard Mumford Jones on *The Theory of American Literature* and Richard Ohmann's *English in America* (*ALS 1976*), but neither one studies in such detail the sociological implications or the class backgrounds, the role of universities, along with other social institutions such as the press, publishing houses, and book reviewing. I think we could learn a great deal from such an analysis.

I am always amazed by how frequently recent criticism is the subject matter of current criticism, but I think the new record in that regard has been set by William C. Dowling in *Jameson, Althusser, Marx: An Introduction to 'The Political Unconscious'* (Cornell), a book-length exposition of a work originally published in 1981! Dowling claims that "Jameson is the only one working in English who writes as the peer of the French post-structuralists" (p. 10), but the main reason for his writing this book is not Jameson's importance but his difficulty. He is certainly correct about the latter claim, although the source of the difficulty is neither Jameson's Marxism nor his poststructuralism but an unwillingness he shares with Derrida to "come out and say what he means" (p. 11). Dowling justifies Jameson's obscurity by stating that he rejects plain style because it is "the limpid style of bourgeois ideology where there is no need for obscurity because all truths are known in advance," a form of rationalization that I find neither convincing nor attractive. He goes on to say that "a genuinely Marxist style, then, will be one that produces what Jameson calls (in *Marxism and Form*) a sense of 'dialectical shock,' that as the price of its intelligibility again and again forces the reader out of customary and comfortable positions and into painful confrontations with unsuspected truths" (p. 11). With such reasoning how can you ever be sure you are not merely justifying poor writing?

Still, the book is worth looking into, precisely because it manages to do what Jameson has not done: it comes out and says what Jameson means. Jameson *is* an important thinker and writer about literature, who *can* write clearly (read his book on Wyndham Lewis), and his theories about how works of literature express ideology are worth trying to understand. Dowling presumes a knowledge of Marxist texts, including those of Louis Althusser. He explains the key terms used by Jameson and Althusser, and he makes Jameson's ideas accessible.

Western Marxism since Lukács's *History and Class Consciousness* (1932) is studied in Martin Jay's brilliant book, *Marxism & Totality: The Adventures of a Concept from Lukács to Habermas* (Calif.). Jay distinguishes between Western Marxist thought and the more orthodox Eastern variety, dating the latter from the acceptance of the Second International and *Das Kapital*. The more recent discovery of Marx's early manuscripts shows him to have been the Hegelian that Lukács claimed he was, and it is this lead that is followed by many theorists about whom Jay writes. Because the book is only peripherally concerned with literature, I shall not discuss it at length, but it includes lucid discussions of Antonio Gramsci, Ernst Bloch, Herbert Marcuse, Lucien Goldmann, Jean-Paul Sartre, Louis Althusser, and Jürgen Habermas. This is probably the standard work in English on the subject.

Frank Lentricchia's newest book, *Criticism and Social Change* (Chicago), is fundamentally a study of Kenneth Burke in the light of Deconstruction, in which the author uses Burke to develop a theory of political and social criticism that relates rhetoric to ideology.

Lentricchia desires an engaged criticism that is aware of what De-construction teaches us about the arbitrariness of language (he crit-icizes Paul de Man for the political futility of his theory). He says he is writing this book "to set forth and elaborate a number of key con-cepts which I take to be required tools for the literary intellectual who would be a social force" (p. 19), but he is hampered by a lin-guistic skepticism concerning the nature of rhetoric and its relation to a dominant ideology, or hegemony. What makes Burke, for all his insight into social activity, a weak source for a theory of social action is the persistent irony that undercuts his own positions and his Modernist conception of the ultimate dominance of form. Any book by Lentricchia is an event, and this one certainly challenges post-Structuralist critics to leave their linguistic double bind to engage the world. As interesting as the book is, however, it does not succeed in showing us how to break out of that double bind as long as we believe that language is inherently arbitrary and unable to state what it means.

Brief mention goes to an expanded edition of Robert Weimann's *Structure and Society in Literary History: Studies in the History and Theory of Historical Criticism* (Johns Hopkins), the earlier version of which I discussed in *ALS 1977*. This is an important theory of his-torical criticism, particularly its effort to describe its social dimension. The main expansion is a lengthy chapter entitled "Text and Historical Epilogues, 1984," that confronts Derrida and the post-Structuralists claiming that their seeming deconstruction of all history is logically flawed.

v. Theory of Fiction

Perhaps the most active genre in contemporary criticism is the theory of fiction, or narratology. Many leading figures contribute to this genre, and some have written the books I shall cover in this section. Robert Alter, whose *Partial Magic* (*ALS 1975*) is an important recent book on narrative, has published a collection of essays, *Motives for Fiction* (Harvard). Most are specific readings of authors and their novels, but the following have theoretical interest for students of nar-ratology: "Mimesis and the Motive for Fiction," "History and the New American Novel," "The American Political Novel," and "Literature and Ideology in the Thirties." All essays in this volume are occasional, often produced as review essays for such journals as *Commentary*,

New York Times Book Review, American Scholar, and *New Republic.*
Alter writes with almost journalistic lucidity. But he is more than a
facile writer; he is constantly stimulating and thoughtful, and he
wears his erudition easily.

John Barth's collection of essays and other writings about fiction,
*The Friday Book or, Book-Titles Should be Straightforward and Sub-
titles Avoided: Essays and Other Nonfiction* (Putnam's), is full of both
gems and laborious *jeux d'esprit.* In keeping with the high spirit of
his novels and the 18th-century parodistic style he often employs,
Barth presents a hilarious stream of prefatory essays and other materials: "The Title of This Book," "The Subtitle of This Book," "Table
of Contents," and "Epigraphs." By doing this Barth almost fictional-
izes his first book of nonfiction, asking us to question the irony and
authenticity of the narrative voice. The book is a lot of fun to read,
with such topics as "Some Reasons Why I Tell the Stories I Tell the
Way I Tell Them Rather Than Some Other Sort," "How to Make a
Universe," "More on the Same Subject," and "Historical Fiction, Fictitious History, and Chesapeake Bay Blue Crabs, or, About About-
ness." But lest *ALS* readers think this is only a book for the Barth
insider, let me add that the book is worth owning if only for two
essays that are classic studies of recent fiction: "The Literature of
Exhaustion" (1967) and "The Literature of Replenishment" (1980).
The former outlines Barth's theory of the end of the novel, reflecting
a dominant mood of the period, whereas the more upbeat 1980 essay
defines postmodernism and redefines his earlier essay as having really
been about the end of modernism, not the end of the novel. These are
two of the most brilliant statements I know about the literature of the
recent past, and they demonstrate effectively that Barth is one of our
strong critics.

More a work of philosophy than narratology, J. M. Bernstein's *The
Philosophy of the Novel: Lukács, Marxism, and the Dialectics of
Form* (Minnesota) starts from the theoretical work of the young
Lukács and goes from there to a brilliant reading of Marxist aesthetic
theory. Bernstein deals with philosophical topics that issue from both
Theory of the Novel and *History and Class Consciousness,* emphasizing Lukács's view that the novel is the principal dialectical form representing the external world. Bernstein ties Lukács's work to a larger
philosophical perspective that includes Kant and Marx as well as
poststructuralism. The book assumes a knowledge of the philosophical tradition, particularly German Idealism, and deals with traditional

Marxist categories such as reification, alienation, praxis, and totality. There is a particularly good concluding section on Marxism and modernism. Increasing attention is being focused on Lukács, a thinker much neglected in this country until recently. I reviewed two books on him last year, and more translations and paperback editions of his works are coming into print.

Another book from the active University of Minnesota Press is *Story and Situation: Narrative Seduction and the Power of Fiction* by Ross Chambers, volume 12 of the Theory and History of Literature series. Chambers writes primarily about the short story, with essays on such authors as Poe, Balzac, de Nerval, Flaubert, James, Joyce, and Saki, but students of the theory of fiction will want to read the first two essays, "Story and Situation" and "Self-Situation and Readability." In these pieces the author describes narrative as a "transactional phenomenon. Transactional in that it mediates *exchanges* that produce historical change, it is transactional, too, in that this functioning is itself dependent on an initial *contract*, an understanding between the participants in the exchange as to the purposes served by the narrative function, its 'point' " (p. 8). The transaction is defined as having an element of seduction; to describe this seductiveness Chambers uses a distinction exploited by Roland Barthes, between writerly and readerly texts. The writerly text tends "to realize itself as a seductive *object*, one very largely dependent, that is, on the willingness of its readership to be seduced, as opposed to the seductiveness of the readerly text, which is much more strongly centered in a sense of its own power to take the initiative and to develop an *active* seductive maneuver" (pp. 13–14). The analytic essays employ the theory well, and the concluding general essay, "Authority and Seduction: The Power of Fiction" rounds out the book with a good piece of metatheory.

I wish to mention an interesting collection of essays connecting the work of Jacques Lacan with a theory of narrative: *Lacan and Narration: The Psychoanalytic Difference in Narrative Theory* (Johns Hopkins), edited by Robert Con Davis. This collection was originally published as the December 1982 number of *Modern Language Notes*. It was Lacan who claimed that the unconscious is a text and that we should also read fictional texts as if they were expressions of the unconscious. These essays explore many implications Lacan offers us about reading fictional texts, and it is a welcome addition to the growing literature interpreting Lacan for American audiences and for students of narratology. Contributors include some relative newcomers as well as names familiar to students of French literary theory such as Shoshana Felman, Jeffrey Mehlman, and Richard Macksey. I found particularly useful two essays by the editor, "Introduction: Lacan and Narration" and "Lacan, Poe, and Narrative Repression," as well as Shoshana Felman's "Beyond Oedipus: The Specimen Story of Psychoanalysis."

A major topic this year is that of metafiction, or post-Modern fiction. In *Reading (Absent) Character: Towards a Theory of Characterization in Fiction* (Oxford) Thomas Docherty discusses the impact of the *noveau roman* and its concept of character on our reading not only recent fiction but also, retrospectively, the fiction of the past. The phenomenological basis of Docherty's theory is made clear by such statements as "By concentrating on the process of characterization in the activity of reading and writing, rather than on the established product of character, the theory will allow for the possibility of change or mobility in the meaning of character (and equally of the writer and reader) as the text is reproduced in the reading" (p. xiv). The author writes well about the breach between not only the Realist conception of character and that of the Modernists, but also between characterization in high modernism and that of post–World War II writers. "The radical break comes in fiction when we see the psyche of the reader, a real human, being probed through a more radical involvement of his or her position and perspective in the creation of the fictional text, and also in the very creation of subjectivity" (p. 30). Docherty discusses the traditional topics of fictional discourse, including names, time, plot, and motivation, and although he starts from the point of view of the *noveau roman,* most of his discussion centers on works in English, primarily British novels. The book is lively to read and is free of jargon.

A work that concentrates on recent American fiction is by Jerome Klinkowitz, *The Self-Apparent Word: Fiction as Language/Language as Fiction* (So. Ill.). By "self-apparency" Klinkowitz means that the word draws attention to itself rather than fading into the background of a story line because of simply assumed meanings it might have in conventional discourse. This is a variation on the signifier/signified split captured by critical discourse from the writings of de Saussure. Much recent notice has been taken of the congruence between fictional practice and theoretical insights which point out the arbitrary connection between signifier and signified. For 20th-century writers words become instruments of play and plasticity. The post-Modernist authors on whom Klinkowitz focuses include Walter Abish, Ronald Sukenick, Robert Coover, Donald Barthelme, Gilbert Sorrentino, and Stephen Dixon. The author does not break new theoretical ground, but he provides a good introduction to a group of problematic novelists.

Whereas for Klinkowitz the play of words is more important than events in the novels, Alan Singer, in *A Metaphorics of Fiction: Discontinuity and Discourse in the Modern Novel* (Florida State) sees all plottedness in recent fiction as being fundamentally ironic. Mimesis is a metaphor; but metaphor is also a form of mimesis, and both character and plot are rhetorical. Singer's readings of Barnes's *Nightwood*, Hawkes's *Second Skin*, and Beckett's *How It Is*, work well in light of this theory. My only problem is with the density of Singer's prose which like much contemporary criticism tends to strangle on its own tropes.

Brief mention goes to Allen Thiher's *Words in Reflection: Modern Language Theory and Postmodern Fiction* (Chicago), which also argues that 20th-century theories of language have undermined our beliefs in representation, signification, and narrative unity. It is these theories that lay the intellectual ground for post-Modern fiction. The thinkers on whom Thiher focuses are Wittgenstein, Heidegger, de Saussure, and Derrida; the novelists include Joyce, Borges, Beckett, Faulkner, and Nabokov.

Brief as it is, Patricia Waugh's *Metafiction: The Theory and Practice of Self-Conscious Fiction* (Methuen) may be the most useful of all these books on postmodernism. Part of the New Accents series, this work is intended as an introduction, but it is an erudite, detailed, serious approach to the field. Waugh's thesis is that "metafiction is a tendency of function inherent in *all* novels" (p. 5), making it possible to apply the insights gained from recent fiction to reading works of the past. Waugh succinctly lays bare the structure of the metafictional novel: "Metafictional novels tend to be constructed on the principle of a fundamental and sustained opposition: the construction of a fictional illusion (as in traditional realism) and the laying bare of that illusion" (p. 6). All plottedness becomes self-conscious; every narrative is inherently a fictional illusion; the purpose of fiction is then not merely to create the illusion of its own self-sufficiency but also to expose that illusion in the process of creating it. Waugh focuses most heavily on 20th-century American and British fictional texts. Her theorists are the familiar Continental Europeans.

vi. Theory of Literature

In this section I shall review those books I believe will make the strongest contribution to literary theory, along with works by well-known theoreticians. A major recent discovery has been the Russian critic Mikhail Bakhtin, best known for his theory of dialogism and intertextuality. Bakhtin's life has been something of a mystery, with long periods of nonpublication, and rumors of Siberian exile and censure by the Soviet authorities. Some of these mysteries have been cleared up in *Mikhail Bakhtin* (Harvard), by Katerina Clark and Michael Holquist, a biography that also introduces Bakhtin's work and thought. I have mixed emotions about recommending this book—even though it is necessary to understanding how Bakhtin's life relates to his work and intellectual environment—for it is turgidly written and uninspiring. I find Bakhtin's work fascinating, but I would never have read it had I read this biography first. Still, for those already interested in Bakhtin this book is essential, for it is the first to explain the circumstances of not only the life but also the confused authorship of the earlier works.

A more consistent, well-done work is Tzvetan Todorov's *Mikhail Bakhtin: The Dialogical Principle* (Minnesota), volume 13 of the Theory and History of Literature, trans. Wlad Godzich. This is probably the right introduction to Bakhtin's work, even though it is somewhat disfigured by Todorov's hagiographic tone, which states quite directly that Bakhtin is "the greatest theoretician of literature in the twentieth century" (p. ix). The book is basically a summary of Bakhtin's ideas with lots of quotations. Todorov emphasizes the principle of dialogism, or intertextuality, and he chooses his quotations no matter what the topic to mirror this aspect of Bahktin's thought. This technique often makes Bakhtin seem the creature of a single idea. Even so, Todorov is quite skilled at making us understand Bakhtin's complex vocabulary. One should of course read Bakhtin's works first—particularly *The Dialogic Imagination*—but I recommend keeping Todorov's discussion within easy reach.

Christopher Butler's *Interpretation, Deconstruction, and Ideology* (Oxford) studies the various schools currently competing in the critical marketplace. A literate, closely reasoned analysis, it looks at the various ideologies as paradigms and explores their viability. Butler believes that criticism is in crisis. "I wish to ask in what follows," he says, "how far new theoretical models for criticism reflect the type of intellectual upheaval which occurs when the paradigms for common practices change, and how far the shifts of methodological allegiance amongst teachers and students may be directed to further pragmatic ends. I interrelate and criticize linguistic, structuralist, deconstructive and Marxist approaches to the text, which have previously tended to be discussed separately" ("Introduction"). Butler is concerned not with the philosophical consistency of a theoretical position so much as with whether the theory works when applied to a literary text. To test the theories, Butler examines the works of a number of authors, including Camus, Conrad, and Yeats. His own position is revealed at the end as being "radical-liberal," by which he means that he basically accepts the Marxist critique of bourgeois society. The book is dispassionate and reasonable, but one longs occasionally for a more astringent critique of some of the theories.

William Cain's *The Crisis in Criticism: Theory, Literature, and Reform in English Studies* (Johns Hopkins) is a work of both theory and pedagogy. Cain believes that English studies needs reform and that theory should serve as the basis for that reform. "We need," he states, "to reclaim the role that has been lost, changing our self-conception from academic teacher/critic to man or woman of letters or, better still, 'intellectual worker.'" The job of the intellectual worker is to "give voice to 'the powerful language of resistance,'" to question "established practices" instead of taking them for granted (pp. 8, 9). Although Cain examines the work of many theorists, the ones on whom he most strongly focuses are E. D. Hirsch, J. Hillis Miller, and Stanley Fish. He is most interested in placing critical theory against its social and historical background, treating the relationships intertextually. This is the book's strong point.

It is Cain's program that I find disappointing, for it seems somewhat vague and unfocused after his astringent analyses of various post-Structuralist and hermeneutic critics. "We need to return the canon to history. . . . How have we come to perceive these texts as we do? What values do they embody? How did they serve the society within which they were written, and how is this history related to our own?" (p. 262). It isn't clear to me, however, whether "we" are the critics and teachers or whether "we" are our students. Can we ask the students to seek answers to these questions before we are sure they can, in fact, read the text? This solution sidesteps the issue raised by Deconstruction's belief that any consistent, coherent reading of a text is impossible. Nor does Cain's conclusion—impressive though its rhetoric may be—help us understand how best to change the literature curriculum: "And when we interpret texts, we should do so not in order to uncover and affirm literary value but rather to perceive inter-textual relationships, social and political problems that the language exposes, ideological gaps it helps to uncover" (p. 274). Nonetheless, this is a stimulating book, the kind we need more of in this transitional period, because the future of literary studies will always be closely bound to our theories of language and literature.

I wish to mention the last book Paul de Man prepared for publication before his death, *The Rhetoric of Romanticism* (Columbia). This volume collects all the author's essays on romanticism except for "The Rhetoric of Temporality," which was recently reprinted in the new (1983) edition of *Blindness and Insight*. De Man's topics include Rousseau, Wordsworth, Hölderlin, Shelley, Yeats, Kleist, the Romantic Image, autobiography, and anthropomorphism. Particularly useful are translations of a few early essays, and most fascinating of all is the publication of a brilliant long excerpt from de Man's Harvard Ph.D. thesis, entitled "Image and Emblem in Yeats." As one might expect, the quality of these essays is high, the substance demanding.

Jacques Derrida's newest work in translation is *Signéponge/Signsponge* (Columbia), a book that is fundamentally unreadable by someone unfamiliar with the poet Francis Ponge. Derrida is, however, the topic of two books that I shall discuss briefly. The first is *Derrida on the Mend* (Purdue) by Robert Magiola, a rather strange book that discusses Derrida's work and basic insight in relation to Far Eastern thought. In that regard it is something like Fritjof Capra's *The Tao of Physics*. Magiola sees Derrida's intertexts as including Heidegger and Taoism, with connections between the Deconstructive method and the Taoist way. There is some merit in the argument, although each text becomes a metaphor for the other rather than an explanation. A very good opening chapter explains the work of Derrida. The second book is a collection of essays called *Taking Chances: Derrida, Psychoanalysis, and Literature* (Johns Hopkins), ed. Joseph

H. Smith and William Kerrigan. These essays emanate from a Forum on Psychiatry and the Humanities of the Washington School of Psychiatry, the main subject being the confrontation between Derrida's analytic method and the "age of psychoanalysis." Contributors include a number of people already known as interpreters of Derrida or Freud, including Derrida himself, Samuel Weber, Alan Bass, David Carroll, and J. Hillis Miller. There is an excellent essay by Derrida, on himself; and by Weber, on Freud. From Derrida you learn the most about Derrida; from the others you learn the most about Freud.

The Skeptic Disposition in Contemporary Criticism (Princeton), by Eugene Goodheart, is not a survey of Deconstruction and other forms of contemporary criticism but a critical reading of it and its overall implications. The author starts from the premise that Deconstruction is a form of ultimate skepticism about whether there is any coherence or meaning beneath the surface of "reality" or the text. "The skeptic disposition," he says, "with which I am principally concerned is of the anti-theological dogmatic variety, which dominates literary study today. I speak of a *disposition* in order to suggest that what is at stake is not merely a matter of cognition. The conviction of certainty or of uncertainty is rarely the conclusion of an argument, however rigorous its logic; it is rather the result of a temperamental or willful need to see the text and world in a certain way. Doubt or certitude, the conviction of emptiness or fullness, are anterior to logic and evidence" (pp. 13–14). In an excellent opening chapter the author discusses Matthew Arnold as someone who uses literature as a substitute for religion. Goodheart then plays off Arnold against Barthes, Derrida, de Man, and Fish. There are good chapters on Barthes and Derrida and an interesting one entitled "Literature as Play." I found the conclusion, on "Deconstruction and Social Criticism," to be weak. Endings are always difficult.

Another one of the New Accents series is Robert C. Holub's *Reception Theory: A Critical Introduction* (Methuen), which discusses German reception theory (reader-response theory) with particular emphasis on the School of Constanz and its chief exemplars, Hans Robert Jauss and Wolfgang Iser. Holub describes the program of reception theory, discusses precursors of the current theorists (such as Roman Ingarden and Hans-Georg Gadamer), presents a detailed exposition of Jauss and Iser, and explores some alternative models such as the Marxist, communication, and empirical reception theories. Holub is a critical analyst as well as a presenter and, while his writing tends at times to be a bit dull, it is straightforward. This is as good a place as any to learn about an important critical approach.

Brief mention goes to an important book that I received too late to read all the way through: *Revolution in Poetic Language* (Columbia), the first translation into English of Julia Kristeva's doctoral thesis (1974). Primarily a semiotic study, it is more formalistic than Kristeva's other works, its theoretical bases lying in linguistics, the philosophy of language, phenomenology, and psychoanalysis. The book is described as a work of metalinguistics, and the "revolution" in the title refers to the overturning of poetic language in Modern literature to the point where language becomes self-examining and self-referential. Kristeva is a leading theorist, and for anyone interested in studying her work, this book is essential.

In *The Deconstructive Turn: Essays in the Rhetoric of Philosophy* (Methuen) Christopher Norris performs Deconstructive readings of both philosophical and critical works, including such writers as Wittgenstein, Kierkegaard, and John Livingston Lowes. The analyses are written under the assumption that "deconstruction has its own kind of philosophic rigour" and they "are all concerned with philosophies or arguments which actively *resist* deconstruction, to the point where its effects are all the more striking for having taken hold of their text, so to speak, against all the odds" (p. 3). Norris's opening chapter, "Deconstruction and 'Ordinary Language': Speech versus Writing in the Text of Philosophy" is one of the better brief exegeses of deconstruction.

Students of the New Criticism and of the history of American criticism will be interested in the *Selected Essays of John Crowe Ransom* (LSU), edited and introduced by Thomas Daniel Young and John Hindle. This collection of Ransom's best essays is impressive for its range and variety; there are pieces on "The Aesthetic of Regionalism," "Criticism as Pure Speculation," "Wanted: An Ontological Critic," "The Literary Criticism of Aristotle," "Humanism at Chicago," two on "The Concrete Universal," as well as many others on diverse topics. Many titles are by now familiar masterworks of 20th-century criticism. Two of the best-known essays, "Criticism as Pure Speculation" and "Wanted: An Ontological Critic," seem quite contemporary and remind us of how many problems in critical theory are not at all new. A good introduction defines Ransom's career and explains his major concerns.

William Ray's *Literary Meaning: From Phenomenology to Decon-*

struction (Basil Blackwell) studies the development of recent literary theory as primarily concerned with both reading and meaning. While introducing the reader to contemporary criticism, the book critically analyzes many important thinkers. Ray traces a progression from Poulet, Sartre, and Blanchot to Derrida, Barthes, de Man, and Fish, with many other critics discussed as well—all of them engaged in reader-response criticism. Moving through such categories as "The Phenomenology of Reading," "Subjective and Objective Criticism: Psychoanalytic and Hermeneutic Theories of Meaning," "Structuralism and Semiotics," and "Three Models of Dialectical Criticism," Ray has in fact written a critical history of contemporary theory. His style is lucid but a bit dry. I would rank this book among the middle rank on the growing shelf of advanced introductory texts in literary theory.

Another book doing a similar task for contemporary theory is *Criticism and Objectivity* (Allen & Unwin) by Raman Selden, which attempts—in reaction to David Bleich's *Subjective Criticism* (*ALS*, *1978*)—to reconcile the critical paradigm of deconstruction with the British tradition of empiricism and objectivity. Selden believes that deconstruction has taught us that "the critic cannot finally interpret texts, because they are necessarily decentered. . . . The decentering of the text and the displacement of the subject as origin and source of meaning does not leave us with a chaotic field of arbitrarily conflicting or interweaving codes but with a more completely structured discourse and a less unified concept of meaning" (p. 157). This well-written book is free of jargon, and while it is well reasoned, it is not systematic.

Because any book by George Steiner is an event, I wish to mention briefly the publication of two books by him. The first, *Antigones* (Oxford), traces the figure of Antigone in literature from Sophocles to the present, tracing its use in various literary and dramatic forms, including opera. The book is brilliant, the prose dense. I give it only brief mention because it is less a contribution to theory than a work of scholarship, history, and speculation. It is probably more useful as a reference work, but for those interested in the topic, it will reward a thorough reading. The other work is *George Steiner: A Reader* (Oxford), an excellent collection of the essential writings of someone who is a cultural resource. In the preface Steiner provides a good overview of his own work. There are selections from such books as *Language and Silence, Tolstoy or Dostoyevsky, The Death of Tragedy, On Dif-*

ficulty, In Bluebeard's Castle, and *On Babel.* Also reproduced here is the brilliant essay from the *New Yorker* on Anthony Blunt, the art critic arrested for espionage; it is also a study of the British intellectual establishment.

vii. Residue and Final Thoughts

The following books came into my hands after I had begun to write this chapter, and so I have not had time to read or even skim them with much care. Because they all appear to be of potential interest to *ALS* readers, I wish at least to acknowledge their existence. In some cases I might report on them next year. In American Literature are Stoddard Cartin, *California Writers* and Carl S. Smith, *Chicago and the American Literary Imagination.* In Women's Studies are Mary Kelley, *Private Woman, Public Stage: Literary Domesticity in Nineteenth-Century America* (Oxford), and Wilma Garcia, *Mothers & Others.* In Theory of Fiction are Peter Brooks, *Reading for the Plot: Design and Intention in Narrative* (Knopf); Paul Ricoeur, *Time and Narrative,* volume 1 (Chicago), trans. Kathleen McLaughlin and David Pallauer; and F. K. Stanzel, *A Theory of Narrative* (Cambridge), trans. Charlotte Goedsche. In Literary Theory are Lynette Hunter, *Rhetorical Stance in Modern Literature: Allegories of Love & Death* (St. Martin's); Joseph P. Strelka, ed., *Literary Theory & Criticism. Festschrift in Honor of René Wellek. Part I: Theory* (Peter Lang); and Elizabeth Wright, *Psychoanalytic Criticism: Theory in Practice* (Methuen).

A number of valuable books were published this year. I am particularly impressed with the increased number of books in women's studies, with the growing sophistication of that field and the theory of fiction, and with the growing interest in modernism. A number of books have already been announced that suggest that 1985 will see increased efforts toward developing a new theory of literature and toward applying that theory to a study of modernism, fiction, and the teaching of literature in our colleges and universities.

University of California, Davis

21. Foreign Scholarship

i. East European Contributions

F. Lyra

The quality of the studies of American literature here, as probably elsewhere, does not quite square with their quantitative increase, necessitating the application of more stringent criteria of selection for the annual review than in preceding years. I regret that a certain number of articles could not be obtained. Some of them, especially those published in the Soviet Union, might be interesting if not stimulating. The best I can do is list the titles and places of publication to show the full scope of the present state of study of American letters there.

The bulk of the material reveals continuing preoccupation with 20th-century literature, with that of the 1970s dominating. As for earlier writers, in sheer amount of print, 1984 belonged to Poe, at least in the Soviet Union where the propensity for commemorating anniversaries—in this case Poe's 175th birthday—elicited one major work and several articles. Of these, two may be mentioned outright: B. Berman's "Edgar Allan Poe. Fakty i legendy. 175 let so dnya rozhdenia amerikanskogo pisatela" [Edgar Allan Poe: Facts and Legends. The American Writer's 175th Birth Anniversary] (*V Mire Knig* 1:84–85) and V. Cherednichenko's "Aristokrat intelektu" [An Aristocrat of the Intellect] (*LGr* 4:164–75).

a. **19th-Century Literature.** With *Young America* (1971), *Herman Melville and American Romanticism* (1971), numerous articles on American literature of the first half of the 19th century, and now the monograph *Edgar Allan Po. Novelist i poet* [Edgar Allan Poe: Short Fictionist and Poet] (Leningrad: Khuthestvennaya Literatura), Yurij Vital'evich Kovalev has emerged as a Soviet authority on American romanticism. His latest contribution is the first book on Poe in the Soviet Union; for that reason alone it deserves an extensive review, but there is space here for comment on only a few of his points.

The Soviet scholar regards Poe as a consummate American Romantic who had many features in common with Emerson, Thoreau, Hawthorne, and Melville; each in his own way was investigating the roots of his countrymen's "collective dispositions and social disharmony." Poe shared with them the belief in the Ideal, in the opportunity of the American to become a new man provided he underwent a revolution of consciousness; like Emerson and Thoreau he believed in the individual, the self; like Emerson he was exploring the relationship between "society and solitude," and he was close to Emerson as a Symbolist. Like the American Romantics, Poe was disturbed by the chasm between the Ideal and reality, the direction of the progress of bourgeois civilization. Poe's pessimistic and tragic *Weltanschauung* was typical of late American romanticism. Kovalev also points out some differences between Poe and his fellow Romantics, although he is less specific in this area. He fails to say anything about Poe's conflicts with them. Consistent with the limits announced in the title of the book, Kovalev refrains from discussing Poe's criticism, *The Narrative of Arthur Gordon Pym*, and *Eureka*, to which he makes only a few passing remarks. Kovalev does not inform us that Poe's greatest aspiration was to become an influential critic, but he presents an efficacious account of Poe as a poet and short fiction writer.

Considering the proliferation of esoteric readings of Poe, Kovalev's study appears refreshingly rational. He discusses the selected works thematically in the light of Poe's aesthetics, and demonstrates, on the one hand, Poe's closeness to the contemporary literary currents, and on the other, his ambitious exertions toward originality and experimentation. Kovalev pays considerable attention to Poe's interest in the various faculties of the mind and psychological processes, particularly the dark sides of the human soul. Recognition of Poe's preoccupation with the psychological aspects of consciousness, says Kovalev, is essential for understanding his poetry and most of his tales. Kovalev asserts—too strongly perhaps—that Poe's "concentration on psychological processes was something totally new" and was not properly understood. With their tendency to interpret his work biographically, many readers and critics saw it as a madman's work about himself. So intense was his interest in the workings of the mind that he "circled around the subconsciousness." "Had he been born fifty years later, he might have become busy working on a theory of the function of the subconsciousness in poetic creation."

Among the tales Kovalev has chosen for a lengthy analysis is the rarely discussed "The System of Dr. Tarr and Prof. Fether" (pp. 193–

97) in which he discerns several meanings. Recognizing the humorous side of the tale, he ascribes to it a weighty intent on Poe's part: the exploration of one of Poe's favorite themes, the difficulty in distinguishing between the sick and the healthy mind. According to Kovalev, Poe deals here with three types of consciousness embodied in Monsieur Maillard, the narrator and the author. The story, says Kovalev, is "a serious criticism of the contemporary American mind, or, if you wish, the mind of the New Adam embodied in the narrator." I am not sure whether his interpretation of "The System" is original, but I find the reference to the New Adam a bit farfetched and inconsistent with what he tells us about him elsewhere in the book.

Kovalev leaves no doubt as to which side he takes in the antipodal opinions about Poe. For instance, he sides with Edmund Wilson against Joseph Wood Krutch when declaring that Poe was not alienated from the spirit of his times. His partiality declared, he still succeeds in providing a sense of objectivity to his judgments because he looks at Poe in the context of the literary and ideological circumstances, historical and contemporary, that produced them. Kovalev emphatically refuses to read Poe's work biographically, although in the comments on Roderick Usher he comes close to doing just that. He repeatedly stresses Poe's engrossment with aesthetics, but predictably protests strongly against those who hail Poe as a forerunner of the art-for-art's-sake school. Relating Poe's art to nonaesthetic factors, he demonstrates, for example, how Poe's frequent use of death can be accounted for historically and culturally and how he transformed his contemporaries' fascination with the rule of death and the past over the living into an aesthetic and psychological category. At the same time, however, by stating that "death in Edgar Poe's poetry . . . was to *a large extent* [emphasis mine] the product of his poetic imagination" (p. 130), Kovalev provides a tantalizing suggestion.

Much of the attractiveness of the study consists in the "obvious" solutions the scholar proposes to the various controversial and contradictory opinions that abound in Poe criticism. If, for example, the critics cannot agree about the meaning of "Al Aaraaf," Kovalev says why: there is no use in looking for meaning in the poem (and in some other works) because Poe, thorough Romantic that he was, deliberately made "vagueness the supreme law of the poetic structure of this work" (p. 99).

Kovalev precedes the discussions of "The Poet" and "The Short Fiction Writer" (pp. 67–283) with two biographical chapters, "The

Legend" (pp. 4–23) and "The Man" (pp. 24–64). The tone in these
chapters is apologetic, yet he exercises restraint and tact in blaming
social and economic factors for the writer's tragic life. But he applies
even more restraint in describing Poe's character flaws, chiding biographers for distorting Poe's life and personality. Kovalev tends to exaggerate some of his virtues and guesses at others: "He never did
hack-work" (p. 57); "There was another side . . . to his life during that
year [1829–30] hidden before the outside world, not documented, yet
far more important than his wanderings between Baltimore, Philadelphia and Richmond. Young Poe was working, working as if possessed" (p. 42). He says nothing about Poe's flirtations, his two engagements after Virginia's death, his self-destructive urges. The Soviet
scholar's sympathy toward Poe is contagious, it may beguile the un-
wary reader, but the specialist, even the most favorably biased, including Kovalev, knows better.

Most of the short studies of 19th-century literature concentrate on
individual authors. One of the better contributions, if not the best, is
Agnieszka Salska's essay on "Emily Dickinson's Lover" in *Studies in
English and American Literature: In Honour of Witold Ostrowski*
(Warszawa-Lodz: Panstwowe Wydawnictwo Naukowe; pp. 135–40).
Unlike Rebecca Patterson, John Cody, and some other critics and
Dickinson scholars who have dealt with the well-known riddle of the
poet's life, Salska does not look for a solution in psychoanalysis, "sentimental romancing," or the poet's overt biography. Her reading of some
of the baffling love poems, such as "Wild Nights–Wild Nights!" "With
thee, in the Desert–" "A Wife–at Daybreak I shall be–" convinces, but
I am not quite persuaded by the interpretation of "Come Slowly–
Eden!": "The intensity of the she-flower's (or his own) ecstasy anni-
hilates the bee. The fact that he is 'lost in Balms' looks more destructive than creative, more like a case of murder or suicide than
like conception." Salska's overall conclusion, however, is credible,
though—like so much else in Dickinson's poetry—not fixed: "Emily
Dickinson's lover as he appears in the poems is a version of, a metaphor for 'the other' which both catalyzes the mind into creativity and
threatens to submerge it in inarticulate intensities. The situation of the
erotic encounter, whatever its biographical background, is used by the
poet to test the possibilities and limits of consciousness as it impinges
upon 'the challenging unknown—the intellect's greatest need.' "

Emerson's name appears frequently in Soviet general studies of
American literature, but there has not been a Russian book on his

work since 1912 (*Representative Men*) and he is very rarely the subject of single publications. Under such circumstances even a short article on him seems noteworthy. Such is the case with E. F. Osipova's "Traditsia neoplatonizma v tvorchestve R. Emersona" [Neoplatonic Traditions in R. Emerson's Works] (*VLU* 3,xiv:43–47). The subject matter of the article is, of course, vintage; it is the calm and understanding with which Osipova writes about Emerson's idealistic beliefs that is striking. She criticizes him for having "limited the possibilities of knowledge," for not having "explored the dark side of the human soul, the dark depths of the subconsciousness and the irrational." In passing she makes a rather surprising statement: "Probably the first who questioned the validity of the teleological approach to history was Edgar Poe." Osipova also has published an article on Melville's Bartleby and the crisis of the philosophical fundamentals of American romanticism (*Zarubezhnaya Literatura* 2:35–41), which I was unable to procure.

The Melville specialist will have to decide whether, or to what extent, Khalil Husni's "The Confidence-Man's Colourful-Colourless Masquerade: Melville's Theatre of the Absurd 'In Black and White'" (*SAP* 17:219–31) is original or yet another redundant piece on color symbolism in Melville's work. Husni's tortuous style does not make the task easy: "This iconoclastic presentation of the two polar archetypes, of what is white and what is black, what is good and what is evil, what is benevolent and what is malevolent, what is heavenly and what is infernal—not only results in a universe without norms, standards, or measures in which blackness is the obverse side of whiteness, and where the counterpart of Christ is the Devil, but also reflects the irresoluble complexity of the Confidence-Man who is often associated with whiteness and blackness, and whose first two appearances as the 'man in cream-colours' and Black Guinea are respective embodiments of the two poles of colour."

N. I. Nakaznyuk is to be complimented for the short contribution on an extremely rare topic in Soviet studies of American letters, deficient though his assumptions are—"Grazhdanskaya voyna v poezii Germana Melvilla" [The Civil War in Herman Melville's Poetry] (*VLU* 4,xx:61–66). Half of the article deals with Melville's philosophical and aesthetic views in the 1850s, the rest—a discussion of *Battle-Pieces*—is founded on the wrong premise that "only now first steps are being taken" to appreciate Melville's war poems properly, to reverse the received opinion that he was a bad poet because of "the

unnatural marriage of prose and poetry . . . his disregard of the laws of
poetry." Just the opposite opinion seems to prevail among literary historians: they measure Melville's defeat as a poet by what he failed to
learn from Whitman.

Interested *ALS* readers might find a way of getting hold of two
other Soviet contributions in American romanticism which were
beyond my reach: I. M. Popova, "Russkaya kritika ob amerikanskom
pisatele (D. F. Kuper—marinist v russkikh zhurnalakh 1830kh)"
[Russian Criticism on an American Writer (J. F. Cooper—Sea
Novelist in Russian Periodicals of the 1830s)] in *Problemy razvitia
literaturnoi kritiki* [Problems of Development of Literary Criticism]
(Dushambe; pp. 22–26); and S. D. Pavlychko, "Otsenka romantizma
SSHA XIX veka v sovremennom amerikanskom literaturovedenii"
[The Evaluation of U.S. 19th-Century Romanticism in Contemporary
American Literary Scholarship] (*Vestnik Kievskogo Universiteta.
Romano–Germanskaya Filologia* 18:106–08).

b. 20th-Century Literature. Yasen N. Zasurskii's *Amerikanskaya literatura XX veka* [20th-Century American Literature] (Moskva: Iz-
datel'stvo Moskovskogo Universiteta) first appeared in 1966. A comparison of the present second edition, which purports to be "corrected
and enlarged," with the earlier text might disclose the range and
nature of the modifications. It would be instructive to find out whether
Zasurskii, a leading Soviet Americanist, has in any way qualified his
thinking about American writing over the last 20 years. Unfortunately
I was unable to get hold of a copy of the first edition. In a brief author's
note Zasurskii forewarns that he does not present "an exhaustive survey of 20th-century American literature." He proposes to study only
"aspects of the literary process which perceptively reveal the specificity of American literature" consisting in "above all the dynamic development of realistic literature" (p. 3). Zasurskii, however, does not
identify factors generating the "dynamism." He asserts instead that
"the development of realistic literature has been complicated by a
strong pressure of apologetic bourgeois ideas, conformism, the influence of Freudianism, and Modernist tendencies." Exactitude is not
his virtue. He displays an unsavory inclination to compound the
tangled estate of 20th-century writing by neglecting to substantiate
qualifiers or to analyze complexities; for instance, "Eugene O'Neill's
work in the '20s was romantic, naturalistic, symbolist, and expres-
sionistic; nevertheless it was moving along toward realism" (p. 136).

The book abounds in sweeping generalizations which are likely to put off a knowledgeable reader. The organization of the work and the direction he has given to the development of American literature suggest that socialist realism is the pinnacle of that development. "Socialist Realism in American Literature: Theory and Practice" (pp. 452–77) is indeed the last section, not counting the ritualistic "instead-of-the-conclusion" chapter entitled "The Contemporary Ideological Struggle and American Literature" (pp. 477–93). But considering the thin content of the chapter, the suggestive conclusion runs against Zasurskii's intention. The chapters "Crisis and Proletarian Literature in the 1930s" (pp. 250–67) and "New Features of Critical Realism of the 1930s" (pp. 268–83), which make up the body of his book, are ideologically sound but meager in substance, too. The student of the Red Decade will still have to reach for Walter B. Rideout's *The Radical Novel in the United States, 1900–1954* and Daniel Aaron's *Writers on the Left*, Zasurskii's opinion about them notwithstanding: "They distorted the process of the development of the literature of socialist realism in the United States, disconnecting it from the national bedrock; they belittled the ideological-esthetic potentialities and perspectives of its development, applying for this purpose the unscientific terms 'radical literature' (Rideout) [and] 'American literary communism' (Aaron)." Zasurskii takes note of the nonrational forces in American literature, but does not go far beyond the recognition of Freudianism. He makes short shrift of New Criticism and of the Symbolist and myth movements, subjecting some of their practitioners and theoreticians—especially Lionel Trilling, Leslie Fiedler, and Richard Chase—to scathing criticism based, regrettably, on a very narrow selection of their works, sometimes on a single article. He also applies this procedure to many socialist writers. Such practice undermines the value of the study, as do other kinds of sloppiness as, for instance, the indiscriminate application of the terms "epoch," "stage," "era."

With one notable exception Zasurskii unequivocally rejects all Modernists on the ground that they are not concerned with the American qualities of American literature. His resentment of modernism reaches far indeed: "Modernism, irrespective of the subjective aspirations of its individual representatives, objectively serves anticommunist purposes, acts against the development of realistic art, corrupts the artistic intelligentsia" (p. 413). Faulkner is the only Modernist Zasurskii grants immunity from the contagion of the trend, because Faulkner's talent was so great that in the course of time, he was capable of redeeming himself. Zasurskii gives an entire chapter to *The Sound and the Fury* (pp. 222–50), making no secret of his admiration for the novel despite his disapproval of the stream of consciousness technique. Zasurskii seizes the occasion to point out that V. V. Ivasheva was the first critic to comment on the novel and to recognize Faulkner's talent (p. 249). If he means there were no other critics outside the Soviet Union who had written about Faulkner and his novel prior to December 1933 (when his article was published), then his statement must stand as a major factual error. Zasurskii intimates that the writer's work has enjoyed steady attention in the Soviet Union since the appearance of Ivasheva's article. This is not the case. He might at least have hinted at the reasons for the 20-year-long hiatus that existed in Soviet criticism of Faulkner and for the absence of any Russian translation of a novel of Faulkner's until 1961 (*The Mansion*). The Soviet scholar eulogizes Faulkner for the trilogy, "a great victory of realism. The writer, who symbolizes Modernist literature, at the end of his road arrived at realism, created realistic works" (p. 428). Zasurskii chooses not even to mention *A Fable*.

Since Zasurskii fails to provide specific criteria of selection, his book contains several surprises, one of which is his extensive treatment of Gertrude Stein. He devotes 11 pages to her only to arrive at the arguable conclusion that "she left no important traces in the history of American literature" (p. 176). Few of the numerous writers he discusses have been presented so comprehensively, and none of the proletarian authors. He is justified in striking at the anti-Sovietism of some writers, but the upshot of his anger against Allen Drury, Mickey Spillane, Grace Metalious, and a host of other "boulevard belletrists" is overkill: their "trashy fiction defines the general atmosphere of contemporary American literary life" (p. 386); so does, he maintains, that of such "avantkitsch" authors as Terry Southern, William Burroughs, and Hubert Selby. Even a novel like *Love Story* should be condemned as "it became a serious weapon of political propaganda and ideological expansion" (p. 417). Zasurskii does not allow for the operation of the pleasure principle in the reader's contact with belles lettres.

Zasurskii follows a strict chronological order in dealing with his subject matter, but he is inconsistent in his approach to the material; descriptive sections alternate with analytic ones, and some are discursive and simply overwritten. He is at his best in the analytic chapters on *The Sound and the Fury*, Dos Passos's novels up to the last volume of *U.S.A.*, *The Grapes of Wrath*, and part of that on *For*

Whom the Bell Tolls which, incidentally, he analyzes in the original, for the novel had not been translated at the time of Zasurskii's writing. The inconsistencies, though, never obscure his focus on realism, which in his view is the only artistic creed capable of saving the Americanness of American literature, a property seemingly of no value anymore to either American readers or critics, which in the Soviet Union, however, by dispensation remains as important as ever.

Zasurskii's chief theoretical issue is taken up by I. V. Fedosyonok but reduced to a discussion of John Gardner's *On Moral Fiction*, in "Realizm protiv modernizma (esteticheskie i etichiskie vzglyady Dzhona Gardnera v knige O nravstvennoi literatura)" [Realism against Modernism: John Gardner's Esthetic and Ethical Views in *On Moral Fiction*] (*VMU* 6:20–26). Gardner's anti-Modernist views are "persuasive because they have been pronounced by one of the most prominent American writers of our age who feels profoundly the complex dialectical connection between the many-sided character and the revelation of harmony in the external chaotic world." Fedosyonok finds Gardner's opinions close to those of Alfred Kazin (*Bright Book of Life*), Hugh Kenner (*A Homemade World*), and Irving Howe (*Decline of the New* and *The Critical Point*).

A few earlier American Realists are discussed by the late Petr S. Balashov in his posthumous *Pisateli-realisty XX veka na Zapade* [Realist Writers of the 20th Century in the West] (Moskva: Nauka), which contains, besides 11 articles on British and German authors, four essays on as many American writers: Ambrose Bierce, Upton Sinclair, Erskine Caldwell, and Philip Bonosky. These are fugitive pieces, unequal in quality and scope. A bias toward Bierce prompts Balashov to overlook his artistic deficiencies. In tracing "Upton Sinclair's Evolution" (pp. 202–20) Balashov conveniently stops in the '30s when Sinclair was still an admirer of the Soviet Union. Whether Balashov inflates Maxim Gorky's influence on Sinclair, I leave for the comparatist to decide. Balashov is generous toward Caldwell (pp. 220–40) whose literary career he follows up to the appearance of *Around About America* which, along with the earlier *Jenny by Nature* and *Close to Home, Georgia Boy*, "mark[s] the writer's return to important social problems." Balashov tactfully omits his and other Soviet critics' earlier misgivings concerning *Tobacco Road* and other less successful works. He lavishes praise on Bonosky (pp. 241–50), especially on *Burning Valley* and *The Magic Fern*.

Among American Realists the greatest share of attention this year

was accorded John Steinbeck, thanks to Sergei S. Baturin's book
Dzhon Steinbek i traditsii amerikanskoi literatury [John Steinbeck
and the Tradition of American Literature] (Moskva: Khudozhestvennaya Literatura). The title is misleading. Aside from the few references to earlier American literature scattered throughout the book,
Baturin does not show Steinbeck's writings in historical perspective.
"The Tradition of American Literature" probably refers to the last
100 pages taken up by two articles devoted to Dreiser (pp. 252–305)
and Cooper (pp. 306–50). Baturin does not make the slightest attempt
to integrate the three studies. As far as I can tell, no other American
author in the Soviet Union has yet been privileged with a biography
of such warmth. But writing only about his best traits, Baturin produces a flat profile; he even treats Steinbeck's Vietnam episode with
generous understanding. He also assumes an uncritical attitude toward Steinbeck's literary achievement. The biography reveals no
traces of the vigorous controversy that marked his reception in the
Soviet Union for almost 40 years after 1937, when his work was first
discussed there.

By contrast with the biography of Steinbeck, Baturin's profile of
Dreiser exudes no warmth, and there is hardly a hint at the complexity
of the man and his work. He presents Dreiser's career as a steady
process of ideological growth culminating in his application for membership in the Communist party. The critic acknowledges his leaning
toward individualism, his interest in Quakerism and other ideologies
(not the pessimism, though), but he either sidesteps their explanation
by implying that they were peripheral, or accounts for them prag-
matically. Thus *The Bulwark* "is a history of a few generations of a
Quaker family; it deals with a problem as eternal as the world—relations between father and sons. At the same time, however, the novel
is about the influence of capitalist society upon man, and as such, it
is related to Dreiser's other works, in the first place to *An American
Tragedy*."

The article on Cooper is a factual description of the writer's work
in chronological order. Baturin demonstrates Cooper's literary versatility but forbears a critical evaluation of his fiction. Cooper appeals to
him above all as a critic of America from the position of a democrat
rather than from that of a landowner or Christian moralist. Consequently he hurries through the Littlepage trilogy and the last five
novels, but he discusses at some length most of his earlier works, even

making a few pertinent remarks about the little-known *Autobiography of a Pocket Handkerchief*. He points out correctly that Cooper preferred the rule of landed aristocracy to that of financial and commercial bigwigs. Baturin misses no opportunity to demonstrate that Cooper was free of racial prejudices; his treatment of Scipio (*The Red Rover*) should convince the skeptics.

Two leftovers from 1982 provide a convenient transition to a review of the study of American literature in the '70s. Being excessively concerned with literary process, Soviet scholars have found the decade an expedient time frame to observe its operation. In their view the '70s initiated a new literary period for which, admittedly, they have no name yet. In "Sut' peremen: iz opyta tendentsii amerikanskoi prozy" [Roots of Change: Experimental Tendencies of American Prose], an essay published in *Novye khudozhestvennye tendentsii v razvitii realizma na zapade, 70-e gody* [New Artistic Tendencies in the Development of Realism in the West: the 1970s] (Moskva [1982]: Nauka; pp. 201–30) N. A. Anastas'ev announces the decline of the avant-garde. "The books of Hawkes, Pynchon, Brautigan, which not so long ago were accepted as prophetic discoveries and bold challenges to prevailing moral norms, have suddenly lost their authority not only with the readers, but also with the critics, though their pathos of nihilism is still being practiced" (pp. 204–05). There is a revival of "feeling for human dignity and responsibility for the present and the future of the country, the world" (p. 206). In many novels of the '70s Anastas'ev discerns a renaissance of the American Dream and concurrently the emergence of reality from under the layer of the dream. He substantiates his diagnosis by looking closely at three works: Gardner's *October Light,* Joan Didion's *A Book of Common Prayer,* and Toni Morrison's *Song of Solomon*. Anastas'ev considers Gardner a key figure in today's American literature. "He does not only dream about the ideal, *he creates it*" (p. 208). *October Light* presents "an organic complexity of the dream and reality." Didion's book marks a new stage in the development of American literature after a period of artistic inertia. *Song of Solomon* draws Anastas'ev's high praise for the original resolution of man's confrontation with an antagonistic world. He writes eloquently about Morrison's artistic relationship with Faulkner and Thomas Wolfe.

Anastas'ev's general conception of contemporary American literature is shared by M. M. Koreneva in "Golos avtora—golos deistvitel nosti" [The Author's Voice—The Voice of Reality] (pp. 231–64), but she regards the '70s from a broader perspective against the '60s and from a different angle. For one, Koreneva is less irritated by the experimentation of the '70s which in her view did not always produce bad results, especially with authors who are "by instinct" Realists, for example, Vonnegut and Albee. But such experimenters as Hawkes, Pynchon, and others distorted reality and therefore should be considered "antihumanists." The '70s brought a change in the social climate and with it a change in aesthetic norms which postulate a break with subjectivity; the image of the world should be determined by reality and not by the author's voice. Koreneva discusses appreciatively, though briefly, the work of Joyce Carol Oates, Larry Woiwode, and Preston Jones, who exemplify—with various degrees of artistic success—"the return to the poetics of realism." But her highest praise is reserved for Styron's *Sophie's Choice;* it is "a synthesis of different poetic layers of artistic means—documentary, confessional, autobiographical, experimental prose—and a deep exploration of the relationship of characters and history." She pronounces the novel "the top achievement of the '70s."

Georgii Zlobin has done a sweeping review of the current novel in "Boyazn' istorii. Strannitsy sovremennogo amerikanskogo romana" [Dread of History: Pages of the Contemporary American Novel] (*Inostrannaya Literatura* 3:174–87).

The Polish critic Lech Budrecki does not share the Soviet view of American postmodernism, contrary to what the title of his excellent essay "Wyczerpanie neo-awangardy" [The Exhaustion of the Neo-Avant-Garde] (*LitSw* 9:323–46) suggests. "The American neo-avant-garde did not fall apart during the '70s. On the contrary, it became stronger and continued to expand." It acquired respectability. No post-Modernist author renounced his convictions or abandoned innovative fiction, but none has produced a masterpiece, though outstanding works appeared. Since the veritist novel prospered too, the '70s may be said to have brought about a "polarization" of American fiction. Some post-Modernists "compromised," for example, John Irving (*The World According to Garp*) or Tom Robbins (*Another Roadside Attraction*). Budrecki's article highlights a more extensive interest in American innovative fiction, at least on the part of the monthly *Literatura na świecie*. During the year the periodical published translations of the prose of Harry Mathews, Raymond Federman, Ronald Sukenick, and Gilbert Sorrentino as well as lengthy biographical notes on a few post-Modernists and interviews with William Gaddis (1:178–89) and Sukenick (9:263–72). Federman's work was also the subject of a review article by Marek Wilczyński, "Surfiction as a Theory and Practice of Fiction: The Novels of Raymond Federman" (*KN* 31,iv:117–40), which unconsciously demonstrates the solipsistic nature of surfiction.

Of all the contributions to the study of the decade's fiction, I find Zoltán Abádi-Nagy's "New Wine in Old Bottles: The 'Nature-Versus-Civilization' Dichotomy as Reconsidered in the American Novel of the 1970s and 80s" (*HSE* 17:7–47) the most instructive. He proves that a traditionally thematic approach to the fiction of a period can still be rewarding. Skilfully avoiding the pitfalls of bromides, Abádi-Nagy gives a meaningful comprehensiveness to the complex diversity of philosophical attitudes and artistic creation. He discusses the subject matter under five headings: "(1) the ecological novel; (2) the back-to-nature idea reconsidered (the sociocultural aspect); (3) the theme of re-engagement with nature (the psychological aspect); (4) a differentiated look at civilization; (5) the Freudian aspect." The classification does not in the least affect the flexibility of his approach to the neatly integrated material which chronologically ranges from Peter De Vries's *Let Me Count the Ways* through James Dickey's *Deliverance*, Lisa Alther's *Kinflicks,* and other novels and writers, to Saul Bellow's *The Dean's December* and John Barth's *Sabbatical.*

By way of concluding the survey of the study of fiction I want to mention three Russian items which were not available for comment. Two of these were printed in a collection of articles, *Printsipy funktsionirovania yazyka v ego rechevykh raznovidnostyakh* [Principles of the Function of Language in Its Speech Varieties] (Perm): N. P. Vit, "Lekschiskie sredstva vyrazhenia avtorskoi i personazhnoi tochek zrenia v novellistike Flanneri O'Konnor" [Lexical Devices Expressing Points of View of Author and Character in the Stories of Flannery O'Connor] (pp. 109–15); and N. V. Tkhov, "Tsvety v proze Karson Makkallers" [Flowers in the Prose of Carson McCullers] (pp. 115–23). The third contribution is on Robert Penn Warren, whose name appears frequently in Soviet discussions of American literature but who is rarely the subject of individual studies: A. L. Savchenko, "Problema chelovecheskogo otchuzhdenia v romane R. P. Uorrena *Pridi v zelyony dol*" [The Problem of Human Alienation in R. P. Warren's

Novel *Meet Me in the Green Glen*] published in the collection *Obraz geroya—obraz vremeni* [The Image of the Hero—The Image of Time] (Voronezh; pp. 128–36).

The yield of poetry studies was infinitesimal. Maya Koreneva published an essay on Denise Levertov (*Inostrannaya Literatura* 12:198–202) in which she dwells extensively on how Levertov transforms political views into emotionally effective poems. In Poland Leszek Engelking wrote a comprehensive, well-informed essay on a rare subject—Vladimir Nabokov's poetry (*LitSw* 4:308–20), and Jadwiga Węgrodzka gave us a superfine reading of a poem by E. E. Cummings under the most unpoetic title "Organizacja superkodu w wierszu 'All in Green Went My Love Riding' E. E. Cummingsa" [The Organization of the Supercode in 'All in Green Went My Love Riding'] (*KN* 31,iv: 441–54). Węgrodzka draws out and elucidates the rich texture and superb construction of the poem, demonstrating that Cummings wrote it "in the tradition of the religious lyric." From Lewis Leary's invaluable *Articles on American Literature, 1968–1975* we learn that Cora Robey expounds the same poem in the *Explicator* (September, 1968). Cummings's poem might be appreciated even better if Węgrodzka's analysis were compared with Robey's (I have no access to it here), or with the readings of others—if there are any.

Drama fared as poorly as poetry; but there were a few contributions on theatrical art, of which two are from 1983; they were published in a collection of articles, *Zarubezhnaya dramaturgia. Metod i zhanr* [Foreign Dramaturgy: Method and Genre] (Sverdlovsk): V. Ya. Mizetskaya, "Instsenizatsia kak zhanr sovremennoi amerikanskoi dramaturgii" [Stage Production as a Genre of Contemporary American Drama] (pp. 76–86); V. M. Paverman, "Problema khudozhestvennogo metoda E. Olbi v sovetskoi kritike" [The Problem of E. Albee's Artistic Method in Soviet Criticism] (pp. 101–13). The Hungarian scholar Zoltán Szilassy has written a valuable article in this field, "The American New Performance Theories of the Nineteen-Sixties" (*HSE* 17:37–47). Contrary to the title, Szilassy writes about the vigorous practice of the theater rather than theories. The article is awash in facts and happenings, producing an effect that matches the nature of the actual theatrical life of the decade, which he himself compares to "a confusing kaleidoscope."

The death of Tennessee Williams occasioned an important article by M. Turovskaya, "V stronu Tennessi Uil' yamsa" [Looking at Tennessee Williams] (*Teatr* 4:138–56) which no one interested in the Soviet reception of American drama can afford to ignore. She expertly combines biography with analysis of his plays and Russian performances—they started in Moscow in 1961 with "Orpheus Descending." Turovskaya calls special attention to Chekhov's influence on Williams and minimizes that of D. H. Lawrence.

A minor "shock of recognition" has been occasioned by a short, competent study of Thornton Wilder's plays, "Mif i prichta v dramaturgii T. Uaildera" [Myth and Parable in T. Wilder's Plays] (*VMU* 3: 38–43). Wilder is yet another author whose name shows up often in Soviet discussions of American literature, especially as the author of *The Eighth Day* and *Theophilus*, novels highly regarded by Soviet critics; but prior to the first Russian translation of *The Skin of Our Teeth* and *The Bridge of San Luis Rey* in 1970 and 1971 respectively, he was considered "a decadent reactionary." Even with the change in attitude, however, he is still very seldom the sole subject of studies. I. I. Samoilenko, author of the article, examines *The Skin of Our Teeth* and *The Alcestiad* to point out the functions of and relationship between myth and parable in the plays without granting them any transcendental or metaphysical significance; the emphasis is on their universal humanistic values. Samoilenko's analysis inadvertently demonstrates the generic nature of Wilder's art which allows different readings with no loss of the writer's message for Everyman, Humanity. Samoilenko maintains that Wilder's message is optimistic. His argument sounds convincing with regard to *The Skin of Our Teeth*, less so with *The Alcestiad*. The story of the Antrobus family appears to Samoilenko as a parable in which "the biblical myth" functions as "an auxiliary element that raises a family's problems into universal significance. . . . Endowing the protagonists with mythical and realistic images, . . . Wilder gives them philosophical depth." But the scholar reduces the relationship between Antrobus and his son Henry to a generational conflict. His historiosophical reading of the play runs counter to the widespread assumption that it demonstrates Wilder's cyclical concept of history. Samoilenko denies the existence of any mystical proto-Christian elements in *The Alcestiad*. Alcestis's self-sacrifice has a purely human dimension: "The only force which determined her choice was the force of love, Eros." Wilder's question, "how to conquer death," should be read "how to overcome fear of death." According to Wilder, says Samoilenko, Alcestis's immortality consists in the prolongation of life in the memory of people; every man preserves and passes on to others a particle of eternity: eternal love, goodness, reason.

c. Miscellaneous. F. D. Abilova traces John Dos Passos's visit to the Soviet republic of Dachestan (*Sovremenny Dachestan* 6:71–73); V. Bykov writes on "Dzhek London, ego druzya i revolutsia v Rosii 1905–1907" [Jack London, His Friends, and the Revolution in Russia, 1905–1907] (*Novaya i Noveishaya Istoria* 4:148–62); the article includes Bykov's reminiscences about his meeting with Anna Strunskaya in 1959. I was unable to ascertain the quality of S. Prigodii's article "'Natsia natsii?' 'Strana ravnykh vozmozhnostei?' Sovremennaya khudozhestvennaya proza i polozhene natsionalnykh menshinstv SSHA" [Nation of Nations? A Country of Equal Opportunities? Contemporary Artistic Prose and the Condition of National Minorities in the U.S.A.] (*Raduta* 4:149–53).

There have been, however, weightier contributions in this category, both on the study of myth. Aleksandr S. Kozlov's *Mifologicheskoe napravlene v literaturovedenii SSHA* [Mythological Trends in American Literary Scholarship] (Moskva: Vysshaya Shkola) is meant to be a textbook for university students of philology. Apart from brief illustrative and exemplary quotations, however, the publication provides no texts of American myth critics, thus falling short of its chief heuristic purpose: "The success of the struggle against bourgeois ideology depends in large measure on versatile knowledge of the ideological positions of the adversary" (p. 4). Actually, the tone of the book suggests that Kozlov treats American myth critics as colleagues rather than adversaries. With few exceptions he does not even engage in polemics. He suggests that some Soviet scholars are not against myth criticism as such; what they object to—as do numerous American critics—is the "mythomania" that bends creative fiction to the dictates of Freudian and Jungian psychology, anthropology and symbolism producing "fantastic," i.e., chimerical and absurd readings. Consequently, Soviet scholars prefer to practice "criticism of myth" rather than "myth criticism." Composed as a survey, *Mythological Trends* is packed with names and facts.

Zsolt Virágos's "Versions of Myth in American Culture and Literature" (*HSE* 17:49–84) is an erudite, superbly documented contribution to the study of myth; its evaluation, however, must rest with the specialist in the field. But it seems to me that Virágos handles too much substance within the limits of an article. "In Section I, which treats the connection between ancient myth and literature, I will primarily concentrate on the following issues: the authenticity of mythical prefigurations, the nature of the mythical comparison, methodological consideration regarding the 'discovery-and-evaluation' routine and what I call the 'jumping-the-queue' procedure. This section is also concerned with the ideological reasons for the so-called 'large demands' upon myth, and an attempt is made to suggest the outlines of a theory of artistic synthesis. . . . Section II offers a broad treatment of American cultural myths, while an attempt is also made to highlight the main structural and functional relationships of the various inherent aspects of myth" and much else. The compressed load affects the author's style, occasionally producing convoluted sentences which obstruct appreciation of the content. My objections notwithstanding, the specialist will find stimulating observations in the article. With a little exaggeration perhaps, this much can be said about some, if not the majority, of the current publications on American literature in this part of the globe.

University of Warsaw

ii. French Contributions

Marc Chénetier

Were I to plan my own obsolescence as French *ALS* reviewer, the task would be from this year on greatly simplified. A very important tool was made available to all researchers in Anglo-American studies at the very beginning of 1985; I must mention it a bit early as it may serve a useful purpose. As a collaborative project between the Société des Anglicistes de l'Enseignement Supérieur (SAES) and the French Association for American Studies, under the aegis of the Mission Interministérielle de l'Information Scientifique et Technique (MIDIST), the trial issue (No. o) of a *Catalogue Descriptif des Périodiques Français d'Etudes Anglaises et Américaines* [Descriptive Catalogue of French Periodicals of English and American Studies] has been published and is available free of charge from the Service des Publications, Université de Montpellier III, B. P. 5043, 34032-Montpellier-Cedex, France. It lists 39 periodicals and will in the next issue list several more, among which many have to do with American literature. A much-needed instrument, it should simplify the work of colleagues who despaired of finding their way through the increasingly dense jungle of French publications in this field.

a. **Critical Theory.** One book and one collection may be of interest this year to literary theorists. The first issue of *Tropismes* (Revue du Centre de Recherches Anglo-Américaines de l'Université de Paris X-Nanterre) is dedicated to "Hermeticism." Robert Silhol published *Le Texte du Désir: La Critique après Lacan* (Lausanne: L'Age d'Homme, "Ecrits/Cistre"), a book that attempts to sort out the varieties of Lacanian approaches and affirms the possibility of a new kind of literary anthropology. Even though the literary works analyzed here do not belong to the American corpus, this effort by a French Americanist to renew the discourse of psychologically oriented criticism is more than worth mentioning.

b. **General Works.** Three contributions on general subjects draw attention this year. Pierre Deflaux's *Aspects Idéologiques du Roman Américain de la Deuxième Guerre Mondiale* (Paris: Didier Erudition) is a massive (683 pages, plus microfiche bibliography) piece of work, covering fictionalized universes inspired by World War II from the earliest Mailer and Jones to the more recent novels of Heller and Vonnegut. Beyond the specific questions raised by World War II, Deflaux inquires into the nature of "war novels" in general, feeding on Cooper and Melville as well as on Crane. The first part (pp. 2–92) constitutes a theoretical and historical attempt at placing the specificities of World War II as fictional subject matter. The second and third sort out novelistic production according to a rough ideological watershed. "Le roman nationaliste et conservateur" (pp. 93–238) reviews rather minor and ill-known novels of the '40s and '50s, from that of Vincent McHugh to Irwin Shaw's *Young Lions*, insisting on the gamut of patriotic values and hagiographic writings illustrated for example by Wouk's *The Caine Mutiny*. "Le roman libéral et progressiste" (pp. 239–476) refines the analysis of liberal reactions to the war, attempts a typology of "the enemy," turns to a study of American internal political themes, and devotes separate chapters to Norman Mailer, James Jones, and Joseph Heller. The variety of reactions is emphasized in Deflaux's conclusion, where he suggests that the war novel claims all the classical missions of writing and provided a refuge for speculations on the "revised humanism of this century."

Ginette Castro's *Radioscopie du Féminisme Américain* (Paris:

Presses de la Fondation Nationale des Sciences Politiques) properly belongs to the realm of American Studies but must be mentioned here for reasons other than its outstanding quality and completeness. Its sixth chapter deals with feminist literary criticism and chapter 11 with the varieties of "parallel institutions," among which are feminist art movements.

Finally, in *Espaces Américains* (*Cahiers Charles V*. No. 5, ed. Philippe Jaworski and Michel Gresset), Jeanine Parot published a paper on "Images de la ville et espace romanesque: réflexions sur quelques romans américains" (pp. 121–50) in which she studies representations of the city in their relation to the space of writing in such texts as Crane's *Maggie*, Dreiser's *Sister Carrie*, Lewis's *Babbitt*, John Rechy's *City of Night*, and Dashiell Hammett's *Red Harvest*.

c. 18th Century. A scanty, rather than red, harvest it is this year in 18th-century studies, a state of affairs that should not last long as Europeans are gearing up for the 1986 Conference of the European Association for American Studies on "the Early Republic" to be held in Budapest; a number of publications are in the works.

"Andrew et André: quelques variations sur le thème du 'self-made man' chez Saint-John de Crèvecoeur" (*From Rags to Riches*, pp. 9–22), by Bernard Chevignard, is the only French contribution on this period in the volume, which also contains a paper by Robert F. Sayre: "Charles Herbert: the Revolutionary Prisoner as 'Self-Made Man'" (pp. 23–35).

The CRAA published its "Séminaires 83" as *Annales du CRAA* (ed. J. Béranger et al.). It includes, among many pieces dealing with Canada, Michel Gauthier's "Relation de Voyage et Emigration dans le récit de James Morris Birkbeck 1817" (pp. 119–38).

d. 19th Century. Yves Carlet, one of our foremost specialists on transcendentalism, came out with three articles: a general one entitled "Continents, Planétes: les Transcendentalistes et l'espace" (*Espaces Américains*, pp. 39–60), where he studies the avatars of space in Channing, Brown, Emerson, and Thoreau; one on "Emerson et le succés, ou les métamorphoses du 'commerce'" (*From Rags to Riches*, pp. 37–56), where he deals with Emerson's notion of success in its relation to self-reliance; and one on Emerson's iconoclastic positions in "L'espérance contre la mémoire: ambiguités de l'iconoclasme emersonien" (*Hagiographie*, pp. 65–82).

Edgar Allan Poe received quite a bit of attention. An analysis of his concept of the short story is the theme of Francis Berces's "Poe and Imagination: An Aesthetic for Short Story Form" (*Les Cahiers de la Nouvelle*, No. 2, January 1984, pp. 105–14), while Bertrand Rougé deals more specifically with one story ("La pratique des corps-limites chez Poe: la vérité sur le cas de 'The Man That Was Used Up' " (*Poétique* 60: 471–86) and Jean-Louis Magniont with another (" 'The Cask of Amontillado' ou la Comédie Dérisoire") in the second issue of a new journal entirely given to the short story in English (*VisC* 2:27–36). As far as Poe's verse is concerned, Thomas Bernard-West deals with the "eloquence of Edgar Allan Poe's poetry" in "Unparticled Matter and the Space Between Atoms" (*Espaces Américains*, pp. 61–76). Meanwhile, the theoretical debate goes on, illustrated by Henri Justin's rejoinder to Françoise Lévy on narrative structures, which provides the occasion for a critical survey ("The Fold is the Thing: Poe Criticism in France in the Last Five Years," *PoeS* 16[1983]:25–31).

In *VisC* 1:47–58, Monique Pruvot assesses "L' 'Imposture' de Hawthorne dans 'The Prophetic Pictures,' " delving into the regressive techniques of the use of paintings in the tale. Claude Richard's "La Pornographie Ecarlate" (*RFEA* 20:185–94) stresses the staging of woman's pleasure in *The Scarlet Letter*, estimating that it is the source of the "fathers' " wrath and that the "porné" triggers their ruthless upholding of the law.

Twain is the author Jacques Chouleur chose to illustrate the concerns of the 1983 Grena colloquium on myth and values, using him, among other writers, to document the legendary qualities of the Mormon leader in "De Mark Twain à Fawn Brodie: le prophète mormon Joseph Smith face à ses hagiographes et ses détracteurs" (*Hagiographie*, pp. 107–24).

Melville receives varied treatments. While Gilbert Schricke ("Melville: 'The Encantadas' or the Deceitfulness of Appearances," *Cahiers de la Nouvelle* 2:147–54) and Patricia Bleu (" 'Benito Cereno' de Melville ou le fantôme de la subversion," in *Le Voyage Austral* [Grenoble: Ellug], pp. 125–37) refined an abundant body of commentaries on two well-explored stories, Barbara Lemeunier opted for a stylistic exploration of *The Confidence-Man* (and more particularly Melville's use of irony) in "Coconut Shy on the Mississippi: Melville's Style in *The Confidence-Man*" (*Hagiographie*, pp. 7–30). The most stimulating piece on the subject this year again is undoubtedly Philippe Jaworski's "Le départ d'Ismaël. Exercice d'Approche" (*Espaces Amér-*

icains, pp. 77–88) which explores the many meanings of the notion of departure in *Moby-Dick,* from "beginning" to the "oceanization of space," in all cases an expression of the quest for the open.

Patricia Bleu had an article on Henry James in *Trames* (Limoges) 6(1983):105–11, which I forgot to mention last year. Two other interesting ones have to be added now. Laurent Souchu's analysis of *The Bostonians* ("Le Texte à Trous," *RFEA* 20:195–207) proposes a mode of access to James's underlying eroticism in the novel, suggesting, through the study of a key passage, that James deciphers the discursive evasions of hysteria while exploiting them to elaborate a "gappy," poetic text. Also dominated by a psychoanalytical approach is Nancy Blake's study of *The Wings of the Dove* ("L'Hystérie ou 'La beauté et la Dignité de l'Ar,'" *Dires* [Montpellier] 2:51–66), where the dove is shown to become gradually a portrait of the artist, all the more so as hysteria questions, by its very nature, the line separating the sexes.

There were, finally, two contributions to Bierce studies in 1984, all the more noticeable as Ambrose Bierce has not been studied much of late. A comparison of the treatment of time in two stories by William Sansom and Bierce constitutes Suzanne Dutruch's article ("Temps et durée dans 'Among the Dahlias' et 'An Occurrence at Owl Creek Bridge,'" *VisC* 1:35–46); as for Gilles Menegaldo, his attention is claimed by "narrative traps" ("Les pièges de la narration dans 'The Suitable Surroundings,'" *Trames* 7:27–38).

e. Drama.   Contributions are few here, but of great documentary interest. Colette Gerbaud, in "La Femme et le Temps, ou Mémoire, Mort et Solitude" (*Coup de Theatre* [Dijon] 4:19–26) studies the plays featured in *The New Women's Theatre* (Vintage, 1977), ed. Honor Moore, and, while stressing the interesting feminine qualities of these works, pleads for a disengagement from feminist militancy that might well jeopardize artistic forms.

Geneviève Fabre's "New and Ancient Myths and Images in Recent American Mask and Puppet Theatre" appeared in a collection of essays published in Germany, *Modern Drama and Society* (Carl Winter; pp. 141–54) and concentrates on the recent work of Eric Bass and Julie Taymor.

f. Poetry.   The most sizeable item here is Françoise Delphy's *Emily Dickinson* (Paris: Didier Erudition). This "thèse d'Etat," one of the

last to appear since the doctoral set-up is now being modified in
France in favor of less weighty dissertations, revolves around the
question of the self in the New England poet. "The self" is the center
of the first part (pp. 17–209), where the manifestations of the self are
simultaneously tracked down thematically and stylistically; this is prolonged by a second part dealing with its loss (pp. 210–338) where the
body and psychologically treated manifestations of ecstasy, despair,
time, and space feature prominently, in all their rich ambiguities, de-
bouching into an analysis of narcissism and violence. The third part
(pp. 339–500) delves into what Delphy calls "the guarantees of the
self"; nature, love, and God are thus in turn the subject of minute
thematic explorations, where the materiality of images is given privilege, after the lessons of Gaston Bachelard, Jean-Pierre Richard, and
the critics of the so-called Geneva School. A final part explores the
inheritance of Emily Dickinson, "our contemporary."

Eric Riewer has given an excerpt of his work-in-progress on
Charles Olson to *Espaces Américains* (pp. 151–65), an excerpt entitled "A Sense of Locality: Olson in Gloucester." In *Tropismes,* Anne
Lecercle has an essay on T. S. Eliot seen under a psychoanalytical
light (" 'Tuer l'Enfant ou la conjuration de la faille': lecture de la
dernière strophe de 'The Waste Land,'" 1:75–90). Finally, I wrote
yet another essay on Vachel Lindsay in which I endeavor to make
plain the modernity of a poet whose ground-breaking and prophetic
innovations must be reassessed over and against the hackneyed image
of the jingleman ("Vachel Lindsay: Modernity and Modernism," in
American Poetry: Between Tradition and Modernism (1865–1914)
[Regensburg: Friedrich Pustet], ed. Roland Hagenbüchle, pp. 197–
207).

g. Early and Mid-20th-Century Fiction.   Let us open this rich section on a lighter touch, due not so much to the very serious and competent treatment Thurber receives at the hands of Suzanne Dutruch and
Roland Diot, but because of the permanently endearing nature of the
author's humor. Rolande Diot is a seasoned expert on 20th-century
American humorists and her work on Perelman and Thurber is known
for its excellence. In *Trames* (7:49–66) she explores Thurber's strange
lexicon and classifies it after the rules of a sort of Buffo(o)n of words:
"Nouvelle Histoire Naturelle ou le Monde des Anti-Mots de James
Thurber" makes lovely reading for fans of "The Wonderful O" or
"The White Deer." Suzanne Dutruch, an "anglicist" by trade, launches

another American foray in *VisC* 2 (subtitled "Le Jeu/Les Jeux") and mockingly echoes a Marivaux gone sour in "Les Jeux de la Haine et du Hasard dans 'A Catbird Seat' de James Thurber" (pp. 81–88).

Another punster was Gertrude Stein, even though this is not the only aspect of her work Jacques Darras studies in a contribution to *Espaces Américains*. His brief "Rosaire de la prose" (pp. 167–70) owes as much to Darras's pyrotechnics as to Gertrude's. Jean Marcet, in " 'This Must Not Be Put In A Book': Les stratégies érotiques dans l'écriture de Gertrude Stein" (*RFEA* 20:209–28), explains how, in order "to cope with the problem of actual censorship and to satisfy the demands of her own 'almost puritanic' reticence" about sex, Stein relied on concealment and transfiguration. He tries to identify the mechanisms involved in a process "that leads from a defensive and euphemistic approach in her early fiction to an unqualified celebration of sexual delight in her erotic poetry." In "Politique et Poétique de la Ville" (*Cycnos* [Nice] 1:59–72) Marcet also published "Paris, France: le Paris de Gertrude Stein."

The only piece on Fitzgerald appearing this year, before we leave this "génération perdue," is that of Christiane Johnson, and it deals with Fitzgerald's stay in Hollywood ("F. Scott Fitzgerald et Hollywood: le rêve américain dénaturé," *RFEA* 19:39–52).

Even though I do not feel compelled this year as I did last to open a special Faulkner section to accommodate an incredibly abundant production, it must be said that the majority of articles published this year on early-20th-century American literature deals with southern authors among whom Faulkner cuts his usual towering figure. Jacques Pothier writes of landscape and margins in "L'arriére-pays appalachien comme marge de l'espace faulknérien" (*Espaces Américains*, pp. 107–20). Besides coediting *Faulkner and Idealism: Perspectives from Paris* with Patrick Samway (Miss.), Michel Gresset brought still another "perspective" in *International Perspectives on Faulkner* (Miss.) with his " 'The Old, Fine Name of France,' or Faulkner's Western Front from 'Crevasse' to *A Fable*." Other contributions on Faulkner include Michel Bandry's "Et Sutpen créa Sutpen . . ." (*From Rags to Riches*, pp. 83–94) and "Jefferson et Memphis dans l'Oeuvre de Faulkner" (*Cycnos* 1:49–58). But Bandry, a Caldwell specialist, also has written two pieces on his favorite author. One deals with the perverse sexuality in the novels ("Le pays de Caldwell, ou des hommes dans des corps d'animaux," *RFEA* 20:229–42) and the other with "Erskine Caldwell in Hollywood" (*Hollywood*, pp. 42–63). The relationship between literature and the movies seems to have been of particular interest this year, since both *RFEA* 19 ("Hollywood au miroir," ed. Michel Ciment) and the most recent GRENA publication dealt with the theme. The latter includes in particular a paper by André Muraire on Steinbeck's *The Grapes of Wrath* ("Radicalisme et Subversion dans *The Grapes of Wrath* de John Ford," *Hollywood*, pp. 64–78).

Wrapping up this section requires mention of George-Michel Sarrotte's "Carson McCullers et son groupe" (*Masques*, Spring 1984, pp. 46–49); of Sylvie Mathé's "De la subversion à la séduction: la rhétorique du discours affectif dans [J. D. Salinger's] *The Catcher in the Rye*" (*Hagiographie*, pp. 41–54); and of a paper that conveniently links this period with contemporary production: in "Sex vs. Text: From Miller to Nabokov" (*RFEA* 20:243–60), Maurice Couturier argues that "the representation of sex has always been a critical problem in American fiction" and that, when the latter gets explicit, it tends to "overpaint the erotic scenes," as in Henry Miller, or makes "uproarious fun of them" (Coover, Roth). To his eyes, the only nonromantic, nonironic, but "poerotic" approach of this sort of material has been Vladimir Nabokov's.

h. Contemporary Fiction. Nabokov is also the subject of Didier Machu's "De Mona-Lisa à Lola-Lola: *Laughter in the Dark*," appearing in a lovely-looking and very promising new journal, *Autrement Dire* (Nancy) 1:69–90.

Even though several such pieces are in the offing, the only general and theoretical piece to appear on contemporary American fiction this year was my "The Soporific Adventures of Neo and Post: An Insomniac's View" (in *Neo-Conservatism: Its Emergence in the USA and Europe* [Amsterdam: EAAS Series], ed. Rob Kroes, pp. 110–29), in which I reflect on the sterile vogue of prefixes used to tag ill-identified phenomena. In particular, I dispute the validity of an ongoing collapse of "post-Modern" into "post-Modernist," which leads critics to talk indiscriminately of literary objects belonging to the period following the (disputable) demise of modernism as an aesthetic movement and of a set of ideas and attitudes that can legitimately be ascribed to authors and philosophers going as far back as Hegel. This plea for lexical hygiene is one that relays previous speculations on modernism and modernity. I also prefaced and presented a collection of contemporary American short stories in translation, ed.

Philippe Jaworski (*Bas de Casse* 7:5–10), which includes work by Walter Abish, Raymond Carver, Guy Davenport, William Kotzwinkle, Steven Millhauser, and Grace Paley.

But the major contribution in the field for 1983 is undoubtedly Pierre Gault's book, *John Hawkes: La Parole Coupée* (Paris: Klincksieck). Prefaced by Maurice Nadeau, thanks to whose earnestness John Hawkes has begun to cut somewhat of a figure in France, this beautiful book is an example of what can be done when a theoretically sophisticated mind applies itself to major poetic texts without ever pedantically flaunting its theoretical sources. A highly idiosyncratic book, it is all but epigonic and actually manages to reveal the more or less conspicuous mechanisms of an exceptional kind of writing. The first part, on "Narrativity: Reader, Narrator and Character" (pp. 9–66) relies heavily on *The Lime Twig*, opening *in medias res*. The second ("Strategies and Figures of Hawkesian Rhetoric," pp. 67–130) dwells on *Death, Sleep and the Traveler* and *The Passion Artist*, in which Gault highlights respectively the processes of enumeration and Hawkes's predilection for the oxymoron. The third part ("Access to Interpretation," pp. 131–232) first deals with *The Beetle Leg* and *Second Skin*, in which desire, frustration, and incest provide the thematic backbone; he then goes on to analyze the figure of the narrator in *The Blood Oranges* and quantitative aspects of *Death, Sleep and the Traveler*. All in all a masterful narratological study.

In the same collection, Claude Lévy published a book on Saul Bellow that has many of Gault's qualities. *Les Romans de Saul Bellow* (Paris: Klincksieck) is as humble a book as its title suggests. But beneath this unprepossessing surface lies a most penetrating analysis best summed up by the subtitle: "Tactiques narratives et stratégies oedipiennes." Narratological and psychoanalytical in scope and method, the author endeavors, with great success, to read with an uncommonly acute and informed eye eight of Saul Bellow's novels. He never falls into the vaguely humanistic generalities too often generated among Bellow's critics by an *oeuvre* of great topical import. Evading a debate of opinion is the book's explicit program. A "deliberately empirical and immanent method" allows Lévy to examine narrative and psychological strategies, to discern under apparently sleek and even surfaces an impressive array of modes of dissimulation and selective memory. In turn, *Dangling Man, The Victim, The Adventures of Augie March, Seize the Day, Henderson the Rain King, Herzog,*

Mr. Sammler's Planet, and *Humboldt's Gift* are submitted to a rigorous
scrutiny that reveals subterranean obsessions lurking under the discourse of Bellow's characters and narrators.

Claude Lévy also edited the issue of *DeltaES* (No. 19) dedicated
to Bellow's work. He does not appear in the table of contents, leaving to a variety of European and American colleagues the task of
further exploring his pet subject. An interview with Saul Bellow by
Pierre Dommergues opens the issue (pp. 1–28). Among other French
contributors are Robert Silhol, whose "*Augie March* et les balance-
ments délicats d'un moi à la recherche de soi" (pp. 93–108) shows
Augie hesitating between Europe and the United States; Marie Pierre
Kerneur with an essay on "Herzog et les Machiavels" (pp. 109–30),
where she documents Herzog's struggle with the "reality-instructors";
and Rachel Ertel, a well-known French specialist on the Jewish novel,
who describes *Mr. Sammler's Planet* as a "Roman de Mémoire et
d'Histoire" (pp. 155–69).

Among other Jewish novelists more properly belonging in this
section than in the ethnic literature department is Bernard Malamud.
Antoine Halff has chosen to compare some of his gamblers with those
of a British author ("Portrait du Nouvelliste en Joueur: Figures du
Jeu dans quelques nouvelles de W. Somerset Maugham et de Bernard
Malamud," *VisC* 2:5–18).

Several studies on a wonderful southerner also belong more properly here. They are on Eudora Welty; all appear in the third issue of
Cahiers de la Nouvelle and are authored respectively by Marc Amfre-
ville and Anne Wicke ("'Acrobats in a Park': secret d'une représentation, représentation d'un secret," pp. 119–26); Danièle Pitavy-Souques
("Optique-Erotique: 'A Memory' de Eudora Welty," pp. 127–38); and
Claudine Verley ("B.A. ou parcours initiatique: structures narratives
et sémantiques dans 'A Visit of Charity' de Eudora Welty," pp. 139–
52).

Thomas Pynchon's *The Crying of Lot 49* was on the syllabus for
Agrégation this year (1984–85) and there should be quite a harvest
of pieces on him in our next report. But three interesting articles already appeared in 1984. Simone Vauthier wrote her "*Gravity's Rainbow* à la carte: notes de lecture" for *Fabula* (No. 3, pp. 97–118), while
Georgiana Colville, another "Strasbourgeoise," gave her "L'Alchimie
de Pynchon dans *The Crying of Lot 49*" to the local *RANAM* (17:213–
18). At the other end of France, Claude Richard contributed a fasci-

nating comparison between the same novel and the paintings of Vermeer, "Oedipa Regina," to *Dires* (Montpellier), pp. 67–84.

Fabula also published (No. 3: 77–96) a study by Claudine Thomas, "Norman Mailer et le Discours du Roman." Finally, a brief report on "The Novels of Edmund White" (*QL*, 15 Apr., p. 5) by George-Michel Sarrotte and an article by John Dean on Thomas Berger ("Thomas Berger's Fiction: Demystification without Demythification," *Hagiographie*, pp. 55–64) are worth mentioning. Nancy Blake also wrote a short contribution on William Gass: " 'Out of time, out of body': An Erotic Map of *The Heart of the Heart of the Country*" (*RFEA* 20:264–73).

i. **Ethnic Literature.** Issue No. 19 of Michel Fabre's *AFRAM Newsletter* (Paris III) came out in September and is its usual thorough, informative self. It now runs close to 50 pages and contains reviews, summaries of dissertations, brief articles, and notes on Afro-American and Third World literature in English. Fabre concentrated on the works of Ralph Ellison in several publications, editing in particular a special issue of *Focus* (Paris) and one of *DeltaES*. The *Focus* number on Afro-American literature includes Fabre's own panorama of contemporary writers (pp. 12–16), a thorough and pithy piece in which well-known (Reed, Kelley) and lesser-known artists (Murray, Major) are presented to the French public; a survey of black literature in the U.S. from its origins to World War II by Marc Saporta ("L'Histoire de la littérature romanesque Afro-Américaine," pp. 1–8); a study by Robert G. O'Meally ("Le Roman Invisible de Ralph Ellison," pp. 9–11); and another by Robert Stepto ("L'épanouissement d'une littérature," pp. 17–20). *DeltaES* No. 18 was an issue on Ellison, featuring a piece by Ralph Ellison ("Remembering Richard Wright," pp. 1–14), and three French studies of *Invisible Man:* Simone Vauthier's " 'Not Quite on the Beat': An Academic Interpretation of the Narrative Stances in R. E.'s *Invisible Man*" (pp. 69–88), J. de Romanet's "Musical Elements in *Invisible Man* with Special References to the Blues" (pp. 105–18), and Fabre's essay entitled " 'Looking at the Naked Blonde—Closely' (or Scrutinizing Ellison's Writing)" (pp. 119–31), where he endeavors to isolate characteristics of Ellison's style. But Fabre did not stop there, adding two more pieces to his impressive bibliography on the subject: "Ralph Ellison's 'Black Rite of Horatio Alger'; or, The American Dream Revisited" (*From Rags to Riches,* pp. 109–19) and "Ecart et Totalisation: Pour une Lecture Symbolique d'*Invisible Man*" (*EA* 37:54–66). By the same prolific author are worth noting "Chester Himes in direct" and "Bibliographie de Chester Himes" (*Hard-Boiled Dicks* [Dec. 1983], respectively pp. 5–21 and 63–74) as well as a piece given to Le Monde Diplomatique ("Dix Romans qui ont compté," Oct. 1984, p. 26).

From Rags to Riches also contains a piece in the same field, this time on Booker T. Washington, by Hélène Christol ("*Up From Slavery*: le roman 'algérien' d'un colonisé," pp. 95–108) in which the author's autobiography is read as success story. As for Maya Angelou's autobiography, Jean Cazemajou's study appeared in *Annales du CRAA* 10:71–91 ("L'Autobiographie de Maya Angelou: itinéraires d'une pionnière du mouvement des droits civiques").

Cazemajou also ventured into the field of Chicano literature with "*Hunger of Memory* de Richard Rodriguez" (*FRAN* 1,v:147–65). Chicano literature is the specialty of Marcienne Rocard who added "L'ambiguité ethnique du Chicano: à la recherche d'un discours adéquat" to her completed research (*Le Facteur Ethnique aux Etats-Unis et au Canada* [Lille: Presses Universitaires, 1983], pp. 163–70).

Asian-American literature, a field little explored in France so far, has been the object of Jane Bataille's "Yellow Rage: New Pages of Asian-American Literature" in yet another new journal given to Anglo-American studies (*GRAAT* [Tours]1["Protest and Punishment"]:75–92).

There were finally several contributions on Jewish literature— that is, literature not only written by writers who are Jewish but which also systematically endeavors to convey the specificity of Jewish culture and experience. The special issue of *L'Arc* dedicated to I. B. Singer (No. 93) contains, among others, a paper by Colette Gerbaud ("Gimpel l'Imbécile ou le Conte de l'Egaré," pp. 79–83) and one by Judith Stora-Sandor ("Les Secrets du Magicien, l'humour de l'écrivain," pp. 97–104). But the latter's overarching achievement this year is a book on Jewish humor, *L'Humour Juif dans la Littérature de Job à Woody Allen* (Paris: Presses Universitaires de France), the scope of which obviously goes beyond merely American concerns. In point of fact, only the eighth chapter (pp. 195–254) deals systematically with American Jewish humor, expectedly enough encompassing the works of Malamud, Bellow, and Roth, but also, less expectedly, that of Erica Jong and Bruce Jay Friedman. This is definitely a most valuable handbook for understanding the inner mechanisms of a protean form of humor. Stora-Sandor distinguishes the relationship binding a people to its God and its Law, traditional "shtetl" humor, from a more modern form, concluding her well-informed and well-written essay with a few handy "keys to Jewish humor" (pp. 255–325).

j. Science Fiction and the Fantastic. Last year, I announced the forthcoming publication of the papers gathered after a Nice colloquium on "Images de l'Ailleurs-Espace Intérieur" held in April 1983. The volume is now out, and constitutes Nos. 9–10 (March) of *Métaphore* (Nice). The papers range far and wide and are not on the American illustrations of the genre alone. But a number of Americanists contributed, including Jean Raynaud with "Images de Nulle Part" (pp. 51–60) and John Dean with "The Use of Stars in S.F. Literature" (n.p.). Two papers on Ursula Le Guin were contributed by American critics, one of whom is Robert Scholes.

Another collective endeavor is illustrated by part 2 of *Trames* (No. 7, "Humour et Imaginaire") which contains in particular two essays on Robert Sheckley: "R. Sheckley, *A Ticket to Tranai:* humour, nonsens et utopie" by Jean Raynaud (pp. 107–20) and "Science-Fiction et Parodie: le cas Sheckley" by Gérard Cordesse (pp. 121–35). Other theoretical essays by Raynaud found their way into *Trames* No. 9 ("Valeur et fonction idéologiques des dystopies de science-fiction," pp. 87–98); *Travaux du CIEREC* (St. Etienne) ("Configurations psychiques des paysages d'altérité," 42:143–52); and *Poétiques* (1983) ("Fantastique et science-fiction: essai de différentiation," pp. 89–100).

But what meager interstellar space I have left must be devoted to a presentation of Gérard Cordesse's masterpiece, which received the Prix Spécial du Grand prix de la Science-Fiction Française for 1984, awarded by a jury consisting of science fiction writers, critics, and directors of collections. *La Nouvelle Science-Fiction Américaine* (Paris: Aubier) opens with an analysis of the objective conditions in which science fiction books are produced; the place of and part played by editors, publishers, fans, authors, and literary agents is finely analyzed in the first chapter (pp. 7–22), this being followed in chapter 2 (pp. 23–58) by an analysis of evolution in the publishing world until 1967. The remaining three chapters deal in turn with the "New Wave" of science fiction writing in England and the United States but also as it was made manifest by American expatriates living in Britain (pp. 59–102), with "the theoretical premises of SF" (pp. 103–38) and with the wake, so to speak, of the New Wave (pp. 139–203). The theoretical premises of Cordesse's fourth chapter are varied and sophisticated, ranging from linguistics to semantics and communication theory, the aesthetics of reception and Iuri Lotman's *Structure of the Artistic Text*. The premises *it* holds consist in treating the science fiction text as literature, moving as far as possible away from the merely cosmetic notations of contents and story line summaries *cum* vaguely humanistic banalities that too often strew the field.

In "After the New Wave" (chapter 5), Cordesse introduces us to feminist and minority subtypes of science fiction literature and presents a sizeable variety of confirmed and upcoming authors. For such readers—and I count myself among them—who have never been particularly sensitive to this literary form, Cordesse's book is a must. In it, the deviltries an exceptionally intelligent treatment can play upon our reluctant tastes abound to such an extent that one may well turn to these mountains of unread books after all.

Université d'Orléans

iii. German Contributions

Rolf Meyn

The 1984 report will have to be longer than last year's, since German scholars were very productive. Several *habilitationsschriften* and monographs were published, which—because of the methods they employ and the neglected areas of American literature they cover— need a longer treatment. In addition, I must discuss some important 1983 publications that escaped me last year. In general, comparative studies of literary decades, dealing with genres or themes from both an American and a European point of view, have remained in vogue. In contrast to previous years, German scholars focused at least as much on the 19th as on the 20th century.

a. **Literary Criticism and Theory: Comparative Studies.** Of the books that embrace almost two centuries of American literature and, in addition include critical theories from both sides of the Atlantic plus a comparison with congenial European literature, Helmbrecht Breinig's *Habilitationsschrift Satire und Roman. Studien zur Theorie des Genrekonfliktes und zur satirischen Erzählliteratur der USA von*

Brackenridge bis Vonnegut (Tübingen: Narr) should be mentioned
first. Breinig bases his study of the American satire on five American
writers and some of their works, namely, Hugh Henry Brackenridge's
Modern Chivalry; Herman Melville's *Pierre* and *The Confidence-
Man;* Mark Twain's *The Gilded Age, A Connecticut Yankee in King
Arthur's Court,* and *Pudd'nhead Wilson;* Sinclair Lewis's *Babbitt;*
Kurt Vonnegut's *Slaughterhouse-Five* and, albeit briefly, *Breakfast of
Champions.* With the exception of the first writer and his early example of an American satire, Breinig discusses writers and novels that
have been dealt with over and over again in literary scholarship. Yet
one has to concede that they were only rarely discussed within the
framework of the genre of satire. Especially Breinig's views of *Pierre,
The Confidence-Man,* and *Slaughterhouse-Five* ought to instigate
new discussions of these works. His thesis that *Pierre* should be seen
as a satire because Melville attacked in it the traditional form of the
novel, which in *The Confidence-Man* was carried to "total stimulance
and frustration of decoding at the same time," thereby reducing traditional satire to absurdity, is convincing in the light of his painstaking analyses. Equally stimulating is Breinig's interpretation of
Slaughterhouse-Five, in which he discovers not only a satire directed
against the military establishment and American society as a whole,
but also one against Billy Pilgrim, the escapist, himself. The chief
merit of the book, however, lies in the author's ability to incorporate
the current discussions of the satirical genre into a study of five
American writers. Breinig starts out from a comparison between
the "illusion-producing potential" of the traditional novel and the
"illusion-blocking elements" of the satire. He cogently shows that
American writers from Brackenridge on, time and again, became dissatisfied not only with the society they lived in but also with the novel
as a vehicle for pronouncing their ideas, so that satirical novels also
turned into satires of the novel. In this respect, Breinig is correct in
pointing out a line of development from the beginnings of American
literature into the post-Modern era of a Vonnegut in which, as one
critic after another tries to illustrate, the dissatisfaction of writers
with traditional forms of literature became a dominant issue.

A comparable endeavor in both scope and methodology is Klaus
P. Hansen's *Die retrospektive Mentalität. Europäische Kulturkritik
und amerikanische Kultur* (Tübingen: Narr). The book is a much-
needed corrective to the many recent explorations of utopian and
dystopian literature, a tendency, Hansen holds, that too often neglects

that part of literature in which discontent with the present is expressed by looking for ideals rooted in the past. Following Karl Mannheim, the author defines mentality as a combination of ideas, a basic pattern of thinking producing a world-view. Contrary to Mannheim, however, Hansen does not believe that mentality expresses a fixed ideology, but is flexible enough to allow variations. Hansen sees the retrospective mentality which he mainly examines in 19th-century writers such as Crèvecoeur, John Filson, Timothy Flint, James Fenimore Cooper, Herman Melville, and Mark Twain as part of a European intellectual heritage dating back to Greek and Roman times and Montaigne. Its most important foundations, however, were laid in the Enlightenment, by Rousseau, Chateaubriand, and their contemporaries, when nature became a "manifest of cultural criticism." Two competing images developed—the noble savage and the barbarian, America as the New Arcadia and as the howling wilderness of the Puritans. Both versions were adopted by American writers as well. Hansen discovers a retrospective mentality in the later phase of American Puritanism, from about 1670 to Jonathan Edwards, when the call for a return to the values of the Founding Fathers became louder and louder. Even the American Revolution, Hansen claims, was legitimized retrospectively, not only by its indebtedness to the natural right of the Enlightenment, but as an extension of the English Whig ideology. More important, though, were the retrospective qualities of the American myth. The traditional cultural assets of Europe became sources of corruption for a young nation striving for its cultural autonomy. Yet the "American Adam in Virgin Land" was only an idealistic construction that even in its heyday between 1820 and 1870 was hopelessly outdated. Hansen then deals with three variations of the American myth—the frontier myth, the myth of the noble Indian, and the agrarian or pastoral myth. The latter, he thinks, was discussed at length only in Crèvecoeur's writings. John Filson and Timothy Flint used the historical Daniel Boone for literary purposes, but they were well aware that their idealized natural hermit and his idylls were irretrievably gone. Hansen's main thesis is that in post-Revolutionary America the retrospective mentality entered a new stage, since "the demands of bourgeois liberalism had meanwhile been put into practice." The insistence on social change gave way to the affirmation of the accomplished. Yet Cooper, who according to Hansen led the retrospective mentality to a climax,

was too much a "conservative progressivist" to condemn the degeneration of the present, a vital part of the retrospective mentality, completely. Cooper's model of history was contradictory since it contained two concepts of progress, one based on the moral qualities of
man, the other negative, underlining the shortcomings of the present
with idealized images of the past. Bret Harte and Mark Twain parodied Cooper, thereby signaling the decay of retrospective conventions. Thoreau, like Cooper, believed in a pre-existing world order,
yet his retreat into nature had none of the static qualities of a Leatherstocking but was meant as an interlude of meditation on the essentials
of human existence. Melville presented his South Sea paradise, Typee,
as a place of monotony and stagnation. Billy Budd, his version of a
noble savage, carried the stigma of moral indifference, demonstrating
that the equivalence of morality and nature no longer existed. Twain's
"degenerated nature hermit," Huck Finn, displayed moral helpless-
ness. Instead of retreating into nature, he was able only to retreat
from society. Hansen's "model of the retrospective mentality" is certainly open to some questions. But his approach, the fruit of profound
readings of Karl Marx, Sigmund Freud, Karl Mannheim, George
Boas, Arthur Lovejoy, William Empson, Henry Nash Smith, Leo
Marx, and many others, is a stimulating method which throws a new
light on a large part of American literature.

The development from modernism to postmodernism, including
a definition of the latter, fascinates an ever-growing number of
German scholars. Two bulky comparative studies deserve special mention. Harald Mesch's *Verweigerung endgültiger Prädikation. Ästhe-
tische Formen und Denkstrukturen der amerikanischen "Postmod-
erne," 1950–1970* (München: Wilhelm Fink) is a revised dissertation,
submitted to the University of Munich in 1978. Although the largest
part is devoted to the poetry of William Carlos Williams, Ezra Pound,
Frank O'Hara, Charles Olson, and many others, illuminating chapters
also deal with painting (Jackson Pollock, Franz Kline, Mark Rothko,
Barry Newman, Allan Kaprow, Robert Rauschenberg, Larry Rivers),
with music (John Cage, Free Jazz) and, though marginally, with
prose writers such as Gertrude Stein, William Faulkner, and Jack
Kerouac. Science and philosophy (Descartes, Einstein, Heisenberg,
Whitehead, Wittgenstein) are also heavily drawn upon in order to
illustrate the revolution in Modern thinking, which for Mesch is at the
core of postmodernism. The author observes in all fields the attempt

to redefine the relationship between the world and the self. The loss
of transcendence and the realization of the void, argues Mesch, cannot frighten the post-Modern artist anymore. He severs himself from
metaphysics and reaches a new "solipsistic sensibility" which enables
him to avoid hierarchies—in poetry expressed by bipolaric metaphors.
As Mesch clearly shows, William Carlos Williams and many post-
Modern poets after him refuse to express themselves in metaphors.
Correspondingly, hypotaxis, which per se denotes a hierarchy, gives
way to parataxis—vide Stein, Faulkner, and many post-Modern poets.
Similar phenomena can be found in music, dance, and painting, e.g.,
the dissolution of the traditional theme-and-variation hierarchy in
Free Jazz, the equilibrium of sound and silence in the music of John
Cage, of motion and stasis in dance, and the abandonment of clear
references to objects in painting. Thus, concludes Mesch, a post-
Modern work of art is invariably open, without a beginning or ending and devoid of external, absolute points of reference.

Bernd Schäbler's dissertation, *Amerikanische Metafiktion im Kontext der Europäischen Moderne* (Gießen: Hoffmann, 1983), which
escaped my notice last year, starts out from a similarly broad scope,
though painting, photography, and film are only occasionally taken
into consideration. Much more than in Mesch's book the focus is on
fiction and literary theory, both in America and in Europe. Schäbler's
aim is "to work out the basic principles of modernism and modern art
movements" and "to discuss recent fiction in the context of modern
anti-illusionistic and anti-mimetic art movements." Schäbler begins
with an extensive discussion of literary theory and concepts of art in
Europe—two chapters are devoted to discussions of modernism with
regard to theories of the novel in both Germany and England. Then
follows an interesting chapter on aesthetic reflections on the 1960s,
with a special emphasis on Modern concepts of time and space and
post-Modernist ideologies as formulated by Daniel Bell, Leslie
Fiedler, Jürgen Peper, Theodor Adorno, Harry Levine, Ihab Hassan,
Frank Kermode, to name only a few. The main part of the book
centers on what Schäbler calls "the avant-garde fiction of the 1960s
and 1970s", otherwise labeled "metafiction," "New Fiction," or "surfiction." This body of recent American fiction is contrasted with the
renaissance of documentary fiction ("faction") in the last decades.
Metafiction itself is examined under the aspects of its imaginative
turn, the breakdown of genres, and paranoia. Interpretations of major

novels by Raymond Federman, Gilbert Sorrentino, Kurt Vonnegut, and others conclude the book. Schäbler's basic thesis is comparable to Mesch's: American metafiction as a segment of post-Modern art is not a literature of exhaustion or the death of the traditional novel. It is part of a long development which can be traced to the 1920s, when, as Siegfried Kracauer and Walter Benjamin diagnosed long ago, the idea of the artist as a genius and the work of art as a genuine, unique, and closed product of his mind collapsed.

Our overview of comparative studies in Germany should also assess two brief ones. Wilhelm Füger's essay "Streifzüge durch Allotopia: Zur Topographie eines fiktionalen Gestaltungsraumes" (*Arcadia* 102:349–91) is a proof of the current interest in utopian literature. Though Füger mentions only one American work—B. F. Skinner's *Walden II*—his theories should be of interest to all scholars working in this field. Füger's term "Allotopia" embraces not only the traditional notion of utopia but also fiction dealing with an alternate course of history, a fantasy or visions of horror or escapism. Since criticism of the present is always part of allotopian literature, it can also border on satire or science fiction. Yet in most cases fictional counterworlds are not identical to our own. Mostly allotopian literature doesn't tell us exactly how to reach the alternative world, or it remains deliberately vague. Quite a different theme is tackled in Manfred Pütz's article "Max Webers und Ferdinand Kürnbergers Auseinandersetzung mit Benjamin Franklin: Zum Verhältnis von Quellenverfälschung und Fehlinterpretation" (*Amst* 29:297–310). In his novel *Der Amerikamüde* (1855), Kürnberger made Franklin the scapegoat of an ideology of greed and crude materialism which is violently attacked by the hero of the book. Kürnberger, in order to expose Franklin as the ideological villain, deliberately distorted and misrepresented two of his tractates, "Advice to a Young Tradesman" and "Necessary Hints for Those That Would Be Rich." This hardly matters in a novel that has to be read as a fervent idealist's document of disillusionment. But it is important insofar as Max Weber in his famous essay "The Protestant Ethic and the Spirit of Capitalism" (1904/5) refers directly to Kürnberger's novel and his Franklin quotations. Although Weber had his misgivings about the novel as such, he took over its author's manipulations and omissions, doubtless, as Pütz holds, because he wanted to show Benjamin Franklin as "a representative of an absolute ethics of ends which is materialistic in content, irrational in origin, and contemptible in spirit." Thus, however, Weber overlooked an essential aspect of Franklin's thought "which is rather instrumentalist and technological in fiction."

b. **Literary History.** An important publication that arrived too late for inspection last year is Jürgen Wolter's *Habilitationsschrift Die Suche nach nationaler Identität. Entwicklungstendenzen des amerikanischen Dramas vor dem Bürgerkrieg* (Bonn: Bouvier, 1983). Although there are some books on early American drama, this is the first one written exclusively from an American Studies approach. Wolter concedes in his introduction that from the viewpoint of literary quality there is very little to be found in this area. But looked at as a cultural phenomenon, as literary expression of sociological ambitions and reactions to historical conditions, early American drama is a fascinating field, since it reflects successes and crises of America's search for identity. Wolter bases his study on dramatizations of national incidents and national characters, "pillars of literary nationalism until the Civil War." Representative figures such as the Yankee, the pioneer, the Indian, and the Negro, but also historical figures such as George Washington and Andrew Jackson, all of them crowding the pre–Civil War stage, come under close scrutiny. Wolter begins with a chapter on the drama before 1776, among which anti-British and anti-Loyalist satires (and their pro-British counterparts) stand out. He deduces from his analysis that American drama came into existence when a national system of values could be set off against the British one. This was accompanied by a growing awareness of local materials that could be used dramatically. It led to an American variety of the English comedy of manners in the first half of the 19th century. Wolter sees a continuous line from the beginnings until the Civil War, because two tendencies remained—the patriotic-nationalistic affirmation of an American ideology and the satirical negation of its opponents, both accompanied by a moralizing, didactic tone, a residue of Puritan times. The nationalistic propaganda drama, based on heroic exploits, became the main form. In its wake, historical figures such as Pocahontas, George Washington, and Andrew Jackson were glorified and even apotheosized. The immense popularity of the frontiersman and the Indian, Wolter argues, can be explained by the types' compensative functions. The nation's bad conscience about the treatment of the Indians was either mollified by an emphasis on positive American characteristics or neutralized by apologetic self-indictment and cathartic compassion. This was also true in the case of the stage Negro, whose black mask of the minstrel show was used similarly. The abolitionist drama questioned this strategy, but its more radical variations never appeared on stage and even in them the Negro was never granted real social equality. The historical drama of the 1830s reflected the political crises of this decade. Wolter clearly shows a metamorphosis from a patriotic drama about historical events to an escapist, sentimental, domestic melodrama with only a vague historical background. The search for a national identity continued, yet now the growing rift between ideal and reality was at the core. Those plays which did not follow the turn into melodrama tackled social and political problems of their time—some even criticized the election system of the Jacksonian era. All this proves, Wolter holds, that American society became more complex and its way of seeing itself more differentiated.

Two years after Jürgen Schäfer's *Geschichte des amerikanischen Dramas* appeared (*ALS 1982*, pp. 478–79), there is another survey of American drama. Gerhard Hoffmann's *Das amerikanische Drama* (Bern: Francke) is a collection of essays on various topics, which taken together form a kind of history of modern American drama. Berndt Ostendorf's "Vorformen und Nachbarformen des amerikanischen Theaters: Minstrel Show, Vaudeville, Burlesque, Musical, 1800–1932" (pp. 12–26) pays tribute to the fact that "American theater from the beginning was popular theater. An unpopular one wouldn't have survived, for America lacked those classes which promoted and kept alive European theater: aristocracy and the upper middle class." Klaus Schwank follows with a chapter on American melodrama before World War I (pp. 27–38), which disappeared when film became a mass media, though, as he holds, melodrama remains part of 20th-century mainstream theater. Hartwig Isernhagen follows with an overview of tendencies and organizations of 20th-century American theater (pp. 39–56). Modern American playwrights (O'Neill, Behrman, Albee, Wilder, Williams, Baraka) and their theories are dealt with in Alfred Hornung's essay (pp. 57–75). After these preliminary chapters specific playwrights and theatrical forms are analyzed. Gerhard Hoffmann discusses O'Neill (pp. 76–120), Gisela Hoffmann explores the American verse drama from William Vaughn Moody to William Carlos Williams and Robert Lowell (pp. 121–43), Ulrich Halfmann focuses on the drama of social criticism of the 1920s and 1930s (pp. 144–81), whereas Meinhard Wintgens concentrates

on Thornton Wilder's "epic theater" alone (pp. 182–201). Paul Goet-
sch in his essay "Vom psychologisch-sozialkritischen zum absurden
Drama: Williams, Miller, Albee" sees these playwrights as innovators
who went beyond Ibsen's analytical drama and the crude realism of
the American drama after World War II to a combination of psychological and sociological analysis (pp. 202–39). Horst Grabes concludes the collection with a thorough discussion of the experimental
theater since the early 1960s, taking into consideration not only white
playwrights, but also representatives of other ethnic groups (pp. 240–
72). Hoffmann's *Das amerikanische Drama* is certainly eclectic. But
by putting both the playwrights and the subgenres of the American
drama into a broad sociocultural and historical context, the collection
achieves a compactness not easy to surpass.

c. **Colonial and 19th-Century Literature.** A major contribution to Puritan literature has appeared in Germany with Klaus Weiss's *Habilitationsschrift Grundlegung einer puritanischen Mimesislehre. Eine
literatur- und geistesgeschichtliche Studie der Schriften Edward Tay-
lors und anderer puritanischer Autoren* (Paderborn: Ferdinand Schön-
ingh). Weiss sees the Puritan concept of mimesis, which he mainly
examines in the works of Edward Taylor, embodied in two varieties,
the "imitatio naturae" and the "imitatio Christi." The latter is an act
of spiritual life and, as Weiss repeatedly demonstrates, was set against
the imitation of nature by Taylor and his contemporaries. For them,
the "imitatio naturae" could function only if the order of nature with
its six subsequent stages (divine, angel, human or rational, animal,
vegetative, and elementary) were fully perceived. To clarify their
statements, they often resorted to the method of dichotomy, which
Taylor also applied in his poetry. Essentially for the Puritan, understanding of nature was the differentiation of two levels: on the one
hand pre-existing divine idea, on the other a created copy, both
dichotomically related. "Creature" and "nature" were understood as
imitations by Taylor, William Ames, and other Puritan writers. But
these words also corresponded to terms like "image" and "footsteps,"
signs of divine perfection or ideas of God, a tradition stemming from
Augustine and other medieval thinkers. As for the concept of beauty,
Weiss contradicts Perry Miller who held that the Puritans mainly applied it to handicraft and not to fine arts. Weiss claims that for the
Puritans beauty showed both in nature and in fine arts, e.g., as order
and harmony, in which all things are connected by structural princi-

ples, as "excellency," combining goodness, dignity, and grandeur; as "exactness," meaning precision and perfection; as the "light" of an unfathomable wisdom; and, finally, as the glory and majesty of God radiating from any creature. As regards the "imitatio Christi," Weiss believes the American Puritans less interested than their English brethren, with the exception of Edward Taylor who paid a special attention to Christ as a human being both in his sermons and in his meditations. For Taylor, Christ's humanness was not destroyed by the crucifixion; on the contrary, the unity of human and divine nature remained as inseparable as before. Christ had called all men to enter His succession; hence the Puritans, and above all Edward Taylor, emphasized that man must follow Him by leading a spiritual life, implanted in him by the Holy Ghost or the spirit of Christ. When Taylor wanted to express the strong bond between Christ and his believers, he employed in prose and verse images of fountains, wells, water, and floating. Man's inner growth toward a mystical union went through the stages of "beginning, progress and perfection" and was part of the "vita activa" for all Puritans, because it provided prescriptions for the ethics of everyday life. With regard to Puritan aesthetics, Weiss corrects the common notion that Puritans were essentially hostile to images. Taylor, Ames, and many others frequently dealt with the role of arts and mimetic problems pertaining thereto. Similes and metaphors in Taylor's poetological meditations enclose the registers of painting, ceramics, engravings, forging, and architecture, always functioning as demonstrations of Christ's image-spending acts. "Imagination," "fantasy," and "fancy" were used interchangeably and had a positive connotation for Taylor and his contemporaries. The Puritan concept of mimesis as developed in Edward Taylor's time, Weiss concludes, had a deep impact on later generations from Jonathan Edwards to Ralph Waldo Emerson. Weiss's book is without doubt a major and inspiring achievement in the field of Puritan studies. One can only hope that it will be translated into English as soon as possible. Besides this book, colonial literature is dealt with only in Regina Hewitt's article "Toward a Socio-Literary Perspective: Mather, Hawthorne and the Puritans in Crisis" (*ArAA* 9:147–55). It is a plea for literature as a means of obtaining historical and social evidence of a given period. Kai T. Erikson in his book *The Wayward Puritans* (1966), Hewitt maintains, relied too heavily on records, registers, and ledgers. Cotton Mather in *Magnalia Christi Americana* (1702) and Nathaniel Hawthorne in *The Scarlet Letter*, "Young Goodman

Brown," and "Endicott and the Red Cross" furnished equally valuable insights into the three crises in 17th-century Massachusetts—the
Antinomian controversy, the Quaker persecutions, and the witchcraft
trials. Both Mather and Hawthorne depict 17th-century colonists who
believed in their own separate identity. It is therefore misleading to
look back to England for an explanation of the problems within the
social hierarchy, as Erikson does. The three crises, the reverberations
of which one can easily detect in Mather's and Hawthorne's writings,
weakened the clergy's power and helped to prepare the way to social
stability and a participatory government. Hawthorne's treatment of
history, especially, attests to this fact.

Essays on 19th-century literature will have to begin with a presentation of Brigitte Fleischmann's "Die Darstellung des Indianers im
Melodrama der Jackson-Zeit: 'Metamora; or the Last of the Wampa-
nougs'" (*Amst* 29:311–21), an important appendix to Jürgen Wolter's book. According to Fleischmann, melodramatic plays, the most
popular entertainment of the Jackson era, were "sensitive barometers
of the least common denominator of the age's attitudes and concerns."
In this respect, it was significant that Edwin Forrest, the most popular
actor of his time, offered a substantial sum of money for the best
tragedy in five acts in which the protagonist was an Indian. John
August Stone's melodrama *Metamora*, which was selected by a jury
of experts including William Cullen Bryant, became a raving success
not only because the protagonist's role was tailored to fit the famous
Forrest, but also, as Fleischmann cogently shows, because it was a
product of a special sociocultural situation. In contrast to the noble
savage of Romantic literature, Stone's Indian was a figure of darkness,
though not the vicious and cruel Indian of the captivity story. Metamora's death was presented to the audience as a victory of light over
the forces of darkness. The literature of the Jackson era is also dealt
with in Ulrich Halfmann's "Auf der Suche nach der 'real North
American story'. John Neals Kurzgeschichten 'Otter-Bag' und 'David
Whicher'" (*Link Festschrift*, pp. 213–26). Halfmann sees John Neal
as the first American writer who thought about how to present the
Indian without reducing him to a mere cliché or using him for a subversive glorification of the westward movement. Neal's demand for a
"real North American short story," Halfmann holds, was certainly part
of the period's clamor for a genuine national literature. But for Neal it
also meant an authentic American style and a realistic, critical, and
complex world-view, as two of his best stories amply prove. Another

short story of that period is thoroughly explored in Winfried Herget's "Hawthornes 'Endicott and the Red Cross'. Rekonstruktion und Vergangenheit aus den historischen Quellen und in der fiktionalen Ausgestaltung" (*Link Festschrift*, pp. 227–42). As the title says, the essay contains an interesting comparison between the historical event, as Hawthorne knew it from several sources, and his own version of it. Herget discovers in the sources the "uncertainty and insecurity of political acting, which has to combine devotion to religious principles with pragmatism." Hawthorne, in contrast, interpreted Endicott's rash act as a prelude to the American Revolution, that is, as an act that ultimately helped to change the course of history. Bret Harte, also rarely discussed in German scholarship recently, found a proponent in 1984. Klaus P. Hansen in his article "Francis Bret Harte: Ironie und Konvention" (*ArAA* 9:23–37) is dissatisfied with many critics who question Harte's craft as a writer, accuse him of sentimentality, and place him somewhere between romanticism and realism in literary history. Hansen calls for a reconsideration of this writer, since nobody so far has recognized the deliberate narrative function of his ironic style which operates in three ways: Harte renders his plots in a manner which is too traditionally learned for the triviality of events and characters depicted. Furthermore, he often violates the logic of narration and comes up with surprise endings which frustrate the reader's expectations. In some cases, Harte even destroys the narrative illusion by asking the reader's help in untangling the plot. These forms of irony amount to a considerable distance between the narrator and the world he creates. This fictitious world is modeled after the frontier myth with its emphasis on a harmonious nature and a noble savage. Harte, like Twain several decades later, attacks this myth.

Two classic 19th-century poets are examined from a rather unconventional angle. Kuno Schumann in his "Die Kulturlandschaft—ein amerikanischer Traum" (*Link Festschrift*, pp. 257–72) deals with Poe's landscape fiction and comes to the conclusion that the poet has to be judged in an American tradition, because he like most of his contemporaries believed that the transformation from wilderness into a "cultural landscape" was predominantly a cultural enterprise. In "The Domain of Arnheim," however, the artist replaces the farmer as "tiller of the earth." Poe did not share Whitman's "mythical certainty" that "the United States themselves are essentially the greatest poem." In Poe's opinion, Schumann argues, there was at best some hope that this could be achieved by future generations. An interesting contribution to the Dickinson scholarship is Roland Hagenbüchle's essay "Emily Dickinsons Ästhetik des Prozesses" (*Link Festschrift,* pp. 243– 56). Hagenbüchle examines Dickinson's poetry in analogy to the notion of process, which characterizes so much of 19th-century science. Emerson, influenced by religious and scientific ideas of his time, understood the world as a constantly changing, infinite metaphor. Dickinson, so Hagenbüchle holds, went one step further. Unlike Emerson and Thoreau, she was not content with only registering transformational processes, but interested in understanding processes in regard to the interactions between the observer and the phenomenon. Processes, whether of experience or of nature, were for Dickinson always complicated by the observing consciousness. Thus perception for her became an interactional process, the analysis of which was achieved in the poem itself. Her main goal was to point out the mechanisms of human perception and the structure of human experience. Meaning was nothing but process for Dickinson. In this respect, Hagenbüchle believes, Dickinson's poetry illustrates the transition from the analogical world-view of the Puritans to the "processional-heuristic" perception of modernism.

Two late-19th-century writers are covered in *Die Utopie,* a collection of essays on English and American utopian and dystopian novels from the 19th and 20th centuries. Olaf Hansen in his contribution, "Edward Bellamy: *Looking Backward: 2000–1887* (1888)" (pp. 103–19), compares Bellamy's novel to Thomas More's *Utopia,* in regard to the extent of its influence. Yet in spite of all its influence on political movements at the turn of the century, Hansen argues, one must not overlook Bellamy's deeply rooted conservatism. For him, social reform had to start with a reform of the individual. Bellamy's utopia was ultimately a dreamland contrasted with a nightmarish here and now. He followed the tradition of the parable and the allegorical narrative: his indebtedness to Hawthorne is unmistakable. Hansen does not deny that Bellamy anticipated the technical achievements of our time. Yet, he holds, *Looking Backward* fascinated so many different ideological groups because its abstraction from the facts of everyday life allowed many different readings. Hans-Joachim Lang in his chapter, "Ignatius Donnelly: *Caesar's Column: A Study of the Twentieth Century* (1890)" (pp. 139–60) has far more reservations about this novel. He notes that Donnelly's historical analogies— the French Revolution, the decline of Rome, its deterioration from republican virtues (mirroring the Founding Fathers of the U.S.) to wealth, world domination, and corruption "are not very encouraging." Dystopian and utopian elements are lumped together, with even a plan for reform in the middle of the book. Conspiracy and anti-semitism are also part of the "many preferences and phobias" in *Caesar's Column.* If there is a positive thrust, it is turned backward—to an idealized agrarianism in some remote part of the earth. Donnelly is afraid of the capitalist oligarchy, but he fears the masses even more. Unlike Bellamy, he foresees little of the technological civilization of the 20th century. Yet in one respect Donnelly surpasses Bellamy: he is able to construct the civilization of 1989 out of its mentality—the sensual wants of its arrogant oligarchy. Lang presents a daring thesis: the long-term effect of *Caesar's Column*, he speculates, might have surpassed that of *Looking Backward.* H. G. Wells in his *When the Sleeper Wakes* (1899) constructs a power structure that is almost identical to that of *Caesar's Column.* Huey Long, but even more so Father Coughlin, the two remarkable demagogues of the 1930s, support in their confused ideology a populism that seems to vacillate between Christian socialism and pro-Fascist paranoia, so much resembling Donnelly's that it is hard to believe in a mere coincidence.

d. 20th-Century Literature.   Most essays by German scholars were again devoted to 20th-century literature. Every decade of this century was explored in at least some of its literary productions. Berndt Ostendorf's "Ein Mythos der Versöhnung. Owen Wisters Cowboy-roman *The Virginian*" (*Link Festschrift*, pp. 273–87) is a case in point. Ostendorf sees Wister's novel as "marginal" in three senses. The author, though belonging to the cultural elite of the East and in close contact with such writers as Rudyard Kipling and Henry James, was afraid that the overcivilized East would become soft and decadent. Like Theodore Roosevelt and Frederic Remington, he fled to the West as a place of rejuvenation. But Wister could never become a regional-ist—he experienced the West from a vacationer's viewpoint, with a secure social status and a bank account in the East. His West became a romantic, pastoral region, with the cowboy, hailing from both the North and the South, as a mythic figure of a regenerative region. Second, Wister's aesthetic ideals were also "marginal." His highest literary ideal was realism, but he never managed to come close to it because the melodramatic effects of his storytelling always undercut it. Besides, Wister wanted to mediate between popularity and quality, between popular and high literature. This marginality made him a

trailblazer in popular culture, insofar as, as in *The Virginian,* the
West became an archetypal region with an unstructured society in
which, according to the Social-Darwinist credo, only the best could
win. Where Wister was bent on reconciliation, Jack London, in a
dystopian novel published six years after *The Virginian,* centered on
revolution, counterrevolution, and class war. In his chapter, "Jack
London: *The Iron Heel* (1908)" (*Die Utopie,* pp. 176–95), Wolfgang
Karrer contradicts those critics who see the novel as a forerunner of
Orwell's *1984,* a warning against future totalitarian trends. The novel,
he claims, is as contradictory as its creator's own philosophy of life.
The dialectics of different points of view allow the reader frequent
alternations between identification and distancing. Ernest Everhard
is glorified as a working-class leader both in theory and in practice,
but he disappears in the violent struggle with the oligarchy. It is
largely due to the multiperspective techniques, in no way inferior to
those of Henry James, that the question of how to judge the revolution remains ambivalent.

Hemingway, in previous years a little neglected in German scholarship, is assessed in Kurt Müller's "Literatur in landeskundlicher
Perspektive. Hemingways 'Soldier's Home' im historischen, sozio-
kulturellen und geistesgeschichtlichen Kontext" (*Link Festschrift,*
pp. 323–39). Müller's aim is to demonstrate that even a short story
whose author employed "the technique of omission as main stylistic
device" can be interpreted in a broad cultural and historical context,
in the terms of what in Germany is called "Landeskunde"—roughly
the equivalent of American Studies. Müller plainly shows that Hemingway's story pointedly captured the change of mood from an idealistic and patriotic war enthusiasm to the materialistic, prosperity-
oriented thoughtlessness of the postwar years. As for the sociocultural
context, Müller discovers in the story "typical attributes of a Protestant middle-class culture" which alienates the protagonist, as is demonstrated by his utter passivity and his indifference to religion. His
apathy and indifference are in Müller's eyes signs of a loss of values
that found in T. S. Eliot's *The Waste Land* perhaps its most intensive
literary expression. This poem is taken up by Armin Paul Frank in his
"The 'Personal Waste Land Revisited,' or: What Did Happen in the
Hyacinth Garden?" (*Link Festschrift,* pp. 289–304). Frank is not interested in another overall interpretation of *The Waste Land.* He
focuses on the hyacinth garden vignette, taking up A. D. Moody's assertion that this is "the center from which the entire poem radiates."

Comparing the vignette to two of Eliot's earlier poems, "La Filia Che Piange" and "Entretien dans un Park," Frank comes to the conclusion that all three are concerned with the same imaginative experience, one that is decidedly not homoerotic, as some critics have claimed. Both poems and the vignette describe situations in which a man and a woman are involved, and in each case a promising love encounter is shattered by the man's failure to take the initiative "in order to overcome the woman's fugitive resentment." Eliot the dramatist is examined in Hubertus Schulte-Herbrüggen's "Die dramatische Funktion des Zwischenspiels in T. S. Eliots *Murder in the Cathedral*" (*Link Festschrift*, pp. 305–21). Schulte-Herbrüggen understands *Murder in the Cathedral* not as a historical drama, but as a variant of the mystery play. In this framework, the interlude in the form of a prose sermon, one of many liturgical elements of the play, is given special meaning by stressing the annunciation character of the play. The sermon's aim is to call for a meditation which is not a spontaneous one, but one that includes the whole community of believers as well as the "communio" with God and the saints. The sermon also draws heavily on martyrdom, connecting Christ's crucifixion with the events to come. Ultimately, Schulte-Herbrüggen holds, it is the sermon interlude which emphasizes the similarity between the mass as re-enactment of Christ's suffering and death and *Murder in the Cathedral* as a dramatic re-enactment of Becket's suffering and martyrdom.

Eliot's rival and mentor Ezra Pound is dealt with in Franz Link's *Ezra Pound* (München: Artemis), an introduction to the poet's life and work. As such, the condensed little book doubtless surpasses many of the reader's expectations, since Link succeeds not only in his main goal, i.e., "to interpret the knowledge conveyed as image, myth, and history in Pound's lyrics," but also in incorporating much of the Pound criticism as well as the poet's affiliations with art movements and politics. Furthermore, Pound's poetic techniques are by no means neglected. Link proceeds chronologically, beginning with a chapter on myth and image in Pound's early poetry, in which the focus is on metamorphosis, the influence of Yeats, Pound's definition of myth, his concept of the human soul, the role of the woman as mistress, image, and epiphany. Then follows a concise analysis of *Hugh Selwyn Mauberley*, which Link considers a Menippean satire. The interpretations of the cantos fill the largest part of the book. The poet's attempt to create a "meaningful relation between myth and history" absorbs much of Link's interest in his analysis of the cantos. Link discovers in the middle cantos, in contrast to the earlier ones, a greater interest in history and in the rise and decay of order instead of a presentation of history based on mythic structures. Pound's "order" is always endangered by "USURA." This, Link believes, is one of Pound's major flaws (besides his bizarre devotion to Mussolini), since he attributes all failures of history to usury, i.e., the wrong use of money. For Link, the *Pisan Cantos* are not a continuation of the earlier ones, but the poet's attempt to render an account of his earlier actions. Yet Pound's political blindness remains—the reader is not able to learn anything from his depiction of history. Link is inclined to call Pound's later cantos a long poem in the sense of Whitman's *Song of Myself,* because they contain a record of the poet's individual experiences. A short biography and a brief annotated bibliography conclude the little monograph, which is admirably balanced between well-founded criticism and equally well-justified praise of this poetic innovator.

Modern historical novels caught the attention of quite a few German scholars in 1984. They are collected in Raymund Borgmeyer and Bernhard Reitz, eds., *Der historische Roman II: 20. Jahrhundert* (*A&E* 24). Interpretations of American novels begin with Bernd Lenz's "Geschichte als Bestseller: Margaret Mitchell's *Gone With the Wind* (1936) als Modellfall" (pp. 35–49). Lenz holds that *Gone With the Wind* completely fulfills the criteria that qualify a literary work as a historical novel. It deals with a verifiable historical period which covers the Civil War and the Reconstruction era and, though the main characters are fictitious, evokes the historical dimension by constantly referring to authentic persons, places, and events. The fictitious characters add to the historical qualities since their fates exemplify the consequences of a crisis situation. Although Mitchell wanted Melanie Wilkes to be the heroine of the novel, Lenz sees nothing surprising when the reader turns to Scarlett O'Hara as the main character, because she personifies the clash "between the old form, the Southern Lady, and her antagonist, the New Woman," which illustrates the historical change of the South. Lenz attributes the novel's status as an immediate best-seller and its unbroken popularity ever since to three facts: its historical relevance; its actuality at the time of another crisis, the Great Depression; and its archetypal and ahistorical qualities in regard to human conduct.

Another historical novel, published almost simultaneously, comes under scrutiny in Martin Christadler's "William Faulkners *Absalom, Absalom!* (1936): Geschichte, Bewußtsein und Transzendenz. Das

Ende des historischen Romans" (pp. 51–66). For Christadler, *Absalom, Absalom!* is not a historical novel in the tradition of Scott and Mitchell, but one of the great works of modernism, close to Joyce, Conrad, and Proust. Contrary to some critics who see the novel as an allegory of southern history, Christadler holds that Faulkner was at best interested in different "modes of shaped history"—the idealistic, the mythic, the psychological, and the narrative. Yet the historical panorama, as Faulkner said himself, was only a by-product of his materials. Faulkner was in search of a reality which was beyond the horizon of history. Wolf Kindermann's dissertation, *Analyse und Synthese im Werk William Faulkners* (Frankfurt: Lang), is another example of the interest this writer still elicits in German scholarship. Kindermann's work is an attempt, by no means revolutionary, "to define the main evolutionary stages in Faulkner's thinking." Kindermann discovers seven stages, the first being the generation theme as a metaphor of the old crumbling order, the last, confined to the Snopes Trilogy and *The Rievers,* denoting the succession of generations as part of the ever-changing human experience within the solidarity of the community. Kindermann's method is what he calls "the cognitional triad"—cognitive orientation, ethical structure, and ethic conception. Whether the seven evolutionary stages can be separated from each other as strictly as the author claims may be debatable. Nevertheless, the book is a solid attempt to describe Faulkner's development in terms of "generation" and "community."

In "Thornton Wilders dokumentarischer Weg zu Caesar: *The Ides of March* (1948)" (*Der historische Roman II,* pp. 67–80), Horst Brinkmann interprets this novel as one of the early examples of the fact/fiction tradition, since the reader is confronted not with a biographical tale but with documentary material. This, however, is presented from a multiperspective viewpoint and, in each of the four "books," alternately enlarged and compressed. In spite of Wilder's assertion that everything is freely invented, it is nevertheless obvious that he understands himself as a chronicler of a historical era, with Caesar as its shaping force. Brinkmann thinks that Wilder's portrait of this great Roman is one of the most successful in literature, because it is the product of literary competence, psychological insight, and a unique familiarity with the sources. A rarity in international scholarship is Dora F. Munker's contribution " 'Men are only Men'—Der Held und sein ideales Ich in Mary Renaults Theseus-Roman *The King Must Die* (1958)" (*Der historische Roman II,* pp. 81–95).

Munker believes Renault's position to be vastly underrated. She claims that there are not many authors who are interested in explaining from a psychological viewpoint why historical figures become legendary heroes and what effects their private, inner life has on society. Renault's thesis is that historical changes are the results of individual acts. *The King Must Die* is a study of the dualistic hero Theseus who is unable to overcome the conflicting forces within himself, but whose failure drives him to perform such deeds as the killing of the Minotaurus which have a lasting impact on the course of civilization. For Munker, Mary Renault's achievement has to be seen in her capacity to endow the conventional figure of the heroic leader in popular historical fiction with a realism and a depth hitherto almost absent in this genre.

A parody of the genre, John Barth's *The Sot-Weed Factor*, has retained its attraction for German scholars. Wolfgang Ruth's article, " 'Meager fact and solid fancy'. Die Erfindung der Vergangenheit in John Barths *The Sot-Weed Factor* (1960)" (*Der historische Roman II*, pp. 97–116), is another attempt to come to terms with the relationship between fiction and historical fact in this novel. Ruth points to the epilogue, in which the carefully woven threads of the plot are abruptly torn apart and the characters left to an uncertain fate, as proof that Barth distrusts both historiography and fiction. In Ruth's opinion, the novel is more than anything else an invitation to a whole genre to return to the fictional shaping of reality which in historical novels after Scott had too often been subjugated to supposedly incontestable historical "truths." Hans Galinsky approaches the same problem from a different direction. In his essay "Kolonialzeitliche 'Wirklichkeit' in John Barths Roman *The Sot-Weed Factor*. Die Rolle der Sprache bei der Vermittlung von geschichtlicher 'Wirklichkeit' und 'Wahrheit' " (*Link Festschrift*, pp. 359–86), his focus is on language. The headings of most chapters, Galinsky notices, formulate operations of speech or of listening. They are far more frequent than in Henry Fielding's *The History of Tom Jones, a Foundling,* one of Barth's models. In contrast to Fielding, Barth also includes poetological and rhetorical formalizations of speech acts. Barth's language transmits special aspects of historical reality—the regional economy of a southern colony, the condescending attitude of some Britons, and the literary indebtedness of a culture transplanted overseas which shares the Classical "imitatio" concept. Even more important is that the author reproduces history by using documents and the two versions of an 18th-century verse satire which in turn is modeled after Samuel Butler's *Hudibras*. Thus, Barth's creation of history rests on the foundation of language as an interlocking process. Bernhard Reitz in his essay "'A society of ragamuffins'—Fortschritt und Fiktion in E. L. Doctorows *Ragtime* (1975)" (*Der historische Roman II*, pp. 135–54), after counting himself among fervent defenders of Doctorow's best-seller, places this novel on a level with *The Sot-Weed Factor*. Reitz sees Theodore Dreiser and Harry Houdini as key influences in regard to Doctorow's concept of literature, since both figures wrestle with the problem of realism which the author brushes aside. He freely dabbles with the plot structure of romance, but this is done openly and pointedly so that a mere accident is out of question. Equally obvious is Kleist's Michael Kohlhaas model, which Doctorow refers to several times in *Ragtime*. His collection of historical characters is nowhere a carrier of historical or sociological developments, but embodies highly private obsessions and whims. Similarly, the fates of the three families are not intertwined by historically relevant elements, but by unveiled coincidences. Doctorow, so Reitz holds, deliberately puts fictitiousness above the principle of verisimilitude, the touchstone of a historical novel in the realistic tradition. The succession of images becomes the structural principle of the narrative. Yet despite his "epistemological distrust" Doctorow presents us a narrator who by the ordering of the images provides the reader with a coherent interpretation of an epoch, although a highly subjective one. It is also a negative one, a cyclical interpretation of history in which progress becomes regression.

Essays on dystopian novels after World War II occupy a large part of the collection *Die Utopie*. The first of them is Hans-Wolfgang Schaller's "B. F. Skinner: *Walden Two* (1948)" (pp. 219–34). Schaller sees this book in the tradition of Thomas More's *Utopia*, as far as form and the author's intention are concerned. He judges the message of *Walden Two* quite differently, however. Instead of an "Anti-Anti-Utopia," Schaller holds, the book is much more a dystopian description of a future in which man is reduced to the level of conditioned responses. The highest value is smooth functioning of daily life and a persistent feeling of happiness. But Skinner's model of a society built exclusively on behavioristic foundations leaves many questions open, among them the problem of creative fantasy. Skinner constantly emphasizes the practicability of his model, but too often has his protagonist Frazier present Walden Two as an "accomplished

fact," thereby avoiding further discussion. Even more questionable
is the fact that all power is in the hands of "planners," trained psychologists of the behaviorist school, who are more or less dictators of a
society that in its second generation will become a dehumanized collective, without ethics, consciousness, and history, soulless robots
with contented smiles on their faces. Another dystopian novel, published seven years after *Walden Two,* is analyzed by Hartmut Heuermann in his chapter, "Ray Bradbury: *Fahrenheit 451* (1953)" (pp.
259–82). Heuermann discovers in this novel a strong affinity to
Huxley's *Brave New World* (1932) and Orwell's *1984* (1948), because
all three authors extrapolate symptoms of their times and project
them hyperbolically into the future. Though Bradbury did not personally suffer under the excesses of McCarthyism, there is no doubt
for Heuermann that themes and motifs of *Fahrenheit 451* reflect the
political atmosphere of this era. Bradbury's dystopian society of the
year 2000 is the result of the author's anxieties of the Cold War years.
He shared with many other intellectuals a distrust of television, which
he believed had the power to manipulate and indoctrinate to such an
extent that apolitical attitudes, cultural decadence, and a breakdown
of interhuman communications (as described in the relationship between the protagonist Montag and his wife) was inevitable. The dangers of a nuclear war, hovering above the world since 1950, are still
a part of Bradbury's future, although no political reason is given.
When the catastrophe happens at the end of the novel, it is inescapable and apocalyptic. In Schaller's opinion, Bradbury's main intention
was to describe the growing enslavement of the individual due to
tendencies and manifestations of American mass society. High
technology and a totalitarian regime enter an alliance that inexorably
crushes all cultural traditions and those who still cling to them. Yet
in contrast to Orwell's *1984* there is still hope at the end of the novel.
The protagonist survives the catastrophe, and with him an eschato-
logical ideal of man. This is also the tenor of Peter Freese's chapter,
"Kurt Vonnegut: *Cat's Cradle* (1963)" (pp. 283–309). Freese calls
the book an "anti-novel," in which fully drawn characters are absent.
It is neither a utopian sketch of a positive counterworld nor a dystopian warning against the consequences of developments already
underway or a science fiction extrapolation of an imminent end of the
world, but a "realistic fantasy *sui generis.*" The title metaphor points
to the characters of the book who are unable to find any sense in a
senseless world, but it also refers to the whole novel as an epistemo-

logical exercise in the tradition of postmodernism. This is not to say that *Cat's Cradle* is without values or ethics. The opposition of science versus religion is also one of evil versus good, despite the fact that Vonnegut ironically undercuts religion in the form of "Bokonism." Man must try to shape reality by concepts, though, as in the case of Bokonism, they may be lies. This, for Freese, is one of the central concerns of Vonnegut's novel. Heinz Tschachler's contribution, "Ernest Callenbach: *Ectopia: A Novel About Ecology, People and Politics in 1999* (1975)" (pp. 328–48), deals with a work that, in Tschachler's words, is a "utopian romance," albeit in form a synthesis of diary notes, journalistic columns, popular-scientific essays, tractates, and narrative parts, demonstrating again how in modern American literature the barriers between high and trivial literature are disposed of. The novel, however, follows the 19th-century tradition of this genre— the hero in search of a better life has to overcome a severe personal crisis before experiencing a break-through to a new identity. Tschachler sees in the novel a continuation of the national pastoral myth. The coexistence of civilization and wilderness provides for a permanent frontier, but this does not mean regression. Callenbach believes in a balance between life close to nature and technology. According to Tschachler, *Ectopia* may well mark a change in the history of utopian literature. Callenbach does not project an anti-utopia to be understood as a warning, but depicts a world that is more or less a conglomeration of ideas that have had a deep impact on politics and society for the last 20 years. It remains to be seen, however, whether Callenbach's "ecological imperative" will contribute to a national change of mind. The renaissance of the "pioneer mentality" of recent Reagan years may well be more than a last flare-up of "obsolete norms and values."

Utopia from a feminist viewpoint is the theme of Theresia Sauter-Bailliet's chapter, "Marge Piercy: *Woman on the Edge of Time* (1976)" (pp. 349–70). Sauter-Bailliet discovers in this novel a basic structure that is similar to that of *Fahrenheit 451* and *Cat's Cradle*— an alternation between analysis of the present and projection into the future. The starting point, as in all of Piercy's works, is the abuse of power in order to dominate men and women and the individual's rebellion against it. The psychiatric clinic symbolizes the modern American Dream turned into a nightmare. Yet, so Sauter-Bailliet holds, Piercy's novel must not be read as an expression of resignation, but as one of stubborn belief in the "positive potential" of man. It comes to life in the portrait of the feminist utopia of Mattapoisett, which is anarchic, race- and classless, governed only by communication and sympathetic understanding. Modern technology, as in the case of genetic manipulation, is as positive as closeness to nature, since it liberates woman from her traditional role and enables her to meet the male counterpart on equal terms. Although Piercy's utopian society belongs to the tradition of matriarchal cultures of the past, Sauter-Bailliet cautiously raises the question of whether the feminist vision of the 20th century will not be stronger than the utopian ideas of the century before.

Women's literature, discussed by female critics, seems to catch on in German scholarship. Waltraud Mitgutsch in "Women in Transition: The Poetry of Anne Sexton and Louise Glück" (*ArAA* 9:131–45) argues that Sexton and Glück "share a female self-consciousness rather than a feminist consciousness." Their poetry is ambiguous and explores some kind of departure from a world which is largely male-oriented. Yet both poets are unable to achieve a complete liberation. The collective consciousness against which they rebel allows them only a position of defiance. Mitgutsch, however, perceives a striking difference between the two women. Sexton often expresses an identification with nature, projecting her sexuality on natural phenomena. The male lover can be a life-giving force, but also a brutal enemy, in which case natural phenomena such as the moon or the sea, all of them archetypal images of the female, become a healing force. Glück, Mitgutsch thinks, is more radical. With her, nature is mostly part of a hostile universe. Her landscapes are projections of her inner self, on the point of becoming an ice-locked world. Her poetry is also more radical in its description of love, which is at best an ensnaring bondage. Glück's anger is that of a younger generation refusing to compromise. Gisela Ecker in her article "The Politics of Fantasy in Recent American Women's Novels" (*EAST* 6:503–10) explores a group of novels that depart from the mode of realism and venture into the fantastic, a trend that for her seems to have increased since the mid-1970s. Employing a sociological and Lacanian psychoanalytical approach, Ecker claims that the structural opposition "real" versus "unreal" can be linked with feminist concerns—women striving to overcome oppressive conditions by "transcending both the material and the conceptual limitations of patriarchal society." The Lacanian notion of desire as expressed through literary fantasy can appear "in form of a loss, an absence, a point of resistance, the creation of an open space." Ecker then briefly discusses Suzy McKee Charna's *Walks to the End of the World* (1974) and *Motherliness* (1978), Ursula Le Guin's *The Left Hand of Darkness* (1969) and *The Dispossessed* (1974), Marge Piercy's *Woman on the Edge of Time* (1976), Joanna Russ's *The Female Man* (1975), and June Arnold's *Sister Gin* (1975). Ecker concludes that the dissolution of habitualized concepts of gender, as in some of these novels, is a "meaningful and political process." A fantasy text cannot be read only as the product of an escapist attitude, but has to be considered in the context of more general feminist debate, opening up a range of hitherto hardly explored reactions connected with fantasizing, the release of the emotions of joy, fear, and desire.

There were two dissertations on modern American "classical" writers. Christiane Maurer in *Die Idee der Liebe. Die Frauen in Saul Bellows Romanen* (Frankfurt: Lang) covers Bellow's portrayal of women from *Dangling Man* to *Humboldt's Gift*. Her theoretical approach is simple but nevertheless efficient. Since the women in Bellow's novels exist only in the minds of the male protagonists and are tied up with their problems, Maurer argues, they belong to the category of "otherness," against which the males strive to define themselves. Hence the women are mostly squeezed into a frame of archetypical, stereotypical, and mythical references, which reduce them to specific types. Maurer discovers five of them: the obedient bourgeois woman, the domineering woman, the enchantress/seductress, the decadent/eccentric woman, and the Mother. Maurer's minute close-reading analyses are never boring or overtheoretical and lead to the correct conclusion that Bellow's male protagonists are in search of a world governed by love, although their experience of reality is often one-sided. In Bellow's later works, their transcendental quests turn toward God. Correspondingly, their idea of love, whether of *agape* or Eros, prevents them from finding love in reality, making their psychic situations tragicomic. Rainer A. Zwick in his dissertation, *Rites de Passage in den Romanen* Why are We in Vietnam? *und* An American Dream *von Norman Mailer* (Tübingen: Narr) begins with a long excursion into cultural anthropology, religion, and American Studies in order to demonstrate what rites of passage exactly are, namely, a three-stage process of man's initiation into social life, as it appears in many civilizations and myths. Zwick mainly uses Arnold van Gennep's three-phase concept of rites of separation, rites of transition, and rites of incorporation, which was several decades later modified and reformulated by Joseph Campbell as a "monomyth" and its stages separation-initiation-return. Zwick sees in *Why Are We in Vietnam?* a structure mirroring Gennep's three phases. As for *An American Dream,* the author claims that the protagonist's final rite of passage, which means a change in social status, ends outside all commitments. Therefore, he concludes, the novel is more what R. W. B. Lewis called a variant of a rite of passage—a *deniation.* Zwick's dissertation suffers from too much theory but is nevertheless a solid study of two of Mailer's most important novels.

Universität Hamburg

iv. Italian Contributions, 1983

Gaetano Prampolini

Whether in terms of quantity or quality there does not seem to have been any sizeable variation in the work done by Italian Americanists in 1983, compared with previous years. One curious feature, though, is the dropping of book-length studies from 13 (1981) and eight (1982) to three. The other 77 items of which this report will give account are all shorter contributions, most of them concentrated in six publications (either special issues of periodicals or monographic collections of essays). Melville and Whitman have been the most studied among the major writers; the Puritan heritage in American culture and literature, and post-Modern fiction and ethnic literatures, the most studied areas.

A double issue (2–3) of *RSA* is almost entirely devoted to the proceedings of the 6th Conference of the Italian Association for North-American Studies, which took place in Bologna in 1981. That the theme of the Conference—"In the Puritan Grain"—was such as to invite the widest spectrum of approaches is already clear from the six papers that were the *pièces de résistance* of the program.

In his tightly reasoned and greatly stimulating "How the Puritans Discovered America" (pp. 7–21) Sacvan Bercovitch discusses the significance and implications of what is, in his view, "the distinctive contribution" of the Puritans to American culture: that Bible-flavored rhetoric which originated from their exegetical feat of discovering "America" in scriptural prophecies and which has been voicing ever since, in so many variants and with impressive continuity, the national myth of consensus insisting on a geographically elastic and history-

proof notion of America as a special land destined for a special kind
of people to fulfill the best of human aspirations. Tiziano Bonazzi's
"Ordine e salvezza nel pensiero di John Cotton" (pp. 80–93) raises an
important methodological question by pointing up the necessity (but
also the objective difficulty) for the modern scholar to take proper
heed of the radical discontinuities existing between his own secularized experience and the Puritan religious one. As his case in point
Bonazzi uses Cotton, whose conduct in public life, generally judged
as wavering and contradictory, appears—once his thought and the
religious experience that nourishes it are examined closely and rigor-
ously enough, which Bonazzi does through a limpid exposition of
Cotton's theology of redemption—to have been wholly consistent with
his stringent views of what the true Christian life should be. In "Dans
le sillage puritain: les vicissitudes du progrès à l'époque transcen-
dentaliste" (pp. 32–47) and "Puritanism and the Problem of Progress:
Hawthorne on Work and Play" (pp. 48–67) respectively, Maurice
Gonnaud and William Wasserstrom employ the concept of "progress"
as a kind of gauge for the vitality of the Puritan heritage in the Romantic period. The former elucidates the correlation between Emerson's changing views of the role and function of progress and the shifts
of his attitude—from impassioned rejection through nostalgic redis-
covery to final rehabilitation—toward the values of his ancestral culture. Challenging current interpretations of Hawthorne's "The Artist
of the Beautiful" as simply another meditation in the Romantic vein
over the plight of beauty and art in an insensitive environment, the
latter argues that this tale is rather a parable most relevant to the
American 1840s, when the wondrous operations of the steam engine
had just started winning over the public mind to the worship of the
machine. Most sagacious if at times slow-paced, Wasserstrom's analysis unravels Hawthornean allegory and irony to reveal how the writer
is here deploring, in the name of Puritan ethics and organicistic
aesthetics, his contemporaries' "debasement . . . at the altar of Progress." In "Puritanism and Romanticism" (pp. 68–79) Larzer Ziff contrasts the meanings that a number of crucial images have, on the one
hand, in William Bartram's *Travels* and, on the other, in the works of
Jonathan Edwards and Thoreau, thus elegantly highlighting significant similarities between Puritanism and romanticism, both of which
he sees as dialectically opposed to the rationalistic sensibility of the
American Enlightenment. In the last (and also the least) of these papers, "Puritanism: the Persistence of a Myth" (pp. 22–31), Leslie

Fiedler flashes a kaleidoscope of hackneyed remarks on Hawthorne's "myth of Puritanism" (and on "the myths of Hawthorne" that have accreted to that primary myth), and then contributes his own mythopoeic mite by making Hawthorne a misogynist (a cryptic one in his fiction, but blatantly so in his impatience with "scribbling women"). Fiedler's case rests on very flimsy and questionable evidence, but, after all, hasn't he sweepingly declared from the start that "the notion of objective and disinterested scholarship" is itself a myth?

This issue of *RSA* also contains 20 of the shorter papers that were read at the five workshops that completed the program of the conference. Here, however, there is room only for a brief mention of those that appear to me to have the best claims on the reader's attention. Two belong to the workshop on "Autobiography and Puritanism" (pp. 94–132): in one Itala Vivan reviews the functions of autobiography as a characteristic form of expression, first of the Puritan and then of the American mind; in the other, Mario Corona sees the evolution of middle-class consciousness from the 17th to the mid-19th century reflected in the different ways in which a Puritan autobiographer, a Franklin, a Thoreau, a Hawthorne, and a Melville cope with what— whether "wildness" within or "wilderness" without—the self senses as evil and threatening otherness. (An enlarged version of this paper is appended to *I Puritani d'America* [Milano: UNICOPLI], a small reader of Puritan texts edited by Corona for the classroom.) The workshop on "Writers 'In the Puritan Grain' " (pp. 133–68) contains Renzo S. Crivelli's analysis of the affinities in subject-matter, technique, and vision between two New England artists, Robert Frost and Andrew Wyeth, and also Annalisa Goldoni's stock-taking of the uses Charles Olson makes of Puritan materials in his *Maximus Poems*. An excellent paper by Mario Maffi on Horatio Alger, Jr.'s novels (which the author sees as powerful vehicles of codes of social control and self-control, updating Puritan, Franklinian, and Defoean values and having wide influence on generations of American writers) stands out in the workshop on "Puritanism and Mass Culture" (pp. 169–201). This workshop also includes Alessandro Portelli's remarks on the relation between work and leisure in Mark Twain's *Innocents Abroad* and Paola Ludovici's on Harriet Beecher Stowe's attitude toward Puritanism in *The Minister's Wooing*. The two remaining workshops are on "Puritan Theology and Culture" (pp. 202–27) and "Hawthorne, James and the Puritan Imagination" (pp. 228–59). The latter groups Vita Fortunati's timely reminder of the problematic complexity of

James's treatment of feminism in *The Bostonians*, Silvia Albertazzi's observations on Hawthorne's use of gothic motifs and properties in his historical tales, and an interesting reading of Hawthorne's "Wakefield" by Leonardo Terzo. He argues that in the narrator's attitude toward Wakefield's self-banishment, overt censure is a way of exorcising secret attraction and that in this tale introspection in the best Puritan tradition ends in an intimation of such symptoms of modern alienation as boredom and anxiety.

It seems appropriate that one half of the essays included in the Pan-American issue of *LetA* (3,xiv–xv [1982]) which bears such a title as "The Whitman Continent," should record the wide, deep, and continuing appeal of Whitman's poetry and personal charisma to Latin American poets, many of whom certainly would have cheered at Pablo Neruda's salute to him as "the first man to possess a genuinely continental voice." Thus, Nicola Bottiglieri (pp. 23–45) concerns himself (rather diffusely) with the long, enthusiastic essay through which, in 1887, Cuban poet-patriot José Martì made Whitman's verse and democratic credo known to the Hispano-American world; Antonio Melis (pp. 117–41) tersely outlines the impact of Whitman's example on the poetics and techniques of 20th-century Nicaraguan poets from Rubén Darìo to Ernesto Cardenal; Alain Sicard (pp. 177–88) defines the nature and the extent of Neruda's Whitmanism; Luiza Lobo (pp. 101–15) and Eduardo Lourenço (pp. 171–76) indicate the ways in which the encounter with Whitman affected the work of two Brazilian poets, Sousândrade and Fernando Pessoa.

Silvano Sabbadini (pp. 185–215) appraises one important aspect of Whitman's legacy to the poets of his own country—namely, the affirmation of the identity of poetry and reality, and of language as the place where a truly democratic conciliation of individual and society is made possible. The discussion of poets more or less directly responsive to Whitman's "affirmative utopia" (Sandburg, Patchen, W. C. Williams, Olson, Ginsberg, but also Pound and Hart Crane) bears out the Marxian interpretation of American poetry that Sabbadini develops on the postulate that the history of American poetry "homologically" reflects the inability of American society to actualize the values proclaimed by the national ideology of democracy. Valerio de Scarpis (pp. 5–21) also deals with Whitman's fortune—more precisely, with the fascination exerted on so many poets, American and foreign, by the image of poet-prophet that Whitman builds up throughout his book. That image, argues de Scarpis, in an "implication" of the revolutionary step Whitman took by placing his own personality at the center of his poetry as the all-absorbing subject-matter of it—a step made possible by Whitman's anticipatory awareness of what current psychology terms "identity."

This special issue is completed by three worthwhile essays on specific aspects of Whitman's work. Focusing her attention on the relation of form to theme in *Song of Myself*, Biancamaria Tedeschini Lalli (pp. 47–72) finds that this poem owes its structure to a pattern of distinctions (oppositions) and integrations (conciliations) which affects and connects all its levels, and points out how this pattern, together with such devices as the shifting functions of the "I" and the abolition of space and time specifications, confers on *Song of Myself* those qualities of ambivalence, elusiveness, open-ended fluidity, and dynamism which pertain to the very essence of its central theme. A systematic reading of the two articles and the profusion of notes that attest Whitman's seriousness in cultivating the study of language enables Marina Camboni (pp. 73–100) to discern a change of focus in the poet's linguistic interests, as he moved from the enthusiastic recognition of the resources of the English language to concentrate more and more on the definition of the features of that democratic American language he envisaged as the only one fit to fully express American experience. While the author seems to go a little too far in crediting Whitman with "a linguistic theory of his own," her essay makes it quite clear how relevant and essential his theoretical interest in language was to his poetic program. Whitman's treatment of the nude is the object of a good many insightful remarks by Andrea Mariani (pp. 143–69), who underlines the liberating effect this aspect of Whitman's poetry had on American painters and sculptors, and notices how the poet's conception of the human body as something intrinsically noble, clean, and beautiful finds its best embodiments when nudity—neither idealized nor made the vehicle for symbolism—appears in postures of self-reliant ease, in blissful communion with the natural environment and free from erotic implications.

In her finely written "Il bestiario di Emily Dickinson" (*Il piccolo Hans* 37:139–54) Marisa Bulgheroni sensitively discusses Dickinson's animal imagery, which she sees as a kind of "language within the language" working in two fundamental ways—either as a stage where the roles enacted by the animals suggest to the speaker momentary, experimental definitions of her own identity, or as a geometric space measured by the motion of the animal only to suggest the immeasurable distance covered by the imagination. A catalogue of the ever-varying meanings conveyed by the most frequently recurring animals indicates how deeply subversive of traditional animal symbologies this bestiary is—a fact that the author, paying perhaps unnecessary dues to current pieties, ascribes to Dickinson's marginal position as a woman in a male-dominated culture.

In Mirella Billi's *Il vortice fisso: La poesia di Sylvia Plath* (Pisa: Pacini) the study of the work of this poet benefits from the author's sensible handling of Structuralist and semiotic methods of analysis as well as from her judicious recognition that, although in Plath's case poetry is neither a symptom nor an immediate, uncontrolled expression of psychic disorder, reference to her biography is indispensable to interpretation (inasmuch as her experience is the mainspring of her imagination and her neurosis the shaper of some of her most characteristic associative processes). Billi examines Plath's macrotext as "a system of relations" whose intrinsic coherence she brings into evidence by studying in turn some significant segments or aspects of it: *The Bell Jar* as an invaluable index to paradigms and structures that reappear in the poems; the "Poem for a Birthday" sequence as the stage for a death-rebirth drama ending in an only provisional, makeshift restoration of the shattered self to integrity; the centrality to the whole system of the idiosyncratic lunar mythology Plath adapted from Robert Graves's *White Goddess;* the inescapability of the "death-circuit" and Plath's unresolved ambivalence to it. The "fixed vortex," combining circularity and immobility, is the image pointed up at the end of the book as the one which best embodies and condenses the oppositions and contradictions of Plath's universe. Although the author conducts her study primarily (and, at times, to the point of redundancy) at the level of forms of content, the homology obtaining between these and the forms of expression is well illustrated through close analyses of some individual poems (those of "Who," "The Moon and the Yew," and "Ariel" are particularly effective) and in a final synoptic description of Plath's style. Thoroughness, clearness, and interpretive acumen make this book one that no student of Plath's poetry should overlook.

The only other item concerning poetry is the brief introduction Giovanni Giudici has written for Aldo Busi's competent version of *Self-Portrait in a Convex Mirror* (*Autoritratto in uno specchio convesso;* Milano: Garzanti), the first of John Ashbery's books to be translated into Italian. While Giudici's claim that Ashbery is the leading figure among the poets writing in English today may surely be disputed, his description of the essential traits of Ashbery's verse is both informative and precise.

Among the contributions on fiction (to which we now turn) we can add Alide Cagidemetrio's fine book on the autobiographies written by pioneers, *Verso il West: L'autobiografia dei pionieri* (Vicenza: Neri Pozza). Instead of the singularity to be expected in one's account of one's life, the author in fact finds stereotypes, clichés, and serial-like homogeneity typical of popular forms of fiction as the distinctive marks common to the 29 texts on which she bases her study. In her investigation of the reasons for such an outcome in what promised to be the ideal form for the realistic representation of the West which romances *à la* Cooper could not provide, Cagidemetrio brings to bear a clear awareness of the "paradoxes" ruling any autobiographical act, an intelligent and unobtrusive use of semiotics as well as a mature understanding of the 19th-century American cultural context. On the one hand, she shows how the rhetoric of the pioneer turned autobiographer cannot avoid being intensely modeled by the conventions of other genres which also deal with the West (romance and dime novel, biography and travel literature); on the other, she points out how western autobiography shares the assumptions of contemporary culture at large, and is sustained by it right through the first two decades of the 20th century. Thus, the myth of the pioneer as the quintessential representative of American democracy sheds the heroic light in which the autobiographer feels entitled to posture (no matter how ordinary his experience); thus, it is the "archetypal national fable" of progress through the wilderness into a promised land that he re-enacts in fashioning the narrative of his life. These texts—in both validating the ideology of "Manifest Destiny" and authenticating the legend of the West—fully satisfy the sense of verisimilitude of their readership. The only fault in Cagidemetrio's book (which is also notable for tautness and restraint) is perhaps an excess of its virtues: the preempting and ruling out of the possibility that there may somewhere exist an autobiography presenting a straightforward, unadorned, true-to-memory record of a frontiersman's experiences.

The term "initiation," of such wide currency in studies of American fiction, has lost any clear denotative efficacy by being made to cover a variety of themes, situations, and forms. From this premise originates *Sigfrido nel Nuovo Mondo: Studi sulla narrativa d'inizia-*

zione (Roma: La Goliardica), a synergic collection of first-rate essays by an interdisciplinary team of the University of Rome-I, which illustrates just how useful the concept of "initiation" can in fact be, both as descriptive category and heuristic tool, once its scope is defined with enough precision. A narrowing of its applicability is the chief aim of the introductory essay by editors Paola Cabibbo and Annalisa Goldoni (pp. 13–51). Taking the tribal rituals of initiation and the pattern of the adventure of the mythological hero as parameters, the authors define a paradigm against which they measure a good sample of "initiation" novels and short stories. This enables them to set down a typology exhibiting systematic analogies between the archetypal model and the literary text but also significant deviations of the latter from the former, and hence to propose the qualified use of the term "initiation" for only those texts in which "the scenario of initiation" figures in a consistent and recognizable way and has a structuring function and where there is an experience of radical transformation taking place within a brief time span.

Theoretical points only touched upon by Cabibbo and Goldoni are elaborated by some of the other contributors through analyses of individual texts. Teresa Pàroli (pp. 53–87) examines Old English and German poetry to draw a distinction between "initiation" and "conversion." Basing his argument on Goethe's *Wilhelm Meisters Lehrjahre* and Thomas Mann's *Tonio Kröger*, Giuseppe Nori (pp. 89–131) defines the fundamental difference between initiation novel and *Bildungsroman* in terms of radical metamorphosis vs. continuing maturation, circular vs. linear movement, "extraordinary" vs. historical time, definitive vs. never-ending process. In the enlarged version of an essay that first appeared in 1977 (see *ALS 1978*, p. 474) Fedora Giordano (pp. 133–52) calls attention to the close affinity existing between the recurrent metaphors of initiation she finds in Jack London's stories and the symbolism pertaining to the Jungian process of individuation. Donatella Izzo and Nori (pp. 153–72) choose an undisputable initiation story, Sherwood Anderson's "The Man Who Became a Woman," to concentrate on the liminal phase of initiation in the light of V. W. Turner's notion of "in-betweenness" and assess the usefulness of the concepts of self and status in accounting for the transformation at the core of the initiatory experience.

Further verification of the viability of the model proposed in the introduction comes from another group of essays which at the same time represent valuable contributions to the interpretation of the works under scrutiny. In the story of the protagonist of Melville's *Redburn*, Izzo (pp. 173–200) sees the point-by-point conformity to the *form* of the anthropo-mythological paradigm and the no less systematic inversion and debasement of its *content* as indicative of Melville's ironic treatment of a narrative code whose very denomination ("initiation novel"), Izzo acutely remarks, is an oxymoron, the two terms of which refer to conditions prevailing in antithetically oriented cultures—the traditional and the modern. Transgressive occurrences—in a parodic key—of the initiation pattern are also noticed by Annalisa Goldoni (pp. 201–08) in the process of "dismantling" undergone by the protagonist of Nathanael West's *A Cool Million*, by Cabibbo (pp. 209–16) in "the making of a mock hero" presented in Richard Brautigan's *Abortion*, and by Christina Bacchilega (pp. 217–35) in James Purdy's *Malcolm* and John Gardner's *Grendel* (in both of which, the author maintains, the initiation pattern is a device intended to set off the disintegration of the self). All of these instances are in keeping with the idea, somewhat cursorily advanced by Cabibbo and Goldoni, that in presenting initiations that more often than not finish up not with the initiand's reintegration into society but with his separation from it, American literature deconstructs the initiation model that American culture has always cherished as a means to describe itself, and explodes the contradiction inherent in the latter's devotion to the mutually incompatible imperatives of a perennial "start anew" and incremental progress. The only "successful" initiation that appears in this volume—and one conforming precisely and substantially to the archetypal model—is that of Ike McCaslin in Faulkner's "The Old People," studied by Cabibbo (pp. 237–49). But what the young hero is initiated to, stresses the author, is a mythic, ahistorical view of the world. The inability to come to terms with the actualities of history is, on the other hand, offered as the main cause for Quentin's failure as initiand in *Absalom, Absalom!*, where Andrea Dimino (pp. 251–76) sees initiation performed through narration (the passive receiving of Sutpen's story from "tribal elders" being Quentin's novitiate; his active reshaping of it, his initiatory trials). But Dimino's argument appears at times overingenious and marred by a relapse into that connotative and metaphoric usage of "initiation" which Cabibbo and Goldoni are, quite rightly, so eager to discredit.

Mariella Di Maio's "Jules Verne e il modello Poe" (*RLMC* 35 [1982],iv:335–54) is a rather diffuse assessment of the influence of the American writer on the Frenchman. It makes clear, however, how

Verne respected Poe's work as a kind of lodestar throughout his career—from his early elaboration of the concept of "extraordinary"
fiction to his late *Le Sphinx des glaces* where, once more, he employed
Poe-derived motifs to supplement a rationalistic explanation of the
mysterious ending of *Arthur Pym*. But the big event of the year concerning Poe is the appearance of a new translation of the whole corpus
of his tales (*I racconti di Edgar Allan Poe;* Torino: Einaudi), superbly done by Giorgio Manganelli in three volumes of a handsome uniform series which presents "writers in writers' translations." In an
instructive translator's note Manganelli succinctly indicates some of
the solutions he has devised to meet the challenges of his text—in
particular, to render what he distinguishes as the three tones (horrid-
grotesque, argumentative, and visionary) of Poe's style.

Whatever the originality of their respective conclusions (on which
I will not venture to pass judgment, not being *au courant* with the
unrelenting flow of recent Melville scholarship and criticism), the
essays gathered in *Melvilliana*, ed. Paola Cabibbo (Roma: Bulzoni),
provide painstaking and probing analyses of Melville's language and
techniques, but also recommend themselves as intelligent and fecund
applications of principles, methods, and procedures derived from that
area of literary theory stretching from early structuralism to semiotics
and deconstructionism. The idea of Melville that inspires and informs
them does not appear too dissimilar from the one that Giorgio Mariani
(pp. 257–80) recognizes as characteristic of American Deconstructionist criticism, of which he gives a clear and sober overview: a kind
of philosopher of language, Melville never ceases, while writing about
the world, to question himself about the possibility and meaning of
writing.

In the four essays grouped in part 1 the interpreter's task consists
in going beyond the letter of his text, by taking hold of clues concealed
within it—a move most clearly seen in the three that deal with works
in which Melville's narrative strategy requires the reader to transcend
the limitations of the narrator's or one of the characters' point of
view. Of these essays, two—Paola Cabibbo and Paola Ludovici's (pp.
43–59) and Mario Materassi's (pp. 79–107)—have been published
elsewhere, in 1979 and 1970 respectively. The third is an essay in
many ways complementary to another she published on the same
novel in 1980 (see *ALS 1980*, pp. 568–69). Donatella Izzo (pp. 13–
41) limpidly identifies in the text of *Typee* the elements that invite
the reader to go beyond the interpretations of facts on the part of both

Tom the protagonist and Tom the narrator, and to realize that the
corruptive contact with Western culture Tom so much dreads for
the Typees has already taken place and has produced its first effects
with his sojourn in the Edenic valley. The fourth, an attentive and
perceptive study of "The Encantadas" by Annalisa Goldoni (pp. 61–
77), highlights two important aspects of Melville's work: the epistemological concern with the elusiveness of reality under myriad appearances, and the role played by imagination in performing the
semantic enrichment and transformation of referential data.

The five essays grouped in part 2 concentrate on what the editor of
this volume calls Melville's "negative strategies" (structural and
rhetorical devices meant "to conceal rather than convey meaning, . . .
to delay and even block communication"), which support an image
of Melville as avant-garde writer, antagonizing the readers of his
time by a deliberate frustration of their expectations. Completing her
dyptich on *Redburn* with an essay focusing on the discourse of this
novel (as the one collected in *Sigfrido nel Nuovo Mondo* focuses on its
story), Izzo (pp. 111–31) persuasively argues that, far from being
evidence of the writer's haste and immaturity, the extensive and often
gratuitous digressions, the narrative discontinuities, the destabilization of meaning in the ending, the use of disparate codes, are all parts
of a plan to disorient the reader, to render his progress through the
novel homologous to Redburn's disappointing and ineffectual voyage.
This homology—inscribed in that crucial chapter 31 where Izzo de-
tects a *mise en abyme* of the rules of production and fruition of the
text—is seen as Melville's way of making the point that literature,
not unlike Redburn's guidebook, is unreliable when conceived as
purveyor of pat certainties, and, not unlike travel, valuable only as
space for a cognitive quest indefinitely in progress. The expansions of
discourse in *Billy Budd*, so largely predominant over the story, are
minutely and perspicaciously studied by Giuseppe Nori (pp. 215–55),
and found to be the agents of the destabilization, deconstruction, and
disintegration of meanings that reveal Melville's self-ironical stance
as to the possibility of reaching or even searching for truth, and which
suggest the necessary relativity and in(de)finiteness of any interpretation. The category of "the Neuter" as defined by Roland Barthes
(not neutrality but firm refusal of the world's injunctions to take a
stand, annulment but also complex coexistence of polarities, replacement of an "either/or" by a "both/and" or an "in turn" logic, etc.)
offers Cabibbo (pp. 133–62) a very apt hermeneutical key to "The

Piazza," which—through her most elegant and enlightening reading—proves to be a capital instance of Melville's struggle to eschew the authoritarianism of any binary paradigm and also of his exploration of absence (silence, darkness, immobility, void, and so on) as the most likely repository of truth.

The two remaining essays are less convincing, possibly because of the exuberance of their authors' associations. In the "etymologies" she traces in "The Lightning-Rod Man" and "Bartleby" (including the anagram of the name of the latter's protagonist into "art" and "byble") Ludovici (pp. 163–88) sees evidence of how the letter of a Melvillean text may allude to and, at the same time, conceal the spirit of those great sources and fathers, religious and literary, with which Melville felt any modern writer should reckon and which he himself aspired to emulate before deciding in disillusionment that he too had better "give up copying." Aiming to redeem "The Bell-Tower" from critical disrepute, Goldoni (pp. 189–214) brings to light the complex interplay of symmetries and dissymmetries through which Melville makes an affirmation of the absolute rights of artistic creativity coexist with (and undermine) the endorsement of the punishment of pride expressed in the epigraphs and the closure of this tale. Giuliano Gramigna's "Il Capitano Amasa Delano, traduttore" (*Il piccolo Hans* 39:23–33) is primarily a discussion of the (im)possibility of translating based on both psychoanalytical hermeneutics and Walter Benjamin's pronouncements on the task of the translator, and concerns "Benito Cereno" only inasmuch as it assimilates Delano's myopic construction of what he sees aboard the *St. Dominick* to the work of a translator, "faithful" to the surface of his text but helplessly blind in front of those "untranslatable" flashings of the text's "true" sense.

On James there are only two short contributions this year: Rita Ferrara's "La figura dello scrittore nei racconti di Henry James" (*Il ponte* 39,vi–ix:668–77) and an excellent postscript by Agostino Lombardo to Marcella Bonsanti's translation of *The Sense of the Past* (*Il senso del passato;* Milano: Garzanti). Dealing with 15 stories (from "Benvolio" to "The Velvet Glove") in which James dramatized the writer's struggle to protect his artistic and moral integrity from the exactions of life and the allurements of society, Ferrara shows how a paradigmatic life/death opposition and several homological variants of it create a system of metaphors which underlines the evolution of the main theme through the whole corpus. But too much has been crammed into this eight-page article, and the author's conclusion—

that the Romantic primacy of the writer over his work comes to an end with James—appears somewhat desultory. Lombardo points out how what originally had been conceived and begun in 1900 as the story of an "international ghost" became, in 1914, a quite different and more complex work whose true theme is the meaning and value of the past. The view of history as a nightmare that *The Sense of the Past* shares with contemporary works by Eliot and Joyce confirms the 20th-century quality of James's later fiction, while—Lombardo concludes—the excellence of the finished parts of this last of his novels, as well as his passionate dedication to its planning, suggest that for James, too, art was the only sustenance against the insidiousness of the past and the horrors of the present.

In his amiably rambling and ingeniously argued "Mark Twain: in fondo al pozzo" (*Paragone* 402:3–30) Guido Fink interprets several features of Mark Twain's work as symptoms of a dissatisfaction with the written (and printed) word that this writer came to feel all the more acutely as he became fascinated in his later years with so much faster "languages," such as telepathy, dreams, and thought. Indications of his search for a fuller and more immediate transmission of his intuitions, and for a way out of the prison of the book, are seen by Fink in *The Mysterious Stranger*, of which he notices the cinematographic techniques and other suggestive affinities with D. W. Griffith's *Intolerance* and T. Ince's *Civilization*. In "*Dark Laughter* di Sherwood Anderson: il contrappunto temporale come tecnica narrativa" (*Annali* [Fac. Lettere, Univ. di Perugia] n. s. 18[1980–81]:57–71) Maria Rita Maddio makes a bid for a better rating of this novel. Although her use of Gérard Genette's categories and terminology is not impeccable, and her idea of the relationship between technique and meaning rather simplistic, her main point—that Anderson's "contrapuntal" handling of time is meant to suggest how the protagonist's search for innocence and authenticity is doomed to failure—seems to deserve consideration.

A good deal of attention has been given to post–World War II fiction—as witness one full-length book, a whole issue of *Calibano* (7[1982]), and one essay. Franco La Polla's *Un posto nella mente. Il nuovo romanzo americano, 1962–1982* (Ravenna: Longo) opens with a discursive, freewheeling review of the main features of the New Fiction. Most of the points touched upon in these first 48 pages are reiterated in the second section of the book, where La Polla discusses representative novels by writers he distributes under two headings: "some fathers" (Kesey, Gass, Barthelme, Berger, Hawkes, Barth) and "some sons" (Brautigan, Coover, Hjortsberg, D. E. Westlake, Kosinski, D. "Sunset" Carson, Alvin Greenberg, and a group of novelists from the San Francisco Bay area). But the rationale for this subdivision (why, e.g., Barthelme should be a "father" while Brautigan and Coover are "sons," why neither Nabokov nor Burroughs appears among the "fathers") is nowhere explained, and the quality of the discussions is uneven: there is a perceptive reading of *Omensetter's Luck* as a novel staging man's futile attempt to recover the Edenic unity between subject and object, the self and Nature, but most of the pieces on the "sons" betray a certain journalistic hastiness. The last section of the book, collecting La Polla's interviews between 1979 and 1982 with such writers as John C. Batchelor, Jerome Charyn, Walter Abish, Rob Swigart, Peter S. Beagle, Gerald Rosen, Keith Abbott, Joe Cottonwood, and Stephen Schneck, may prove the most useful—along with the bibliography listing the works of 124 writers, many of whom as yet very little known even in the United States. The fact that large parts of this book have appeared independently over the years may account for its fragmentariness and redundancy. But its haziness seems rather to depend on La Polla's lack of concern with defining more accurately the scope and goals of his study and with developing it within some precise methodological framework.

The advisability of having at least a working hypothesis of what post-Modern fiction can be seems on the other hand clear to Guido Carboni, whose essay in *Calibano* (pp. 58–85) starts by constructing a model post-Modern novel. This model would gravitate as near as possible to the center of "a field of forces" defined by such polarities as representation / fabulation, structuring order/destructuring fragmentation, author/reader as textual functions, and would also be characterized by the "ambiguous vision" Tzvetan Todorov assigns to fantastic literature as well as by the "double reference" of photorealism and illusionistic sculpture. Of the five novels examined in the second part of the essay, Pynchon's *Crying of Lot 49* is thus the one that most closely approaches the requirements of the model. Mailer's *Armies of the Night* and Barth's *Lost in the Funhouse* occupy symmetrically opposite positions on the periphery of the field, while more recent works such as Mailer's *Executioner's Song* and Barth's *Letters* are even farther removed, signaling a partial turning away from typically post-Modern concerns. Carboni may not greatly modify current views, but he certainly provides a more cogent and comprehen-

sive definition of post-Modern fiction than the one the reader can get
from the wordy and meandering piece by Barbara Lanati (pp. 9–38),
which should have served as an introduction to the whole issue.
Lanati's views on postmodernism become somewhat clearer in her
other contribution (pp. 118–54), centering on the analysis of Stanley
Elkin's "The Making of Ashenden." Her inability to see any logic in
the shift of narrative focus in the second section of Elkin's long story
leads Lanati to a rather idiosyncratic reading of it, but her extended
parallel discussion of Faulkner's "The Bear," Mailer's *Why Are We
in Viet Nam?*, and "The Making of Ashenden" contains a good many
penetrating remarks on the profound changes that have taken place
in the way the American fiction writer sees his cultural role and practices his art. Alide Cagidemetrio (pp. 39–57) concerns herself with
some of the most provocative aspects of Coover's poetics and achievement. Her observations on "hyperrealism" and the performance metaphor in *The Public Burning* seem particularly insightful, but excessive compression and elliptical transitions make it at times almost
impossible for the reader to follow her reasoning. More rewarding,
therefore, are the essays contributed by Rosella Mamoli Zorzi and
Bianca Tarozzi. Dealing with Coover's ironic-parodic use of the fable,
Mamoli Zorzi (pp. 86–98) distinguishes three different methods of
composition in the "post-Modern fables" of *Pricksongs and Descantes:*
juxtaposition and blending of traditional fables within the same text
(as in "The Door"), manipulation of one single fable (as in "The
Gingerbread House"), or deployment of the generic conventions of
the fable within an original text (as in "The Magic Poker"). Tarozzi
(pp. 99–117) concludes her thoroughgoing and lucid reading of John
Gardner's *Grendel* by noticing a split between the structure and the
texture of this novel—i.e., between Gardner's nonparodic treatment
of the mythic pattern (so unlike Barth's and, also, prefiguring Gardner's strictures on postmodernism in *On Moral Fiction*) and the splendid language which characterizes the monster as a clownish "everyman" in whom the post-Modern reader is likely to recognize *son
semblable.*

Annalucia Accardo and Igina Tattoni's *"The Crying of Lot 49* e
Slaughterhouse Five, due romanzi contemporanei" (*CeS* 22:86–98)
may be of some interest as a diligent (although not always descrip-
tively accurate) inventory of modes, themes, and techniques typical
of the New Fiction. The only item on an earlier post–World War II
fiction writer is "La Bibbia di Bernard Malamud" (*Nuova antologia*

552,viii:168–79), in which Gigliola Sacerdoti Mariani reviews this writer's characteristic themes and devices from the perspective offered by *God's Grace*. At times overly appreciative and on the whole not very original, this article is made interesting, however, by the author's suggestion that the complex father-son relationship emerging from the Abraham episode of Genesis may furnish an important key to the meaning of Malamud's novels as a whole.

The study of ethnic literature also has fared well. Welcome, first of all, is the launching of *In Their Own Words* (Venezia: Lib. Ed. Cafoscarina), the biannual "European journal of the American ethnic imagination," whose first issue—sampling the manifold possibilities of investigation (theoretical, methodological, interpretive) that the present state of this field offers—can be considered, on the whole, a promising start. In his thoughtful and thought-generating essay Werner Sollors (1:17–28) advocates the study of ethnic literatures as a viable means of defining "Americanness" but also warns prospective writers of polyethnic literary history against the dangers of making ethnicity the only or decisive taxonomic criterion in grouping writers, of mindlessly equating ethnicity and (lower) class, and of giving in to that form of self-defeating cultural relativism which is "biological insiderism." Less impressive is the other theoretical contribution, in which Christer Mossberg (1:57–67) takes the literature written by Scandinavian immigrants in their native languages as his model case to discuss the circumstances that may favor the growth of any immigrant literature before it subsides into silence, once the assimilation of the immigrant subculture into the dominant American culture is completed. Mossberg is certainly right in invoking a better knowledge of immigrant literatures and in rejoicing at the current awakening of scholarly interest in them, but do texts not written in English (even if written in America, and no doubt important in the study of American culture) really belong to American literature, or are they not to be viewed rather as transoceanic appendixes to the literatures of the immigrants' native or ancestral countries? William Boelhower (1:29–45) defines the Jewish-American variety of immigrant autobiography in terms of the "paradigm of absence" which he sees underlying the seeming heterogeneousness and the specific uniqueness of his five texts (Edward Steiner's *From Alien to Citizen,* Marcus Ravage's *An American in the Making,* Rebekah Kahut's *My Portion,* Abraham Cahan's *Education,* and I. B. Singer's *Lost in America*): both Old World and New World Jewish environments—although they represent cultural spaces where the autobiographical self can preserve its ethnic identity—are in fact only "makeshift versions" of that ideal homeland, the never-ending, repetitive quest for which is what distinguishes the Jewish-American immigrant autobiography from those of other ethnic groups. Through the notes made by Mario Materassi (1:47–55) when he met the writer in 1968 and again in 1977, Henry Roth explains his long literary silence as the effect of a psychological impasse caused by the loss of that sense of cultural continuity he was then to recapture only on visiting Israel. By calling attention to the "Hibernian" folk elements and ardent nationalism surfacing in a handful of stories and poems written by actor-playwright-journalist John Brougham (1810–60), Pat M. Ryan (1:3–15) challenges the "nativist, amalgamationist and ethnosynthetic" views of those literary historians who seem to ignore the existence of ethnically conscious Irish-American writers. Mario L. Togni (1:69–81) provides the English version and the rather bland commentary which accompany his little anthology of emigrant folk songs from eight Italian regions.

Three items specifically concern the literature of the American Indians. In a postscript to his own version of Charles A. Eastman's *The Soul of the Indian* (*L'anima dell'Indiano;* Milano: Adelphi) Franco Meli clearly outlines the intellectual and spiritual career of a writer who indeed deserves more attention than he has so far received, and points out the significance of this book as a reflection of the situation of Indian cultures in the transition from "the old ways" to acculturation, but also as an anticipation of certain modes and themes of the Indian Renaissance of the late 1960s. Laura Coltelli has sensitively translated a selection of Leslie Marmon Silko's stories (*Raccontare;* Milano: La Salamandra), which inaugurates a uniform series presenting significant works of Indian writers to the Italian reader. In her introduction, after stressing Silko's deeply felt ties to the Laguna Pueblo cultural heritage and the crucial importance of her conception of storytelling, Coltelli offers a sound thematic reading of the stories. The volume also contains the most complete bibliography on Silko to date. Issued as a companion to an itinerant exhibition of the traditional art of the Plains Indians, *I cerchi del mondo. Proposte di lettura* (Genova: Comune di Genova) is an elegantly printed bibliographical guide to the study of the Indian cultures of the plains. It furnishes a virtually complete catalogue both of what has been written in Italy and of what has been translated into Italian on the subject. The entries relating to Italian comic strips and late 19th-century pulp magazines will be of considerable interest to the student of European stereotypes of the Indian.

One item concerns the black American novelist and poet Al Young, whose literary aims and achievement are assessed (and slightly over-valued) in Luciano Federighi's introduction to his own lively trans-lation of Young's second novel, *Who Is Angelina?* (*Chi è Angelina?;* Milano: Jaca Books).

A brief mention, finally, of this year's only contribution to the study of the cultural relationship between the United States and Italy. In-cluded in *Le relazioni Italia–Stati Uniti dal 1943 al 1953: Storia, Eco-nomia, Cultura* (ed. Elisabetta Vezzosi, Fac. Scienze Politiche, Univ. di Firenze) which collects the papers of a conference held in Florence in 1980, Rolando Anzilotti's "L'influenza americana sulla cultura let-teraria e teatrale italiana" (pp. 155–74) is a well-informed survey of the penetration of American literature in Italy in the post–World War II years, offering a number of stimulating observations on the influ-ence it exerted on contemporary Italian writers.

Università di Firenze

v. Italian Contributions, 1984

Maria Vittoria D'Amico

On taking over this Italian section I thought I was aware of the dif-ficulty of the task but have come to realize the full extent of the problem only while trying to carry on the tradition of accurate, subtly ironical criticism which Rolando Anzilotti initiated, and which Gae-tano Prampolini faithfully has continued for so many years, achieving results that it would be hard indeed to equal. I was not able to foresee (in spite of Orwellian premonitions) that 1984 would turn out to be such an *annus mirabilis* for American Studies in Italy: the season of academic "concorsi" has fatally pushed the number of publications up to leviathan-like proportions (and not only in the field of American Studies!).

So across a boundless ocean I started my voyage, choosing to fish out the critical works of Herman Melville, who is the subject of two book-length studies and of several essays and introductions. Mario Corona's *Prima del viaggio, Per una lettura di Moby Dick* (Bologna: Pitagora) seems to deserve priority for scope, learning, and for an original framework. The plan had appeared *in nuce* in a pervious essay on the title of Melville's masterpiece (see *ALS 1980*, p. 569) illustrating how the title might contain and veil the hidden meanings and themes of the book (cosmic, phallic implications). It is a stratified text, built layer upon layer, according to various critical approaches which the author deliberately uses to probe in many directions. The main intention is to "recognize in Melville a writer and an intellectual who faces the problems common to the Western world at a time of rapid industrialization." It is achieved through the use of the Lukácsian categories and of various critical works of historical interest, while the structural analysis of the text is mainly based on psychoanalytical criticism. The variety of critical viewpoints is puzzling for those looking for a uniformity of vision. Only the initiated reader, to whom an enormous body of notes and scholarly references (with even corrections of the official translations of *Moby-Dick*) is addressed, will be able to harpoon this whale of a critical text, which, with its rich, annotated bibliography, constitutes an important step forward in Melville studies in Italy.

Completely different for its simplicity and clarity of exposition is Giuseppe Lombardo's study (*Through Terror and Pity: Saggio su* Battle-Pieces and Aspects of the War *di Herman Melville* [Univ. of Messina: Magistero]) on the 1866 Melville work. On the assumption that already in the *Battle-Pieces* one may find the creativity of the major sea narrative or of "Bartleby," Lombardo's analysis aims at stressing "the high ideological temperature of Melville's vision of the war and also the writer's opinion on the causes and effects of the Civil War" which is thematically framed within Melville's usual good/evil dichotomy. This critical analysis successfully avoids the excesses of fashionable semiological or structural approaches, and its major merit is to be found in its rich critical references and in its searching comparisons with similar works by Melville's contemporaries. The same critical characteristics are to be seen also in a short essay by the same author on a *Timoleon* poem (" 'After the Pleasure Party' di Herman Melville: le fonti, la struttura, l'arte della memoria," *Nuovi Annali* 2 [Fac. Magistero, Univ. Messina]: 369–402) where, while using biographical sources and referring to already accepted critical works (links with Shakespeare and with Tennyson, critical studies by Howard Vincent and by Alfredo Rizzardi), he achieves remarkably original results.

On its way toward greater and greater recognition *The Confidence-*

Man finds two estimators in Sergio Perosa and Luciana Piré. Perosa re-edits his masterly translation of the work (published in 1961 by Neri Pozza [Venezia]) with a new exhaustive postscript (*L'uomo di fiducia;* Milano: Feltrinelli). His excellent interpretation takes into account all the major Melvillean themes and techniques which culminate in the pessimistic vortex of the work. Here Perosa shows how gesture and action are transformed into language and philosophy, in the same way that the comedy of ideas can become comedy of action through particular technical procedures. Perosa has the critical learning and ability to express the very essence of Melville's work in metaphorical terms. His criticism functions at two levels: the realistic level of all the references to popular Western sources (or to the learned genre of anatomy), and the metaphysical level through the mesh of philosophical statements on Melville's implicit and hidden themes (attraction for man's darker side, satire of American everyday life or of Emersonian self-reliance). Hence we see that like the work itself this critical piece clearly shows how entangled by this ambiguous Melvillean text a reader may be, and this is just the case with Piré's essay on "Le confusioni della verità: *The Confidence-Man* di Melville" (*Annali* [Bari: Facoltà di Lettere] 27–28:337–64), where the author gives voice to a series of acute elucubrations to show how the Melvillean silence may well be generative of the most ambiguous truth: his use of peculiar ethical and metaphysical codes bears evidence to the folly of all order and the pre-eminence of falsehood over truth. Piré seems astonishingly involved in her critical adventure: the Confidence Man is still exerting his power to an incredible degree.

Claudio Gorlier's introduction to *Billy Budd* (Milano: Bompiani) is shrewd and exhaustive. His admirable synthesis interprets the character triangle (Billy-Claggart-Vere) shifting from the acknowledged connection victim-victimizer (with any related biblical implication) to a vast display of various archetypal characters (including above all the Handsome Sailor) before going on to evaluate the Melvillean ideology also in the light of existing critical works. Within this happy Melville season may be included an essay by Chiara Briganti ("Quattro racconti gotici di Melville," *SA* 25–26[1979–80]:37–52). Unlike other critics, quite originally she does not explore the gothic element in any of those Melville works traditionally considered gothic (*Benito Cereno* might be a case in point) but, on the assumption that Melville "may be considered a gothic writer in a broader sense, for his belief in a mystery at the foundations of reality," she analyzes some tales ("Bartleby," "Tartarus of Maids") where she observes how gothic devices and imagery enhance his vision of evil and strengthen the celebrated power of blackness.

In 1982(see *ALS*, p. 515) Gaetano Prampolini remarked how the interest of Italian Americanists in the work of James was "steady year after year." This year's work strongly supports this opinion. Two fine items are Attilio Brilli's introduction to *Ore Italiane* (Milano: Garzanti) and Sergio Perosa's to his own version of *The Sacred Fount* (*La fonte sacra*; Torino: Einaudi). Despite the fact that Brilli begins by classifying his subject as travel literature he quickly recognizes its autonomous position: it gives, in fact, impressions and memories of Italy not in the form of a diary or of a mental return to a country whose beauties he loves (Goethe and Stendhal are quoted among others), nor even of a Baedeker, but of an exercise of the memory written at a distance. Brilli's elegant prose introduces us immediately to what he calls "James's verbal simulation of pictorial art," by finding all possible connections with the great masters of watercolor, and focusing on the apparent present problem of James as an artist: an obsessive attraction to the artistic past of Europe unconsciously filtered through his Puritanical vision of history. Perosa gives us penetrating commentary on *The Sacred Fount*, a novel of James's late phase, which the critic defines as muddled, elusively frustrating, a novel within the novel, an antinovel *ante litteram*. A solid Jamesian critic, as Perosa is, may venture this negative criticism, because starting from that premise he not only illustrates the author's creative method and his themes, but he also demonstrates, through an original reading mechanism, how James's experiments, realized through an unreliable narrator, set him closer to experimentalists such as James Joyce. In spite of James's bad luck as a dramatist, after Sergio Perosa's and Giovanna Mochi's essays it would appear that the dramatizations of his works have been remarkably successful. Sergio Perosa also provides us with a close analysis of Benjamin Britten's operatic adaptation of *The Turn of the Screw* and examines film versions of the same work. He includes a highly professional musical criticism of the opera and some original comment on the similarities between Britten's music and James's verbal ambiguity (*"Il Giro di vite:* Dal Racconto di James all'opera di Britten," *LAmer* 4(xvii)[Spring 1983]: 5–16). Giovanna Mochi analyzes the text of *The Aspern Papers* adapted for the stage by M. Redgrave (1959) from a semiotic perspective in "Punto di Vista e Rappresentazione: Riflessioni su una

Riduzione Teatrale di *Aspern Papers* di Henry James (*LAmer* 4(xvii) [Spring 1983]:17–48). She stresses the main problems of transcodification (from narrative to dramatic text) with an open preference for the narrative version and a rather suspicious attitude toward the Redgrave adaptation and the semantic coherence of the characters. Although an essay mostly directed to theater enthusiasts, it is still a noteworthy contribution to the studies of James's narrative art.

Three more essays are devoted to James—all of them in *SA* 25–26 [1979–80]—and all linked to a structural approach: Camilla Pagani's "Immagini in *What Maisie Knew*" (pp. 93–116) still observes the theatrical quality of the Jamesian text, commenting on all dichotomies related to the rich world of images; Yury Lotman's semiotic studies overwhelmingly influence another essay on *Maisie* by Igina Tattoni (pp. 71–92) and a critical piece by Francesco Marroni on *The Portrait of a Lady* (pp. 53–70). The former is attractively written and softens the rigid Lotmanian spacial categories with a sociological analysis of the text; the supine subservience to Lotman's patterns and frames makes the latter essay aridly aseptic, although there are some fruitful remarks on the correspondence between the novel's topography and the psychology of the characters. With his customary subtlety and culture Agostino Lombardo introduces us to the peculiarly obsessive themes of the past ("Henry James e l'incubo del passato," in *I piaceri dell'immaginazione: Studi sul fantastico*, ed. B. Pisapia; Roma: Bulzoni; pp. 261–74). This piece gives a lucid account not only of the writing "conditions" and of the preliminary project of this particular "ghost story," but also interesting parallels between the American quality of Jamesian horror and that of Emily Dickinson or of Poe. In addition, Lombardo's sharp critical insight focuses very perceptively on that celebrated Jamesian concept of salvation through art, showing us how the creative act can be the only true antidote against an obsessive past and war nightmare. Thinking of James one cannot refrain from recalling the term "lesson of the master": Agostino Lombardo's masterful lecture on "The American Dream of the American Artist" (*Impressions of a Gilded Age: The American Fin de Siècle*, ed. M. Chénetier and R. Kroes; Amsterdam: Amerika Inst., 1983; pp. 96–113) is precisely this. Beginning and ending in the name of James this essay is brilliantly constructed through a chain of associated themes and enriched by innumerable quotations from 19th- and 20th-century authors. It illustrates not only the difficult road the American artist must tread but also, with refreshing originality, the positive spinoffs of the artist's outcast status. We discover how the artist, excluded from the American Dream, is able to build at the same time a dream of his own in which the negative solipsistic connotation may paradoxically turn into a positive one. In that magically conquered new area, the written page, as on a new stage, the artist may live his role and his democratic individualism freely.

The fantastic as a genre seems to polarize the attention of many Italian Americanists. As wittily remarked by Biancamaria Pisapia, as the editor of *I piaceri dell'immaginazione* (see above), the fantastic is an archive of our imagination which we often visit; on this premise she edits a rich collection of essays on the genre (in both English and American literature) that show distinct family ties. Two theoretical essays are contributed by Luigi Punzo ("Intersezioni dell' immaginario letterario," pp. 13–35) and by Armando Gnisci ("Reale, immaginario fantastico," pp. 36–62) and a rich critical bibliography by Armando Scarsella (pp. 277–338).

For its acute theory and subtle analysis of excerpts from Hawthorne, the essay by editor Pisapia deserves particular attention ("Il laboratorio del 'romancer,' " pp. 193–211). By a rather sensual use of language and at a dreamlike pace Pisapia transports us into the romancer's laboratory: her route runs along the border between empirical and arcane reality, and the sometimes puzzled reader has to follow rather blindly the critic's seductive revisitations of that dreamy no man's land where romance is created. By this path and with Pisapia's guidance the romancer's language and technique are no longer obscure to us. Charles Brockden Brown, Twain, and Hawthorne are the subjects of three other essays. To Igina Tattoni we owe an original research on Brown's ethical stance, discovered through an examination of the contrasting dichotomies of *Memoirs of Carwin the Biloquist* (pp. 153–66). "I *Mysterious Stranger Manuscripts:* un esperimento nel fantastico" (pp. 232–60), the title of the essay by Maria Ornella Marotti, hints at the aim of this piece: the analysis of the imaginary and of the structural tendencies in Twain's work as evidence of the author's experimental efforts. It is no easy task, considering Twain's acclaimed realistic style, but the critical attainment is noteworthy. The political meaning of Hawthorne's "Young Goodman Brown" is, according to Giorgio Mariani (pp. 212–31), the clue to all the other elements of the story, which are centered on Brown's appalled discovery of the deep interconnections linking his "civilized" settlement and the wilderness. Due homage is paid to Edgar Allan

Poe by Ugo Rubeo, who in a rather Genette-oriented essay aims at detecting Poe's deliberate use of the fantastic genre even in the so-called tales of ratiocination (pp. 167–92).

Of wider scope is Stefano Tani's "L'esperimento del Professor Hawkline: case stregate e sogno americano da Brown a Brautigan" (*Miscellanea* 5, Ser. 3, xiii:46–79) in which the traditional gothic-fantastic theme is linked to a peculiar concept of American topography and architecture: the haunted house and the forest are seen not only as an extension of the American self but also as a mirrorlike projection of the haunted conscience of the American Dream. The survey of this pattern, including mostly southern and New England authors, is lively although somewhat repetitive and riddled with plot descriptions, but the critical achievement is unique and exempt from too fashionable a critical approach. Despite its very general title, "Temi e funzioni nei racconti americani dell'Ottocento" (*Letterature* 6[Genova: Facoltà di Magistero, 1983]:159–91), Piero Mirizzi's essay, as he says in his introduction, focuses above all on the function of deception to be found in many 19th-century short stories. Scholarly and extremely rich in references from 19th-century authors (Irving and Hawthorne, among others, and Twain—of this latter Mirizzi is a prominent specialist in Italy), the essay not only examines various recurring narrative patterns but also pinpoints and comments on with pleasing originality several technical devices in Poe's and Hawthorne's tales.

Akin, to some extent, to the essays already discussed are two studies picked out from the huge collection in *Studi Americani* 25–26 (1979–80): Paola Gallo Mastrodonato's analysis (" 'The Fall of the House of Usher': il paradosso del narrare," pp. 7–36) attempts to stress the predominance of form and structure over theme in the tale; the critical path seems somehow discontinuous and overridden with Genette's terminology but the final synthesis helps to focus the reader's attention on the original assumption of the story *montage / demontage*. Stefano Tani's competence in John Hawkes's fiction is clearly seen in his beautifully written analysis of "Plot Structures in the Fiction of John Hawkes: from *The Cannibal* to the Sexual Triad" (pp. 263–93), although space limitations on the essay regretfully impose the concentration of so many critical data that we lose something of the overall assessment of the work. In "Il doppio paradigma ideologico di *The Pearl* di John Steinbeck" (pp. 199–223) Mario Materassi finds a complex homology among the various social systems described in

the story. The result of this analysis is innovative and countertra-
ditional, and stresses with incontestable precision how in perfect correspondence with the complex ideological system of the novelette
there is to be found an equally complex sign mechanism in which,
Saussure-like, *tout se tient*. Theodore Dreiser and Kurt Vonnegut are
the subjects of the essays by Oriana Palusci ("Due strategie narrative
a confronto in *An American Tragedy*," pp. 117–34) and by Annarita
Scalesse ("Kurt Vonnegut: La conquista dei mondi interiori," pp.
405–22), while three different essays deal with nonfiction topics:
Giuseppe Gadda Conti offers a well-informed and -documented survey of the presence of "William James e Theodore Roosevelt nella
stampa italiana" (pp. 135–77); while Fedora Giordano's research
deals with the first American studies and interest in Freud's and
Jung's theories and is supported with literary examples from the fiction of Jack London and Waldo Frank (pp. 179–98). This essay constitutes a valuable starting-point for any further study on the subject,
as does Giorgio Mariani's investigation of the Indian press in the
1960s and 1970s (pp. 423–50). Mariani's article provides excellent
documentation on the various stages of the complex relationship between the American government and the Indians from Custer's death
on; this study shows with great subtlety how the new Indian press did
not question the validity of the ancient culture but knew how to create
a rejuvenated and flexible identity which, interestingly, found a means
to unity in the use of the language of the white dominators. The remaining four essays are centered on poetry: Paola Gaddi's piece on
James Agee (pp. 225–62) reveals a mainly biographical and thematic
approach; Bernadette Falzon analyzes "The Images of the Poet's Personae in Sylvia Plath's *The Colossus*" (pp. 295–330) with critical insight far beyond any trite feminist approach, focusing on the theme
of Plath's dual personality and on her search for a definite identity.
In "La poesia di Frank O'Hara" (pp. 331–72) Carlo Giacobbe examines all great influences, both literary and artistic, on the creative
technique of the New York poet. In "Defending the Groves: Gary
Snyder's Poetry of the Earth" (pp. 373–404) Giuseppina Cortese emphasizes the multicultural influences of Snyder's poetry; if her reading of the poems is mainly linguistic, her full recognition of the
various influences working upon Snyder makes her essay a complete,
round analysis of that poet's work.

Starting from the linguistic analysis of the borrowings and recurring French-Canadian lexicon in the works of Francis Parkman, An-

gela Giannitrapani centers on the strong links that bind Parkman to the frontier world and to the world of nature in *Francis Parkman e la fleur de lis* (Napoli: Bibliopolis). This long and exhaustive study gives us not only a highly complex topographical picture but also a rich comparison with texts of other authors concerned with the theme of nature. Although very helpful to those who may wish to go deeper into the natural and even pictorial aspects of frontier writers other than Parkman, this work, because of its innumerable digressions, seems rambling. American nature re-emerges overwhelmingly in the original work of Andrea Mariani, *Scrittura e figurazione nell'Ottocento Americano da Horatio Greenough a Elihu Vedder* (Napoli: Società Editrice Napoletana), who, while analyzing the literary essays *per se* of a group of American painters, introduces us most ably to their paintings as well. It is an original and sophisticated study, austere and unsensational in style, which skillfully reveals American nature through a refined filter of literary and art criticism. William Boelhower's study, *Through a Glass Darkly: Ethnic Semiosis in American Literature* (Venezia: Helvetia), covers different topics, and cutting across several disciplines—cultural geography, anthropology, semiotics, cartography, cultural history—traces an interesting map of American ethnicity. The whole work is structured around and based on a spatio-temporal perspective: in fact the topological system presents a series of "binary isotopies" (Old/New World: presence/absence; dwelling/nomadism) which are lucidly explored. The abundance of critical approaches (most frequently along the lines of French and Italian semiotics) and the bulky content (which even deals with postmodernism) tend at times to baffle the reader, who is expected to draw out an overall assessment from the threads of this complex work. The myth of America in the Italian literary imagination and memory is the main concern of Giuseppe Massara's *Americani* (Palermo: Sellerio). More suitable as a study for Italists than for Americanists, the text is an intelligent critical foray into immigration literature as a theme, mostly envisioned within the pattern of the acceptance or rejection of the imperishable American Dream. The research behind this work is exhaustive and detailed and makes the text, enriched by well-informed notes and an ample bibliography, an important work. Two works linked with Massara's book are concerned with the vision of Italy in the imagination and observation of American travelers in Italy: *Americans in Rome, 1764–1870* (2 vols.; Roma: Centro Studi Americani). *The Descriptive Catalogue* (vol. 1; ed. A. Pinto Surdi

and C. Penteriani Rossetti) is an intelligent and rich commentary on
102 works exhibited in the Palazzo Antici Mattei during the 1984
EAAS conference; *Rome with Hawthorne and James* (vol. 2; ed. P.
Ludovici and B. Pisapia) is an interesting anthology comparing texts
by Hawthorne and James concerning the same Roman sites. In the
field of comparative studies two short essays by Marilla Battilana,
who shows a highly individual competence in comparisons between
figurative art and literature, stand out. In "La narrative gotica
dall'Inghilterra all'America: un confronto" (*Museum Patavinum* 1:
151–61) the author deals not only with the salient gothic characteristics in general (as seen even in the cinema and in the figurative
plastic arts) but also with the characteristic American gothic traits,
scrutinizing with particular acumen concepts of the wilderness and
the frontier. Her second essay ("Interscambi culturali anglo-veneti
nel '700" in *Miscellanea di Studi in Onore di Vittore Branca* 4:205–19)
examines the influence of Palladio and Palladianism in England and
America, where this style became via neoclassicism the first official
style of the Confederation (observable also in New York and Philadelphia, and in the works of Charles Brockden Brown). The interre-
lation between music and literature is demonstrated in a compact
essay by Gigliola Nocera on John Cage's indebtedness to Thoreau's
experience and writings ("Henry David Thoreau e il neo-trascen-
dentalismo di John Cage," *Le forme e la storia* 4[1983]:83–115). The
direct line connecting Thoreau's perception of the sounds of nature
and Cage's environmental music (silences included) is illustrated
through a series of quotations, both musical and literary, that indicate Nocera's high musical competence. In the comparativist field
T. S. Eliot has stimulated the critical imagination of two poetry
specialists: Tommaso Pisanti and Massimo Bacigalupo. "La poesia
minore per T. S. Eliot" (*Atti:* "Il Minore nella storiografia letteraria";
Ravenna: Longo; pp. 437–50) is a dense and learned report on the influences of the so-called minor poets (from the Italian, English, and
American traditions) on Eliot and on the significance of minor or
secondary poetry. In spite of its brevity, this article is highly recommended for its scholarly documentation. In the short "'Hieronymo's
Mad Againe': Eliot, la *Waste Land* e *Hamlet*" (*Paragone* 35(June):
46–59) we have Massimo Bacigalupo at his best: brilliant, knowledgeable, sarcastically aggressive towards other critics. The analogies running from *Hamlet* to *The Spanish Tragedy* to *The Waste Land* are

used to show both Eliot's mythical method and the vengeance theme as a pivotal knot in the three works.

A pungent (or maybe just whimsical) wit seems somewhat excessive, especially when some Italian critical interpretations of Ezra Pound (a god on Bacigalupo's Olympus) or of T. S. Eliot are concerned. Bacigalupo's worship of Ezra Pound (and his almost unique acquaintance with his art) is further evidenced by his edition of *Omaggio a Sesto Properzio* (Genova: Edizioni S. Marco dei Giustiniani) which opens the poetry section of this review. It is the very first annotated edition of Pound's poem, translated into Italian by the editor, sometimes moving away from the usual English edition and basing his version on Pound's original typescript (hard and strange work indeed: an Italian version of the English *pastiche* translation Pound did of Propertius's Latin poem). In the long introduction we learn almost everything of this poem's genesis and of Pound's initial, politically pacifist intentions, which led him to translate from the Epicurean Propertius in a very free, almost surrealistic and sacrilegious manner, which Bacigalupo pinpoints both in the introduction and in the notes. Although on a minor work of Pound, it is likely to be considered the Poundian event of the year.

Many good articles about or introductions to American poetry are published alongside translations or anthologies, variously conceived and framed. Tommaso Pisanti's *Poesia dell'Ottocento americano* (Napoli: Guida) offers an intelligent selection of 19th-century poets, and in the elegantly written introduction, a lucid and necessarily brief evaluation of the authors dealt with (a soft spot for Poe is evident) which may also serve as a valuable guide even for the non-specialist reader. A symposium organized at Fano (May 1982) gave birth to an interesting volume, *Poesia della metamorfosi*, ed. F. Doplicher (Fano: STILB), which founds its collection of translations and essays on the concept of "transcultural parallels" among the poetics of different countries, starting from the assumption that poetry by its very nature may be considered the most reliable mirror of the tensions of our age. The Anglo-American section includes an excellent collection of poems representative of contemporary tendencies and of particular schools such as the Beats, the San Francisco Renaissance, the Black Mountain group. It is compiled by Caterina Ricciardi ("Scuole e tendenze," pp. 556–61) who offers some beautiful translations of poems (the ones from Gary Snyder and Frank O'Hara are excellent). In the same collection Andrea Molesini ("Eccentricità e classicismo," pp. 578–81) and Cecilia Miniucchi ("I nuovi Americani," pp. 589–91) seem to favor the eccentric poets of the new wave or those with rather "European" connotations. The two critics offer some very good translations of lesser-known poets but it is a pity that their introductions are at times too journalistic in tone. Equally eccentric is the structure of *Poesie americane: i giochi e la fatica* (Torino: Tirrenia) by Guido Carboni and Barbara Lanati, which is a critical-methodological excursus into the world of American poetry stemming from teaching experience at the University of Turin. The students' tastes and preferences have strongly influenced the methodological commentaries of Carboni and the sometimes impressionistic critical interpretations of Lanati, but on the whole this is a valuable critical anthology and constitutes an innovation for Italy.

Roberto Sanesi has re-edited his beautiful 1966 translation of Hart Crane's *The Bridge* and *White Buildings* with a new note enlarging his long introduction to the work (*Il ponte;* Milano: Garzanti). Bianca Tarozzi's interest in contemporary and Modernist poetry is demonstrated once more in three essays: "I travestimenti di Marianne Moore" (*AIV* 142:293–303) are for the critic the disguises veiling Moore's self and the metaphors she adopted for her poetry. Under the rough skin of elephants and rhinoceroses or other animals is hidden, in Tarozzi's view, a poetical self longing for a perfect form of poetry. The existentialist interpretations seem questionable but the connections and links with Moore's contemporary poetry notably enrich this work. The other two essays are introductions to the work of poets whose poems are included in translation: the brief introduction to "Tre poesie" by Robert Lowell (*Linea d'ombra* 5–6:39–40) plays successfully on double dichotomies: the England/America opposition as a mirror of the double family life of Lowell and of the two-sided— Classical and Modernist—quality of his poetry, subtly analyzed by Tarozzi, who is a well-known Lowell specialist. "La strada e il paradiso" (*In forma di parole* 5,ii:247–73) is a note to the good translation of *The Book of Ephraim* by James Merrill, who, according to the critic, is the ideal version of the poet envisaged by Auden: "passionately in love with words," a true artist of the 1940s more concerned with form than with content. The elitist periodical *In forma di parole* published two more articles on American poetry: Franco La Polla comments on his own and F. Meo's translations of some of Wallace Stevens's poems in a short essay ("Stevens, Eliot e l'identità della sirena," *In forma di parole* 5,ii:172–80) focusing on the poetical identity of Stevens silhouetted against T. S. Eliot. Against the moralistic appraisal of the latter's poetry, La Polla re-evaluates the "shrinking," peculiar art of Stevens.

Marina Camboni's deep interest in women's studies is evident in her "La donna nata a metà" (*In forma di parole* 5,iv:164–71), an afterword to her beautiful translations of poems by Adrienne Rich, where she displays a very good capacity for introspection. Camboni summarizes and emphasizes the salient qualities of Rich's poetic essence as those of a woman writer whose work becomes especially precious because of her attention to language as a creative instrument *per se*. Another standard-bearer of feminist literature is the subject of a booklet-length essay by M. Carmela Coco Davani, "Anne Sexton: la mappa perduta" (Quaderni dell'Istituto di Lingue, Palermo). The Structuralist background of the author is clearly reflected in this analysis, which achieves an overall assessment of the poetic art of Anne Sexton when it rises above structural details. The best part of this essay is the intelligent cataloguing of all the items and themes connected to the "witchcraft of art." Although it is above all concerned with the complex relationship between Sexton's inner and outer egos, only cursory attention has been given to the painful problem of her suicide. We have an openly feminist interpretation in Emanuela Dal Fabbro's afterword to Edith Wharton's *Estate* (Milano: La Tartaruga), which she sees as the true summer counterpart of *Ethan Frome*'s wintry moralism. This contrast of winter and summer introduces a succession of opposing dichotomies that for Dal Fabbro lead us to the main principles of the sphere of feminine action. The interpretation is shrewd and penetrating, if at times obsessively feminist in its use of such terms as identity, space, and initiation, which are repeated so often as to give it a ritualistic tone. Together with the fine translation of "Beatrice Palmato" (a distinctly *osé* unpublished fragment by Wharton) Dal Fabbro offers an important contribution to the re-evaluation process of Wharton's work. In *Dialogue in Utopia: Manners, Purpose and Structure in Three Feminist Works of the 1790's* (Pisa: ETS) Liana Borghi compares Mary Wollestonecraft's *Maria*, George Imlay's *The Emigrants,* and C. B. Brown's *Alcuin,* starting from the critical assumption, as theorized by Northrop Frye, that utopian elements are present in almost all educational and social models. Borghi's analysis, however, is not carried out on the lines of a sociological study as might have been expected, but through

careful and subtle examination of the structure of the novels from
the point of view of form and content, both of which are clarified for
us in this original contribution to the study of women in literature.

Moving away from the feminist field and bringing us closer to
modern times are three studies on two highly intellectual authors who,
though detached from their social milieu, are very different from each
other: Henry Adams and William Faulkner, to whom modern American thought, with its historical and literary background, owes so
much.

The close relationships between scientific and literary methods
and the subtle links between historical and political ideals and the
field of aesthetics are underlined in the long introduction to my Italian
version of Henry Adams's *Democracy* (*Democrazia: Un romanzo
americano;* Pisa: Nistri-Lischi). The essay is meant to be more than
a single preface to the novel, which I consider a true Watergate novel,
clarifying the position of this work in Adams's oeuvre. Through close
examination of Adams's other literary works and many of his historical, political, and scientific essays, I show the novel to be indicative
of the way a rare symbiosis of life and art can come about.

Agostino Lombardo offers us in his "Faulkner in Italy" (*Faulkner
IP,* pp. 121–38) an unparalleled exposition of the way the southern
author, even more than Joyce, may be viewed as a sort of catalyst
for Italian literary culture and suggests that Italians have been much
more appreciative of his art than American critics. Lombardo reviews
all the Italian intellectuals and critics who have shown particular interest in Faulkner, giving us some innovative critical perspectives on
both Faulkner's fiction and Italian studies: with keen discernment he
pinpoints how the translation of Faulkner's works into Italian may be
considered an "instrument for the introduction of new linguistic elements in the texture of Italian narrative prose." The publication of
Flags in the Dust—almost a century after *Sartoris*—is an "important
event" in Mario Materassi's words: the publication of the Italian version (*Bandiere nella polvere;* Milano: Bompiani) seems an important
event too. This translation of Douglas Day's edition includes his introduction, a preface by Agostino Lombardo, a short contribution by
Mario Materassi, and a translator's note (the book was translated by
one of the best Italian translators, Pier Francesco Paolini) commenting on some linguistic aspects and problems in translating Faulkner.
Rich in information and examples, Lombardo's preface ("Il romanzo

sommerso di Faulkner," pp. v–xi) shows his great familiarity with
Faulkner's fiction and the problems presented by the figure of the
artist as they appear not only in the plot of the work itself but also
through a widely noted comparison between *Sartoris* and this 1927
novel, which is considered an Ur-*Sartoris*, a pre-text to *Sartoris*. In the
short space of his comment ("Da *Sartoris* a *Bandiere nella polvere*,"
pp. xii–xvi) Mario Materassi presents an enlightened study of the
complex structure of this novel with all its contrasts, showing that the
work can be considered the keystone of all Faulkner's production because we find outlined in it his global pattern already complete from
the point of view of form and ideology.

The critical reading that two scholars propose for Fitzgerald's
The Great Gatsby (Paola Cabibbo and Donatella Izzo, *Dinamiche
testuali in* The Great Gatsby; Roma: Bulzoni) takes us very far from
the studies examined above. The aim of their analysis is to show "how
the text works as a complete system" and "a new perception of the
relationship of the novel with the literary system and modern and
post-modern areas." As is to be expected, semiological and Structuralist approaches are very much to the fore in this scheme. In fact Fitzgerald, or Gatsby, is fragmented and dissected to such an extent that
he fades into the background or may even be completely forgotten
by his readers, who instead learn all about fragmentation, disjunction,
flexible structures of the text, and so forth. There are two very good
sections in the study: the one considering the semiosis of the optic
elements and images of sight in the text ("Caleidoscopio," by Donatella Izzo) and the one on "Rites of Passage" (by Paola Cabibbo).
Enriched by a vast, up-to-date bibliography, this is the most important
recent Italian contribution to the field of Fitzgerald studies.

Post-Modern trends in American fiction are the subject of a book-
length study by Guido Carboni, *La finzione necessaria* (Torino: Tirrenia) and of an anthology edited by Peter Carravetta and Paolo
Spedicato, *Postmoderno e letteratura* (Milano: Bompiani). Carboni
picks up the threads of a critical discussion hinted at in *Calibano*
(1982), developing its theoretical and philosophical dimension with
a rich bibliography and enriching it with plentiful examples taken
from the visual arts (especially photography) and from American
literature. Some of his connections (for example that of "l'identità
bisociata" of hermaphroditism and post-Modern writing) seem a
little far-fetched but the work offers some very lively criticism and

some original ways of dealing with the so-called monsters or archetypes of popular culture.

The critical anthology edited by Carravetta and Spedicato is undoubtedly the most useful and complete Italian text for anyone who
wants to find out more about the post-Modern current. All the golden
calves of the new culture are included (from John Barth to Ihab Hassan, from Paul Bové to Gerald Graff), divided into sections covering
criticism and creative work. Spedicato's introductory essay ("Nel
corso del testo, nel corpo del tempo," pp. 9–36) is a first-rate survey
of all the best in post-Modern literature. The competence of the critic
shows up not only in the subtle analysis of single essays contained
both in the text and elsewhere, but especially in the way he tackles
the various philosophical schools that provide the foundation for the
post-Modern framework—from Heidegger to Nietszche, from Kant
to Bataille. Carravetta's splendid essay ("Malinconia bianca: l'inter-
mundium di Yale," pp. 183–227) embraces and integrates the whole
of the American literary landscape. The critic gives a sensitive analysis
of the reactions and interpretations put forward especially by the
Deconstructionist critics of the Yale school, thus indirectly providing
us with a panoramic view of contemporary American criticism.

Although its title hints at a "short trip" in the American critical
province, Remo Ceserani's book, *Breve viaggio nella critica americana* (Pisa: ETS), appears as a very significant (and lonesome) study
on the subject published in Italy. It is pleasant to read, thanks to a
rich supply of anecdotal material, and it informs us on various critical
milieus, both in and out of the official magazines and in and out of the
campuses and provides us also with an up-to-date bibliography.

Besides the few contributions we examined in the field of Henry
James studies, very few Italian specialists have researched the American stage. We might believe that there is a "conspiracy of silence" as
far as the popularity of American theater in Italy is concerned. The
statement is witty—just as Guido Fink, its author, is—and it seems
perfectly founded since even the publication of such an important
monographic collection on the subject as *Quaderni di teatro* 7,xxvi
(Nov.) was unknown to me until the very last minute. In his introductory piece the editor, Guido Fink, with his customary brilliance,
summarizes the Italian life of American theater, from both the bibliographic and the dramatic points of view, adapting a critical performance for us in "Una commedia in tre atti" (pp. 3–10), which shows us

the various stages of Italian reactions to and acceptance of American theater. This is, more or less, the main subject of the different essays of the collection, all critically valuable and dealing with various topics. Thornton Wilder, the only American playwright ardently loved by generations of Italians (O'Neill occupies second place) has only one essay in the collection devoted to him (Rosalba Spinalbelli's "Il *caso* Thornton Wilder," pp. 40–55). Others are "Quel teatro venuto d'oltre oceano" by Paolo Emilio Poesio (pp. 17–21); "Grattacieli Made in Italy" by Leonardo Gandini (pp. 56–61); "L'*illegittima tragicità* di Visconti" by Giulio Cesare Castello (pp. 62–68); "Arbasino: America come teatro" by Roberto Barbolini (pp. 69–77). Two studies are very technical and useful to initiates: an annotated bibliography from the theater magazine *Il dramma* (1929–42), compiled by various authors ("Quando l'America si chiamava Irlanda," pp. 22–39) and "Teatro commerciale e teatro sovvenzionato negli Stati Uniti d'America" (pp. 117–34) by Duccio Faggella. David Mamet monopolizes the attention of two critics. Guido Almansi deals with "Il caso David Mamet" (pp. 92–105), stressing all the author's characteristics and the connotations of his dramatic language and code with critical subtlety. Roberto Buffagni offers us his criticism of and commentary on "American Buffalo" (pp. 106–16). Ruggero Bianchi is obviously one of the group, his interest having been engaged in this field for a long time: "L'invenzione dimenticata" [The Forgotten Invention] (pp. 78–91) is in this case the Living Theater's adaptation of Jack Gelber's work, which now seems rather classical and superseded by new, experimental adaptations. This analysis by Bianchi, who as usual shows an extraordinary firsthand knowledge of his material, starts from that premise to illustrate the new experimentation as a trial of "global scenic writing" not to be considered as a representation of verbal text. From this perspective, he notices how receptive the Italian experimental theater is towards American innovations that are often adapted and performed on Italian stages first.

In 1984 Ruggero Bianchi contributed two other essays; one is "Interfuit il testo imperfetto: *Of Mice and Men* e il modello del *play-novelette*" (*LAmer* 4,xvii[Spring 1983]: 71–108). It exhibits a perfect critical performance by the author: through a Structuralist approach he envisions different versions of Steinbeck's text (dramatic, narrative, scenic) and analyzes their interactions, giving prominence to the performance section which is brilliantly dealt with. In "L'essere in se

del passato: Kantor e l'avanguardia americana" (*Kantor: Protago-
nisma registico e spazio memoriale*, ed. L. Gedda; Firenze: Libero-
scambio; pp. 25–46), Bianchi's third essay, the critic studies not only
various stage adaptations of "The Dead Class," but also reactions to
Kantor, and his influence in the American experimental theater; all
functional devices (spacial diagram, author's double role) are painstakingly screened by Bianchi, whose essay is essential both for Kantor
studies and for methodological studies on scenic space in general.

The theatrical adaptations of *Uncle Tom's Cabin* since 1852 are
dealt with by Luigi Sampietro in his brilliant and well-documented
essay "*Uncle Tom's Cabin*, il più grande spettacolo del mondo"
(*LAmer* 4,xvii[Spring 1983]:49–70). It underlines all the leading elements of Romantic and Christian myth in Tom's story and shows all
the absurd and melodramatic aspects of these adaptations, supported
by the strength of Romantic rhetoric. The wit of the essayist and the
rigor of the scientist give us as readers that gift of *le plaisir du texte*
which is virtually unknown in the large majority of our critics.

Before closing, a few items strongly deserve mention. Marisa
Bulgheroni reviews the Italian version of Robert Coover's *A Political
Fable* (*Alfa-Beta* 67[Dec.]:19) with her extraordinary competence
in contemporary American fiction, making the best use of every
nuance of her seductive critical language. She preciously synthesizes
all clues to Coover's fiction—myth and history, stressing the author's
ability as a fabulating historian whose method relies on the power of
language. "Lo stile paranoico" (*Azimut* 9-10,iii:93) would be, according to Luciana Piré, the main feature of many works by New York
intellectuals from the 1930s to the 1960s, which she perspicaciously
reviews also on the ideological level.

Some translations (in addition to those already mentioned) are
noteworthy on account of their introductions: Giuseppe Lombardo
translates (and briefly introduces) a minor work by Melville, *Rip
Van Winkle's Lilac*, directly from the original manuscript at Harvard's
Houghton Library (*Il lillà di Rip Van Winkle*; Messina: Facoltà
di Magistero). Marilla Battilana offers an elegant Italian version of
Sarah Kemble Knight's diary (*Il diario di Madama Knight*; Padova:
Cleup) in its first appearance in Italy, where it must have many an
admirer, since it was followed by a different version after five months:
Il viaggio di Sarah Kemble Knight, ed. Piero Sanavio (Milano: Serra
e Riva).

University of Catania

vi. Japanese Contributions

Hiroko Sato

If the academic achievement of a year should be measured by the number of books on individual writers, then 1984 may be called a lean year. Even in the study of fiction, no critical appraisal or biography of an individual novelist came out in book form. However, looking at the year's production from a different point of view, 1984 can be regarded as fruitful. There was an abundance of general surveys of literature, of certain periods of time, and studies of women writers or clusters of certain racial groups.

The most important among these kinds of works is a book simply called *Shosetsu II* [Novel, Volume II] (Taishu-kan).[1] This book is the ninth volume of a series titled *Eibei Bungakushi* [The History of English and American Literature]. The range covered by this volume is the English and American novel in the 19th century, with two chapters on the American novel. Chapter 5, "The Emergence of the Nineteenth Century American Novel," and chapter 6, "The Development of the Nineteenth Century American Novel," are by Taro Shimada and Toshio Watanabe respectively. Though the main purpose of the book is to supply general and prevalent views on the novels of that period, both Shimada and Watanabe go deeper than that. Shimada divides his chapter into eight sections: "General Survey," "Charles Brockden Brown," "Washington Irving and the Knickerbocker Group," "James Fenimore Cooper," "Edgar Allan Poe," "Simms and Southern Writers," "Nathaniel Hawthorne," and "Herman Melville." Shimada, by viewing these writers in terms of allegory and symbolism, succeeds in explaining the origin of "ambiguity," the most prominent characteristic of American romanticism. Shimada says that allegory is possible only in a homogeneous society in which a rigid social hierarchy exists. Since such a society is alien to America, its literature has developed so as to suit its heterogeneous and fluid society. To capture the truth, American writers in the first half of the 19th century had to resort to symbolism, in which one thing could indicate several different things; hence, the ambiguity. Shimada deals with the works of the above-mentioned writers from this point of view, and proves how this symbolism can be an advantage as well as

1. When no place of publication is indicated, one should assume the place of publication to be Tokyo.

an impediment to these writers. For example, toward the end of his life Hawthorne came to fear the ambiguity of imagination and to long for a world in which the existence of allegory was possible. This fear caused the decline of his creativity. The fact that both Hawthorne and Melville came to deal with the loss of innocence and the significance of experience in their later works is an indication of their attempt to restrain their rampant imagination. Shimada thinks that this attitude is what connects the literature of romanticism with that of realism. Watanabe's chapter on realism shows quite a different approach from that of Shimada. If Shimada tries to show the general characteristics of the writers of romanticism through the analysis of individual writers, Watanabe begins with the general theory and then proceeds to the particular. Watanabe's chapter also consists of eight sections, "The Theory of American Realism," "The Establishment of American Realism," "Howells and the Sentimental Novel," "Mark Twain—a Writer of 'Conscience,'" "Henry James—a Writer of 'Consciousness,'" "The Responsibility of the Writers of Realism," and "Some Aspects of American Realism." Watanabe begins with the definition of "reality" and then proceeds to that of "realism." He chooses only three novelists, Twain, Howells, and James; he attributes "the correspondence theory of realism" to Twain and "the coherence theory of realism" to James, borrowing Damian Grant's definition, with Howells in between. The correspondence theory of realism does not contain any inherent value judgment, but the theory forces writers to function as the "conscience" of the society. According to the coherence theory of realism, on the other hand, the function of realism is to deal not with human conscience but with consciousness. This theory admits the function of imagination in presenting "truth" to the reader. Watanabe's analysis of the works of Twain and James on the basis of these two points is quite convincing. He also rightly appraises Howells's contribution to the development of the American literature of this period. Both Shimada and Watanabe, with their definite conception of American literature, present not only a reliable general survey of American fiction of the 19th century but also a solid scholarly analysis of it.

Another important achievement in a similar vein is *Eibei Bungaku Koza, Vol. 13* [*Lectures on English and American Literature*] (Kenkyu-sha). This volume, the last of a series which began in 1961, deals with modern literature on both sides of the Atlantic, mostly after the 1960s. Seven chapters are apportioned to American literature:

"The American Novel" (Yokichi Miyamoto), "American Poetry" (Rikutaro Fukuda), "American Drama" (Hiroshi Narumi), "American Criticism" (Minoru Hashiguchi), "The Scholarly World in America" (Hikaru Saito), "Black Literature" (Takeo Hamamoto), and "Science Fiction" (Koji Numasawa). These articles as a whole give reliable information on these respective fields, and the last three chapters are especially welcome because they deal with fields that are usually neglected in this kind of book. Saito's article on the activities of scholarly societies in America and on the publications of university presses, for example, provides information that is difficult for us to come by. Interest in black literature after Richard Wright has been displayed in this country for some time. Hamamoto's chapter is valuable, for he places contemporary black literature in a historical perspective, beginning with Jupiter Hammon and Phillis Wheatley and slave narratives. Science fiction has attracted a great deal of attention as a form of entertainment, but has never been treated as serious literature. Numasawa's article is the first, belated attempt to give this charming genre legitimacy.

Three books either on women writers or on women in American literature came out this year. Motoshi Karita's *Amerika Bungaku to Josei* [American Literature and Women] (Yashio-shuppan) is a collection of essays Karita wrote in the 1950s and '60s on American women writers and poets such as Emily Dickinson, Edith Wharton, Gertrude Stein, Willa Cather, Katherine Anne Porter, Eudora Welty, and Sylvia Plath. Karita's pioneering work in this field is to be admired. However, quite a few critical and biographical studies of these writers have been made in the past decade or so; consequently, some of these essays are dated. For example, we cannot discuss Edith Wharton's life and work without referring to R. W. B. Lewis's *Edith Wharton* (1975). In *Amerika Bungaku no Hiroin* [Heroines in American Literature] (Riberu-shuppan), ed. Iwao Iwamoto and Takeshi Morita, 16 articles by 16 scholars on the same number of American writers are collected. The writers selected here range from such 19th-century writers as Poe, Hawthorne, Melville, and James, through Dreiser, Hemingway, Faulkner; Jewish writers such as Bellow, Michael Gold, and Malamud; and the playwrights O'Neill and Williams to such recent writers as Salinger and Joyce Carol Oates. In a way, the title of the book is misleading, for most of the articles demonstrate the absence, and not the presence, of heroines in the works of the chosen writers. Though this book therefore gives an impression of lacking consistency, it is an interesting accomplishment if we view it as a collection of critical essays on these writers and playwrights as seen in terms of their conception of women. *Gendai Amerika Josei Sakka no Shinso* [The Depth of Contemporary Women Writers in America] (Kyoto: Minervashobo), ed. Michiko Naka and Kazuko Watanabe, is a collection of nine essays on nine American women writers by nine women scholars. The writers dealt with here are Ellen Glasgow, Zora Neale Hurston, Anaïs Nin, Eudora Welty, Mary McCarthy, Susan Sontag, Joan Didion, Joyce Carol Oates, and Alice Walker. These essays share two themes which give the book coherence: how the traditional myth of the domesticity of women affected the psychology of these women writers, and how they treated the male conception of the double role women have played toward men—as a haven and as a destructive power in their dreams. All the essays in this book show how these women writers try to break through the social barriers that have had crippling effects on their creativity. Though short, each essay presents a clear, moving portrait of the struggle of these writers to keep their creativity alive and to establish their own worlds in societies averse to their activities.

One of the fruits of the ever-increasing interest in Jewish writers was a special issue in the fall of 1983 of *Eigo-Seinen* [The Rising Generation] wholly devoted to Jewish writers. This year, Shigeo Hamano's *Yudayakei Amerika Bundaku no Shuppatsu* [The Beginnings of Jewish-American Literature] (Kenkyu-sha) has made a valuable addition to the shelf of studies of Jewish writers. Using literary works and statistics as evidence, the author begins by presenting the lives of the Jews who came to America from Russia. Hamano chose this specific group of Jewish people because he believes that the characteristics of American Jewish writers should be traced back to their own or their ancestors' experiences of pogrom and immigration to the Promised Land—America. Consequently, his book deals with Abraham Cahan, Mary Antin, Anzia Yezierska, Michael Gold, Samuel Ornitz, and Ludwig Lewisohn. This very informative and stimulating book has one dubious point: the fusion of the world of fiction and historical events. Though this can be a great weakness when a strict critical theory is required, Hamano's forceful presentation of Jewish experiences is nevertheless quite persuasive.

Other books that cover a wide range of writers are Shigetoshi Katsurada's *Manazashi no Mochifu* [The Motifs of Gazing] (Kindaibungaku-sha) and Tamotsu Yagu's *Amerika Bungaku ni miru Pyuri-*

tanizumu no Isan [The Heritage of Puritanism in American Literature] (Yoru-dan-sha). Katsurada's book can be called a declaration of a personal credo in literature. He uses four American writers—Hawthorne, Melville, James, and McCullers—to illustrate his belief that the charm of reading is to see the writer's gaze behind what he expresses and to hear what he does not say in words. Katsurada's attitude could be called dilettante, but this is a very charming book. Yagu's study of Puritanism in American literature is in a vein similar to the work done by Bercovitch and Brumm. Using the typological theory of the Puritans, Yagu deals with the works of Hawthorne, Melville, Faulkner, O'Neill, Arthur Miller, Fitzgerald, and Mailer, and tries to see how the Puritan belief in the millenium affected these writers' conceptions of the American Dream. Yagu, who is erudite in theology, presents an especially convincing analysis when dealing with *The Scarlet Letter* and *Moby-Dick*.

As I mentioned at the beginning of this article, very few books were published on individual writers in 1984. Only four books on 19th-century writers and poets came out. The most noteworthy of these is *A Melville Lexicon* (Kaibun-sha), comp. Shigeru Maeno and Yoshiaki Inazumi. This painstaking work forms a pair with *A Melville Dictionary* by Maeno (see *ALS 1976*, p. 456). This present dictionary contains about 8,000 items; terms of maritime affairs and nearly 4,000 words of Melville's own coinage are explained. This book will be a necessary tool for Melville scholars in exploring his complicated world.

Henry David Thoreau and his close relationship to nature is almost self-evident. However, according to Joichi Okuda, no one has ever attempted to examine seriously Thoreau's responses to the seasonal changes in Concord. Okuda, in his *Thoreau Bungaku ni okeru Fudosei—Kisetsu* [The Climate in Thoreau's Works—Seasons] (Hokusei-do), tries to establish a relationship between Thoreau's philosophy and the seasons. Okuda states that Thoreau refers to the four seasons in this order of frequency: summer, winter, spring, and fall. Okuda asserts that summer and winter are the contending forces in nature—the former expressing the flourishing of the life force, and the latter, the suppression of it, demanding abstinence, and that this struggle influenced the formation of Thoreau's philosophy. Though nobody who is acquainted with Thoreau's work can deny Okuda's point, his hasty linking of the seasonal features and Thoreau's ideas of life seems a bit superficial.

Two books on 19th-century poets were published in 1984. One is Haruo Shimizu's *Rairakku no Uta—Whitman no Kyosetsu* [The Song of Lilacs—Whitman's Doctrine] (Shinozaki-shorin), an attempt to understand the poet's philosophy by explicating such ideas as nature and the universe, body and soul, death and life, sex, freedom, equality, fraternity, and democracy. Shimizu asserts that the "Lilac Elegy" is the poem that presents all these central ideas of the poet. An interesting study of Stephen Crane's poetry and its relation to his prose writings is done by Zenichiro Oshitani. *Stephen Crane no Shi* [The Poetry of Stephen Crane] (Kyoto: Yamaguchi-shoten) is divided into two parts: the first half is an analysis of his poems, while the latter half is wholly devoted to the translation of his poems. In his analytical study, Oshitani establishes the spirituality shown in Crane's poetry and thinks that this quality should be taken into consideration when we examine Crane's prose works.

No critical work in book form on 20th-century American novelists was done this year. However, two books on William Faulkner, *William Faulkner no Mississippi* [Mississippi in William Faulkner's Work] (Seiji-sha), ed. Tokiya Nakajima and Shigeo Machida, and Shozo Kashima's *Faulkner no Machi nite* [In Faulkner's Town] (Misuzu-shobo), were published. The former is a kind of guidebook to the locale of Faulkner's fictional world, while the latter consists of personal reflections on Faulkner's novels evoked by Kashima's own visit to Oxford, Mississippi.

As for playwrights, a small but valuable book on Arthur Miller came out. Masanori Sata's *Arthur Miller: Gekisakka eno Michi* [The Road to a Playwright] (Kenkyu-sha) deals with such Miller juvenilia as "No Villain," "Honors at Dawn," and "The Great Disobedience" and points out that Miller started to develop the themes and techniques of his later, mature plays in these plays written while he was a student at the University of Michigan.

As for periodicals, *Eigo-Seinen* has apportioned a great deal of space to American literature again this year. This magazine ran a special feature on the literature of the 1930s in its April issue (130: 10–19): "Reconsidering American Literature in the 1930s." Five articles, "A Reappreciation of the Literature of the '30s" (Kenji Inoue), "Southern Literature—the Dawn of the Southern Renaissance" (Kyoichi Harakawa), "The Literature of the Minority—On the Literature of the Ghetto" (Hajime Sasaki), "Criticism in the '30s—Permanence and Mutability" (Tsuneharu Mori), and "Literature and Movies" (Hisao Kanaseki), constitute the feature. The literature of the 1930s has been labeled with such epithets as "naturalistic," "proletarian," "Marxist," and "social-minded," and less attention has been paid to its artistic side. The purpose of this collection of essays is to view the literature of the '30s in historical perspective and to try to see its relationship to and its influence on American literature after World War II. These articles point out that, in order to deal with the unstable social and economic conditions of the time, the literature of the '30s had to invent the modernistic techniques which the writers in the '60s and '70s have since inherited and elaborated.

Among other articles appearing in *Eigo-Seinen,* three are especially worth mentioning. Hideyo Sengoku's "The Return of Ishmael—an Introduction to *Moby-Dick*" (130:54–57) is an attempt to examine the double role Ishmael plays in the novel—as the narrator and as one of the participants of the great drama. Sengoku thinks that when the novel begins with "Call me Ishmael" and ends with "The drama is done," this framework makes the whole drama into something that exists only in the talk of the narrator; hence, Ahab's "catastrophic disappearance" at the end of the drama. What Melville tries to show through this reduction is the void of the world, Sengoku asserts. Takayuki Ogawa's "Edith in the Land of Time: an Approach to Edith Wharton" (130:366–70) is an ambitious attempt to deal with Edith Wharton's concept of time and its relation to her art of fiction. Through the analysis of *The House of Mirth, Ethan Frome,* and *The Age of Innocence,* Ogawa indicates how closely Wharton's concept of time is connected with the formation of her fictional framework and her characterization. Misako Koike's "Women in American Drama" (130:218–20) clearly outlines the changes in the female characters in American drama since the 1960s. Comparing the heroines created by Corinne Jacker, Beth Henley, and others with the women in O'Neill's and Williams's plays, Koike points out some new themes of these plays—women's independence attained through the spiritual killing of mothers, women's identity acquired through cooperation with other women, and so forth. *Eigo-Seinen* also continued to run, in installments, a very interesting study by Shunsuke Kamei, a noted Whitman scholar, titled "Sex and American Culture." This serialized essay has been running since 1983 and is still continuing in 1985. This study will be duly noted when it comes to an end. Also, quite helpful textual criticisms of major works by Hawthorne (Taro Shimada), James (Tsugio Aoki), Faulkner (Kiyoyuki Ono) and Emily Dickinson (Takao Furukawa) have appeared this year in that journal.

Among the articles appearing in academic periodicals, Koji Oi's article in *Amerika Kenkyū* [The American Review] (No. 18), "The Fate of the Adamic Hero in the Early American Novel" (pp. 27–46), is outstanding for its brilliance and its wide perspective. This is written for a special feature of this periodical, "The Individual and Collectivity." Through an examination of early American novels from William Hill Brown's *The Power of Sympathy* to James Fenimore Cooper's novels, Oi aptly points out that the American novel has always acted as critic of the paradigm of the Adamic hero who denies tradition and social restraint. Throughout its history, the American novel has shown its readers the impossibility of human existence without social restrictions. Oi proves this by contrasting the early American novels with the attitude of American people in the early part of the 19th century which led to the election of Andrew Jackson, an Adamic hero, as their president.

The role of the narrator seems to be of great interest among young scholars here. Two articles in *Studies in American Literature* (No. 21) can be categorized in that group. In "The Great Art of Telling the Truth—a Study of Herman Melville's 'The Bell-Tower'" (pp. 1–16), Shoji Noma compares "The Bell-Tower" with Hawthorne's "The Artist of the Beautiful" and tries to prove that, by telling the story of Banadonna through an unreliable narrator, Melville succeeds in creating the ambiguity of a confidence man. Though most critics have had a low estimate of "The Bell-Tower," Noma asserts the importance of the story in its relation to later works. Suzuko Shindo's "On the Narrator of 'A Rose for Emily'" (pp. 35–50) is a more straightforward study of Faulkner's story. Shindo suggests that if we move our viewpoint slightly, this story can be seen not only as a story of Miss Emily Grierson's weird life, but also as that of the narrator, who represents the collective body of white, middle-class males of the South.

The question of the narrator is more elaborately treated in the prize-winning article by Takayuki Tatsumi—"Violence about the Sovereignty of the Text: An Essay on *The Narrative of Arthur Gordon Pym*"—appearing in *Studies in English Literature* (61,ii:253–68). This essay was awarded the prize for young scholars by the English Literary Society of Japan. Tatsumi explains the transferring of sover-

eignty from the narrator Pym to the writer Poe and then to the omni-
present novelist himself and proves that this move corresponds with
the loss of power of the act of writing and the ascendency of language
into the place of dominance. This means the revenge of the inhuman
text on the human point of view; hence, the text deceives its reader
and deprives him of the absolute point of view by creating the uncertainty and ambiguity of the story.

The same line of argument can be observed in Ikuko Fujihira's
"From Voice to Silence: Writing in *Absalom, Absalom!*" in the English number of *Studies in English Literature* (pp. 75–91). This study
seems to be an extension of an earlier article on *The Sound and the
Fury* by the same author (see *ALS 1982*, p. 469). Fujihira analyzes the
uses of the written word in letters and "ledgers" in the novel and
points out that these written documents stimulate the imagination of
the narrator and create the multiple layers of meaning of the novel.

Mention should also be made of two articles on contemporary
American poetry. One is Keiko Kondo's "T. S. Eliot and His American
Contemporaries, Wallace Stevens and Marianne Moore," in *Studies
in English Literature* (English number, pp. 55–74). This is an attempt to show how Eliot's Americanness and his Puritan heritage
drove him to rigidity and to his longing for "intellectual maturity and
historical consciousness," while the same qualities created a free and
individual imagination in Moore and Stevens. Sachiko Yoshida's
"From Particular to General and from General to Particular—the
Social and Private Visions of Allen Ginsberg and John Ashbery" in
The American Review (pp. 106–33) is a study of poets' social commitment, seen through two poets whose life-styles form a sharp
contrast.

In conclusion, I'd like to refer to two books in the line of comparative literature and culture. One is Shoichi Saeki's *Nichibei Kankei no
nakano Bungaku* [Literature and the Japan-U.S. Relationship] (Bun-
geishunju-sha). Saeki, a noted literary critic and scholar of American
literature, observes the reactions to World War II on both sides of the
Pacific through an examination of literary works. His emphasis is on
Japanese literature, but his deep interest in American literature, which
started on the eve of that unhappy war and which was strengthened
by his personal contacts with America and its people and culture after
the war, helps him to show clearly the similarities and differences of
the two cultures. Kichinosuke Ohashi's *Anderson to Sannin no Ni-*

honjin [Anderson and Three Japanese] (Kenkyu-sha) is a study of the influence of American literature of the 1930s, especially Sherwood Anderson, on the formation of proletarian literature in Japan.

Tokyo Woman's Christian University

vii. Scandinavian Contributions

Mona Pers

It was an active year in Scandinavia in American literary scholarship, especially as regards book-length studies dealing with 19th- and 20th-century poets and prose writers: Herman Melville, the Norwegian immigrant writer Hjalmar Hjort Boyesen, Joyce Carol Oates, and the poets T. S. Eliot, who has long been a favorite with Swedish scholars, and John Berryman. Articles on recently published novels by Mark Helprin and Marilynne Robinson, Willa Cather's heroines, immigrant novels, Lafcadio Hearn's nonfiction, and again T. S. Eliot were written in both English and the Scandinavian languages.

To honor seniority, I will commence with the book on Melville. The aim of Mary-Madeleine Gina Riddle's study, *Herman Melville's "Piazza Tales": A Prophetic Vision* (Göteborg: Gothenburg Studies in English), has been to show how the final arrangement of previously published sketches with the addition of the introductory tale that became *The Piazza Tales* is nothing less than "a representation of the author's prophetic vision." Since it "correlates with the progressive complexity of the historical, political, and social development of slavery," Riddle feels justified in calling Melville's book "a socio-historical myth that also contains a prophetic warning." Riddle's discussion is based on a meticulous scrutiny of assorted primarily sociopolitical references and allusions, which she relates to pertinent biographical and historical facts. She proposes that "the many historical references indicate that one is dealing in part with submerged and political themes," and that a study of the interrelatedness to be found within the tales suggests "a social allegory that makes evident Melville's hatred of oppression."

Riddle recognizes that numerous critics have already taken a sociopolitical approach to the analysis of Melville's writings. Her own contribution she claims is to "consider not only each of the short tales as an entity unto itself but also as an integral part of the unified collection in which they were finally published." Preceding her discussion of the individual tales, to each of which she devotes a separate chapter, is "a brief overview of Herman Melville's socio-political background and a number of his major works." It is mainly in the conclusion that Riddle consistently "considers the collection as a unified, larger new tale." Although at times she falls into the trap of overstating her case and tends to become repetitive in her use of quotations, with her "entry into the labyrinth of Melville's references" Riddle has on the whole been successful in her endeavor to "add to a greater understanding of *The Piazza Tales* as a unified whole." Barbara A. Kathe's essay on Cather, "The Influence of the Past: Metamorphosis in Willa Cather's Heroines (*AmerSS* 16:37–43) is by comparison a less successful venture. Although its mere existence is a welcome sign that Cather's attraction for Scandinavian scholars may be widening, this essay adds nothing new to our understanding of the author or her work. With its many factual errors, facile generalizations, and rehash of already over-used critical material, it fails to argue persuasively the proposed thesis that "Cather's obsession with past values and memories, coupled with her didactic purpose, distorted her portrayal of the past, the land, and its pioneers."

Portrayal of the past is the theme also of two other essays, one on Lafcadio Hearn and one on Marilynne Robinson. In "Lafcadio Hearn och den döende kreolkulturen" [Lafcadio Hearn and the Dying Creole Culture] (*Artes* 3:77–88), Gunnar Harding explains Hearn's fascination with the cooking, folk medicine, and language of the Creole people and with Afro-American music, and evaluates his efforts to preserve for posterity a sense of a colorful way of life doomed to extinction. The Creole culture of the South of his childhood, closer to his heart than the modern American world, afforded Hearn the escape he needed. In "Escaping this World: Marilynne Robinson's Variation on an Old American Motif" (*MSpr* 78:211–16), Gunilla Florby discusses another form of escape, arguing that Robinson's new novel, *Housekeeping*, is a variation of the theme of pastoralism ubiquitous in American literature from the 17th century to *The Great Gatsby*. Even though Robinson's novel "deviates from the classic two-stage pattern of withdrawal from society followed by a turning towards nature," since here "the turning away looms larger" than usual, Florby still sees Ruth, the protagonist of the novel, as "one of the last in a long succession of American seekers." In her heroine's pondering of images reflected on the surfaces of lakes, windows, and mirrors, Florby maintains that the author "fleetingly touches the question at the core of her version of the pastoral. When the trappings of civilization have been left behind, when the distractions have been peeled away and the self is alone with itself, what dreams may come? Can there be an end to peeling?" Florby wonders at the conclusion of her essay.

The problem of social and emotional isolation, the inevitable result of withdrawal, is at the core also of Torborg Norman's book, *Isolation and Contact: A Study of Character Relationships in Joyce Carol Oates's Short Fiction, 1963–1980* (Göteborg: Acta Universitatis Gothoburgensis). Its aim is to "examine and discuss the nature of certain fundamental types of character relationships . . . in varied communicative situations" in order to "capture the creation of character as a process of mainly verbal interaction." To this end Norman selected a hundred-odd stories from ten of Oates's collections of the '60s and '70s, leaving out *The Hungry Ghosts* and *The Poisoned Kiss* because they did not fit her conceived format. Focusing on "that aspect of the text in which characters are made to speak . . . in dialog and monolog, in direct or reported form," Norman endeavors to "follow the interaction of the characters in their conversation as it appears to move between the psychological extremes of isolation and contact." The types of interaction she investigates are limited to such situations as involve the individual with public authority (chap. 3, "Official Authority and the Individual Voice"), with family members (chap. 4, "Familial Bonds"), and with love partners (chap. 5, "The Connection between Men and Women"). To "facilitate" her discussion Norman unfortunately decided to adopt "certain terms" from speech act theory. Most of chap. 2, "The Conversation of Characters," is a presentation of various theories of interpersonal perception that the author deems "adaptable and applicable to literary texts." She may be right in theory, but she made a mistake in trying to put it into practice. Her study is infinitely more readable when she forgets about speech practices, which fortunately happens frequently, and uses her own words to analyze the texts.

Bo Gustavsson's *The Soul under Stress: A Study of the Poetics of John Berryman's* Dream Songs (Uppsala: Almqvist & Wiksell International) is a good example of how effective a tool simple, straightforward language is for untangling even the most intricate problems. It is an acknowledged fact that *The Dream Songs* presents a number of special difficulties. Gustavsson's aim has been to "eliminate some of them" by examining the poetics of this complicated poem. It is

Gustavsson's contention that "the understanding of John Berryman's new kind of writing requires an understanding of his poetics." Because Berryman writes a "workshop criticism" it is Gustavsson's opinion that his critical essays should be regarded as "an integral part of his activity as a poet." In order to investigate Berryman's mature poetics Gustavsson has correlated the essays with his interviews and also, especially in chapter 1, "Contexts: Cultural and Critical," taken into account the relevant criticism of his poetry. Establishing the poetics of *The Dream Songs* by means of this contrapuntal approach, Gustavsson has been able to realize his aim of contributing significantly to the understanding of the poet's *magnum opus.* Gustavsson's thesis is that Berryman in *The Dream Songs* "evolved a postmodern poetics that enabled him to fully express his sensibility." In chapter 2, "Towards *The Dream Songs*," he traces the poet's development towards the dream song mode "through his earlier poetry and a group of essays, where he clarifies his poetic ideas." In chapter 3, "The Poetics of *The Dream Songs*," which is the key chapter of the book, he explains why an essay the poet wrote on Whitman is crucial for the understanding of *The Dream Songs*, developing in chapter 4, "The World of *The Dream Songs*," the idea that Berryman's undertaking "to record fully the soul under stress" is a "Whitmanian project" because "Song of Myself" has both determined the craft of *The Dream Songs* and shaped its content. As a point of departure for his discussions of the separate books constituting *The Dream Songs* Gustavsson has chosen to investigate the epigraphs, his reason being that "they offer the thematic contexts for an understanding of the poem." This approach, he maintains, enabled him to find "the rationale for the heterogenous material of *The Dream Songs* that other critics, because they failed to see the significance of the epigraphs, have overlooked." Chapter 5, "*The Dream Songs* and the Poetry of the Last Years," concludes this penetrating and illuminating study.

　　Only one American poet besides Berryman has attracted the attention of Scandinavian scholars this year. T. S. Eliot's animals have inspired two studies, one being Johannes Hedberg's "T. S. Eliot, Old Possum and *Cats*" (*MSpr* 78:97–105), a short article explaining the poet's love of cats, the meaning and application of the word "Possum," and the origin of *Cats*, the other being Marianne Thormählen's *Eliot's Animals* (Lund: CWC Gleerup). In the introduction to her book Thormählen gives an amusing account of her fruitless "search for a tenable approach" to the structuring of her material. After realizing that both the "context" and the "symbolic image" were unsatisfactory as a recurring motif, she decided to abandon "all pretence to methodological consistency" and "allow the metaphorical function of each animal image the scope it seemed to call for." As a result her presentation of Eliot's animals "follows the simplest of outlines. Chapter by chapter, different animal categories proceeding from one representative to the next [follow] in roughly chronological order": dogs, cats, birds (the longest chapter), small creatures, rats, fishes, and in the last chapter the miscellaneous. This loose structure serves Thormählen well. It affords her ample scope for references to other works and authors (her knowledge of German, French, and Italian literature is impressive), and to other Eliot critics. The entire book is in fact like an open-ended, challenging discussion with other Eliot critics and scholars, the purpose of which is clearly to inspire questions and suggest answers rather than to dogmatically prove her own points. Disturbed by the lack of recognition for the achievement of others that she has often spotted in Eliot criticism and scholarship, she goes out of her way to give credit where credit is due, sometimes to the point of breaking the flow of her own discussions. This does not prevent her book from being a joy to read, however, and its extensive, informative footnotes will no doubt prove a gold mine for future research on Eliot.

Of the three studies by and about immigrants Per Seyersted's book is of particular value. It is on a 19th-century critic and writer who was also professor of German at Columbia University. *Hjalmar Hjort Boyesen: From Norwegian Romantic to American Realist* (Norway: Solum Forlag) makes available to the English-speaking world a wealth of hitherto inaccessible material written in Norwegian. "Largely on the basis of this untapped . . . material, I arrived at a view of Boyesen that differed from that presented by other critics," says Seyersted. To "correct and amplify the picture of Boyesen" given by two recognized scholars in the field, Clarence A. Glasrud (to whose 1963 bibliography Seyersted's own is intended to be a supplement), and Marc L. Ratner (who wrote the appreciative foreword to Seyersted's book), Seyersted published his findings in a series of five articles. They all appeared in Scandinavian periodicals, with the deplorable result that until now they have remained unknown in the U.S.A., even to Boyesen scholars. Seyersted's collected essays give an incisive, sad, but unsentimental picture of the life and work of a man belonging to two countries but ultimately feeling at home in none.

The interest in ethnic literature is spreading in Scandinavia as elsewhere in Europe. In her survey article, "Draumen om fridom og jord: Biletet av utvandringa til America i nokre emigrantromanar" [The Dream of Freedom and Land: The Image of Emigration to America in Some Emigrant Novels] (*Samtiden* 93,iii:47–51), Ingeborg R. Kongslien demonstrates how the major novels of four prominent writers of immigrant life, the Swede Wilhelm Moberg and the Norwegians Ole Rølvaag, Johan Bojer, and Alfred Hauge, together have shaped the Scandinavians' idea of what it meant to emigrate. Their importance for historical and social research is only now beginning to be recognized; their common theme, the dreams and trials of immigrants, is as urgent as ever today. Mark Helprin's recently published book, *Winter's Tale*, is about an immigrant son left to fend for himself in Manhattan. Anna Marie Agaard's essay, "Allt ska bli bra: Om Mark Helprin och visionen av fullkomlig, helt rättvis värld" [Everything Will Be Fine: About Mark Helprin and the Vision of a Perfect, Completely Just World] (*Vår Lösen* 3/4:204–11) focuses on the writer's poetic language as a means of discovering a new reality, and traces the similarities in tone of what Agaard calls Helprin's "fable" and the Italian film, "La notte di San Lorenzo."

University College at Västerås, Sweden

22. General Reference Works

J. Albert Robbins

Because they are highly selective and authoritative, reviews-of-research-and-criticism volumes are of highest significance to specialists. This year has given us a much-needed volume, *The Transcendentalists: A Review of Research and Criticism,* ed. Joel Myerson (MLA). The volume falls into three parts: general essays, individual Transcendentalists, and response to the movement. The five general essays treat the movement, the times, Unitarianism, communities, and periodicals. The roster of Transcendentalists runs to 28 persons, from the most important, Emerson (32 pages), to such minor followers as Charles King Newcomb (one and two-thirds pages) and Samuel Johnson (two and one-third pages). "The Contemporary Reaction" examines several major writers outside the movement: Lowell, Hawthorne, Melville, Poe, and Whitman—and various lesser contemporaries. More on *The Transcendentalists* will be found in chapter 1 and other relevant chapters, above.

Another important review-of-research volume is the updating of *Fifteen American Authors Before 1900: Bibliographical Essays on Research and Criticism,* ed. Earl N. Harbert and Robert A. Rees, editors also of the original 1971 volume (Wisconsin). The two chapters on southern literature have been dropped in the revised edition, and the increase in size has been held down to slightly over 100 pages. See relevant chapters, above, for further notice of this new edition.

The bible of documentation and physical format of typescript work has, for the MLA, been the modest booklet, *The MLA Style Sheet* (1951), then the more elaborate, prescriptive *MLA Handbook for Writers of Research Papers, Theses, and Dissertations* (1977), and now the 2nd edition called *MLA Handbook for Writers of Research Papers,* ed. Joseph Gibaldi and Walter S. Achtert (MLA). Its principal innovation is the death of the citation footnote—that beloved (and overused) badge of Germanic scholarship. There are two reasons for the change: simpler forms of citation are just as clear and are, in this

age of high costs, far cheaper. *PMLA* shifted at once to the new parenthetical and works-cited format. Most of the other learned journals
have yet to reform their ways.

It is all explained in chapter 5, "Documenting Sources." Actually,
there are five documentation forms described, with parenthetical form
described first (pp. 136–61). The others are the author-date system
(pp. 161–63); the number system (pp. 163–64); full information in
the text (pp. 165–66). The last and least favored is the traditional
form: citations in footnotes or endnotes—the documentation to which
we have for so long been accustomed (see pp. 166–81).

The *Handbook* principally addresses the student population. A
somewhat enlarged version which presumably speaks to the professional audience, *The MLA Style Manual* (MLA, 1985), will be noticed
in *ALS 1985*.

Of all the student guides to works on American literature the
granddaddy is Clarence Gohdes and Sanford E. Marovitz, *Bibliographical Guide to the Study of the Literature of the U.S.A.* (5th ed.,
Duke). This is the first time that the guide has had a coauthor. Since
the first edition in 1959 its 102 pages have grown to the present 256
(and its price from $2.50 to $29.75). New subjects since the 4th edition
in 1976 are computer aids, women's studies, film studies, science fiction, and Chicano studies. One topic, regionalism, has lost its separate
status but is absorbed under other headings. A new feature is a list of
principal biographies of 135 American authors.

The work shows care in selectivity and citation but there are a few
oversights. For example the new edition cites Joe Weixlmann's *American Short Fiction Criticism, 1959–1977* (item 24.86) but not its twin,
Jarvis Thurston's checklist of short fiction criticism, 1800–1858 (item
24.19 in the 4th edition of Gohdes's *Guide*). An even more egregious
omission is a completely new medium: the online database. Instead of
telling us (in a note to item 3.31), "The MLA has computerized its
annual bibliography," it would be more useful to know that the *MLA
Bibliography*, as of 1984, was available for the years 1968–84 online
in file 71 of the DIALOG system (Dialog Information Services, Inc.,
Palo Alto, Calif.). DIALOG also has online Magazine Index (file 47,
back to 1959), Book Review Index (file 137, back to 1969) and Dissertation Abstracts Online (file 35, back to 1861). The section called
"Computer Aids" in the Gohdes-Marovitz volume consists of books
on the subject. Well and good, but bibliographers of American literature must commence citing the computer databases themselves.

A new landmark reference work is Gerald Bordman's *The Oxford Companion to American Theatre* (Oxford), not to be confused with *The Oxford Companion to the Theatre* (*ALS 1983*, pp. 376–77). A *Companion* on the American drama and theater is yet another (but overdue) acknowledgment that our drama and theater are of international significance.

There are three new genre guides. Patricia L. Parker has compiled *Early American Fiction: A Reference Guide* (Hall), a bibliography of books and articles about American fiction before 1800. She records studies of 28 writers of early fiction. Harriet Semmes Alexander has prepared *American and British Poetry: A Guide to the Criticism, 1925–1978* (Swallow), alphabetical by poet and by individual poem. Patricia Marks contributes *American Literary and Drama Reviews: An Index to Late Nineteenth-Century Periodicals* (Hall), a useful finding list of elusive materials.

A growing "regional genre" is scholarship on western writing. Jon Tuska and Vicki Piekarski have edited *The Frontier Experience: A Readers' Guide to the Life and Literature of the American West* (McFarland). The "life" part embraces the ethnic element, religion, traders and commerce, law and the lawless, the military frontier, trails, and such. Approximately one-third deals with "literature": commentary on major and minor writers (such as Owen Wister, Bret Harte, Helen Hunt Jackson, Zane Grey); popular magazines (such as *Argosy* and *Wild West Weekly*); assessment of major critical works; films and television programs.

During the year Gale Research Company produced ten volumes in the *Dictionary of Literary Biography* series—works of high quality and rapidly growing scope. There were three volumes of interest to scholars of early letters—all noticed above in chapter 11: *American Colonial Writers, 1606–1734* (DLB 24), *American Colonial Writers, 1735–1781* (DLB 31), and *American Writers of the Early Republic* (DLB 37). Emory Elliott edited all three. Clyde N. Wilson edited *American Historians, 1607–1865* (DLB 30), with essays on three literary figures: Washington Irving, William Gilmore Simms, and Elizabeth F. Ellet.

Last year *American Newspaper Journalists, 1873–1900* (DLB 23) was published, with Perry J. Ashley as editor. This year he has edited *American Newspaper Journalists, 1901–1925* (DLB 25)—with sketches of such writers as George Ade, Irvin S. Cobb, Ben Hecht, and Ring Lardner. Ashley also has edited the succeeding volume, *American*

Newspaper Journalists, 1926–1950 (DLB 26), including such next-generation persons as Franklin P. Adams, Heywood Broun, Walter Lippmann, and H. L. Mencken.

American Screenwriters (DLB 26), ed. Robert E. Morsberger, et al., includes 65 professional film writers, but not such occasional film writers as Fitzgerald and Faulkner. One does find here such writers as James Agee, Zöe Akins, Ben Hecht, Sidney Howard, Anita Loos (author of over 100 films), and Clifford Odets. A second volume of screenwriters is in progress.

Thadious M. Davis and Trudier Harris have edited *Afro-American Fiction Writers after 1955* (DLB 33), with essays on 49 authors—all but two living. Darwin T. Turner contributes "Afro-American Literary Critics: An Introduction," pp. 309–16. Daniel Walden's *Twentieth-Century American-Jewish Fiction Writers* (DLB 28) covers the work of 51 authors from Nathan Asch to Anzia Yezierska—33 still living. Of the 33, 12 are women. Finally, John Cech has edited *American Writers for Children, 1900–1960* (DLB 22; Gale, 1983)—welcome attention to an often overlooked genre.

From time to time we have called attention to such Gale series of reprinted criticism as *Nineteenth-Century Literary Criticism, Twentieth-Century Literature Criticism,* and *Contemporary Literary Criticism.* Yet another was born in 1984: *Contemporary Authors: Autobiography Series*—another series of reprinted material, one would be prone to assume. Wrong. Gale has requested original autobiographical recollections from living writers. Of the 23 authors in the first volume, 18 are American—the best known of whom are Vance Bourjaily, Kay Boyle, Erskine Caldwell, Marge Piercy, James Purdy, and Diane Wakoski.

Following the yearbook formula, *DLB Yearbook 1983* (published 1984), ed. Mary Bruccoli and Jean W. Ross, updates some previous author essays (four) and presents new entries (24); includes articles on "The Public Lending Right in the United Kingdom" by Brigid Brophy (pp. 15–21) and on "The Public Lending Right in America" (pp. 22–28) with statements by authors and a short piece by William B. Goodman ("PLR and the Meaning of Literary Property"); essays on the year in literary biography, drama, poetry, fiction; lists of literary awards and honors; and obituaries. The concept of "public lending right" is an offspring of the computer age. Now that library circulation systems are widely computerized it is possible and economical to compile statistics on the number of borrowers of specific volumes. And that makes it possible to charge a royalty fee on the quantity of borrowers—a windfall for authors, but death to the centuries-old concept of the free public lending library as basic to the common welfare.

Joel Myerson recalls the first volume of Jacob Blanck's classic *Bibliography of American Literature* and reviews the most recent (7th) volume in "How Stands the Cause? The *Bibliography of American Literature* after a Quarter of a Century" (*PBSA* 78:45–56). The 7th volume (Yale, 1983) advances the coverage from James Kirke Paulding to Frank Richard Stockton and, after Blanck's death late in 1974, was completed and edited by Virginia L. Smyers and Michael Winship. In his review essay Myerson reminds us of exactly what Blanck set out to do, as announced in his preface to volume 1. The work, now so close to completion, is still unique and indispensable.

Indiana University

Author Index

Subject Index